Selected works of Jawaharlal Nehru

FROM LEFT: JAYAPRAKASH NARAYAN, KAMAL JUMBLATT OF LEBANON, NEHRU.
AT THE ANTI-NUCLEAR ARMS CONVENTION, NEW DELHI, 16–18 JUNE 1962.

Selected works of Jawaharlal Nehru

SECOND SERIES
Volume Seventy Seven (1 June – 19 July 1962)

Editor

MADHAVAN K. PALAT

Jawaharlal Nehru Memorial Fund
New Delhi

PUBLISHED BY
Jawaharlal Nehru Memorial Fund
Teen Murti House, New Delhi 110 011

ISBN : 0-19-949476-2
ISBN : 978-0-19-949476-7

DISTRIBUTED BY
Oxford University Press
YMCA Library Building, Jai Singh Road, New Delhi 110 001
Mumbai Kolkata Chennai
Oxford New York Toronto
Melbourne Tokyo Hong Kong

PRINTED AT
Aditya Arts,
I-66, Jadunath Enclave,
Sector 29, Faridabad-121008

CONTENTS

I. GENERAL

II. NATIONAL INTEGRATION COUNCIL

III. POLITICS

(a) Indian National Congress

(b) Social Groups

(c) Laws and Administration

(d) States

(i) Andhra Pradesh

(ii) Bihar

(iii) Goa

(viii) Madras

(ix) Mysore

(x) Northeast

(e) Media

IV. DEVELOPMENT

(a) Economy

(e) Education

(b) Anti-Nuclear Arms Convention

(c) Moscow Peace Congress

(d) USA

(h) Tibet

(i) Pakistan

(j) Africa

(k) Nepal

FOREWORD

Jawaharlal Nehru is one of the key figures of the twentieth century. He symbolised some of the major forces which have transformed our age.

When Jawaharlal Nehru was young, history was still the privilege of the West; the rest of the world lay in deliberate darkness. The impression given was that the vast continents of Asia and Africa existed merely to sustain their masters in Europe and North America. Jawaharlal Nehru's own education in Britain could be interpreted, in a sense, as an attempt to secure for him a place within the pale. His letters of the time are evidence of his sensitivity, his interest in science and international affairs as well as of his pride in India and Asia. But his personality was veiled by his shyness and a facade of nonchalance, and perhaps outwardly there was not much to distinguish him from the ordinary run of men. Gradually there emerged the warm and universal being who became intensely involved with the problems of the poor and the oppressed in all lands. In doing so, Jawaharlal Nehru gave articulation and leadership to millions of people in his own country and in Asia and Africa.

That imperialism was a curse which should be lifted from the brows of men, that poverty was incompatible with civilisation, that nationalism should be poised on a sense of international community and that it was not sufficient to brood on these things when action was urgent and compelling—these were the principles which inspired and gave vitality to Jawaharlal Nehru's activities in the years of India's struggle for freedom and made him not only an intense nationalist but one of the leaders of humanism.

No particular ideological doctrine could claim Jawaharlal Nehru for its own. Long days in jail were spent in reading widely. He drew much from the thought of the East and West and from the philosophies of the past and the present. Never religious in the formal sense, yet he had a deep love for the culture and tradition of his own land. Never a rigid Marxist, yet he was deeply influenced by that theory and was particularly impressed by what he saw in the Soviet Union on his first visit in 1927. However, he realised that the world was too complex, and man had too many facets, to be encompassed by any single or total explanation. He himself was a socialist with an abhorrence of regimentation and a democrat who was anxious to reconcile his faith in civil liberty with the necessity of mitigating economic and social wretchedness. His struggles, both within himself and with the outside world, to adjust such seeming contradictions are what make his life and work significant and fascinating.

As a leader of free India, Jawaharlal Nehru recognised that his country could neither stay out of the world nor divest itself of its own interests in world affairs. But to the extent that it was possible, Jawaharlal Nehru sought to speak objectively and to be a voice of sanity in the shrill phases of the 'cold war'. Whether his influence helped on certain occasions to maintain peace is for the future historian to assess. What we do know is that for a long stretch of time he commanded an international audience reaching far beyond governments, that he spoke for ordinary, sensitive, thinking men and women around the globe and that his was a constituency which extended far beyond India.

So the story of Jawaharlal Nehru is that of a man who evolved, who grew in storm and stress till he became the representative of much that was noble in his time. It is the story of a generous and gracious human being who summed up in himself the resurgence of the 'third world' as well as the humanism which transcends dogmas and is adapted to the contemporary context. His achievement, by its very nature and setting, was much greater than that of a Prime Minister. And it is with the conviction that the life of this man is of importance not only to scholars but to all, in India and elsewhere, who are interested in the valour and compassion of the human spirit that the Jawaharlal Nehru Memorial Fund has decided to publish a series of volumes consisting of all that is significant in what Jawaharlal Nehru spoke and wrote. There is, as is to be expected in the speeches and writings of a man so engrossed in affairs and gifted with expression, much that is ephemeral; this will be omitted. The official letters and memoranda will also not find place here. But it is planned to include everything else and the whole corpus should help to remind us of the quality and endeavour of one who was not only a leader of men and a lover of mankind, but a completely integrated human being.

Indira Gandhi

New Delhi
18 January 1972

Chairman
Jawaharlal Nehru Memorial Fund

EDITORIAL NOTE

One of the grand themes of this volume is the Integration Conference which was close to Nehru's heart and had been prompted by the series of communal and linguistic clashes in 1960 and 1961. His efforts were energetic and wide-ranging, but they continued to haunt him, not the least because what happened in East Pakistan had repercussions in India. Punjab is surprisingly quiescent, at least so far as Nehru's correspondence is concerned, but the northeast is very alive on the questions of Nagaland, A.Z. Phizo, the All Party Hill Leaders' Conference, Assam Oil Revenues, and movements of people across the borders of Tripura. At both a personal and political level Nehru suffered a grievous loss when B.C. Roy died unexpectedly. Foreign affairs follow their usual trajectory with as many as twelve parliamentary debates devoted to the China question. Of especial interest is the discussion over the purchase of MIG aircraft from the Soviet Union and the surprisingly sharp reactions from the UK and the USA. Nehru managed to get two well-deserved holidays, one in Kashmir, and the other in the Nandi Hills in Mysore, but they yielded more than their fair share of correspondence, a species of catching-up. However, Jayaprakash Narayan at least commented that he looked well rested.

Some of the speeches have been transcribed; hence the paraphrasing, punctuation, and other such details have been inserted. Words and expressions which were inaudible or unintelligible have been shown by an ellipsis between square brackets thus: [...]. When no text or recording of a speech was available, a newspaper report has been used as a substitute. Such a newspaper report, once selected for publication, has been reproduced faithfully; other information has been added only by way of annotation. Most items here are from Nehru's office copies. In personal letters, and even in official letters composed in personal style, the salutation and concluding portions were written by hand; such details are not recorded in the office copy. Therefore these have either been inserted in Nehru's customary style for such persons or his full name has been used, but the editorial intervention is indicated by square brackets. Information on persons may always be traced through the index if it is not available in the footnote. References to the *Selected Works* appear as SWJN/FS/10/..., to be understood as *Selected Works of Jawaharlal Nehru*, First Series, Volume 10.

In the case of the Second Series, it would be SWJN/SS/.... The part and page numbers follow the volume number.

Documents, which have been referred to as items, are numbered sequentially throughout the volume; footnote numbering however is continuous only within a section, not between sections. Maps of the boundary between India and China have been reproduced from official documents and are placed at the end of the volume.

Nehru's speeches or texts in Hindi have been published in Hindi and a translation into English has been appended in each case for those who might need or want one.

A large part of Nehru's archives is housed in the Nehru Memorial Museum and Library and is known as the JN Collection. This has been the chief source for items here, and has been made available by Shrimati Sonia Gandhi, the Chairperson of the Jawaharlal Nehru Memorial Fund. Unless otherwise stated, all items are from this collection. The Nehru Memorial Museum and Library has been immensely helpful in so many ways, and it is a pleasure to record our thanks to it. The Cabinet Secretariat, the secretariats of the President and Prime Minister, various ministries of the Government of India, All India Radio, the Press Information Bureau, and the National Archives of India, all have permitted us to use material in their possession. We are grateful to *The Hindu*, the *National Herald* and *Shankar's Weekly* for permission to reproduce reports and illustrations.

Finally, it gives me great pleasure to thank those who have contributed to preparing this volume for publication, most of all Geeta Kudaisya and Fareena Ikhlas Faridi. The Hindi texts have been edited by Mohammed Khalid Ansari, and the translation from the Hindi was done by Chandra Chari.

Madhavan K. Palat

LIST OF ILLUSTRATIONS

I. GENERAL

1. In New Delhi: Press Conference[1]

Jawaharlal Nehru: Shall we put down the subjects on which you wish to ask me questions.

Subjects suggested: Laos, ECM.

Question: How are you now? Have you recovered fully?[2]

Jawaharlal Nehru: What do I look like.

Question: You look all right.

Jawaharlal Nehru: Then I am all right. I am quite all right.

Question: Your holiday programme?

Jawaharlal Nehru: I can holiday here in Delhi.

Question: You'd like to say something about MIG.

Question: Are you visiting Paris and Bonn after your trip to London for the Commonwealth Prime Ministers' Conference?[3]

Jawaharlal Nehru: I did read something about it in the newspapers, I haven't heard of it. I think highly unlikely.

Question: Kashmir. Now that the debate in the UN is coming up again, we would like to ask some questions.

1. Vigyan Bhavan, New Delhi, 13 June 1962. Two versions are available: (1) *Press Conferences*, GOI, MEA, External Publicity Division, pp. 24-48, (2) PIB. Both have been used and what is missing in the MEA version is printed in bold type.
2. See SWJN/SS/76/items 81-82, 85-86, 510, 536. See also Sarvepalli Gopal, *Jawaharlal Nehru*, Vol. 3 (Delhi, India: Oxford University Press, 1984) p. 266.
3. For meetings of the Commonwealth Conference, see SWJN/SS/78.

Jawaharlal Nehru: What am I to say about Kashmir. I do not know.[4]

Further subjects suggested:

Tibet, Steel Targets and the Bokaro Scheme, poor progress of the Third Plan generally and iron & steel crisis, election of Deputy Leader, high altitude tests.

Jawaharlal Nehru: The election of the Deputy Leader will take place at a lower altitude.

Question: I would like to put a question in Hindi and I would like the answer in Hindi. What is the policy of language to be used by AIR.

(Comment by Correspondent: He is taking the place of Swami Rameshwaranand[5] here?)

Further subjects suggested:

National Integration,[6] Anti-nuclear Conference in Delhi,[7] Speech in the Lok Sabha two days ago by Vishwanath Singh Gahmari about the Eastern UP.[8]

Question: Will you like to say something?

Question: What will happen after the expiry of India-China Treaty?

Jawaharlal Nehru: After its expiry, it does not function.

Question: What will happen then.

LAOS

Jawaharlal Nehru: It is very comforting to know that after nearly a year's continuous tussle, some kind of settlement has been arrived at among the three

4. See item 409 and appendices 38 and 44.
5. Lok Sabha MP, Jan Sangh, from Karnal, Punjab.
6. See section II on National Integration.
7. See item 360.
8. See items 202-204.

Princes. You will have noticed that the Geneva Conference practically was prepared for a settlement long ago.

The difficulty arose not in the Geneva Conference. All the parties there were in favour of a settlement but in Laos itself between the three Princes.[9] Now, for various reasons, they have agreed and it is a very good thing not only for Laos but round about because these countries of South East Asia are intimately connected: if one goes wrong, the situation in another is affected. The only principle that can satisfactorily apply to these countries is the principle of—I use the word without liking it—neutrality. Any other attempt to pull one way or the other immediately brings conflict and it must be realised that the military way is not the way to settle problems in South East Asia. I am not talking about the rest of the world for the present but in South East Asia certainly.

Well, I shall go on to the European Common Market.

Question: The latest is that Mr Khrushchev has said that it may be a turning point in the relations viz. settlement of various issues. Do you agree with him? He has sent a message to Kennedy about this.

Jawaharlal Nehru: I hope it will be a turning point. It is. It was an extraordinary case. It appears so easy and the Geneva Conference was called to meet for a few weeks, four or five weeks, I thought, but it dragged on nearly a year now because, behind the apparent ease of it were all kinds of other problems and certainly it may well be a turning point in South East Asia and South East Asia itself will affect the larger situation.

Question: The cold war between North Vietnam and South Vietnam is on the increase and you must have seen there is some accusation about the International Supervisory Commission also taking a partisan attitude.

Jawaharlal Nehru: The cold war is bad but we could put up with it. But it becomes hot war often there. Yes, the International Commission received numerous complaints and was asked to report on them. It has reported criticising the action of both, on the one hand, the North Vietnam and on the other, South Vietnam and the United States. It has spread out its criticism evenly on all. The International Commission does not judge. It has to judge according to the terms of reference that have been given to it and that is, has there been a breach of the Geneva Agreement or not? According to that, it has held that there have

9. The three Laotian Princes were Souvanna Phouma, Souphanouvong, and Boun Oum.

been breaches on both sides, on the American side, the landing of troops and material there and on the other side, in other ways.

Question: You received some communications from President Ho Chi Minh and President Ngo Diem.[10] Was it with regard to the functioning of the International Commission or was it some personal communication?

Jawaharlal Nehru: I forget now whether they were purely personal messages or something else. I have a vague idea that they were of a personal kind. Something must have happened. I might have sent some congratulatory message on their birthday and replies to them might have been received. Well, I do not quite remember it now.

Question: There is a report that the Polish representative has declined to sign this Report of the International Commission.

Jawaharlal Nehru: Well, the Polish representative has not agreed with part of the Report. I do not think I should go deeper into it because when the Report comes out, you can see it.

Question: Under the new Laos agreement, the prerogatives of the Commission to supervise have been extended. Could you give us some idea of the commitment, that is, what use the Indian forces would be made of by the Commission?

Jawaharlal Nehru: No. Which agreement?

Question: With the formation of the coalition government, the powers of the International Commission have been expanded, as I understand it.

Jawaharlal Nehru: Well, there are no Indian forces in any number.

Question: That is what I mean, who is going to police the new Government. Will India be willing to send troops for supervision, etc.

Jawaharlal Nehru: There has been no question of India sending any further troops to South-East Asia. We have got a small number to look after the Commission itself. The idea is that the Governments concerned help the Commission.

10. See SWJN/SS/76/appendices 22 and 46. For Nehru's responses, see SWJN/SS/76/items 486-488.

EUROPEAN COMMON MARKET

Well, now something about the ECM. The very name implies that it is the European Common Market. But because these relations are interrelated, we are naturally affected by any decision that might be made, by England or by the Commonwealth. Directly, we are interested in our exports not being hit. That is very important for us. Indirectly, we are interested in the other consequences of the Rome Treaty. It is our effort to see that arrangements are arrived at so that our exports would not be hit. We have some hope that we shall succeed. With regard to the Rome Treaty business, this may be considered a preliminary to further steps to be taken according to the Rome Treaty of the ECM powers—which means some kind of political coming together also. We are rather concerned with that. It is not for us to come in the way but a political coming together, according to us, would be good or not good in terms of the policy it pursues. If it is a liberal policy, not in economic terms, but in political terms, then it may be a good thing. Otherwise, it may help reactionary elements and forces.

> Question: It is supposed to be a rich men's club. The entry of neutral nations is taboo. Will it have any political repercussions on the Commonwealth tie?

Jawaharlal Nehru: It is difficult to say. There are some repercussions, of course, because the economic relations of the Commonwealth countries are one of the strongest bonds between them. If they are affected, it is bound to have some effect on the Commonwealth. How far, I cannot say at present, it depends on the circumstances because no member of the Commonwealth, to my knowledge, wants its ties to weaken. They attach some value to them, but on the other hand, circumstances are weakening them.

> Question: You have said that you expect as a result of the Common Market that our exports will not be affected, but I think the only assurance so far we have is that our textile exports may not be very heavily taxed. Otherwise, there is no sign of any encouragement.

Jawaharlal Nehru: Yes, may be.

> Question: There is one aspect of ECM and I wonder whether you would care to comment on that and that is the present community as well as the enlarged possible community's relationship with Africa, especially in view of the fact that the Brussels negotiations seem to be proceeding

with the hope that a fairly large part of the present Africa and the British Commonwealth probably, would be getting associated with the Community. For example, Nigeria, Tanganyika, etc. may get associated with the ECM.

Jawaharlal Nehru: Do you mean the relationship between the emerging countries in Africa and the Common Market?

Question: Yes, Sir,

Jawaharlal Nehru: Naturally these countries require help for their development and this help can be in the sense of aid or trade or both. If impediments are put in the way of their trade and exports, then instead of helping them you hinder them.

Question: Do you envisage that Britain's joining the European Common Market means the death knell of the Commonwealth? Or shall I put the question the other way and say what is the value of the Commonwealth politically and economically if Britain joins the ECM and puts all her interests in Europe.

Jawaharlal Nehru: I have just answered that question in a sense. I have said that undoubtedly Britain joining the ECM would injure to some extent the cause of the Commonwealth. I would not call it a death blow, but it would weaken the links.

Question: How do you view the reports in the Press that there has been a lot of American pressure on Britain to join the ECM?

Jawaharlal Nehru: I have not quite understood it.

Question: There have been reports in the Press that the Americans are pressing Britain to join the ECM. How do you view those reports?

Jawaharlal Nehru: Yes, I have seen such reports and I believe to some extent they are correct.

Question: In your Lok Sabha speech, you criticised the political aspects of ECM. Since then, have you received any assurances from Britain or other countries that it would not be so bad?

Jawaharlal Nehru: No. I have received no assurances and I am hardly likely to receive assurances because that is in the future. How can any country assure me as to what might happen in the future, when it is wholly out of its power?

MIG

Then, we go on to MIG. We had felt for some considerable time that our Air Force was relatively weak, that is, the machines, etc. more especially after some much later type of aircraft was given as aid to Pakistan.

The demands on our Defence Forces, as you will realise, have increased greatly both because of the occasional crises that occur in the Indo-Pakistan relations and on our northern border. So, we felt that we should really manufacture the type of aircraft that we required. We are now manufacturing transport aircraft, we thought we should manufacture other types. It is not so much a question of buying aircraft from any country but manufacturing it with their help, of course. And in order to manufacture it, we thought of a new model. We have not come to any final decision or agreement about it yet. We are considering all aspects, and even in the Soviet Union, we have to consider many aspects and talk to them about it. But it is true that the enquiries we have made thus far have been pretty thorough by our experts—that is by our Air Force experts—into the various types of aeroplanes from different countries, about the aircraft that might suit us. We have been inclined to think that the MIG is the most suitable for two or three reasons. We looked upon it, first of all, from the facility of manufacture, and it seemed to us that the MIG was the stout, simple type, not a sophisticated, complicated one as others are. It is much more difficult to manufacture these highly sophisticated aircraft here. But the MIG was relatively simple and good for rough wear. That is one thing in its favour, and an important thing from the point of view of manufacture. And secondly, the price factor and presuming so far as performance is concerned, they are about equal to others planes. And in regard to the price factor, the price was less, apart from being paid for, probably, in rupees. But these things are not settled. We are still enquiring about various matters.

Question: Has there been a firm offer by the Soviet Union to sell India these aircraft?

Jawaharlal Nehru: I do not think so. The fact of the matter is that our Air Force people went to the Soviet Union for another purpose, to buy some engines in order to have the engines made here. When they were there, some two or three months ago, they were interested—our Government was not thinking of it even—they were only interested in these MIGs and they asked the Soviet people to show to them the latest types of MIGs and they showed them all round and talked about them. There was no regular offer made by them or offer made by us. But we did gather that they would be willing to come to some agreement with us about it. It is all rather informal but it was the report of our Air Force officers that interested us in this because they spoke rather highly of it, especially in regard to facility of its manufacture in India. That is what we are concerned with. Our people have done remarkably well in manufacturing aircraft—they have made—like the AVRO. The AVRO has been made from scratch by Indian mechanics and by some people it is supposed to be better than the prototype in England.

Question: Is there any pressure from Britain or America that we should not get these MIGs?

Jawaharlal Nehru: There is no pressure at all from America. You might read it in the newspapers but there is no pressure from the Government at all. There were some enquiries from Governments like the UK and USA about it.

Question: It has been reported that one of the aspects about which India might be concerned in making any agreement with the Soviet Union is that she should be fully free, that she should enjoy full freedom in the deployment of such MIG fighters against China.

Jawaharlal Nehru: Well, as I have been laying stress before you, we are after manufacturing them, not buying them—we may have to buy a few of them to begin with, to carry on till we manufacture. But if we manufacture anything, surely we should be completely free to use them without asking anybody's permission. But the question has not arisen at all; nobody has mentioned it, but it is obvious, that we must have complete freedom to use any aircraft or any weapon as we like.

Question: Has China got these supersonic MIGs?

Jawaharlal Nehru: I do not know; I think they had not got it previously but I do not know recently what has happened.

Question: Have politics at any time played any part in the purchase of our defence equipment, and why these things are brought in now, the political aspect of the deal in the negotiations going on?

Jawaharlal Nehru: Politics, to some extent, always colours one's thinking; politics lead to certain results. But politics should not according to us come in the way of any important policy that we may wish to adhere to. **You cannot just ignore politics.**

Question: Have there been any offers from any other country to collaborate in the manufacture of aircraft?

Jawaharlal Nehru: I believe. You see, in other countries, in most of them—though they may encourage you—we have to deal with private firms. The Government of that country may encourage you but you have to deal with private firms, and we have discussed this matter pretty fully with private firms in other countries where such aircraft are produced. One difficulty or inconvenience is that one has often to deal with a number of private firms to get the full article while in the Soviet Union one deals with one party who is responsible for every part of the undertaking.

Question: May I know, Sir, whether after getting the MIGs India will be superior, in air force, as compared to Pakistan?

Jawaharlal Nehru: There is no question of superiority or otherwise. One does not know precisely in what weapons the United States is superior to the Soviet Union.

Question: But why not get the superior ones from them...

Jawaharlal Nehru: No, you cannot because whatever we get are really second rate weapons compared to the high standard which they require. Probably in many weapons the United States is superior to the Soviet Union, in some weapons the Soviet Union may be superior. They are constantly changing them and getting what they consider better weapons. In fact, all these tests etc. are meant to help them to find out what superior weapons they can use, apart from the big bombs.

Question: Were the inquiries about the MIG by the United States and the United Kingdom, as you mentioned, of a casual nature or of a more serious nature to find out what we are doing?

Jawaharlal Nehru: Even serious things are put casually.

Question: The manufacture of the MIG, I believe, would take place after about two, three years, what about the immediate future?

Jawaharlal Nehru: That is another point. The manufacture of the MIG is supposed to be a feasible proposition here within a short term of years because it is a simpler aircraft. The others take much longer and some planes which come earlier, which we buy earlier if we buy them, are supposed to fill a certain gap.

Question: By the time we begin to manufacture these MIGs, within two or three years it is quite possible these MIGs will become out of date.

Jawaharlal Nehru: It is not quite possible. It is more than possible. It has always happened, this kind of thing. This MIG is 21—this is the latest type.

Question: Along with the manufacture of these, we will be buying initially a number of these aircrafts.

Jawaharlal Nehru: Yes, to begin with one has to buy them even for the sake of manufacturing them and also because there is a gap which we wish to fill.

Question: Could we have some idea of the price even in terms of percentages that Russians talk about it?

Jawaharlal Nehru: I do not know because we have not discussed this matter in any detail.

Question: We have been depending for our military equipment and other ammunition on Britain. With this MIG purchase, shall we interpret that this is now a bit of a change of policy?

Jawaharlal Nehru: You will realise that even now we are making here British aircraft like the AVRO, like the GNAT, two British aircraft that are being made herein our factories from their blueprints. So we have a large connection with British equipment being supplied to us.

Question: In considering this MIG purchase, did you personally consider the ideological or political aspect of it, that it would ruffle friends elsewhere in the world. I can see now that there is interpretation in America that aid is being withheld on account of this ideological purchase?

Jawaharlal Nehru: These are the possible consequences you are pointing out. You see we want to be friends with all countries. And we have, I must say, succeeded in a large measure. But the moment there are pressures from one side or the other, that friendship becomes slightly tainted and those pressures may be exercised at any moment affecting our policies.

As a matter of fact, in this particular matter, although there has been some reference in the press, foreign press, no such pressures have been brought to bear on us by any Government.

Question: Leaving aside the question of justification or pressures, is it your opinion that the purchase and manufacture of MIGs by India will affect the relationship between India and Britain and the United States?

Jawaharlal Nehru: I don't think so. As a matter of fact, we have purchased big transport planes from Russia and helicopters. They did not attract any particular attention. We purchased them simply because they were the most suitable for our high altitude work but we have always taken care to keep the different types of aircraft from different countries entirely separate from the others, that is, for reasons of secrecy and the rest. Neither party wants its own machines to be examined by the other, just like the British would not like the Russians to see their machines here, so the Russians, and we have to give an assurance to both that this will not be done. They will be kept in different air fields completely. There will be no overlapping.[11]

KASHMIR

Question: In case some other countries might bring forward a resolution to the UN asking India and Pakistan to negotiate or mediate or both, what will be the stand of India on this resolution?

Jawaharlal Nehru: That depends on the resolution but we are prepared always to talk to Pakistan, but not for any mediation. Our position is completely clear in regard to it. Only it gets rather covered up by years of subsequent happenings. People seem to forget that the original complaint was one of aggression, aided by Pakistan on Kashmir. That is why we went there. Much has happened since then which cannot be ignored. Anyhow we do not believe in the solution of this or any other major problem by war. I think it would be most unfortunate if there was such a development and we hope that there will not be. That applies to the northern frontier too. One has to take precautions; that is a different matter. But we do not want to be entangled in a war anywhere, least of all in these high mountains. Although the situation appears to be difficult, and it is difficult, I don't give up hopes of some peaceful settlement. As you perhaps know, we have repeated an old offer to the Chinese Government about withdrawal behind certain lines of both parties.[12] I think that is an eminently fair and reasonable

11. On the MIG purchase, see items 370, 373 and 432 pp. 708-710.
12. For India's note of 10 May 1962, see *White Paper VI*, pp. 96-97, and in this volume appendix 8 (b).

offer. It is a temporary one, that is, it is meant to produce conditions for talks and negotiations. It is not correct to say that we are against negotiations with China as they often say but negotiations can only lead to fruitful results if they start in the right atmosphere. And it is in order to create that right atmosphere, we have suggested withdrawal of both parties.

It is true that that withdrawal largely applies much more to the Chinese than to India, but the principle is the same for both, I repeat this because there is sometimes in foreign papers and others loose talk of war. We are not conditioned that way to jump into a war. Of course, if we are attacked we have to defend, we will defend.

Question: Lately in the so-called Azad Kashmir, there is much bellicose talk of resort to war and other matters to settle the Kashmir dispute. If there is a conflict, will it remain confined to Kashmir or will the theatre of conflict be extended?

Jawaharlal Nehru: It was stated long ago that any conflict in Kashmir would not be considered by us as confined to Kashmir. It depends on the nature of it of course, but we wanted to make that quite clear.

Question: Some of your statements have been interpreted about Kashmir that you are prepared for the settlement of Kashmir dispute on the present ceasefire basis, with minor adjustments. From these statements, some people have concluded that you are prepared for a settlement with China also so far as Ladakh is concerned on the same basis. Would you agree with that?

Jawaharlal Nehru: No, Kashmir and the northern frontier stand on a different footing.

Question: You have referred to your offer again made to China. Is it true that their reply is in the negative?

Jawaharlal Nehru: Yes, more or less, the reply is in the negative.

Question: In continuation of the same question, apart from the China question, is it true that the Government of India would be prepared to settle the Kashmir issue on the basis of the ceasefire line?

Jawaharlal Nehru: I suggested that some years ago, because of our extreme desire for a peaceful settlement. It was not accepted, although it was a natural thing, that is, accepting the position as it is, but because it was not accepted the matter lapsed. And, if we have to argue this matter, we argue on fundamentals that Pakistan has committed aggression in Kashmir which it has.

Question: Does that offer still stand?

Jawaharlal Nehru: It has lapsed.

CHINA

Question: How do you distinguish between India's charges of aggression against China and against Pakistan? Could you elucidate on that? What was the distinction between the two forms of aggression?

Jawaharlal Nehru: The differences are obvious. Pakistan committed aggression on us and there was a local war for sometime and ultimately there was a ceasefire. And broadly speaking, the ceasefire line is a line of division between the part occupied by Pakistan and us. On the other side, China has committed aggression. It has crept across Ladakh a good deal, without the slightest justification. And you will see that the whole background, the whole historical sequence and the facts are different. I can understand China saying that the frontier in one particular place is not quite clear, let us clarify it. But we do not talk about this kind of frontier. Frontier may mean half a mile this way or half mile that way. But you do not consider this frontier dispute where hundred miles forward is concerned. It is quite absurd. It is not a frontier dispute; it becomes a dispute about large sections of territory. You will remember that repeatedly both in writing and orally we complained to the Chinese Government about their maps. And every time their answer was that these maps were old maps and that they would see to it that they were rectified and we will settle it peacefully. But even that answer can fit in with the rectification of the border—half a mile this way or that way or some such petty things. But how does it fit in with 150 miles of march across the border? So, it is patent that our position in regard to the frontier was dead clear. We have put it before them. We have absolutely clear maps which we have put before them with latitudes and longitudes etc. marked. They knew that we possessed these lands and claimed them. They could not have come there under any mistake. They might have said that your claim to it is less than ours. That was a different matter. But knowing that, they came over there and took possession of them. I find it very difficult to understand this. And then those officials —the Chinese and Indian officials who considered this question brought out a big report or two reports.[13] I think anyone who reads those reports will find quite enough justification for the Indian stand. In fact, after the officials' reports the next step should have been a consideration by the two Governments of those reports. Unfortunately, that has not taken place; it may take place in future. That would be a proper way of considering this problem.

Question: Mr Chou En-lai's complaint against you is that the officials' report was not followed by a meeting between the Heads of two Governments.

Jawaharlal Nehru: He did not quite say that, although he did mention something to that effect. It is not that; the Heads of two Governments can meet but they cannot sit down and consider the report of a thousand pages. In fact, that report was not published in China till recently.

Question: On the Chinese border discussion, in the earlier stages of negotiations did you get the impression at any time that the Chinese were thinking in terms of any final settlement or just a provisional settlement. Did they have any mental reservations on this subject?

Jawaharlal Nehru: We have not discussed this matter with them, rather we have discussed very little except when Premier Chou En-lai came here. We sent long letters and communications to each other. That is not the way to discuss anything. Naturally letters and communications on either side are couched in a strong language and all that. It is difficult to say about what one has at the back of one's mind, but I do think the impression I have got is that the Chinese

13. SWJN/SS/66/Supplement.

Government would like a settlement with India. What the settlement may be, I cannot say. But they are not happy over our present relations.[14]

CHINESE ATTITUDE TO KASHMIR QUESTION

Question: Did they recognise dispute between India and Pakistan in regard to Kashmir and it is the border territory that is concerned, that whatever agreement they reach with us, if they desire one at all, can only be provisional.

Jawaharlal Nehru: Their attitude in regard to Kashmir, although we have taken strong exception to it as we have every right to—has not varied much. I mean to say that even some years back—it was not put very clearly—there was always a loophole in it. It was quite different from the Soviet attitude, which is quite clear. It did give us the impression at the time that they were supporting our case on Kashmir, but on later examination, we found that there was always a loophole.

TIBET

Question: What was the value of the trade with Tibet before you withdrew the Indian Trade Agencies in Tibet?[15]

14. On this issue, a meeting of the Consultative Committee of Parliament on External Affairs on 15 June 1962 was reported thus: "Prime Minister Nehru is understood to have told members of the Consultative Committee of Parliament attached to the External Affairs Ministry today that the Chinese did not seem to like the present relations with India because the Chinese reputation had been 'injured'.

    Pandit Nehru was replying to questions by members who wanted to know how he got the impression as stated at his recent press conference that China would like a border settlement with India and that the Chinese were not happy with the present ties.

    When members drew his attention to the strongly worded notes of China, the Prime Minister is reported to have told them that even behind the strongly worded notes there was another line of thinking.

    Analysing the background of his impression, the Prime Minister is reported to have referred to the general economic recession in China, increase in population, and lack of food.

    He is reported to have stated that India was much better placed on the border than two years ago. That did not mean that India was posing for a war, he is reported to have said.

    The meeting which lasted one hour also discussed the political aspects of the European Common Market, and the implication of the settlement arrived at between the three princes in Laos with particular reference to the situation in the entire south-east Asia region." See the *National Herald*, 16 June 1962, p.1.
15. See also item 387.

Jawaharlal Nehru: The value of trade in the last few months has been very considerable, because realising that trade was going to stop, all the merchants and others rushed to do what they could do within these months. But previous to that the trade was lessening, dwindling, because of restrictions put upon it.

Question: What is the position of places of pilgrimage in Tibet like Kailash, Manasarovar and others, whether Indian pilgrims would be allowed to go and under what conditions?

Jawaharlal Nehru: We do not recommend people to go there, but it is up to the Chinese authorities to give them facilities or not.

Question: They will go there, but will they come back?

Jawaharlal Nehru: Pilgrims are a hardy race. They go and come back. They should be compared to people who try to go up these high mountains. Thousands have gone this year and have come back.

INDO-NEPAL RELATIONS

Question: Would you say something about Indo-Nepal relations in the light of your discussion with the King?

Jawaharlal Nehru: I made it clear to him that we had no desire to interfere at all with his internal happenings, nor do we want Indian territory to be used for any kind of attack on Nepal, raids on Nepal. But according to our laws, peaceful agitation could be carried on here.[16] It is a little difficult for people to understand a rule of law in a country. Some people do not understand that. For instance, it is very difficult for us to explain to China that there is a rule of law and that the Press is free to say what they like. In the same way, in Nepal, although totally different, there was this difficulty to understand this. I think that, to some extent, they understand our bona fides in this matter.

DEPUTY LEADERS OF PARTY

Question: What are the functions of the Deputy Leaders of the Congress Party?

16. For Nehru's talk with Mahendra, see SWJN/SS/76/item 472.

Jawaharlal Nehru: The function is to preside when the leader is not there.

Question: Anything else?

Jawaharlal Nehru: And to look after the general organisation of the party.

Question: What is the function of the Deputy Leader in the Rajya Sabha and Lok Sabha? Will they be officiating for the leader when he is not there?

Jawaharlal Nehru: No.

Question: Then, who will do that?

Jawaharlal Nehru: The Leader of the House, whoever he may be.

Question: That means, you will nominate another person, another Minister, when you go out?

Jawaharlal Nehru: Well,I may or may not. But that has been the practice all along. For instance, there is the leader of the Rajya Sabha. He need not be the Deputy Leader of the Party. But he will be the leader in the Rajya Sabha. He is responsible or any senior man is responsible, whoever he may be. But the Deputy Leader is not automatically responsible for guidance in the Lok Sabha or the Rajya Sabha. As a senior man, he will be consulted. That is a different matter.

Question: I find a constitutional anomaly in what you say. According to the Constitution, the President takes note of the leader of the majority party. Now, suppose you are away and some emergency arises, will the President call the Deputy Leader of the Congress Party in the Rajya Sabha and the Deputy Leader in the Lok Sabha.

Jawaharlal Nehru: The President?

Question: Yes.

Jawaharlal Nehru: Where does the President come into the picture?

Question: Because in an emergency....

Jawaharlal Nehru: For the last twelve years such an emergency has not arisen.

Question: When you were away attending the Commonwealth Prime Ministers' Conference, the Assamese delegation came on the question of the Nunmati refinery and it was Maulana Azad who decided it. A similar situation can arise even if you are away for a week or ten days.

Jawaharlal Nehru: Maulana Azad decided it, no doubt because he was an outstanding figure in the Congress Party, and not because he was the Deputy Leader. I am sorry, I mean, he was not Deputy Prime Minister as Sardar Patel was. But all these things do not go by the labels you put upon them but by the fact that Maulana Azad was recognised, and as such his advice was taken.[17]

Question: What is the position now? You have the Home Minister,[18]you have the Finance Minister[19] and a Minister without Portfolio.[20]In any issue, who will be recognised a senior colleague in the Cabinet?

Jawaharlal Nehru: I have got all those....

Comment by Correspondent: All of them hold durbars also.

Jawaharlal Nehru: The biggest durbar now is the President's. Although personally, I think it is a very good innovation. The President was good enough to mention it and I strongly encouraged him to do so.

Comment by Correspondent: Many people do not get time and they complain later on. What about the complaints which he receives?

Question: On the question of the Deputy Leader, I wanted to ask this. While I wish you a long life, I want you to provide the answer to the great question mark which is writ large on the faces of the people after your recent illness, namely: Who leads after Nehru?

Jawaharlal Nehru: That question is out of date. Now the question is why should'nt Nehru take the great decision and retire and leave because the question who after Nehru does not arise.

17. In 1953, Nehru issued a directive to this effect before leaving for London, see SWJN/SS/22/pp. 289-291.
18. Lal Bahadur Shastri.
19. Morarji Desai.
20. T.T. Krishnamachari.

Question: The complaint against you made is that Gandhiji took great care to train leaders and he also named one who could take charge after him.

Jawaharlal Nehru: Gandhiji did nothing of the kind. You know nothing about Gandhiji, and you talk about him. Gandhiji did that at the height of the non-cooperation movement. He was not thinking in terms of Prime Ministers and others. And he was good enough to give me the privilege of making me No. 2, No. 1 being Vinoba Bhave, and to lead the civil disobedience movement.[21]

Question: You have no number 1 and 2 according to your view?

Jawaharlal Nehru: No. 1 and 2? First of all, I want you to appreciate that Gandhiji never thought in terms of officers in Government. The question did not arise before him.

Question: Who presides at the Cabinet meetings in your absence?

Jawaharlal Nehru: The senior member. The Finance Minister is the senior member.

Question: Gandhiji called you a jewel among men, you have not called anyone a jewel?

Jawaharlal Nehru: You see those are extravagant descriptions. They were all right, if I may say so, at the time of constant conflict with the Government, the British Government, of the day. It is another atmosphere, another thing in which we function. And Gandhiji said those things.

CONGRESS PARTY

Question: You must have come across an opinion being expressed that the present composition of the Cabinet has led to an increased ideological conflict within the Cabinet.

Jawaharlal Nehru: The ideological conflict is inherent to some extent in the Congress and to go further than that, the country. The Congress represents that country. And Government represents the Congress, that is, it has a certain

21. Nehru is referring to the individual satyagraha when Mahatma Gandhi chose Vinoba, Nehru and Patel to be the first, second and third satyagrahis, see SWJN/FS/11/pp. 160-161, 182-183, 192-199.

ideology, very definitely but it is opposed to sectarian methods or sitting on those who don't disagree with it. While it has a clear ideology, it tries to convert others, to take that into its fold rather than to push them out. It is a fundamentally different way of approach. We think and discuss these matters in European terms, that is, in terms of European politics. Our background has been different under Gandhiji. Under Gandhiji, people of differing outlooks functioned together because there was something in common under his leadership. In a sense, we functioned together because we have a great deal in common. In some matters we don't agree, that is, ideologically but there too we find a common way, a middle way, and we function accordingly. We do not believe in class conflict. Although we do believe there is conflict between classes, we do not believe in encouraging class conflict. There is conflict obviously between a zamindar and his tenants, and a capitalist concern, there is conflict of interests. We want to remove conflict in other ways instead of crushing this or that. The whole approach is different.

Question: Do you mean to suggest there is no ideological conflict in the Congress so far as ideological questions are concerned.

Jawaharlal Nehru: That is exactly what I mean to say. Of course not, it is very difficult to have ideological compactness between two intelligent human beings. Our party has got very clear principles and ideologies declared in our Manifesto and everybody by and large in the Congress is supposed to adhere to it. But in adhering to it, he may be inclined one way or the other, you cannot be rigid about It.

Question: What is the machinery envisaged for selection of the future leader?

Jawaharlal Nehru: Future leader of what?

Question: Future Leader of the Party and therefore of the Government.

Jawaharlal Nehru: Party of course will have to elect him.

Question: The organisation or the Parliamentary Party or will there be a combination of the two?

Jawaharlal Nehru: It has ultimately to be done by the Parliamentary Party. Why did I become the Prime Minister?

Question: Because the All India Congress Committee passed a resolution, not the Congress Parliamentary Party.

Jawaharlal Nehru: I became the Prime Minister because at the time I was the Congress President and the then Viceroy sent for me because I was leader as Congress President of the Congress Party. If I had not been that, perhaps somebody else might have been selected. That thing went on then. But it is true as it may well be that the leader of the Congress Party may not be important. By and large, those in the Congress Party, if they produce a leader, he will represent them but he can only do so with effect if he is accepted by the Congress organisation or possibly ignore [ignores] it. If they ignore it then the whole Congress Party goes to pieces.

Question: According to you what does right or left represent in your Cabinet? Is it some personalities or views because Mr Morarji claims to be something more than a socialist because he believes in Sarvodaya but generally speaking he is regarded as a rightist.

Jawaharlal Nehru: Those terms do not fit in. They give some vague indication. They don't really fit in with Indian politics. They are historically derived from Europe and our conditions are somewhat different. For instance, I have come across even now a person who considers himself extreme left who, according to me, is a hopelessly conservative individual, in social matters he will talk broadly of communism and socialism but in his personal social life, he will be as conservative as anything. These are conflicts. We in India are a very mixed lot having had a mixed past and for us to label each other or groups simply left or right, has no peculiar meaning. Of course, you can analyse them and see in some matters they are left and in some matters they are right.

Question: What are the considerations on which you appoint a Minister? Sometimes it is said that Deputy Ministers are not even personally known to you.

Jawaharlal Nehru: I think every Minister I have appointed is known to me, he may be known a little more or a little less. I also take the advice of my colleagues about them because one consideration apart from quality or merit is some kind of geographical distribution and in that I have to take the advice of colleagues.

Question: In this distribution...Assam and Madhya Pradesh did not appear...

Question: Recently when the Council of Ministers was announced by the All India Radio, it was mentioned that they took their oath according to the Order of Precedence. Precedence comes in, as first you and then Mr Desai and then I believe Mr Jagjivan Ram etc...

Jawaharlal Nehru: The order of precedence largely goes by the date of the appointment etc.; to some extent not. For instance, Mr T.T. Krishnamachari, on his recent appointment, took his place which was his before he left the Government, he did not start at the bottom of the ladder but he took his former place—fifth or thereabouts. The Cabinet Secretary placed him thereafter consulting me. That is what we think is right; normally it is that. There have been exceptions to this, as in the case of Pantji when he came he was given a much higher place;[22] he was not placed at the end of the list of Ministers, because he was senior, very much so.

Question: That means these rankings do have some meaning then.

Question: In New Delhi at least.

Jawaharlal Nehru: Yes, you may say that it has some meaning.

Question: Recently, Sir, some persons including Mr Jayaprakash Narayan have been busy giving you the generous advice that you should step down from office and ...

Jawaharlal Nehru: I just said that the question "After Nehru who?" is completely out of date because they have given up hope of waiting till after Nehru. So a quicker change is desired.

Question: One question about Deputy Leadership? Why not allow this issue to be resolved by the party by allowing the members to exercise their right of free choice? Otherwise, the information now gathered is, that whereas the party was in favour of choosing a senior member you just came in the way.

Jawaharlal Nehru: I am sorry I did not follow the question at all.

Question: In the matter of Deputy Leadership, why not allow the party to decide it by a free vote?

22. Govind Ballabh Pant was appointed Home Minister in January 1955.

Jawaharlal Nehru: Why not allow the party? Certainly the party will decide it. Who else will decide it? Of course, the party always decides it and will decide it this time too.

Well, let us go on to the next subject; I have got to be in the Parliament soon.

HIGH ALTITUDE TESTS

Jawaharlal Nehru: All I can say is that I express my deep regret that any tests and especially high altitude tests should take place. I see that the Secretary-General of UN has expressed regret to these tests taking place.

NATIONAL INTEGRATION

Jawaharlal Nehru: I think the recent meeting of the Council was a helpful and useful meeting. It does not perhaps function in a dramatic way but in a good solid way, it is very helpful.

> Question: Yesterday, Mr Munshi[23] met you. Is there any special significance attached to that?

Jawaharlal Nehru: Yes, yes, he met me yesterday or the day before. I do not quite remember what he said to me. It was not that important that I should remember every word that he said.

> Question: Rajaji[24] is coming to the Anti-Nuclear Arms Conference. Is any meeting possible between you and him? Was that point discussed with you by Mr Munshi.

Jawaharlal Nehru: That was not even mentioned. Rajaji is coming to the Anti-Nuclear Arms Conference. We shall, of course, meet in the conference.

> Question: No separate meeting?

Jawaharlal Nehru: I have not thought of it, it may be.

23. K.M. Munshi, of the Swatantra Party, and founder president, Bharatiya Vidya Bhavan, 1938-71.
24. C. Rajagopalachari, leader of the Swatantra Party.

> Question: Recently the Home Minister made a statement about the Jamaat-i-Islami in the Lok Sabha. We would like to know if you consider the RSS as dangerous as Jamaat-i-Islami is and, if so, whether any action is being contemplated against the members of the RSS by the Government?

Jawaharlal Nehru: I have not seen the Home Minister's statement about the Jamaat-i-Islami, and it is rather difficult to compare two organisations in this way. They are based differently although they are both, I think, very narrow in their outlook, and therefore harmful to the idea of national integration.

Jawaharlal Nehru: Somebody asked me about the Eastern UP districts.

> Question: Before you come to that, may I ask what do you propose to do about the DMK's continued demand for Dravidisthan?

Jawaharlal Nehru: First of all, we ignore it. Secondly, we have to take steps where necessary. The demand is so unreal and artificial that it is a little difficult even to consider it seriously. Nowadays wherever you may be, the thinking, is, the drift is in favour of larger aggregates. In the ECM it is gradually Western Europe taking political shape as an aggregate. One does not think in terms of cutting off what one has got.

Then, somebody delivered a speech about the Eastern UP districts.[25] Well, I think he exaggerated somewhat, but basically he was right, that is, the Eastern UP districts are among the poorest in UP and, therefore, in India. It is essentially an agricultural area, overpopulated, with all the burdens of a heavy population and backward agriculture. To some extent, cane cultivation has helped it and also sugar factories.

> Question: Do you propose anything, in this respect, for the development of these backward areas?

Jawaharlal Nehru: That is one of our principle headaches. We should like to do something; we continually consider it, and I think we are going to do something, but it is difficult to pull them out of the rut they are in. It takes a little time. It is not difficult ultimately but it makes time. Whatever good we do naturally flows towards these who can take advantage of it more. Those who cannot take advantage of it easily, remain left behind. But I do believe that they are going to come up.

25. See item 203.

ANTI-NUCLEAR ARMS CONFERENCE

Jawaharlal Nehru: It represents an idea which is very important and to which I am much attached. But I have not the least notion what it will do. Of course it can pass a resolution and all that. Apart from that, what it will do I do not know.

Question: Sir, you invited Rajaji to attend this conference and was it at the initiative of the organisers of this conference?

Jawaharlal Nehru: That is correct. The organisers told me that Rajaji was not very anxious to attend the conference but hinted that he might come if I wanted him to attend, I wrote to him and said that I would be very happy if he came.[26]

HINDI OF AIR

Question: Can we have your views on the proposal to change the Hindi of AIR.

Jawaharlal Nehru: I do not quite know but I have been thoroughly dissatisfied with the Hindi of the AIR as it used to be. I think I know Hindi fairly well but it was beyond me—the Hindi of the AIR.

Question: How do you like its English?

(No reply)

Question: When it was beyond you, how was it tolerated for ten years under Dr Keskar's regime?

Jawaharlal Nehru: Because we are a very tolerant people.

Question: What about Dr Gopala Reddi?[27] Is he adopting a new policy with regard to language in the AIR at your instance?

Jawaharlal Nehru: At my instance? Well, I did suggest to him to look into this matter. And his Deputy Minister[28] is interested too.

26. See items 357-363.
27. B. Gopala Reddi, Minister of Information and Broadcasting.
28. Sham Nath, Deputy Minister in the Ministry of Information and Broadcasting.

Question: Would you like to see to it that there is onset of languages which will be equally acceptable to people in Punjab, Kashmir, the South and Bengal? What is intelligible to one is unintelligible to another.

Jawaharlal Nehru: The difficulty is that people take pride in not understanding anything.

Question: If you change Hindi of the AIR today, we will have to change the Hindi of the Constitution tomorrow?

Jawaharlal Nehru: You are quite right. We will have to. We propose to. It is a continuing process of a developing language. The development can be impeded by certain rigid ways of approach. As a matter of fact a language doesn't develop according to what some Hindi enthusiast or some Urdu enthusiast or I might say, it only helps it this way or that way. The real language develops if it is in touch with the people, not in touch with some literary academies only.

Question: Can you throw some light on Phizo's activities?

Jawaharlal Nehru: Mr Phizo? First of all, I do now know where he is. I have, of course, seen some reports about his having left Pakistan for the Western world, I am not sure at all. I think we worry ourselves too much about Mr Phizo and some newspapers in London give him far greater importance that he deserves.

Question: What is the interpretation that can be put on the escape of these people? Would it be some indication that these groups have broken up and each one is trying to escape aid behave in its own way or is there any organised movement behind it.

Jawaharlal Nehru: There are many explanations. One is that pressure on them is considerable and they want to escape that pressure or they wanted to meet Phizo in Pakistan.

Question: In view of the misunderstandings about your personal religious faith, would you like to elaborate this point?

Jawaharlal Nehru: I have written something about it in my books and I have written articles and I speak too. But I could hardly use a press conference for propaganda or for views on religion. Well, thank you.

2. To Taufiq Ahmad Nizami: Clarifying Ideology[29]

June 26, 1962

Dear Mr Nizami,[30]

Your letter of the 9th June came some time ago. I am sorry for the delay in answering it.

I do not like rigid and fixed dogmas about socialism and economic structures. Society is ever changing and, therefore, any approach that we make to it must be a flexible one. The Industrial Revolution has changed the face of life all over the world, and chiefly in the industrialised communities. With the coming of the atomic era and jet travel etc., vast changes have taken place and are going to take place.

Therefore, I feel that Marxism, though it throws some light on certain historical processes, is as a whole out of date today. As a matter of fact, Communism that is practiced in some countries is itself a marked variation from Marxism. It is natural for us to realise that a definition of society which was made over a hundred years ago and before the Industrial Revolution had developed, must be inadequate today.

I do not try to define socialism because any definition would make it rigid. I would say, however, that the objective to aim at is equal opportunity for all. Further, that this can only be attained by adopting modern techniques in science. This leads to a large measure of State control, and it is opposed to private monopolies and private concentration of wealth.

I do not know if this gives you an idea of what I think. I speak frequently on these subjects. Naturally in speaking to large crowds I have to make myself understood by them, and use simple language.

Yours sincerely,
Jawaharlal Nehru

29. Letter ; address: 3 English House, Aligarh Muslim University. PMO, File No. 2(285)/58-64-PMS, Vol.I, Sr. No. 41-A.
30. Nizami, an undergraduate student of AMU at this time, later taught political science in AMU and abroad, 1966-2006; Director, Centre for Nehru Studies, AMU, 2000-2006.

3. To Chief Ministers[31]

July 10, 1962

My dear Chief Minister,

It is almost eleven months now since I wrote to you what was supposed to be a fortnightly letter.[32] This long break has made it difficult for me to pick up the old threads again. I feel very guilty at this lapse of mine because I have always attached importance to the fortnightly letters I wrote to you and those which you wrote to me. We meet each other from time to time and occasionally write to each other on special subjects. Nevertheless, the sending of these fortnightly letters did create an additional bond between us which I valued. Therefore, the break that has occurred has been most unfortunate and something which I regret very much.

2. Why has this long break occurred? There was the election campaign[33] and then the elections themselves. Subsequently other matters followed; the formation of a new Government at the Centre, the election of the President and the Vice-President, and the formation of new Governments in the States.[34] Unfortunately, I did not keep well during this period and suffered from an indisposition which, though not serious, did affect my working capacity. And so month after month passed without my usual letter to you. There was, I think, some reason for my not keeping up my old routine, but none of the reasons I have indicated was adequate if I had really been anxious to write. The fact is that somehow the urge to write to you became much less and I could not easily develop the mood to do so. And so, heavily occupied as I was, I made this an excuse for not writing. You will forgive me, I hope. I see no point in sending you a letter full of trivial details which have no importance. I do not want to tell you of my programme and what I have been doing, nor do I want to repeat the news that appears in the papers. A letter, such as I want to write to you, if it has any relevance, should deal with matters which are not obvious, or should try to indicate the importance of something that has happened. It should be a link and a bond between us and our minds.

3. We talk of integration and consider it rightly as something of vital importance in India. That integration has to take place at all levels; beginning

31. Letter to Chief Ministers of all States and the Prime Minister of Jammu and Kashmir. PMS, File No. 25(30)/62-PM, Sr. No. 2 A. Also available in G. Pathasarathi (ed.), *Jawaharlal Nehru. Letters to Chief Ministers, 1958-1964,* Vol. 5 (New Delhi: Jawaharlal Nehru Memorial Fund, 1989), pp. 500-511.

32. On 5 August 1961, see SWJN/SS/70/item 8.

33. See SWJN/SS/74/items 66-91 and SWJN/SS/75/items 8-24.

34. See SWJN/SS/75/items 25-82 and SWJN/SS/76/items 14-41.

from the top between you and me and our respective Governments, in our Party structures, where there is often too great a tendency to form groups, and so on down to the mass of people.

4. Perhaps it was my indisposition, added to many other factors, that led to a certain unease in my mind and this again came in the way of my writing letters to you. I did not wish to convey the sense of unease to you, as a letter is likely to do to some extent.

[Personal Health]

5. First of all, I shall refer briefly to a subject of no great importance and yet one which has been talked about a great deal during the past few months. That is my health. I am sure that nothing serious has been or is the matter with it and doctors have assured me of this. I have always taken good care about it and led a fairly regular life. It is true that I tend to overtax my system by putting too much of a burden on it. My body has reacted well to this during all these years. Ultimately, however, the continuing strain brought about an accumulation of fatigue which led to my indisposition. This has been a warning to me not to overdo things in future. I have a dislike for ill-health. I do not like the idea of not keeping fit. I think it is everyone's duty to do so and not to complain all the time of ailments and weaknesses. In India, we are apt to talk a great deal about these ailments and one's ill-health. The whole atmosphere thus becomes rather depressing. One of my chief troubles during the last few months has been people asking me about my health and showing great concern about it.

[Importance of Development]

6. These last few months have been full of new developments which are noteworthy. I do not propose to weary you with an account of what has happened. Indeed I shall only refer to some important aspects of these developments. This letter is more to break this long period of not writing and to try to get into stride again. I hope to be more regular in my letters in future but I shall put a somewhat lesser aim before me, that is, instead of sending you fortnightly letters I shall try to write at the beginning of every month.

7. Among the many problems, national and international, that face us, the most important is that of our development according to the plans laid down for it. There is I find an element of disappointment even among our friends at the slow pace of progress and the many bottlenecks that have arisen. Those who are not our friends, whether in India or abroad, point to our failures and difficulties. Undoubtedly, there are these difficulties which make our burden all the heavier.

But I see no reason for dismay at the outlook, provided always that we remain stout of heart and do not waste our energy in internal conflict. We have set out on a journey and are well advanced on the way. I do not think anything that can happen can effectively stop our progress; it may occasionally delay it. We have learnt by and large to plan and to plan well. We have to learn to implement our plans equally well. Thus implementation and good administration are the bases of our progress. Good administration necessarily includes an administration at all levels which works with integrity and efficiency.

8. I should like to lay stress on this because on this depends the atmosphere we create for our work. Unfortunately, our administration, though very good in parts, is not uniformly so and there are far too many complaints of lack of integrity.[35] Our critics rejoice in repeating this all the time and perhaps they exaggerate a good deal. But because they exaggerate we should not take things lightly and remain complacent. We have to work with all our strength and energy to root out corruption and inefficiency, wherever they may exist. All Ministers, whether, at the Centre or in the States, have a special responsibility to this end.

[Foreign Aid]

9. Any rapid development necessitates a good deal of investment. The money for investment has largely to be raised in the country and partly, in the case of underdeveloped countries, by aid from abroad. There is no other way. The aid need not be free grants but should consist of loans and credits. That is how we have been progressing thus far and our people have borne this heavy burden. We must also express our gratitude to many friendly countries who have helped and aided us in many ways. The fact, however, remains that the main burden must be borne by our own people. The moment we shirk this burden and imagine that others will carry it for us and thus grow complacent, we have basically lost the race.

10. Apart from the fact that too great a dependence on others is dangerous even for our independence and freedom of action, real progress depends upon the spirit we create in the country on self-reliance.

11. I refer to these matters because we are faced with a set of circumstances which may materially reduce the aid we might get from abroad. This will add to our difficulties and yet perhaps, from a long-term view, this may be for our good because it will force us to think in terms of doing things ourselves rather than relying on others. Fortunately, we have advanced industrially and technologically enough almost to make everything that we need here. It may

35. For example, see SWJN/SS/76/items 141-142, 163, 165 and appendix 8.

be that what we make will be a little more expensive. Even so, if we make it in our own country, it is more advantageous for us. So I am not altogether unhappy at the greater difficulties we have to face in regard to foreign aid. Of course, I would like to have as much of it as we need. But the price for it will be too great if we lose our sense of self-reliance and begin to depend too much on others.

12. This dilemma faces us at every step. We have naturally and rightly, tried to get as much aid in the shape of long-term loans and credits from friendly countries as possible. We have made it clear that this aid must have no strings attached to it. But it is equally clear that where there is financial dependence, this might affect our larger policies to some extent. I think it is true that those who have helped us have not attached any strings to their aid and we must be grateful to them for the help they have given. It is not right that we should feel annoyed if that help does not come when we expect it or is less than our expectations. Whatever is given to us with goodwill, we should be thankful for it. Our Finance Minister[36] has gone abroad to explain our position to those who might help and I am sure his visits will produce some results. What these results are likely to be, I cannot say. It is clear, however, that we cannot barter our freedom of action for the sake of aid. That would be losing something very valuable which cannot be measured in terms of financial aid. Our Finance Minister fully realises this, as we all do.

13. Another point with which the Finance Minister will deal is the question of the European Common Market and its effect upon us if the United Kingdom joins it, as it is likely to do. It is not for us to advise the United Kingdom but we are entitled to point out the consequences on us in case our export markets are limited. We talk of aid, but trade is much better than aid. The Finance Minister will be meeting the countries of the European Common Market. It is right that we should deal with them directly and not merely through the United Kingdom.[37]

[MIG Purchase]

14. This question of aid has arisen rather unexpectedly in connection with the proposal by us to buy Russian supersonic fighters, the MIGs. We have not made any definite proposal about this matter but, owing to pressures on us because of the policies adopted by Pakistan and China, our Defence Advisers are anxious that we should strengthen our position. To buy modern weapons is

36. Morarji Desai.
37. About his visit abroad in 1962, see Morarji Desai, *The Story of My Life*, Vol. II (Delhi: Macmillan India, 1974) pp. 181-184.

an expensive undertaking and we cannot indulge in it for too long. Therefore, we thought of manufacturing them ourselves and it was the relative ease of manufacturing the MIGs in India that turned our attention to them, apart from their comparative cost. This has created a furore in the United Kingdom and in the United States. I did not expect this as I thought that foreign governments cannot object to a commercial transaction which we consider favourable to us. But the fact is that the political aspect of this transaction has affected these countries greatly. We have made it clear to them that we cannot limit our choice because of these political considerations when we are thinking only of a commercial transaction. However, we have sent a team to England to enquire what they have to offer and the terms of their offer. The important aspect continues to be facility of manufacture in India. It is possible that our expert team may subsequently go to Russia to find out what the possibilities there are. After investigating all the proposals we shall have to come to a decision. That decision will take into consideration all the factors and will inevitably be based on what is good for India in the short run as well as the long run.

15. This involves the possibility of financial aid and credits being cut down even to a great extent. This will be hard on us, but I have no doubt that there is no other choice for us. If we change our broader policies because of pressures from abroad, that may well mean a basic change in those policies which we are not prepared to accept, even though the consequences may be hard for us.

16. When this was mentioned in Parliament by me, there was almost unanimous approval of what I said.[38] That was gratifying. There was a tendency also to blame or at least to criticise the USA and the UK for their pressure upon us in this matter as well as for the attitude they had taken up in regard to Goa and Kashmir. We feel strongly on these subjects and are convinced that we are in the right. Nevertheless, I hope that the friendly relations which exist between the USA, UK and ourselves will not be affected by these developments. I want to lay stress on this because it is not right for us to blame others if they do not help us according to our wishes. They have helped us greatly in the past and we should be thankful to them for it. Unfortunately, an element of the cold war creeps in when we fall out in any matter with other countries. I would earnestly hope that we should resist this temptation and continue to have friendly feelings with these great countries even though they might not fall in with our wishes occasionally.[39]

38. See item 432 pp. 708-710.

39. On the MIG purchase issue, see items 381-382.

[China and Pakistan]

17. This element of the cold war is already very much in evidence in our relations with China and Pakistan. With China, there has been a spate of strongly-worded statements on both sides; with Pakistan also our present relations are greatly strained. Believing as we do that we are completely right in our attitudes towards China and Pakistan, I am convinced that we should avoid the language of cold war in dealing with them. In no event does that help and we have to take special care about this matter. After all, the only sensible thing to aim at is for a solution of our problems with these countries and peaceful relations. We may get angry occasionally on what they do to us. But still we have to keep the ultimate objective in view. We have to strengthen our military position when they threaten us. Even so, we must realise that it will be a tragedy for us to have military operations against each other. While we keep our powder dry and are ready for emergencies, we should strive for a peaceful settlement. Anything else with Pakistan would be a tragedy not only for the two countries but for the peoples of these countries who are so closely allied to each other. With China, our contacts are not great, but the consequences of our conflict are very far-reaching.

18. But apart from these considerations, I thank that the policy we have pursued or attempted to pursue is essentially based on always trying for peaceful solutions and of avoidance of war. Peaceful solutions are not furthered by the language of war which is embodied in what is called the cold war. We have seen this on a much larger scale on the world's stage. It is the cold war which has bedevilled every attempt to find a solution of world problems. Behind the cold war lie fear, suspicion, distrust and anger. We must try not to fall a victim to these emotions and passions while, at the same time, doing everything to protect our national interests. Even from the point of view of national interests, a peaceful approach is obviously desirable.

19. We have recently seen in our relations with Pakistan how one bad act leads to another from the other side and something much worse happens. This again leads to excitement on our side and something undesirable happens which produces its own reactions in Pakistan. If this kind of thing is allowed to continue, then the situation might well get out of hand on both sides of the Indo-Pakistan frontier and produce disastrous results. A special responsibility, therefore, lies on political and other leaders as well as newspapers to prevent these deplorable happenings and developments and to realise that there can be no such thing as reprisals against innocent people.

20. On our frontier with China-Tibet, we have gradually been building up our position and increasing our outposts in Ladakh etc. The building of

mountain roads, which is still going on, has helped us. The result is that we are in a somewhat more advantageous position than we were a year or two ago. Even so, it would be unwise for us to indulge in any action. The Chinese Government, realising that we are strengthening our position and weakening theirs, has lately become more aggressive in tone in its statements made to us. I do not know what this signifies, and we have to be wide awake and careful.

21. But I would repeat that, apart from any high morality, it is the strictest practical good sense for us not to fall into the trap of cold war in regard to Pakistan and China. Even if Governments are, we must not think that the people are our enemies.

22. In Pakistan, strange things are happening. The coming up of the new Constitution, very limited as it is, has opened the flood gates of criticism and agitation. A military rule and such agitations are not compatible. The position is, therefore, essentially a fluid one. In East Pakistan, more especially, there is discontent. Some authorities there want to turn people's minds to anger and hatred against India in order to lessen this discontent against themselves. We must not fall into this trap and act in a way which creates ill will between peoples.

23. Looking round to our neighbours, we should feel thankful that we have escaped many of their troubles. We have a Constitutional Democratic Government functioning with a large measure of success. We have plans for development which already have produced good results and which promise greater results in the future inspite of the difficulties that face us. This can hardly be said about our neighbours. We have goodwill for these neighbour countries of ours and wish them progress. Our progress certainly is not dependent on their remaining backward.

24. Meanwhile, it should be remembered that the most important question of all is that of disarmament. Unless some effective results are achieved by the Disarmament Committee at Geneva, the outlook for the world is bleak indeed. Thus far the only success achieved is in drafting a preamble which, as far as it goes, is satisfactory. But obviously much more is needed. Peace congresses are held and I suppose they do some good work. But there appears to be an attempt in them to gain a political advantage and the quest for peace is often connected with warlike language. Yet we must hope that peace will triumph in the end.

Yours sincerely,
Jawaharlal Nehru

4. To Mohan Singh: Succession to Nehru[40]

July 15, 1962

Dear Shri Mohan Singhji,

Thank you for your letter of the 13th July which I have read with interest.[41] I confess I do not understand all this gossip as to who will succeed me. I cannot help this talk even though it appears quite pointless to me.

We have all to think of the future. Indeed, all our planning is for the future. But the future is the outcome of our present-day activities. Therefore, what we do in the present is important. I have no intention at present of retiring, and I believe I am quite fit enough to carry on for some time. What will happen after I leave is more than I can say. But I have faith in the Indian people, and there are many competent men who can undertake responsible positions in India.

Your suggestion for me to appoint a team to shoulder my responsibilities has no particular meaning. As a matter of fact, my responsibilities are shared by members of my Cabinet, each one of whom is not only in full charge of his portfolio but also shares in the formulation of general policy. That is the essence of Cabinet Government which we have. As for my work in the international sphere, that is an outcome of my work for India. I cannot separate the two. If we succeed in India in any measure, that will have its effect on the influence we exercise on the rest of the world. Otherwise my personality will not make much difference.[42]

Yours sincerely,
[Jawaharlal Nehru]

40. Letter to the Deputy General Manager, Punjab National Bank Ltd, Parliament Street, New Delhi. Sent from Nandi Hills, Mysore State. NMML, T.T. Krishnamachari Papers, File 1962. Also available in the JN Collection.
41. See appendix 62.
42. See item 5.

5. To T.T. Krishnamachari: Succession to Nehru[43]

July 15, 1962

My dear T.T.,

I enclose a letter from Mohan Singh, the Deputy General Manager of the Punjab National Bank.[44] I do not quite remember who he is, although I must have met him.

I am sending this letter to you as well as a copy of my reply, as I thought these might amuse you.[45]

Yours sincerely,
Jawaharlal Nehru

43. Letter to the Minister without Portfolio. Sent from Nandi Hills, Mysore State. NMML, T.T. Krishnamachari Papers, File 1962, Auto.
44. See appendix 62.
45. See item 4.

II. NATIONAL INTEGRATION COUNCIL

6. Verbatim Report—I[1]

A-1 to A-2[2]

Jawaharlal Nehru: Friends, I am grateful to you and especially to those who have come from other parts of India to Delhi for this Council meeting. Delhi is not in good climatic condition at the present moment, and it must be a trial for some of you for turning up here and for staying here for a day or two. Also, I must apologise to you for the great delay in holding a meeting of this Council. It is seven months or thereabouts since we held a meeting of the Integration Council. Well, the reason for the delay was obvious. The elections intervened, and it was considered a little difficult to hold this Council meeting then. It might perhaps have been held; it would have been good if it had been so held. But we thought it better to hold it after the elections were over. This is the main reason for the delay. There are other minor reasons too. Anyhow, we meet today. And apart from the members of the Council who have been nominated some time ago, I have invited two or three others who technically are not members of the Council but whose presence here, I think, we shall all welcome. One is the General Secretary of the Hindu Mahasabha, Shri Bishanchander Seth.[3] The political parties which have been included in the Council are specifically said to be in Parliament. And in Parliament, the Hindu Mahasabha, at the time when this appointment took place, hardly had a party—one representative—and so, he was not made a member of the Council. But he represents a certain group of thinking in this country, and so I invited him here today. Then, Shri Asoka Mehta[4] is another who has been invited. He is not in Parliament now. A colleague of his, Shri Ganga Sharan Sinha,[5] is a Member. And I thought that Shri Asoka Mehta's presence here would be helpful.

1. Verbatim record, 2 June 1962, of the discussions held at Vigyan Bhavan from 9.30 a.m. It was chaired by Nehru; following the editorial practice of this series, his name has been substituted for Chairman. MHA, File No. 6/36/62-OL.
2. Centred sub-headings A-1 etc. indicate the pagination of the original.
3. Seth was elected to the Lok Sabha in 1962 from Etah, UP, on the Hindu Mahasabha ticket. The spelling of his name, as given in *Lok Sabha Who's Who 1962* (p. 473), has been retained throughout this document.
4. PSP leader.
5. Rajya Sabha MP, Independent, from Bihar.

A-3

Now, I do not know how you would like to proceed with our work. The last meeting of the Conference laid down certain general prepositions and specific things too which we wanted to do.[6] Something to that effect has been done, but I do not know how far it has been satisfactory. The Secretariat has prepared some papers which have been distributed. The papers are supposed to give facts, etc., not opinions. I think you would like to know what the facts are. And I imagine that most of us have got the experience of the general election, and it is generally agreed that certain trends in this general election were not satisfactory from the point of view of integration, apart from other points of view. Stress was laid on destructive factors and so on. I imagine that we have one or two proposals in the shape of resolutions that have been sent to us, or suggestions. I think we might have a general discussion about the developments since we last met and lay particular stress on particular points this morning, and towards the end of our morning session, we might determine the rest of the agenda—what are the things we should take up. If you agree, we shall proceed in this way. Is that more or less agreed to?

Members: Yes.

Jawaharlal Nehru: Shri Ramaswami Aiyar.[7]

C.P. Ramaswami Aiyar: Mr Prime Minister, I am grateful to you for having summoned this meeting after the general elections because they have furnished some examples of what may be called the right political procedure. I do not mean to say that there have been no complaints regarding the election and the methods pursued during the election but, by and large,

A-4

I think it can be stated without fear of much contradiction that the country at large has displayed an equanimity and poise which are worthy of all praise. And talking generally, the elections have demonstrated that the experiment of democracy has really found firm foundations in this country. I do not

6. See SWJN/SS/71/item 68.
7. C.P. Ramaswami Aiyar, Chairman of Hindu Religious Endowments Commission, 1960-62.

propose to enlarge on that topic much further but there are few general observations which may be pertinent in this connection which, with your leave, I shall advance.

The first point that I desire to make is that judging from the papers that have been placed before us and the discussions in the press and on public platforms, there is a certain amount of impatience manifested in many quarters regarding what is called the question of emotional or national integration. I think myself that the problems now facing the country are long-term problems and not problems which can be disposed of almost with a kind of all-embracing topical enthusiasm. Let me analyse the factors that are present in the country. It cannot be forgotten that it used to be called in the language of the law "status as opposed to contract"; the status was profoundly modified in this country and the emergence of personality, of individuality and of ideals like self-determination and self-expression became evident and plain immediately before the formation of the new Constitution of India, and the processes are continuing thereafter. Now, that undoubtedly made a tremendous change in what may be called the general complexion, political and social, of the country. The breakdown of the Hindu Joint Family System, the legislative, and other efforts are now bringing what may be called the cult of personality into a very sharp perspective. These factors are there and cannot be ignored or forgotten. While that process has been going on, another parallel, but not wholly parallel, process

A-5

is also in evidence arising from problems like those arising from the socialistic pattern of society and what may be called the reallocation of patterns of society along new lines of conception of human ingenuity and human progress and human evaluation. Now, therefore, we have had two violent changes—or three changes—facing the country, firstly the changes in the domestic law, the changes in social and political pattern arising from the emergence of a democratic ideal and along with that, the cult of personality. A great philosopher, Hume, has stated that the present day is an age which is the crisis of the individual soul.[8] That crisis was very much in the forefront in the beginning of the era which culminated in the foundation of the Indian Constitution and similar Constitutions in various other newly started democracies in the world. But soon afterwards

8. David Hume.

the idea of socialism began to develop, which required a new coherence, a new building up of society. And these are the conflicts which are now facing the country. In this posture of affairs, my own feeling in the matter is—and I advance my feeling with great hesitation and with a view more to invite discussion than to dogmatise—is that the problems of today are long-term problems which can be solved only by the proper organisation of two things, namely, the press and the educational agencies—the press, by which I mean all methods of popular dissemination of knowledge—the press, the platform, the television, the radio, all that kind of thing. These have to adjust themselves towards a new harmony, free from all passions and free from all subversive and retrogressive ideals.

B.1

The second aspect of the matter which I wish to present for a moment is that the problems of today can only be solved by a reorganisation and reorientation of education, meaning by education the widest possible way to disseminate the true and right values of humanity, through school, college and all like sources of public dissemination of information and enlightenment.

Having said this and having posed therefore that these problems cannot be approached in a spirit of impatience or of haste but must be through a kind of a generally well designed and well-conceived programme of enlightenment of the press, and by the press and by the reorientation and reorganisation of education, I wish to say no more except this that we have perceived quite recently some subversive forces rearing their heads. That again, to my mind, is a temporary phenomenon. A similar phenomenon has arisen in my part of the country. Before this, really some seven or eight centuries ago, we have had similar processes of what may be called apparent subversions threatening the foundations of society, which have had some kind of vogue for some time, but the general common sense and the equipoise and balance which have characterised Hindu society all through have counteracted those influences. I am not therefore a pessimist; I am an irredeemable optimist, and I would say that the problems before this Council are problems of education and of popular instruction and dissemination of the right values and the right poises of life.

Thank you.

B.2

Jawaharlal Nehru: Perhaps those who speak might, apart from any general observations, discuss what has been done and what has not been done.

C.D. Deshmukh:[9] Sir, what I have to say is, I think, largely procedural. To begin with, I should like to congratulate the Ministry concerned for following up some of the suggestions which were made in the meeting of the National Integration Conference in the time that has elapsed since the Conference was held because they have been impartially utilised in placing before us a picture of the implementation that has been attempted, and when we take up the agenda I have no doubt that we shall go through each of these items individually. But what I think is lacking is a kind of general assessment of the situation. I do not know who would be considered responsible for making such an assessment. I should imagine that if all the Chief Ministers are members now of this Council, I hope they will give us some picture of what their reading of the present situation is because I think it is very essential that as the Council proceeds with its work, it must survey the current position in order to be able to reappraise either the facts of the situation or revenue the remedies to that we are going to adopt.

There was some reference made by you, Sir, to the undesirable trends which were apparent in the recent elections. The precise connection with national integration or otherwise, I think, should be brought out by someone who is generally in possession of the facts, or has observed the situation there.

As a result of what was said in the Parliament there has been a certain amount of apprehension in

B.3

regard to a new direction in which these disintegrating tendencies have shown themselves, namely the desire for certain parts of the Union to secede. No one believes that in the form in which the proposal was put forward, it can ever be regarded as a practicable proposition, but what the Council might be interested in would be the inwardness of the situation from that part of the country, why exactly it is that such a claim is made or such a proposition is even incidentally brought forward in the legislature.

9. Former Finance Minister, now Vice Chancellor of Delhi University, and President of the India International Centre.

I was wondering whether the Chief Minister of Madras[10] would be able to shed some light on this particular matter.

The third thing which is connected with the assessment of the situation is this: I think special efforts should be made to arrange projects of research, not through political channels but through the universities or cultural bodies, projects of research which would concern themselves again with investigating the situation as it exists, in regard to national integration or disruptive forces, and to present the findings. It is essentially a matter of team work, that is to say, it will not be taken up by any particular person of a university and therefore it is likely to be overlooked. In any case each university faculty or department has its own current project of research, which means that they are engaged in some of the more traditional academic projects for the next year or two, and it seems to me that the Planning Commission ought to give special attention to this as a special project. It may be that they might find someone in the universities or a body of people in the universities or in a university which would take it up or, say, four universities in a

B.4

region, or it might be undertaken by a body even like the India International Centre. They have set up a Research Council and I feel—here I speak as President of the Centre—that if they are assisted, they would be able to organise a research project on national integration or what the sociological or psychological situation is, or what people feel about it, what they say so that we shall have many more facts than just qualitative impressions of what is happening or what are almost automatic reactions of something abnormal that happens from time to time, like the demand for secession on behalf of the DMK. It seems to me that it is only then that a process is set at work and the country seems to awaken again to the problem, whereas what I am arguing is that there should be a study of all the factors involved.

Then there is the question of regional development on which the Planning Commission have given us a note. I know that in the Faculty of Economics of the Delhi University Dr Ganguli[11] has made a special study of some of these things. I was wondering whether the Planning Commission could not assign to him a special study from an academic point of view of what the implications of this question of regional development are.

10. K. Kamaraj.
11. B.N. Ganguli.

So these are some of the procedural matters which I thought I would raise.

Then another matter is the sentence here which says that the Secretariat does not know but it presumes that the Sarva Seva Sangh has taken action in regard to a mass campaign for signing a pledge. I think they ought to take a little more active

B.5

interest in this; in other words they should have addressed the Sarva Seva Sangh and asked them whether they proposed to do this, when they proposed to do it or whether they have dropped the idea. It has to be pursued a little more actively. In other words that brings me to the question of what sort of secretariat the National Integration Council has or whether it is just done, whether it is taken in the stride by officials of the Home Ministry or whether someone has been specially asked to look after this work, that is to say, whether there is a cell which will concern itself specifically with matters connected with the affairs and the deliberations of the National Integration Council.

That is all that I would like to say at this stage.

Jawaharlal Nehru: A new secretariat has come into being which is really the Home Ministry and some officials function there as a secretariat.

As for what you said, as for the general assessment of the situation, the idea was that the Chief Ministers and other members of the Council should give their assistance.

C.D. Deshmukh: I am suggesting that, that when they speak they would try and give some general assessment of the situation.

E.M.S. Namboodiripad:[12] Sir, I have given a note to the Secretary[13] underlining the need and the urgency to tackle the communal problem. This, to my mind, is the most important and dangerous development that has taken place during the last few months. As a matter of fact, this had become

12. Former Chief Minister of Kerala and now CPI, General Secretary.
13. The Home Secretary, V. Viswanathan.

B.6

a serious problem even at the time when the National Integration Conference met in September and reported.[14] You will remember that in the speech delivered by Mr Ajoy Ghosh[15] he had underlined the importance of this and he had also called at the end of his speech for a nation-wide mass campaign for the unity of the country and against communalism. Unfortunately nothing could be done at that time. But immediately after that Conference certain dangerous developments took place, I believe in Aligarh, Moradabad and certain other parts,[16] and recently, during the last few weeks, certain dangerous developments have also taken place in Malda.[17]

C-1

Now, I am of the view that this should not be lightly brushed aside because, on the one hand, this creates difficulties in our own country—this is slowly spreading to other parts also—and worse than that, it is also worsening the relations between India and Pakistan. The Malda developments were followed by Rajshahi developments.[18]

Sir, I do not think it would serve any useful purpose by saying that the incidents in Rajshahi were worse than those in Malda. There is no use comparing the two. But what happened in Malda and what happened in the other parts of India before that are sufficiently serious. I would, therefore, suggest that priority should be given to these problems like language, education, etc. At the present moment, of course, this appears to be the most important problem.

When I come to the merits of the question, I feel that this should be tackled at the political level. I am afraid that the papers circulated to us by the secretariat show a tendency of tackling the problems at the administrative level. Of course, many of these problems have to be tackled at the administrative level, I do not deny the need for them. But problems like communalism, separatism, etc., cannot be tackled by the administrative officers or the Ministers alone. Here is, for example, the mechanism for

14. 28 September to 1 October 1961 at Vigyan Bhavan, New Delhi. See SWJN/SS/71/item 68.
15. General Secretary of the CPI, 1951-January 1962.
16. See SWJN/SS/72/items 60-71 and appendices 7 & 16.
17. See items 44-45, 49-51.
18. See items 51-53, 70-71.

implementation of decision from national integration proposed here. That is, in the States the Chief Minister is assisted by the Chief Secretary, who in his turn, will be assisted by a Special Officer. This is the mechanism suggested. Such a mechanism, of course, is all right in so far as the question pertains to the extent to which the three-language formula and other things in the educational fields are concerned.

C-2

For these things this is necessary. But when you tackle such problems as communal tension or tendency towards separatism, etc., these cannot be tackled by such a mechanism. I think it is necessary that on the one hand bodies like that Integration Council should be formed at the State and lower level as well; besides that I would also suggest that some steps should be taken at the organisational level, as between the representatives of the various political parties and social organisations, to have such problems tackled in greater detail. These are some of the suggestions that I would like to make at the moment.

Zakir Husain:[19] Mr Prime Minister, I have heard with great interest the observations that have been made so far, and I am in full agreement with the remarks made by my friend, Dr Deshmukh, about the need for impartial research in problems of integration. But as I agree with that proposal, the thing that occurs to me is the sense of urgency in this matter. That is most important. Research is very good. It is essential. And for the dissemination of the objectives that you will have to follow, that would be very useful; but a greater sense of urgency, I think, is needed in regard to this problem of integration.

At the moment, after the Conference on integration, it seems to me that we have supplied to the people a slogan which helps them to escape thinking, which also helps them to escape action. It has begun to speak of integration without meaning much. They are today thinking even differently about this problem. That seems to me to be obvious from some of the things that I have seen in these reports. For instance, the matter is put into such a wide context that the real objective of

19. Vice-President of India.

C-3

integration is forgotten. As Sir C.P. Ramaswami has said, education is of absolute importance in this behalf. Now, going round the country my own feeling is that education today is not helping us at all in the creation of any outlook on life. It is an absolutely colourless, mercenary sort of activity that is going on. It gives us absolutely no colour in life at any stage, primary, secondary or university.

Now there are proposals to revise text books. Welcome steps have been taken by the Ministry of Education to do that. But that problem also has been set in a very general setting. If you read the proposals about the revision of text books, you will find that they are proposals which would be taken up by any country which is absolutely integrated, which has no problem of disintegration, which is not facing any definite problems in that behalf. It is a general education problem of relating text books to the curriculum, of revising the curriculum and so on. There is not even a mention about the slogan "integration" except of the vertical integration, which is integration of the curriculum of one class to the class above. It has nothing to do with the problem of integration. Therefore, I feel that if we had urgently taken up this matter in every text book, in the teaching in University and school organisation, we would have proceeded in a different way and probably achieved better results.

Also in the matter of communal tensions, in the matter of languages, I find that everything is said to be all right. With regard to language, I am afraid, it is not. People are very sensitive about it, sometimes sentimental wrongly, absolutely, misinformedly, but they are sensitive. And unless you take it up seriously and remove that misapprehension, you have not done anything with regard to

C-4

integration. It might be perfectly all right on paper that orders have been issued, but what have those orders resulted in? Therefore, if there is a greater sense of urgency about the thing, we would tackle problems a little differently. I would plead for that.

K.M. Munshi:[20] Mr Prime Minister, Sir, I am very much oppressed with the fact that the question of integration is being discussed very eloquently

20. Swatantra Party leader; founder president, Bharatiya Vidya Bhavan.

on paper and in newspapers but the process of disintegration is proceeding apace in the country. During the last few months such of us as have had occasion to tour the country and see the way that disintegrating factors were thrown up during the elections and exploited by all parties—I do not want to share the blame—for the purpose of winning elections, they show clearly that it is rather dangerous to take an optimistic view of integration being achieved as a long term process.

The slogan of secession which has come up is the logical extreme which we should have expected of the regional chauvinism which has been rampant in this country throughout in most of the States, and though the Chief Ministers are anxious to do their best in the interest of integration, the pressures of regional chauvinism coming up from the party from below is so great that in actual administrative practice they are not able to resist them. It may be all right in reports submitted to the Governments or to the Chief Ministers, but at lower levels there has been considerable encouragement to disintegrating factors. But more than that the point which the Vice-President has just now made, I may elaborate a little.

C-5

To my mind, the greatest problem of integration revolves round the fragmentation of the academic world in India today. The national consciousness in India, let us be frank, is not inherited from ages past. It has been the product of the unity of the educated Indians in English medium Universities for 150 years, and it was there in the academic world which gave not only national consciousness but national values and to a large extent gave us the potentialities to win freedom in course of time. Now, within fifteen years of freedom, the Universities have seen to it that the intellectuals of this country re-fragmented. I am putting it in rather strong terms. Apart from official reports I can give you instances of my own experience in such parts of the country which I have seen. Today a graduate of one University is a stranger in another University. There was a time when we English-knowing people from one end of the country to the other used to feel one. Take my friend, Sir C.P. Ramaswami. When we were students we never felt strangers to each other because of the English and the Sanskrit that we knew. We never knew that one was a Madrasi and the other was a Gujerati or a Bombayite. Today a graduate from Gujarat feels isolated from a graduate of Bombay within two years. I am only giving an instance. I do not want to blame anybody. The fact remains today that having taken care to drive out English and having replaced it by all kinds of experiments of English and Hindi, of one thing or the other, we are going towards a stage when we would like to have fourteen sub-nations and not one nation. I have seen new graduates coming up. They have nothing in common. The graduate of Gujarat, when he goes to Bombay or transfers himself from one college to another, feels entirely a stranger because of the absence of English medium. There

[TEACHING ENGLISH IN REGIONAL LANGUAGES]

You Said It

By LAXMAN

I knew someone was bound to come up with that suggestion. He's saying, ". . . . English is essential, I admit, but ways and means should be found at once to teach it in the regional languages . . . .!"

(From *The Times of India*, 3 July 1952, p. 1)

C-6

is complete absence of English in the University of Gujarat. Similarly with regard to Hindi I do not want to say anything. But these things are happening all over the country. Now what will happen if a graduate from Madras University is not able to feel anything in common with the graduate from the Delhi University or from Punjab or anywhere else. Therefore, the first and most urgent problem is the problem of grappling with the idea of hurriedly displacing English by Hindi or other regional languages. We have had the Radhakrishnan Commission. We have had numerous suggestions. I appeal to you, please do not displace English hurriedly. Displace it by Hindi whenever the time comes for it. In the process of displacing English we have created a complete fragmentation of the academic world of India. Unless we restore it integration is not possible.

Sir, riots and tensions are not created by the ignorant layman. It is created by the educated man. It is fostered by the educated man. It is fostered by the graduate who is brought up in an atmosphere of regional chauvinism. Therefore, the first problem is not merely education—it can be a broader viewpoint—integration will only depend upon the unity and the solidarity of the University, educated men in this country. It is through him that will flow the other unities. Therefore, my first submission to this Integration Council is that they should take up this question first.

The University Grants Commission has a provision already that policies could be laid down by the Centre and could be followed by the UGC in respect of universities. What is the use of appointing commission after commission to consider the same question over and

C-7

over again? I am for Hindi as anyone else in this country. My views are very well known. I was one of the small groups who fought for a place for Hindi in the Constitution. I do not despair to say that we shall see Hindi some day as the national language. But new questions have arisen and if we pursue this policy of giving liberty to the universities of adopting Hindi or English or regional languages, you can take it from me that there will be two countries, if not more, in this country, one Hindi-speaking belt and the other English-speaking or regional speaking belt and you will not have the solidarity that you are striving for. That is my clear perception which I want to put before this Council.

The next point which I would like to touch upon at this stage is about the position of this National Integration Council. What is going to be the position of the Council?

D-1

It is an all-party instrument, national instrument for the purpose of fostering integration. When that is so, integration must be made into an all-party platform. That is my submission. We should remove the issue of integration from the battlefield of party politics. Unless we do that, we will not be able to secure what we want. For instance, take the question of secessionists in the South. It is a very sinister movement. I am not inclined to take it as a light affair which will not catch if proper steps are not taken. I am only giving you one instance. Therefore, Sir, the question of integration must be removed from party platforms to the platform of the Integration Conference or the Council as the case may be. This must be above party politics. If that had been done, we would have achieved a great success in achieving integration. For instance, today the Council cannot merely become a registering body and it cannot be said that the Home Ministry sets up certain things and such a body has done this. But what is the Conference supposed to do? It must in its own way survey the integrating and disintegrating forces, of course with the material supplied by the other people. It should discuss frankly and freely things with the Chief Ministers, not as Chief Ministers but as members of some national body, as to how deviations are being made and how they can be resisted and, above all, we can release an atmospheric pressure which will enable the Governments, the Administrations and the Chief Ministers to resist the chauvinistic pressure and all that.

Something has been said about caste and communal passions. They are there and we are not going to remove them. Elections have shown that they are living factors so much so that about panchayats the note says clearly

D-2

that they are a real danger but you cannot remove them because they are deeply embedded in our social and political life. Such communal and caste passions can only be stopped if the integration forces in the whole country are so powerful that one feels ashamed to call oneself a member of a particular caste or a particular creed. It was so during the Gandhian days, I remember very well. One was ashamed to call oneself belonging to a particular creed or caste. That was so because a moral atmosphere was created in favour of national unity. Now unless that is created without delay and on that level, it is very difficult to pass resolutions and get rid of communal passions. This is a long-term process and communal passions can be overcome by constant law and order forces and educational and other forces. But more dangerous than them, I think, is the regional chauvinism which is leading and which is going to lead to greater disasters unless we wake up in time. That is my submission. Thank you, Sir.

Asoka Mehta: Mr Prime Minister, Sir, almost immediately after our Conference we had serious communal disturbances in Uttar Pradesh. At that time I had written to the Home Minister requesting him that a meeting of the Council be called. I had made that request because I felt it was necessary for us to sift whatever evidence was available and assess as to what the forces were that were responsible for the outbreak of those riots. If I remember aright, Sir, even in the UP Legislature more than one assessment was offered and it appeared as if the responsibility was either of the Administration or of certain political parties. In matters of such paramount importance where

D-3

party positions are taken up and it becomes well-nigh impossible to find out who really was responsible for this kind of dangerous disturbances, I think this Council should have the opportunity to step in, really look into the matter and find out where the fault lies, not so much to blame anyone but to see that such faults are corrected. It was an important occasion but, Sir, I am sorry that it was not fully availed of to make this Council more effective.

Sir, we have to approach this problem, as has been pointed out, in three ways. There will be administrative measures; there will be educational measures and cultural measures; and there will also have to be political measures. Now that the elections are over we have an opportunity to find out to what extent political forces are responsible for fostering either national integration or national disintegration. Administrative measures, cultural and educational measures, we can think of even after six months or one year. Of course, they have to be thought of as early as possible, but it may not always be possible to find out what political forces are at work. Probably the elections every five years provide us the best opportunity for an incisive political assessment to find out what political measures can be taken or administrative measures need to be taken. There is no doubt that just on the eve of elections in order to help certain parties in the elections certain forces were stirred up. In the elections also caste or communal or certain other disintegrating forces were supported or strengthened. We had tried to amend our electoral law to see that such mischief did not go unpunished but even that electoral law has not helped us. If such political forces had not been stirred up, then we need not have bothered about them.

D-4

I should think this particular meeting should devote more of its time in a frank manner to see why these forces came up, what they did, what mischief they did and what we have done about it and whether our law can do anything in the matter. If the law is powerless—I do not think the law can be powerless—then what are the other methods at our disposal? On the last occasion, Sir, we drew up a fragmentary code for political parties. That code is of a negative character. I say it is of a negative character for this reason that it lays down certain suggestions whereby a political party can be prevented from doing certain things which might stir up serious trouble in the country. But perhaps it may be useful to consider whether a positive code is not possible. Law by itself will not succeed unless we have that kind of a positive code. I agree with Mr Munshi when he says that ultimately the forces of disintegration can be held at bay only if this Council is able to release the forces of integration which are stronger. And at least in the last seven months we have not been able to do that. Whether administrative measures and educational measures alone will be able to counter the rot that has set in is a matter that needs to be considered. I believe it is something like that paradox—what is woven in the day is unwoven in the night. To a considerable extent the other forces seem to be unweaving it. I do not know whether the Council at a meeting like this ought to have any sub-committee which will come to grips with the problem. Whether it is a problem of organisation or whether it is a problem of communal tensions or of regionalism, in the last analysis these problems seem to get aggravated because of the tremendous strength they derive from the political climate. To what extent, therefore, the political climate has to reorganise itself is a matter to which we could not give much attention in the last conference. I do not think we can do

D-6

that even on this occasion. But I feel that however difficult and however uninviting the subject may be, this subject is of crucial importance and it is a very difficult subject. I would request once again to see whether some machinery can be delivered whereby we can look into this matter. Thank you, Sir.

Sampurnanand:[21] Sir, I agree that the situation to which Mr Munshi has referred exists but it seems to me that sometimes in trying to tackle problems of this kind we involve ourselves in a kind of vicious circle. All that Mr Munshi has said about the great service rendered by people who have received English education is correct. No sensible person asks for any immediate elimination of English from our courses of study, particularly at the university stage. But we must be clear in our minds about what we feel about it. We, I mean the Central Government, the State Governments, this Council or this Conference, are not the only people who are any kind of final authority on this question. There is the general public and we must take cognizance of the feelings and the sentiments which have swayed in the post-independence period. There has been and there is still going to be a very considerable expansion of primary education leading to expansion of secondary education. Then there are members of the Legislature, and I am sure there will be pressures about giving a more important place to regional languages and Hindi. These pressures cannot easily be resisted by Governments or by this Conference. We cannot ignore those pressures. Then, Sir, it has often been urged that at some distant date when the regional languages have shown that they are properly equipped they can replace English. A very good proposition, but what is the criterion of proper

D-6

equipment of a language? If on any particular day there are 500 good books in Hindi or any other Indian language, there will surely be more than 500 books in English on the same subjects and any one can turn round and say that the regional language is not properly equipped. Although I am sure a number of good books are being published every year, a number of useful books for the general reader, the number of books fit for university education is small, and understandably so, because the books for university students are bound to be of a highly technical nature. And where is the publisher who can afford to lock up his money in the publication of such books, when there is no one to read them?

21. Former Chief Minister of Uttar Pradesh.

BLANK BOARD

(From *The Times of India*, 29 June 1962, p. 1)

E1

If the universities and colleges are not going to adopt Hindi or the other regional languages as the medium of instruction, if they are not going to put a deadline, so to say, and say that from such and such a date we shall have Hindi, Marathi or Bengali as the medium of instruction, whatever be the medium of instruction, no publisher will possibly publish the necessary books and there will be a stalemate. So, we have to be clear in our minds as to what exactly we mean. Then only can we take the necessary steps in this direction.

A good deal has been said about the various disintegrating factors. Unfortunately they are there. Perhaps it was fortunate that the general elections brought them up prominently before our eyes. We are now aware of them better than what we might otherwise have been and possibly we will be in a better position to deal with them.

A number of remedies have been suggested, but I would beg of you to think of one aspect of the question. While during all these years we have been paying every attention to bring about the material advancement of the people, we have almost completely ignored the emotional aspects of the matter. We have not created the necessary emotional atmosphere, with the result that with all our efforts, planning, etc., we have not been able to evoke that spirit of self-sacrifice which is needed for the success of these efforts. I think it is time that greater attention was paid to this subject. We should evolve some kind of philosophical basis for our activities. We are taking every effort through publicity and other ways to give a picture of the new

E2

world which we want to create, but so far we have paid very little attention to give the people an idea of the new man who is going to live in that new world. I think it is high time that we did so. If our efforts are bent in this direction, it might be possible to secure the co-operation of the various parties, social or political, which are engaged at this time in carrying on their activities some of which are definitely harmful. I have been harping on this tune for a number of years. I can only say that to my mind this is a matter of supreme importance.

I have little more to add, but before I stop I should like to bring to your notice an example of the extent to which regionalism or domiciliary restrictions can go. In the course of our visit to various parts of India, the members of the Emotional Integration Committee came across a curious state of affairs in Andhra. The Osmania University, as you know, was set up by the Nizam and one of the rules is that only "Mulkis" can study in that University. Now, the Hyderabad and Osmania Universities are in the Andhra State and they are a part of the Andhra State. But the definition of "Mulki" covers only a small number of people who happen to inhabit what is the Telengana area of the old Hyderabad State. The result is that a person coming from any other part of Andhra Pradesh, however brilliant he may be, cannot get admission to the Osmania University. Many brilliant boys are turned out. So far as I know, the University authorities do not want this state of affairs to continue, but there is a peculiar political situation. It seems that at the time of the merger, there was some kind of agreement, as a result of which the members of the Andhra

E3

Legislature, elected from the Telengana region form some kind of a Regional Committee and the views of the Regional Committee are paramount in these matters. Although the matter has come up before the Osmania University, the problem has not been solved. This gives an example of the extent to which such things can go.

This is all I have to say.

Mohanlal Sukhadia:[22] Sir, many points have been raised so far. I would like to bring to the notice of this Council only two or three points particularly. One is about the medium of instruction in different Universities. I think at present this matter is being discussed in the press and other circles also and some sort of finality is absolutely necessary in this matter, because generally we find that the idea is going round that the medium of instruction in the Universities also should be in the regional language. Now, as was pointed out earlier, I also feel that if this process goes on developing, the result perhaps would be that there would no unifying force left in the higher academic circles also. It is necessary that the policy about the medium of instruction at the University level should be decided as early as possible. One fact we have seen is this. The national forces were best united against the British Government at that time. When we were fighting the battle of independence, there was an urge for having a national language, so whether it was South or North, under the leadership of Mahatma Gandhi, everywhere the feeling was that we should have an Indian language as our national language. Now, perhaps we are slowly drifting from that.

E4

Sometimes we talk of English. Sometimes we talk of the regional language. Perhaps the general impression which is going round is this that we cannot think in terms of having an Indian language as our national language. I am not pleading for any particular language to be the national language, but at least all the political parties in different regions should come to a decision that we should have some national language, and which may be later on introduced in the Universities and other places also. At present we find the fear is there about the higher services. On the one side we are deciding that we should have more all-India services. Last time

22. Chief Minister of Rajasthan.

we decided to have medical, engineering and the forest services on the all-India pattern. On the one side, we are having all-India Services. On the other side, the medium of instruction in the Universities would be in the regional language. I do not know how far it will fit in later on when this process goes on further.

The second point which I wish to impress upon you is this. We are thinking of having text books and other things, which may lead to integration and an all-India feeling. But then there are certain organisations which are working at present in India, particularly among schoolboys. At their tender age, the minds of these schoolboys are poisoned, more or less, with communal feelings, anti-democratic feelings and so many things. I think the text books alone will not solve the problem. If such feelings are put into their heads at this young age, then later on I think the situation would be more difficult. It requires a strong decision. If we do not take a decision on that, we will find that after some time these communal feelings would be more rampant amongst the

E5

educated persons. Then, there would be more difficulty in solving this problem of communal feelings. At present the greatest advantage is the tradition we have derived due to our national struggle and other things. It has given us a background for the unity of the country. This is a strong force in our favour. I think with the lapse of time, in view of certain forces which are working in the country, it is just possible that we may lose our grip. It may even be that the disintegrating forces may gain an upper hand. Therefore, this should be kept in view. If we are alive to all these things, if the political parties, all of us here agree that at least at the school stage—these boys who are going to the schools should not be drawn into this. They may be voluntary organisations or other types of organisations, but the communal feelings should not be instilled into their minds.

Frank Anthony:[23] Mr Chairman, the discussion has shown how the approach of each one of us perhaps is conditioned by certain predilections. It is valuable because it helps us to set ultimately our approach in the correct perspective. Dr C.P. Ramaswami Aiyar said that he felt that essentially the problem is now of a long-term character. Dr Deshmukh was partly right when he said that we must not forget the qualitative and the research

23. Lok Sabha MP, nominated from the Anglo-Indian community.

approach. Dr Zakir Husain was equally right when he expressed impatience only with the research approach. Mr Namboodiripad[24] emphasised what was merely a facet of the larger problem of general disintegration in the country, a problem which affects a large minority in the country. Mr Munshi put his finger on one of the problems

E6

that face us, namely, educational fragmentation. What I feel is this that the problems that face us are multipronged. Our approach will have to be equally multipronged. Some of the problems are long-term; others are urgently short-term. And it would be for us to attempt to analyse and evaluate these problems. Mr Munshi talked of educational fragmentation. I agree with him. But that is only one of the major problems that face us. I agree also with the viewpoint that Mr Munshi has expressed, viz., unless we are able to do something to put some kind of brake on this process of disintegration in education, the bonds of administrative unity, the bonds of emotional integration at least among the educated sections, among the leaders of thought and action in the country, to that extent, will disappear. But that is not the only bond that is worth preserving. The leaders of thought and action may be a small elite against the emergence of primary education and secondary education in the regional languages. In the final analysis—they may only represent an ineffective political elite—it is necessary to maintain that bond among the educated sections of the country.

Then, one of the speakers referred to regional chauvinism. That, to my mind, is one of the greatest dangers. There again, there is a fear that we may approach the problem ad hoc, because it is underlined by the DMK, by the DMK's plea. My own feeling is that this regional chauvinism will have to be met in some basic context.

F-1

We will have to deal with it ad hoc. We will have to see in Tamil Nadu it has a special context, the context of a people with a rich and proud cultural and civilisational heritage; but that problem faces us basically in Nagaland in the whole of the North-eastern area. The promptings, the impetus may be different but the challenge is the same. So we will have to deal with this regional chauvinism in that way. Nobody has underlined

24. CPI leader and former Chief Minister of Kerala.

what I feel is the immediate problem, and that is the caste and sub-caste chauvinism. That I feel, Sir, is a problem which will have to be set on many fronts, administrative, I do not know to what extent, educationally, but certainly politically, and it is a problem which we will have to face squarely. It is no good saying that we made a mistake and we gave hostages to caste and sub-caste when we created linguistic States. I agree with that. I do not want to be mistaken. I will give an example. I was always against the reorganisation of the States. I said immediately that we were giving hostages to regional and linguistic chauvinism but look at the caste lobbies we have created. Take the example of the Reddys of Andhra. I am giving it as an example. I do not mean to be offensive. I said one thing; if we did not have unilingual or a sort of uni-caste States, there would be checks and balances. In multi-lingual Madras the Reddys were a dispersed unorganised political community. With the creation of Andhra they have become a solid consolidated caste lobby and today the caste lines are set fiercely between the Reddys and the Khammars [Kammas]. In the same way the caste lines are set among the dominant castes; in Mysore between the Lingayats and Vokkilagars [Vokkaligas] and the history repeats itself. That is there. What we can do to blunt that edge of casteism I do not know because casteism

F-2

today is identified with political and economic power. People may ridicule me but I am a little afraid that if we do not create the necessary conditions but if we make same blunders this will magnify itself a thousand-fold in the villages through the panchayats. I am not denigrating our village people. They are very good people. A leading journalist was telling me the other day. In the UP he wanted to stand for election. He was a Chaturvedi and certainly he was the ablest person for the panchayat in that area. So he proposed himself but when the others met they said, 'there is no second Chaturvedi to second your proposal'. And what they did was they deliberately coolly calculated in numerical terms the castes and sub-castes and in terms of the numerical position they said, you will be the sarpanch and so many of these will be panches. Of course, we are certainly committed to decentralisation of the democratic process but let us also remember this that with the decentralisation of the democratic process there has been a proliferation of caste and sub-caste consciousness and if we drive that down into the grass roots of our village life then there will be same edge. I do not think caste is an evil socially today, not to that extent; its edge is political today but if we drive it down into our village life it will become an evil socially because people will be living with their elbows on one another's ribs and the elbows will have the same kind of political edge. Therefore I feel that we might consider this educational approach; we might consider the approach to the regional challenges in a general context not only with regard to the DMK, and above all, we ought also to consider this challenge of caste and sub-caste.

F-3

Bhai Jodh Singh:[25] My friend Mr Munshi has raised an important question and he has reminded us of the good old days when English-knowing people could communicate with one another as there was a concord among the educated people. But in those days if I remember correctly we used to gather at our annual gatherings, and pass resolutions but could not accomplish anything. It was when the masses were roused through their own language or Hindustani to a certain pitch of action that we got independence. English has got its value in science and in technology but you cannot educate 30 crores of people through English. I think during the 200 years of rule over India the percentage of people who could speak English correctly or communicate with one another in that language was not above one or two per cent, if I remember correctly. It may be a little more. We have now to enthuse the masses and we cannot do that through English.

Some remarks have been made about elections especially by my friend, Mr Anthony, if I remember right. Now, Sir, I would make a proposal which may sound very novel. We have tried another method of election in the panchayats, what we call the three-tier system where you have panchayats, then gram panchayats and then zilla parishads. If we can introduce that system also in the Assemblies and higher bodies, that will lessen the appeal to the caste on a large scale. What I found during these elections in the Punjab was—of course I did not stand for any assembly membership or any other membership—that people appealed to caste and sub-caste only when there is a large number of people in that vicinity belonging to that section but if we did as we did in panchayats—we elected panchayats sometimes unanimously in most of the villages—there was no appeal to caste. Especially

25. Sikh scholar , Vice Chancellor of Punjabi University, Patiala, 1962-66.

F-4

when several castes came together in zilla parishads there was no appeal to castes. I do not know how the population is distributed in Andhra and other places. As far as Punjab is concerned, I know there are some caste villages but when several of those castes come together they cannot appeal to any caste in particular because every party wants power and as yet they have not been able to check themselves from appealing to whatever brings them the membership. Therefore I feel that if we had indirect election that evil will be to some extent minimised.

As for the development of the regional languages, in the first place we cannot force the hands of the clock back. We have set before the people a certain ideal and they have taken to it and if we now say that instead of regional languages we will have a foreign language as medium of instruction—which I think is nowhere to be found on the face of this earth in independent countries—then I think we will be rousing an opposition which will be much more than what we are facing now. Therefore, I think we should propose remedies—not what should be or what we think to be correct—but taking all the circumstances into consideration in the light of what we have done so far we should remove those defects and not try to wipe out wholesale what we have done so far and begin with a clean slate. That is impossible in any country I think. These are the few remarks that I wanted to make.

Binodanand Jha:[26] Sir, a few topics of current importance have been introduced in the debate which make it more comprehensive than the agenda provides scope for. For instance about this caste business in the elections let me point out to you one thing.

F-5

Casteism has not travelled from the villages to the capital. It is the other way round. It has travelled from the capital to the villages. And why is it so? Let me point out to you again another factor. And that is in connection with the elections. These days in many places the level of the caste and the possession of a jeep are the two inevitable instruments to give a man a lead in the election. We may call it the caste-bred or the jeep or helicopter-bred election and for this state of affairs more or less every

26. Chief Minister of Bihar.

party ought to be blamed. We publish the names of our candidates only a few weeks before the date of the election, just two or three weeks before. The result is, there is no other conveyance except a jeep to produce success in the election and these jeeps too we want to move them at a speed of about 100 miles per hour. This procedure which is adopted more or less by every party for fighting the elections is responsible for introducing all the unnecessary heat, unnecessary wastage and at the same unnecessary dependence on extraneous considerations such as caste and other things. But let me assure you that all these factors are dying down. There is one fact to which Shri Namboodiripad drew attention this morning and we should recognise it. If you take the instances from 1947 right up to 1962, over all these 15 years the ratio is not on the increase; not only that, the instances are numerically fewer still. And the most encouraging aspect of this is that the sympathetic movements associated with particular places are not there now. If there would have been Aligarh in 1947 it would have been very difficult to save Delhi or towns near about from Aligarh but today Aligarh is isolated because there is no sympathy elsewhere for such things. It is only a local happening; mostly the reason is something local whereas

F-6

formerly that was not the case. So we should not give weight to this communal business out of proportion. It is a dying phantom. The real reason why people even today go the caste way or the communal way is not so much due to their love for or leanings to the caste or community but because they think that would give them some job here and there or give them some political position or some clerical position. That is the main reason. Sir, in other words it is an inevitable symptom of a country where the economy is changing, where we have got a backward economy which is gradually giving place to a forward modern economy. In these conditions such things are inevitable. The real unity today is being forged in the factory areas, in the townships, in the urban areas. Let anybody go and speak to those people about communal tension or caste tension and he will get the reply in a proper way.

G1

The old symptoms were mostly associated with that India. As I have pointed out, it is a legacy of the past. But the new India is also being forged, the unifying force is also being generated. The point is that the speed should be accelerated. Its momentum should be more and more so that it may outnumber and overwhelm the disintegrative forces. We do not fight shy of what is happening today. Here and there some simple situations have arisen, but there is no doubt that a better India is coming out of it. For example, take Bakr Id. At no time during the past fifteen years in my State were we free from any trouble on that occasion. But this year we were free from troubles. I am pretty sure next year nobody will be troubled on that account. The only trouble is this. The emphasis has shifted to some other quarters, viz., trouble-makers from other countries are there. There are spies who want to make trouble here. The incidents are localised. They cannot create now chaos and disturbances throughout the State or even in a big part of the State. So, the fundamental thing is this. The line of progress, the line of development that we have chalked out, the country has before it, would surely lead to more and more unity. But there are certain discordant features to which I should like to draw your attention. Shri Munshi pointed out that a graduate from the Gujarat University has got scant respect if he goes to Andhra. I may point out to him that he need not travel so far. We have got four Universities in Bihar and the day is not distant when a boy from the Patna University will be treated as a foreigner in the Ranchi University.

G2

Each University is adopting a policy of autonomy and autonomy is a big thing, a very pious thing, for the purpose of bringing in narrow ideologies, narrow attitudes. Autonomy now means, admission limited to the particular locality, appointments of professors and other staff to be limited to the particular region and similar things. It means you arrange the faculties in such a way that a boy studying in a Muslim College will have very little to do with the Bhagalpur College. So, the problem has to be tackled by the University Grants Commission with a view to bringing about one uniform standard instead of the diversities. Diversities are there, but there must be a standard, which should be an all India standard. It should be the national standard. I have no doubt in my mind that this too will be solved in due course.

Therefore, we are confronted not with a basic problem, but with some of the facets of a problem which is dying out. We have got to build up the new forces. With diligence and energy, I have no doubt in my mind that with your leadership and co-operation of all the members of the different political parties it would be possible for us to avoid the pitfalls which we have often been facing in our onward march.

G3

अटल बिहारी वाजपेयी:[27] सभापति जी, मैं इस बात का स्वागत करता हूँ कि आपने हिन्दू महासभा के प्रतिनिधि को इस परिषद् में शामिल होने के लिये निमंत्रण दिया है। सचमुच में यह काम पहले ही होना चाहिये था। इस का अर्थ यह नहीं है कि हिन्दू महासभा के विचारों से मैं सहमत हूँ। इस चुनाव में भारतीय जनसंघ को जिसका मैं एक प्रतिनिधि हूँ, यदि सब से अधिक विरोध किसी दल की ओर से सहन करना पड़ा है तो वह हिन्दू महासभा है। हिन्दू महासभा की दृष्टि में हम एक मुस्लिमपरस्त पार्टी हैं। हमने कहां कहां मुस्लिम उम्मीदवार खड़े किये, इसकी एक लम्बी सूची बना करके हिन्दू महासभा की ओर से सारे देश में बांटी गई। मैं स्वयं अगर चुनाव में हार गया,[28] मेरे कांग्रेसी दोस्त मुझे माफ करें, तो कांग्रेस की वजह से नहीं और न कम्युनिस्ट पार्टी की वजह से जिसने मेरे क्षेत्र में कांग्रेस को जिताने के लिए सारी ताकत लगा दी। मैं अगर हार गया तो हिन्दू महासभा की वजह से हार गया। मेरे खिलाफ हिन्दू महासभा के दो उम्मीदवार खड़े थे[29] और उन्होंने यह प्रचार किया कि मैंने दिल्ली में होने वाले हिन्दू सम्मेलन का विरोध किया था।

बिशनचन्द्र सेठ: मैं यह पूछना चाहता हूं कि जो विषय हमारे सामने है उससे यह प्रश्न किस तरह से सम्बन्धित है?

[Translation begins:

Atal Bihari Vajpayee:[30] Mr Chairman, I welcome the fact that you have invited a representative of the Hindu Mahasabha to be part of this Council. As a matter of fact, this should have been done much earlier. That does not mean that I am in agreement with the ideas of the Hindu Mahasabha. If the Bharatiya Jan Sangh of which I am a representative has had to face the utmost opposition from any Party, it is from the Hindu Mahasabha because in their perception, we are a pro-Muslim Party. A long list was

27. Jan Sangh leader.
28. Vajpayee lost his Lok Sabha seat to Subhadra Joshi of Congress from Balrampur, UP, in the Third General Elections.
29. The other three candidates were Ahmad Nasir Usmani of Swatantra Party, Swaroop Nath of Hindu Mahasabha and Vishwa Nath Agrawal, an Independent, see *RECI*, p. 61.
30. See fn 27 in this section.

prepared of constituencies in which we had put up Muslim candidates and it was circulated by the Hindu Mahasabha all over the country. If I have lost the election myself,[31] forgive me my Congress friends, it is not because of the Congress, and even because of the Communist Party which put all its efforts into the Congress victory. But if I lost, it is because of the Hindu Mahasabha. Two Hindu Mahasabha candidates opposed me[32] and they were doing propaganda that I had opposed the Hindu Sammelan to be held in Delhi.

Bishanchander Seth: I wish to ask how this is relevant to the subject being discussed here.

Translation ends]

Pattom Thanu Pillai:[33] Sir, neither the question nor the answer is understood.

Atal Bihari Vajpayee: I was under the impression that my Hindi speech was being translated into English.

Jawaharlal Nehru: Mr Vajpayee of the Jan Sangh congratulated me on inviting a representative of the Hindu Mahasabha here and then he was proceeding to say something apparently about the differences between the Jan Sangh and the Hindu Mahasabha, to

G4

which the representative of the Hindu Maha Sabha [Mahasabha] asked whether this meeting had been called to consider the question of differences of the two parties—Jan Sangh and Hindu Maha Sabha [Mahasabha].

अटल बिहारी वाजपेयीः यह ठीक है कि यह मीटिंग इसके लिए नहीं बुलाई गई है। लेकिन जो बात मैं कहना चाहता था, उसके लिए यह भूमिका ज़रूरी थी कि राजनैतिक मतभेद रखने वालों को भी हमें यहां पर बुलाना चाहिये और केवल हिन्दू महासभा नहीं, मैं तो एक कदम और आगे जा कर कहना चाहूंगा कि अकाली दल और मुस्लिम लीग को भी बुलाना चााहिए। अगर इस मंच का उपयोग हमें विचारों का परिवर्तन करने के लिए करना है तो फिर सब को निकट ला करके ही यह परिवर्तन किया जा सकता है।

31. See fn 28 in this section.
32. See fn 29 in this section.
33. Pattom A. Thanu Pillai, Chief Minister of Kerala.

G-5

और अगर हम यह मान कर चलें कि कुछ दल हमारी दृष्टि में सम्प्रदायवादी है और उन्हें सुधारा नहीं जा सकता है, अपने प्रभाव से उनके विचारों को बदला नहीं जा सकता है तो फिर राष्ट्रीय एकीकरण की दिशा में प्रगति बहुत ही मुश्किल होगी। लेकिन इसके साथ यह भी आवश्यक है कि यह परिषद् इस बात पर विचार करे कि साम्प्रदायिकता क्या है। कौन से दल साम्प्रदायिकता की श्रेणी में आते हैं। हमारे गृह मंत्री जी[34] भी अभी तक संसद में इस प्रश्न का स्पष्ट उत्तर नहीं दे सके हैं कि किन दलों को हम साम्प्रदायिकता की सीमा में बांधते हैं। क्या यह प्रश्न एक राजनैतिक प्रश्न है? चुनाव में जो भी प्रचार हुए मैं उनका उल्लेख नहीं करना चाहता। हमारे बारे में जो कुछ कहा गया वह किसी से छिपा हुआ नहीं है। शायद हमने कुछ गल्तियां की होंगी लेकिन जो कांच के घर में बैठ कर हमारे ऊपर पत्थर फैंकने की भूल करते हैं उनसे हम बड़ी विनम्रता से कहना चाहते हैं कि आप हमें बतायें कि हम किस ढंग से सम्प्रदायवादी हैं, हमारी कौन सी गतिविधि, हमारी कौन सी नीति राष्ट्रीयता के मार्ग में बाधक है ताकि हम उस पर विचार करें और हम उसे सुधारने के लिए तैयार हैं। लेकिन अगर इसे एक राजनैतिक सवाल बनाया जाएगा, हमारे विरूद्ध जनता को उभारने की कोशिश की गई तो फिर हम उसका मुकाबला करेंगे। जब से भारतीय जनसंघ मध्य प्रदेश में, उत्तर प्रदेश में थोड़ी सी सीटें प्राप्त करने में सफल हुआ है तब से देश में एक हवा पैदा करने की कोशिश की जा रही है कि भारतीय जनसंघ देश की एकता को तोड़ना चाहता है। अगर यह बात सच है कि हम एकता को तोड़ना चाहते हैं तो, प्रधान मंत्री जी, इस परिषद् में हमारे लिए कोई जगह नहीं है, फिर आप कह दीजिए कि हम यहां से चले जाए। जहां तक मेरा व्यक्तिगत सम्बन्ध है, मैं ऐसे दल से

G6

सम्बन्ध नहीं रखना चाहता हूँ जो एकता को तोड़ना चाहते हैं। हां, एकता किस तरह से पैदा की जा सकती है इसके बारे में हमारा अपना दृष्टिकोण हैं और बड़ी शांति से, विनम्रता से हम उस दृष्टिकोण को देश के सामने रखने की कोशिश करते हैं। मैं जो हिन्दू महासभा से अपने मतभेदों की चर्चा कर रहा था वह इसी संदर्भ में कर रहा था, फिर भी मैं उनके आने का स्वागत करता हूँ क्योंकि मेरे विचारों से बहुतों को मतभेद हो सकता है और कल यह मांग हो सकती है कि भारतीय जनसंघ के प्रतिनिधि को राष्ट्रीय एकता सम्मेलन में शामिल करने की ज़रूरत नहीं है। मैं इस मांग को रोकने के लिए हिन्दू महासभा के प्रतिनिधि को सम्मेलन में शामिल किए जाने का स्वागत

34. Lal Bahadur Shastri.

नहीं कर रहा हूँ। लेकिन हमारा मत है कि यदि हम एकता के बारे में राष्ट्रीय एकता के आधार पर विचार करना चाहते है तो फिर हमें पार्टीबन्दी और दलबन्दी को अलग रखना होगा। हम मिल कर इस बात का फैसला करें कि साम्प्रदायिकता क्या है और क्या नहीं है लेकिन इस तरह का अभी कोई प्रयत्न नहीं हुआ और इसलिए बड़ा भ्रम पैदा हुआ है। चुनाव में इस भ्रम को बढ़ाने की कोशिश की जाती है। मैं नहीं जानता कि गृह मंत्रलय ने जो पोस्टर्स और पैम्फलेट्स इकठ्ठे किये है उनसे किस बात का संकेत मिलता है लेकिन, प्रधान मंत्री महोदय, मैं आपके ध्यान में एक बात लाना चाहता हूं, आपका ध्यान एक बात की ओर खींचना चाहता हूं। एक ऐसी बात चुनाव में कही गई - शायद राष्ट्रीयता, राष्ट्रीय एकता भी उससे पीछे पड़ जाती है - और वह बात यह थी कि देश में कुछ ऐसे लोग हैं कि जो महात्मा गांधी की तरह से

G-7

आत्महत्या [हत्या] करना चाहते हैं। यह बात मंच से कही गई, सार्वजनिक रूप से कही गई। मेरे पास एक पोस्टर है जो पंजाब में कांग्रेस की तरफ से दीवारों पर लगाया गया, जिसमें चित्रों में यह बात दिखाई गई है कि जब गांधी जी की हत्या हो गई तो मिठाईयां बांटी गई और एक नेता है जो आजकल अपने अनुयायियों से कहते हैं कि तुमने गांधी जी को मार दिया और तुम्हें अब नेहरू जी को मारना चाहिए। मैं गृह मंत्री जी से जानना चाहूंगा कि क्या यह बात ठीक है? देश में कोई ऐसा दल है, कोई ऐसा व्यक्ति है जो आपको हानि पहुंचाना चाहता है? यह बात राष्ट्रीय स्वयंसेवक संघ का नाम लेकर कही गई। राष्ट्रीय स्वयंसेवक संघ के विचारों से आपका मतभेद हो सकता है लेकिन मैं बाल्यावस्था से राष्ट्रीय स्वयंसेवक संघ के संपर्क में हूं और मैं दावे के साथ कहता हूं कि यह बात गलत है और अगर यह सही है तो मुझे बताया जाए। कोई आपको मारना चाहे और मैं उस संस्था के साथ सम्बन्ध रखूं तो मैं चुल्लू भर पानी में डूब कर मर जाना अच्छा समझता हूं। लेकिन चुनाव में सार्वजनिक मंचों से इस प्रकार का हम प्रचार करें ओर फिर हम आशा करें कि देश में एकता का वातावरण पैदा हो सकता है? नहीं, इस तरह ऐसा वातावरण नहीं पैदा हो सकता। ऐसे संगठन समाप्त किये जाए, ऐसे व्यक्तियों को जेल में बन्द होना चाहिए लेकिन हम चुनाव के दिनों में ऐसे प्रचार करते है। मैं जानता हूं कि हमारी तरफ से भी चुनाव के प्रचार में गलती हुई लेकिन ऐसी कोई बड़ी गलती हमने की है तो हमें बताईये, हम अपने अनुयायियों के खिलाफ कार्यवाही करेंगे और उन्हें निकाल देंगे। अगर उनको निकालने में सफल नहीं हो सका, अगर मेरी आवाज़ इस बारे में संगठन में न सुनी गई तो मैं उस संगठन से अपना सम्बन्ध तोड़ लूंगा। सार्वजनिक रूप से इस तरह की हवा पैदा की जाए और फिर यहां सम्मेलन में बैठ कर यह

G-8

सोचें कि देश में एकता कैसे हो? मैं बड़ी विन्रमता से कहना चाहता हूं कि हम इस बात पर शान्ति से, गम्भीरता से विचार करें कि सचमुच में एकता के मार्ग में कौन सी बाधायें हैं। राजनीति को अलग रख दें। राजनैतिक, आर्थिक तथा सामाजिक प्रश्नों पर हमारे बीच में मतभेद हो सकते है, मतभेद होंगे, लेकिन क्या उन मतभेदों की वजह से हम राष्ट्रीय एकता के सवाल पर भी एक दूसरे से मिल नहीं सकते? अगर हम परिणाम पर पंहुचे कि नहीं चल सकते तो फिर राष्ट्रीय एकता के लिए ऐसा सर्वदलीय प्रत्यन करने का कोई अर्थ ही नहीं रहता है। लेकिन मेरा दृढ़ विचार है कि अगर खुल कर बातें कहीं जाए तो हम सफल होंगे। अगर किसी दल के खिलाफ कोई बात आती है तो उस दल के प्रतिनिधियों को बुलाया जाए, उनकी जबावतलबी की जाए। आप केवल कांग्रेस के ही नेता नहीं है, आप हमारे राष्ट्र के नेता है। कोई दल गलती करता है तो उस दल के नेताओं को बुला कर कह सकते है कि यह क्या बदतमीज़ी हो रही है लेकिन मुझे अफसोस है कि आप सार्वजनिक मंच पर कहते है और हमें बुला कर नहीं कहते। क्या हम देश के नागरिक नहीं है? हम भी देशभक्त है। शायद कुछ लोग इसको मानने से इंकार कर सकते है और करते है लेकिन अगर हमारी देशभक्ति में शक किया जाता है तो फिर हमारे बीच में कोई मिलने की भूमि नहीं है। लेकिन, मैं समझता हूं कि हम इस विचार को ले कर चलें कि हम सब देश की भलाई चाहते हैं। भलाई किस ढ़ंग से हो सकती है इसके बारे में अलग राय होगी, लेकिन अभी एक मुख्य मंत्री महोदय ने कहा कि छोटे छोटे बच्चों के दिमागों में साम्प्रदायिकता का ज़हर भरा जाता है, तो अगर यह बात सच है तो गलत बात है, इसे रोकना चाहिए। लेकिन वह साम्प्रदायिकता का ज़हर क्या है? मैं

G-9

समझता हूं कि उनका मतलब शायद आर. एस. एस. से था। आर. एस. एस. छोटे बच्चों में भी काम करता हैं। आर. एस. एस. हिन्दुओं का एक संगठन है। आप उसके विचारों से मतभेद रख सकते हैं मगर आप हिन्दुओं के इस अधिकार को नहीं छीन सकते कि अपने बच्चों में संस्कार डालें, मै अपने बच्चों में इस बात का अभिमान पैदा करें कि वे हिन्दू है। इस देश में हर एक मज़हब के मानने वाले अपने मज़हब के मानने वालों को अपने मज़हब में तैयार करते है फिर हम हिन्दुओं से इस अधिकार को कैसे छीन सकते हैं। क्या सैकुलरवाद का, साम्प्रदायिकता का मतलब यह है कि इस देश में हिन्दू कोई नहीं रहे, सब अहिन्दू हो जाए? मैं नहीं समझता कि ऐसी मूर्खता की बात कोई कह सकता है। हमें इस बात को सोच कर चलना होगा कि आखिर हम जिस साम्प्रदायिकता की निन्दा करते हैं वह साम्प्रदायिकता क्या है। जब यह निश्चित हो जाये तब सारे देश को, सब को उस साम्प्रदायिकता को रोकने

के लिये सर्वदलीय आधार पर कोशिश करनी चाहिए और उसको कम किया जाना चाहिए। अगर राष्ट्रीय स्वयंसेवक संघ के कुछ काम ऐसे है जो कि गलत काम है तो आप उनको बुला कर बता सकते हैं, उनके नेताओं को कह सकते है और अगर वह न मानें, न सुनें, तो उस आधार पर सारे देश के जनमत को उनके विरुद्ध जागृत कर सकते हैं लेकिन एक चुनाव जीतने के लिए, या चुनाव के बाद जनता ने जो चुनाव में फैसला दिया है उस फैसले से अपना रोष प्रकट करने के लिए अगर हम एक हवा खड़ी करें तो मैं नहीं समझता कि यह हवा खड़ी करने में किसी का कल्याण हो सकता है। हां, कुछ दलों के राजनैतिक उद्देश्य पूरे हो सकते है। तो इस हालात में हम फिर उसी राजनैतिक आधार पर बातें करते हैं और तब हमें राष्ट्रीय एकता की बातें करने का अधिकार नहीं रह जाता है।

G-10

सभापति जी, मैं कहना चाहूंगा कि जब कभी साम्प्रदायिक दंगे होते हैं तब मेरी पार्टी का नाम लिया जाता है। मगर बार बार हम कहते है कि इन दंगों की अदालती जांच कराइये कि उसमें कौन लोग फंसे हुए है। दंगा एक लॉ एंड आर्डर का सवाल है और जांच के बाद जिम्मेदार लोगों को सजा मिलनी चाहिए। जबलपुर में दंगा हुआ[35] और उसकी अदालती जांच भी हुई लेकिन उसकी जो रिपोर्ट है वह अभी तक नहीं प्रकाशित की गई। हमने कहा कि अलीगढ़ में, मेरठ में जो साम्प्रदायिक दंगे हुए उनकी अदालती जांच कराई जाए। अभी मालदा में दंगा हुआ। मुझे ताज्जुब हुआ कि उस दंगे के साथ जनसंघ का नाम कैसे नहीं जोड़ा गया। कुछ हमारे ऐसे मित्र हैं जो बाद में जोड़ सकते है या जोड़ रहे हो, मगर अभी तक खुले तौर पर कह नहीं सकते है। ये दंगे ऐसी चीज़ तो नहीं है जो कि छिपा कर रखी जा सकती है। अगर कोई दल दंगा कराता है, अगर किसी दल के व्यक्ति दंगे के साथ सम्बन्धित हैं तो उनके खिलाफ कार्यवाही होनी चाहिए।

H-1

उस दल के नेताओं को बताना चाहिए और अगर आप इस परिणाम पर पहुंचें कि केवल इने गिने दो चार व्यक्ति नहीं बल्कि सारा दल एकता के मार्ग में बाधक है, देश को गढ़े में डालना चाहता है तो फिर उस दल पर आप पाबंदी लगा दीजिए, उसको गैर कानूनी घोषित कर दीजिए लेकिन उससे पहले बातें साफ सफाई से कही जाय। हम यहां समझने के लिए आए हैं, अपना अपना पक्ष रखने के लिये आये हैं लेकिन हम गोलमोल बातें करेंगे तो फिर राष्ट्रीय एकता के उद्देश्य को पूरा नहीं किया जा सकता।

35. In February 1961, see SWJN/SS/66/item 34 and SWJN/SS/67/items 26-37.

बिशनचन्द्र सेठः मैं चाहूंगा मुझे थोड़ा सा मौका दिया जाए।

[Translation begins:

Atal Bihari Vajpayee: It is true that this meeting has not been called for this purpose, to consider the question of differences between the Jan Sangh and the Hindu Mahasabha. But this introduction was essential as a background to what I wished to say, that is, the representatives of parties with differences in political ideology should also be invited here, and not only from the Hindu Mahasabha. I would go one step further and say that even the Akali Dal and the Muslim League should also be invited; if we are to use this forum to bring about a change in mindsets, then it can be done only by bringing everyone closer.

And if we assume that from our point of view some parties are communal and cannot be reformed, nor can their ideology be changed through our influence, then progress on the national integration will be extremely difficult. But at the same time it is also essential that this Council should debate what is communalism and which are the parties which fall within this category. But our Home Minister[36] has not been able to give a clear answer to this question in Parliament as to which parties may be defined as communal. Is this a political question? I do not wish to mention the kind of propaganda that was carried out during the elections. Whatever was said about us is not hidden from anyone. Perhaps we might have made some mistakes. But we would like to politely ask of those living in glass houses and throwing stones at us: please tell us in what way we are communal, which actions or policies of ours have been obstructive to nationalism, so that we may ponder and prepare to change them. However, if this is turned into a communal issue and efforts are made to instigate the people against us, then we shall challenge that. Ever since the Bharatiya Jan Sangh succeeded in winning a few seats in Madhya Pradesh and Uttar Pradesh, a move is afoot to create an atmosphere in the country that Bharatiya Jan Sangh is trying to break up national unity. If this is true, then Mr Prime Minister, there is no place for us in this Council, and you should ask us to leave. So far as I am concerned personally, I do not wish to align myself with any Party which seeks to break up the unity of the country. Yes, we have our own viewpoint on how to forge national unity and we try to place that viewpoint very peacefully and very humbly before the country.

36. See fn 34 in this section.

I was referring to those differences between us and the Hindu Mahasabha in this context, and even then, I welcome their joining the Council because I realise that many would have vast differences with my ideas and it is possible that there may be a demand that there is no need to include a representative of the Bharatiya Jan Sangh in the National Integration Council. I am not welcoming the inclusion of the representative of the Hindu Mahasabha in order to preempt the demand for our exclusion. But it is our opinion that if we wish to look at unity from a national perspective we should keep partyism and groupism at bay. We should all get together to arrive at a consensus about what is communalism and what is not. However, no such attempt has so far been made and that has created a great confusion. During elections this confusion is sought to be confounded. I do not know what do the posters and pamphlets, collected by the Ministry of Home Affairs, indicate but, Mr Prime Minister, Sir, I want to attract your attention to something that was said during the elections and which leaves the issue of communal harmony far behind. And that was, it was said openly, publicly that there are some people in this country who wish to assassinate like Mahatma Gandhi. I have a poster which was put up on the walls in Punjab by the Congress which had pictures showing sweets being distributed when Gandhiji was assassinated. And there is a leader who is telling his followers, you killed Gandhiji and now you should kill Nehruji. I want to ask the Home Minister whether this is right. Is there any Party or any individual in the country who wants to harm you? This was said with reference to the Rashtriya Swayamsevak Sangh. You can have differences of opinion with the Rashtriya Swayamsevak Sangh but I have been in touch with them since my childhood and I can say categorically that this is wrong, and I should be corrected if I am wrong. I would prefer to die rather than be associated with an organisation which wants to kill you. However, during elections, if such propaganda from public platforms is done, how then can we hope to create an atmosphere of unity in the country? No, this is not how a spirit of unity can be created, such divisive organisations should be shut down and such individuals put in jail. But such propaganda during elections is not right. I am aware that mistakes have been made during election propaganda from our side also. But please tell us if we have committed such a huge mistake and we will take action against our followers and expel them. If I do not succeed in expelling them or if my voice is not heard in this matter in the Party, I shall break off my allegiance to that Party. Let us create a general atmosphere of amity and then sit together in conference to debate how unity can be forged. I would like to say in all humility that we should debate and analyse peacefully and in all seriousness as to what are the real obstacles in the way of national unity. Let us leave politics aside. There may be differences of opinion over political, economic and social issues but can we not come together over the issue of national unity in spite of those differences? If we reach the conclusion that we cannot have a consensus, then there is no meaning in making an all Party effort like this at all. But it is my firm belief that if we discuss things openly we will succeed, if anything comes up against any Party, then its representatives should be sent for and questioned. You are the leader not only of the Congress Party but the leader of the nation. If any Party makes a mistake, you can call its representatives and reprimand them for unacceptable behaviour. But I regret that you talk about all this in a public forum but do not talk to us directly. Are we not citizens of this country? We too are patriots. Perhaps some people may refuse to accept this and do refuse but if our patriotism is questioned then there can be no common meeting ground between us. But I feel that we should proceed on the assumption that all of us have our nation's interests at heart. There may be different opinions about how we should do good to the country. But just now one Chief Minister said that young children's minds are being filled with the poison of communalism. If that is true, it is wrong and should be stopped. But what is this poison of communalism? I feel that he meant the RSS. The RSS works among the very young. The RSS is a Hindu organisation. You may have differences of opinion with its ideology but you cannot snatch away the right of the Hindus to teach their children about our culture and values and create a feeling of pride in being a Hindu. In this country, followers of every religion bring up their children according to the tenets of their religions. How then can you deprive the Hindus of the right to do so? Does secularism or communalism mean that there should be no Hindus in the country, that everybody should become non-Hindu? I do not think anyone can say something so foolish. We must ponder over what communalism implies and once a consensus is reached on that, an attempt should be made on an all-Party basis to root out such communalism. If the RSS does something wrong, you can call them and point out their mistake, you can talk to their leaders, and if they do not listen or agree, then on that basis you can muster public opinion in the entire country against them. But to do so in order to win an election or to express anger against an electoral verdict of the masses, and to arouse public opinion and create an atmosphere of hostility, is something which I do not think is likely to benefit anyone. Yes, it may help some Parties to achieve their political goals. In such circumstances if we are to talk on political grounds, then we do not have the right to talk of national unity.

Mr Chairman, I would like to point out that whenever there are communal riots my Party is blamed. But we repeatedly say that there should be a judicial inquiry into the riots to find out who was actually involved in them. Riots are a law-and-order issue and after the inquiry, those who are responsible should be punished. There were riots in Jabalpur[37] and there was a judicial inquiry also but the report of that inquiry has not been published till today. We asked for a judicial inquiry into the communal riots in Aligarh and Meerut, there has been a riot in Malda. I am surprised that the Jan Sangh has not been named in connection with these riots. It is possible that there may be some friends who may do so later or are doing so but are not coming out openly. After all, riots are not something which can be kept hidden. If any Party incites a riot, if members of any Party have been involved in a riot, action should be taken against them, the leaders of that Party should be informed about this.

If you reach the conclusion that it is not just a handful of individuals but an entire Party that is obstructing integration, wants to push the country into an abyss, then you can place restrictions on the Party or declare it illegal. But before doing that, things should be clearly spelt out, we are all here to understand the issues involved and to present our point of view. But if we talk in a roundabout manner, then the goal of national unity cannot be achieved.

Bishanchander Seth: I would like a chance to say something.

Translation ends]

H-2

Jawaharlal Nehru: Mr Vajpayee has been asked a question as to what was communalism. His whole speech was in defence of his own organisation, that is, the Jan Sangh and the Rashtriya Swayamsevak Sangh which are alleged to be communal. That is the main purport of his speech. They are accused of this, and he has produced a poster issued in Punjab, presumably by the Congress during the elections, which says something about the persons who were guilty of murdering Gandhiji and who are now thinking in terms of putting an end to me. He took strong exception to that and he said that if any organisation with which he was connected said anything of this kind, he would leave it. So he said that these charges should not be made,

37. See fn 35 in this section.

and if they are made, they should be enquired into. He defended the RSS on that basis. It is rather difficult for us to go into an attack or defence of any group or party here, because that will lead to interminable arguments. We meet here presuming that we, all of us, want the integration of India, of the people of India. Now we have no proper idea of what communalism is, just as some people call the RSS or even the Jan Sangh as a communal organisation and they deny it. In other words, there is some difference as to the meaning of the word "communalism" or the interpretation of it in action. It is difficult for us to go into that, we will lose ourselves in perpetual debate.

May I say that in an adjoining room here there is some kind of exhibition of election posters issued in the General Election? They have been shown in some room here. So members of the Council may profit by a view of them as to what was said at that time.

H-3

बिशनचन्द्र सेठः आदरणीय सभापति जी, मैं सबसे पहले इस ओर आपका ध्यान दिलाना चाहता हूं कि हमारे आदरणीय मित्र वाजपेयी जी ने जिस प्रकार से अपना व्याख्यान शुरू किया मैं उसको इस मीटिंग के लिये उपयुक्त नहीं मानता। कारण बड़ा स्पष्ट है कि यहां पर हम एक चीज के सुधार के लिये बैठे हैं। हमारा व्यक्तिगत या किसी के ऊपर कटाक्ष करने का कोई भी लक्ष्य नहीं होना चाहिए। जहां तक कि जनसंघ और हिन्दू महासभा के संबंध में यह कहा गया कि हिन्दू महासभा के कारण जनसंघ की हार हुई और हमारे वाजपेयी जी हार गये, मैं इसे व्यक्तिगत प्रश्न मानता था और उसको यहां लाना मुनासिब भी नहीं था। लेकिन चूंकि उन्होंने इसकी चर्चा की है तो मैं सही जबाव देना चाहता हूं कि अगर आज जनसंघ अपनी पोजीशन क्लीयर कर ले कि वह सचमुच अपने में एक आरगेनाइजेशन नहीं है बल्कि आर. एस. एस. का एक पार्ट है तो शायद ये डिफिकलटी देश के अंदर नहीं रहे। आज पोजिशन यह है कि सचमुच आर. एस. एस. के साथ जनसंघ एक बंधी हुई चीज़ है और सारा कार्यक्रम आर. एस. एस. की तरफ से आता और ये जनसंघ वाले अपने को अन्नैसेसरी शो [unnecessary show] करने की कोशिश करते हैं कि हम डिफरेन्ट आर्गेनाजेशन हैं। और दूसरी डिफिकल्टी यह है कि सारे देश के अंदर जितने जनसंघ के अनुयायी हैं उनके सामने जो पोजीशन आज तक रखी गईं है वह और है और उनके दिमाग में कुछ और है। पोजीशन यह रखी गईं है...

अटल बिहारी वाजपेयीः हमारे संबंध में क्या आपको ज्यादा पता है?

बिशनचन्द्र सेठः पोजीशन यह रखी गईं है कि हम हिन्दू कल्चर, हिन्दू भावना को

लेकर आज देश में कार्य कर रहे हैं। परन्तु उनके करने का जो ढ़ंग है वह इस प्रकार का है कि वे अपने आप को कांग्रेस से अधिक सैक्यूलर

H-4

साबित करके आपको या होम मिनिस्ट्री की आखों में पर्दा डालना चाहते हैं। यह सत्य है और मैं इस संबंध में केवल इतना ही कहना चाहता हूं।

इसके बाद में जो स्पीचेज़ अभी हुई हैं उनके संबंध में मैं यह जरूर कहना चाहता हूं कि शिक्षा का जहां तक संबंध है उसमें एक बड़ी मौलिक बात की ओर मैं आपका ध्यान दिलाऊंगा। जैसा कि श्री के. एम. मुंशी ने कहा, हो सकता है उनकी बात सही हो परन्तु उस सत्य से मुख नहीं मोड़ा जा सकता कि जितने प्रान्त हैं उनमें अगर आज इस प्रकार का वातावरण निर्मित किया जाये कि सारे देश की शिक्षा प्रणाली एक बोर्ड के अंतगर्त काम करे और उस बोर्ड के अंदर मान लीजिए सोलह स्टेट यहां हैं तो चार चार जो शिक्षा विशारद हैं उनको मिलाकर एक बड़े बोर्ड का गठन किया जाये और उनके सारे देश का शिक्षा कार्यक्रम रखा जाये तो हमारे देश में बहुत सी बातें हल हो सकती हैं। आज ईमानदारी की बात यह है और मेरा पन्द्रह सालों से यह अनुभव है कि आज प्रान्तीयता का बोलवाला है, प्रान्तीयता का इतना जोर है कि अगर कोई भी सज्जन किसी विशेष प्रान्त के हों और कहीं अफसर बन कर चले जाते हैं तो उस प्रान्त के सारे के सारे आदमी कल्पना करते हैं कि हमारा काम बन जाये। जो जिस जात से या क्षेत्र से संबंध रखते हैं उनसे यह आशा करते हैं कि हमारा काम बन जाएगा। यह विचारधारा परखने के कारण में मैं नहीं जाना चाहता किन्तु इस सत्य से मुख नहीं मोड़ा जा सकता है।

इसके बाद मैं होम मिनिस्ट्री में अपने परम मित्र का ध्यान इस और आकर्षित करना चाहता हूं कि आज देश के अंदर जितने कानून बनाये जाते हैं, अगर ईमानदारी से सोचा जाये तो कानून बनने के बाद में प्रेक्टिकल शेप

H-5

में नहीं आने पाते। आज कानून बनता है और दूसरी ओर कानून का उल्लंघन करने के लिये अनेक प्रकार की चीजें मैदान में दूसरों के दिमाग में आती हैं। उसी की वजह से यह दिक्कत है कि हम अपने उद्देश्य तक पहुंच नहीं पाते। आज अगर एक केस लान्च होता है जिसमें पन्द्रह बीस दिन या महीने में सजा का या छूटने का फैसला हो सकता है तो वह केस पांच पांच वर्ष, तीन तीन वर्ष चलता है और इस तरह केस का असली स्वरूप नष्ट हो जाता है। मैं केसेज़ का नाम नहीं लेना चाहता लेकिन हमारे सामने देश के अंदर अनेक केसेज़ हैं जिनमें बहुत ज्यादा डिले कर दी जाती है। यदि आप सचमुच देश में एकता स्थापित करना चाहते हैं तो सबसे पहली चीज मैं आपके सामने निवेदन करना चाहता हूं कि आपका कानून इस प्रकार का हो कि

जो इमीडिएट एफैक्ट करे। आज सारे देश में इन्कम टैक्स से लेकर नार्मल लाइफ में एक अजीब आफत मची हुई है। मैं आपको बताना चाहता हूं कि आज पुलिस की क्या हालत है। कहीं मर्डर होता है तो केस को ऐसा बना दिया जाता है, कुछ न कुछ ऐसा स्वरूप कर दिया जाता है कि केस ही नहीं चलेगी। डकैती का केस है तो चोरी का कर देते हैं और अगर चोरी हुई तो कुछ और कर देते हैं। मैं जानता हूं हाउस का वक्त बहुत कीमती है और मैं ज्यादा नहीं कहना चाहता हूं। सिर्फ मैं अपने इलाके का एक हवाला देना चाहता हूं। मैं एटा से इलेक्शन लड़ा और एक जगह इलेक्शन के सिलसिले में गया। वहां एक बुजुर्ग एम. एल. ए. आए, उन्होंने कहा मैं आपकी मीटिंग का प्रेसीडेन्ट बनना चाहता हूं। मैंने कहाः मुझे इससे ज्यादा खुशी क्या होगी। उन्होंने एक वाक्या सुनाया कि एक चमार की लड़की या बहू को वहां के रहने वाले मुसलमानों ने तंग किया और जब वह रिपोर्ट लिखाने वाले को लेकर थाने में गई तो देवसंयोग से वहां दारोगा एक मियां थे और उन्होंने बजाय उसकी रिपोर्ट लिखने के उस आदमी को खूब मारा पीटा। मैं सिर्फ आपको यह बताना चाहता हूं कि आज पुलिस की हालत यह है कि ईमानदारी से केसेज़ नहीं लिखे जाते। क्राइम एक्चुअली कम नहीं हुआ है बल्कि बढ़ा है। अगर प्रापर लिखापढ़ी नहीं होती और उस पर प्रापर कार्यवाही नहीं होती तो फिर कोई उपाय नहीं रह जाता है। यह एक बड़ी लम्बी चीज है। मैं आपको केवल इतना ही बताऊंगा कि आज हमारे देश में कानून को इस प्रकार से बरता जाए कि कोई आदमी ग़लत काम करे तो कानून को दस प्रंदह रोज के अंदर की उसको सजा देने में कामयाब होना चाहिए। आज हालत यह है कि अगर एक आदमी

H-6

रुपया खर्च कर सकता है और उसका इन्फुलेन्स हो तो अपराध करने के बाद वर्षों तक उसको कुछ होने का नहीं।

एक चीज़ ग्राम पंचायतों के बारे में निवेदन करूंगा। उनके संबंध में अभी किन्हीं मित्र ने कहा, और मैं बिल्कुल अक्षरशः उसको मान्यता देता हूं। चूंकि मेरा देहात से लगाव है और मैं देहात से ही लड़कर आया हूं इसलिए मैं यह कह सकता हूं कि एक गांव में अगर ठाकुर वहां ज्यादा हैं तो कोई सोच नहीं सकता कि दूसरा कोई आदमी वहां पंच बने। आज हमारे देश में बहुत अधिक जातपात का बोलबाला है। गांवों की हालत सबसे बुरी है। जब मैं छोटा था, अभी मैं 56 वर्ष का हूं, तो जिस शहर में मैं पढ़ता था वह बीमारी चली और उस समय हम गांव चले गये। तब हमारे बाबा कहा करते थे कि गांवों का जीवन बड़ी सादगी और संतोष का है।

J-1

आज गांवों के हालत यह है कि किसी भी मालदार आदमी की या किसी की भी बहू बेटी की इज्ज़त सुरक्षित नहीं है जब तक कि उसके साथ दस लठबन्द न हों। अगर उसके पास ताकत है तो वह गांवों के अंदर अपनी इज्ज़त बचा सकता है। अगर उसके पास ताकत नहीं है, अगर वह लठइत [लठैत] नहीं है, झगड़ालू नहीं है तो उसकी इज्ज़त नहीं बच सकती है। आज यह हालत हो गई है। मैं इस इलेक्शन में दो चार सौ गांवों में गया और मैंने एक गांव भी ऐसा नहीं देखा जहां पार्टी बन्दी न हो। अगर कहीं मैं एक पार्टी के लोगों के पास बैठ गया तो दूसरी पार्टी ऑटोमेटिकली खिलाफ़ चली गई। हमारे देश का इतना बड़ा ह्रास हो गया है। मैं सोचने लगता हूं कि इस कांफ्रेंस में बैठने के बाद अगर हमारे प्रधान मंत्री ने कोई फंडामेंटल चीज़ नहीं की जिससे वस्तुतः गांवों के जीवन में, जिस पर हमारा देश आधारित है, कोई परिवर्तन लाया जा सके तो आपकी इस कौंसिल का कोई पर्पज़ सर्व होगा ऐसा मैं विश्वास नहीं करता।

इन्हीं शब्दों के साथ मैं वाजपेयी जी से कहूंगा कि मैंने कोई पर्सनल अटैक नहीं किया। आपने एकदम लठ मार दिया, इसलिए मैंने भी यह गुज़ारिश कर दी।

[Translation begins:

Bishanchander Seth: Honourable Chairman, Sir, I would first of all like to draw your attention to the fact that I do not consider the manner in which our respected friend Vajpayeeji began his speech to be appropriate for this meeting. The reason is pretty clear that we are here to deal with one issue. Our intention should not be to attack any individual. As far as the Jan Sangh and the Hindu Mahasabha are concerned, that it was said that the latter was responsible for the former's defeat and Vajpayeeji also lost, I consider this a personal issue and it was not appropriate to drag this into the discussion here. But since he did raise the issue, I would like to give the right reply, and that is, perhaps all these difficulties will go away if the Jan Sangh were to make its position clear that it is not really a separate organisation but only a part of the RSS. Today the position is that in reality the Jan Sangh is tied to the RSS and its entire programme comes from the RSS and the Jan Sangh tries to unnecessarily show that it is a different organisation. The second difficulty is that the position that has been kept before the followers of Jan Sangh is quite different from what their thinking is. The position that has been put before them is…

Atal Bihari Vajpayee: Do you know better about us?

Bishanchander Seth: The position that has been put before them is that we are trying to work for the nation on the basis of Hindu culture and identity. But the manner of their functioning is to prove that they are more secular than the Congress and in this manner wish to bamboozle you and the Home Ministry. This is the truth and I wish to say only this.

I would certainly like to say something about the speeches that were made after that, and that is, as far as education is concerned, I would like to draw your attention to a very basic fact. As Shri K.M. Munshi said, and it is possible that what he is saying is right, but you cannot ignore the fact that if we were to create an ambience in all the States that the country's entire education system works under one single board, and a big board is constituted by mutual consent, many problems in the country could be solved. The honest truth is, and it has been my experience for over fifteen years, that provincialism is dominant, so much so that if an individual belongs to a particular State and becomes an officer in another state, the entire population of that state thinks that its work will get done. The expectation is that the officer of a particular caste or state will oblige his kinsmen. I do not wish to go into why there is such a mindset but this truth cannot be ignored.

After this I wish to draw the attention of my very good friend in the Home Ministry to the fact that whatever laws are made in the country today, they do not take a practical shape after being passed, if you think about it honestly. Today a law is passed and immediately various loopholes to contravene that law are conjured up. This is the reason that we are unable to reach our goals. If a case is launched today which could be settled within fifteen-twenty days, a month, to sentence or acquit, that case actually drags on for years, three years or even five years, and in this manner, the real purpose of the case is lost. I do not wish to name the cases but there are innumerable cases in our country over which there is inordinate delay in the courts. If you really wish to aim for national integration, I would like to request that the first thing to be done is that the law should be enforced with immediate effect. Today there is a great deal of chaos in normal life over the matter of income tax. I want to tell you what the status of the police is all about today. There is a murder and the case is made so complicated and given such a shape that the case cannot be tried at all. Dacoity is turned into theft and if there is a theft, it is turned into something else. I know that time for this house is very valuable and so I do not wish to say much, I merely wish to give you an account of what happened in my area. I fought the election from Etah and went to the constituency in that connection. There a very senior MLA came and said he wanted to chair my meeting, I said nothing would make me happier. He related an incident when the daughter or daughter-in-law of a chamar was harassed by Muslims and when they went to register a case at the police station, where by some strange coincidence, the daroga [station in-charge] was a Muslim and instead of registering a case he beat up the man mercilessly. I merely want to point out that the situation today is that the police does not register cases honestly, and the crime rate has actually not come down, but increased. If there is proper paper work and then proper action is not taken, then it leaves no other option. This is a very long drawn out thing. I shall merely tell you that we should promulgate laws in the country in such a way that if there is any crime committed, within ten-fifteen days the law should be able to punish the accused. Today the situation is such, if an individual has money and influence then he can go scot free even after committing a crime.

I will urge something about village panchayats. Just now as one of the members said and I give full credence to what he said because I am attached to the rural areas and have won the election from those parts, I can say that in any village if there is a majority of Thakurs, then nobody else can even dream of becoming a panch. Today the caste system has too strong a hold on the country, it is worse in the rural areas. Now I am fifty-six years old and when I was very young and studying in the city an epidemic broke out and we went back to the village. Our elders used to say then that life in the villages is very simple and happy.

Today the situation in the rural areas is such that the women folk of no family is safe unless they are surrounded by ten armed men. Those who have the power can save the honour of themselves and their women; those who have no power or cannot fight for themselves, their honour is not safe. Today the situation is, as I saw during my tour of a few hundred villages, that one could not find a single village which is not caught up in partisan politics. If I sat with members of one party then automatically the other party would turn hostile. This is the tragedy of our country today. I am beginning to think that after we have met at this Conference, unless our Prime Minister is able to do something fundamental which would bring about real transformation in our rural areas on which the country is based, this Council would not have served any useful purpose.

With these words I would like to tell Vajpayeeji that I did not make a personal attack. Yours was the first blow and hence I made my plea.

Translation ends]

J-2

Jawaharlal Nehru: Mr Bishanchander Seth, General Secretary of the Hindu Mahasabha, who had just been speaking, first of all dealt with the Jan Sangh and the RSS. In brief, he said that the real difficulty arose because they pretended to be two different organisations.

A.B. Vajpayee: They are.

Jawaharlal Nehru: They really are one with two faces. I won't go further into that.

Then, he said something about education, that if there was one All India Board, there would be uniformity of education, one Board in which all the States would be represented. And he finally said that the conditions in the villages had deteriorated greatly ever since his youth, and now no person could keep his honour or self-respect unless he could protect it with some people with lathis round about him and if a Thakur went there, nobody else would be there to stand up. Well, these are really not directly under the subject we are discussing and we lose ourselves if we go into that. But I did not wish to stop either Mr Vajpayee or Mr Seth from saying what they wished to say.

A.B. Vajpayee: May I say that we have come here with the presumption that all of us want national integration? But the moment we go out we accuse each other of fomenting national disintegration. If this process is to continue, how can national integration be achieved? I do not think that the remarks offered by me are irrelevant, they are entirely relevant.

J-3

Bishanchander Seth: The same is the case with me also.

Jawaharlal Nehru: It is obvious that there are differences between parties. I am not talking about political or economic differences but differences on the question of communalism itself. And if we enter into those points, the purpose of this Council meeting will not be served and we will be lost in some other things. The presumption under which we meet here is that all of us who meet here and those whom we represent want national integration. It may be that their idea of national integration may be different somewhat but essentially they want it.

C.D. Deshmukh: I was wondering whether a small sub-committee should consider these questions like what exactly is communalism or how exactly it expresses itself in the actions, unwittingly even, of some parties, and whether some kind of code could not be drawn up in regard to this. Similarly, the other question is of regional chauvinism. It may consider what are the things which are to be postponed and what is permissible in the pursuit of the development of a particular region, which is a sort of legitimate object. And another sub-committee may go into the question of medium of instruction. These three or four issues seem to come up again and again. Now, it is obvious that no State can solve them by a general discussion in a large body like this. But if we want to bring the pros and cons together, would a sub-committee serve any useful purpose? I just interject this. I do not know whether it is the proper stage at which to do so.

J-4

K.M. Munshi: There are a number of committees.

C.D. Deshmukh: Whether a small committee of this Council could prepare the material for any final resolution that we might wish to pass in this regard—that is what I meant.

K.M. Munshi: The more important question is whether this Council is to have any kind of effective operational activity or rest content with merely discussing what other people have done or carry out a debate on academic questions. The scope of function of this Council must first be to enable us to know exactly how we stand. For instance, take the suggestion that integration should be considered a non-party issue and the propaganda should be on behalf of the Integration Council. It should be considered whether it is possible, whether it is feasible and whether it should be done and what shape should be given to the activities of this Council. Otherwise, you will disperse after two days' meeting and after six months you will discuss the reports of the various committees. Therefore, first of all, we must concentrate on the scope of the functions of this body—what you propose to do, what is going to be placed in national life and how it is going to help national integration.

Jawaharlal Nehru: We can hardly give executive functions to this Council. But there are the representatives of all the parties here who will agree with them. Presumably, they will influence their parties. There are the Chief Ministers here who will presumably give some executive shape to what they agree to here.

How can you give power to this Council?

K.M. Munshi: Suppose there are deviations, then would they not be brought before the Council? Suppose, for instance, some policy is adopted...

J-5

Sanjiva Reddy:[38] We will point it out at the next meeting. If anything happens in a particular area in the country, we can certainly point it out here.

K.M. Munshi: It can only come up for discussion.

Sanjiva Reddy: If you take the question of education, it must be left to the universities, for implementation.

K.M. Munshi: Particular universities have not implemented.

Sanjiva Reddy: You can discuss it with them and bring them round.

K.M. Munshi: That must be discussed by this Council. Otherwise, it will be merely idly passing of resolutions, whether they are implemented or not.

Jawaharlal Nehru: You cannot. This Council as such cannot take any executive action. That must be made quite clear. It just cannot. You cannot convert it into some kind of super government sitting all over India. But, nevertheless, it can have a great deal of influence on governments, on political parties and on the general public. If we decide on something, apart from the publicity value of it, it should be implemented. The Chief Ministers are here; presumably, they will try to carry it out, not 100%, may be 50% or 75%, whatever it may be. And political parties and those who represent them here, will publicise them.

C.P. Ramaswamy Aiyar: Although, as you have rightly said, this Council cannot function as a kind of overall executive and administrative body, nevertheless, it is open to this Council to have sub-committees for dealing with the particular

38. N. Sanjiva Reddy, Chief Minister of Andhra Pradesh.

J-6

points which have given rise to disintegrating results. Those sub-committees—in which I take it that the Chief Ministers will be represented—may confine their attention to the main points which in the opinion of each sub-committee would be producing disintegrating factors. Take for instance the question which was raised by Mr Munshi with regard to the fragmentation of educational work. The question of what may be called the feeling of foreignness among the educated community is there, and whether that question can be dealt with at all effectively and, if so, how—by the joint work of the universities or otherwise—may be dealt with by a committee. Another committee might deal with what may be called certain subversive factors which have demonstrated themselves or manifested themselves during the election. One of those aspects may be taken up and concentrated upon. While these committees will be essentially what may be called co-ordinating bodies, nevertheless there may be some kind of spade work done by which it might be useful later on to have a discussion in this Council.

Zakir Husain: That would be for our own guidance; those investigations are for our own guidance and decisions may be taken.

C.P. Ramaswami Aiyar: If on the basis of the recommendations of those committees, we make any statement or issue any manifesto, it might have some effect upon public opinion in general because this Council is a kind of cross-section of Indian life, administrative and non-administrative.

Jawaharlal Nehru: You have in effect to some extent supported what Dr Deshmukh has said about the appointment of sub-committees.

J-7

C.D. Deshmukh: In order to avoid misunderstanding, all I meant to say was that because of the practical inconveniences of trying to resolve these in a plenary session of this Council, a sub-committee (or committees) which means a smaller member of people who know more about the subject and who feel more keenly about it may be formed and they may sit for two or three hours and produce a report which should be dealt with in the same session; that is to say, before we disperse. I did not have any standing committee in my mind. That work should be disposed of in this particular session and I thought that might be a convenient procedure. If it cannot be disposed of, it might come up later, but essentially it is part of the procedure of this session of the Council.

Jawaharlal Nehru: Oh! Yes, that can be done.

C.D. Deshmukh: For instance, I have a lot to say about the medium of instruction. I cannot go on repeating this or making speeches again and again. It comes up again and again. Some speakers speak about it. Then there is another speech on that. It will go on. Actually, this matter was dealt with exhaustively in the Education Committee of the last Integration Conference. Well, maybe there are some points to be clarified or something to be added. I thought that if it was continuation of the same process that might be helpful. But finally, this Council should issue its conclusions at the end of the session and not leave matters to be dealt with through standing committees. This is without prejudice to any discussion that we will take up on Mr Munshi's resolution. I am not now speaking indirectly against that.

K.L. Shrimali: I may inform the members that the Government has recently appointed a Committee under the distinguished Chairmanship of one of the members of this Council, Dr Ramaswami

J-8

Aiyar. And this Committee is going to survey the whole field of university education including the medium of instruction, and we will make a copy of the report of this Committee available to this Conference also. I hope that the interim report will be available within a period of six months. It will take some time for the full report to be finished because they will have to go into all the aspects of university education, and I do not think it necessary to appoint another committee to go into this question. This whole subject could be dealt with very exhaustively by this Committee which we have recently appointed.

K-1

K.M. Munshi: May I suggest that two or three subjects might be selected for which, as Mr Deshmukh suggested, there might be a sub-committee to deliberate on them and convey their views, which may perhaps be generally acceptable to this Council, because the Council must go to the country with some kind of conclusions which naturally of course should be consonant with what all has gone before.

Jawaharlal Nehru: Some subject was discussed, the code of conduct for the political parties, etc. This perhaps may be a suitable thing for this Council …

C.D. Deshmukh: We have still to consider it.

Jawaharlal Nehru: We might like to appoint committees for that thing, to the question that has arisen as to what communalism is and what should be avoided. That might be. The medium of instruction thing is, I should imagine, too big a subject to be dealt with in the course of an hour's meeting in the afternoon.

C.D. Deshmukh: Matters have been brought to the point of issue, that is to say, one knows now the pros and cons. That is the stand we took and we perhaps had a certain amount of misunderstanding cleared. It would really be following up that paragraph in the conclusions of the National Integration Conference. It has said a great deal about the medium. What I mean is this, that in view of that it is perhaps a matter of surprise that some more points should have been raised in regard to the medium of instruction, because we thought that there was general agreement. Obviously there is some feeling that what was said last time is not complete or adequate. If so, those who held that view and that included the Chief Ministers as well as

K-2

the special conference of which Dr Sampurnanand was the head. He agrees generally with the findings of the Education Committee, and a view of a body, say, like the University Grants Commission Seminar. Now one might have something to say about the medium that might clear the air and that was all my hope.

D.S. Kothari: There is the Committee which had recently been appointed …

C.D. Deshmukh: That might give guidance. We are still open to conviction if they bring forward some other points of view.

K.M. Munshi: The country would expect the Council to give some lead. It will not be satisfied if we discuss the situation here and then disperse.

Sampurnanand: We have the general lead given by the Emotional Integration Committee and by the Zonal Councils.

K.M. Munshi: Take the other question of subversion which Dr Ramaswami Aiyar mentioned just now. The country expects some lead to be given.

Sampurnanand: About communalism, that subject can come before the sub-committee.

Jawaharlal Nehru: How shall we proceed? Do we appoint any sub-committee?

Ganga Sharan Sinha:[39] But which are the subjects which will be considered by the sub-committee? For example, communalism or the medium of instruction, are we going to refer it to that committee or not?

Jawaharlal Nehru: We may appoint a sub-committee to deliberate on communalism, what, in their opinion, communalism is, and how it should be avoided.

N. Siv Raj:[40] That committee should be non-communal.

K-3

Ganga Sharan Sinha: What are the issues that we refer to the committees? That we should decide. Still it appears that there are differences of opinion regarding the issues to be referred to the committee.

Dr A. Ramaswami Aiyar:[41] Just two points which might be considered—one, the emergence of what may be called communal or caste factors either in administration or in public life. The other is the idea of regional separatism. Those are the two points which are very much in the public eye now. Is the Council going to say anything on that? Is the Council going to give a lead on the subject and, if so, have we got the materials for giving the lead, and if we have got the materials, some committee may consider those materials and see whether there is any basis for the complaint of regional bodies asking for separation. Is it possible to harmonise those views? Is it possible to convince them that they are going on the wrong lines? Are

39. Rajya Sabha MP, Independent, from Bihar.
40. Member of the Republican Party of India; Mayor of Madras, 1945-46, and Independent MP in the Second Lok Sabha from Chinglepet (SC), Madras.
41. Apparently a transcription error for C.P. Ramaswami Aiyar. A. Ramaswami Aiyar does not appear in the list of participants in Appendix I of item 8 published on pp. 223-225 of this volume.

we going to take any line in regard to that aspect? Are we going to take a line in regard to what may be called the emergence of sub-communities and sub-castes as factors in public administration and executive actions? These are matters on which the Council may be expected to give some pronouncements or take some kind of a stand. That is the aspect, I take it, which Dr Deshmukh and Dr Munshi are indicating? Am I right?

N. Sanjiva Reddy: I think that is very important.

K.L. Shrimali: Last time's Resolution is still before us. We have written to the State Governments to implement that recommendation and we have appointed another committee recently under the Chairmanship of Dr Ramaswami Aiyar. There is no point in appointing still another committee to go into this question and

K-4

add to the confusion. I do not think the matter is so simple as Dr Deshmukh has suggested. Even in this there are sharp differences of opinion with regard to the medium of instruction for college education and the whole thing will have to be gone through very thoroughly and exhaustively by a committee of educationists, for we really want to have consensus of opinion in this matter.

Jawaharlal Nehru: But we never get the educationists to agree to anything.

C.D. Deshmukh: Medium of instruction has political aspects also which affect our attitude towards our national integration. It is not a province left exclusively to educationists.

N. Sanjiva Reddy: From this angle we will have to discuss it.

C.D. Deshmukh: There is also this point which I made, namely that the National Integration Conference has actually given a lead in regard to the medium of instruction. What I said was that either the regional languages are bound to come as media of instruction…

A Member: At what stage?

C.D. Deshmukh: At the university stage. I am talking of the university stage. I am not discussing anything about the secondary education stage where there is less difference of opinion. But at the university stage it says that they are bound to come and that due preparations acceptable to that academic world should be made in regard to this. Now, whilst academically that might be supported, it does raise this very important point, particularly important from national integration, that the nation will lose or have a weaker link in regard to intercommunication. Now that could be either Hindi ultimately or English in a transitional period. Then

K-5

the Integration Conference said that for the time being it must be English, because Hindi will take about as long to develop as the other regional languages. It is not as if Hindi is like French or German or Russian which can immediately replace English, should that be the intention. Therefore, till that stage comes along, we shall have to phase, if necessary, although that part of the Resolution said that the phasing period need not be as long as was feared. You may phase supplanting of English as medium by a regional language or Hindi as the case may be, and side by side you must place considerable emphasis on the teaching of Hindi and English throughout the university stage, Hindi because we wanted a national link, and English because we wanted an international link plus an instrument to enable us to develop our own languages as fast as we can. Obviously, unless you keep the window open to the world and find out what is happening, it cannot be done through translations, you will not be able to develop your own language. It means you will want to be familiar with the new concepts as you go along. Therefore it seemed to me that it is agreed all over the educational world that the emphasis on English must not weaken; if possible, it must be reinforced.

Jawaharlal Nehru: When you talk about the emphasis on English, you don't mean that English should be the medium.

C.D. Deshmukh: It need not. That is the point. It need not be; it should not be. Gradually it will cease to be. This is one point and nothing has happened in the last six months because the Universities and States are taking decisions all the time. All this I should have said in the sub-committee. Naturally I have got

K-6

to take up time here because I want to explain to the Education Minister about the urgency of this matter. Delhi University is beginning now optional Hindi in economics, political science and history in its constituent colleges in the B.A. Pass course; that is on the certificate of the heads of the departments that a sufficient number of good standard text books are available in Hindi in these subjects for that stage, namely the B.A. Pass stage. Now the Delhi University has already a system under which option is given to the students to answer in Hindi questions which are set in English, the medium of instruction being so far English, and 33 to 40% of the students are already taking advantage of this option in history, economics and political science. Then they find that about 80% of the teachers are prepared to teach in Hindi if required. Well, it may be 80 or it may be 75%, but there is large number of teachers who are prepared. The other 25 or 20% say that they will not be because obviously they are not drawn from the Hindi-speaking areas. Now the arrangement that is proposed is that complete option will be given to the constituent colleges as well as students to choose whichever medium they want. Every college will have two mediums. English will continue, but if you want a Hindi section it is there or if the Hindi section is larger, then there will be an English section. It may be that in some colleges the number of students who want Hindi or the number of teachers—which is more likely—is not enough, then by exchange of students between

K-7

colleges it may be possible to set up well equipped classes or sections both for Hindi and for English. Now an experiment of this kind does not imperil anything so far as the authorities of Delhi University are able to make out ...

C.P. Ramswami Aiyar: Except inter-university mobility.

C.D. Deshmukh: No, because English still continues to whoever wants English and more necessary emphasis and considerable emphasis continues on English itself as a language of comprehension and expression. [Interruption] Yes, of course, that goes back to the secondary course of education where for seven years we want that English should be properly taught, not the language of Chaucer or *Fairie Queene* or Emerson, but modern English for the purpose of comprehension and for expressing oneself in regard to the modern environment. I am sorry, but that is what I had in mind in regard to the medium of instruction.

Frank Anthony: Are we anticipating Mr Munshi's item?

C.D. Deshmukh: This is a permanent committee. Mine was to enable us to discuss the matter. For instance the report will come up before the plenary session. That is the usual expedient in meetings like this.

Jawaharlal Nehru: Well, after hearing Dr Deshmukh, would you like to appoint a committee to report by tomorrow?

L-1

Jawaharlal Nehru: You wish to confine it to the medium, not to the fact of language being made really compulsory?

C.D. Deshmukh: It is part of the process.

Jawaharlal Nehru: There is considerable difference between English being the medium and English being the compulsory language.

C.D. Deshmukh: It will have to be dealt with by the committee for medium of instruction at the university stage.

Chairman: We can appoint a committee. We will have to sit in the afternoons to meet for two hours by arrangement.

D.S. Kothari:[42] It is going to be the same committee as last time with the same terms of reference. Please do not confine it to the limited aspect of medium of instruction. Let it confine itself to the broad aspects of education, discuss the progress made in the light of the resolutions adopted last time and suggest further things.

K.L. Shrimali: Resolution No. 18 on page 18 is a comprehensive resolution.

42. Chairman, UGC.

Frank Anthony: We will come to a broad agreement. May I suggest on the lines of Mr Munshi's resolution? In paragraph 15 we have already come to a broad sort of decision about the medium of instruction in universities.

D.S. Kothari: The general thinking in the universities is, if I may say so, very much on the lines of the resolution we adopted at the last conference of Vice-Chancellors. There are two basic points in this. Firstly, if there be a regional language, which is the language of a large number of people, that language must find a place in the university, otherwise that language will not be viable, because even if text books for schools are to be written they will have to be written by people of the universities

L-2

very often. The language must develop and must have some place in the universities. The university must make some contacts with the community. It is, therefore, that the language of the community must occupy a place in the university.

Jawaharlal Nehru: What do you mean by "place"?

D.S. Kothari: I will come to that shortly.

Secondly, as the school education is in the language or the region, we cannot have a sudden switchover in the medium of instruction between the school stage and the university stage. I am not at the moment going into the merits of it. Having decided right or wrongly—perhaps rightly—that at the school stage, there will be difficulty for students speaking the language of the region, having decided that, it follows immediately that at any rate at the early stages of the university education the medium of instruction must be the same as at the school stage. Even now, Sir, in most of the universities in India the medium of instruction is English. Even so teachers find it very difficult to convey the ideas in the regional language to the First Year students, whereas through the medium of English they find it easy. Though in most of the universities, officially the medium of instruction is English, but for the facility of students in the earlier classes they have informally to use Hindi or whatever the language of the region may be to convey the ideas to the students.

So, at the university stage, at the early stages of degree course, we have to be bilingual, English and the language of the region. In other words, it is to be the same as at the school stage. The basic point is that there cannot be a sudden switchover in the medium of

L-3

instruction between the school and the early stage of university education. There has to be a continuity in the medium of instruction. As the student advances higher and higher up, when he goes to the post-graduate stage, the medium of instruction also tends to be more and more in English because he has to consult more and more books in English as he advances higher up. Therefore, at the end of the undergraduate study, while the medium of instruction may be the regional language, the student will have a good knowledge of English. I am saying this because in most of the universities the medium is English. If we do so it will have an advantage because it will make for the students to apprehend a subject more fully. At the moment the drawback with our students is that their apprehension of the subject is very feeble indeed and we cannot take the students ahead unless they learn through the same language with which they have learnt in the school stage. Therefore, at the end of the undergraduate stage it will be an advantage to have English as a compulsory language where regional language is the medium of instruction, a compulsory language for everyone to study because his apprehension of the subject will be better. With medium of instruction being the regional language, he will be able to save a little time from that and devote more to the study of English language.

Further, by adopting modern methods of teaching English—we may be wrong in our conception—we expect that the student will have better fluency in expressing himself in the language and better grasp of the English language so that when English is made compulsory at the undergraduate level, when he goes to the post-graduate stage, there the teaching will have to be in the English language.

L-4

Thus, Sir, two languages will be used at the university stage—regional language as the medium of instruction and English language as the compulsory language. Every graduate thus, who comes out of the university, will require enough proficiency in the English language to understand the expressions when he comes to the post-graduate stage when the medium of instruction will also become very largely English. This will serve a double purpose. There will be academic mobility at the universities and the students will be better equipped for post-graduate research and it will also make students better educated in their subjects.

Bijayananda Patnaik:[43]What happens to Hindi as the national language?

D.S. Kothari: We expect every school student to learn Hindi so that every matriculate must know enough Hindi for the purpose of inter-communication on the common level.

Bijayananda Patnaik: Enough Hindi, enough regional language and enough English. It is rather heavy.

D.S. Kothari: He has to know language of the region, English and Hindi.

K.M. Munshi: That is my resolution too that I may move. As Dr Kothari suggested, by the time a man becomes a graduate he must have sufficient working knowledge of English to be able to have a community of outlook throughout the whole of the country. More or less the same idea has been expressed in my resolution. That simply carries out paragraph 15 of the Conference Resolution. It was felt that the link must ultimately be Hindi. Hindi like any other language must some time take over from English. Till such time English will continue to be the link. That is the main object with which I moved this resolution. The idea is that it should be uniformly enforced in the country.

L-5

Jawaharlal Nehru: I do not think any university has banned English as the medium of instruction.

K.M. Munshi: We are discussing here at a theoretical level but the things are different when we come to practical things. For instance, take the universities with which I have something to do. In the Gujarat University, first the idea was to teach Agriculture and Engineering through English medium. Suddenly within six months you started teaching them in Hindi. There were no Hindi text books. The teachers themselves did not know anything except English, and Animal Husbandry, Chemistry, Biology, Engineering have to be taught. This is what is happening. Experiments are being made every day by people who think they know about education.

K.L. Shrimali: The universities are not responsible for this decision. We take full responsibility for this. The Radhakrishnan Commission—Dr

43. Chief Minister of Orissa.

Radhakrishnan, the Vice-President was also a member of the commission—has recommended that ultimately federal or regional languages must become the languages of these areas. We have been trying to implement it.

K.M. Munshi: I am not finding fault with what you say. We have got this charter. I am not departing from it but I must say that it has not been enforced or recognised by the different universities. I want the authority of this Council to go to the country and say, "Well, this is the standard norm which every university is expected to follow."

K.L. Shrimali: This Resolution is there. We have been impressing on the universities to implement it.

K.M. Munshi: But it is not being implemented.

L-6

D.S. Kothari: This Resolution was communicated to the Vice-Chancellors' Conference and as far as I know the Vice-Chancellors are in agreement almost entirely with this Resolution.

Frank Anthony: May I say, Sir, that I had some kind of a resolution to be put down in my name? I do not know whether Mr Munshi had the same thing in mind. I had in mind the elimination of English by an order of the Gujarat University Senate. Now, I wanted to bring to the notice of this Council two matters. We have in paragraph 15 of our statement indicated what we feel should be the general approach. Ultimately the regional languages will be the medium of university education but there must be the national link that may be Hindi. In the transition period it will continue to be English and, in any case, English will be used for purposes of teaching science and technology.

I wanted to go further. Within paragraph 14, you gave certain guarantees to linguistic minorities. You said there that in future where any colleges or even lesser educational institutions are run through the medium of minority language, if they have no facilities to affiliate locally, they will affiliate outside. Now, two things follow from the Gujarat University Senate decision. It may be said that they have the right; they are autonomous body to introduce Gujerati so far as their own Government colleges are concerned. But they have this embargo to follow. They have said that minorities that are running English medium colleges shall not do so. It is a breach of the guarantee that is given to the linguistic minorities. I put this question to the Home Minister and he said that they had given an assurance

L-7

to important linguistic minorities, Bengalis, Tamilians etc. and because of that they are going to amend the Constitution. To that effect the Prime Minister has also given assurance that English will be the alternate language for an indefinite period. Now, I want to pose two questions. If English is to be the alternate language for an indefinite period how can anyone say to a linguistic minority institution that they shall not teach through the medium of English? That is precisely what they have said. What is the factual position? For instance, how can anyone say where Hindi is being taught in a non-Hindi region that they shall not teach Hindi. Immediately the legal point will be taken up. But it is the national language. Then, will not that apply almost equally to the alternate official language? English is the sole medium of entry to the superior services.

M-1

It is the sole medium of examination for the Defence Academy. At least the Bengalis, Tamilians and Gujeratis will say "We want our children to go into the superior services; we want to enter Khadakvasla and NDA. How can you prevent us from pursuing higher education in English?"These are all legal matters. The question is that the Conference has already said that this should be the link. Secondly, minority institutions should have the right to affiliate. If we demur at giving any kind of direction, let us guarantee that minority institutions will have the right to affiliate and Dr Shrimali can help us. [Interruption]

Jawaharlal Nehru: Are we going into this particular controversy? Now would you like to have a sub-committee to say something more than what we have done in the last resolution about this question of medium, about the position of English and Hindi and other regional language in university education? [Interruption]

C.D. Deshmukh: I did not say more. What I said was that I was surprised that certain views were expressed here in the course of the morning which went against the findings of the National Integration Conference.

Y.B. Chavan:[44] You have expressed even outside.

C.D. Deshmukh: Here.

Y.B. Chavan: Individual expression of opinion does not affect the general agreement.

C.D. Deshmukh: During the meeting of a body like the Council for the first time there are important people who have said that they are not very happy about this or that.

K.L. Shrimali: Sir, I think it would be better for the sub-committee to see how this can be implemented, etc.

C.D. Deshmukh: I am not trying to anticipate the decisions of the committee at all. For instance there is this curious report

M-2

from Annamalai. Here we are worried about the link. When asked whether they would take some students from outside, the Annamalai University said that would not take other students at all. That seems to go to the very root of the idea of integration. Similarly I heard in Madras that in the three-language formula, although it does not refer to university education, the number of marks given to Hindi is 50 and they do not count for the final examination marks, with the result that everyone is proud to boast that he got zero in Hindi. I do not know in what circumstances people there will ever learn Hindi, even for the next generation. I have not been able to verify this.

K.L. Shrimali: This committee could advise further steps for the implementation of its recommendations.

C.D. Deshmukh: That is the only limited purpose of this.

Jawaharlal Nehru: Well, the idea is that we have a sub-committee to report on what has been done in furtherance of that Resolution and what should be done further. Is that agreed to?

44. Chief Minister of Maharashtra.

Pattom Thanu Pillai: Sir, in matters like these there cannot be complete unanimity of opinion. Certainly we must act upon the maximum amount of agreement that is possible. On the basis of some difference of opinion if we go on changing the decisions already taken, there will be no end.

Jawaharlal Nehru: We are not changing anything. We are asking how it has been implemented and what further should be done about it. Then what about the personnel of it? I think it should be as follows:

Dr Deshmukh
Dr Kothari
Dr Munshi
Dr Jivraj Mehta
Dr Sampurnanand
Mr Frank Anthony
Bhai Jodh Singh

Dr Sampurnanand will be the Chairman. The Committee will consider what is being done in regard to the Resolution

M-3

on the subject and what more should be done.

Now what about the committee on other subjects?

Communalism.

Bijayananda Patnaik: You might have a DMK man.

Jawaharlal Nehru: There is none. What about another committee?

C.P. Ramaswamy Aiyar: If a Committee is going to be appointed with regard to these aspects of communalism and regional chauvinism, that cannot possibly report by tomorrow morning, because it is a tremendous amount of material. We have not got any representative of one of the organisations which we have in mind. So we must have more time to look into them and the report can only be presented at the next session of this Conference.

Jawaharlal Nehru: Communalism and regionalism—what exactly is meant by it? What do we want to avoid?

C.D. Deshmukh: We have already said a lot about this in the Integration Conference. Now to say that we do not really know what we mean by it …

K.M. Munshi: What should be done about it? We have already condemned it.

Indira Gandhi:[45] Every time it happens we say it is a bad thing, but there should be certain steps. This is really linked up with the suggestion made by Shri Asoka Mehta about the creation of a force, the necessary integration force.

Jawaharlal Nehru: The other committee may report at the next meeting of the Council which is presumably three months later. What should be the terms of the Committee?

N-1

What should be the term of reference? Should it be for communalism or regionalism or for both?

N. Siv Raj: Not necessarily.

K.M. Munshi: Then we will have two committees.

C.P. Ramaswami Aiyar: It is only a question of reporting on the disintegrating effects of communalism and regionalism as they have been recently manifested, and suggest some remedies.

N. Siv Raj: Does regionalism necessarily mean separatism?

C.D. Deshmukh: Communalism has a religious and political concept. The people who would be able to shed light on it might be different sorts of people. Their feelings might be different. It should be rather a bigger committee or a different committee.

C.P. Ramaswami Aiyar: It would be wise to enable that Committee to co-opt people who are not represented in this conference who might represent the

45. Chairman of the National Integration Committee of the Indian National Congress.

opposite point of view and who could present their point of view before the council.

Jawaharlal Nehru: First thing is, should we have one or two Committees?

C.P. Ramaswami Aiyar: One committee will be able to deal with it, with power to co-opt.

Indira Gandhi: Although they can be dealt with by one Committee but there are two levels of urgency.

Regionalism is a very long way off but communalism is urgent.

C.P. Ramaswami Aiyar: I do not think Mr Nadar[46] will give the same emphasis.

Jawaharlal Nehru: By a resolution we are not going to put an end to it.

C.P. Ramaswami Aiyar: That committee may sub-divide into two, one dealing with this subject of immediate importance.

Zakir Husain: Then what is the advantage in having one

N-2

committee. There are ugly manifestations.

Sadiq Ali:[47] You need different types of personnel.

बिशनचन्द्र सेठः मैं तो एक कमेटी की बात को गलत मानता हूं। वो बिल्कुल अलग अलग आसपैक्ट्स हैं जो कि आप डील करना चाहते है। ये बिल्कुल दो चीजें है और मैं नहीं समझता कि आप इनको कैसे मिलायेंगे। जब वे जुदागाना चीजें तो फिर आप उनको कैसे एक में मिलायेंगें। मेरा कहना है कि अलग अलग कमेटी होनी चाहिए और उनके मेम्बर भी दूसरे होने चाहिए क्योंकि कुछ ऐसे है जिनको कि एक मसले पर अपने आप को एक्सप्लेन करना है।

46. K. Kamaraj Nadar, Chief Minister of Madras.
47. General Secretary, AICC.

[Translation begins:

Bishanchander Seth: I consider having one committee would be absolutely wrong. I cannot understand how you can mix up different aspects which you wish to deal with. They are separate issues, how then can you mix them up? In my opinion, there should be separate committees with different members because there are certain people who would need to give an explanation for one issue or the other.

Translation ends]

Indira Gandhi: We may have two small committees which could sit together.

Y.B. Chavan: That can split itself into two.

K.M. Munshi: It is better to have small committees, dealing with one subject rather than have a bigger one. It will lead to more quick disposal.

Zakir Husain: Would it be all right if we appoint two committees and ask them to give one report?

K.M. Munshi: One may be done earlier. The other may take time.

Jawaharlal Nehru: Let us have two committees which can function together as one. Who will members of these? Will you be one C.P.?

C.P. Ramaswami Aiyar: I shall be glad to serve but I shall prefer to be on the regional committee. Kamaraj and myself will work together. The other is more Northern.

Indira Gandhi: The caste problem will come into the other.

Jawaharlal Nehru: What about Kamaraj?

Kamaraj Nadar: I do not have time.

C.P. Ramaswami Aiyar: He must be there otherwise I will not serve on that.

N-3

Frank Anthony: Is there anyone from North East Frontier? I find the regional challenge there and somebody who has a contrary view to the Assam Chief Minister may be there.

Jawaharlal Nehru: The following people will be on the Committees:

REGIONAL COMMITTEE:	COMMITTEE RE: COMMUNALISM:
Shri C.P. Ramaswami Aiyar	Shrimati Indira Gandhi
Shri Kamaraj Nadar	Shri Vajpayee
Shri Y.B. Chavan	Shri B.S. Seth [Bishanchander Seth]
Shri B. Patnaik	Shri Sadiq Ali
Shri Asoka Mehta	Shri Namboodiripad
Shri B.P. Chaliha	Shri Mujeeb[48]

C.P. Ramaswami Aiyar: We may say, with power to co-opt not more than two.

Jawaharlal Nehru: They can have joint or separate sittings and should present the report to the next meeting of the Council.

O-1

What are the terms of reference?

C.P. Ramaswami Aiyar: Problems arising out of the agitation for regional autonomies and problems arising out of the agitation in regard to that matter.

Zakir Husain: There are other problems also, problems of distribution of developmental resources.

Asoka Mehta: We should not confine ourselves to the challenge from the DMK alone. Even apart from these separatist tendencies there is a feeling in every State that they have been neglected and such assertions are made in different parts of the country and the parts are trying to be greater than the whole.

48. Mohammad Mujeeb, Vice Chancellor, Jamia Millia Islamia.

C.P. Ramaswami Aiyar: Anything of fractionalisation or separatist tendencies arising out of the demand for regional autonomy.

Zakir Husain: For instance the development of State citizenship.

C.D. Deshmukh: We might say to examine and report on all aspects of integration and communalism.

Jawaharlal Nehru: Separatism is only a small aspect for this Committee—the DMK aspect. It does not arise anywhere else except in Nagaland.

Partap Singh Kairon:[49] We need not go very deeply into it now. Representations might be received; memoranda may come in and papers might start talking about it and possibly instead of putting the cobra in the basket we might be releasing it.

Jawaharlal Nehru: Why not we just say, national Integration and regionalism and for the other one, national integration and communalism.

C.P. Ramaswami Aiyar: Yes; that will be all right.

Jawaharlal Nehru: Since we have appointed Committees to consider some of the matters, those particular matters will not

O-2

be considered by us any further.

Indira Gandhi: What about convenors for the Committees? Possibly we might have Chairman-convenor. Asokaji[50] is there for the Communal Committee.

Jawaharlal Nehru: Yes; what about the Regional Committee? I suppose Mr C.P. Ramaswami Aiyar will be the Chairman-convener.

After some discussion the Council decided to adjourn now and reassemble after lunch at 3:00 p.m. to consider the other items of the agenda and it was also agreed that the Committees might meet after the Council's afternoon session.

49. Chief Minister of Punjab.
50. Asoka Mehta was chairman of the committee on integration and communalism as given in the proceedings, item 8 p. 220, though in this verbatim record, his name does not appear on this committee.

P-1

The Council reassembled after lunch at Three Of The Clock with The Prime Minister in the Chair.

Jawaharlal Nehru: We shall take up item 3. There is a paper among those circulated as appendix 1. This, I gather, was placed before the Conference last time. I shall read through that:

(Reads out Appendix I)[51]

After this the Conference said in its statement:

"The Conference was of the opinion that in order to foster and develop national integration, it was necessary to have a code of conduct in respect of political parties, the press, students and the general public."

If we treat this as the basis, we can proceed to consider anything else which might be added on to it.

C.D. Deshmukh: It strikes me that there is a lacuna here which does not define the relation between the Party and its members. That is, if a member violates any of these provisions then what is the duty of the party vis-à-vis the offending member? It would often happen that these things are committed by members and not by the parties as such.

Jawaharlal Nehru: There is reference to that in regard to violence.

C.D. Deshmukh: Yes only for that. It does not say that the Party just use some sanction or dissuade its members from doing so. For instance I was told that in the elections in one place very offensive slogans were used by members. One would not be able to hold the party responsible. They would say:"Sorry, we did not authorise this."

51. Appendix I of the Proceedings published here within item 8 is a list of Council Members, see pp. 223-224. Appendix II is a draft code of conduct for the Press; Nehru is probably referring to this document. It is possible that there is a difference between the documents in use at the meeting and the document tabled in Parliament which has been published in this volume of SWJN. See pp. 225-226.

Jawaharlal Nehru: The Party should dissociate itself and condemn the person.

C.D. Deshmukh: That is what I mean some reference to sanction against the member should be there, if he violates the code of discipline.

P-2

C.P. Ramaswami Aiyar: Is it not within the party's disciplinary jurisdiction?

Zakir Husain: It should be expressly mentioned in this.

Q-1

Sadiq Ali: In the States of Maharashtra and Madras the various Parties met to evolve a common code of conduct. In Maharashtra we had a meeting for two or three days …

C.B. Gupta: Ultimately during the time of the elections they were observed more in their breach.

Asoka Mehta: We did not incorporate other items in the code because it was suggested that there would be a separate meeting or a separate effort for drawing up a code for election. Therefore, all those things pertaining to the election were kept out. Things of general usefulness alone were included in the code that was drawn up. Otherwise those things were before us at that time also.

Sadiq Ali: The State code has mostly no reference to election. There was no meeting at the all-India level.

Asoka Mehta: That was why it was not included.

K.M. Munshi: The code is there all right even as it is.

Asoka Mehta: Representatives meet at the State level and national level where these matters would be brought up. It was there in the report.

Jawaharlal Nehru: Do we confirm this and repeat what we have said in paragraph 23?

Asoka Mehta: Unless the machinery is set up the code remains on paper.

C.P. Ramaswami Aiyar: With reference to what fell from Mr Deshmukh—"for immediate adoption by political parties and for its effectual implementation in relation to individual members thereof"—what is our view?

C.D. Deshmukh: "Effectual implementation on the part of the members of the parties concerned".

Jawaharlal Nehru: Shall we add something like this at the end of the preamble, or we may leave the whole thing as it is, confirm the preamble and add if you choose to add.

Q-2

Asoka Mehta: One more thing I would like to add if it is possible. The suggestion has often been made that in elections people from one part of the country might contest in another part. I do not know if political parties would agree that if any one offers himself as a candidate like that, they would not like to raise the question of his being an outsider, because if that issue is raised, this effort on the part of the persons to contest outside the linguistic area or linguistic region will become very difficult. Odd individuals might say what they like, but responsible political parties may not make this an issue. The political parties are represented here. The code was drawn up with the consent of the political parties. Even if he is an independent person, the question is whether this issue should be raised by the political parties.

A.B. Vajpayee: The question is whether this should be considered as an additional qualification, simply because an appeal should be made to the people that he has decided to contest from a different place.

Asoka Mehta: I am only saying that responsible political parties should not raise this as an issue. Otherwise we are inevitably confining people to their own place. Regarding what individuals might say, that is already covered by the additional clause which is added. He has every right to reach out in whatever way he likes.

Jawaharlal Nehru: Is this important enough to be mentioned? A man may say, for instance: he is a town-dweller, what does he mean by representing us in the villages; he does not know anything about villages.

Asoka Mehta: I think the linguistic thing is much bigger than the question of town-dweller.

Jawaharlal Nehru: A person says that he does not live in the constituency.

Asoka Mehta: I was only referring to the linguistic aspect. I only confine myself to that.

Q-3

K.M. Munshi: Generally the feeling is that this would help in the process of national integration.

Indira Gandhi: Do you think it will make any difference?

Asoka Mehta: The suggestion has often been made that this should be a definite policy. I have heard various people suggesting that the Prime Minister should not contest from only one particular constituency or one particular State. Responsible people have said this before the elections. Recently the Prime Minister in a particular by-election said that he was happy that somebody from North India was contesting from South India and that it was a step in the right direction; something like that. I thought that this was a policy which one wanted to encourage. Then necessary precautions have also to be taken. We should not encourage something on one side and undermine something on the other.

Y.B. Chavan: We would be happy if you put it in a positive way.

Q-4

बिशनचन्द्र सेठः मैं तो ऐसा समझता हूं कि यह सम्भव नहीं है क्योंकि अलग अलग रीजंस की अलग अलग लेंगुएजैज़ है। जो आदमी उस इलाके की लेंगुएज को जानता नहीं है तो फिर वह अपने को कैसे एक्सप्रेस करेगा। अगर साउथ का आदमी यू. पी. में खड़ा कर दिया तो वह अपने आप को वहां लोगों के सामने एक्सप्रेस नहीं कर सकेगा, अपनी बात एक्सप्लेन नहीं कर सकेगा। तो यह चीज़ प्रैक्टिकल तौर पर डिफिकल्ट है।

इसके अलावा अगर एक आदमी दूसरे शहर का भी खड़ा किया जाता है तो उसी में उलझन पड़ती है और लोग कहते हैं कि यह तो यहां आउटसाइडर आ गया है। इसलिए मैं समझता हूं कि यह कारामद स्कीम नहीं होगी।

जवाहरलाल नेहरुः बहुत कम ऐसा होगा लेकिन जहां ऐसा हो उसके लिये यह कहते हैं।

बिशनचन्द्र सेठः मैं तो यह गुजारिश करूंगा कि यू. पी. में हमने बहुत बाहर वालों को मौका दिया है। और किसी प्राविंस में तो हम ऐसा देखते नहीं है।

जवाहरलाल नेहरुः आपने अच्छा किया।

बिशनचन्द्र सेठः मैं यह चीज़ इसी एग्रीमेंट के प्वाइंट आफ व्यु से ही तो कह रहा हूं कि और प्राविंस वाले तो इसको आवजर्व नहीं करते हैं।

[Translation begins:

Bishanchander Seth: I do not think this is possible because different regions do have separate languages, how can someone who does not know the language of that region be able to express himself ? If an individual from the South is made to stand from UP he will not be able to express himself to the masses there, nor can he explain his point of view. This is rather difficult from the practical point of view.

Apart from this, even if an individual from another city is put up as a candidate, then people start saying an outsider has come in. That is why I think this is not a practical scheme.

Jawaharlal Nehru: Perhaps it may not be done in too many places but he is talking about instances where it is possible.

Bishanchander Seth: I would urge that in UP we have given many opportunities to people from outside but we have not seen this happening in any other province.

Jawaharlal Nehru: You have done well.

Bishanchander Seth: I am saying this from the point of view of this agreement that it is not being observed in other provinces.

Translation ends]

Q-5

Jaipal Singh:[52] I do feel that what my friend, Mr Mehta, has suggested is absolutely untenable. It is a fact that person is an outsider. Why are you

52. Lok Sabha MP, Jharkhand Party, from Bihar.

trying to muzzle the people by telling them to their face that he is coming as an outsider? He is an outsider, that is a fact. You know it yourself. The thing is, gradually if political parties can develop a practice whereby we shall invite more and more outsiders, then the problem would be met. But to say that we must not say that he is an outsider—I think I have every right to say that the Prime Minister is an outsider coming to my area, have I not?

Asoka Mehta: But he is not an outsider if he goes there to contest.

Jaipal Singh: I am sorry he is misunderstanding my point. Here he raised the question of political parties undertaking that they shall not treat a man who does not belong to that place as an outsider. Similarly other arguments can come in that an outsider comes to plead for a local man. Why should he do so? You see there is no end to this chain of argument. I think we have just got to face it. He is an outsider after all. Let the political parties present the case and see that he gets there. It is not merely a question of a candidate standing but a whole battalion of people from outside coming to fight for a particular candidate, to electioneer for him. The same argument crops up. Why are outsiders coming for pleading for A, B, or C? It is not a question of the candidate himself as such. You have to extend the same argument to other facts of election, not merely one fellow.

Indira Gandhi: Certainly in our part there is a demand for outsiders to come. People see that this is an opportunity to see the national leaders.

Q-6

Jaipal Singh: I am glad I am being supported in what I am saying. Let us not object to outsiders coming. They say it is quite a different thing. Here is a man who is going to represent people. It is not a question whether he is an outsider or not but how much he knows of the local problems, the language, and so on, which are relevant.

R-1

Indira Gandhi: But you suddenly pick up some man and you put him up in a highly educated constituency. It is entirely different. But where there are backward people, you can put up anybody there. The people do not know what that person stands for. If you happen to influence them, you can get into it. That is not democracy.

Jaipal Singh: I really do not know what democracy is. People vote for him whom they like. That is democracy.

Indira Gandhi: If they vote under a misapprehension, it is not democracy. If they fully realise themselves what he stands for and they approve of it, then they will vote for him. How many people are going to come from outside places?

A.B. Vajpayee: They go because of other considerations, not because they want to further national integration.

Y.B. Chavan: If they want to go like that, we should encourage them to do so for the purpose of national integration.

A.B. Vajpayee: Simply because an outsider has come, the local candidate will be asked not to stand?

Y.B. Chavan: People will not go only because of that; there will be other considerations.

C.D. Deshmukh: The question is, who is an outsider? That is to say, are we thinking in terms of different states or different districts of the same state? You can describe as an outsider anyone who does not belong to that district. Now, the Constitution, so far as the election to the Central Legislature is concerned, permits of any one being a candidate, who is registered anywhere. Now, that expresses, so to speak, the

R-2

spirit of the Constitution-makers that you are a citizen of India. You are registered as a voter somewhere and therefore, you are entitled to represent a party if that party chooses any constituency for you in India. What is suggested is that the other parties should not make capital of the fact that such a choice has been made and fling this into the face of the candidate every time that here is a rank outsider. What does he know? He may be there just on merit. You may even say that being an outsider, he really is not fully conversant with the local conditions. That is an argument. But merely to say that he is an outsider is something which goes against the spirit of integration.

Jawaharlal Nehru: That is true but how to distinguish between these two, that he is an outsider and he does not know the local conditions, and he is not an outsider.

C.D. Deshmukh: What I mean to say is, the outsider must acquaint himself with the conditions of the constituency he is going to represent.

Bijayanand Patnaik: That will not cut much ice unless all the political parties agree to have one outsider from each of the parties to contest there. Then only will it be possible.

Jaipal Singh: It should not merely be at the parliamentary level, it should be at the assembly level also, and also at the local bodies level, all along the line.

Jawaharlal Nehru: The fact of the matter is that the conception of a candidate is becoming narrower and narrower.

Sadiq Ali: In the United States it is done like that.

Zakir Husain: It should not be an argument which absolutely denies the right of an Indian citizen, if anyone wants to contest an election from any place he should have the chance to

R-3

do it.

Sadiq Ali: Only the outsider must make himself acceptable to them.

K.M. Munshi: It is not practicable to enforce. Local consciousness is so much that even if one resides on the other side of the river, he will not be able to contest.

Partap Singh Kairon: Let some outside candidates be put up for Parliament. All the parties should be asked to bring in persons from other States.

Indira Gandhi: If an outsider wants to come there, what prevents him from going there ahead of time and making the people know about him?

K.M. Munshi: There are practical difficulties.

Sanjiva Reddy: It should be left to the political parties.

K.M. Munshi: Let this Code be worked for some time, instead of adding something which will not be of practical help to us.

Jawaharlal Nehru: Well, anyhow, shall we add what Dr Deshmukh suggested? It might be added separately.

C.D. Deshmukh: "…political parties even if they … only on the ground that …"

C.P. Ramaswami Aiyar: I merely intended to say "Wherever a person stands as a candidate, he must know the constituency…"

Jawaharlal Nehru: "The Council confirms …."

C.P. Ramaswami Aiyar: "And would urge on the political parties effectively to implement these recommendations in relation to their individual members."

R-4

Jawaharlal Nehru: "….confirms this and would urge on political parties effectively to implement these principles in relation to the members of such parties."

Jaipal Singh: I would like to know what "before exhausting all methods of conciliation and mediation" means. Suppose you have a State somewhere, there is linguistic issue. Take my own State or Assam or anything like that. With whom do these people conciliate or mediate? I have not understood what that terms means.

Jawaharlal Nehru: It waters it down very much.

Jaipal Singh: With whom do I conciliate and mediate?

Indira Gandhi: I think that there should be some kind of a committee at the State level with whom people could get in touch.

Jaipal Singh: That committee does not exist. I thought I would include the word "religious" also. We have mentioned everything—"communal, caste, regional, linguistic"—and the word "religious" should be added somewhere, because that does come in every now and then. In fact, that is one of our headaches.

Jawaharlal Nehru: Shall we add the word "religious" there?

Members: Yes.

Jaipal Singh: I think it is very necessary.

C.P. Ramaswami Aiyar: May I suggest the word "available" to be added? That means, you contemplate the setting up of suitable bodies, conciliatory or arbitral bodies.

R-5

C.D. Deshmukh: We do not want to make it dependent upon the setting up of bodies. All that means is, there are, in respect of any issue, constitutional methods available for setting them up or recourse to authority before whom you can urge your case. Suppose there is a religious issue, you will of course go to the district officer, you may go to the Law and Order Ministry; you can have recourse through the regular constitutional channel. But it is only when you despair that you cannot be helped in that way that you may resort to agitation. That is all that it means. There is always someone available. Mediation for instance does not require any law. You have to choose the kind of person who you think might help you to settle the case. Somebody might come to an individual like Sir C.P. Ramaswami Aiyar and say, "We do not agree…."

C.P. Ramaswami Aiyar: That is why I suggest the word "available".

C.D. Deshmukh: "available" is all right but you extend "available" by saying that it would refer to the machinery that we would set up. No separate machinery is necessary. It may be better to have it in some cases wherever a large number of such cases crop up. But it should not be dependent on the setting up of a machinery. That is what I mean.

C.P. Ramaswami Aiyar: Either personally or through a machinery.

S-1

C.D. Deshmukh: I am not objecting to “available”.

Jawaharlal Nehru: I think the addition of “available” improves it.

C.D. Deshmukh: Yes, certainly, except that it denotes a search for possible methods; it is a kind of indication.

Frank Anthony: May I indicate two points which I feel we might consider here? They are rather important. These are so vague. We formulated these before the elections and I do not think they had the slightest impact on the conduct of any of the parties. But two major problems have been underlined in the Lok Sabha in the matter of whether we can do anything to regulate the conduct of the parties. One is that the last elections, more than any other, underlined the fact that democracy is practically disappearing and that in fact we are setting up a plutocracy, that the cost of fighting the elections will become so increasingly prohibitive that people of ordinary means, people with character, people with ability, will have no place in the so-called democratic set-up. It was cynically suggested—I do not know if it was cynically suggested but it was suggested by the Law Minister—that we should abolish all returns for elections expenses because—he says—we may still concede that 9 out of 10 returns are false. Why make the candidates put in false returns when we know that few honest candidates observe this Rs 25,000 or Rs 30,000 limit. Now whether we can put down something in the code to sort of counter-balance …

Jawaharlal Nehru: It is an important question no doubt, but I do not think it comes in

S-2

here. We may consider the question of elections separately.

Frank Anthony: It is a vital matter. If you create plutocratic conditions, what kind of democracy can you have?

Jawaharlal Nehru: It did not come in here. When considering the question of elections its place is there.

Frank Anthony: You could put in a general clause and I have suggested it. That would particularise the offences so as to create some kind of brake on exploitation of caste and community. Even then there should be some indication to the party that it was not advisable—being an offence—openly to canvass for candidates. [Interruption] But there should be something here. We put in things so vague; it means nothing and the malpractices will continue; they would still be there. I gave out the suggestion, that two things strongly emerged, two major problems were posed in the last elections—exploitation of caste and community and the tremendous emphasis on money.

Zakir Husain: There is clause (1) of this.

Bijayananda Patnaik: That is covered but it is all wishful thinking in the absence of a disqualification clause.

Zakir Husain: We are stating what we want. But sanction is a different matter. It is covered by clause (1)...

Bijayananda Patnaik: Then the other clause also is not punitive. This was drafted before the General Elections to give an indication that the political parties should behave in this manner. Nobody observed

S-3

it and we might still think it not binding in the absence of a certain amount of ban or a certain amount of disqualification.

A Member: This is part of the election law. It finds a place in the election law.

Binodanand Jha: In the matter of industrial disputes if the two parties agree to an arrangement and the union goes in for unauthorised strikes the office-bearers of the union take action against such strikes. It is a workable method and they have banned unauthorised strikes. If any union without giving notice...

A Member: It is a voluntary act.

Binodanand Jha: It becomes legal in the sense that as the Labour Department was a party to it, the Labour Commissioner takes note of that.

Bijayananda Patnaik: But here are things which are bad for national integration, and there is no remedy against it.

Binodanand Jha: A code like this has two objectives. First of all, it creates public opinion to assert that these disintegrating influences have got to be checked in such and such a way. That has a general educative value and secondly, if you want to implement it in all seriousness, and if you think that such implementation is necessary, then the good offices of the parties themselves have to be resorted to, and when they agree to the general principles, how can they get out of the fact that its implementation has got to be done.

C.D. Deshmukh: I wanted to point out that this code was really not for election at all. This was for inter-election conduct, and it was specifically stated

S-4

here in paragraph 24 that the code of conduct to be observed during the forthcoming General Elections would be evolved. Now we are trying to regard this as a code for elections, which is not correct.

Jawaharlal Nehru: It is not.

C.D. Deshmukh: It is for the inter-election period. [Interruption] No, no, these were the general patterns of behaviour, political behaviour apart from elections.

Bijayananda Patnaik: But we are discussing this, that "political parties should desist from creating obstructions" etc.

C.D. Deshmukh: At other times than elections. To the extent to which meetings take place during elections, certainly this should apply. After all you cannot say: I will not disturb the elections but I will only disturb the meetings during elections. That is not the intention. All I say is that it was in our mind then, that we want a specific code for elections.

Jawaharlal Nehru: I think we should not put specifically election meetings in this. Well, then, shall we leave out the word "available" and leave it as it is?

So we take it that the Council confirms this and urges on the political parties effectively to implement these principles in relation to members of their parties.

C.P. Ramaswami Aiyar: You may say: "implement these principles in the matter of regulating the conduct of the members of those parties".

Jawaharlal Nehru: Is that agreed to?

(There was no dissent)[53]

S-5

Jaipal Singh: I would like to know when the comprehensive codes will be formulated. The first sentence is: "It is not possible to formulate comprehensive codes on all these matters without further consultation with the interests involved." When are the interests going to be consulted? And when will the comprehensive codes come into being?

Jawaharlal Nehru: This is a matter of detail. We might go on adding to this, and we added the word "religious" before "communal". There is one thing in the Conference statement. It ends up—paragraph 24—saying: "The question of fasts for political and other purposes should also be considered by the Council."

Then there is the question of evolving a code of conduct for the students as well and that the Council should consider the question of fasts by students, but for the present we are not saying anything about it. It is Appendix II and this I understand from Dr Shrimali has been prepared by the Education Ministry. This requires to be considered more carefully.

C.P. Ramaswami Aiyar: In dealing with this matter, Mr Prime Minister, it seems to me that the real origin of the trouble is not in the students so much as in the teachers. It is because of the frustration of teachers and it is the example set by the teachers that infects the students and which practically provokes their conduct. From personal experience I may say that, generally speaking, the students, left to themselves, are much more amenable to even strong disciplinary measures against them where they are wrong.

T-1

Their main difficulty arises because the teachers are mostly bitter themselves and convey the spirit of frustration and bitterness and rebellion to the students. At the present moment a great deal of work has been done

53. In the original "dissension."

by the Education Department to improve the status and the remuneration of teachers in certain institutions. How far that has really refracted itself in relation to the students I cannot say just now. But I think a code of conduct for the teachers is as important as a code of conduct for the students.

Zakir Husain: That would be in addition to this.

K.L. Shrimali: At the last Conference we had agreed that we must adopt a code of conduct for the students as well. Therefore, we have tried to draft this code.

C.P. Ramaswami Aiyar: Take a simple case. Supposing the teacher begins a fast. If you ask the student not to undertake a fast, he says his teacher is doing so. Therefore, he should also do it.

Bijayanand Patnaik: All this advice to the students to undertake a fast must be coming from the teachers.

K.L. Shrimali: Improvement in the conditions of their service and better qualifications will have a healthy effect on the educational atmosphere. That is really the main thing. I think we had better drop this for the time being. Since the conference has recommended that we should draw up a code of conduct for the students as well we have attempted.

Indira Gandhi suggested the deletion of 4(a).

T-2

K.L. Shrimali: I am in favour of deletion of 4(e) and not 4(a).

Sanjiva Reddy: A student is an elective politician.

C.P. Ramaswamy Aiyar: In one of the Universities with which I was associated a student of MA succeeded in getting elected to the Vidhan Sabha and he realised that his engaging in studies was rather of minor importance as compared to other activities which were of greater advantage to him.

Jawaharlal Nehru: Shall we have a code of conduct for students or not?

Some Members: It should be dropped.

C.D. Deshmukh: Students' behaviour is relevant inside the campus or outside the campus. Now, most of the student indiscipline that has happened in this country happens inside the campus. That has only very distant connection with national integration. There are other countries, for example, whether it is Hungary, Korea, Japan or Turkey where student unrest has occurred outside the campus and has resulted in even the overturn of governments. Now, that is not a matter within the control of university authorities. In 1960 I visited Japan. The university authorities there, I found, took no notice of what the students did outside the campus for the simple reason that they could not control their behaviour outside the campus. They said that was a law and order problem, and that they were only responsible for what they did inside the campus. In respect of the latter they were very severe. But so far as their marching or slogan-shouting outside the campus was concerned, they said that was a matter between the law and order authorities and the students. But from the point of view which is pertinent to us, it is that conduct which is material. In other words,

T-3

students may destroy public property, go on the rampage etc. Therefore, some authority is needed to tell the students that this is the code of conduct. That authority cannot be teachers or authorities of the universities for the reasons that I have stated.

C.P. Ramaswami Aiyar: I am constrained to disagree with Dr Deshmukh in this matter. Supposing students conduct themselves in an improper manner outside the campus. To suggest that there is no jurisdiction vested in or exercisable by the authorities in the university in relation to their conduct outside the campus is to abdicate the whole doctrine of the relations between the teacher and the students, between the institution and the students, because after all, a Sanskrit scholar like Dr Deshmukh would know, that the Sanskrit word the student is "Antevasi", that he is part of a great household with the teacher, and as such he is subject to a definitely firm jurisdiction of the teacher in relation to his whole conduct during his pupilship, during his student career. That is my interpretation of it.

Binodanand Jha: A code of conduct for students will have some good effect. The idea is that political parties should keep their hands off the students.

Partap Singh Kairon: That is not possible. Some other people may be responsible.

Bijayanand Patnaik: We ourselves should agree as political parties not to interfere with students.

K.M. Munshi: The point which Mr Patnaik made required some consideration, for generally in all these matters some political party or the other is making the students instrument for some trouble or the other. The use of students by party purposes is something very reprehensible.

T-4

Partap Singh Kairon: Let us put it wherever we are having a code of conduct for political parties. Even in religious processions pupils are being dragged in for shouting objectionable slogans.

K.M. Munshi: You cannot stop them from doing so. Of course, we can say that political parties should not make use of students for political purposes; that would be something consistent with it.

Bijayanand Patnaik: I think we political parties should restrict ourselves.

Indira Gandhi: We made a mention of this in our regional report that came out some time ago. We said therein that every section of the public must have responsibility in this matter of national integration. And because students are an important section of the public, they also have a responsibility.

K.M. Munshi: It is not suggested that the code for students should not be there.

K.L. Shrimali: If we delete (e) and keep (a) to (d) that will meet our purpose.

U-1

The operative part is 4 and I suggest that (e) should be deleted.

C.D. Deshmukh: This is coming from a gathering which includes political leaders as well as those who represent them. [Interruptions]

Indira Gandhi: We are considering only point No. 4 which is at the bottom of the page. We are deleting (e).

A.B. Vajpayee: Part (b) is very comprehensive and all-pervading. It says "or is aimed at defying the authority of the teacher". [Interruption]

C.P. Ramaswami Aiyar: May I ask this question? Supposing you lay this down. Then does it not mean that really you are asking the students to refrain from certain things which normally speaking the college or university authorities would ask them to refrain? In reality are you not really exhorting students from a distance without allowing the students to deal with this mater as a matter of domestic arrangement between the teachers and the students? That is, if they take part in any activities creating feelings of ill-will and if they resort to agitation, the university or college authorities will say "You have not done the right thing according to the Code which regulates the university or the college and so you get out". [Interruption] I think we are not trying to find out on whom we should lay squarely the responsibility of good behaviour of the students. I say you put the responsibility squarely on the shoulders of the university authorities and teachers; and the students, as a part of the body-politic of that university or institution, should be dealt with by the authorities of the college or the university and not by this body.

Indira Gandhi: We have no dealing with them.

C.P. Ramaswami Aiyar: We only exhort them.

U-2

Binodanand Jha: The students are under their control only for six hours. For the remaining 18 hours they are not under their control. And it has been observed that they even manhandle the teachers. It is wrong to think that every time the student acts on the inspiration of the teachers. It is quite correct that on many occasions he works under the influences of political parties.

C.D. Deshmukh: I think we should formulate this and we send it to the universities to persuade the students' unions to accept this code of conduct.

A.B. Vajpayee: That would be proper.

C.D. Deshmukh: We formulate it as a desirable thing.

C.P. Ramaswami Aiyar: I can well understand the suggestion that you send this kind of thing to the universities and ask them to take pledges from the students. But I am rather loathe to legislate directly to the students over the heads of the institutions. That is what I feel. One would have no objection to say that this is a desirable thing to do—this code of conduct. It is hoped that the universities and other educational authorities will enforce it on the part of the students by taking pledges from them or taking such measures as they may adopt. That I can understand.

Jawaharlal Nehru: You are addressing not only the students but also the teachers and the institutions. The approach is slightly different, although the content may be the same. Could we approach them directly and the students through their educational authorities?

C.P. Ramaswami Aiyar: If there is a code of conduct laid down for teachers and for students in two grades and the whole of that code would be sent to the various institutions, in order to give effect to that both on the part of the students and the teachers, we might have to redraft it.

U-3

Jawaharlal Nehru: Then what type of students? College, university or high school students?

C.P. Ramaswami Aiyar: It is more important to deal with university students form one point of view because they know the risks they are running. The real trouble arises today in the case of young careless secondary school and primary school students who run out to various meetings and take part in processions and slogans. My friend, Mr Kamaraj, will know the kind of shouting slogans, hostile to certain groups or whatever it is... [Interruptions]

Jawaharlal Nehru: I think whatever we may adopt, we have to somewhat redraft it for this purpose.

C.D. Deshmukh: The noisiest lot are the school students. What we are discussing now is the core of the code. It would be useful if the educational authorities ...

Jawaharlal Nehru: All that means that the code has to be somewhat redrafted. The way of our approach is to consult them, to confer with them, the students, especially the elder students.

C.D. Deshmukh: That is how it could be clothed.

Bhai Jodh Singh: My experience is that if the teachers are not with the political parties, students would not be disturbed.

C.P. Ramaswami Aiyar: It seems to me that the whole matter will have to be reconsidered from the point of view of different treatment of teachers and various grades of students and the responsibility laid on the institutions primarily before we deal with these categories of students separately.

Jawaharlal Nehru: Well then shall we appoint some committee for this purpose?

W-1

The Committee will consist of:

Dr C.P. Ramaswami Aiyar
Dr Deshmukh
Dr Kothari
Bhai Jodh Singh
Dr Shrimali

Would they send the draft to the Universities straight and send it here?

Lal Bahadur: It should come before this Council?

C.P. Ramaswami Aiyar: It would be useful and tactful to consult the University before we finally adopt the draft.

Zakir Husain: You send this suggestion to them and let them do what they like.

Indira Gandhi: I want to make one point to be included for the University level students. That is an appeal to them as responsible citizens not to be swayed or exploited by political parties or anybody and they have some responsibility too.

Jawaharlal Nehru: The draft will refer to teachers, students and political parties and the draft may be sent for consultation to Universities.

Next is Code of Conduct for the Press. This requires consultation more than the others with the press.

C.P. Ramaswami Aiyar: Re[ference] this proposal to evolve a code of conduct for the press. I feel very strongly that the recommendation of the Press Commission on which I had the honour to serve with re[ference] to the Press Council should be first brought into operation because the whole idea of the Press Commission was that the press will never improve its own status and be alive to its responsibilities unless they have a domestic tribunal which will judge all infractions, not from the point of view of a censor but from the point of view of a friendly counsel and friendly exhortation. I do not wish to say anything more than this that some of us who served on the Press Commission—there are at least two here—attached the most basic importance to the early formation of a Press Council as

W-2

the most powerful instrument for regulating their uniform code of conduct of behaviour and of maintaining their tradition which should be dear to the press and to avoid the monopolistic tendencies to which reference is made now. It seems that the Code should really be evolved by a Press Council for the Press through the instrumentality of a domestic body of that kind. I feel very strongly that step is called for now and the sooner it is taken the better.

Jawaharlal Nehru: Why was not your proposal given effect to? I was told that a Bill was actually drafted.

C.P. Ramaswami Aiyar: Because other recommendations of the Press Commission have been more or less fragmentarily adopted or brought forward before the Legislature; but to my mind, speaking as one who devoted considerable attention to this subject—I have tremendous evidence and Dr Zakir Husain and Shri Jaipal Singh would bear me out—I would say that the press itself was extremely anxious to start on those lines. Nevertheless I find that the price page schedule and other things have been brought forward but not what I consider to be the basic recommendation of the Press Commission.

Jawaharlal Nehru: That was in effect the recommendation to the press?

C.P. Ramaswami Aiyar: It was an appeal to the press to organise a Press Council with the active encouragement and co-operation of the Govt. which would give the Press Council certain powers which are necessary to enable the Council to operate effectively and it seems that most of the ills which now afflict the press viz., the evil of monopoly, evil of sweating, evil of the manager-editor or managing proprietor trying to be the man who writes leading article as well as to deal with the financial future of his organisation—all these evils would be dealt with effectively by this as it has been dealt with by the Press Council of England. In fact the Press Commission did me the honour

W-3

to ask me to go to the England and interview the press barons. I did that and I came to the conclusion that the inauguration of the Press Council with the whole-hearted cooperation of the press and with the concurrence and encouragement of the Government would be the solution to many of the evils which now afflict the press. I commend that very strongly to the Prime Minister and to my fellow colleagues on this Council.

Jawaharlal Nehru: In England they have not solved the problem yet and there are great difficulties. The monopoly has grown much more than before and only a few papers are left which can carry on.

C.P. Ramaswami Aiyar: In fact after the recommendation of the Press Commission the evils that were so obvious then have been accentuated.

Jawaharlal Nehru: I am sorry that our Minister[54] is not here. I asked him to come.

C.P. Ramaswami Aiyar: My suggestion to the Prime Minister is, he may invite the attention of the Minister concerned to the importance of dealing with domestic regulation of the press through a Press Council.

Jawaharlal Nehru: Mr Sham Nath[55] is here.

Sham Nath: This question of Press Council was taken up and probably there were short [sharp] differences of opinion as to its composition and so the Bill which was passed once at the Rajya Sabha was not taken up in the Lok Sabha, but we will take it up and do something about it. It is receiving the attention of the Ministry.

54. B. Gopala Reddi.
55. Lok Sabha MP, Congress, from Chandni Chowk, Deputy Minister in the Ministry of Information and Broadcasting.

C.P. Ramaswami Aiyar: The sharp differences that he refers to are on the part of those who suffered most by the initiation of the Press Council. Dr Zakir Husain will bear me out when I say that we found as a matter of fact that people who were illiterate were actually appointed Assistant Editors on Rs 1750 in some journals. The old aged aunt of a particular owner was made the Assistant Editor in order to lessen the profit and in order not to give bonus to employees. We mentioned that

W-4

in the report. In another case a lawyer was paid Rs 7½ per month to be foreign correspondent.

Jawaharlal Nehru: In our country?

C.P. Ramaswami Aiyar: Yes. He never went beyond India?

B. Patnaik: Why Rs 7½?

C.P. Ramaswami Aiyar: Do not ask me. That is the evidence. He invented the whole thing but the poor man was getting probably Rs 20 in the profession and Rs 7½ extra was not a negligible factor. Dr Zakir Husain knows that and he knows the place where that evidence came from. I suggest a code of conduct for the press. This was investigated and my impression is that the Press Council itself should lay down that code. That is what has been done in America and England.

Zakir Husain: That is only natural. You want the code for political parties with the agreement of the political parties. Similarly for this.

C.P. Ramaswami Aiyar: The Press Commission report says what the function of the Press Council should be, what the function of the Government should be and what they could do in the matter of laying down a code for their guidance and to avoid some of the deleterious tendencies which are now a feature of the Press.

Sham Nath: Will it not be better that a committee be appointed with some representatives of the Press to examine the best code and make recommendations. The Information Ministry has submitted a draft code. Probably the formulation of a Press Council might take some time—two to three months. We have to wait till then. The alternative suggestion is we might appoint a committee consisting of some representatives of the press and some other eminent people.[56]

W-5

C.P. Ramaswami Aiyar: Whenever I travel to various parts, the Press meets me and says: "Why is the Press Council not yet started?" I have heard that from the press in Hyderabad, Madras, Bombay and other places. They have been saying this for the last five or six years.

Jawaharlal Nehru: Shall we say that the code of conduct for the Press should be framed by the Press itself or in consultation with the press?

C.P. Ramaswami Aiyar: It should be formulated by the Press in close consultation with the Government.

Jawaharlal Nehru: Yes, and in this connection attention is drawn to the recommendation of the Press Commission which suggested that a Press Council should be established.

C.P. Ramaswami Aiyar: I suggest that the Minister concerned should call conference of press in this matter and should stress before them the importance of framing a code for themselves and placing it before the Government of acceptance. The Government will have to make the final choice no doubt because they legislate on that.

Jawaharlal Nehru: Do you say that the Press Council does it?

C.P. Ramaswami Aiyar: The Minister should call a conference of Indian Press and place before them the importance of having a Press Council and giving it the jurisdiction for Code of Conduct. They are themselves prepared to do that. There was not a single dissentient note through the whole course of the two years of the work of the Commission on their part except one person[57] in Madras which took certain curious line of its own.

56. B.V. Kesker, former Minister of Information and Broadcasting, clarified the position in a letter to Nehru on 4 June 1962. See appendix 16.
57. In the original "one person" appears as "aper" which seems to be a typing error. It could have been "a person".

X-1

Is it not so, Dr Zakir Husain?

Zakir Husain: Yes.

C.P. Ramaswami Aiyar: They were practically unanimous. The members of the Press were unanimous that they would themselves work out a code of conduct and they will apply it to themselves. They said they would be glad to do that. It was pointed out that the Bar Council does that; the Medical Council does that and the Press Council may also do that for the Press.

Jawaharlal Nehru: What do you suggest? How should we proceed now about it?

C.P. Ramaswami Aiyar: We might invite the attention of the Minister concerned to the importance of having a Press Council and having a code of conduct formulated by the Press Council when it is brought into existence. My point is this. You must not provoke opposition from the Press. If you simply say that this is the code of conduct that I prescribe for the Press you are going to get a tremendous tornado of criticism but if they themselves formulate a code of conduct for themselves as they have undertaken to do, then you would disarm opposition.

Bijayanand Patnaik: You need not say to the Press that you do this or that. You can say, these are the difficulties and say that the Press might consider evolving a code of conduct on that basis. You can point out the difficulties in the way of national integration and tell them to evolve a code of conduct.

Jaipal Singh: Of course it would have been wrong to impose anything on them and therefore we felt that after our report was submitted, the Government should make up its mind about the necessity for a Press Council, but the initiative would lie with the Press themselves who have been almost unanimous on this matter. I do not

X-2

know what has been happening but nothing has been done so far. As far as this Council is concerned if we make a particular reference to this particular item in the Press Commission's Report that should suffice and the Government can go ahead.

Jawaharlal Nehru: One difficulty is that the Press is represented by various groups, I mean to say, proprietors, editors, sub-editors and so on …

A Member: And working journalists.

Jawaharlal Nehru: … who do not agree as they have conflicting interests.

C.P. Ramaswami Aiyar: As a matter of fact, that matter also was considered by the Press Commission. This question of what may be called the conflicting interests between the proprietor, the managing editor and other editors was also considered and the interests of the actual compositors were also considered and a kind of modus vivendi was arrived at as you will find from a perusal of the Press Commission's report.

Jawaharlal Nehru: May I suggest that you might draft something for us to pass on the lines of what you have said?

C.P. Ramaswami Aiyar: I shall be glad to do so by tomorrow morning. I hope someone would send me a copy of the Press Commission's Report.

Sham Nath: We will send it.

C.D. Deshmukh: I have one suggestion to make somewhat on the lines of what Mr Patnaik is saying. We can certainly say that when we came to the consideration of working out a draft code of conduct for the Press we felt that it was primarily for the Press to do so and in that context we recalled that the Press Commission had made the recommendation that the Press Council should be established. It was not clear why there was this much delay in the establishment of such a Press Council but either through

X-3

the Press Council or through some other representative body of the Press we hope this matter will receive due consideration. And we might say that in that context we felt that it lay in the power of the Press to take many positive steps to promote national integration as well as to refrain from taking certain actions which will lead to disintegration. For instance, they could take active steps to develop a feeling of unity. That would come under No. 1. They could for instance refrain from doing something and that would come under publication of inaccurate reports and so on. One could lay down what we feel should be an ideal Press without arrogating to ourselves the role of actually laying down a code of conduct. One could indicate all those without giving it the label of a code of conduct. We can say that these are the matters to be covered and we think that the Press can do it; we think that the Press can refrain from doing such and such things and it is for the Press to decide what exactly they would do.

Jawaharlal Nehru: Is that all right? Would you keep that in mind when drafting?

C.P. Ramaswami Aiyar: Yes, I shall.

Jawaharlal Nehru: Item (4), shall we take it up? Proposal to evolve a code of conduct for elections including Panchayat Raj elections.

Indira Gandhi: I think the representatives of the various parties should state their views.

Jawaharlal Nehru: Yes; about Panchayat Raj elections would the party representatives give their views?

K.M. Munshi: So far as the Swatantra Party is concerned, it has decided not to participate in panchayat elections.

Kamaraj: In Madras they have contested.

X-4

K.M. Munshi: We passed a resolution only recently, and …

K. Kamaraj: In Coimbatore recently some days back they have contested.

K.M. Munshi: … I am authorised to say that it will be implemented.

A.B. Vajpayee: There was some news to this effect.

A Member: There is a difference between Panchayati Raj and panchayat.

E.M.S. Namboodiripad: In Kerala our party has decided to follow the general principle laid down for all India that panchayat elections should be on non-party lines but unfortunately the Congress and the PSP have decided against it. They have decided to contest on party lines. With regard to other parties at the all India level I cannot say.

Pattom A. Thanu Pillai: If all parties genuinely agree—and I say that deliberately—that political parties as such should not contest the elections there would be no difficulty but then we know what has been happening in Kerala and what will happen in Kerala. So I cannot now positively undertake to say that the parties will not fight the panchayat elections. There is one difference between the Kerala panchayats and panchayats in other States. A panchayat in other States would consist normally of less than 2,000, or 3,000 persons but in a panchayat in Kerala the population would be anything between 10,000 and 25,000 and sometimes 30,000. It is a much larger body and therefore so far as Kerala is concerned the panchayat election is not such a simple thing as it is in other States. That fact we cannot ignore. And we are now only thinking of forming panchayat samitis. The idea is

X-5

that a number of panchayats coming under one development block would come under one Panchayat Samiti. We are only going to pass legislation to constitute those samitis. Here so far as panchayats are concerned also we have got this difficulty. I represent only the PSP so far as these matters are concerned. I must consult my Congress friends. I do not know if the Congress leaders here can speak on behalf of the Congress in Kerala. I think it will be premature for me to say anything definite about it. I have no doubt that Shri Namboodiripad's party has probably formally decided that it need not be on a party basis. Anyway I cannot say anything definite about it at this stage. Personally I would very much like to see that no party contests as party and these elections proceed on the basis of the requirements of the particular panchayats. If the generality of people in a panchayat put forward an individual unanimously, in that case we should try to avoid contests. I do not know what will happen in panchayat elections in other States, the panchayats there being very small. If we can avoid contests that will be the best thing. But as things are today in Kerala I doubt very much if that will be possible. That is why we have adopted this principle of fighting on party basis. That is the position.

Y-1

A.B. Vajpayee: We have already taken a decision to the effect that panchayat elections should not be fought on a party basis and we are trying to adhere to it.

P.C. Seth:[58] It should not be held on a party basis. It is quite correct.

Binodanand Jha: We are trying to solve this question since 1950. As a matter of fact, our State probably was the first State where the PSP and the Congress both came to an agreement not to contest the elections on a party basis. There the Communists differed. Then, Karyanath Sharma[59] and his lieutenants captured a few panchayats on party lines. What happened later on was this. The non-interference by political parties was so much appreciated by the panchayat people that if any party other than those who were in agreement wanted to enter the panchayat polls on a party basis, all of them combined to bring about the defeat of the other party. Hence that party which had disregarded this general approach on its own fared very badly at the polls. We took this decision very deliberately, because the panchayats are not only deliberative bodies. They are also executive bodies charged with judicial functions and if a party man sits there, whatever be the party he may belong to, to pronounce judgment as a party man, it would be a very ridiculous position. It would offend against the whole concept of the judicial system in the country. So, we deliberately took this decision. What happened later on was this. As the political parties came out of the field, the elections were contested by nondescript and particularly anti-

Y-2

social elements. They all came forward to capture the panchayats—bad characters, robbers at some places. They stood for election as "mukhias", as "sarpanches"—persons convicted for serious offences. They rallied round them a band of persons. So, merely walking out of the field would not complete the whole task, which the political parties are charged with in this matter. We have now decided that we should not be content with a negative approach to the problem. We must see that the panchayat elections

58. This must be B.C. Seth, that is, Bishanchander Seth, of the Hindu Mahasabha.
59. Most likely, Karyanand Sharma, peasant leader, who led the CPI in Bihar after Independence.

go on uncontested and the best men selected. It will now be the duty of every Congress Committee to do this. Other political parties are also falling in line. Our men are moving in the interior, touring the areas, to see that the election takes place uncontested. When it is uncontested, the best men are generally elected. If you leave the whole field, by merely a directive that the political parties should not enter into it, they might abide by the order. But the result would be more dangerous. They will terrorise a whole village people and it will create a bit of complications. So, in order to complete the task, we must take a vital responsibility on us. It is for all the political parties to see that there are no contests and that panchayat elections are uncontested.

We have defined in law what is an uncontested election. Any mischief-maker can put in his nomination. Nobody can prevent it. But if a man gets the majority votes, if he gets 80% votes, then

Y-3

we say that it is an uncontested election. The law provides that whenever the panchayat election is uncontested, that panchayat is classified as Class I and it is given more powers. Wherever there is a contest, it is classified as "B" class panchayat and its powers are curtailed. The law provides for that. So, we have decided it is the law that there may be uncontested elections.

Y.B. Chavan: When it is uncontested, would there be any voting?

Binodanand Jha: Voting is there. Three persons can force an election, can force a voting, viz., the proposer, seconder and the nominee.

Jawaharlal Nehru: Well, as we have appointed two Committees, which are going to meet now, we might adjourn now and meet tomorrow morning at half past nine of the clock.

The meeting then adjourned for the day.

7. Verbatim Report—II[60]

A-1

Jawaharlal Nehru: Dr C.P. Ramaswami Aiyar has given us the draft on the subject of the Press. Now only a few copies, I am afraid, are available at present.

C.P. Ramaswami Aiyar: If I am permitted by you, Sir, I shall just read it. I have got only eight copies.

Jawaharlal Nehru: I am going to suggest that you might read it. We might take that item first.

(C.P. Ramaswami Aiyar read the draft)

(Copy placed below)

C.P. Ramaswami Aiyar: That is my report. As a matter of fact two whole pages of the report are devoted to the professional code, and that might well form the basis of further discussions and investigations.

Jawaharlal Nehru: Shall we proceed with this? I am sorry every member here has not got a copy of this document. I can read it paragraph by paragraph.

C.P. Ramaswami Aiyar: May I suggest that perhaps the best plan would be, pending the circulation of this document, that this Council may consider the question of the necessity of framing a Press Code and of setting up by representatives of this Council a committee or something of that kind with some representatives of the Press so that at least a tentative code might be promulgated as early as possible.

A-2

Item 3(b) of the agenda deals with the proposal to evolve a Code of Conduct for the Press. This item is the sequel to a statement issued by the National Integration Conference, which recommended that this Council

60. Proceedings, 3 June 1962, of meeting held at Vigyan Bhavan from 9.30 a.m. It was chaired by Nehru; following the editorial practice of this series, his name has been substituted for Chairman.

Centred sub-headings A-1 etc. indicate the pagination of the original.

should take steps to evolve such a Code of Conduct. It is rightly pointed out that the Press has a vital role to play in national integration in the way of promoting a feeling of national unity and solidarity, by setting its face against disruptive forces and by exercising a due restraint and sense of responsibility in dealing with matters likely to create tension or promote antagonisms or animosities.

In pursuance of the above idea, the Ministry of Information and Broadcasting has placed before this Council a draft Code of Conduct which is on right lines and, so far as it goes, worthy of acceptance by the Press and other interests concerned.

In this connection, the Council is constrained to observe that no action has, so far, been taken on the Report of the Press Commission which was constituted in September 1952 and made its recommendations in July 1954. The Commission, after taking evidence from all parties interested and after having dealt at length with the standards and performance of the Press and taking into account the right of freedom of expression, investigated specially some question relating to accuracy and fairness, to right methods of presentation of news and views, and to a sense of responsibility in news reporting and in comment. The Commission paid specific attention to the topics of yellow journalism and sensationalism as well as to malicious and irresponsible attacks, including attacks on communities and social groups and on individuals, and also to many other questions ranging from indecency and vulgarity to

A-3

astrological predictions.

The Commission came to the unanimous conclusion that the establishment of a Press Council was a matter of fundamental importance, not only to safeguard editorial independence but the objectivity of presentation of news and views. They were also of the definite opinion that the Press Council will have the responsibility of fostering the development of the press and protecting it from external pressure. Following the example of the Royal Commission on the Press in the United Kingdom, the Commission stressed the importance of promoting proper functional relationships amongst all sections of the press; and paragraph 955 of the Report sought to vest the Press Council with jurisdiction over matters relating to ethical standards and professional etiquette, change of objectionable publication (of news, comments and advertisements), infractions of journalistic ethics or professional codes. In fine, the Commission stated in paragraph 957 that the formulation of a Code dealing with the rights and responsibilities of the press will be one of the prime duties and obligations of the Press Council when it is established. Special attention was paid to certain principles that should find a place in the Code of Journalistic etiquette. They are set out below:

(1) As the Press is a primary instrument in the creation of public opinion, journalists should regard their calling as a trust and be ready and willing to serve and guard the public interest.

(2) In the discharge of their duties, journalists should attach due value to fundamental human and social rights and shall hold good faith and fair play in news reports and comments as essential professional obligations.

(3) Freedom in the honest collection and publication of news and facts and the right of fair comment and criticism

A-4

are principles which every journalist should always defend.

(4) Journalists shall observe restraint in reports and comments which are likely to aggravate tension likely to lead to violence.

(5) Journalists shall endeavour to ensure that information disseminated is factually accurate. No fact shall be distorted and no essential fact shall be suppressed. No information known to be false or not believed to be true shall be published.

(6) Responsibility shall be .... [claimed] for all information and comment published. If responsibility is disclaimed this shall be explicitly stated beforehand.

(7) Unconfirmed news shall be identified and treated as such.

(8) Confidence shall always be respected and professional secrecy preserved, but it shall not be regarded as a breach of the code if the source of information is disclosed in matters coming up before the Press Council, or courts of law.

(9) Journalists shall not allow personal interests to influence professional conduct.

(10) Any report found to be inaccurate and any comment based on inaccurate reports shall be voluntarily rectified. It shall be obligatory to give fair publicity to a correction or contradiction when a report published is false or inaccurate in material particulars.

(11) All persons engaged in the gathering, transmission and dissemination of news and commenting thereon shall seek to maintain full public confidence in the integrity and dignity of their profession. They shall assign and accept only such tasks as are compatible with this integrity and dignity; and they

A-5

shall guard against exploitation of their status.

(12) There is nothing so unworthy as the acceptance or demand of a bribe or inducement for the exercise by a journalist of his power to give or deny publicity to news or comment.

(13) The carrying on of personal controversies in the Press, where no public issue is involved, is un-journalistic and derogatory to the dignity of the profession.

(14) It is unprofessional to give currency in the Press to rumours or gossip affecting the private life of individuals. Even verifiable news affecting individuals shall not be published unless public interests demand its publication.

(15) Calumny and unfounded accusations are serious professional offences.

(16) Plagiarism is also a serious professional offence.

(17) In obtaining news or pictures, reporters and press photographers shall do nothing that will cause pain or humiliation to innocent, bereaved or otherwise distressed persons.

Having regard to the adequate and comprehensive treatment of a Code of Conduct for the press outlined in the Press Commission's Report and recommendations, this Council desires to stress the importance of implementing the above recommendations as early as possible. If, however, as has been pointed out by the Ministry, it will take about two years to have such a Press Council set up, this Council recommends the setting up of a smaller committee to confer with important Press representatives and to examine and formulate a Press Code with due advertence to the Press Commission's recommendations aforesaid.

B-1

Jawaharlal Nehru: Is the committee to be formed by this Council?

C.P. Ramaswami Aiyar: Yes. It is either a question of legislation on the basis of a Press Council or if that legislation is likely to take some time—and I have no doubt that it will take some time—some work has to be done by this Council in relation to this matter which is of real importance. This Council may bring into existence a small committee of three or five who may be empowered to consult the important press interests concerned, and there may be a tentative code which may be made public and which may then elicit public criticism, and at all events, the matter will be kept pending before the public. They would realise what the duties and obligations of the press should be and what the rights of the public vis-à-vis the Press are.

Jawaharlal Nehru: It is being typed out. Perhaps we will pass on to something else till it comes.

Sampurnanand: We shall place our full report in the afternoon.

Asoka Mehta: Yesterday we did not reach any conclusions regarding panchayats.

Jawaharlal Nehru: We shall take it up and discuss it later on. Yesterday, so far as I could gather, the general remarks of the members were in favour of panchayat elections being run on non-party lines but some difficulties were pointed out.

C.B. Gupta: So far as UP is concerned, the State Congress Committee at its Executive Committee meeting has decided that it will not participate in these elections on party lines and the same view has been expressed by the

B-2

members of the UP Legislature Congress Party. There are some other parties which have also decided like that but the Socialist Party is very much opposed to it. They are not agreeing to this. There are three parts of these panchayat elections. One is the election to the membership of the Gaon Sabha; the other is the election to the Kshetriya Samiti—election to the Pramukh's position—and the third is the election to the Zila Parishads. So far as the election to the panchayats are concerned, even in the last elections certain parties had decided that they would not participate in the elections on party lines, and they did not participate. But at certain places, the Socialist Party did not agree and they put up candidates. Now, the elections to the Kshetriya Samitis and especially elections to the offices of Pramukhs are pending, and elections will be taking place very soon. Our position both as a party and as members of the organisation is that we will not participate in those elections on party lines. But so far as the elections to the Zila Parishads are concerned, the matter is still pending. Formerly, the Act had envisaged that there would be elections to the Zila Parishads for certain members by direct election. Only recently, Shri Jayaprakash Narayan[61] was there and he addressed a meeting of the members of the Legislature Party, and he expressed very strongly that there should not be direct elections. The matter was considered by our UP Legislature Congress Party as well as by the Congress Executive, and they have come to the conclusion that we should make an amendment of the existing Act and that we should have the method of indirect elections.

Jawaharlal Nehru: To the Zila Parishads?

B-4

I suppose there are different patterns everywhere.

Y.B. Chavan: Not only is it in regard to the power for the Zila Parishad. In our State, a little more power is shared by the Zila Parishad and there, the feeling is that it is better to have direct elections only. We have completed the process of direct elections last week, and I must say that there is fundamental difference of opinion about direct and indirect elections. Their power is exercised by the represented people.

Jawaharlal Nehru: Direct elections of?

Y.B. Chavan: Of Zila Parishad Members.

Jawaharlal Nehru: What about the ex-officio members like pramukhs?

Y.B. Chavan: Not pramukhs, we are not allowing members of the legislature to sit as ex-officio members.

Zakir Husain: The entire electorate took part in the election?

Y.B. Chavan: Yes.

61. Sarvodaya leader.

N. Sanjiva Reddy: How does the panchayat come into the picture? It does not come at all. The village level panchayat does not come in at all.

Y.B. Chavan: They are; of course, the representatives elected by the panchayats are also there and also the members of the Zila Parishad in that area.

N. Sanjiva Reddy: In the Zila Parishad, the panchayat is not represented.

Y.B. Chavan: It is directly elected.

Bijayanand Patnaik: That is a separate sphere of administration.

Y.B. Chavan: There is a lot of co-ordination. In a block samiti the members of the Zila Parishad representing that area and also members indirectly elected from the panchayat sit. That is, that link is there.

B-5

Bijayanand Patnaik: The panchayat?

Jawaharlal Nehru: How is it elected?

Y.B. Chavan: By the members.

N. Sanjiva Reddy: In our State, they automatically become members.

Y.B. Chavan: The co-ordinating link is there.

C.B. Gupta: Is your panchayat like our Gaon Sabha?

N. Sanjiva Reddy: Yes, it may be 1,000 or 2,000; 5,000 or 6,000 at certain places and I think that 30 or 40 of them are elected as presidents for the Panchayat Samiti, and that president becomes the ex-officio member of the Zila Parishad. These people co-opt five members from the cooperatives and others.

C.B. Gupta: We have given the right of representation to the cooperative societies. They can nominate their own men. We have given that right.

N. Sanjiva Reddy: Here, these elected members co-opt others.

C.B. Gupta: The Bharat Sewak Samaj and the women's organisations, they too have been given representation.

N. Sanjiva Reddy: There is a lot of overlapping between the panchayat and the Zila Parishad and also between the panchayats.

Binodanand Jha: If you have one tier for district development only, another tier of independent local body for the Block Development Committee and a third tier of a local body for panchayats, all these would result in difficulty. The obvious result would be that carrying out the developmental work from the district right up to the village level would be impossible. Formerly, the district boards were not in the picture because they were not

B-6

charged with developmental work. Their functions were very limited, collection of the road cess for the district board roads or cess for schools, etc. Now, the development work is going to be entrusted to these bodies and the possibility of conflicts will be there. But so far as the question of integration is concerned, if we decide that the panchayat elections should be held on non-party lines then every effort should be made to secure that object.

Zakir Husain: Do I understand it aright that it is possible to have in your District Parishads members none of whom would be connected with the panchayat at any stage? Is it politically possible?

Y.B. Chavan: Coordination is there. They are elected by a smaller electorate consisting of about 15,000 voters. The panchayat is a statutory body. It does not send any representative to the Zila Parishad.

Binodanand Jha: There is the likelihood of a person who is not very well disposed towards the Samiti or the Zila Parishad going there and there will be a conflict.

N. Sanjiva Reddy: The Panchayat Samiti is the most important factor regarding roads, schools, minor irrigation, etc. Therefore, if the person representing that area in the Zila Parishad does not see eye to eye with someone else, there will be some sort of a conflict.

Y.B. Chavan: There will be co-ordination between the panchayat and the Zila Parishad. We have transferred much of their functions, development activities, to the Zila Parishads. There is much transfer of power to the Zila Parishads. So, the authority for their own purpose will be nearer the district and the real coordination will be done at

B-7

the Block level. There, of course, the representatives of the panchayats do come into the picture. It will be very effective.

C-1

Zakir Husain: Would you really mean that those elections are not on party lines? Even if there is one political organisation that chooses to run its elections on party lines, I think automatically everybody should do so unless in fact we all agree on a set procedure.

Chavan: It is one thing to say that we accept indirect elections, that we are not fighting the elections on party lines, but really speaking, it is not followed in practice, and if at all they want to, they will certainly try to take very effective interest in the panchayat elections themselves. Really speaking, to say that we fight elections indirectly is a negation of the principle that we do not want to fight on party lines. It happens in fact that every party does take interest because otherwise it means defeat for them.

Zakir Husain: There is the talk of non-party elections but it is not a reality.

A.B. Vajpayee: Taking interest in the elections and fighting the elections on party tickets cannot be put on the same footing. Individual members do so.

N. Sanjiva Reddy: Personal rivalries also.

A.B. Vajpayee: In UP party symbols are not being allotted.

C.B. Gupta: In UP 80% of the elections were also unanimous; the candidates were selected unanimously.

Bijayanand Patnaik: That is everywhere.

N. Sanjiva Reddy: In the Telengana area they wanted to contest it on party labels whereas in Andhra Pradesh there was no such contest. It is individual members in the villages; no party. It is between X and Y. No ideology is there at all.

C-1

Jawaharlal Nehru: I suppose we can hardly go into this question. When we are discussing how far these elections can be run on non-party lines we get into deeper waters as to the manner of the election, and since in every State there are some differences we can hardly go into all that.

A.B. Vajpayee: Should we not try to evolve a uniform pattern throughout the country?

Jawaharlal Nehru: No, because in most States, as it is, legislation has been passed and is being acted upon, and it is difficult to hold up everything till new legislation is passed. I suppose we could express our opinion in regard to the panchayat elections, that as far as possible elections on party lines should not take place. It is a general advice.

Bijayanand Patnaik: As far as possible it would be there.

N. Sanajiva Reddy: It should be non-parties. Why divide the village again on these lines. This subject is there for the Congress Working Committee to discuss tomorrow. Other parties may also discuss this, and if they agree, the village should not be divided on party lines.

Bijayanand Patnaik: In fact it is divided even now.

Asoka Mehta: Yesterday, there was a considerable amount of consensus as far as the panchayat—that is the Gaon Sabha—was concerned, but even yesterday the Chief Minister of Maharashtra had made it clear that he was not favourably disposed to the idea of extending it to the Panchayat Raj—that is, to the higher level. Now today it appears, as he pointed out again, that even if we have indirect elections for the higher level—Panchayat Raj—directly or indirectly, parties do come in, because they constitute ultimately the

C-3

electorate. In the past, five years back, we were only concerned with panchayat elections—that is elections to the Gaon Sabhas, and we rightly agreed that political parties should be kept out. Now the Gaon Sabhas have become either constituencies for higher bodies, or are linked, in some way or the other, with the higher bodies which go right up to the district which has substantial powers as he pointed out. Therefore whether political parties can withdraw from the higher structure as a whole or they can withdraw only from the village level, and whether the withdrawal would be genuine, as Shri Pattom pointed out, are matters to which I cannot give an answer offhand. It is rather a complicated picture now.

Jawaharlal Nehru: It is not only a complicated picture but it is rather difficult for us in the Council to upset all the legislation, every law that has been passed. We may give an indication if we like …

Asoka Mehta: But at what level?

Jawaharlal Nehru: At as many levels as possible.

Asoka Mehta: But that becomes very difficult because—can I have your attention Mr Chavan?—in Maharashtra now there are not two levels of administration—the State and the unit level—but three levels of administration—am I right? Now, if political parties function at two levels, why should they not function at the district level? His contention is that he had separated the village level completely. At village level the parties in Maharashtra or the Government of Maharashtra would say: "At the village level political parties may

C-4

keep themselves out." But at the district level and State level there are political parties. When we come to Andhra, the position becomes difficult; the district level is directly based upon the elections that have taken place at the Gaon Sabha level. Therefore the distinction which is possible in Maharashtra is not possible in Andhra.[62] That is a difficulty that arises when

62. The original script has "Maharashtra", which does not make sense and appears to be an error.

once you have a three-level administration or a two-level administration. Really at the fourth level, at the Gaon Sabha level, we all agree, the majority of the people here agree. But the real question is what do we do at the third level. The first and the second levels are allowed to function but at the third level, would it be advisable that it should be kept out? If that is so, do we think that the third level is nearer to the fourth level? In Maharashtra the Chief Minister seems to argue that the third is closer to the second. He says now the headquarters will go to the district rather than to the State if I understood him correctly. Therefore the whole position is: What is the status of the third level, the district level? Can political parties remain confined…

Jawaharlal Nehru: And the third level varies in different States. Sometimes it is the outcome of the second level and sometimes it is independently constituted.

Asoka Mehta: And it is substantial; in Maharashtra, for instance, a District Council will have a budget of Rs. 2½ crores or Rs. 3 crores per year. Now can it be left to people who are unconnected with political parties, and will that not lead to the same kind of difficulty that was pointed out by the Chief Minister of Bihar, at the panchayat level? These are questions

C-5

that will have to be gone into before we give a general advice.

Jawaharlal Nehru: We agree that at the fourth level there should be no party. Is that right?

C.B. Gupta: Gaon Sabha is the fifth level. Kshetra Sabha is the fourth. Gaon Sabha is one unit of administration. Kshetra Sabha is another unit of administration. Then there is the Zila Parishad as a unit of administration. Then comes the State and then the Union. There are five units in all.

N. Sanjiva Reddy: Apart from the State and the Central levels there are the district, block and village levels; these are everywhere. We are having direct elections for the village level. Should we have direct elections for the Block level again? How many times are you going to divide the village?

Binodanand Jha: Our concept of election procedure was that as far as possible we should have only two elections in the country, one for the panchayats and another for Parliament or the State, and the remaining bodies we should constitute by indirect election.

Y.B. Chavan: They are also to have elections, the cooperative societies for example. When they are getting more and more economic power, certainly democracy should function there and elections also. How can we run away from elections?

N. Sanjiva Reddy: Panchayats must be elected and then, later on, they must be allowed to manage. The intention of Panchayati Raj—the name itself indicates that panchayats would be an important factor there in the higher levels.

Y.B. Chavan: As you yourself said, it is A versus B. Instead of A and B it is better to allow some programmes to fight.

C-6

[Interruption] It ultimately becomes so, even under indirect elections, it is noticeable; though we do say that we are not fighting the elections on party lines. Once it becomes the electorate for the higher levels, it becomes a fact that it is on party lines.

Bijayanand Patnaik: It does become.

Y.B. Chavan: Unless we accept Shri Jayaprakash Narayan's conception of democracy that it should be one without parties …

N. Sanjiva Reddy: I have discussed it with him also. You allow freedom at the panchayat level. Then they are elected.

Bijayanand Patnaik: It is to be right down on programme lines.

Jawaharlal Nehru: Even when you do not set up candidates on party lines, individual members of a party will no doubt exercise their influence.

Bijayanand Patnaik: Oh, yes, that is what is happening.

Jawaharlal Nehru: It does make little difference whether you put up a party candidate if an individual member of a party chooses to contest.

Asoka Mehta: There is the further difference as the Chief Minister of Bihar[63] pointed out. If the attempt is there that the election should be uncontested by political parties, then the other less organised parties came in. Then the question of prestige comes up. If a party puts up a candidate it will not withdraw it. Individuals belonging to different parties probably living in the villages can operate. So from that angle parties not coming in formally will be helpful.

C-7

Binodanand Jha: There they abjure the temptation to come into the Panchayats.

Asoka Mehta: If people are indirectly elected to the panchayats or anyone can be elected to the Samities.

Binodanand Jha: The present position is ambiguous. There are the Village Samitis and they are elected and the panches become ex-officio. There are others also. Some are elected by the cooperative societies. There are a few representatives from non-official bodies. It is like that.

Asoka Mehta: But the whole character becomes different. In Maharashtra primary political workers will take charge of the district administration. Here only a mukhiya will be in charge of the district administration. So places are bound to vary very much.

Binodanand Jha:[64] Now there is the developmental work and the District Committee is charged with making totals of the budgets of the Panchayat Samitis. The Panchayat Samiti wants to do so many things. You total it and a certain percentage will be reserved for district developmental works. Otherwise the District Committee is a calculating body. It is not charged with the duty of interfering with the Panchayat Samiti's work but they are given the power of audit, the power of inspection to see that there are no lapses on their part and if there are, proceed against that body subject to the wishes of Government. The Zila Parishad will have a non-official, an officer of the rank of ADC.[65]

63. Binodanand Jha.

64. In the original, "Bihar" which is represented by Binodanand Jha.

65. It is not clear what this acronym means. In this context it could possibly be Additional District Collector, implying thereby Additional District Magistrate.

Bijayanand Patnaik: That is everywhere.

Binodanand Jha: We have to accommodate the worn-out District Boards.

D-1

C.D. Deshmukh: May I say something? In regard to the procedure we are asked to consider whether it is possible to have an agreement among the parties to keep out of panchayat elections. Well, an exploratory discussion has disclosed that although there are a number of arguments in favour of and against political parties participating in elections, it does not appear that there is sufficient evidence yet to show a confidence, that is to say, whether the consequences feared by those who argue one course are taking place, or whether there is greater evidence of materialisation of the fears on the other side. In any case, in the absence of any experience it seems that the States have taken different actions in regard to the precise local arrangements. In the circumstances, it seems it is premature to try and have an agreement amongst the parties. The Council could, I think, recommend that the situation be kept under observation and we have reports, say, every year or every six months so that when the time is ripe one may then in accordance with that get the parties to agree to some kind of desirable solution. This subject should be deferred. We cannot take a decision today.

Jawaharlal Nehru: It is difficult for us to take rigid decisions. Because the State Assemblies have passed legislation it is very difficult to foresee a broad picture. We may, if we so wish, generally express ourselves in favour of one-party elections, especially at the lower levels.

C.D. Deshmukh: We could say that the consensus of opinion seems to be in favour of keeping out political parties as such from the lowest levels.

Pattom Thanu Pillai: May I make one observation? To me it appears that if you allow parties to set up

D-2

candidates or to participate as parties at the higher level than it is better that it is allowed at the lowest level as well. Suppose, for instance, the proposal is to constitute a panchayat samiti in such a way that the members will be elected by the panchayats. For instance, suppose we make an arrangement that the Panchayat Samiti will consist of the presidents of the panchayats coming under that samiti. It is quite a reasonable arrangement.

N. Sanjiva Reddy: That is what we have done in Andhra.

Pattom Thanu Pillai: In that case if you allow political parties to function at the level of the Panchayat Samiti, is it not necessary that you have the parties at the level of the panchayat itself and to higher bodies also. In Kerala the panchayat has a fairly big area with the population going up to 30,000 persons. Now, a panchayat consists of 7, 10 or 11 members. If you agree that at the panchayat samiti level parties cannot function, it follows that on the Panchayat Samiti level also parties should not be allowed to function. Not that I am dogmatic about it. To me it is not clear how the arrangements can be reconciled with the view applying it to the lowest

[INTEGRATION WITHIN INTEGRATION]

You Said It

By LAXMAN

I wish to express, Sir, that our State would like a national integration of our own!

(From *The Times of India*, 8 June 1962, p. 1)

level. Then we must make it possible to keep out parties at higher level also. That is not possible. Therefore, I fully agree with Dr Deshmukh that this matter may be allowed to keep pending for further consideration at a later stage or freedom should be given to States or parties to adopt the course that is suited to them.

Partap Singh Kairon: The freedom is there.

Pattom Thanu Pillai: We cannot have a single pattern.

Binodanand Jha: The whole issue involved will confuse the distribution of powers and the distribution of work at panchayat samiti level and Zila Parishad level. Most

D-3

of the States have concentrated their attention on developmental work. At panchayat level there is no limit to the transference of power to the people. We have transferred the police powers. We have transferred the magisterial powers. We have transferred the municipal powers. We have raised a police force, which is called Raksha Dal whose number is 1,06,000. They have uniforms. They are a statutory force. If you introduce political parties at that level it means you have got a sub-inspector of police who is a Congressite or a PSP or a Communist and you have got a magistrate there who is a Congressite or a PSP or a Communist. Will that inspire confidence and will that go for the proper functioning of the institution? That is the point. We all agree on one thing, whether you want to transfer power to the people, whether that transference would be followed by the political complexion. Now, the question is how to protect them from political influences. That is the main point. So we are most anxious that at the panchayat level things should be protected and politics should not percolate to them. If at Panchayat Samiti and Zila Parishad level, if anybody wants parties to come in, let them have them.

Sampurnanand: What are the powers?

Binodanand Jha: The magistrate has got third class magisterial powers. They can put to jail for certain offences.

Jivraj N. Mehta: So far as village panchayats are concerned, we have direct elections in Gujarat. Then, there is the taluk panchayat which consists of the presidents. At the tehsil or taluk level we have sarpanchas of various panchayats. That means direct elections. They automatically form the tehsil panchayat. At the Zila Parishad level we have half the members elected from the taluk

D-4

panchayats and half by direct elections in which the cooperative societies also participate. That is the arrangement that we have. We have not been so generous in the distribution of powers as police recruitment etc. to the gram panchayats.

M.L. Sukhadia:[66] I think we should take a general decision that at the village level parties should not participate in the elections because it is not only a question of dividing the village only once but it will defeat the very purpose that we have in view that the villagers should give more cooperation for the development of the village. That purpose will not be achieved. If the members of the panchayat are elected on a party ticket, the other party would try to run him down. In the villages that sort of atmosphere would continue. So, at least at the village level I think all parties should come to this decision that they may not run the elections on party lines. If that is done, I think at the block level or at the Zila Parishad level that bitterness would not exist. We can save at least the villages and those who are elected by the villagers from the evil influence. They can join block samitis and panchayat samitis. In Rajasthan, Andhra and, perhaps, UP we have an indirect system of election where the sarpanch of a village automatically becomes a member of the block samiti or the Panchayat Samiti and the pradhan of that Panchayat Samiti automatically becomes a member of the Zila Parishad. In our State, of course, the Zila Parishad is an advisory type of body. The real statutory power lies in the Panchayat Samitis. In Maharashtra the position is different. In Andhra and Rajasthan the basic units are Panchayat Samitis. At panchayat level if elections are fought on party lines, I think other parties will not be able to keep themselves away from that. During

66. Chief Minister of Rajasthan.

D-5

the elections we have found that the panches who are elected in different village panchayats have exercised a lot of influence. So, naturally, if the MLA or the MP finds that some other party is interested in getting their nominees elected, he would not keep himself aloof; he would also be active. If there is general agreement, it would be in the interest of Panchayati Raj and also, perhaps, in the interest of political parties.

As regards the question of casteism, our experience has been that one need not have so much fear about caste factors. In the panchayat elections we have found that if the majority belongs to a particular caste the villagers have elected somebody else as their sarpanch. Therefore, the question of caste may be only a passing phase. There is nothing to fear about caste.

Partap Singh Kairon: Besides that, in the village there is no single caste which is in majority. Probably the single majority group may be 40% or 25%. And as the members to be elected are 5, 7 or 9, hence no single caste men will get elected on their own caste because there will be two or three people coming in for competition and naturally the votes will be divided. We have seen that even the minority caste has become predominant because they have good relations with other caste. So caste has no fear. In Punjab in the recent elections a very strong political party put up a strong candidate and said that they are going to fight elections. The other parties announced that they will not participate as parties. The election was to go on for five, six days. The result of the first day showed that all their strong people were defeated because of jealousy among villagers and ultimately the political parties came out with an announcement that they are not going to

D-6

fight the elections on party basis. So, so far as the gram panchayats are concerned I am afraid—about Kerala I do not know because I do not know about the conditions existing there—in the rural areas no party will dare to put up their candidates.

In the Panchayat Samitis there are all the sarpanches as its members, there are six or seven more, and three are co-opted Harijans and three are co-opted women and one or two from the cooperatives. They elect people for Zila Parishad. The people in the Zila Parishad co-opt two women and two Harijans. That is how the thing is going on. Sometimes political parties do wish to take part in Zila Parishad elections because they cannot dictate at the gram level. Therefore, we have to see whether we can fight elections to Zila Parishad on party basis or not.

E-1

I think that is the only place where we should decide about it. Otherwise people will learn to their woe how difficult the thing would be.

We can generally say that at the village level elections should not be fought on party lines.

Jawaharlal Nehru: Could we take as a basis for further consideration Dr Deshmukh's suggestion? This is a new experiment of Panchayati Raj and we should like to further watch it. Prima facie we feel that they should not be run on party basis, especially at the lower level.

Bijayanand Patnaik: We should not say that, because that means we justify their being run on party lines at the higher levels. Some States have not done that; they have deliberately kept out right through.

Ganga Sharan Sinha: I would like that we accept Dr Deshmukh's suggestion. Up till now the experience was entirely different because gram panchayats were not linked with the parties. We must not fight on party lines but because of this transfer of power and because of this linking up of gram panchayats with the higher bodies I think that matter requires further consideration. Besides that, Sir, as our Chief Minister has said, he made this experiment in Bihar and the PSP and the Congress Party both did not fight the elections at the panchayat level, but the result was not very encouraging. Ultimately the people who came were worse than the party candidates. He made this experiment and this experiment was not very happy.

Binodanand Jha: As I pointed out yesterday, we are going to weed out such elements and we are going to have uncontested elections in the majority of panchayats this time.

E-2

Ganga Sharan Sinha: This suggestion that parties must not fight in gram panchayats is a negative attitude. My experience is that even in the citizens' committees they fight. We should not forget that there has been transfer of power. Therefore I suggest that this question requires further consideration with the transfer of power.

Binodanand Jha: Have you got any objection if at the village level they should not be run on party lines?

Ganga Sharan Sinha: I am in agreement with this suggestion. Emotionally I feel that way, but my apprehension is that it will not work if we are going to have direct elections and transfer of power. I think in regard to this particular matter political parties should come together because it is not so simple a matter as it appeared five or ten years ago. Therefore it requires further consideration.

Jawaharlal Nehru: Have you generally agreed to the suggestion of Dr Deshmukh? I shall ask him to put it down in writing.

Deshmukh: I will try to do that. The point is this. We feel that the balance of advantage seems to lie in parties keeping out of panchayat elections but where participation is unavoidable, they should at least agree to moderate to the greatest possible extent the virulence of party politics. [Interruptions]

Ganga Sharan Sinha: If we are going to have direct elections, then it will be very difficult.

E-3

बिशनचन्द्र सेठः मैं थोड़ी सी बात कहना चाहता हूं। जहां तक पंचायत राज का सवाल है, थोड़े दिनों के बाद में ही सारे देश में पंचायतों का एलेक्शंस वगैरह होगा। तो मैं ऐसा मानता हूं कि अलग अलग प्रांतों के जो विधान इसके लिए हैं वे एक तरह के होने चाहिए। इसमें चाहे विलम्ब हो जाये, साल दो वर्ष इसमें चला जाए, लेकिन उसको यूनिफार्म कर दीजिए। पार्टीज़ तो इसमें जरूर ही आयेंगी चाहे वह डाइरेक्ट तौर पर आयें या इनडाइरेक्ट तौर पर, सच्ची बात तो यह है। यह बेसिक चीज़ है और वहां से ही आप सारी कंट्री का स्ट्रक्चर बनाना चाहते हैं। ....

[Translation begin:

Bishanchander Seth: I want to say a few words. As far as the issue of Panchayati Raj is concerned, elections to the panchayats are going to be held in the country shortly. Therefore it is my belief that the constitution of these panchayats in the different States should be made uniform, no matter how much it delays, even if it takes a year or two, make the rules uniform. Parties will of course come into this, whether directly or in an indirect manner and this is a fact. This is a basic thing and you need to structure for the entire country on this basis.

Translation ends]

Bijayanand Patnaik: Indirect election, indirect infiltration.

बिशनचन्द्र सेठः फिर दूसरी बात यह है कि बिहार वाले दूसरी चीज़ बता रहे हैं, महाराष्ट्र वाले दूसरी चीज़ बता रहे हैं। तो जिस तरह से आल इंडिया का जेनरल एलेक्शन होता है उसी तरह से यह एलेक्शन भी होना चाहिए। यह कम वैल्यू की चीज़ नहीं है। तो मैं निवेदन करूंगा कि सारे देश में जो इसके लिए अलग अलग प्रांतों में अलग अलग लेजिस्लेशंस है उन सब को एक समान बनाना चाहिए। इसमें विलम्ब हो जाए और नेक्स्ट फाइव ईयर में हो जाये तो भी कोई बात नहीं है लेकिन ऐसा होना चाहिए। साथ ही साथ में यह भी कहूंगा कि यह सोचना कि पार्टीज़ नहीं आयेंगी, बेकार है। मैं ऐसा नहीं मानता हूं। किसी न किसी फार्म में वे आयेंगी ही चाहे वह सामने से आवें या पीछे से आवें।

जवाहरलाल नेहरुः इसमें भी कुछ फायदा है कि दिखाई नहीं पड़ें।

बिशनचन्द्र सेठः लेकिन कम से कम कानून तो एक ही शक्ल में होना चाहिए।

जवाहरलाल नेहरुः बात यह है कि गांव में यह अंदेशा है कि कहीं वहां इतना जोश न

E-4

चढ़ जाये कि वहां कत्ल हो, लोग एक दूसरे को मारने लगे। फिर उनको काबू में नहीं रख सकते। तो यह नुकसानदेह हो सकता है।

बिशनचन्द्र सेठः मगर सब कानून एक माफिक होना चाहिए। अलग अलग स्टेट्स में ड़िफ़रेन्ट डिफ़रेन्ट कानून होना मुनासिब नहीं है।

जवाहरलाल नेहरुः क्यों?

बिशनचन्द्र सेठः सारा बेसिस जो है वह आपकी पंचायत ही है।

जवाहरलाल नेहरुः बेसिस तो पंचायत राज है और उसमें कोई फर्क नहीं हो। कैसे हो, कैसे करें, इस पर अलग अलग सोच सकते हैं।

बिशनचन्द्र सेठः मेरा जो ख़्याल है वह मैंने अर्ज कर दिया।

[Translation begins:

Bishanchander Seth: Secondly, the problem is that Bihar is asking for one thing and Maharashtra another. Therefore just as general elections are held for all of India, these elections should also be held in exactly the same manner. This is not something which is of less value. So I shall request that the different legislations being passed in the different States in the country should be made uniform. Even if there is delay in this matter and if it happens in the next five years, it does not matter at all, but it should happen. At the same time I will also point out that it is useless to think that parties will not be involved. I do not believe that. They will be involved in some form or the other, whether it is directly or indirectly.

Jawaharlal Nehru: I do not see any advantage in this.

Bishanchander Seth: But at least the laws should be uniform.

Jawaharlal Nehru: The fact of the matter is that there is an apprehension in the rural areas that passions may mount so much that there may be murders, that people might start killing one another. Then they cannot be kept under control. In that event this can prove harmful.

Bishanchander Seth: But the laws should be made uniform, it is not feasible to have different laws in different states.

Jawaharlal Nehru: Why?

Bishanchander Seth: The entire basis is the Panchayat.

Jawaharlal Nehru: The basis is Panchayati Raj and that will not be different. There can be different ways of thinking how it should be done and what should be implemented.

Bishanchander Seth: I have expressed my views.

Translation ends]

Deshmukh: We can say something like this:

"This Council discussed at great length the suggestion to evolve a code of conduct for elections for the various levels of Panchayati Raj. The discussion disclosed a great diversity of statutory arrangements in force as well as of the extent of devolution of power in the actual conduct and tone of elections from State to State. In the circumstances the Council felt that while there appeared to be some balance of advantage in keeping party politics out of panchayat elections at the village or primary level, it was advisable to defer taking a decision to a future session. The Council decided that in the meanwhile the situation should be kept under careful review."

E-5

Jawaharlal Nehru: Mr Deshmukh, simply say "balance… at the village level."

E.M.S. Namboodiripad: We have not got village panchayats in Kerala.

C.D. Deshmukh: To suit Kerala we have said "at the village or primary level."

Jawaharlal Nehru: So, do you agree with Dr Deshmukh's suggestion?

(No dissenting voice)

Jawaharlal Nehru: All right, we agree to it.

F-1

We go back to Dr C.P. Ramaswami Aiyar's draft which has been circulated. I will read it.

Item 3(b) has no more any significance.

C.P. Ramaswami Aiyar: We may say, in connection with the proposal.

Jawaharlal Nehru: Yes. (Reads)

"The proposal to evolve a Code of Conduct … animosities."

Agreed except for the first line or two.

(Reads) "In pursuance ... interest concerned"

C.P. Ramaswami Aiyar: It is very truncated but so far as it goes there is no objection. My own view is that the 17 para Resolution of the Press Commission should be regarded as a tentative code for further discussion and for placing before the country.

Zakir Husain: That is much more comprehensive than our terms of reference. We are concerned only with integration. There are some items there which are relevant to us and others which are not.

Jawaharlal Nehru: Is it necessary to have the second para?

C.P. Ramaswami Aiyar: That code is before us.

Jawaharlal Nehru: We may say: The Council considered a draft code of conduct which has been placed before it.

"In this connection ... 1954".

Is it quite correct to say that no action has been taken?

C.P. Ramaswami Aiyar: As a matter of fact action has been taken on price page schedule but the Supreme Court decided that it is ultra vires. So the legislation has become infructuous. My suggestion is that you might drop the next para and start with para 1 on page 2.

"The Press Commission came to the unanimous conclusion..."

This is historical more than anything else.

Asoka Mehta: All other references to the Press Council

F-2

are irrelevant for our purposes. Even what is there on page 2 could be compressed.

Jawaharlal Nehru: We leave out the third para on page 1.

Coming to the first para of page 2, can it be shortened as Mr Mehta suggests?

We state:

> "The Commission stated that the formulation of a Code was the responsibility and prime duty of the Press Council when it is established …"
>
> Sham Nath: Can we say: "The Council agreed with the unanimous recommendation etc.?
>
> Bijayanand Patnaik: We may say that the Council agreed with the Commission's views.

Jawaharlal Nehru: Whether the Council agreed or not can be stated at the end. It is desirable to state what the Commission stated. Suppose you start from the middle of the page:

> "The Commission came to unanimous conclusion that the establishment of a Press Council is a matter of fundamental importance and stated that the formulation of a Code dealing with the rights and responsibilities … obligations … special attention was paid to the principles."

These principles might well be stated. Nobody will look into the book.

> C.P. Ramaswami Aiyar: I think so. Nobody has looked into it and nobody is likely to.
>
> Indira Gandhi: You say "this Commission". Nobody knows what Commission it is.
>
> C.P. Ramaswami Aiyar: The Press Commission whose report was published in 1954, stated …

Jawaharlal Nehru: Shall we keep all these?

> C.P. Ramaswami Aiyar: It will be useful to keep all these 17 recommendations before the public. There are certain matters which could be disclosed or have to be disclosed to that Council under legislative provisions. For instance, in other countries legislative provisions have come into existence enabling people even to mention the names of correspondents only for certain disciplinary purposes

F-3

and there are certain protections also in those acts.

The Press Council had judicial powers.

Jawaharlal Nehru: It will not be regarded as breach of confidence, or against professional conduct.

We go further.

"Having regard to the adequate … two years."

C.P. Ramaswami Aiyar: That might go. We might say: For the present the Council recommends etc …

Jawaharlal Nehru: Who is to form this Committee?

C.P. Ramaswami Aiyar: The Council, naturally, because it had to be so that some code may be brought before the next Council pending legislation. I think on the whole this Council has before it the proposal to have a code of conduct. Therefore the Council may form a Committee or recommend to the Ministry.

Jawaharlal Nehru: It is very difficult for a Committee formed by us to do it.

G-1

Bijayanand Patnaik: Already something has been drawn up here. Why not we recommend the same thing to the Press pending legislation?

C.P. Ramaswami Aiyar: The real difficult is this. At the time when the Report was published care was taken to consult a certain number of interests. Between 1954 and 1962 new phenomena have appeared in the Press. New monopolistic tendencies and new conglomerations and agglomerations of power have come into existence. The people whom you have to consult today are different. Moreover there has been a great increase in the language newspapers which was not a phenomenon which we observed in our days. So these language newspapers, smaller newspapers, must be consulted. Most of the magazines which were then in existence have disappeared.

Jawaharlal Nehru: Confer with representatives …

Sham Nath: We might say Press interests.

Jawaharlal Nehru: Representatives of the Press. I am not interested in the interests. I am interested in the representations. I object to the word "interests".

C.P. Ramaswami Aiyar: As a matter of fact the Commission itself found that there was a great conflict between Press interests and Press representation.

Jawaharlal Nehru: For the present the Council recommends the setting up of a smaller Committee by the Ministry of Information and Broadcasting.

Ganga Sharan Sinha: Why not say by "Government"?

A Member: It is better to say specifically the Ministry concerned.

Jawaharlal Nehru: … to confer with representatives of the Press.

C.D. Deshmukh: Apart from conferring with representatives of the Press the Committee itself should include representatives of the Press.

Ganga Sharan Sinha: I would like to say "by the Government"

G-2

because it is for the Government to do it. How is this Council aware which Ministry will handle it? So far as we are concerned, it is for the Government to decide. We might simply say "Government".

Jawaharlal Nehru: It is a matter of general knowledge.

Ganga Sharan Sinha: I think it is always better to refer to the Government than to the specific Ministry.

C.P. Ramaswami Aiyar: The whole point is, the question of a code has been examined by the Press Commission and they have made certain recommendations.

Asoka Mehta: We might just say a Committee; why do we say a smaller

Committee? When we make a suggestion to the Government or to the Ministry it is for them to decide what the size should be.

C.D. Deshmukh: There is a question I would like to ask. The existence of the Council would mean due implementation of any code that might be evolved? What I meant was that it is not only for the purpose of accepting the Code as it exists but if will also take steps to see that the code is observed by journalists and that there will be sanctions which it will exercise against offending journalists. If that is so, if there is delay in the setting up of the Press Council, merely the adoption of a Code will not be a very effective step.

C.P. Ramaswami Aiyar: It is true but this is what was done elsewhere in other countries. There the Press more or less as a voluntary act accepted the Code and it was thereafter that legislation came into force which incorporated that Code and added further provisions and gave disciplinary jurisdiction and formed a Press Council. That has been the example of other countries. That is why it may be useful to have the Code first. During the course of deliberations of the Press Commission we found that there was general agreement to accept something by way of a Code.

C.D. Deshmukh: Then there is a positive advantage in having a Committee and getting a Code formulated and accepted by the Press so that it can serve as a basis for future legislation. And I think a sentence to this effect saying that it is a positive advantage in favour of appointing a Committee could be added.

Jawaharlal Nehru: I don't think such a sentence is necessary. We say here, this Council desires to stress the importance of implementing the above recommendations as early as possible. For the present this Council recommends to the Government the setting up of a Committee including representatives of the Press to examine and formulate a Press Code with due regard to the Press Commission's recommendations aforesaid.

Is that all right?

Member: Yes.

Jawaharlal Nehru: Paragraph 3 goes out completely. "The Press Commission whose Report was published in 1954 came to the unanimous conclusion", etc.

etc. Then it goes on—those 17 points. At the end, "having regard to the adequate and comprehensive treatment of a Code of Conduct for the Press outlined in the Press Commission's Report, this Council desires to stress the importance of implementing the above recommendations as early as possible." For the present … shall we say, "In the meanwhile…"

C.P. Ramaswami Aiyar: Yes,"in the meanwhile".

Jawaharlal Nehru: "In the meanwhile this Council recommends to Government the setting up of a Committee …"

C.P. Ramaswami Aiyar: May I interrupt for a moment? When you say including representatives of the Press, does it

G-4

adequately bring out the necessity of consulting representatives because we found this difficulty that the important or larger newspapers took one view which was almost diametrically opposed to the smaller newspapers and to the language newspapers. To my mind consultation with variegated interests, with variegated representatives is important.

Jawaharlal Nehru: We have laid stress on consultation with various interests.

H-1

C.P. Ramaswami Aiyar: Suppose you have two or three papers with a very large circulation on the Committee. They say: "This is the Code". They might completely ignore what might be called the needs of the smaller press, the weaker press, the language press. That aspect must be taken into account.

Jawaharlal Nehru: "In the meanwhile, this Council recommends the setting up of a committee, including representatives of the Press, to confer with the interests concerned …"

C.P. Ramaswami Aiyar: "After such consultations as they may decide upon". May I suggest this expression "confer with all sections of the Press …" That might be better than the word "interests". "Interests" might involve proprietary interests.

Jawaharlal Nehru: Shall we say: "...to confer with different sections of the Press"?

C.P. Ramaswami Aiyar: Yes.

Jawaharlal Nehru: Is that agreed to?

Bijayanand Patnaik: We should add: "This Council urges on the Government the need to form the Press Council quickly".

Jawaharlal Nehru: You want to expedite the formation of the Press Council.

Bijayanand Patnaik: We have not said it anywhere.

C.P. Ramaswami Aiyar: We are in favour of implementing the recommendations as early as possible.

Jaipal Singh: You say: "to confer with different sections of the Press", but not represented on the Committee.

Jawaharlal Nehru: The Committee need not have members of the Press on it.

C.P. Ramaswami Aiyar: Not necessarily so.

C.D. Deshmukh: I thought that the Committee should have representatives of the Press on it.

C.P. Ramaswami Aiyar: We found a tremendous amount of veiled, if not open hostility between the various sections of the Press and there was no question of dictation by one section of the Press to the other. So, a particular Code might involve greater practical difficulties for adoption than if we merely consulted and were not included in the body. We found, as Shri Jaipal Singh will recollect, that there was a tremendous and vocal discontent. If there is a Code, they do not want it to be laid down by so and so. They mentioned a particular newspaper. The proprietor of that newspaper should not be allowed to lay down the Code; that was the kind of evidence given before us.

C.D. Deshmukh: The Press Commission contained representatives of the Press.

C.P. Ramaswami Aiyar: Yes, in a way. Not many.

C.D. Deshmukh: I have no strong views on the matter.

C.P. Ramaswami Aiyar: I think you may leave it to the Government. If you take one representative of the Press on the Committee, you will have to take representatives of different sections of the Press.

C.D. Deshmukh: Anyway, the position is open. It may mean that, without giving prominence to it.

H-3

C.P. Ramaswami Aiyar: On the Press Commission there were Dr Patwardhan[67]—representing the Maharashtrian language press—Mr T.N. Singh[68] and Mr Chalapati Rao.[69] There were certain difficulties. It became a kind of duel between some of the members of the Press Commission.

C.D. Deshmukh: Anyway, I am not pressing this.

Jawaharlal Nehru: In paragraph 2 I suggested some change. It reads:

"The Council considered that the Draft Code of Conduct placed before it is on right lines and so far as it goes worthy of acceptance by the Press."

Humayun Kabir: It is for public information. The suggestions should also be included. Otherwise, people would not know what the Draft Code is.

Jaipal Singh: The Code of Conduct so far as it goes is worthy of acceptance by the Press … etc. I do not agree to the words "which is on right lines".

Jawaharlal Nehru: You take out the words "on right lines".

"The Council considered the Draft Code." We want to refer to these things.

C.D. Deshmukh: After the words "… by the Press and other interests concerned", you should add the following sentence:

67. P.H. Patwardhan also known as Rao Saheb Patwardhan.
68. Journalist, Lok Sabha MP, 1952-62, and Member, Planning Commission, 1958-March 1967.
69. M. Chalapathi Rau, editor of *National Herald*.

"The Council felt, however, that this is a matter which must be decided by the Press itself." It has already appeared in the papers this morning that this was your decision. Then, you go on to say: "In this connection ..."

H-4

C.P. Ramaswami Aiyar: In other words, the efficacy of any such Code will depend on the general acceptance by the Press. That is the real aspect.

Jawaharlal Nehru: I shall add that sentence:

"The efficacy of such a Code will depend upon its general acceptance by the Press."

C.D. Deshmukh: That is why we are not finally saying that this is the Code we accept. We say it is worthy of acceptance. We do not say anything beyond that.

Zakir Husain: Why don't you put in the words: "Spontaneous cooperation." What is the harm in it?

Humayun Kabir: I suggest that you enumerate the 17 principles and then after that welcome to the last paragraph. You might say: "The Council also considered the following principles of the Draft Code which was placed before it."

Para 2 should come as the last paragraphs.

Jawaharlal Nehru: It comes in well enough here.

Bijayanand Patnaik: You might say: The following Draft Code was considered by the Council and is worthy of acceptance by the Press.

Where will the code of conduct be placed?

J-1

Jawaharlal Nehru: It depends upon the efficacy of the code. It will be an appendix.

Ganga Sharan Sinha: We may have the points in the body of the statement itself. You have mentioned the items of the Press Commission in the body of the statement, and for this to be an appendix it does not look nice.

Bijayanand Patnaik: We are recommending to the Government to set up a Committee to consider a Code of Conduct in consultation with the Press, and this Council suggests the Code of Conduct for their consideration. It can come as the last paragraph. We are suggesting a Draft Code for their acceptance.

C.P. Ramaswami Aiyar: The Ministry is confronted with the Press Commission's Report and must take some action on it. We the Members of the Council suggest to the Government the formation of a committee to deal with the Code of Conduct put before the Ministry of Information and Broadcasting. We place before them a pointed reminder that there has been a Press Commission which has made some recommendations. We ask them in reference to both those factors to appoint a Committee to deal with this question. That is the position.

Humayun Kabir: I suggest that the draft also should be in the body of the text itself. That would be better.

Bijayanand Patnaik: You can make them appendix 1 and appendix 2. Then the statement will become very short.

Jawaharlal Nehru: Both these may be put as appendices.

Ganga Sharan Sinha: I hope that does not require any change in the wording. After putting this also in the appendix it may require some verbal changes here and there.

Jawaharlal Nehru: Then, regarding item 3, Dr Sampurnanand's report, we are not ready for it. It will come in the afternoon. We may take up the proposal of Mr Munshi for appointment

J-2

of a sub-committee to investigate the question of encroachment, legislative or administrative, on the fundamental rights of citizens as regards residence, service, education, trade, business and property throughout the country.

K.M. Munshi: Mr Prime Minister, there is a long note of the Ministry which to some extent supports the necessity for taking some kind of action whether as suggested by me or as it might be suggested by anyone else. I would draw attention to page 5 of the note about education particularly:

Read from "Almost all State Governments appear to have introduced domicile rules" to "virtual ban on the mobility of trained personnel".

On page 6 read from "The main argument in favour of imposition of restrictions" to "meeting of the Chief Ministers of States and Central Ministers".

Sir, my submission is this. We have got to look at this question not from the point of view of the States but from the point of view of integration as a whole. I emphasised yesterday that the mobility of teachers and students in universities, colleges and other institutions is a sine qua non for national integration. Whatever may be the merits or demerits of this kind of discrimination or imposition, they must be removed in some particular way. To enable students from all parts of the country on their merits to get admission anywhere should become the general policy for integration. I may only mention here an instance, it is a very notable example. In the Pawai Institute set up by the Government of India, I understand that more than 10,000 students appeared for the entrance examination from all over India belonging to every community and every caste, and 500 were to be selected. This means that the institution is the greatest unifying factor in the whole of India. Recently they held an examination for entrance for qualifying people called from all parts of India. That is what I call

J-3

an integrating factor, that is, students from all parts of India can join. There are one or two colleges, technical, engineering and others, where students are taken from all parts of India on the strength of a merit examination. Now that system should be followed as a matter of policy for integration. There may be local difficulties. For instance, I may mention my own State of Maharashtra. The engineering colleges are few and the number of seats are not commensurate with the population. Therefore, naturally Maharashtra does not want to give any seats to outsiders, but the better way in my opinion would be to allow outsiders to come to Maharashtra and give Maharashtra additional seats in other States so that this may be compensated. But the restriction of the educated mind that he belongs to a particular State and therefore he is in a privileged position or is going to get a certain concession is, I submit, a disintegrating factor.

The other matter to which I would draw your attention is, whatever happens at the graduation stage, so far as post-graduate departments are concerned, most of them are supported in some way or other by the UGC. So far as scholarships for post-graduate students are concerned, they should be open to competition to the whole of India in every university. That is the second suggestion.

There are other discriminations of residence, service, etc. If necessary, with the assistance of the Ministry, I can place more facts on them. There are imperceptible administrative discriminations of a character which sometimes appear to be very small, but the aggregate effect of it is to disintegrate. To quote only one example in one State—not my State of Maharashtra—the order went out that all eating houses and restaurants must have a board in the regional language. The result is that if a Bengali has to go to a restaurant, he must first know

J-4

the particular language of the region before he can enter the place. I am just giving this by way of instance, and I am sure the Commissioner will be able to tell us many more instances. Therefore, these little things require to be enquired into. Under article 19 of the Constitution there is freedom to reside in and move throughout the whole country as a fundamental right. That is basic to the common citizenship and unity of the country. Therefore, any restriction or any encroachment either by the higher officials or the lower officials or by particular local boards should be closely looked into and corrected by drawing attention to it. I am sure if the Commissioner can tell us all that he knows which is not in his report, it will be very revealing. I understand that very often in one State neither the Chief Minister nor the Chief Secretary received him when he went there to enquire. That kind of thing is going on in many States. There are some notable exceptions—I do not say that there are none—but this thing is a very important matter. If the fundamental rights given in article 19 are restricted by administrative or departmental action in different States, you will have the integration of the country disturbed very seriously. That is why I move the resolution. It may be accepted in any form or it may be sent back to the Home Ministry for further consideration—I have no objection to it—but I thought that this was a grave menace particularly with regard to the mobility of students, and I consider it absolutely necessary that this matter should be considered from the all-India point of view. No students from any part of India should be prevented from joining an institution whatever provision you may make with regard to finances or accommodation. That is my submission. Otherwise it may come to this that there may have to be more universities or institutions of the Centre, which may be a costly affair,

J-5

the unifying factor of a common educational agency may be utilised for the purpose of integration. But that is a roundabout way of doing things.

K-1

C.B. Gupta: May I suggest an amendment to the resolution proposed by Shri Munshi? It is this. Instead of allocating seats for all India students or for students coming from other States, let us allocate seats, at least 50%, to students who come from the area in which that institution is situated and the remaining 50% may be allocated on an all-India basis.

K.M. Munshi: How the resolution should be improved is left to you. I only put before you the national goal which should be there.

Humayun Kabir: It is not only in Bombay, there are other institutions also. There is the Indian Institute of Science, Bangalore, where admission is on an all-India basis, without any consideration of their State. And the candidates take a common entrance examination. There is a common entrance examination to the Institutions at Kharagpur, Kanpur, Bombay and Madras. The difficulty is other way round. We do not get a sufficient number of students from outside the western region in Bombay City. We do not get a sufficient number of students from outside the eastern region and part of UP for the Kharagpur Institute.

Jawaharlal Nehru: When you say that there is a common entrance examination for the four Institutes, do they indicate that they will only go to one particular Institute?

Humayun Kabir: They have to indicate their preference.

Jawaharlal Nehru: Preference is all right, but it is not exclusive preference.

Humayun Kabir: In every Institute, there is an admixture of different students. For example, out of the 300 admissions to the Kharagpur Institute, I would say that about 160 would be from the eastern region. Then you have the regular

K-2

institutions which exist today in every State. They are existing in 10 States and the other States will be covered during the Third Plan and there, the scheme is in this way that 50% of the seats are for students from that State, 30% for other students as decided by the All-India Council of Technical Education and 20% is on all-India competition. In every State there is such an institution. Most of the technical institutions, engineering and polytechnic, almost every one of them is receiving Central grants and no institution receiving Central grant can refuse admission to anyone on the basis of domicile or that kind of thing. What happens is, there are not applicants. I had also some correspondence with Mr Chavan. They only replied about the university.

Then, so far as post-graduate studies are concerned, there is a guarantee of scholarship. Every student is entitled to get scholarship. There is no question of any State coming in. But the difficulty is that the State Governments are finding it difficult because their means are limited. Even the full quota of 30% for other States is not filled. The students also have their first preference for a college located in their own State and it is only when there is an over-riding desire for a particular course that they want to go outside.

Y.B. Chavan: The very fact that the All-India Institutes hold a common entrance examination shows that they are not prepared to accept the university degrees as they are. Even one university does not accept the candidate of another university. When we say that students from other States should be considered on merits and should be allotted seats, on what basis are you going to accept the merit? That means, for admission to all these colleges, there should be all-India examinations. So far

K-3

as Maharashtra is concerned, we go by the results of the universities in the State. We do not go by domicile of the person concerned. So far as the students of the universities in the State are concerned, they are taken on merit, absolutely on merit. But suppose somebody from the other universities is to come, on what basis is merit to be considered?

K.M. Munshi: The question is that there should be a certain modicum of students from outside the State.

Y.B. Chavan: It is not only a question of national integration, it is a question of giving more facilities to the people of that area also. That also should be considered.

D.S. Kothari: There is one general question and one particular question. There are some universities in India, for admission, they require the students to produce a domiciliary certificate. There is one university of which I know definitely, which requires the students to produce a domiciliary certificate of continuous residence in that area for fourteen years, not of the parents, but of the student. What actually happened was this. This is a fact. A student who passed the BA Examination and stood first in that university sought admission to the MA course in the same university, he was not admitted. Why? Because in the MA class the students are limited and students who produced domiciliary certificates were taken in. But the student who studied in the same university could not get admission. The point is, where there are such restrictions, it goes against the very spirit of the university. From the Vice-Chancellor down to the post-graduate students they resent it. But these restrictions have been imposed by the State Government and I am told, with the support of the Zonal Council.

K-4

So, this is so important that I would respectfully submit that there is no time to waste. This Council should decide here and now that the university should not be required by the Government to ask for a domiciliary certificate. Let then ask for merit but the university should not be asked by the Government for a domiciliary certificate.

N. Sanjiva Reddy: Even the Government cannot help it …

D.S. Kothari: It is against the very spirit of the university.

N. Sanjiva Reddy: I entirely agree.

K.L. Shrimali: The UGC has suggested that no Central grant should be given to the particular universities which impose this restriction against anybody. The law will have to be amended.

D.S. Kothari: What is the result of that?

N. Sanjiva Reddy: I would very much like the Zonal Council to go into that.

D.S. Kothari: Why I am stressing that we should take some decision now is this. Firstly, it is counter to the very spirit of the university, which must be the unifying influence. If one university imposes this restriction, another university in the same State will start to impose the same restriction, and it will start a chain reaction. We must abolish it.

K.L. Shrimali: The law must be amended.

N. Sanjiva Reddy: It should not be on a regional basis. If they say that you do not belong to a particular community and therefore you have no seat, it is also equally bad.

D.S. Kothari: The point is that the Government should not force the university to do like that.

K.M. Munshi: We should have an all-India policy, an integrated policy of education for the whole country.

K-5

D.S. Kothari: In the field of education, when we are concerned with the university, the Government should not force the university to do something which is entirely against integration.

Zakir Husain: Do you think that the universities are allowed to do like that? They should not be allowed to do that.

N. Sanjiva Reddy: Even if they want to do that, they should not be allowed to do that.

D.S. Kothari: You are going a step further. What I am suggesting is, so far as university education is concerned, there is no question of caste, creed or religion. That is what we want. It is the State Government which requires them to ask for a domiciliary certificate. But you are suggesting now that at least we should take this up with the State Government and ask them not to ask the universities for a domiciliary certificate.

Humayun Kabir: As I said, so far as the All-India institutions are concerned, there is no difficulty. But with regard to the State institutions, there was a lot of discussion. There was a consensus of opinion that up to about 25% of the seats in each institution in the State might be thrown open to people from other States. That is a very long step forward.

Zakir Husain: But that has not been done.

Humayun Kabir: So far as the All-India institutions are concerned, I think we do not have much complaint from anybody.

K.M. Munshi: May I say that there is one university, the Annamalai University, where nobody is permitted from outside? All I want is a uniform policy throughout India.

K-6

D.S. Kothari: All we want is that admission should be made irrespective of these considerations.

Frank Anthony: I would strongly support Mr Munshi's suggestion. I mean, it is not only a single question as indicated by Dr Kothari. It takes on many forms.

L-1

My friend Mr Kabir said that there are no restrictions so far as the All-India institutions are concerned, but so far as I am aware, the All-India institutions only touch the fringe of the demand for technical education. The difficulty is with regard to other institutions and there are the domiciliary restrictions, and as my friend Mr Reddy has said, the communal reservations, and members of the minority communities who do not say that they are backward, rather who do not say that they belong to backward classes, well, they just cannot get any admission. Just by way of illustration let me say that one member belonging to my community, a boy, a B.Sc. (Hons) who stood first in his university, well, cannot get into "Delhi" because he is under-aged. For one year he has been trying to get into every university in India. He cannot, because of these local conditions. Either they have domiciliary restrictions or they say there is the communal G.O.[70] as was the case in Madras, which, of course, has since been withdrawn. Otherwise among 60% or 70% or 80% there is this scramble to get into the Backward Classes. Now they may be III class or not even III class, something like a Negro[71] or something like that. They form 85% and there is nothing left for the people who are even domiciled, if they are a self-respecting minority and if they say: "We do not want to be Backward Classes."That is the difficulty.

N. Sanjiva Reddy: In Mysore there were the Lingayats and they were saying they were backward.

Frank Anthony: That is happening. With political power you have given educational privileges and the most powerful communities become backward

L-2

so far as education is concerned and they are patronised. What I feel is—I am not pointing my fingers at anybody—that a committee would be appointed to go into all the different respects of this matter because there are very serious difficulties faced by others, particularly with regard to technical education, in the matter of entering into medical and engineering colleges. The whole question, as Mr Munshi has pointed out, is that they were becoming more and more fossilised along regional directions. There is no question of mobility. It is now becoming a question of deliberately immobilising our people mentally and educationally. See what has happened to the proposal for judges. Dr Roy[72] is not here and so I do not want to say it in his absence. To the States we suggested that one-third of their judges should be from other States, but Bengal said: "No, not at all; we never allow anybody who is not a Bengali in our judiciary", and that is happening everywhere. So there is trend to, sort of crystallise this

70. Communal GO (Government Order), introduced in Madras Presidency, provided caste-based reservations in government jobs and college seats.
71. In the original "Negro tod" but possibly Negritoid.
72. B.C. Roy, Chief Minister of West Bengal.

immobility. I feel it is a very vital matter and we can have a committee to go into it.

B. Malik:[73] On this point there is a slight difference between the language of article 16 and article 29 of the Constitution. Whether it is deliberate or by accident, I do not know. While in matters of the Services there can be no distinction on the grounds of place of birth or residence, those words are omitted from clause (ii) of article 29. I pointed it out in my first report and every subsequent report. The result is that certain universities take

L-3

advantage of this omission and say that in matters of admission to our universities or our educational institutions we are entitled to differentiate between people who are residents of the State and others. Now this matter has been pursued by me, by the Ministry of Home Affairs and by the Zonal Councils, and I am glad to report that now, I think there are only one or two universities which still persist. Now, if you want to root it out completely you will have to amend the Constitution, or make education a Concurrent Subject. Otherwise we are doing our best every time the Zonal Council meets and in the meetings of the Chief Ministers this matter is brought up. But there are one or two universities which still persist, as has been pointed out in the note. But the matter is being seriously pursued.

D.S. Kothari: Is it the universities that persist or the Government?

B. Malik: It is the Governments.

D.S. Kothari: Let us make it clear that the universities do not want this. That is the point.

B. Malik: But as I said, this was several years ago when many universities persisted in this discrimination. Now the number has come down to one or two.But there is this lacuna in the Constitution itself.

Jawaharlal Nehru: Mr Munshi's proposal is an all-embracing one—not only education but many other things—and it should be a sub-committee which would largely discuss the question of education. And Dr Kothari has pointed

73. Commissioner for Linguistic Minorities.

out one particular thing, which appears very objectionable. He says that we need not wait for a committee but that we should give a decision about this particular matter, that there is no question of

L-4

law about this. We are not a legislative body. We make a strong recommendation. Dr Kothari, will you put this down on paper, what you would like? What do you say to the appointment of the committee as suggested by Mr Munshi? That committee will deal with so many subjects. It would rather get lost. I think, if you want to confine it to education, let us have it so. One thing I may point out with your permission. In places like the Nagaland there are all kinds of restrictions on people who would be going there, who would like to carry on business there. I think they are very right restrictions. It is so in NEFA too, because otherwise they upset the economy of the place, the profession of petty shopkeepers and others. Not only economy, they create social problems there and introduce all kinds of customs and ways of living which are not suited to that place.

K.M. Munshi: Exception is made in the case of such areas in the Constitution, that there can be discrimination.

Jawaharlal Nehru: Is there?

K.M. Munshi: That is my impression; I am speaking from memory.

A.B. Vajpayee: So far as Kashmir is concerned there are the restrictions.

Jawaharlal Nehru: There are standing orders so far as Kashmir is concerned. In Kashmir nobody can acquire land unless he has a certain lease of Kashmir residence. Though I might be called a Kashmiri I cannot get land there. That was, I think, a very good provision made by the old Maharajas and they are continuing it now, as otherwise Kashmir would have been flooded with English people, they acquiring part of the land, and

L-5

by some rich people from Calcutta, Bombay, etc. buying up the remaining land. In that case the whole nature of the place will be changed; it will not be an agreeable place to live in. They are now slightly relaxing the restriction, relaxing it very slightly. Those are rather special cases.

D.S. Kothari: It may be something like this; it can be worded better. "The Council notes that the universities can and should exert a powerful unifying influence in the country. In this connection the Council strongly recommends that admission to universities should not be based on considerations of domicile, caste or creed but should be determined on the basis of academic merit." I mean to say, that is our opinion and we recommend that.

K.L. Shrimali: It is subject to the provision that seats should be specially reserved for the Scheduled Castes and Scheduled Tribes.

Kothari: Yes, subject to that.

K.L. Shrimali: Subject to their reservations.

B. Malik: May I suggest one change? The word "domicile" is not the proper word. It should be "place of birth or residence".

Kothari: Yes, it may be like that : … "on considerations of place of birth" ….

Jawaharlal Nehru: Would you agree to Dr Kothari's proposal?

Bijayanand Patnaik: It raises the question of universities.

L-6

बिनोदानन्द झाः एब्स्ट्रैक्ट के ऊपर, प्रिंसिपिल के ऊपर तो कोई एतराज हो नहीं सकता है, आप मान सकते हैं लेकिन सारी चीज़ को देखते हुए मैं यही कहूंगा कि जो तगड़े हैं वह और तगड़े हो जायेंगे और जो हम लोगों में कमज़ोर है व और भी कमज़ोर हो जायेंगे। जहां तक आर्ट्स कालेज़ेज की बात है उसके लिये तो कोई दिक्कत नहीं है लेकिन टेकनिकल कालेजेज़ बहुत कम है और सारी मार टेकनिकल कालेज़ेज के ऊपर है और इसी के लिये सारी दिक्कत है। तो ऐसा रखा जाए कि एडमिशन तो खुला रहे लेकिन जिस स्टेट के लड़के का दूसरी स्टेट के कालेज में एडमिशन हो वह स्टेट उसके लिये कम्पेनसेटरी ग्रांट दे। एडमिशन में आप कोई डिफिकल्टी न रखिये, जो भी जावे वह हो जाये और चला आवे, पहले वह चला आवे लेकिन जब भर्ती हो जाये तब, जिस स्टेट का लड़का हो उससे उस स्टेट को जहां कि वह गया है एक कम्पेनसेटरी ग्रांट मिले।

[Translation begins:

Binodanand Jha: There can be no objection in the abstract to the principle, you will agree. But taking everything into account I will certainly say that those who are powerful will become more powerful and those of us who are weak will become weaker. There may be no problem as far as the Arts Colleges are concerned. But there are very few technical colleges and all the attack is on the technical colleges and that is the biggest problem. So there should be a rule that admission may be kept open, the State from which a student gets admission in a college in another State should pay a compensatory grant to that State. You should not place any difficulty in the way of admission, let the students go wherever and take admission in any state. But once he gets admission, the State from which a student goes to another State should pay a compensatory grant to the State in which he gets admission.

Translation ends]

Bijayanand Patnaik: Just like Sainik Schools.

Humayun Kabir: We fought to abolish it four or five years ago. To go back on it will be perhaps a retrograde step.

Zakir Husain: In this matter of reservation of seats, if Bombay gives ten seats in the engineering college these ten seats should be allocated to ten States. They should have one each from there, two each from there.

Humayun Kabir: Most of the seats outside the State remained unfilled and …

Zakir Husain: It is very irritating …

Humayun Kabir: We had been pressing for a number of years. The particular case mentioned by Mr Anthony would be covered by that. Students have to apply now to a number

L-7

of institutions in different parts and sometimes sit a number of examinations. We have been requesting the State Governments and telling them that we are conducting the All-India examinations for the All-India institutions and requesting them that they may accept our examination as an examination common to the States as a whole. What happens now is that a student does not get admission in a college and he does not know that in another college two seats are remaining vacant and at the last moment inferior students are taken in to fill the two vacant seats and the other student does not know that there is a vacancy there. A student cannot take so many examinations. There should be a common entrance examination for every State. That would itself be a long step forward. Mr Chavan's objection to that was: My University has a common examination and I go by their marks. But then he himself says: How can I equate the examination by, say, the Poona University with the examination by the Annamalai University? I would ask him: How can you equate the Poona University with the Aurangabad University or the Marathwada University? Therefore, if you have a common examination.

Y.B. Chavan: Let all the universities be open for all the colleges and let the Bombay people flood all the colleges all over the State. The question Binodanandji raised is a sociological question. But there are backward areas. Even the educational standards are a little lower. What do we do to them? Shall we say: You are still backward and you will remain backward for years to come.

Humayun Kabir: That is why in the regional colleges…

Y.B. Chavan: First Class students of all the universities should have …

L-8

K.M. Munshi: In several States the standards differ and there is a race for giving more First Class marks in order to get their students admission.

Y.B. Chavan: It has given rise to the demand for more facilities.

K.M. Munshi: I am not apportioning blame. I am setting out the state of things which require to be rectified by this body.

Y.B. Chavan: There is another state of things …

Humayun Kabir: Two things have to be done. In the All-India Council we went into the question in detail. On the one hand we have to see that the best students are not denied opportunity. On the other hand we have to see that the kind of situation mentioned by Mr Jha and Mr Anthony is not created. That is why, for example, you show some special considerations for some; I mean the Scheduled Castes and the Scheduled Tribes are given some concessions. This is of course gradually disappearing. But we have to give that. Otherwise students from certain areas and belonging to certain communities would not be able to come into the institutions at all. We have therefore this 50%, 30% and 20%. A few years ago Punjab raised this question.

M-1

They wanted reservation for certain territorially backward areas students. They wanted 100% reservation. We gave them 70% reservation to be reduced by 5% every year. In fourteen years there will be no reservation. We took advantage of the difference between article 19 and article 16. So you have to give a little weightage to various areas, to various groups for a period so that they can come up and the differences do not become greater.

Y.B. Chavan: More facilities should be made available for students of the same State in the State itself.

D.S. Kothari: Universities should not determine admission on the basis of birth. They should be free and should not be forced to determine admissions on the basis of caste, creed and place of birth. That is one thing. The second is that there are certain areas which are backward. It will be very wrong for us even in the long run because education is so vital for economic progress, to reduce disability between different areas. Educational facilities have to be taken to backward areas to reasonably comparable levels in other areas of the country. This action is required at the level when we come to certain All-India institutions and so on. For that purpose All-India examinations should be held. We cannot have All-India examinations for every university. But where All-India institutions are working at a very high level, for specialisation and so on, for that we can have All-India examinations.

Jaipal Singh: Bihar is getting so progressively industrialised that the question of integration has become a very serious problem, that is to say, factory after

M-2

factory springing up and everybody else coming in excepting the people of the locality. If you are going to make it All-India level and say that everybody should come in, I am afraid these areas are going to get un-integrated. I warn you against that step. You have got to go out of the way to make sure that while industrialisation is growing at this tempo people there are able to take some advantage out of this. I am not talking here about Scheduled Castes or Scheduled Tribes. I think the Chief Minister knows what I am referring to. All our engineering colleges are outside that area. Unless and until you have a few technological institutes springing up there it will roughly mean that as far as technical education is concerned, they will have been completely left out of the technical advancement. Unless they are in a position to take advantage of these developments I am afraid we are going to work against the interest of national integration. I think we have got to go out of our way for reservation or safeguards, unpleasant though they may be, but the facts are there.

D.S. Kothari: So far as Mr Kothari's proposal[74] is concerned, it does not preclude the Bihar Government from reserving seats in colleges for particular castes such as Scheduled Castes and Scheduled Tribes. That is a Constitutional obligation and there is nothing to hinder that provision.

Jaipal Singh: I am suspicious about Mr Munshi's move. Here we have only highlighted the subject of education. His resolution relates to All-India citizenship. In the Constitution certain safeguards have been given but he is stressing this question of common citizenship which roughly means he is making an attack on the safeguards which are given in the name of national integration. He is trying to attack the safeguards that are already provided. It means that, I want to be blunt about it.

M-3

Jawaharlal Nehru: We are considering Dr Kothari's resolution which is much more limited and even there the Constitutional safeguards for the Scheduled Castes and the Scheduled Tribes are there. The Council knows that universities can and should exert a powerful unifying influence in the country. In this connection the Council strongly recommends that:

74. As in the original but probably it should read "Mr Munshi's proposal."

"Admissions to universities should not be based on considerations of place of birth residence, caste or creed except in so far as any reservation is required by the provisions in the Constitution, but should be determined on the basis of academic merit."

Humayun Kabir: Reservation should not be denied to anybody on this account.

M.L. Sukhadia: I do not know what is the aim of this resolution but let us not do something which will harm the interest of the local students. For example, we are opening medical colleges in Rajasthan with a view to be some day in a position to fill up the shortage of doctors at present in Rajasthan. Now, if you open admissions on All-India basis, there are chances that persons may come from outside. They would get their admission there. After passing their examination they will go away; they will not be interested in remaining in Rajasthan and develop that place. That thing will have to be taken into consideration. Similarly, the students' standard in Rajasthan cannot be compared with the students of Bombay and other places. It would mean indirectly that the institutions would be run with the finances of the particular State and there are chances that the advantage would be taken of by certain advanced States. I am, therefore, in agreement that you can reserve a certain percentage in each college. There is no harm absolutely in that. Give that much number of seats in certain other

M-4

States so that the particular number may be completed. If you are going to have merit-basis, the backward States are definitely to pay for it. This is wrong. The total expenditure is born by the UGC or the Government of India in the first instance. But after the one-plan period, when the next Plan comes, more or less it becomes State expenditure. For a medical college we have to run the whole hostel and certain other things. And then I do not know what would be the ultimate result.

D.S. Kothari: This point is covered. We are suggesting here the admission should not be based on place of birth and so on but we are saying "academic merit" and in academic merit one can give preference to students of one's own university or State.

M.L. Sukhadia: That way the objective that you have in mind will not be fulfilled. Why can you not say that in lieu of certain admissions here you will provide the same number of admissions to our students in other States, and the Centre should finance them.

Jawaharlal Nehru: This is nothing to do with the Centre. This is bad in principle. I do not understand any university denying admission to students from other States. You may reserve seats to some extent for your people but the problem is more a theoretical one. The Resolution reads:

"The Council recommends that universities can and should exert a powerful unifying influence in the country. In this connection the Council strongly recommends that admission to universities should not be denied on considerations of place of birth, residence, caste or creed except in so far as any reservation is required by the provisions in the Constitution but should be determined on the basis of academic merit."

The result is that apart from everything else you bring down the levels of education. If you insist on taking

M-5

second and third class in preference to first class it will bring down the whole level of education.

M.L. Sukhadia: While starting an engineering college you have reserved 50% of the seats for the students from that particular State because you think that after a certain number of years the responsibility is ultimately that of the particular State. Now, here you are saying that more or less all the colleges should be opened on merit.

Humayun Kabir: It says, "It should not be denied".

M.L. Sukhadia: "Should not be denied" means "it should be open".

Humayun Kabir: Even in the case of regional colleges the students from other States are not prepared to come. In a regional college 70% to 75% of the students are from within that State alone.

N-1

M.L. Sukhadia: In Calcutta I am told students from other States are not given admission in colleges.

D.S. Kothari: This is a very simple question. The point is this. If I have sufficient merit, I should not be denied admission in any university in the country. Any institution should be open to me, no matter where I am residing. I only want that to be there. [Interruptions]

M.L. Sukhadia: Now, naturally, you cannot expect that the academic standards of a student of a backward State would be the same as those of a State which is far advanced. The result would be that they will not get admission at all if you follow this policy. You are giving safeguard to Scheduled Tribes and Scheduled Castes but there are others who may belong to other communities but still because of certain reasons they have remained backward.

बिनोदानन्द झाः इसके अलावा सेम यार्ड स्टिक नहीं है। जो डिग्री एक जगह के कालेजों से मिलती है और जो डिग्री दूसरी जगह के कालेजों से मिलती है, क्या उनको एक ही यार्ड स्टिक से नापा जा सकता है? नहीं मापा जा सकता है।

[Translation begins:

Binodanand Jha: Apart from this the yardstick is not the same. Can the degree given by the colleges of one State and that given by colleges of another State be measured by the same yardstick ? It cannot be done.

Translation ends]

Humayun Kabir: I think something should be done even more strongly that the university students shall not be denied the opportunity of pursuing further studies…

Jawaharlal Nehru: No, no. That is an absurd thing. That is covered by this. I think as framed by Dr Kothari this is totally unexceptionable. This does not prevent us from making certain reservations …

Zakir Husain: Only those which are under the Constitution.

Humayun Kabir : In the case of employment territory is no consideration; in the case of education territory is not mentioned. On academic consideration . . .

Zakir Husain: It is a political consideration. If Rajasthan wants its people to be educated and has no opportunity, it would have to encourage its people.

N-2

D.S. Kothari: Before independence we had the opportunity to go to any part of India, which was a great thing for us. What we are suggesting is this, that a student, if he has sufficient academic merit, should not be denied admission in any part of the country.

Zakir Husain: That is covered in the first part of the Resolution that no one should be denied admission on the basis of residence.

D.S. Kothari: Then you can delete the second part.

Zakir Husain: Nobody should say "Because you are not a Rajasthani, you are denied admission."

Jawaharlal Nehru: So it is like this:

"In this connection the Council strongly recommends that admissions to universities should not be denied on considerations of place of birth, residence, caste or creed except in so far as any reservation is required by the provisions of the Constitution."

Ganga Sharan Sinha: The last portion does not meet his difficulty. I feel that exchange of students will be a better arrangement than this.

D.S. Kothari: He can say that a student from a university outside Rajasthan must have secured 70 per cent marks irrespective of the fact whether he is a Punjabi or a Maharashtrian. He can say that such a student must have secured 60 per cent of marks.

Ganga Sharan Sinha: There again the question of discrimination will arise that there are less marks for Rajasthani students and higher marks for other students. I personally think that exchange of students will be better than this.

Bhai Jodh Singh: How many students in Rajasthan come from outside and how many of them have been denied

N-3

admission? I think, Sir, we are discussing this only theoretically because most of the students will not leave their States if they can help it.

Jawaharlal Nehru: One thing is relevant here. We are rather afraid of ghosts and shadows, that we want to encourage education in a particular place. But this Resolution, if you examine it properly, cannot come in your way. Now this is meant really to lay down an absolute principle. Now I think it is scandalous that a person should not be admitted, however good he may be on merits, because he lives somewhere else or things like them—fourteen years' residence in that place. Now we are having big institutions opened, technological plants and iron mills. Hundreds of people from all over India work there. Sardar Partap Singh Kairon wanted to know. I can tell him there are a large number of Punjabis in these institutions. Now the question arises that they have lived there.

Bijayanand Patnaik: They are nice people.

Jawaharlal Nehru: Where are their children to be educated? How can their sons and daughters—grown-ups—go back to Punjab and get themselves educated? If you take the numbers, they are not very many ultimately but it does cause not only great inconvenience and disturbance to the life of the people but it is also bad from the point of view of integration. A man works there but his child cannot go into a college there.

Bijayanand Patnaik: That is not correct.

Zakir Husain: The sons and daughters of the officers of the Government of India do not go to the colleges there; they are told that they are not domiciled.

N-4

Bijayanand Patnaik: That is not so.

K.L. Shrimali: If that is so, then there can be no objection to this Resolution.

Bijayanand Patnaik: I have no objection; I do not know what it is about.

Jawaharlal Nehru: Then we agree to this point leaving out the last part.

मोहन लाल सुखाडियाः अब सर्विसेज़ वाला प्रश्न इग्ज़ामिन किया जाये तो अच्छा है। कोंस्टिट्यूशन आने के पहले से जहां रेस्ट्रिक्शन लगे हैं, वहां के लिए इजाज़त है कि वे रेस्ट्रिक्शन चालू रखें। लेकिन जहां नये नये रूल्स बने हैं, वहां कोई रेस्ट्रिक्शन नहीं हैं।

[Translation begins:

M.L. Sukhadia: Now it would be a good thing if the services issue were to be examined. Wherever restrictions have been placed since before the adoption of the Constitution should be permitted to keep those restrictions. But there is no restriction wherever new rules have been framed.

Translation ends]

For example in Rajasthan we have no restrictions in respect of language but in many other States they have restrictions.

Secretary:[75] There are no restrictions except in Andhra Pradesh, Manipur and Himachal Pradesh.

C.D. Deshmukh: Sometimes there are devices whereby disproportionately large number of marks are given for interviews and discrimination is practiced against the higher caste students. I do not know whether that condition exists now anywhere but that is more insidious than any kind of rules.

Jawaharlal Nehru: That is fraud.

C.D. Deshmukh: It used to be practised. Take for example the Brahmins from Madras. [(Interruption)] In interviews they were given less marks.

K. Kamaraj: No, no. In the medical and engineering colleges you will find 50 per cent of them even after interviews.

75. The Home Secretary, V. Viswanathan.

O-1

Jawaharlal Nehru: Mr Munshi, what do you say about a Committee to deal with education?

K.M. Munshi: We have no All-India picture of what is being done. That is why a Committee is required. We have only got a few aspects before this Council but if we have a Committee which could go into it and give us a report, it will be helpful because it does not fall within the jurisdiction of the Linguistic Minorities Commission.

Jawaharlal Nehru: I do not know whether the Committee would be able to do much. If you like you can send it to the Education Ministry or the University Grants Commission.

K.M. Munshi: The University Grants Commission can take it up.

Zakir Husain: I think it will be better if you take it up and tell us what is happening in the Country.

Jawaharlal Nehru: There is one matter I would like to mention. We decided previously about the All-India Services being spread out all over. Somebody mentioned Judges in the Calcutta High Court—about one-third being from outside the State etc. We mentioned also that there should be additional All-India Services. Of course they are integrating influences. I do not know what progress has been made. I think it is not much.

Lal Bahadur Shastri: A scheme has been sent to all State Governments but I would like to urge that the replies should be sent as early as possible. A resolution

O-2

has already been passed in the Rajya Sabha and we want to introduce legislation in the nest Session and if we get the comments of the State Government, it will be welcomed.

Jawaharlal Nehru: This afternoon we shall consider the report of Dr Sampurnanand's sub-committee. Is that alright?

Indira Gandhi: What has happened to the other parts of Mr Munshi's Resolution about property etc?

Jawaharlal Nehru: Let us confine it to education. We meet at half past three.

(The Council then adjourned for Lunch till Half Past Three of the Clock).

P-1

The National Integration Council reassembled after Lunch at 3:30 p.m. at Vigyan Bhawan, New Delhi, on Sunday, the 3rd June 1962 with the Prime Minister in the Chair.

Jawaharlal Nehru: We shall take into consideration the Report of Dr Sampurnanand's Committee which has been circulated. Would Dr Sampurnanand like to say something about it?

Sampurnanand: This Report is not a unanimous one because unfortunately our colleague Mr Anthony does not agree with what we have said here. As I understood him, his objection is based on the fact that according to him we have departed to some extent from the conclusions arrived at by the Chief Ministers' Conference.[76] We tried to point out that this Council is really bound by paragraph 15 of the Statement issued by the National Integration Conference. Our report is based on our understanding and interpretation of this paragraph. After all, as all the Chief Ministers were members of the National Integration Conference we can take it that they are parties to what is said in paragraph 15. Anyway, as I said, Mr Anthony thinks otherwise and he will probably explain his point of view. On the whole we think that this Report that we have submitted to your will be a fair solution of the question that we were asked to consider. As you know, there were strong expressions of opinion by several Members, Mr Munshi, Dr Deshmukh, Bhai Jodh Singh and others. I am happy to say that this Report places before you conclusions which have the support of all these gentlemen and which would reconcile all the different points of view from which this question might be looked at and I hope this Council will accept it.

76. For the Statement issued by the Chief Minister's meeting, see SWJN/SS/70/item 63.

P-2

Frank Anthony: Mr Chairman, Sir, I am really sorry that I could not agree entirely with my distinguished colleagues because I felt there was a point of view that should be considered somewhat carefully by the Council in the context of what the Chief Ministers had agreed upon and also in the context of our own agreement at the National Integration Conference. I felt, Sir, that there is a radical departure from the decision of the Chief Ministers' Conference. I do not know whether all members have got an extract of those decisions before them but in the agenda that was circulated with regard to Mr Munshi's Resolution you will perhaps find an extract from the decisions of the Chief Ministers' Conference. If you would turn to that you will find first Mr Munshi's Resolution regarding teaching of English and then there is an extract from the recommendation of the Central Advisory Board of Education and on the next page there is an extract from the statement issued by the Chief Ministers' Conference at the conclusion of their conference on August 10, 11 and 12, 1961. The extract reads as follows:

"18. The question of the medium for university education was discussed at length. The tendency of regional languages to become the media for university education, though desirable in many ways, may well lead to the isolation of Universities from the rest of India unless there is a link in the shape of an all India language. Teachers and students will not be able to migrate easily from one University to another, and the cause of education will suffer for lack of a common link between Universities in different linguistic areas. The importance of such a common linguistic link between Universities was emphasised. Such a common link can only be English or Hindi. Ultimately it will have to be Hindi, and it is necessary, therefore, that every attempt should be made to

P-3

make Hindi suitable for this purpose. The change-over to Hindi and generally to a regional language as a medium of education will only be effective when such language has adequately developed for the purpose of modern education, and more especially for scientific and technical subjects. Every effort should be made to develop Hindi and other languages for this purpose. Till such time as this happens, English may be continued. It may also be possible and desirable for the change-over from English to Hindi or a regional language to be phased or divided up into subjects. Thus, scientific and technical subjects may be taught, for as long as necessary, in English while other subjects may be taught with Hindi or the regional language as the medium. In any event, the standard of teaching both in Hindi and English should be improved and maintained at a high level in schools and colleges."[77]

Now, with great respect I submit that to me the meaning is fairly clear that there was some kind of an inclination to a single medium, either English or Hindi but the Chief Ministers said that inevitably it must be Hindi. Then they went on to say that before there could be a change-over either to Hindi or to the regional languages, these languages must be equipped for the purpose of modern education and then very clearly it has been said that certain subjects including scientific and technical subjects may continue to be taught in English and then it goes on to say that when the change-over is made it may be made to Hindi or the regional language. Now, my friend, Dr Sampurnanand has said that this is in accordance with our own agreement in paragraph 15 of the Statement of the National Integration Conference but paragraph 16 has also to be read First let me read out paragraph 15:

> "15. As regards the medium for University education while a plea was made for the use of Hindi as the medium on an All-India basis, the general view was

P-4

> that the regional languages are bound to replace English as the medium of instruction as soon as the necessary preparations for the change-over could be made acceptable to the academic world. But it was agreed that in such an arrangement, there would be the necessity of a link in the shape of a language understood all over India. It was felt that this link must ultimately be Hindi, but since Hindi like any other regional language will take some time for its full development, English will continue to be such a link. This implied that Hindi must continue to be taught as a second language as in the secondary stage of education, where necessary; and it also implied that English, apart from continuing as a transitional link, will remain as a language of

77. See also SWJN/SS/70/item 63.

> international importance for the enrichment of our languages in regard to science and technology."

Q-1

Then, paragraph 16 reads:

> "The Chief Ministers had expressed the view that phasing of this change-over from English to Hindi or a regional language according to subjects would be necessary but if, as recommended by themselves and the University Grants Commission, all technical and scientific common words, including well known international terms, are included in the technical terminology based on international usage and are common to most of the India languages, then such phasing may not be necessary."

What I felt was this. Whether we agree or not with the Chief Ministers, whether we call them decisions or conclusions arrived at by the National Integration Conference, to my mind the position is very clear. First of all, a certain stage was contemplated during which time these languages would be equipped and a certain norm was prescribed. Then, there would be a change-over either to Hindi or the regional language. Now, what we have sought to do is this. I think I am not incorrectly representing my friend, Dr Sampurnanand. When I asked him: "Is this a departure from the Chief Ministers' decision?,"he said "Yes." This represents second thoughts now. If it represents second thoughts, let the whole Conference have second thoughts on this matter. I agree with the first thoughts as they were set out by the Chief Ministers at the National Integration Conference. The implications here are two-fold. First, you almost enjoin on Universities to introduce the regional language. Perhaps we have already said that that is inevitable. Here there is an injunction. As far as I can make out, there is no latitude. There is a provision that in isolated cases they may allow English. But there is no latitude given to a university which may say: "Well, we would like to continue English."

Q-2

That is my own reading of this thing. Secondly, there is no latitude given to them. I do not know whether all the Universities want to have Hindi. So, in two radical ways we have departed from the previous decision. There is an injunction that you should efface English. Then, you say have Hindi in all the regions where Hindi is not there. This, to my mind, is a radical departure and I felt that I could not subscribe to it, unless the Conference felt that we have advanced to that extent. These are second thoughts—whether or not the regional language must be immediately made the medium in the Universities.

Another position that I would like the Conference to consider is this. There has been an adverse reaction from the linguistic minorities. We have come some distance from the old provision in the Constitution. The Prime Minister in the troubled days in the Lok Sabha gave an assurance that English would continue as the alternate official language. That very largely allayed the misgivings particularly of the Tamils and Bengalis. They said that at any rate they would have the English language as the alternate language. Now, what has been done here is this. In effect, you practically enjoin on the regions to introduce immediately the regional language. You also more or less tell them that except in rare instances they shall efface English. The question I pose is this. Whatever your prejudice may be against English – whether it is a foreign language or anything else – as long as you have this provision, you have to follow it. The Prime Minister has said that it has to be put in the Constitution that English shall be the alternate official language.

Q-3

How do you honour your assurance to the non-Hindi speaking people or to the minorities who do not speak the regional language, whose mother tongue is not the regional language? The assurance was that in any case you will be able to fall back on this alternate language. You do not provide for it. That is my interpretation. You say except in rare instances, which means that they may allow certain colleges here and there. If you do to allow a university to say that as a matter of right they can continue with English or continue largely in English, then, what will be the reaction of the linguistic minorities? Where will they go? Dr Kothari put forward his view very eloquently that if you want a first class nation, it must be a nation which thinks in its mother tongue. More than that you must have communication between the intellectual elite and the common people. I am prepared to subscribe to all that. But remember that these considerations do not apply to millions of linguistic minorities. Even in Madras – was looking at the figures the other day – in Madras City 60% of the people are non-Tamils. Now, for them it is a meaningless cliché to say that they will study in Tamil, that that it is their mother tongue. I do not say that the Madras

State would do that. I doubt very much whether they would say, under this injunction, we will only have Tamil. We feel that this injunction would wipe out English. The injunction not to have Hindi will be an assurance to the linguistic minorities. You have also enjoined on the Universities to efface English. Then, what is the point of keeping this provision to have an alternate language? If they cannot pursue their higher education at least in English, then, what is the point in keeping English as an alternate official language?

Q-4

Then, another position is this. We will have to consider whether as long as English is the alternate language, can any Government say it will not provide facilities for teaching in English? Even can the Gujarat State say to its Gujarati people that you shall only pursue your higher education in Gujarati? With great respect I say "No". No civilised country accepts an injunction of that kind. You cannot dictate to anyone in which language he may want this child to be educated, particularly at the University stage. That is axiomatic in all civilised democratic communities. Now, we are doing four things. First of all, we are enjoining the effacing of English. Secondly, we are eliminating Hindi. Thirdly, we are saying to the linguistic minorities, despite this continuing guarantee in the Constitution, you will not have the alternate language available to you in the University stage. Fourthly, we say that it is the right of the State to dictate to the parent the language in which he shall educate his child in the University stage. All these things I say are not only wrong, but in law they would not be tenable. I feel that the Chief Ministers' decisions were very carefully taken. They met every point of view. What is the reason now, after a few months, for jettisoning that decision? This briefly is how I see it.

Sampurnanand: Mr Anthony seems to be working under a delusion that our Report, which he bases on paragraph 15 of the statement issued by the National Integration Conference is at variance with the decision of the Chief Ministers' Conference. I beg to submit that this difference is only apparent and not real. What

Q-5

the Chief Ministers said might be interpreted as Mr Anthony interprets it, that either Hindi or the regional language might replace English. I am sure that that was not the intention of the Chief Ministers. In any case, there was perhaps this possibility of interpretation of the language. When the National Integration Conference met in September I had before it the resolution of the Chief Ministers. All that it did was to clarify the position. It said clearly that it did not ban the use of Hindi as the medium of instruction in any particular State, in any particular University. If a University came to the decision that it would adopt Hindi, it can do so. It took the commonsense view that in any conceivable set to circumstances, the Universities would naturally adopt as the medium of instruction the language of the region in which they were situated. That was the view which the Conference took. In its decision in paragraph 15 it merely made explicit what was really implicit in the resolution of the Chief Ministers. It explained clearly what the intention of the Chief Ministers was, that the regional language would naturally replace English. So, I beg to submit that there is no real difference between the two.

Again, Mr Anthony said that we have issued an injunction against the adoption of English. We have not done anything of the kind. We have only made clear what the Chief Ministers themselves have said in that last conference. At the same time, I admit that most of us visualise the day will come—perhaps not in the very distant future—when English will be replaced by the regional language. That is true. There is no question of issuing any injunction. It is simply taking a common sense view of things.

Q-6

As we see things developing in India, as we see public opinion developing in India, as we see the regional languages and Hindi developing in India, we cannot but come to the conclusion that the day is not very far off when the place of English will be taken by the regional language. We are not in favour of making a hasty change-over. Mr Anthony read certain sentences from the Chief Ministers Conference Statement. We have also said the same thing. We have said:

> "….every care should be taken by universities to ensure that the transition is made without jeopardising the quality of education, and after careful preparation, etc., the cooperation of teachers and the availability of good standard books written by university teachers or other experts for which every incentive should be provided by the authorities concerned."

We are not saying that the change-over to the regional language or Hindi should be sudden. We have taken every care to define the conditions under which the change-over should be made. Mr Anthony says that we have no right to say that in the present circumstances English shall be completely banned in any University. Any University should be permitted to allow the use of English as the medium of instruction. We have not said that. In fact, in the last sentence we say:

> "With the adoption of regional languages as media of instruction the Council sees no reason why any university should forbid the use of English as medium of instruction in some colleges within its jurisdiction. Indeed, it foresees that in some special circumstances the establishment of such a college might become a desideratum."

We have not said that any University should not be permitted to allow the use of English in certain colleges in some special circumstances.

R-1

I do not really see what objection Mr Anthony can possibly have as a man who comes from a Hindi-speaking area and who himself loves Hindi. I am very grateful to him for the solicitude he has shown to Hindi, but I think that the purpose which he has in view would be served completely by his agreeing to the adoption of this report which, I think, meets all points of view. It takes care to point out that there should be no hasty change-over, that English should continue to be taught in our universities and colleges, that the standard of English should be such that there should be absolutely no difficulty in teachers and students moving from one university to another and in students following lectures, that the standard of Hindi should be good so that Hindi can form a definite and proper link between the various universities in India. I really do not see in what respect this report falls short of Mr Anthony's expectation.

K.L. Shrimali: Mr Anthony may say what statements in the report are at variance with the previous report of the Chief Ministers because this is merely an explanation of what has been effected by the previous conference. In fact, if we look at the last two paragraphs, they meet Mr Anthony's point of view fully. In fact the spirit of the resolution which is proposed to be moved is incorporated in the last two paragraphs. I do not think that there should be any objection to this report. If he could kindly point out any specific statements to which he objects, then probably this could be considered.

Jawaharlal Nehru: Or Mr Anthony could suggest the specific changes in the report to bring out his point of view, because we are rather arguing in the air at the present moment. Both Mr Sampurnanand and Mr Anthony apparently aim at the same thing, but he says that he does not bring it out in his report, and he says that he does. If he would point out specific changes which could be considered, it would be easier.

Frank Anthony: What I felt was this. He says that there is no

R-2

departure. Then let us adopt the phraseology that has been adopted in the last eight lines of the Chief Ministers' report. To my mind that makes the position absolutely clear. If there is no difference, then what objection is there to adopt that language? That is what I said. I subscribe to the first part, the need for the regional language, the need for communion between the common people. But I said that so far as the Chief Ministers are concerned they had, I think, set a rather different pattern. I say, all right, if you think that there is no difference, then adopt the Chief Ministers' language. I do not know whether you have got paragraph 18 of the Chief Ministers' report. It has been set in the printed booklet. You will find it said that ultimately it will have to be Hindi and that it is necessary therefore that every attempt should be made to make Hindi suitable for this purpose, that the change-over to Hindi and generally to regional languages as a medium of instruction will only be effective—and so on, till the end. If Dr Sampurnanand says that there is no difference between this and that, then I say let us adopt this.

Sampurnanand: Why cannot we keep the language of our own conference?

Frank Anthony: My own view is that it is a radical reversal of the policy announced by the Chief Ministers.

Sampurnanand: In that case we are all parties to this radical departure.

Frank Anthony: My objection is that there is radical departure.

Indira Gandhi: This sentence about Hindi which Mr Anthony read out—ultimately it will have to be Hindi ...

Frank Anthony: The whole of the last paragraph reads very clear.

K.M. Munshi: May I make a suggestion? The fear entertained by Mr Anthony is this that at the time when English is replaced by the regional language there may be some people

R-3

wanting to have a college with Hindi medium. He thinks that by this resolution all that is prevented. That is not so according to us. What I suggest is that in the last but one paragraph we may say that with the adoption of the regional language as medium of instruction the Council see no reason why a university should forbid the use of English as medium of instruction in some colleges, English or Hindi—that would meet his point of view. His fear is that by reason of the first paragraph this may be read as excluding the possibility of Hindi medium.

Jawaharlal Nehru: I do not think that is his point.

C.D. Deshmukh: If I understood him correctly, what he said was that English could continue as a medium of instruction in a university, not in a college. I am just trying to understand whether the distinction is that under the old dispensation English could be the medium of instruction of the university as a whole, and that now under the new dispensation it could be the medium in a university and not in a college. That is the basic change which is sought to be made.

Frank Anthony: You are practically saying to a university that it may not, even if the wants to—although I do not suppose that we can dictate to them—continue it as the medium of university education. You may have it in an isolated college here and there, and it may not have Hindi also, I do not know. Dr Deshmukh may persuade the Maharashtra University to have Hindi. But why do you preclude people from having either Hindi or English?

Sampurnanand: How could English be a medium in a university if it is not the medium in colleges also?

Zakir Husain: English would be the medium of instruction for the university to the extent that it is in the colleges.

D.S. Kothari: Whatever you may decide, the question as to what medium of instruction a university must adopt must be a matter

R-4

which should be entirely left to the university. It should not be dictated to by any agency or any organisation including the Government. It is a matter primarily to be determined by the university. We can give any advice or suggest certain considerations and so on. So far as universities are concerned, we shall never submit to anybody dictating to us what should be the medium of instructions, because basically the medium of instruction may be determined, must be determined on grounds which should accelerate the progress of the country. What we have said here is, even if a university decides on its own, there can be no question of compulsion whatsoever to adopt regional language as medium of instruction. Even so we suggest to the university that there may be colleges where the university should permit English to continue as a medium of instruction. Even when a university has adopted the regional language, we say that it should still permit Hindi or English to continue as medium of instruction in special colleges. One word more. We feel that in India a man cannot be considered as educated unless he is able to do things, that is unless he is able to communicate with his fellowmen in the country, and unless he can keep his window open to outside knowledge which means he must have some reasonable knowledge of Hindi apart from the regional language and he must have a good knowledge of English. Everywhere we have laid stress that the essential condition of the whole educational programme is that there must be a continuing stress on English not only as an interim measure but for a very long time, in fact for all time to come, because we want to keep our window open to outside knowledge. We are saying that a university, if it so desires, may adopt the regional language as the medium of instruction because, so far as understanding of a subject is concerned, it is best acquired through one's own language through which one has made his first conception familiar. But so far as the link is

R-5

concerned, we suggest that there must be a link, otherwise he cannot have communion with his fellowmen. The links must be two: Hindi and English. For the common man English should be adequate.

Humayun Kabir: All that I wanted was that in the fourth line of the least but one paragraph if four or five words are inserted, that will meet his point: "With the adoption of the regional language as medium of instruction the

Council sees no reason why any university should forbid the use of English as the medium of instruction for the university or for some colleges within its jurisdiction". That would leave the option to the university either to have the medium for the university as a whole or for some colleges. Even if the university adopted a different medium, some colleges could adopt English or Hindi as the medium. That would meet his point and also that of Dr Kothari. It is for the university to decide what its medium will be.

Bhai Jodh Singh: Sir, I differ from this suggestion because for the present our universities are teaching through the medium of English.

A Member: Not all.

Bhai Jodh Singh: All the universities are teaching. They are simply permitting the use of regional language in certain subjects. Officially in their calendars the language of the universities is English. So, if they change to the regional language, they change of their own accord. Nobody is going to compel them to change to the regional language. Therefore, when they want to change to the regional language, why should we say that even if they want to change to the regional language, they must teach in English? I see no reason for it.

S-1

Humayun Kabir: It does not compel anyone to do anything. The option is left to the universities. If a university wants to continue the medium of English, it can do so. I think that if Mr Munshi had the idea of having one university in Bombay with the medium of instruction in English and another wanted to have another university with the medium of Hindi, there will be no bar to it.

Frank Anthony: I want you to adopt the language of the Chief Ministers' Conference. If you say that there is nothing objectionable in it, then you accept that language. I accept it.

Pattom Thanu Pillai: We would say that if any university wants it, it should be permitted to each in the English medium. I think that is what has now been suggested.

Jivaraj Mehta: If they wish so.

Pattom Thanu Pillai: According to me, it practically changes the whole position. If you agree to that, much of the difficulty is obviated and the penultimate paragraph will have to be changed. Here it is written— "with the adoption of regional languages as the media of instruction, the Council sees no reason why any university should forbid the use of English as the medium of instruction for that university or for colleges." You must reconsider the whole sentence. Otherwise, what is the meaning of saying "with the adoption of regional languages ..."

Humayun Kabir: It would be like this: "It would be a matter for the university to decide what the medium of instruction will be ... the Council sees no reason why certain colleges ..."

S-2

Pattom Thanu Pillai: I fully agree. Let us have it that way.

Humayun Kabir: If you accept Dr Kothari's suggestion that it should be considered as an academic question and we should leave the choice of medium of instruction to the university, it will go a very long way.

Bijayananda Patnaik: The universities are all autonomous bodies, independent bodies. If Government tries to adhere to the national policy requirements, they may resist it. It is our duty to arrive at certain conclusions. I have still to understand the position.

D.S. Kothari: We should respect the decision.

Bijayananda Patnaik: The nation says so and the university must follow the national instruments of policy.

D.S. Kothari: Certainly. That is why it is put there.

Bijayananda Patnaik: It is no use of your saying that the Government is compelling the university. You have been saying from the morning that the university should not accept the Government's decision.

Humayun Kabir: Nobody has questioned the general view that the regional languages are bound to replace English as the medium of instruction. There is more or less common ground amongst us. Therefore, the fear which Mr Patnaik raised is probably not a very genuine one.

Bijayananda Patnaik: It is a point to be decided here. I am trying to extend the point. English language is the window of the world. Some university says that they want only the window of the world and they would profit by it.

C.D. Deshmukh: There was one small point which Mr Anthony forgot to refer to, and that was that the words

S-3

"generally speaking" were added as a result of the discussion with him when we were considering the draft—that is on page 2 in the second paragraph.

We thought that the words "generally speaking" would provide for exceptions. Then, I personally go on to say that there might be circumstances in which, apart from individual colleges, there might be universities using Hindi or English as the medium of instruction. I had in mind the new idea of the Centre starting some so-called National Colleges in various regions. Some such proposal is in its very preliminary stages, is under consideration in Delhi itself. But it may be that in future the Centre might decide to establish a few colleges, for whatever reasons it may have, or universities where the media of instruction would be one Hindi and the other, English. Now, it is not our intention that anything that we say within these three pages should come in the way of the establishment of such universities with Hindi or English as the medium. And we did offer Mr Anthony that we were prepared to insert some sentences to show that in special circumstances, the universities might either retain English or have English as the medium or Hindi as the medium. Therefore, really there is no intention to put an embargo. Indeed, my own conception is that this is not legalistic. That is to say, we are not as a National Council authorised to legislate. We are authorised to reason and that is what we are trying

S-4

to do. We have given the argumentation. According to our argumentation, it seems to us that the best results would be obtained by a university or a college using the regional language as the medium. But there may be other countervailing advantages, and in certain circumstances, the balance may be in favour of some other medium. We would not be so unreasonable as to shut the door against the exercise of any such discretion. Now, if this is taken as the intention, then I would suggest that we relieve Mr Anthony of his apprehensions.

Frank Anthony: Not an apprehension. It is a fact that in the Gujarat University they have outlawed English. They say that they will not teach in English. It happened. What is the good of it? I did not want to refer to it. It is sub-judice. It happened. They have outlawed English. The minority community in Gujarat says that this is the only language we know but you say that you will not teach English.

Jivraj Mehta: I do not think there is any minority college as such in Gujarat. The Gujarat University was started ten to twelve years ago with the intention of teaching in Gujarati or Hindi. The St Xavier's College came into existence later in Ahmedabad. Only with a view to attracting certain kinds of students, they have thought of teaching in English and the position is entirely different. There is no minority college in Gujarat wanting to have English as the medium of instruction. There are 1,482 students in that college. Out of that 1,362 are Gujarati-speaking. The only community that may be called a minority community is the Christian community. There are 31 students. Twenty out of them

S-5

speak Gujarati, their mother tongue is Gujarati, seventy-nine students from outside are non-Gujaratis. To call it a minority college is entirely a misuse of words.

C.D. Deshmukh: I was going to say this. On page three in that paragraph beginning with "With the adoption of regional languages … forbid the use of English", the words "or Hindi" be added. That is my own personal suggestion. We treat them on the same level as English or Hindi. Then at the end, instead of the amendment suggested by Professor Kabir, I would expand it. At the end I would say, "Moreover, if after considering all possible aspects any university chooses to continue English or to replace it by Hindi instead of the regional language, its decision should be respected, as a university be free to decide such matters in its own discretion."

Whether it will satisfy Mr Anthony or not, I do not know.

Jawaharlal Nehru: Why not say it at the beginning?

C.D. Deshmukh: Yes.

Humayun Kabir: I have got something in writing. It may perhaps help.

"While it is natural that regional languages would generally become the media of instruction at the university stage, the Council sees no objection why there should be any bar to the use of English or Hindi as the medium of instruction in the universities or some colleges. In a university where the medium is different, it foresees that in some special circumstances, the establishment of such a college might become a desideratum."

I change the first sentence only.

Jawaharlal Nehru: For a slight change, I would like to ask two questions. It has nothing to do with this. Can we have French as the medium of instruction in Pondicherry because we have agreed to it? It is a matter of international agreement and it is also our desire. I just want to know how it would fit in with this.

S-6

C.D. Deshmukh: If the university decides to have it as the medium, it can have it. It is an exception to the general rule.

Jawaharlal Nehru: Therefore, it should be made clear to the universities. I do not know what Urdu is considered to be. Is it considered a regional language? It may be a more widespread language than is supposed to be. Can Urdu be the medium of instruction?

C.D. Deshmukh: If somebody wants to start some university and can get the State Government to agree to finance it, I do not see why they should not teach in Urdu.

Jawaharlal Nehru: The Jamia Millia has Urdu as the medium of instruction. It is now given the status of a university.

C.D. Deshmukh: Aligarh also has Urdu.

A.B. Vajpayee: But Urdu is the medium of instruction in Jammu and Kashmir.

Zakir Husain: In Aligarh, it is English.

T-1

C.D. Deshmukh: We are dealing here with the generality of cases as we see them.

Jawaharlal Nehru: I merely pointed out that it should not be excluded.

C.D. Deshmukh: We should not say anything which would amount to our forbidding exceptional cases. I think what Mr Kabir has suggested seems all right. It is very short and it expressed the meaning.

Jawaharlal Nehru: It is not very short.

C.D. Deshmukh: It is not short because it is a repetition of the same paragraph in a modified form. That is why it looks long.

Jawaharlal Nehru: Where does it come in?

Humayun Kabir: The first sentence of the last paragraph on page 3. "While it seems natural that regional languages would generally become the media of instruction at the university stage, the Council sees no reason why there should be any bar to the use of English or Hindi as the medium of instruction in a university or in some colleges in a university where the medium is different."

Jawaharlal Nehru: The last few words "where the medium is different" are unnecessary.

C.D. Deshmukh: If that is acceptable to Mr Anthony it is all right.

Jawaharlal Nehru: This takes the place of the first sentence. What about the University's right to determine the medium of instruction?

Humayun Kabir: That, I think, was earlier generally accepted in a way.

Bhai Jodh Singh: May I suggest a change which will meet the whole point? Instead of saying "regional languages" we may make it singular. "When a university decides to adopt the regional language as the medium of instruction, the

T-2

Council sees no reason why that university should bar the use of English" etc. etc.

Jawaharlal Nehru: It is a good principle that the university should determine it.

C.D. Deshmukh: That is very important. The University Act itself includes a clause regarding the medium of instruction. No Act goes to the extent of prescribing the medium.

Jawaharlal Nehru: We come back to this paragraph on page 3, the penultimate paragraph. Should it begin by saying something to the effect that a university can determine its medium of instruction? Is that right?

D.S. Kothari: Yes.

Jawaharlal Nehru: What will be the language?

D.S. Kothari: It is primarily for the university to decide on academic considerations; it is primarily a matter for the universities. [Interruption] No university can function unless it enjoys the fullest support of the Government. Therefore, whenever anybody suggests that a university fights the Government, it makes no sense at all because a university, if it has to function, if it has to serve its purpose, must enjoy the fullest confidence of everyone concerned.

Jivraj Mehta: If a State wants to set up a college in a particular region it can do so by an Act of the Legislature laying down that the medium of instruction shall be so and so.

Humayun Kabir: The question of medium should be primarily the concern of the university to be decided on academic grounds.

Jawaharlal Nehru: Could we have that in the beginning: "The question of the medium of instruction should primarily be one for the university to determine on academic grounds."

T-3

Bijayananda Patnaik: If that is so, will it not go against the decision of the National Integration Conference? How can an individual university be more competent to decide on a general issue like this then the National Integration Council?

Jawaharlal Nehru: I think it is. It may be; the Council may not be. I think it may well be a little more competent than, say, a legislature. It may not necessarily be, but it may be because they know about the educational standards and about educational matters.

Y.B. Chavan: The medium of instruction should be left to the universities to decide on academic considerations.

Jawaharlal Nehru: It is ultimately a question of timing, phasing, etc.

Y.B. Chavan: But the legislature also comes into the picture and they are also competent to decide on the medium of instruction. It is not that it can be said that it is the primary concern of the University only.

D.S. Kothari: Yes, a university's primary concern is the maintenance of standards. For example there is pressure on some universities to switch over to the regional language.

Jivraj Mehta: "Change of medium of instruction" you can mention.

Indira Gandhi: Mr Anthony was thinking in terms of the minorities. I mean, there may be very few people in Gujarat. It does not take care of it in this particular university. Now will that change?

Humayun Kabir: By making an amendment in the Act you can start another university.

B. Malik: To support Mrs Gandhi may I say something

T-4

about the minorities. Now the terms of reference to the committee were only these, the committee to review the action taken for the implementation of the Resolution passed by the National Integration Conference as regards the place of English, Hindi and the regional language in university education. That is why the other question about the linguistic minorities was not allowed to be raised in our report, or was not put in the report. Now the Council decision here should to give the impression that where there are minority colleges—in Rajasthan there are Sindhi colleges—they must now change over and give up their own language. There are minorities who have got their own language schools and colleges, and as the Prime Minister knows, this matter cropped up in Bihar, and through his intervention luckily it was decided in the proper way. The question came up in regard to the Ramakrishna Mission College at Jadavpur. So this decision to confine it only to English and Hindi should not mean that if there are any minorities in a State and they have a college of their own with their language as the medium of instruction, that they cannot have it. The terms of reference refer to these three languages, English, Hindi and the regional language, the terms of reference of the committee.

Jawaharlal Nehru: Of the three languages I take it that the third language is a modern Indian language.

B. Malik: But then if you say that it may allow the use of English or Hindi as the medium of instruction in a university or in some colleges, some States might start interpreting it to mean that besides English and Hindi no other minority language would be allowed.

T-5

B. Patnaik: Except the regional language where it is situated.

B. Malik: Regional language does not come in. I am talking of a minority language, and this problem is a pending problem in some States. It had arisen in Bihar but it was decided there in favour of the minorities.

Jawaharlal Nehru: It arises in bilingual areas.

B. Malik: And most of the areas are bilingual. It arises in such areas where the minorities are in large numbers and can afford to have schools and colleges of their own.

Humayun Kabir: One suggestion was made in the case of such colleges or institutions that they may be affiliated to some other university or board for recognition and for purposes of examinations, even outside the State. To that many of the Chief Ministers replied that they would set up such Boards themselves.

B. Malik: They can affiliate only if they exist, and if they are not allowed to exist, how can they affiliate?

Zakir Husain: The States have reported that there is provision for this.

B. Malik: The terms of reference of the committee mention only English, Hindi and the regional language.

Humayun Kabir: There may be a separate paragraph.

Sampurnanad: There are certain States where the difficulty arises.

B. Malik: Why not say "any other language" instead of English and Hindi?

U-1

जवाहरलाल नेहरुः डा. कोठारी, क्या कहा था आपने?

[Translation begins:

Jawaharlal Nehru: What did you say Dr Kothari?

Translation ends]

D.S. Kothari: I said, change-over of medium of instruction is primarily a matter for the university to decide.

Jawaharlal Nehru: I will read it:

"The change-over in the medium of instruction in a university is primarily a question for the university to decide. While it seems natural that regional languages would gradually or generally become the media of instruction at the university stage, the Council sees no reason why there should be any bar to use English or Hindi as the medium of instruction in a university or in some college in the university."

Humayun Kabir: English and Hindi is an All-India problem. I was thinking that we add another small paragraph where we do not go into the question in detail. We say there is also the problem of minority language. The question of their continuation and development is being treated separately.

Jawaharlal Nehru: Shall I add:

"There is no reason why there should be any bar to the use of English or Hindi or any other language as the medium of instruction or in some of its colleges."

Bhai Jodh Singh: It would be better if you "in some colleges affiliated to it". Otherwise there would be inconsistency.

Jawaharlal Nehru: It would stand as:

"The change-over in the medium of instruction in a university is primarily a question for the university to decide. While it seems natural that the regional languages would gradually become the media of instruction of the university at the university stage the Council feels there is no reason why there should be any bar to the use of English and Hindi or some other language as a medium of instruction in a university or in some of its colleges."

एम० एल० सुखाडियाः पूरी फ्रीडम अब हो गई है।

[Translation begins:

M. L. Sukhadia: Now there is total freedom.

Translation ends]

U-2

Jawaharlal Nehru: I said "French in Pondicherry" or for the matter of that, Urdu in another region or any other language in bilingual regions.

एम० एल० सुखाडियाः मेरा कहने का मतलब यह है कि कांग्रेस को यह सब कहने की ज़रूरत नहीं है। यह सब पहले ही कहा जा चुका है और उनको फ्रीडम है।

ज़ाकिर हुसैनः अगर खुल कर यह हो कि सिर्फ रीजनल लेंगुएज हो तो फिर आप किसी को भी दूसरी लेंगुएज पढ़ने नहीं दें। यह हो सकता है। लेंगुएज के बारे में कोई

रूकावट नहीं होना चाहिए। कालेजेज को खोलने में और उसमें लेंगुएजेज की पढ़ाई करने में रूकावट नहीं हो। अगर कहीं ऐसा करना हो तो वह हो सके।

[Translation begins:

M.L. Sukhadia : What I mean to say is that it is not necessary for the Congress to say all this. All this has already been said and they have freedom.

Zakir Husain: If it is openly admitted that only the regional languages shall prevail, then you will not permit anyone to study other languages. It could happen. There should be no barriers in the matter of languages or in the matter of establishing colleges or teaching different languages wherever possible this should be done.

Translation ends]

Humayun Kabir: It will not be able to stand without the support of the Government. A university cannot last a day without the support of the Government.

Jawaharlal Nehru: The question of "other language" is important in bilingual areas.

वाई० बी० चौहान : यह कहने से और झगड़े पैदा होंगे। कांग्रेस के जरिए से कहना ठीक नहीं है।

[Translations begins:

Y.B. Chavan: Saying this with create more problems. Saying this through Congress will not be right at all.

Translation ends]

One can understand if there are exceptional cases which can be tackled on merit.

जाकिर हुसैनः जो झगड़ा पैदा होता है उसकी अगर दवा दें तो वह भी ठीक नहीं है। उसको तो हल करना है। जहां कोई ऐसी ज़रूरत हो तो फिर दूसरी लेंगुएज भी हो सके, यही मतलब है।

[Translation begins:

Zakir Husain: When there is conflict, it is not right to do some short term treatment. The problem must be solved, wherever it is necessary, other languages should also be taught. This is what I mean.

Translation ends]

Jawaharlal Nehru: It is in exceptional cases like French in Pondicherry.

Y.B. Chavan: Those areas also one can consider. Bilingual areas as such are not sanctioned here.

यहां कांग्रेस में यह कहना कि और लेंगुएज़ज हो सकती है उससे झगड़े पैदा हो सकते हैं। अंग्रेजी और हिन्दी जो कहा है वह तो ठीक है लेकिन और लेंगुएज़ेज की बात नहीं कहें।

[Translation begins:

In this context, for the Congress to say that other languages can be taught can create dissension. It is alright to talk about English and Hindi but other languages should not be mentioned.

Translation ends]

U-3

Zakir Husain: It would be valid only in places where the situation comes up.

Y.B. Chavan: The interpretation can be validly made for other areas also. In a cosmopolitan city like Bombay where there may be a lakh of population speaking one language, it may give rise to confusion. I think we are going too much in detail. I think we should adopt some broad policies.

D.S. Kothari: Perhaps we may leave it at that.

Jawaharlal Nehru: But you must remember that this question arose in exceptional cases like Pondicherry. It does slightly arise in the case of Urdu also. But in the main it arises in bilingual areas.

Y.B. Chavan: A university should have Hindi and English, English to be replaced by Hindi progressively. Bombay is a cosmopolitan city. There we should certainly encourage English and Hindi to be used as medium of instruction.

C.D. Deshmukh: In Mysore, in Belgaum, there is the Parvati Bai College where Marathi is used as the medium and it is at present affiliated to the Karnatak University. What is more, the Vice-Chancellor says that he will allow the use of Marathi as a medium of instruction but the college does not get on.[78] Well, it may be for other reasons and they have been asking the Bombay University to affiliate.

Jawaharlal Nehru: Well, it would read thus:

"The change-over in the medium of instruction in a university is primarily a question for the university to decide. While it seems natural that the regional languages would gradually become the media of instruction at the University stage the Council sees no reason why there should be any bar to the use of English or Hindi as the medium of instruction in a university or in some of its colleges."

Agreed to.

W-1

K.M. Munshi: There is another resolution on making education a Concurrent subject. It might stand over till the next meeting.

Jawaharlal Nehru: Mr Munshi suggests that one of the Resolutions is on education being made a concurrent subject. Do you mean university education?

K.M. Munshi: University education. As a matter of fact it was suggested that it could stand over till some committee reports on it.

Lal Bahadur Shastri: The Committee has been appointed by the Education Ministry.

Jawaharlal Nehru: Is it not a Concurrent subject now?

78. As in the original.

K.M. Munshi: The position today is that standard of education and determination of standards and co-ordination is a Central subject but in the Radhakrishnan Report[79] it has been suggested that education, particularly university education, should be made Concurrent. At the last meeting of the Integration Conference also there was a strong volume of opinion that it should be a Concurrent subject. During the last two days we have seen how many difficulties are cropping up because university education is not a Concurrent subject.

Jawaharlal Nehru: Shall we say in the proceedings that this matter was raised but was deferred till the next meeting, and meanwhile the Chief Ministers may be consulted?

K. M. Munshi: Yes, this should be postponed?

Jawaharlal Nehru: Now there is a letter which Indira Gandhi has received on behalf of a number of film producers—five top-most producers of India. Bimal Roy, Raj Kapoor, Chopra,[80] Rajbans Khanna and Dilip Kumar have agreed to form themselves into a group for this production of a series of documentaries and short films on subjects relating to integration. They have asked us to take some notice of it.

W-2

If we have to refer it to somebody for consideration, we may refer it to the Ministry itself.

Humayun Kabir: We announced last year in different Indian languages with regard to India's unity and the response had been much beyond anything we expected. [Interruption]

Jawaharlal Nehru: Shall we say that we welcome the proposal for the production of documentaries in furtherance of national integration and this may be forwarded to the Ministry concerned?

Humayun Kabir: Many people have sometimes been writing and it is obviously one of the most powerful forces.

79. Report of the University Education Commission also known as Radhakrishnan Commission, 1948-49.

80. Probably B.R. Chopra.

Indira Gandhi: These people very actively helped in Jubbulpore and so on.

Jawaharlal Nehru: We are not mentioning their names.

Indira Gandhi: We should have some idea of the next meeting of the Council.

Bijayananda Patnaik: It should be held somewhere outside Delhi at different places.

Jawaharlal Nehru: Certainly we can hold it somewhere also – in the Southern region.

S.R. Kanthi: At Bangalore.

Jawaharlal Nehru: Is it agreed that we hold it in some other place, preferably Hyderabad or Bangalore?

Pattom Thanu Pillai: In the extreme south.

Jawaharlal Nehru: Hyderabad or Bangalore.

Well, it appears that we have more or less finished our agenda. It seems to me that we have not discussed the subject this time—the administrative services consist, as they should, of All-India men and they can exercise a great deal of influence towards national integration. We suggested that some administrative services should be made All-India, but we are still consulting the States

W-3

about it. It will come up next time. Well, shall I take it that this is all for the present?

Well, roughly speaking when should we hold our meeting? I think one should try to hold it quarterly—in September. September is the month when I shall probably have to go to the Prime Ministers' Conference. So, end of September or early in October.

(Somebody: Nagaland.)

Indira Gandhi: I think Nagaland should be considered very seriously because they have no opportunity of seeing anybody except the military there. It does not help any integration.

Jawaharlal Nehru: Do you mean to say that they will be impressed by our presence there? Well, in Foreign Service examinations one of the Examiners reported—there are about 7, 8 or 10 officers who go for interview to the Foreign Service—that they were most impressed by two Nagas who had passed the examination; from the personality point of view they were most impressed by them. I think one was a woman—I am not quite sure. They were very impressive people—personality and all that.

Well, the meeting comes to a close. Thank you very much.

(The meeting then terminated)

8. Proceedings[81]

The National Integration Conference convened by the Prime Minister which met at New Delhi from the 28th September to the 1st October, 1961, decided to set up a National Integration Council thereon.[82] The composition of the Council is as follows:

(1) Prime Minister as Chairman.
(2) The Union Home Minister.
(3) Chief Ministers of all States.
(4) Seven leaders of political parties represented in Parliament.
(5) Chairman of the National Integration Committee of the Indian National Congress (Shrimati Indira Gandhi).
(6) Chairman, University Grants Commission.
(7) Two Educationists.
(8) Seven persons nominated by the Prime Minister.
(9) Commissioner for Linguistic Minorities.
(10) Commissioner for Scheduled Castes and Scheduled Tribes.

81. Proceedings of the first meeting of the National Integration Council, June 2 and 3, 1962. MHA, File No. 18/11/62-OL.

These proceedings are, in fact, a report on the discussions of the National Integration Council. The verbatim record is published separately as items 6 and 7.

82. For the Statement issued by the National Integration Conference, see SWJN/SS/71/ item 68.

2. The first meeting of the National Integration Council was held in the Vigyan Bhavan at New Delhi on June 2 and 3, 1962. A list of persons who attended the meeting of the Council is given in Appendix I.[83]

3. The Prime Minister in his opening speech welcomed the members. He explained that the delay in holding the meeting has been caused by the fact that general elections had intervened in the early part of the year. A paper outlining the progress of implementation of the recommendations made by the National Integration Conference was circulated to the members. The Prime Minister indicated that during the general elections, certain undesirable trends had manifested themselves and some disruptive factors had come into evidence in the course of the election campaign.

4. The members of the Council then entered upon a general discussion regarding trends and developments since the meeting of the National Integration Conference held in October last, with particular reference to the action to be taken for the preservation of the unity of India and against communalism. Several members took part in this general discussion and made a survey of the developments during recent months. As a result of these discussions, three main problems presented themselves for further and closer examination.

5. The first problem was the place of English, Hindi and the regional languages in university education, with particular reference to the need for the preservation of a link language between the Universities and the teaching of English as a language of international importance for the enrichment of the Indian languages in Science and Technology. A Committee was appointed to consider this problem and to report to the Council on the 3rd June, 1962. The Committee consisted of :

1. Dr Sampurnanand—*Chairman.*
2. Dr C.D. Deshmukh.
3. Dr D.S. Kothari.
4. Shri K.M. Munshi.
5. Shri Frank Anthony.
6. Bhai Jodh Singh.
7. Dr Jivraj Narayan Mehta.

6. After considering the report of the Sampurnanand Committee, the Council adopted the following Resolution:

"The Council reaffirms the conclusions set out in paragraph 15 of the Statement issued by the National Integration Conference in September-October,

83. See pp. 223-224.

1961. The Council recalls that these conclusions did not differ materially from the decisions in regard to the medium of instruction at the University stage arrived at by the Chief Ministers Conference in August 1961, as also that they had since been accepted by the Emotional Integration Committee in its preliminary report.

The Council observes that the policy in this respect is being implemented in varying measures by different Universities, but it is of the view that its implementation should be more purposeful. In the Council's view, the change is justified not so much by cultural or political sentiments as on the very important academic consideration of facilitating grasp and understanding of the subject-matter. Further, India's university men will be unable to make their maximum possible contribution to the advancement of learning generally, and (science and technology in particular, unless there was a continuous means of communication in the shape of the regional languages between its masses, its artisans and technicians and its university men. The development of the talent latent in the country will also, in the view of the Council, be retarded unless regional languages are employed as media of instruction at the university stage.

The Council considers that while generally speaking the replacement of English as medium was thus an inevitable end which should be actively pursued, every care should be taken by universities to ensure that the transition is made without jeopardising the quality of education and after careful preparation, *e.g.,* the co-operation of teachers and the availability of good standard books written by university teachers or other experts for which every incentive should be provided by the authorities concerned.

The Council lays stress on the importance of teaching English as a compulsory subject, whether in any transitional scheme of the adoption of regional languages as medium of instruction, or even after the replacement has been fully carried out at a future date. In the transitional stage, English will serve as the link among university men and between university and university in respect of exchange of professors or migration of students; whilst, at all times, as a language of great international importance, English would furnish, a link with the outside world, constitute an indispensable tool for further study and assist in the development of the regional langauges.

The Council hopes that while English would thus be an international link at all times, its place as an internal link will gradually be taken by Hindi as it develops. The Council therefore urges that at the university stage, the students should be equipped with a progressively better command of Hindi in addition to a good working knowledge of English such as would enable them to follow lectures delivered in that language.

In the light of these considerations, the Council reiterates the recommendation of the Chief Ministers' Conference[84] that the standard of teaching both in Hindi and English should be improved and maintained at a high level in schools and colleges.

The change in the medium of instruction in a university is primarily a question for the university to decide. While it seems natural that regional languages would gradually become the media of instruction at the university stage, the Council sees no reason why there should be any bar to the use of English or Hindi as a medium of instruction in a university, or in some of its colleges. Indeed it foresees that in some special circumstances the establishment of such a college might become a desideratum.

In this connection, the Council urges that there should be a provision in every university permitting the use of Hindi or English as an option to the regional language for answering examination papers.

7. The two other main problems which emerged and which called for further examination were the problem arising out of the agitations for regional separatism in certain parts of the country and the problem of communalism. Two Committees were appointed to deal with (a) the problem of national integration and regionalism and (b) the problem of national integration and communalism. The problems entrusted to these Committees have certain aspects in common and it was, therefore, expected that the Committees may function together whenever they considered it appropriate to do so. The Committees were also authorised to co-opt not more than two members each if they considered it necessary. It was realised that the work of these two Committees may take some time and they were, therefore, requested to make their report to the next meeting of the Council. The following members were appointed to the two Committees :

1. Committee on national integration and regionalism :

    1. Shri C.P. Ramaswami Aiyar—Chairman.
    2. Shri K. Kamaraj.
    3. Shri Y.B. Chavan.
    4. Shri B. Patnaik.
    5. Shri Asoka Mehta.
    6. Shri B.P. Chaliha.

84. For Chief Ministers' Conference, see SWJN/SS/70/item 63.

2. Committee on national integration and communalism:

   1. Shri Asoka Mehta—Chairman.
   2. Shrimati Indira Gandhi.
   3. Shri A.B. Vajpayee.
   4. Shri Bishanchandar Seth.
   5. Shri Sadiq Ali.
   6. Shri E.M.S. Namboodiripad.
   7. Prof. M. Mujeeb.

'Come And Be Shot'

The National Integration Council has set up four committee to go into the factors that militate against integration.

(From *Shankar's Weekly*, 10 June 1962, p. 5)

8. The Council next considered the question of evolving codes of conduct for (a) political parties, (b) students and (c) the Press. The Council reaffirmed the code which had been recommended for adoption by political parties by the National Integration Conference last October. The Council urged the various political parties in the country effectually to implement these recommendations in regulating the conduct of their members.

9. The Council was of the view that it would be desirable to evolve a code of conduct not only for the different grades of students but also for the teachers and the various educational institutions and political parties. In drawing up such a code, there should be the fullest consultation with universities and

educational institutions. A Committee was set up to examine the question further. The Committee would consult the universities and educational institutions while preparing the draft code which it would submit to the Council at its next meeting. The following were appointed to the Committee:

1. Dr K.L. Shrimali—Chairman & Convener.
2. Shri C.P. Ramaswami Aiyar.
3. Dr C.D. Deshmukh.
4. Dr D.S. Kothari.
5. Bhai Jodh Singh.

10. The proposal to evolve a code of conduct for the Press was considered by the National Integration Conference in October last. The Conference had recommended that the Council should take steps to evolve such a code of conduct. The Press has a vital role to play in national integration by promoting a feeling of national unity and solidarity, by setting its face against disruptive forces and by exercising due restraint and a sense of responsibility in dealing with matters likely to create tension or promote antagonisms or animosities.

11. The Council considered a draft code of conduct for the Press placed before it (Appendix II).[85] The Council felt that the draft code was worthy of acceptance. The efficacy of such a code would, however, depend on its willing acceptance by the Press.

12. The Press Commission, whose report was published in 1954, had come to the conclusion that the establishment of a Press Council was a matter of great importance not only to safeguard editorial independence but also for ensuring objectivity in the presentation of news and views. The Press Commission had stated that the formulation and implementation of a code dealing with the rights and responsibilities of the Press will be one of the primary duties and obligations of the Press Council when it is established.[86] Special attention was paid to certain principles that should find a place in the code of journalistic etiquette. These are set out in Appendix III.[87]

13. Having regard to the adequate and comprehensive code of conduct for the Press on the lines indicated in the report of the Press Commission, the National Integration Council desired to stress the importance of implementing those recommendations as early as possible. In the meanwhile, the Council recommended to Government the setting up of a Committee to confer with

85. See p. 225.

86. For former Minister of Information and Broadcasting B.V. Keskar's explanation on Press Council, see appendix 16. See also appendix 53.

87. See pp. 226-227.

the different sections of the Press and to examine and formulate a Press Code with due regard to the Press Commission's recommendations.

14. The Council considered a proposal to evolve a code of conduct for elections including Panchayat Raj elections. It discussed at some length the proposal to evolve a code for elections to the different bodies at various levels in the Panchayat Raj scheme. It was revealed that there was considerable diversity among the different States as regards the statutory provisions for elections to the Village Panchayats, the Block Panchayat Samitis and the Zila Parishads as well as in the extent of devolution of functions and powers to these bodies. In the circumstances, the Council felt that while the balance of advantage lay in keeping party politics out of the Panchayat elections, particularly at the village or primary level, it was advisable to defer further consideration of the question to a future session. The Council desired that in the meanwhile the situation should be kept under careful review.

15. The Council considered a suggestion by Shri K.M. Munshi that the question of encroachments, legislative or administrative, on the common citizenship rights as regards residence, service, education, trade, business and property throughout the country be examined. The discussion centred in the main on the question of admission to universities and educational institutions in different States. The Council noted that universities can and should exert a powerful unifying influence in the country. It, therefore, strongly recommended that admissions to the universities should not be denied on considerations of place of birth, residence, caste or creed (except in so far as any reservations have been provided under the Constitution).

16. Certain film producers had conveyed a suggestion to the Council that they may undertake production of a series of documentaries and short films to further the cause of national integration. The Council welcomed the proposal and decided that it may be referred to the Ministry of Information and Broadcasting for further consideration. The Ministry was requested to make a report on the subject at the next meeting of the Council.

17. In his concluding remarks, the Prime Minister referred to the question of the constitution of All India Services. He observed that the setting up of All India Services would help in furthering the cause of national integration. He expressed the hope that the State Governments would give early consideration to the proposals already sent to them.

18. It was decided that the next meeting of the Council may be held at some place outside Delhi, preferably at Hyderabad or Bangalore, towards the end of September or the beginning of October, 1962.[88]

APPENDIX I

List of Members of the Council and Special Invitees.

The Prime Minister Chairman.

The Union Home Minister.

Chief Ministers of States: —

Shri N. Sanjiva Reddy, Andhra Pradesh.
Shri B.P. Chaliha, Assam.
Shri Binodanand Jha, Bihar.
Dr Jivraj Narayan Mehta, Gujarat.
* Bakshi Ghulam Mohammad, Jammu & Kashmir.
Shri Pattom A. Thanu Pillai, Kerala.
Shri B. A. Mandloi, Madhya Pradesh.
Shri K. Kamaraj, Madras.
Shri Yeshwantrao Balwantrao Chavan, Maharashtra.
Shri S.R. Kanthi, Mysore.
Shri Bijoyananda Patnaik, Orissa
Shri Partap Singh Kairon, Punjab

88. On 4 June 1962, while placing the draft of the proceedings of the National Integration Council meeting, V. Viswanathan, the Home Secretary, wrote : "After the draft has been passed, it will be printed up and copies supplied to the Members of the Council and also made available to the public."

On this, Nehru instructed:

> "You may get this draft printed. I think that at the end of it, you should give the names of all the members of the Council who were present. Also, names of the two or three special invitees.
>
> 2. I should like to place copies of the proceedings of the National Integration Council on the Tables of the Houses of Parliament. The Lok Sabha is adjourning about the 22nd of this month."

* [Did not attend the meeting].

Shri Mohan Lal Sukhadia, Rajasthan
Shri C.B. Gupta, Uttar Pradesh.
* Dr B.C. Roy, West Bengal.

Leaders of political parties represented in Parliament :—

Shri Sadiq Ali.
Shri Asoka Mehta (By special invitation).
Shri Ganga Sharan Sinha.
Shri E.M.S. Namboodiripad (in place of Shri S. A. Dange).
Shri K.M. Munshi.
Shri A.B. Vajpayee.
† Shri Jaipal Singh.
Shri N. Siv Raj.
Shri Bishanchandar Seth (By special invitation).

Chairman of the National Integration Committee of the Indian National Congress—Shrimati Indira Gandhi.
Chairman of the University Grants Commission— Shri D. S. Kothari.
Educationists :

* Dr. H. J. Bhabha.
Prof. M. Mujeeb.

Seven persons nominated by the Prime Minister, namely:—

Dr Zakir Hussain.
Shri C. P. Ramaswami Aiyar.
* Shri Jayaprakash Narayan
Dr Sampurnanand
Shri C. D. Deshmukh
Shri Frank Anthony
Bhai Jodh Singh.

Commissioner for Linguistic Minorities—Shri B. Malik.

* [Did not attend the meeting].
† Did not attend in the afternoon of June 3, 1962.

Commissioner for Scheduled Castes & Scheduled Tribes—Shri A. K. Chanda.

Central Government—Special invitees

1. Dr. K. L. Shrimali, Minister lor Education.
‡ 2. Shri Humayun Kabir, Minister for Scientific Research & Cultural Affairs.
3. Shri Sham Nath, Deputy Minister for Information & Broadcasting.

APPENDIX II

Draft Code of Conduct tor the Prfss

The Press shall

(i) take all active steps to develop a feeling of unity, solidarity and cohesion in the hearts of the people and to create a sense of common citizenship and a feeling of loyalty to the nation:
(ii) subordinate group loyalties based on caste, community, religion, region, or language to national interests;
(iii) condone no move of any person, party, or group to divide the country, or to create tension between its peoples;
(iv) condemn unreservedly incitement to violence or any advocacy of violence as a means of settling conflicts;
(v) withhold publication of unverified news which would tend to create discord, and refrain from giving prominent display to such news;
(vi) contradict or rectify all inaccurate reports or comments relating to such news;
(vii) highlight all activities, whether of the State or of the public, which promote the progress of the nation and unity of the country.

‡ Did not attend on June 2, 1962.

APPENDIX III

(1) As the Press is a primary instrument in the creation of public opinion, journalists should regard their calling as a trust and be ready and willing to serve and guard the public interest.

(2) In the discharge of their duties, journalists should attach due value to fundamental human and social rights and shall hold good faith and fair play in news reports and comments as essential professional obligations.

(3) Freedom in the honest collection and publication of news and facts and the right of fair comment and criticism are principles which every journalist should always defend.

(4) Journalists shall observe the restraint in reports and comments which are likely to aggravate tension likely to lead to violence.

(5) Journalists shall endeavour to ensure that information disseminated is factually accurate. No fact shall be distorted and no essential fact shall be suppressed. No information known to be false or not believed to be true shall be published.

(6) Responsibility shall be assumed for all information and comment published. If responsibility is disclaimed, this shall be explicitly stated beforehand.

(7) Unconfirmed news shall be identified and treated as such.

(8) Confidence shall always be respected and professional secrecy preserved, but it shall not be regarded as a breach of the code if the source of information is disclosed in matters coming up before the Press Council, or courts of law.

(9) Journalists shall not allow personal interests to influence professional conduct.

(10) Any report found to be inaccurate and any comment based on inaccurate reports shall be voluntarily rectified. It shall be obligatory to give fair publicity to a correction or contradiction when a report published is false or inaccurate in material particulars.

(11) All persons engaged in the gathering, transmission and dissemination of news and commenting thereon shall seek to maintain full public confidence in the integrity and dignity of their profession. They shall assign and accept only such tasks as are compatible with this integrity and dignity; and they shall guard against exploitation of their status.

(12) There is nothing so unworthy as the acceptance or demand of a bribe or inducement for the exercise by a journalist of his power to give or deny publicity to news or comment.
(13) The carrying on of personal controversies in the Press, where no public issue is involved, is un-journalistic and derogatory to the dignity of the profession.
(14) It is unprofessional to give currency in the Press to rumours or gossip affecting the private life of individuals. Even verifiable news affecting individuals shall not be published unless public interests demand its publication.
(15) Calumny and unfounded accusations are serious professional offences.
(16) Plagiarism is also a serious professional offence.
(17) In obtaining news or pictures, reporters and Press photographers shall do nothing that will cause pain or humiliation to innocent, bereaved or otherwise distressed persons.

9. To Sampurnanand: Panikkar and Emotional Integration[89]

June 26, 1962

My dear Sampurnanand,
Your letter of the 17th June.[90] I am a little surprised and somewhat distressed to read of what Panikkar is reported to have said. He is a man with considerable ability, but also a good deal of conceit. His saying that I did not know anything about your committee, was, of course, absurd. I know about it, but what I did not know at the time was that the committee was meeting in Srinagar. Probably he took advantage of a statement of mine to this effect and thereafter made the remark he did. The committee was good enough not to trouble me in Srinagar as they thought I was resting.

Yours sincerely,
Jawaharlal Nehru

89. Letter to the Chairman of the Emotional Integration Committee and Governor of Rajasthan. PMO, File No. 2(397)/61-70-PM, Vol. III, Sr. No. 109-A.
90. Appendix 36.

10. To B. Malik: On National Integration[91]

July 10, 1962

My dear Malik,

Thank you for your letter of June 30th with which you have sent me a note about national integration. I have read this note with interest and I find myself largely in agreement with it. I am arranging to send copies of the note to all the Chief Ministers as well as Ministers of the Central Government.

Yours sincerely,
[Jawaharlal Nehru]

11. To K. Ram: Malik's Note on National Integration[92]

I am sending you a letter and a note by Shri B. Malik, Commissioner for Linguistic Minorities. I should like copies of this note to be sent with my compliments to all the Chief Ministers of States and Ministers of the Central Government. You can head it: "Note on national integration by Shri B. Malik, Commissioner for Linguistic Minorities".

91. Letter to the Commissioner for Linguistic Minorities; address: 26, Hamilton Road, Allahabad. Sent from Pahalgam, Kashmir.
92. Note, 10 July 1962, to the PPS. Sent from Pahalgam, Kashmir.

III. POLITICS

(a) Indian National Congress

12. To M.C. Davar: Standing from the Chittur Seat[1]

June 2, 1962

My dear Dr Davar,

I have your letter of the 2nd June about the Chittur seat. You will appreciate that these seats in a distant constituency and another State have largely to be decided on the advice of the local Pradesh Congress Committee. The choice was therefore of the Pradesh Congress Committee. The one case in which a person from North India has stood for a South Indian seat was due to the fact that the PCC recommended his name.[2]

I am afraid that if you stand for election there and oppose the Congress candidate, this will not be a good thing. You will appreciate also that in any such context, the knowledge of the language of the place is important. I would, therefore, not recommend your standing for this seat.

Yours sincerely,
Jawaharlal Nehru

13. To Gulzarilal Nanda: Chief Ministers' Meeting[3]

June 3, 1962

My dear Gulzarilal,

I have your two letters and notes. It would certainly be a good thing to have a meeting of Chief Ministers. But I really do not know when we can have it. Tomorrow is pretty full. The day after tomorrow is the AICC meeting. I do not know how long this meeting will last and whether it will go on till 6th June. Perhaps, you could have your Chief Ministers' meeting on the 6th June afternoon if they are still here.

Yours sincerely,
[Jawaharlal Nehru]

1. Letter to a homeopath and Congressman ; address: 32 B Block, Connaught Place, New Delhi. NMML, M.C. Davar Papers.
2. A.P. Jain was elected to the Lok Sabha from Tumkur in Mysore state in a bye-election; see item 166.
3. Letter to the Deputy Chairman of the Planning Commission, New Delhi.

14. To G.D. Gadre: Will Not Canvas for Rajya Sabha Seat[4]

June 3, 1962

Dear Gadre,

I have your letter of May 28th. I am afraid you have asked me to do something which I have not done for anyone. I do not go about canvassing for people to be made candidates. When the matter comes before me, I give my opinion. At present I do not even know if any elections are taking place for the Rajya Sabha soon.[5]

I have just seen your letter of June 3rd asking for an interview. Tomorrow morning I cannot see you. If you like, you can come on the 5th early at 9 o'clock to my house.

Yours sincerely,
[Jawaharlal Nehru]

15. To Ram Ratan Gupta: Gonda Election[6]

June 3, 1962

My dear Ram Ratan,

Your letter of the 28th May has only today reached me. I have read it. You have been correctly informed that there has been a great deal of criticism about your election in Gonda. I have been much worried about it because the criticism has sometimes come from persons who have no reason to be against you in any way. Now that an election petition is taking place, I imagine that true facts will come out.[7]

4. Letter to a Fellow of the Gandhi Peace Foundation; address: 18/3 Arya Samaj Road, Karol Bagh, New Delhi 5.
5. See also SWJN/SS/76/item 52.
6. Letter to Lok Sabha MP, Congress; address: 14 Windsor Place, New Delhi.
7. In the Third General Election, Gupta won the majority of votes, see *RECI*, p. 61. But the Election Tribunal countermanded the result when the recount in Gonda revealed that nearly 2000 ballot papers cast for the Swatantra Party candidate had been tampered with. Paul R. Brass, *Factional Politics in an Indian State, The Congress Party in Uttar Pradesh* (Bombay: Oxford University Press, 1966), pp. 77-78 and 175 citing *Citizen*, 29 August 1964. See also SWJN/SS/65/items 83-84 and appendix 57; SWJN/SS/68/ items 124-125, 131; SWJN/SS/69/items 134, 137, 143, 145 and appendices 9 and 17.

I am sorry I cannot see you for a few days as I am heavily occupied. Perhaps afterwards I may be able to see you.

Yours sincerely,
Jawaharlal Nehru

16. To T.T. Krishnamachari: Swearing In[8]

June 4, 1962

My dear T.T.,
Would it suit you if we had the swearing-in ceremony on the 8th June morning at 9.30? After I hear from you, I shall write to the President about it.

Yours affectionately,
Jawaharlal Nehru

KRISHNA'S ROLE

(From *The Times of India*, 13 June 1962, p. 1)

8. Letter to the Lok Sabha MP, Congress, and former Finance Minister; address: Claridge's Hotel, New Delhi. NMML, T.T. Krishnamachari Papers, File No. 1963, Auto.

17. To S. Radhakrishnan: Ministerial Appointments[9]

June 5, 1962

Dear Mr President,

I am venturing to recommend to you the addition of two MPs to the present Council of Ministers. These are Shri T.T. Krishnamachari to be a Cabinet Minister without Portfolio,[10] and Shri Prakash Chandra Sethi, Member of the Rajya Sabha, to be a Deputy Minister attached to the Ministry of Steel and Heavy Industry. I trust that you will approve of my proposals.

I suggest that their Swearing-in ceremony might take place on Friday, the 8th June, at 9.30 a.m., if this is convenient to you.

Yours sincerely,
Jawaharlal Nehru

18. In New Delhi: AICC Meetings[11]

The All India Congress Committee met at 3.30 P.M. on Tuesday the 5th June 1962 at Sapru House, New Delhi. Shri N. Sanjiva Reddy presided. 234 members were present. The meeting started with the singing of Vande Mataram.

The proceedings of the meetings of the All India Congress Committee and the Subjects Committee held on January 4 and 5, 1962 at Srikrishnapuri, Patna[12] were confirmed.

President's Opening Remarks

In his opening remarks, Shri N. Sanjiva Reddy, the Congress President, said that the results of the Third General Elections, which were on the whole satisfactory for the Congress would have been far more spectacular, had there been no dissensions and factions in the organisation. Elections in some places were not fought on the ideological plane. Communalism, linguism and casteism played an important role in the Election campaign in many places, and some candidates, Independents as well as others, took advantage of such factions. This was not a healthy trend. Linguistic and communal tendencies in the elections

9. Letter to the President. President's Secretariat, File No. 8/62, p.82.
10. See item 16.
11. Proceedings, 5 and 6 June 1962. *Congress Bulletin*, April, May & June 1962, pp. 90-115.
12. See also SWJN/SS/74/items 13-18.

were dangerous for the country. Elections must be fought on political level. In order to check these tendencies it was necessary to educate the voters properly.

The formation of Congress Governments in the States and at the Centre had further increased the responsibilities of the Party workers towards the successful implementation of the economic programmes and policies of the Party. It was the duty of the Congressmen to concentrate upon the problems of rural development and enthuse the people in the rural areas so that they would come forward and extend their cooperation in the developmental schemes. The basic needs of daily life in the villages such as water supply, schools and hospitals, should be given top priority.

Continuing his remarks, Shri Reddy said that the Village Panchayat could play a major role in the social and economic reconstruction of the villages if they were developed on proper lines. It was, therefore, necessary that the Village Panchayats were kept free from the influence of party politics.

The Congress President then informed the members about his resignation which had been accepted by the Working Committee and announced that a new President would be elected during the present session of the All India Congress Committee.

Condolence Resolution

The Congress President then moved the condolence resolution which was adopted by the House, all Members standing. (The resolution is printed separately elsewhere in this issue.)[13]

The Committee next took up the official resolutions for consideration.

General Elections

Shri C. Subramaniam (Madras) moved the resolution on General Elections. He said that, inspite of a different picture that some people would like to depict about the elections, one thing had emerged with a certain amount of clarity—that the people had definitely accepted democracy as a pattern of administration and the goal of democratic Socialist Society. There might have been some traces of reactionary tendencies like communalism, casteism and linguism in the election scenes but they were not predominant. It was satisfactory to note that lesser number of Independent candidates were elected this time and that their numbers were decreasing gradually as judged from the results of the three

13. In the *Congress Bulletin*, April, May & June 1962, on p. 118.

General Elections and it was hoped that their number would further diminish in the next General Elections. This would be progress in the right direction.

The people had conducted themselves commendably in the General Elections and the fact that greater percentage of voters, as compared with the previous elections, had exercised their franchise was encouraging. Doubts were expressed at times about the wisdom of adult franchise in India but the elections had proved that it was a right step.

Referring to the future pattern of electorate Shri Subramaniam said that it would be constituted of a new generation who had not participated in the freedom struggle or even witnessed it. This generation would be an important factor in deciding the fate of the country in future. Unless the Congress Party attuned itself to this new electorate, the youth of the country, the Congress might not be able to move forward. Greater opportunities should, therefore, be given to the younger elements.

The elections had proved that the Congress goal of democratic socialist society and its attainment through planned economy had been accepted by a vast majority of the people. The Third General Elections had also proved that democracy had taken its root in the country. There should be now no impediment to the fulfilment of the promises made to the people, who had reposed their confidence in the Congress.

Shri G.H. Deshpande (Maharashtra) seconded the resolution on General Elections and said that it might be true that there were traces of casteism and communalism in the country, but the voters, the people at large, were not reactionary. This was proved by the results of the General Elections in which the forces of casteism and communalism were defeated. The common man was not affected by such narrow parochial feelings but it was only the work of some interested persons who tried to exploit the feelings of caste. The manner in which the Elections had been conducted was a matter of pride for the people and the country. The defeat of the Congress in some places was due to the lack of unity in the Party.

Referring to the opposition parties, Shri Deshpande said that the Swatantra Party was reactionary in its outlook and had no future. The people had expressed confidence in the Congress and it was now the duty of Congressmen and the Congress organisation to undertake the task of implementing the programmes of the Party.

Shri Radhanandan Jha (Bihar) moved the following amendment:

"That in Para I of the resolution the following be omitted:

> 'While there is room for improvement in the approach of political parties in carrying on the election campaign'."

"and that the following be substituted for the same:

> "Though experience has shown that the general outlook and approach of the political parties and its workers and also the method of canvassing support requites radical change and major improvements".

He said that group rivalries, communalism, regionalism and linguistic tendencies were rampant at the time of the General Elections. It was only the personality of Shri Jawaharlal Nehru and the drive of the Congress President that largely contributed to the Congress victory in the elections.

Shri K.K. Chatterjee (West Bengal) moved the following amendment:

> "The following words in the second sentence be deleted 'while there … campaign'.
>
> and the following be substituted :
>
> 'While the approach of some political parties was very often against the guiding principles of our Constitution and has been undemocratic in method in carrying on their election campaigns'."

Shri Chatterjee said that it was not enough simply to say that the approach of the political parties in the elections needed some improvement. Some definite measures should be taken in that direction.

Shri V.B. Raju (Andhra) moved the following amendment:

> "Add to the resolution the following para (No. 3):
>
> 'To see that the promises made to the people through the manifesto issued on the eve of the General Elections are fulfilled and to watch the progress in that respect, the AICC appoints a Programme Implementation Committee consisting of the following persons'."

Shri Raju said that the Programme Implementation Committee, suggested by him, was necessary for creating confidence among the people. It was true that an important section of the voters had favoured the Congress, but it was not because there was no other party to be voted to power. Some introspection was now necessary in the party and the members of the AICC and the PCCs should be more critical of the Government without any fear.

All the State Governments were not uniformly implementing the programmes laid down by the Congress. Through our achievements the people should be made to feel that the Congress meant business and not promises only.

Seth Govind Das (Madhya Pradesh) supporting the resolution said that it was only a formal resolution and the question of the appointment of a Programme Implementation Committee, as suggested by Shri V.B. Raju, should be left to the Working Committee.

Criticising the Government, Seth Govind Das remarked that it was due to the administrative machinery only that the progress of the country was being slowed down. Government officials should be alive to their responsibilties in executing the plans and the programmes.

Continuing, he said that although the percentage of literacy was low in the country, the way the people had conducted themselves in the elections had shown that their understanding of political issues was keen.

Shri Darogaprasad Roy (Bihar) moved the following amendment:

"After the words 'the Congress' and before fullstop (.), in para II in the fifth line of the resolution, the following be added:

'though the people have expressed their resentment and 'frustration against unusual delaying procedure in the administrative machinery, harassment to the public and growing corruption and unemployment in the country'."

He said that the AICC must take note of the delay caused in the implementation of the development plans and the harassment caused to the people by such delay. It was true that the people had returned the Congress to power, but effective steps must be taken in order to check the growing unemployment and corruption, otherwise it would be difficult to sustain the confidence which the people had reposed in the Party.

Shri Govind Sahai (Uttar Pradesh) said that while the people's faith in democracy was increasing, the strength of the Congress was waning. The people had full faith in democratic principles and had used their franchise very wisely. It would, therefore be an insult to the voters to say that they did not understand political issues and voted merely because of the personality and popularity of Shri Jawaharlal Nehru.

Shri Jagannath Pahadia (Rajasthan) warned the members that they should not remain complacent because of the success of the Congress at the polls. They should be vigilant and take note of the fact that the influence of princely rulers was still strong in the country, and specially in Rajasthan, inspite of the intensive developmental activities undertaken by the Government.

Shri C. Subramaniam (Madras) replying to the debate rejected the proposal for the appointment of a non-official Committee to insure fulfilment of Congress election pledges, as it was not feasible for a non-official committee to function effectively for the removal of all administrative deficiencies.

Replying to the remarks that the popularity of Shri Jawaharlal Nehru was the only factor behind the success of the Congress in the elections, Shri Subramaniam said that the people loved him because he was the embodiment of the Congress principles and ideology. It was unique in the history of parliamentary democracy that the Congress was voted to power successively in three General Elections.

All the four amendments were withdrawn and the resolution was unanimously adopted by the Committee. (The resolution is printed else where in this issue.)[14]

Elections to Panchayats

Shri Y.B. Chavan (Maharashtra) moved the resolution on Elections to Panchayats and said that the aim and object behind Panchayati Raj was to galvanise the rural masses and secure their active participation in the task of reconstruction and economic regeneration of the people.

The village community should not be divided on Party lines in the elections to Panchayats. If they were divided, it would not be conducive to creating a cooperative atmosphere for social and economic advancement. The resolution was intended to give a lead to the nation and to all other political parties in the matter. The Congress was committed to the ideal of having democratic decentralisation for the last so many decades, but this should not lead to the division of the village community on political lines. The elections to Panchayats should, therefore, be held on non-Party lines.

Shri Hardeo Joshi (Rajasthan) seconding the resolution said that experiences in his State had shown that if elections on Party lines were taken to village levels it tended to fritter away the energy of the people in petty political matters.

Smt. Renuka Ray (West Bengal) moved the following amendment:

"At the end of the last line of the Paragraph I, the following lines be added:

'But if the Panchayat Raj is to fulfil its objective, adequate safeguards against the social and economic exploitations of the weaker sections of village society must operate in an effective manner.' "

She said that social disabilities like untouchability still existed in certain places. If proper safeguards were not provided for the upliftment of backward classes these disabilities might continue to be perpetrated.

Shri Bibhuti Mishra (Bihar) moved the following amendment:

14. In the *Congress Bulletin*, April, May & June 1962, on pp. 118-119.

"पचायतों के चुनाव सम्बन्धी प्रस्ताव के अन्त में पेरा-4 जोड़ना चाहता हूँ जो इस प्रकार है - साथ ही यह अखिल भारतीय कांग्रेस कमेटी विभिन्न प्रदेश सरकारों से अनुरोध करती है कि ग्राम पंचायतों के चुनावों मे ऐसी पद्वति का नियतन करे जिससे गावों में ग्राम पंचायतों का चुनाव जाति व पांति के आधार पर न हो और बिरादरीबाद से गांव वंचित रहे।"

[Translation begins:

In the proposal for panchayat elections, I want to add the following at the end as para-4:- This AICC recommends that the State Governments fix a procedure so that the elections to village panchayats are not held on the basis of caste and the villages remain free from castiesm.

Translation ends]

Shri Mishra said that the question of holding Panchayat elections on non-Party lines should have first been discussed with other political parties. If all the parties accepted it, then this resolution should have been brought forward. If the other Parties did not accept the principle of elections to panchayats on non-Party lines, it would prove disastrous for the Congress to accept the same.

Shri Jawaharlal Nehru intervening in the debate said that while he was fully in favour of the Government being run on the basis of political parties, election on party lines at village level should be avoided. The village was such a small unit that elections on Party lines would divide it into numerous small groups. This would be harmful to the interests of the villagers and not help them in carrying out the development and other works.

Opposing the suggestion made in certain quarters for partyless Government or a partyless democracy, Shri Nehru said that this was not feasible. If all the political parties disappeared, undesirable people would come in and dominate the society. These undesirable people, forming themselves into groups, could only be kept out by organising people politically under a party. Political parties with certain principles were very necessary to seek the mandate of the people to run a Government. So a party system of Government was very essential.

Continuing, Shri Nehru said that despite this, the holding of elections on Party lines at the village level would not be proper. In village panchayats, there was a lot of emotion and excitement engendered and people sometimes came to blows. Elections on party lines would aggravate this and villagers would lose sight of the primary cause of uplifting themselves. At the panchayat level, the main thing was carrying out certain programmes for the upliftment of the people. These were set programmes and set tasks which had to be implemented with united endeavour. There was no controversy about these tasks. They had to be carried out for the good of all. But if people quarrelled among themselves on party lines, these tasks would not be fulfilled in the way they should be.

The decision taken by the Congress in this matter was not a mere expression of an opinion but the establishment of a principle for the Congreas organisation. If some other political parties did not agree to it, the Congress should not worry about it. The people in the villages would lean towards those who wanted non-party elections and an approach of common endeavour to fulfil tasks. Even in non-party elections, there would be partymen. If a Congressman fought the elections, even on non-party lines the people would know what he represented.

Shri Nehru concluded his remarks by giving his full support to the resolution.

Shri P.N. Rajabhoj (Maharashtra) supporting the resolution said that backward classes should be encouraged through Panchayats to come up to the level of other sections of the community.

Shri C.M. Stephen (Kerala) suggested that the resolution should lay more emphasis on the functioning of Panchayats on non-party lines rather than on elections to Panchayats on non-party lines.

Shri Sheelbhadra Yajee (Bihar) moved the following amendment :

> "In Para II, line 6, delete the word 'not'.
>
> "In Para III, line 2, delete the word 'not' and delete the words from 'and directs ... to Gram Panchayats'."

Shri Yajee said that non-party elections to Panchayats would precipitate anarchy and chaos.

Shri Rameshwar Dayal (Rajasthan) moved the following amendment:

> "Add the following words in the third para of the resolution after the words 'Party lines':
> 'provided a similar policy is followed by other political parties'."

Shri Rameshwar Dayal suggested that the Congress should be left free to contest the elections to panchayats on party lines wherever it was found necessary.

Shri Jagannath Pahadia (Rajasthan) moved the following amendment:

> "At the end of the resolution, add: 'Panchayat Samitis and Zilla Parishads'."

Shri K.K. Chatterjee (West Bengal) moved the following amendment:

"add at the end of the 3rd Paragraph:

'The AICC however takes note of the possibility of election fights taking place among Congressmen themselves for identical seats in the Gram Panchayats thus weakening the Congress organisation vitally. The AICC, therefore, advises Congressmen to guard effectively against any such situation developing in any election to a Gram Panchayat'."

Shri Radhanandan Jha (Bihar) moved the following amendment:

"After para I of the resolution, the following be added :

'The AICC further appeals to those State Governments, where the scheme of Panchayati Raj has not been implemented into action, to take effective steps to implement it forthwith'."

Shri Ahmed Bux Sindhi (Rajasthan) opposed the resolution. He said that in the absence of party discipline at the lower levels, there would be clashes among Congressmen and that the opposition parties would take advantage of such a situation.

Shri Y.B. Chavan (Maharashtra) replying to the debate said that the resolution did not seek a contract with other political parties to contest Panchayat elections on non-party basis. If the Congress thought that what it was doing was correct, they must give the lead to others. It was hoped that the opposition parties would cooperate with the Congress in implimenting the proposal.

The amendment moved by Shri Sheelbhadra Yajee (Bihar) was put to vote and was rejected by the House. All the other amendments were withdrawn and the resolution was unanimously adopted by the AICC (The text of the resolution is published elsewhere in this issue).[15]

The meeting adjourned at 7.15 P.M.

(6th June 1962: 9. 30 A.M.)

The Committee met again at 9:30 A.M. on Wednesday the 6th June 1962 when the resolution on Disarmament was taken up for consideration.

15. In the *Congress Bulletin*, April, May & June 1962, on p. 119.

Disarmament

Dr B.V. Keskar (Uttar Pradesh), moving the resolution on Disarmament, said that if countries continued to test nuclear weapons, the effect on the present and future generations would be disastrous. It was essential in the interest of humanity that these tests should be discontinued. No single nation should be allowed to have monopoly on nuclear weapons. Talks on disarmament were going on between USA and USSR and there were discussions on the detection and control of atomic weapons, but no results were achieved so far. If there was no check on this atomic race, it might lead to the destruction of the world.

It was hoped that the 18-Nation conference on Disarmament would reach some understanding in the interest of world peace. India, being a member of this 18-Nation committee, should make efforts towards that end.

Shri R. Venkatraman (Madras) seconding the resolution said that the All India Congress Committee had always taken a keen interest in disarmament and that this resolution would find support not only in India but all the world over. It was useless to talk of disarmament and at the same time continue nuclear tests. The two power blocs should come to an understanding on disarmament through negotiations.

To ensure effective disarmament, it was essential that along with the voluntary ban on nuclear testing, a ban should be imposed on trafficking in nuclear weapons. If nuclear weapons were passed from one country to another, it would be difficult to enforce disarmament. After an international agreement was reached on disarmament, an adequate machinery should be set up to ensure its implementation.

Dr Henry Austin (Kerala) moved the following amendment:

> "Add the following para at the end of the resolution: 'The A1CC welcomes the efforts of individuals and organisations in various countries for bringing about immediate suspension and eventual prohibition of the manufacture and testing of nuclear weapons. In this connection the efforts of the Gandhi Peace Foundation to call for an anti-nuclear arms Convention are commendable'."

Shri Rameshwar Dayal (Rajasthan) moved the following amendment:

> "Add the following para at the end of the resolution:
>
> 'The AICC strongly feels that till the stage of general and complete disarmament is reached, strong and effective measures should be taken on international basis to stop nuclear tests and any further increase in armaments for the interim period'."

Shri Babubhai M. Chinai (Bombay) moved the following amendment:

"In Para three, add at the end of the para:

'The AICC also appeals to the more developed nations to create a Development Fund from the savings effected by disarmament with a view to assisting more widely and intensively the underdeveloped countries'."

Dr M. Jamaluddin (Kerala) moved the following amendment:

"Add at the end of Para II:

'The AICC deplores the current series of nuclear test explosions undertaken by the USA in particular at a time when the 18-Nation Disarmament Committee is in session in Geneva. Considering the views of eminent scientists all over the world on probable adverse effects of high nuclear explosions, the AICC 'hopes that the USA will not proceed with the series of high altitude nuclear explosions in the Pacific and will abandon the idea for the safety of whole mankind and posterity'."

Dr Ram Subhag Singh (Bihar) supporting the resolution said that it was an endorsement of the Government's endeavours to bring about complete disarmament and world peace through its view-points expressed in the 18-Nation Committee at Geneva. Atomic Energy was not for destruction but for the peaceful use and welfare of humanity.

The resolution should not be misconstrued as a weakness on the part of India on the question of Chinese aggression. It was true that India would continue to work for world peace, but it was also true that she would not rest until the territories illegally occupied by China were restored.

Shri Bhagwat Jha Azad (Bihar) speaking on the resolution welcomed the deliberations of the 18-Nation conference on disarmament. He said that while disarmament talks were going on, some nations were distrubing their innocent neighbours in order to involve them in war. India never believed in war as the solution of any international problem but had certainly the right to defend her frontiers.

Shri B. Acharya (Uttar Pradesh) said that disarmament was not only an idea but a practical necessity. If the nations possessing highly destructive weapons did not disarm now, a stage might come when the situation would go out of control. Recalling the disaster of Nagasaki and Hiroshima, he urged upon the nations of the world to reach an agreement on disarmament and avert any possible repetition of such disasters in future.

Shri Kamal Nayan Bajaj (Maharashtra) said that the disarmament talks had not succeeded so far, as the atmosphere in the world was charged with distrust and fear. India, as believer in peace, had a great responsibility in removing this tension and making efforts towards world peace.

Shri V.K. Krishna Menon, speaking on the resolution, said that India's countribution towards effecting disarmament had made it very clear that so far as the problem of peace and war was concerned no agreement could be reached until the two great Nuclear Powers—USA and USSR—came together on this matter. India had, from 1954-1955 onwards, repeatedly pushed forward the idea of direct meeting, formal or informal, between these two countries and it was encouraging to note that during the last 18 months there had been more direct discussion between these two countries than ever before.

Another countribution that India had made in this regard was the appeal made in 1954 by Parliament to the nuclear powers to suspend their tests. India's success in winning the confidence of both the Americans and the Russians was chiefly due to the policy of non-alignment and the personality of the Prime Minister. This had been amply demonstrated to the world by India's conduct in the Commission in Korea, in Indo-China and in Gaza.

It had to be realised that the problem of disarmament was not an end in itself but was only a step towards the ultimate objective of a world without war. A warless world was not merely a philosophical idea but a practical problem. It was cynical to think that there was no use in meetings or conferences to discuss the problems of disarmament and peace and that they led them nowhere.

Continuing, Shri Menon said that the most catastrophic part of this nuclear business was that trouble could break out in the world by circumstances which were not of a deliberate character. No nation wanted to plan a war but yet the danger of war was so much that it could come from a false signal, accidental explosion and aberrations of a pilot carrying nuclear bombs. Governments could also come to wrong conclusions from faulty intelligence supplied by espionage agents.

Possession of atomic weapons provided no national security because nations were not competing against nations in arms but a nation was competing against itself, as by the time it perfected a weapon it became out of date. The bombs dropped on Hiroshima and Nagasaki were today considered baby bombs. A 50 megaton bomb had far more explosive power than the explosive used in all the wars in history. Possession of nuclear weapons was, therefore, no guarantee or deterrent against any attack but only an index of human fear and arrogance.

On the suggestion that India should have nuclear weapons Shri Menon said that this was put forward on the ground that had Japan possessed nuclear weapons she would have been saved in the world war. This argument was fallacious because, if Japan had atom bombs, she would have attacked America. It was, therefore, no guarantee for securing national safety. The idea of disarmament was gradually gaining ground, so that it would be possible for mankind to survive not as separate nations but as one human family.

Dr B.V. Keskar (Uttar Pradesh) replying to the debate said that the main object of the resolution was to convey a message of goodwill and support to the 18-Nation Disarmament Conference and it would not be proper to destroy the spirit of the resolution by accepting amendments to it.

All the four amendments were withdrawn and the House unanimously passed the resolution. (The text of the resolution is published elsewhere in this issue).[16]

General Election and the Congress Organisation —Informal Discussion

The Committee next took up the subject of the General Elections and the Congress organisation for informal discussion.

Shri Mahavir Tyagi (Uttar Pradesh) initiating the informal discussion said that the results of the General Elections would throw light on the present state of the Congress. The ideological inspiration was now missing and factionalism was playing a large part in the organisation. Factionalism in the Congress was the result of suppression of free opinion of the members at various levels. Importance of the Congress organisation and Congressmen was lessened to a great extent and no decision was taken in consultation with the members at various levels but a decision was always imposed. This was surely not helpful towards the establishment of a Democratic Socialist Society.

There were serious irregularities in the enrolment of Congress members everywhere and no effective steps were being taken to put a check to such irregularities. The motive behind fictitious enrolment was to strengthen one's own group and get the party ticket as if the Congress was for seeking party tickets only and not for translating its ideology and programme into action. This motive also gave rise to factionalism in the Congress.

After the elections were over, the members did not care to keep in touch with their constituencies and look to the welfare of the people. This attitude was to a large extent responsible in making the electorate apathetic towards the Congress. It was, therefore, suggested that committees were formed in different areas all over the country. The MLAs and MPs concerned should be associated with these Committees which should look into the complaints of the villagers, redress their grievances and ameliorate their condition.

16. In the *Congress Bulletin*, April, May & June 1962, on pp. 120-121.

Regarding the collection of funds by Congress candidates during elections, Shri Tyagi said that many of these candidates never rendered any account of the funds collected by them. It should be made a point that in future none should be given the Party ticket in case he did not render proper account of the funds collected by him. If any Congress candidate collected funds privately for his election, it should be treated as an embezzlement of the Party fund and disciplinary action should be taken against such persons.

It was high time that the Congress did some heart-searching now and took remedial measures so as to justify the people's faith in the Congress.

Shri Maniklal [Manikya Lal] Verma (Rajasthan) said that all sorts of elements were now infiltrating into the Congress and becoming legislators. During the tenure of office of Shri U.N. Dhebar as Congress President, there were directives to the legislators of the Congress Party for submitting their reports at regular intervals, but very few of them had complied with such directives. Only those who were true to the ideology and programmes of the Congress should be given Party tickets.

Speaking of the administration, Shri Verma pointed out that many of the Government servants were against the Congress. This attitude of the Government servants was likely to go against the interests of the country. This aspect should, therefore, be carefully studied and necessary steps taken.

Referring to the Congress goal of a Socialist Society, he said that ceiling on income and land was a necessary step towards the removal of difference between the rich and the poor. By not imposing this ceiling, the Congress surely did not take a practical step towards socialism. The cry of socialism or any "ism" without practical steps would only create discontent in the country.

Regarding the selection of candidates, Shri Verma pointed out that persons who had contested against the Congress in the past were given party tickets. This was sure to create some feelings in the rank and file of the Congress. Some serious thinking was necessary in this direction and it would be better to impose some ceiling on the incomes and assets of the office-bearers of the Congress at all levels.

The youths of the country were our future strength, but there was no set programme for them and they could not be organised properly. Some new fields of activity should, therefore, be opened out for the younger generation in the Congress.

Regarding the parties which were run on caste and communal lines, Shri Verma said that a ban should be imposed on such parties as these forces were endangering the unity of the country and the forces of disintegration were active under their banners.

Shri Shyamnandan Mishra (Bihar) participating in the informal discussion said that some members had requested the Congress President for a discussion on General Elections and the organisation. This was the first time that such a discussion was requested for. Other main political parties also had discussed the General Elections at length. The AICC should also have given more time and opportunity to its members for such a discussion.

India had passed through three General Elections very smoothly and satisfactorily. If the Congress took pride in this, it was a legitimate pride because it was due to the efforts made by the Congress that such a democratic system could be put into practice.

Referring to the results of the General Elections, he said that there was a steady decline of the Congress strength and that the PSP also had lost its strength, compared with the results of the previous elections. It was important to note that the CPI and the Jan Sangh had improved their position while the Swatantra Party had achieved important and remarkable successes in its very first year of participation in the elections as a Party. From the General Elections of 1957 and 1962, it was clear that Socialism became an important issue during the Third General Elections while it was not so in the Second General Elections. The total seats gained by the various Parties wedded to Socialism would prove the truth of this conclusion.

Continuing, Shri Mishra remarked that people had previously thought that Congress Socialism was only rhetoric. Now, having seen the planned progress of the country through the Five Year Plans, the people had come to know that it was real. While the Government was taking necessary steps for the implementation of the programmes towards the establishment of a socialist State, the organisation also had its responsibilities. Though it could be said from the General Elections of 1962, it was so only in those areas having high percentage of literacy and not in other areas.

In many places of Bihar and Uttar Pradesh, public meetings were not organised in the constituencies. The electorates were not acquainted with the party ideology and programmes and the candidates, many of whom did not even address a single public meeting, did not care to study the election manifesto of the Party and acquaint the voters with the same.

While the Congress failed to undertake any educative and cultural activities in the field, other political parties had been doing so during the General Elections. These had their bad effects for the Congress and the country. In UP and Bihar, casteism played an important role in the elections. Caste Mukhyas dominated the election scene. This was surely an unhealthy trend in politics.

Speaking on the results of some State Parties, Shri Mishra pointed out that the DMK's success in Madras was due to the anti-Hindi and anti-North feelings in the South. On the other hand, the failure of the Akali Dal in Punjab to get majority of seats in that State proved that their demand for Punjabi Suba did not have the support of the people.

Continuing, he said that the increase in the percentage of votes polled in the country was due to the spread of education during the post-Independence period. This proved that our democracy was becoming maturer and maturer day by day. It was an important point to note that there was no national opposition even after the three General Elections. It was not a good sign for the successful working of democracy.

Speaking on the expenses incurred by the candidates in their elections, Shri Mishra remarked that these expenses were mounting high. This was likely to give way to capitalism, as funds had to be collected from the capitalist sources in order to meet such high expenses. Some steps should, therefore, be taken in order to curb the election expenses.

It appeared that the capacity of the political parties to set up good candidates was decreasing. This was so, because there was no work in the field. The problem facing the Congress in this regard was also the same. The success of democracy and democratic processes was also dependent upon the fact whether capable men were coming out in good numbers in the elections. The Congress should lose no time in finding out its weaknesses and flaws in its policies and mend the same. Whether the Congress was going to be the Party of the future for guiding the destiny of the country and the people would be decided now by its actions, achievements and services rendered to the people.

Concluding his remarks, he urged that in the interest of the organisation and the country as a whole, the youths and other newcomers should be encouraged to join the Congress and carry out the responsibilities devolving on its members. Congressmen should go ahead in right earnest with full confidence in themselves.

The meeting adjourned at 1 p. m.

The Committee met again at 3.30 p. m.

Election of Congress President

Shri N. Sanjiva Reddy, the Congress President, invited members to propose names for the election of the next President in his place.

Smt Indira Gandhi proposed the name of Shri D. Sanjivayya of Andhra which was seconded by Shri Y.B. Chavan (Maharashtra).

As no other names were proposed, Shri D. Sanjivayya was declared elected as Congress President for the remaining period of the organisational term.

Informal Discussion—(Contd.)

The Committee then resumed the informal discussion on the General Elections and the Congress Organisation. Shri N. Sanjiva Reddy, the out-going President continued to be in the Chair, as Shri D. Sanjivayya, the President-elect was not present in the House.

Shri Shatrughan Saran Singh (Bihar) partcipating in the informal disussion said that selection of candidates was influenced by group considerations. It was disquieting to see that a PCC president had lesser importance in this regard and that the MCCs and DCCs were disregarded. Chief Ministers played more important roles in the matter of selection. The directives from the Centre regarding recommendations of the MCCs and DCCs were rendered meaningless. A wrong type of candidates was selected resulting in the debacle of the Congress in the General Elections in some areas. Candidates should fight elections on an ideological plane and not on group or caste considerations.

At this stage Shri D. Sanjivayya, the President-elect took the Chair and the informal discussion continued.

Shri Raghunath Singh (Uttar Pradesh) suggested that the constituencies of the sitting MPs and MLAs should not be changed at the time of allotment of Party tickets for the General Elections. It seemed that candidates were selected keeping in view the person who would be the Chief Minister. This was a wrong method of selection. Besides the Chief Ministers and PCC Presidents, leaders of all the groups in the States should also be consulted in connection with the selection of candidates.

Shri P.N. Rajabhoj (Maharashta) warned that Congressmen should be careful in criticising the party and the leaders, because this might have serious effects on the public mind.

Shri K.K. Chattetjee (West Bengal) warned that the rightist forces were coming up. This emergence of rightist elements in the body politic of India was a dangerous symptom and Congressmen should no more remain complacent.

Shri Awadhesh Partap Singh (Madhya Pradesh) said that the prestige of the Congress had gone down considerably during the past 14 or 15 years. It was high time that the organisation thought of its defects and took effective measures in order to bring back its lost prestige. The procedure for selection of candidates was defective and it was a matter of regret that the recommendations at lower levels were not respected.

Shri Prabhunath Singh (Bihar) pointed out that the percentage of votes polled by the Congress had gone down in the 1962 elections. This was due to certain weaknesses in the organisation. The Congress should be reorganised properly and the Mandal Committees should be formed on the basis of block Development areas. Besides this, it would be better if some taxes were levied by the Party on the income of Congressmen.

Smt. Indira Gandhi taking part in the informal dabate said it pained her to hear some of the speeches of the members remarking that Congress standards were going down day by day, was not true. The Congress was still a strong organisation, enjoying the support and confidence of the people and the Congress President was held in great esteem in the country. Congressmen should strectly adhere to the principles and policies laid down by the Party and march onward to achieve the goal and show the right path to the people.

Ideological questions should have been the main issue in the General Elections, but during the work of selection of candidates, this was shoved into the background. It might be true that there were defects and weaknesses within the Party and it was good to discuss these points, but with a constructive mind. Had there been nothing good in the Congress, the organisation would have been nowhere, not even in the General Elections. There were varied opinions and views in the Congress but this should not stand in the way of the Congressmen in making a united move, so far as the programmes and policies of the organisation were concerned in the interest of the country. In spite of some dissensions and factions within the Party, the rank and file of the Congress on the Congress on the whole was praiseworthy. Congressmen should not waste time but march on to the field to the district, to the province—and act unitedly. Political rivalry was a universal feature in the world but this should not affect the party policy and the unity in the Party.

Offering thanks to Shri N. Sanjiva Reddy, the out-going President, she said that he took up the Presidentship of the organisation at a difficult time and guided the Party commendably during the General Elections. Shri Reddy did his best with untiring zeal to strengthen the organisation, unite the workers and lead the country towards progress. His cooperation in the organisational matters would be valuable in future.

Referring to the election of Shri D. Sanjivayya as the Congress President, she said that it was a matter of pride that young blood took charge of the organisation. This was viewed as the opening of the door to new ideas and younger generation who would work under the experienced and valuable guidance of the old guards.

Thanks to the out-going President

Shri Jawaharlal Nehru moved the resolution of thanks to Shri N. Sanjiva Reddy, the out-going Congress President, on behalf of the Working Committee. He said that though it appeared to be a formal resolution, it was something more than formal because Shri Reddy had been the President of the organisation during a very difficult period. It was not an easy matter to be the President of the Congress in the face of the criticism that the importance of the President had lessened. It had changed. It was bound to be with the coming of Independence. The general structure of India had changed but the fact remained that the Congress organisation was the back-bone of the country today and if the Congress organisation was the backbone of the country and the Government, then the President of that organisation must necessarily have importance and be respected.

Referring to the question whether the Congress should be a merely Parliamentary Party or a wider Party as in the past, Shri Nehru remarked that it was true that the Congress could not be a Party like the one it was before the coming of Independence because conditions had changed and the Congress was in a position to some extent to control the destinies of India. Obviously the Congress could not function, when it was in authority, as an opposition. So the Congress had to continue as a mass organisation and continue on this basis as a strength-giving element in the country to the Government. There should not be any mistake about the fact that the Congress was and would continue to be the most vital element in India's public life. If that was so, then whatever it might be, the AICC or the Working Committee or the Congress President necessarily were highly important in playing a vital role.

There were criticisms that the AICC only dittoed what the Working Committee placed before it. It was quite absurd to say that the AICC was a body of yes-men and that whatever the Working Committee said was accepted. The resolutions framed by the Working Committee were discussed by a large number of people including those who were not its members but were invited to its meetings. The whole idea was to have as much common thinking as possible in framing these resolutions. The resolutions framed by the Working Committee were necessarily limited by the policies proclaimed by the Party.

Referring to the system of the allotment of Party tickets in General Elections, Shri Nehru said that the system of giving tickets at the last moment was not good. The tickets should be allotted three or four years before the elections in order to avoid bitterness, unpleasantness and group pullings. It would also be better to prescribe a test for those who applied for Congress tickets to find out whether they, understood the Congress ideology and programmes and were able to tell people about the same.

Paying compliments to Shri N. Sanjiva Reddy, Shri Nehru said that, during the tenure of his office as Congress President, Shri Reddy had faced the difficulties boldly and wisely. There was of course the advice of the Working Committee and others but ultimately the burden fell on him. He discharged that burden in a worthy way.

Continuing, Shri Nehru spoke of the glorious history of the Congress during the past 77 years and remarked that it was a matter of pride for all, who belonged to the Congress, to look back to its history where people from all religions, and of varied communities of India came to the Congress and served the great cause of India's freedom.

Concluding his speech, Shri Nehru welcomed and congratulated Shri D. Sanjivayya, the new Congress President.

Shri K. Hanumanthaiya (Mysore) seconding the resolution of thanks to Shri N. Sanjiva Reddy, the out-going President, said that the AICC had done the wisest thing in electing Shri D. Sanjivayya as the Congress President. It was hoped that the advice and guidance of Shri N. Sanjiva Reddy would continue to be available to the organisation in future also.

Shri N. Sanjiva Reddy next addressed the meeting. He said that during the time he had functioned as Congress President he had the opportunity of coming in closer contact with the people and obtain to his province a wiser man enriched by his experience as Congress President.

Shri Reddy offered thanks to the leaders, specially to Shri Lal Bahadur Shastri and Smt Indira Gandhi, who had given him valuable guidance and had shared a great deal of his burden during the hectic days of work in connection with the selection of candidates.

Welcoming Shri D. Sanjivayya as the new Congress President, Shri Reddy said that he was a young man with a spirit of dynamism and it was hoped that he would give the organisation a new outlook.

19. To Cabinet Ministers: Cooperate with T.T. Krishnamachari[17]

June 8, 1962

My dear friend and colleague,

T.T. Krishnamachari became a member of our Cabinet this morning. We welcome our old colleague back and I am sure that his presence in the Cabinet will strengthen the Government.

17. Letter to all Cabinet Ministers. Copy sent to Cabinet Secretary and T.T. Krishnamachari.

He has joined the Cabinet as a Minister without Portfolio and thus far, the work he is supposed to do is rather vaguely described as that of helping in coordination. I have deliberately kept this rather vague at present so that there should be no rigidity about it to begin with. A little experience will define it a little more.

I have suggested to him that he might especially apply himself to coordination in regard to four of our major problems, that is, Steel, Coal, Power and Transport. These are the foundations of our Plan and therefore success in them means success in our Plan.

He will of course receive your full cooperation in the work he is doing. I would suggest that facilities be given to him to see any papers in your Ministry, which will help him in his work.

Yours sincerely,
Jawaharlal Nehru

'It's All Wrong!'

The P.M. is stated to have written to Cabinet colleagues to extend cooperation to Mr. T. T. Krishnamachari in his task of economic coordination.

From left: Cabinet Ministers, Morarji Desai, T.T. Krishnamachari.

(From *Shankar's Weekly*, 17 June 1962, p. 5)

20. To Gulazari Lal Nanda : Krishnamachari for Planning Commission[18]

June 8, 1962

My dear Gulzarilal,
I am asking T.T. Krishnamachari to become a member of our Planning Commission. I think that in his work of coordination, this is necessary.

Yours sincerely,
[Jawaharlal Nehru]

21. For the Lok Sabha Secretariat: Krishnamachari Blameless[19]

I regret I am unable to make a statement as desired by Shri Hem Barua[20] in his Notice under Rule 197. I am not aware of any practice or convention under which I should make such a statement about a Minister I have appointed. It is open to a Member of Parliament to bring a vote of censure on me or on the Government, if he so chooses.

2. I might mention that I made it clear at the time of the enquiry referred to, and afterwards, that in my opinion no blame attached to Shri T.T. Krishnamachari, the new Minister without portfolio. He resigned because in theory he was responsible for what happened in his Ministry.

22. For Tara Chand: Archives on Subhash Chandra Bose[21]

June 8, 1962

Dear Dr Tara Chand,
Kindly refer to your letter dated January 5, 1962 and Shri K. Ram's[22] letter No. 2(417)/61-62-PMS dated January 9, 1962 on the subject of permission to be

18. Letter to the Deputy Chairman, Planning Commission.
19. Note, 8 June 1962.
20. Lok Sabha MP, PSP.
21. Letter from M.L. Bazaz, PS, to the historian ; address; 8 Tughlak Road, New Delhi. MHA, File No. 50/13/61-Poll (I), S. No.6/c.
22. PPS.

given to Shri K.K. Ghosh[23] to look into the records of the Ministries of Home Affairs, Defence and External Affairs for writing a thesis on Shri Subhash Chandra Bose.

2. The matter has been considered very carefully in consultation with the Ministries concerned and it is regretted that for various reasons it is not yet possible to allow access to the relevant records for private research work.

3. The Prime Minister has seen the papers and he approves of the decision taken on Shri Ghosh's request.[24]

4. I am writing in the absence of Shri K. Ram, who is on a short leave.[25]

Yours sincerely,
M.L. Bazaz

23. For Law Ministry: *Political Quarterly* Article[26]

I wonder if you have seen an article which appeared in the *Political Quarterly* of January – March 1962 on "The Indian President".[27] I am sending you a reproduction of it. I should like to have your comments, if any. I should like to have the article back after you have read it, so that I can send it to the President.

24. To Diwan Chaman Lall: Unofficial Committee Preferable[28]

June 11, 1962

My dear Chaman,

Your letter of June 8. I have read it carefully. I can understand that an informal non-official committee such as you suggest might be helpful, but I am not quite clear yet as to how it would function. For me to appoint such a committee would

23. Tara Chand's research student in the Indian School of International Studies, New Delhi.
24. Later K.K. Ghosh published a monograph *The Indian National Army, Second Front of the Indian Independence Movement* (Meerut: Meenakshi Prakashan, 1969).
25. See also SWJN/SS/70/item 300 and appendix 69, SWJN/SS/74/items 93 and appendix 9, SWJN/SS/76/item 93.
26. Note, 10 June 1962, for the Law Ministry.
27. See appendix 66 for this article.
28. Letter to Rajya Sabha MP, Congress; address: 30 Prithviraj Road, New Delhi.

inevitably give it some kind of an official character. But you may yourself have such a committee, which could help on occasions.[29]

Yours affectionately,
[Jawaharlal Nehru]

25. To Sudhir Ghosh: Admission to Congress[30]

June 12, 1962

Dear Sudhir,

I have your letter of today's date.[31] I remember your application for admission to the Congress Party was considered by the Executive of the Party. It was stated then that you had opposed in Parliament Congress policies and programmes on several occasions. It was considered better, therefore, that we should wait for some time before we gave further consideration to your application.[32]

Yours sincerely,
Jawaharlal Nehru

26. In New Delhi: At the CPP[33]

साथियो? अब हम सालाना रिपोर्ट देखेंगे या उसके बाद accounts. आप सभी को पहले से मिल गई होगी रिपोर्ट, इसको Executive Committee ने इसके गौर किया था, और कुछ थोडी बहुत तबदीलें भी की थीं। बाकी मंजूर कर लिय था। तो अब, आपमें से कोई साहब इसके बारे में कुछ कहा चाहें तो कहें। take up तो कर लिया? स्वीकृत किया है, अच्छा। जी, wait a minute. Mr Lingam[34] has some important …

29. It is not clear which committee this refers to.
30. Letter to Rajya Sabha MP, Independent; address: 95 South Avenue, New Delhi. NMML, Sudhir Ghosh Papers.
31. See appendix 29 (a).
32. For Sudhir Ghosh's reply, see appendix 29 (b); see also SWJN/SS/76/item 75 and appendix 11.
33. Participation in debate, 14 June 1962. NMML, Tape No. M 63(i).
34. There are two persons who were called Mr. Lingam. T.S. Avinashilingam Chettiar and N.M. Lingam, both Rajya Sabha MPs from Madras State. It is not always clear who is being referred to.

[Translation begins:

Comrades, we will now take up the Annual Report and then the accounts. You must have got the report in advance. The Executive Committee has scrutinised it and made some changes and accepted the rest. So, now if anyone wants to say something, please come forward. Has it been taken up? Taken up, very well. Yes, wait a minute, Mr Lingam[35] has some important ...

Translation ends]

[Nehru Continues in English]

Jawaharlal Nehru: Mr Lingam has raised some important considerations. They are not exactly relevant to the annual report but they are considerations which you should consider certainly. He has raised two points. One is the respect due to Parliament and as an instance he has shown that on one occasion the Minister in charge of the subject came a few minutes late to the Rajya Sabha. Well, this is to be regretted, unfortunate, but I should have thought that one instance in these many years is rather a remarkable record. It is a very remarkable record, because something happens, people come and go to the Rajya Sabha, they came back a few minutes late, it is not a thing to comment on but rather to say how rare this has been, this accident and the like. I understand that that time the Minister's watch was slow or some such thing happened, I do not know. I take your argument as an invalid argument because you got hold of one odd instance out of hundreds and hundreds and based the argument on it. I think that is not a very valid argument. Of course, the watch being slow is an explanation and not an excuse. If your watch is slow you miss a railway train or something else, if the train is running in time. That is a different matter. What I mean to say, it is admitted, all of us will admit that every time it is not a question of respect. Every respect should be shown to Parliament, and ministers should be present when their subject comes up before Parliament. But if by accident or otherwise there is some slight delay, it is unfortunate; but to make that the basis of an argument is rather extraordinary. Unknown, I believe to all Parliaments elsewhere, we have two Houses and ministers are supposed to function in both. It creates difficulties for particular ministers sometimes, they have to be, they cannot be, in two places at the same time and therefore while entirely agreeing with the basis which Mr Avinashilingam has based his argument on, I do not think much importance will be attached to a lapse of a minister on one occasion out of hundreds.

35. See fn 34 in this section.

There is another aspect to it to which he also referred, the attendance of members even when three-line whips have been issued and all that. The biggest attendance has been short of the total number of members by, I think hundreds, hundreds actually, over a hundred, 150 or so, which is extraordinary. I mean to say, when a three-line whip is issued, one would imagine that every member will be there, except those who [recording indistinct] and generally the attendance in Parliament is fairly low. In no Parliament can one expect every member to be present all the time because he has his constituency, he has other things to do; even in connection with his parliamentary work, he has other things to do. Apart from other work, the relative proportion has been poor here, that has to be thought of.

The other point that Mr Avinashilingam raised was the manner in which legislation is considered and he drew upon his experience of the old Assembly. If you permit me to say so, that experience is wholly beside the point, the old Assembly had no work to do, the old Assembly, the old government, brought some essential measures, they were not a social reform government, they were not interested in a large number of bills, either some rather unimportant bills and some routine administrative bills came up or the bills that created much furore were repressive bills and the like. So there was little work to do and they could well afford to give more time either in the Assembly or elsewhere, in committees. Essentially, being a representative government they had to do something to give a show of consultation. That is not a good example therefore to quote from his experience of the old Assembly as if there the procedure was more representative and more consultative; it was not. The real thing never came before the Parliament to begin with, they were done outside; some measures came and there was some show of consultation. But I agree there should be as much consultation as possible between members of Parliament.

I cannot give any figure, but I am told that every important bill is referred to a committee. First of all, you must remember that the amount of legislation we pass is infinitely greater than in the old Assembly. Every modern Parliament has to face this difficulty, of tremendous legislation, changing conditions, changing world, changing social conditions, constantly legislation has to be brought. And it becomes a little difficult to deal with it. If Mr Avinashilingam would read people's ideas of how the British Parliament is functioning, he will find their inability to keep up to their old leisurely ways: they cannot do it, simply because there is too much work. The nineteenth century idea of Parliament is no longer prevalent. It is unfortunate. That was a good idea, leisurely way, each individual member of Parliament had much greater importance in England, in the sense that he could play a better part than in this rush behaviour of parliamentary life, where one has to do it in time, otherwise they cannot do it. There are proposals in England that large amount of parliamentary work should be taken away from Parliament together, in order to give Parliament time to consider things, and that work to be given to committees, for greater power to committees to decide, except matters of policy. So these difficulties are common everywhere, but I do agree and I am told and that is so, that every important bill and whenever there is a demand for it, it is referred to a committee, sometimes joint committees.

Now we shall proceed with the Annual Report. Come on Mr Sonavane,[36]

देखिए आइन्दा ये बात, ये तो मैं समझता हूँ ये बात generally आमतौर से कोई loan नहीं दिया जाता जब तक कि Executive Committee नहीं उसको sanction करे ये तो एक general election जब शुरू हो गया, तब एक जल्दी कुछ करना है, मुसीबत है, ये गलत है या सही, और हमने इसमें AICC से मशवरा किया। मैं आपसे कह रहा हूँ ये तो ठीक है, 4-5 बरस बाद आप इसपे गौर कर लें क्या आप करें।

[Translation begins:

Now we shall proceed with the Annual report. Come on Mr Sonavane.[37] Now look here, this sort of thing happening hereafter… I understand…Generally no loans are given unless they are sanctioned by the Executive Committee…. when the general elections take place, we have to do something in a hurry, whether it is right or wrong, that is the difficulty. We have consulted the AICC about this…I am telling you, it is right, after 4-5 years you can consider it, well.

Translation ends]

[Nehru continues in English]

Well there is nothing fundamentally wrong about the Party advancing loans and even grants for elections. Surely, this Congress assembly of Parliamentary Party is interested in the success of those who stand. It cannot. The only argument is that Mr Tyagi[38] says, everybody will apply, but no. I am telling you it was this that the Secretary of the AICC sitting in our office was recommending to us. But they were not advanced, they were advances to the individuals, not to AICC. Well, I know if you can lay down some rules ... We realise that, yes, quite right, we took the risk.

मेरी समझ में नहीं आता कि ये उसूल के खिलाफ कैसे हैं और ये जायज़ खर्च क्यों नहीं है। ये और बात है कि हम इसको न करें, लेकिन ये उसूल के खिलाफ नहीं है। एक

36. T.H. Sonavane, Lok Sabha MP from Pandharpur, Maharashtra.
37. See fn 36 in this section.
38. Mahavir Tyagi.

बात मैं नहीं मंजूर करता कि ये जायज़ खर्च नहीं है member को उसके election खर्च के लिये पैसा देना। आइन्दा के लिए आपको तय करने की जरूरत नहीं है क्योंकि कोई हम ऐसे दे ही नहीं सकते बगैर [Election] Executive Committee की मंजूरी के। ये तो उस वक्त एक pressure था और सोचा गया कि मदद करनी मुनासिब है बाज़ लोगों की इसलिए हमने मंजूर कर लिया, वो कर्जं के तौर पर। लेकिन वो तो कायदा ही है कि हम नहीं देंगे किसी को। जी हां: would you answer it?

[Translation begins:

I cannot understand how this is against the rules and how it cannot be considered legitimate expenditure. It is a different thing that we may not always do it, but it is not against the rules. I do not agree that it is not legitimate expenditure to give money to a candidate for his election expenses. You don't have to decide about the future because we normally do not give such loans without the approval of the Election Executive Committee. This was mainly because of the pressure of the moment that it was considered necessary to help a few candidates and we decided to give the money as a loan. But the tradition is that we do not give it to anyone. Yes. Would you answer it?

Translation ends]

A member speaks for a few minutes.

Jawaharlal Nehru: Mr Lingam reminds me that a number of bills were put up before the Executive Committee. There was a meeting, you perhaps were there.

कर्ज के लेने का ये काफी अच्छा है, लोगों ने वापिस दिया है। पिछले election से पहले जिन्होंने लिया था आदमियों ने कहा है हम दे देंगे। अब कोई नहीं दे सकता तो और बात है, उसपे गौर किया जायगा।

Someone: सौ रूपये का instalment दे रहे हैं जिन लोगों को पैसा दिया गया था।

जवाहरलाल नेहरु: अच्छा और कोई सवाल in this report?

[Translation begins:

One good thing is that people have returned the loans that were taken before the last elections. Now, if one or two are unable to do so, that is different. We will consider it.

A member: They are returning the loan in instalments of Rs 100/- each.

Translation ends]

Jawaharlal Nehru: Any other question on this report?

A Member: Leader Sir, before page 24-25 we have got 27 standing committees. If you go through them, only one standing committee had four meetings in the whole year, and three had three times, six had two times, ten only once, and six had no meeting at all. I will suggest Sir.

Jawaharlal Nehru: Standing Committee के member meeting में आया करें ।

We have to consider the Annual Report first of all. Then we can consider the other matters. We will adopt it if you like?

आप Annual Report पर कुछ कहा चाहते हैं या किसी और रिपोर्ट पर। कोई और मज़मून होगा तो आप रोक दिये जायेंगे post office service वगैरा। देखिये ना, कोई invest करने की हमारी संख्या नहीं है। कुछ हम invest करते है, पैसा होता है, वक्त आने पर जरूरत आने पर काम हो। 5 percent की बात नहीं है, वक्त आने पे हमें चाहिए वो। अच्छा साहब,

[Translation begins:

Jawaharlal Nehru: Standing Committee members, please come to the meeting.

We have to consider the Annual Report first of all. Then we can consider the other matters. We will adopt it if you like?

Alright, are there any more questions on this report? Does anybody want to say anything about the Annual Report. You will be stopped if you take up any other issues. Don't you see, ours is not an organisation to make investments in. We invest money so that it may be of use when we need it. It is not a question of 5%. It should come in useful when we need it. All right.

Translation ends]

[Nehru continues in English]

We have to consider the Annual Report first of all. Then we can consider the other matters. We will adopt it if you like.

Any comments on the accounts? So that is agreed to. All right. We have finished the agenda for the day. There is a resolution that a member has sent me.

It seems to me rather odd. The Congress Party in Parliament is of the opinion that the question of the election of the deputy leaders requires closest scrutiny by the Party, on account of the views expressed by the leader. It therefore appoints the following sub-committee. Then there are names of 15 persons, including me, and the mover, some ministers, some non-ministers, etc, to reconsider the constitutional aspects of this question and submit its report at the first meeting of the party during the next session of Parliament. Meanwhile the election of deputy leader is postponed. जी, श्री एम०पी० भार्गव ![39] [Yes, Mr M.P. Bhargava !][40]

Not Worth Fighting For

Any two congress M. P.s may be elected Dy. Leaders of the Parliamentary Party, their office being now only that of presiding over party meetings in the Leader's absence.

From left: Nehru, Lal Bahadur Shastri, V.K. Krishna Menon, S.K. Patil, Jagjivan Ram, Morarji Desai, Gulzarilal Nanda, U.N. Dhebar

(From *Shankar's Weekly*, 10 June 1962, p. 7)

Now the only view that I have expressed is that non-ministers may also stand. There is no constitutional aspect, they can always stand, you will find nowhere in the constitution is it said that the minister will be elected a deputy

39. In fact, M.B.L. Bhargava, Lok Sabha MP from Ajmer, Rajasthan.
40. See fn 39 in this section.

leader. It is only pointing out that something can be done. So I do not know what constitution is going to be examined because of this. It is for the party to elect, ... करेंगे आप मुझे कह दें लेकिन मुझे 6½ बजे राजेन्द्र बाबू से मिलना है जाके, मैं नहीं चाहता कि मुझे देर हो। पहली बात तो मैं ये कहा चाहता हूँ कि जो [It is for the party to elect… you tell me but I have to go and meet Rajendra Babu at 6.30 and I do not want to get delayed. So, the first thing is] what Mr Bhargava has pointed out about Rule 17, I think his criticism is completely correct. According to the rules, frankly I do not remember that rule and as a matter of fact that at just that period I was bed-ridden, I was ill. And it never struck any of us here and Satya Narayan Sinha or the Secretaries, it did not strike them and it was a lapse, and all of us jointly apologise to the Party for this lapse. Although I suppose that it makes no difference because a large number of people were consulted, there is no formal meeting, but there were plenty of consultations and the names were even allowed to be published in the Press so that members may know before formal action was taken. So I am sorry for that. Hence for this resolution, I think this resolution is neither, shall I say, practical nor desirable. In a sense you go back, it is some semi-criticism of the last resolution when we changed our rules. We have done that. We should not go back unless we want to change our rules; that is a different matter. Then to appoint a committee of 13 to consider the constitutional aspects of deputy leader, it seems to me rather extraordinary, all this hubbub. The resolution passed was that there should be no hubbub, that there is too much talk and dispute and this and that.

Now, Mr Bhargava wants to raise everything and create the maximum hubbub about a minor thing. I think practically therefore, it is not desirable and what exactly, here is your Constitution the only part of it which may, I think it is undesirable to do so, which may be done, so we want, last date … that we postpone our election. That too is wrong I think, we cannot make up our minds, and it is bad, that kind of thing. No constitutional matter is involved. There is the rule about who should be elected and not; we postponed the election once last year, as a matter of fact, last session, that was also at the instance of Mr Bhargava, that postponement then. I was just looking it up. And it was right I think then. It is immaterial. And now again postponement. It will make us a laughing stock before the whole public, we cannot make up our minds, we are quarrelling amongst ourselves, and it really is extraordinary that we should take such a step which should put us at the pillory before the public and every newspaper will laugh at us. We cannot possibly do it. But what is and specially reference is made on account of the views expressed by the leader. The view that I have expressed, not formally but informally, are that ministers as well as non-ministers can be elected, it is upto you to elect or not to elect. That is clearly open to the party to elect a minister or non-minister, nobody has challenged that right. That is all that I have expressed. Now what Mr Bhargava apparently from his speech there was once to make clear, only ministers can be elected, that is limit the power of the Constitution, that is changing the Constitution, we cannot do it casually by a resolution of this type. So I do not think this resolution is at all proper and it will bring disrepute to our party, and that is bad. However as it has been proposed and seconded it is up to you to decide. I have got to meet Dr Rajendra Prasad at 6.30. Probably, I think it will be over by then. Yes I know it is.

A member: Mr Leader, I am not anxious for any postponement ... but the function of the deputy leader should be clearly defined.

Jawaharlal Nehru: What happens in Parliament is apart from the Leader, and he very seldom lays down the law, if I may say so, in the House. It is the minister incharge that does so. I doubt in the last many years if the Leader has intervened unless there is some row. What Mr Santhanam[41] says does not follow at all from either the practice that has been observed or the rules. In the old rules it said that the Deputy Leader shall exercise all the functions of the Leader in the latter's absence; that has been omitted deliberately after discussion, because there was some confusion. I do not think, for instance, it is quite possible you may choose me as Leader; but I may appoint the Leader of the House somebody else and not remain Leader of the House, except when I am there, of course I am there, but that is very often done. The Leader of the House, for purposes of the House only, is somebody whom the Prime Minister appoints; it is a common practice in most places. You cannot, I think it will be desirable to nominate somebody who must be leader of the House in the absence of the Prime Minister. Normally, as I said in regard to bills etc. always the person, the minister in charge, deals with the situation as it arises. Well, may I ask you about Mr Bhargava's resolution. Those in favour may raise their hands...just to save time, it takes longer time in argument. One, two, three, ...those against, ... it appears to be more than three. All right thank you. It is lost.

Well, I must apologise to the Party because in the last month or so, how long is the Parliament meeting, about a month and a half, we have not met, and often partly I was away from Delhi, partly I was ill and all that, largely due to my indisposition. Also during the Budget Session, the House sits till late, 6, 6.30, it is inconvenient, but really I was responsible for this. Normally we should meet much more frequently, once a week at least, to discuss various matters and deal with any bills or whatever it may be. I hope in future we shall

41. K. Santhanam, Rajya Sabha MP, 1960-64, from Madras state.

do so. Not that there is very much time left in this session, probably about a week or, a week left.

Yes. अच्छा फिर जयहिन्द ! [Alright, Jai Hind!]

27. In New Delhi: At the CPP[42]

हमारी पार्टी का क्या नतीजा हुआ। अभी Executive Council [Committee] का ठीक नहीं अभी गिना जा रहा। बात तो, अक्सर तो, unopposed हुए। Deputy Leaders, Dr Mahtab,[43] आइये, आइये और श्री सुरेन्द्र मोहन घोष।[44] Yes, Yes, you better come here and sit here. आइये (यहाँ जगह बनाया है।) सेकेट्री तीन: one from Rajya Sabha unopposed R.S. पंचहजारी[45] क्या? And there was an election by members of the Lok Sabha. The two persons elected as Secretaries are Raghunath Singh[46] and C.R. Basappa.[47] आइये रघुनाथ सिंह, कहाँ है? पर्दे के पीछे छिपे है। Treasurer elected Kamalnayan Bajaj[48] अभी formally नहीं हुआ सभी का election declare। After I have announced these, I am told that I ought not to have done so because the results have not been formally communicated to me. So I withdraw.

[Law of Diminishing Leadership]

(From *The Times of India*, 24 June 1962, p. 1)

42. Speech at the valedictory meeting of the party for the current session (see the *National Herald*, 21 June 1962, p.1 col. 3), 21 June 1962. NMML, Tape No. M- 63(i).
43. Harekrushna Mahtab, Lok Sabha MP from Angul, Orissa.
44. Rajya Sabha MP from West Bengal.
45. Rajya Sabha MP from Punjab.
46. Lok Sabha MP from Varanasi.
47. Lok Sabha MP from Tiptur, Mysore.
48. Lok Sabha MP from Wardha, Maharashtra.

अब वापस नहीं भेजेंगे इन्हें। बैठ जाइये। --- कुछ मैम्बरान ने resolutions भेजे हैं। ये कुछ ज़रा अब कारामद नहीं रहे। एक है बाकर अली मिर्ज़ा [49]

"I propose that the nominations to the committees of Parliament like the Estimates Committee be made by the party by election or at least by the Executive of the party". Now these elections have already been held. This resolution can only apply to the future. The one that I have read that the Estimates Committee member should be elected or nominated by the party or the Executive. Well, if you like you can put this up before the Executive Committee for its consideration.

Then there is resolution by N.C. Kasliwal[50] and Jethalal Joshi.[51] "In the opinion of the Congress Party in Parliament Government should enquire into the foreign exchange holdings of ex-rulers and also make an assessment of the free services they receive at the expense of public funds". Government has enquired and is still continuing to enquire into the exchange holdings of ex-rulers. […] I suggest this may be sent, when we have discussed it, [if] we all agree about it, may be sent to the Finance Ministry. The exchange holdings are Finance Ministry—the free services which can be sent to both (Home Ministry).

फिर एक रेजोलूशन है इकबाल सिंह[52] और पन्नालाल बारूपाल।[53] संसदीय काँग्रेस दल की यह राय है कि संसदीय काँग्रेस दल की कार्यसमिति के चुनाव में केन्द्रीय मँत्री तथा उपमँत्री होने के नाते इस चुनाव में भाग न लें। अब ये चुनाव केबाद आये है और ये आये शायद पहले होंगे, नहीं आज ही का है। तो अब जो कुछ है, जो हो गया, अब आइन्दा के लिए चाहे आप इस कायदे को रखे। यानि गलत आप कहते हैं? कानूनी गलत है? नहीं, कानूनी कोई हमारे Constitution के खिलाफ? खैर इसको भी आप Executive Committee में रख दीजिए, गौर करे आइन्दा के लिए। सब तो हो गये।

एक और है विभूति मिश्र जी,[54] गन्ने के बारे में क्या है पढ़ा नहीं जाता आपके हाथ का। गन्ने के बारे मे सुना जा रहा है कि यदि recovery के साथ कीमत जोड़ने की बात सोची जा रही है, कृपया मैम्बरो की बातों को सुनने का कष्ट करें (किसानों की बातों को) समझ में नहीं आता इसका क्या किया जाय, विभूति मिश्र जी के प्रस्ताव का। वो तो ----- मैने कहा, कि विभूति मिश्र जी कहते हैं, गन्ने के बारे में recovery को कुछ जोड़ा जा रहा है, recovery से जोड़ा जा रहा है उसकी कीमत को । तो किसानों की बातें सुननी चाहिए। तो आप में से किसान चुने जाँय जिनकी बातें सुनी जाँय, या और किसानों की बातें सुनी

49. Lok Sabha MP from Warangal, Andhra Pradesh, now in Telangana.
50. Rajya Sabha MP from Rajasthan.
51. Rajya Sabha MP from Maharashtra.
52. Lok Sabha MP from Ferozepur.
53. Lok Sabha MP from Ganganagar, Rajasthan.
54. Lok Sabha MP from Motihari, Bihar.

जाँय, क्या माने हैं इसके। --- विभूति मिश्र जी ने जो कहा मैं समझता हूँ, अच्छा हो जो एस० के० पाटिल साहब[55] से बातचीत करें।

[EVEN FOREIGNERS' ACCOUNTS]

You Said It

By LAXMAN

To tighten the measures further we should ask all foreigners living abroad to submit their bank accounts!

(From *The Times of India*, 13 June 1962)

विभूति मिश्रः अभी सुनने में आया है कि 2.8 जहाँ पर recovery है, उसको रू० 1.62 कीमत दिया जायगा।

जवाहरलाल नेहरुः विभूति मिश्र जी ने जो कहा मैं समझता हूँ अच्छा हो अगर वो इस बात को जो मंत्री है इस विभाग के, श्री एस० के० पाटिल, उनसे मिलके बात करें और रामसुभग सिंह जी भी उनसे करें जाके, समझायें जो कुछ है। एक बात मैं कहना चाहता हूं कि उसूलन, मुझे कोई शक नहीं है इसमें कि उसूलन recovery पे दाम लगाना ठीक है। चल नहीं सकती कोई और बात। और आज नहीं कल, कल नहीं परसों ये करना होगा,

55. Minister for Food and Agriculture.

बदकिस्मती से हमारे यहां recovery में बहुत फर्क है अलग-अलग जगहों में, बिहार और उत्तर प्रदेश, पंजाब और राजस्थान में कुछ कम है और दक्षिण में और महाराष्ट्र वगैरा में बहुत फर्क है। उनमें वहां तो बहुत ज्यादा दाम इस वक्त भी दे रहे हैं, बगैर किसी कानून के। और अगर recovery पे लिया जाय तो इसमें कोई शक नहीं कि थोड़ा सा फर्क होता है, उत्तर प्रदेश वगैरा में, मैं कह नहीं सकता कित्ता लेकिन बहुत कम है। उससे एक inducement होती है, उसको तरक्की करने की बढ़ाने की। देर में उस बहस में नहीं पड़ सकता, लेकिन ये गौर तलब बात है जो उन्होंने कही कि recovery का अन्दाज कौन करेगा सरकारी, मिल के मालिक करेंगे, मुमकिन है धोखा दें, हो सकता है, तो इसका तो इन्तजाम माकूल होना चाहिए। ये गौर तलब बात है, होना चाहिए। तो मेरी तजवीज तो ये है कि विभूति मिश्र जी और इनसे रामसुभग सिंह से बातें करके और उनके साथ मिलके, उनसे एस० के० पाटिल साहब से बातें कहें जो कुछ उनको शिकायतें हैं, और बातें जो उन्होंने कहीं वो तो इसमें उठती नहीं हैं कि क्या तीन आने का [recording indistinct] है वो नहीं खर्च हुआ ये बात सही है, शिकायत सही है। लेकिन इससे ताल्लुक नहीं है, यू० पी० गवर्नमेंट और बिहार का कसूर है, कोई उन्होंने रूपया और कामों में लगा दिया। नहीं लगाना चाहिए उन्हें, लेकिन वो अलग एक बात है। तो अगर आप पसंद करें तो इसको हम सिफारिश करें कि रामसुभग सिंह, विभूति मिश्र, एस० के० पाटिल साहब से बातचीत करें।

[Translation begins:

Jawaharlal Nehru: What were the Party results? It is not clear; yes, the counting for the Executive Council is going on. Most of them have been elected unopposed. Deputy Leaders, Dr Mahtab,[56] please come, and Shri Surendra Mohan Ghose.[57] Yes, yes, you better come here and sit here. Come. There is a seat here. Secretaries—three, one from the Rajya Sabha unopposed, R.S. Panjhazari.[58] What? And there was an election by members of the Lok Sabha. The two persons elected as Secretaries are Raghunath Singh[59] and C.R. Basappa.[60] Please come, Mr Raghunath Singh. Where is he? He is hiding behind the curtain. Treasurer elected Kamalnayan Bajaj,[61] the results have not yet been formally declared ! After I have announced these, I am told that I ought not to have done so because the results have not been formally communicated to me. So I withdraw.

56. See fn 43 in this section.
57. See fn 44 in this section.
58. See fn 45 in this section.
59. See fn 46 in this section.
60. See fn 47 in this section.
61. See fn 48 in this section.

We will not send them back now. Please sit down. Some members have sent up a few resolutions. They are no longer very relevant. What I mean to say is that Bakar Ali Mirza...[62]

"I propose that the nominations to the Committees of Parliament like the Estimates Committee be made by the party by election or at least by Executive of the Party". Now these elections have already been held. This resolution can only apply to the future. The one that I have read that the Estimates Committee member should be elected or nominated by the party or the executive. Well, if you like you can put this up before the executive committee or its consideration.

Then there is resolution by N.C. Kasliwal[63] and Jethalal Joshi.[64] "In the opinion of the Congress Party in Parliament Government should enquire into the foreign exchange holdings of ex-rulers and also make an assessment of the free services they receive at the expense of public funds". Government has enquired and is still continuing to enquire into the exchange holdings of ex-rulers. […] I suggest this may be sent, when we have discussed it, we all agree about it, may be sent to the Finance Ministry. The exchange holdings are Finance Ministry—the free services which can be sent to both (Home Ministry). [These two paragraphs were in English, but have been included here for ease of reading.]

There is a Resolution from Iqbal Singh[65] and Pannalal Barupal.[66] In the opinion of the Congress Parliamentary Party Central Ministers and Deputy Ministers should not take part in the elections to the Executive Committee of the Congress Parliamentary Party in their official capacity. This must have come in after the election, no, it is today's. Well whatever has happened, has happened. We can make a rule for the future. You mean this is wrong? Wrong in law? No, against our Constitution? Anyhow, you can put it up before the Executive Committee and try to frame a rule for the future. I think that is all.

There is one more by Bibhuti Mishra,[67] can't read what it says, it is hand-written, something about sugarcane. If the price of recovery is considered being added to the price of sugarcane, the view of the farmers should be taken into consideration. I don't see what we can do about this Resolution ... I was saying that Bibhuti Mishra feels that if the price of sugarcane is going to be added on to the recovery costs, then the farmers' views should be considered. Do you mean that we should select the farmers among you or we should listen to all

62. See fn 49 in this section.
63. See fn 50 in this section.
64. See fn 51 in this section.
65. See fn in 52 this section.
66. See fn in 53 this section.
67. See fn in 54 this section.

the farmers? What does it mean? I think it would be better if Bibhuti Mishra were to go and talk to S.K. Patil.[68]

> Bibhuti Mishra: Just now we heard that where the recovery is at the rate of 2.8, they will be paid 1.62.

Jawaharlal Nehru: I think it would be better if Shri Bibhuti Mishra were to talk to the Minister concerned Shri S.K. Patil, and Shri Ram Subhag Singh should also go. They should explain it to him. I would like to point out that on principle it is right that the recovery costs are added on to the price. Nothing else can really work. We will have to do it, if not today, sometime soon.

Unfortunately, there is a great deal of difference in the rate of recovery in the different states. It is very little in Bihar, UP, Punjab and Rajasthan, and it is more in the South and Maharashtra. There the prices are very much higher even without any laws being passed. There is no doubt that if the price is fixed according to the recovery, there will be some difference, in UP etc., but it will be very little. It is only an inducement to increase production. Anyhow, I don't want to go into all that, but it is certainly worth noting what he [Mishra] has said about who will decide the amount of recovery. Obviously it will be the millowners who will decide and they may cheat, so adequate precautions should be taken about that. My suggestion is that Shri Bibhuti Mishra and Ram Subhag Singh should meet S.K. Patil and put the case before him. As for his complaint whether the three annas [recording indistinct] were spent does not really arise from this. The complaint is a legitimate one but it is not related to this. That is the fault of the UP and Bihar Governments who have used the money for something else which they should not have. But that is different. If you like we can suggest that Ram Subhag Singh, Bibhuti Mishra should talk to S.K. Patil.

Translation ends]

[Nehru continues in English]

To some extent what I meant not these two only, others too, they can talk to him.

The other point he raised was the question of corruption. That has nothing to do with this. Take even the weight, we know that sometimes weight is wrongly noted down, that has to be properly scrutinised and checked. I was told when I referred to this that the peasants or their unions who bring this are now quite conscious of this fact and they do not allow it to be noted down wrongly. I do not

68. See fn in 55 this section.

know how far it is true, you know better, but they are wide awake to it, it used to be done, but there are plenty, unless there is proper checking and inspection, there is always a danger of the poor peasant being done in the eye. So if Ram Subhag Singh will arrange, or Bibhuti Mishra and others who are interested to talk to the minister about these various matters. About this matter ? Yes. I understand from Shri Ram Subhag Singh that the minister proposes to make a statement tomorrow in the Lok Sabha. Now, I suggest to you that we can carry on these enquiries; let him make the statement. The statement can be varied later or at the most it is not forever and I would suggest that anyhow, that this matter be given a trial, it will give us some information about it. Meanwhile we should discuss fully, because you cannot discuss it overnight or in the morning, because so that the party may not feel that in spite of our sending this matter to him for consideration he has made a statement that will not be fair to the party or to him. I thought I better announce this, but we should carry on our talks fully. Then, Mr Patil, he tells me he is going away tomorrow. Meanwhile Ram Subhag Singh will meet people here and then those who wish to see the minister can see him, a few days later when he comes back. I do not know, Parliament will be rising, I do not know, who will be here then. But that is a matter which you can consider. All the other points raised are really how to check the possibility of corruption, that should be thoroughly discussed anyhow.

What I have received formally about the secretary and the treasurer, it happens to be the same as I announced to you. I have also received that part of the Executive which has been chosen by the Rajya Sabha members, I do not propose to read it out, full Executive will be read out not by Rajya Sabha and Lok Sabha. The other has not come yet, when other comes we will announce.

We have got a new member here today, Mr Ramakrishna Rao.[69] Well you come and present yourself. Come here. Oh, Chief Whip. Chief Whip, का भी कुछ करना हैं। [Something has to be done about Chief Whip.] No, you cannot withdraw the statement, you cannot withdraw the statement but you can make a change, it is not withdrawing a statement, you make another change, not immediately, you cannot do it the next day, that is absurd ...

I am told that this is the sowing season; having regard to the sowing season and the rest, one announcement has to be made. Therefore I suggest to you that it should be made now and if later, later meaning not a few days later, it amounts to this, that this sowing season will be past anyhow, and the next sowing season, the matter might be considered.

69. B. Ramakrishna Rao, Rajya Sabha MP from Andhra Pradesh.

A member: The leader and friends, on the several points have been raised by my.......

Jawaharlal Nehru : This matter has been discussed before the Standing Committee, that is what he said. I do not know he said so. He is a member of it and he is a minister also.

A member : Mr Leader Sir, the point is..

जवाहरलाल नेहरु: अरे ठहरो, the point is this that—मैं आपका पैगाम उनको भिजवा दूंगा। जाहिर है आप समझ सकते हैं कि मेरे लिए बहुत मुश्किल है कोई हुक्मन कोई बात कह देनी, अपने colleagues को। मैं पैगाम आपका पहुँचा दूंगा उनको। कहिए ? दिक्कतें तो पड़ सकती है एक season के लिए ज्यादा नहीं पड़ती । क्योंकि उसके भी तो season का है। लेकिन खैर,

[Translation begins:

Jawaharlal Nehru: Wait a minute, the point is this— I will send your message to him. Obviously, you can understand, it is very difficult for me to order around my colleagues. I will send your message. There may be problems, in one season, it may not be many but the seasons afterwards, will also come. But anyhow !

Translation ends]

[China]

There is nothing else on our agenda here. I was thinking of saying a few words about our frontier situation, because there seems to be a great deal of misapprehension about it, and questions are asked which are rather embarrassing in the sense that normally such questions are not asked, in a matter of this kind. I do not mean to say that the Chinese Government or the Pakistan Government is unaware of their respective frontiers, they are well aware, they know, but still it is another thing for us to tell them what we are doing there. As a matter of fact, some time ago the Chinese Government sent a very strongly worded note complaining of our aggression. Well, the answer to that was obviously that there can be no aggression on our own soil, our aggression, but that was the first indication that the public had, I do not know if many of you grasped that point, but foreigners grasped it immediately and there was some comment in plenty of newspapers in Europe and in America. The point was that the Chinese complaining of aggression on our part meant that the position has somewhat changed and changed to our advantage, otherwise why should they complain, and the foreign people, foreign important people who study these matters, grasped this immediately, and there have been long articles in responsible journals in America and Europe, but very few people in India seem to have understood the position and questions are being asked which are difficult to answer without, well, creating an embarrassing situation for us. Now it is absurd for me to say, wrong for me to say, that we have changed the situation on the frontier tremendously because that depends on many factors, but it is as I said, I forget, in the Rajya Sabha or Lok Sabha today,[70] but it is more to our advantage than it was previously, partly because of both the road communications being built and the check posts there, but that is no, that can be no definite assurance to anybody. How can I give an assurance what the Chinese may do, they might strengthen their position, they might bring large numbers of troops or not, I do not think it is likely, but all this.

[Pakistan]

So far as the Pakistan situation is concerned, well, we have a little incident and people seem to imagine, many Members of Parliament that we are constantly being set upon by the Pakistanis on our borders, they kidnap our people, and they do all this. Oddly enough, the same charges are made in the Pakistan newspapers about Indian authorities being constantly aggressive and seizing hold of them, some kind of charges. There must be some mistake, I mean to say, either both may be wrong or both may be correct, or either may be wrong. The fact is that there is an element of exaggeration and overdoing in these complaints, a large number of them are just things that occur on a border, thievery or robbery, they come across the borders, they steal some cows or cattle or something, go across, that becomes a political incident here. If it occurs anywhere else, it occurs as thievery. And also it is not a thing to be talked about; inevitably on both sides of the border some attempt is made to receive entry and to find out intelligence about the other. It is this that gives trouble and people who may be engaged in this attempt are seized hold of, or anybody who is suspected of it, he is seized hold of, I am merely hinting to you what kind of a thing happens. There is no question of aggression on the border, there is no real aggression. And the third is where there are some still in spite of our agreement with Pakistan about our border, there are still some little areas which are doubtful, the river, not being settled, and all the doubtful

70. Probably, Nehru is referring to his speeches in the two Houses on 20 June 1962, see items 395 & 396.

areas over the river there is some controversy and sometimes some conflict, somebody goes on their side. They say he has come here, we seized hold; we say he has not gone to your area, it is our area; but it is a disputed thing. Apart from this there is no aggression taking place or can take place at the present moment. And when our relations are bad this kind of thing occurs, these petty incidents occur again and again.

[Malda and Rajshahi Conflicts]

Third thing I wanted to mention to you was the new situation that has arisen in East Pakistan, West Bengal border, Rajshahi district and Malda district on our side. I have given full particulars of all that we know about the incidents that have happened on either side. This began by relatively petty incidents in Malda on our side. A Santhal woman who was selling fruit got into an argument with a person who was buying it, a Muslim, and he slapped her. This irritated the Santhals very much and the next few days they attacked the Muslims round about, burnt their houses and killed a few, a little later they again repeated it. This was written about in a great, very exaggerated manner, in the Pakistan and East Pakistan press. If you read what was written in the East Pakistan press, you yourself get very excited, you can understand what these press reports do. People were excited because they were told, thousands, hundreds of thousands of people were being being killed, Muslims were being killed on this side, and the result was, and some speeches were delivered by Pakistan authorities too. There was a powerful reaction in Pakistan in various districts, but notably in Rajshahi district, where the people there, among other many Santhals and others, were killed in large numbers. That is our information, I will not give any figure because it is impossible to give any figure. If you read the Calcutta papers they will say thousands were killed, either side the papers have a tremendous responsibility in this matter because in matters of this kind, passions are easily roused and they act and react on each other. But there is no doubt that large scale killings took place in Rajshahi district, in a railway train that was stopped in one other place, apart from petty incidents in many districts.

About two or three weeks later, the reaction to this took place on the West Bengal side, not on that big scale but still in several districts, and a number of communal troubles took place and a number of people were killed. I forget the exact number but I should say about anything from ten or eleven to eighteen or so odd people here and there and so on; one acts, one reacts from the other side. Now I do not know, we did not know, if anything has happened recently in Rajshahi district, after these incidents, and my impression is that those incidents are so bad the Pakistan Government were rather alarmed at their excesses and were rather ashamed and they had to send a large portion of their army to put them down, you can imagine, East Pakistan Rifles and the army, and which they have admitted. They also did some rehabilitation work, huts burnt etc. have been built afresh. I do not know if anything has happened since then there. When this incident happened which gave rise to some feeling in the Lok Sabha, that some Santhals were trying to cross the river in the middle of the night and they were fired upon. I think that this is one of the least of the incidents that occurred. One of the incidents one can understand, if in the middle of the night, against the rules in force, a crowd suddenly came up on the border, imagine what the police force would feel, will think, and this is the report we have received and they were, when the police came there, bows and arrows and spears were used against them, they fired and there were some casualties which vary from, Pakistan says two, may be seven, I think possibly, children and others.[71]

[Refugees from East Pakistan]

It was a bad show but it was not an understandable show. Now why did the Santhals want to cross over just then. There was nothing that had happened immediately before. Remember that the previous struggle had been with Santhals and probably they decided to come over and took time over it. In fact I am told that they decided to come over secretly in the middle of the night, they had meetings who had to cross the river and all that, it was a deliberate decision. And they have come over and some are coming over from day to day. It is difficult to say how many have come over because contradictory accounts are received by us. Now this raises another question, a very difficult question, what is to be done with them, we have to give them relief of course, but this is a temporary measure, permanently what has to be done? Rehabilitation, one has to do something, how rehabilitation of how many, a few hundred, a few thousand, a few hundred thousands, or a few million? Nobody knows, because the more people cross over from an area where they are in a minority, those who are left behind are in a slightly worse position, and if a big stream like this starts, it becomes an unending stream. One may have to deal with hundreds of thousands of persons. Therefore and it is not to their advantage either to come over. It is true that they have grievances, they are not treated well, but they are in sufficient numbers, there are millions there and they should protect themselves there and gather and work for their gaining their rights. It is not correct to say, I do not think it is correct to say, that the Muslims in East

71. See also section on Social Groups in this volume.

Pakistan want to drive them out in large numbers. Some, a few may, but it is not correct. Now therefore we do not wish to encourage them to come away, both for their sake and for our own sake. As I said it does not matter if a few thousands have come, we will help them of course but if this thing becomes bigger than it is, we sink with it with the weight of the refugees. You see if it is something like that happened in West Pakistan and India we just sink, Bengal sinks, under the weight of this problem.

So, one has to think over this. I do not think, I think some people are coming some people have come, it has remained in the thousand and we should deal with them and try to help them. That is a different matter. Then again it is suggested that we should send them to Dandakaranya. We may. In Dandakaranya we have, what we did was to rehabilitate people, we gave them seven acres of land and all kinds of help to rehabilitate them. Now most people in West Bengal or East Bengal probably have at most two or three bighas of land. No, no, no, I cannot stop them, do not bother, so two or three bighas of land they have. Now the offer of seven acres is a great temptation. I mean to say, if you offer seven acres to anybody who has come from East Pakistan, millions will take advantage of it, not that you have the acres to give millions, but it is too great an attraction, the seven acres of land. Of course seven acres are not very good land and anyhow that has to be developed. So that this business of doing something which is of tremendous attraction to other people who have lived a hard life with two to three bighas of land and rehabilitation and much bigger areas of land and houses being given, it upsets their life there. Quite apart from what the Pakistanis might do to them, it shakes them up and induces to come away if anything happens. Suppose we have, used to have, communal riots in British times, but we never had this migration business then; there were bad riots, nobody thought of running away to another place where they would be looked after and helped to the best of ability. This new problem has got a new shape. I merely wanted to put it to you that at the present moment it is capable of being handled; but if, I mean to say, some newspapers, they think and suggest that we should take responsibility for the nine or ten millions of Hindus there. Well no country can do that, and the result may well be, if this thing increases, this kind of thing, especially newspaper propaganda on both sides, then it may become very difficult, both for the Hindus and the Muslims to live where they are in minorities on the borders specially, and the Pakistanis are communal, their whole base is communal. But let us not imagine that we are not communal. Especially when passions are aroused, we are as communal as anybody else. And this kind of thing grows and the situation grows worse by our speeches, by our newspapers, by talks, it makes it much worse, and I do not think it is likely, but it is a possibility that a situation might be created which really no country or government can handle. I just wanted to give you some idea about this.

This session which is going to be over soon, has not had many meetings of our party. Partly because this is budget session, we sit late, partly this was due to my indisposition or ill-health, various reasons. It is a pity because we have so many problems that we should discuss apart from individual bills or other things just general problems because I [...]

[Socialism]

I am talking about the session before that,[72] I took advantage of one of these meetings to talk about, generally about socialism. And some friends wanted my speech, they appreciated what I said, and wanted my speech to be published in a pamphlet form. When I looked at the report of it I did not like it at all, although it was, I believe taken down as recording; it was not the fault of tape recorder but my own fault. There was this one thing to speak, repetition, this and that and I discarded it.

Now friends and colleagues have asked me to repeat the performance, write it out. It is very difficult to write it out, but my point is that I should like to discuss these matters, they are important matters. People talk about left and right. Now the whole concept of left and right is a European concept in the development of European politics. It does apply to India to some extent of course. But not in that way, and socialism, most people think of socialism as some levelling process. It is not a levelling process because if you looked upon this as a levelling process it means the dead level of extreme poverty, and nothing else. Nobody wants that. The whole concept of socialism as we know it arose, well, about a hundred or little over a hundred years ago. But before that there was what was called an Utopian socialism, that is a desire for people to be equal. That has always been there among people, a desire not to have too great ups and downs in the society, too rich and too poor, but there was no way out in those days.

Socialism is an economic theory, not a sentiment, sentiment is good of course. It is sentiment of people cooperating together. Today a society which has the essence of capitalism, acquisition or raising yourself on the shoulders of others, that is capitalism. Some people raise themselves, others are set upon; that is, at the same time capitalism has performed wonders in the world. So it is no good cursing capitalism. Now look at the countries of Europe today, almost every country in Europe enjoys what is called the affluent society, whether

72. Nehru attended the CPP meeting of 29 April 1962, see SWJN/SS/76/item 80.

it is western Europe, which is a capitalist Europe or Eastern Europe. Russia enjoys now more or less affluence, but not so much, you see the same process in capitalist society and in communist society.

What is the affluent state therefore due to? There is a difference of course in the communist method and in the other method. But what is this affluence due to—to greater wealth production. What is wealth due to? Greater wealth production comes of taking advantage of modern science and techniques. Both people take advantage of that, the communist countries and the capitalist countries, therefore they are rich, they are producing more wealth and even in the capitalist countries the standard of people has risen very greatly. The standard of poor has risen greatly, in spite of the big difference, it has risen. Karl Marx's theory that the difference between the rich and the poor will become bigger and bigger as time goes on has fallen flat, because in America, in England there is no poor according to our standards of poverty. There is none. There are grave differences, grave difficulties there. It is my belief that capitalism had undergone a change and will undergo perceptible change towards greater forms of social control. In America, which is the highest capitalist country, there is more state control than even in India, and we talk so much of socialism, they do not. That is so, but whatever America may have done, it has taken it 100 or 200 years to reach that stage. We can do that, it is impossible for us to remain in poverty and we cannot because of many factors. Therefore for us there is no choice but a socialist method, social controls etc. Of course, beyond this economic theory there is the sentiment of preferring equality, or something approaching equality, to this tremendous difference. And no country in the wide world has such great differences as India, leave out money, that of course; caste system, social strata, now such tremendous differences, you all know it. Elections bring it out; we are the country most sunk, most undeveloped, most backward in this, because of caste chiefly, plus poverty. Any country in the world, no country in Africa, in Asia, and you cannot imagine how nobody in the wide world can understand us, because of the caste system, they do not understand it. They have got class yes, they understand, they do not understand caste and untouchability and all that. Now persons talk bravely about socialism and are sunk in caste. It is, there are social structures they accept that, they are used to it, but they talk bravely of socialism, there can be neither socialism nor democracy in a caste ridden society. You rule that out.

[Producing Wealth]

I am merely mentioning some heads of subject for us to consider, to discuss so that our minds may be cleared. Fortunately there are quite a number of pamphlets which we issued then and we will issue. Now the other day a friend of ours coming from Ghazipur delivered a speech in the Lok Sabha which was really terrifying.[73] He said, and he said this to me later, that in some parts of the district, some parts, not all over the district, the daily wages, two annas and some times even one anna; now I cannot conceive of it. Because there is such a thing as labour going elsewhere. He says go and look at it, there, I do not know how anywhere the wage can be one anna. But whether it is one, two or three annas, the point is that there are certain parts of our country which are terribly backward and among those parts are the eastern districts of UP—Ballia, Gorakhpur, Basti, Ghazipur, Deoria, etc.—and to some extent in Bihar and to some extent in other areas too. Now those areas should be looked after. I cannot say how, but I think I have suggested it to the Planning Commission to have a special enquiry made, not a big-scale enquiry but some competent man to enquire and report and see what we can do. Then another difficulty comes. If we spend our resources as we would be inclined to, in these poverty-stricken areas, we do a little good, but we do not basically change the productive apparatus of the country. Ultimately we can only make good by increasing the wealth-producing apparatus. The wealth-producing apparatus is land, better agriculture, scientific agriculture and factories, big factories, small factories etc. Now, people do not realise that real progress will come only by doing, not by going about giving doles to people, not by going about encouraging things which are help for the moment but do not increase basically the wealth-producing capacity of the people. I have often given an instance here to the party that the Punjab is by and large the State where the per capita income is the highest. The Punjab has no big industry. It has a multitude of small industries and its agriculture is good. Agriculture is the basis of it and wherever you go in Bihar or UP, their bad condition is due to their utterly bad agriculture, bad agriculture which is a shame to see. It is no good. You may go and put up a factory there, big factory as UP Government wants to do. It will do some good to some people, no doubt it will; but ultimately it will not raise the per capita income much, while if there is a slight increase in agriculture productivity, it increases everybody's income immediately. If, as I have often suggested to you, if we can increase our income per capita in India, our production, by one anna per day, a very small amount, I suggest you to calculate when you go home how much difference it makes to India—one anna per day per capita. You get the whole of your five year plan money thereby, and much more. You cannot do that by some big schemes, big schemes are essential; power is essential in order to do that, coal is essential, transport is essential, and so on, steel is essential, but really what is

73. See items 202 & 203.

most essential is good agriculture in India and where there is good agriculture you will find the people better off, even though they may have no big industry. I am very much in favour of big industry, I am not against it but I find there is no state in India with more big industry than certain parts of Bihar. Enormous money in thousands of crores have been invested there; yet Bihar is one of the poorest per capita states in India. It is a very good example. Punjab which has no big industry is flourishing like a green bay tree, and Bihar with all the steel plants and all the industries and this and that, Chittranjan, is poor as church mice. I am suggesting all these things merely to make you think, it is not some kind of magic thing whether it is socialism or whether it is capitalism, you have to increase the wealth-producing capacity. You can ultimately only increase it by adopting methods which have succeeded in the world. Those methods are for agriculture, better tools, fertilisers, and so on so forth. Ordinary methods, there is no mystery about them, but a better plough widely introduced in UP and Bihar will be greater, lead to greater progress than half a dozen big factories. These factories are essential I admit. Well it is 7 o'clock, let us go now.

[Recording indistinct]

Jawaharlal Nehru: Executive Committee के नाम आ गये हैं :

Rajya Sabha - Shrimati Seeta Yudhvir, Shri S.D. Patil (not S.K.), Shri Satyacharan Shastri, Km. Shanta Vasisht, Shri Ram Sahai, Shri S.S.N. (श्याम सुन्दर नाथ) Tankha, Shri N. Sri Rama Reddy, Shri N.M. Lingam, that is eight for the Rajya Sabha.

Now Lok Sabha : Shri Mahavir Tyagi, Shri Ram Subhagh Singh, Shri H.C. Mathur, Shri Bhakt Darshan, Shri Bhagwat Jha Azad, Shri K. Hanumanthaiya, Shri S.K. Patil, Shri P.R. Chakravarty, Shri S.S. More, Shri D. Basumatari, Shrimati Ganga Devi, Shri Gurmakh Singh Musafir, Shri S.C. Samanta, Shri Ravindra Varma, Shri K.C. Pant and Shrimati Renuka Ray. ऐ, क्या करूँ अब। भाई साहब एक बात रह गयी है, Chief Whip का मैंने आपसे कहा है, क्या किया जाय। ऐ ? मै nominate करता हूँ। तो मैं कर दूँगा उसे, आपको मालूम है मैं क्या करूँगा। कौन? yes-जी to me.

[Other Matters]

I appoint Shri Satya Narayan Sinha as Chief Whip.

A member : I have only one small point to make and it is this. Only today in our House Mr Annadurai was speaking. Annadurai, the DMK leader, and he mentioned the backwardness of Madras etc. Now about these backward areas or the theory of backwardness, if some figures statewise are given they will be very helpful for propaganda and our either Planning Commission or some other agency can prepare, the relative backwardness of the different areas, that can give what is really any real grievances there or only I want to know.

Jawaharlal Nehru: I think you will find if you search for it, information about this in various publications. You may, the fact is there is no state in India which has not got backward areas. You can get the figures, complete figures for a state, and you can get within the state. I suppose you will get some area, there is no state which has not got some poverty striken area. All right come here. मेरी राय में मुनासिब हो अगर आप पसंद करें तो कि कुछ पुराने हमारे office bearers को निस्बत कह दिया जाय। कौन कहेगा, पुराने वाले थोड़े ही कहेंगे। मैं तो कह दूँगा। मैं क्या उसमें ज्यादा कहूँ सिवाय इसके कि ये record होना चाहिए कि हमने पुराने office bearers का शुक्रिया अदा किया। So I propose, ऐ, मैं तो आप जानते हैं किसी कदर बेहया हो गया हूँ I suggest for your consideration and adoption, a vote of thanks to the old office bearers of the Party.

Meeting ends.

28. To K.C. Jena: Voting and Party Discipline[74]

June 26, 1962

Dear Shri Jena,

I have your letter of the 26th June. From what you write, there appears to have been a breach of Party discipline. But it is difficult to spot the person who committed this breach by not giving you his first preference vote. The voting was secret. I do not, therefore, see what action we can take in the matter.[75]

As you have written to the Chief Whip of the Congress Party, he will no doubt give thought to this.

Yours sincerely,
[Jawaharlal Nehru]

74. Letter to Lok Sabha MP, Congress; address: 105 South Avenue, New Delhi.
He was elected from Bhadrak Reserved constituency (Scheduled Castes), Orissa, in 1962 elections.

75. This could be a reference to the Executive Committee elections, which had been held in the CPP meeting on 21 June 1962. See item 27 p. 279.

29. To K.M. Cariappa: No Army Officer in Rajya Sabha[76]

June 26, 1962

My dear Cariappa,

I have your letter of the 20th June. I am sorry I have been unable to recommend to the President the nomination of an ex-Army Officer to the Rajya Sabha. The number of those so nominated are very few; twelve in all, and a vacancy occurs every third year. It is a difficult choice, and we recommend scientists, educationists and others to the best of our knowledge.

We know very well that our officers and men of the three services are very good. Our jawans are, as you say, perhaps the best in the world. We also realise that modern warfare demands the latest techniques in weapons. We have, therefore, paid a great deal of attention to the production of such weapons in India. To depend on others is not very safe, apart from its being very costly.

Yours sincerely,
[Jawaharlal Nehru]

30. To K.K. Shah: Seminar on International Youth Movements[77]

30th June, 1962

My dear Shah,

I have your letter of June 28th with which you have sent me a note which you prepared for the President. I have read this note.

I am rather doubtful about the advisability of inviting experts from foreign countries to a seminar on youth movements. We have more or less information about various youth movements in the world and they vary greatly. Their objectives are different. Inviting foreign experts to tell us about what they do does not impress me very much.

As for defining socialism or the socialist pattern of society, I do not think a convention is going to do this. If necessary, a small committee might consider this.

Yours sincerely,
[Jawaharlal Nehru]

76. Letter to the former Chief of Army Staff; address: The Roshanara, Mercara, Coorg.
77. Letter to the General Secretary, AICC.

31. To Sunderlal: No Time for Interview[78]

July 1, 1962

My dear Sundarlal,

I am sorry I cannot find time for an interview during the next day or two, and I am going to Kashmir on the morning of the 4th. Perhaps, after I return, we can meet.[79]

Yours sincerely,
Jawaharlal Nehru

32. Death of Purushottamdas Tandon[80]

Please convey to family of Shri Purushottamdas Tandon[81] my deep sorrow at his passing away. He was one of my oldest friends and colleagues for whom I had great love and regard. He lived a full life devoted to his country's welfare and was a symbol of integrity and simple living. We shall miss him greatly.

Please also send some flowers on my behalf to his house.

33. On Death of B.C. Roy[82]

It is difficult to realise that Dr Bidhan Chandra Roy is no more. He died in the fulness of years and of achievement, and yet he was essentially a young man full of energy and vigour and with youthful enthusiasm. He was full of ideas for Calcutta, for Bengal and for India.

A great man, a giant among men, has gone and left us sad and mourning. We shall miss him greatly of course, and we shall sorrow for that. But let us also remember his great achievement: How he faced the terrible problems of Bengal after the Partition and gradually overcame them. He was indeed the stout pillar of Modern Bengal and indeed of the whole of India.

78. Letter to the chairman, All India Peace Council. NMML, Pandit Sunderlal Papers, File No. 35.
79. Nehru was in Srinagar from 4 to 12 July 1962.
80. Telegram, 1 July 1962, to the District Magistrate, Allahabad.
81. Freedom fighter, MP and Congress President briefly in 1950.
82. Message, 1 July 1962. PMS, PIB.

A beloved friend and comrade has departed and we are left forlorn.[83]

34. At the CPP: Deaths of Purushottamdas Tandon and B.C. Roy[84]

Friends, you may be aware of the purpose for which we have met, I do not think and hardly think it is necessary to deliver speeches on this occasion, though if you want, if you would like to have them you can have a few short speeches. Anything else?

Yes, yesterday saw the death of two persons both of whom had been intimately connected with us, our comrades and friends and both of whom took a great part in the struggle for freedom.[85] Tandonji's death, it might be said, was in a sense expected, he had been ill for a long time. And it was really as relief from pain it must have come to him. As for Dr Roy, some people present here, met him, had a talk with him, day before yesterday evening, one of our ministers was telling us how he saw him day before yesterday evening, in his room he had a talk, and in spite of his fairly ripe age, very few persons struck me as possessing the essential quality of youth as Dr Roy did. What is the essential quality of youth? Enthusiasm, he was full, not only of the present but of the future, building for the future and therefore his death has come as a peculiar, a distressing event and unexpected. He had not been too well for the last few days, but nobody who had seen him expected his death then. Of course, he was obviously a man of great stature so far as India is concerned; but more particularly Bengal, ever since the Partition, has been, you might say, built up by him, and Bengal had more problems probably than many other parts of India ever since it was cut into two. He faced these problems bravely and his dominating personality can be seen in all that has happened in Bengal, during these last fifteen years or so, Even before it was there, but now more so than before. It is a little difficult to speak to him, speak about him, in very moderate language because he was such a giant among men, an outstanding figure and withal, not a distant person; but, as I said, his quality of youthful enthusiasms endeared him to us. It is undoubtedly a loss which is very hard to bear and it can be said with perfect truth that he filled a place which will be

83. On 1 July at 11.25 a.m. the following phonogram had been sent from Nehru: "All our love and good wishes to you. Jawahar Indira." See items 34 & 35.

84. Speech, 2 July 1962, at a specially convened meeting in the Central Hall of Parliament. NMML, Tape No. M 63 (ii). See *The Hindustan Times*, 3 July 1962, p. 6 cols 6,7, 8 and *National Herald*, 4 July 1962, p. 4 cols 7 and 8.

85. Purushottamdas Tandon and B.C. Roy. See items 32-33 & 35.

very difficult to fill in equal measure. Still, such things happen, and all of us, have to be prepared to shoulder the burden when our time comes to shoulder it. I am sure that our comrades and colleagues in Bengal will rise to the occasion, shocked and grieved as they must be, and carry on the work to which Dr Roy devoted his life.

Many events come to my mind. Whenever he used to come here he was so bubbling over with his schemes for Bengal, for Calcutta, he never thought of death cutting short his work for many years to come. And that is a sign of youth and greatness. Anyhow I will not say much about him now; he was a very dear friend of ours, many of us, mine certainly, for the last, I do not quite know, but certainly about 42,43,44 years that I have known him intimately. And all of you know him. I shall now read a resolution that has been drafted, or rather two resolutions:

> "The Congress Party in Parliament is shocked at the sad and sudden demise of Dr Bidhan Chandra Roy, Chief Minister, West Bengal. Dr Roy was a brilliant physician and intellectual giant and an outstanding statesman. He had a valiant record in the national struggle and since independence he had been a pioneer in national reconstruction in India in general and West Bengal in particular. The country has suffered an irreparable loss in his demise."

The second resolution reads:

> "The Congress Party in Parliament is grieved at the sad demise of Rajarshi Shri Purushottamdas Tandon, Ex-President of the Indian National Congress. Rajarshi Tandonji was a man of the highest integrity and sincerity and adhered firmly to the dictates of his conscience. He was an ardent supporter of the spiritual values of life. He was a valiant fighter and rose to the highest position in the organisation. The country has lost one of the noblest sons in his death."

If you agree with those resolutions, we might stand up and pass them. There is a public meeting in the Town Hall of Old Delhi. Such of you as can go there, I hope I will come at 6.30. There is plenty of time, so that is over.

35. In New Delhi: Purushottamdas Tandon and B.C.Roy[86]

मेयर साहब,[87] भाइयो और बहनो,

कल का दिन हमारे और औरों के लिए एक अजीब गुज़रा, कोई साढ़े दस बजे सुबह ख़बर आयी टंडन जी के गुज़र जाने की, फिर दो घंटे बाद साढ़े बारह बजे टेलीफ़ोन आया कलकत्ता से कि बारह बजे लगभग डॉक्टर बिधान चन्द्र राय गुज़र गये।

आप सब लोग जानते थे उन दोनों को, कमोबेश टंडन जी को। टंडन जी के साथ मेरा क़रीब का काम का रिश्ता पचास बरस से ऊपर का था। यों तो उन्हें जानता था और अपने छुटपन में। डॉ. राय से कोई पैंतालीस बरस से मेरी जान पहचान थी, मोहब्बत थी और काम में भी शिरकत थी। तो आप ख़ुद समझ सकते हैं कि इसका असर मेरे ऊपर जैसा कि औरों पर क्या हुआ, एक बड़ा दरख़्त उखड़ता है ज़मीन से, ज़मीन हिल जाती है। तो ज़ाती नहीं रहती, जो इस वक़्त लाखों या करोड़ों आदमी इन कल के वाक़ियात को सुनकर रंजीदा हुए, परेशान हुए तो वो ज़ाती बात नहीं रही, वो तो एक मुल्क की बात हो गई।

टंडन जी की जब मेरे सामने तस्वीर आती है, जब हम चालीस बरस हुए गाँव में फिरा करते थे साथ, ख़ासकर इलाहाबाद ज़िले के और आसपास के ज़िलों के। अक्सर मैं, मेरा उनका इत्तिफ़ाक़ नहीं होता था विचारों में लेकिन कभी उनके साथ मोहब्बत और उनकी क़दर करने में कमी नहीं रही, और असल बात यही होती है कि एक आदमी की सच्चाई की क़दर की जाये, उसकी अक़्ल की क़दर की जाये, ख़ाली ऊपरी हाँ-हाँ करने से कुछ नहीं होता, चाहे हाँ करें, चाहे ना करें लेकिन क़दर होनी चाहिए बड़े आदमियों की। तो बावजूद अक्सर आपस में हमारे बहस किए और कुछ ना-इत्तफ़ाक़ी भी होने के, कांग्रेस कमेटी के अन्दर बरसों का साथ था, अक्सर बहस होती थी। लेकिन जो बात वो कहते थे उस पर हम सब बहुत ग़ौर से विचार करते थे, क्योंकि वो एक सच्चे दिल से निकलती थी, एक विश्वास से निकलती थी।

डॉक्टर राय की निस्बत मैं क्या कहूँ, हर जो बात उन्होंने उठाई उसमें बड़ापन दिखाया और ख़ासकर हिन्दुस्तान के दो टुकड़े हुए, बंगाल के दो टुकड़े हुए, तो बंगाल पर ख़ास बोझा इसका पड़ा, आप जानते हैं, पंजाब पर पड़ा लेकिन पंजाब से ज्यादा बंगाल पर पड़ा, और अजीब हालत बंगाल की थी उस ज़माने में, अब भी बहुत उसका सारा बोझा डॉक्टर राय ने उठाया, हिम्मत से, अक़्ल से और सम्भाला उसको। तो एक बात जो ख़ासतौर से मुझे डॉक्टर राय की सामने आती है वो यह कि बावजूद उम्र अस्सी बरस की हो गई, उनके जज़बात, उनके ख़्यालात बूढ़ों के नहीं थे, जवानों के थे। क्योंकि, जवानी की निशानी क्या होती है? उम्र तो एक फ़िज़ूल चीज़ है, चेहरे पर झुर्रियाँ भी पड़ जायें उससे कुछ निशानी

86. Speech, 2 July 1962, at the Condolence Meeting organised by the DPCC in the Town Hall in Chandni Chowk. NMML, AIR Tapes, TS No. 8879, NM No. 1709. See also *The Times of India*, 3 July 1962, p. 3 cols 5 and 6.
87. Nooruddin Ahmad.

होती है लेकिन असल में इंसान के उत्साह कैसे हैं, जोश कितना है, कैसे वो आगे देखता है या पीछे देखता है, बूढ़े आदमी आमतौर से पुरानी कहानियाँ कहा करते हैं, वो भविष्य को नहीं देखते, मुस्तक़बिल को। डॉक्टर राय इस माने में इन्तहा दर्जे जवान थे, हर वक़्त आगे देखें अब यह करना है, वो करना है, यह बनाना है, कलकत्ते को यह करना, बंगाल को करना है, हिन्दुस्तान को यह करना है। तो एक यह निशानी थी आख़िर दम तक उनका एक जवान दिमाग़ रखने की, जिस्म चाहे पुराना हो जाये।

अभी परसों शाम को उनके पास मेरे कुछ साथी गये थे, हमारे केन्द्रीय गवर्नमेंट के कुछ कैबनिट मिनिस्टर और उन्होंने ज़ोरों से उनसे बातें की, बहस की चन्द बातों की, उनका दिमाग़ भरा था उन बातों से क्या करना है, क्या नहीं करना है और उन बेचारों को क्या मालूम था कि बारह-तेरह घंटे बाद वो गुज़र जायेंगे। ख़ैर, उम्र पूरी करके एक माने में गुज़रे वो, हमारे लिए जल्दी गुज़रे क्योंकि बहुत काम उन्हें करने थे बंगाल में और हिन्दुस्तान में और हमारे लिए एक सूनापन हो गया क्योंकि उनको देखकर और उनकी आवाज़ एक गरजती हुई आवाज़ थी, टेलीफ़ोन पर वो बोलें तो सुनने वाले वो बहरा हो जाता था, क़रीब परेशान होता था। बोलते थे कुछ, क्योंकि उनमें इत्ता एक जोश था वो निकलती थी इन बातों से। ठीक है कि हम अपने बड़े आदमियों की क़दर करें, उनकी याद करें और उनसे कुछ सीखें, ख़ासकर यह सीखें कि किस तरह से काम करने का तरीका है, किस तरह से मिलजुल के जोड़ने की बातें हम सीखें, उखाड़ने की और अलग करने की नहीं। मैं आपसे कहूँ एक इम्तहान है बातों का कि जो बात अलग करती है उसमें कुछ न कुछ ख़राबी है, जो बात जोड़ती है वो अच्छी है। अब हिन्दुस्तान में ख़ासतौर से जोड़ने की जरूरत है। यों तो दुनिया भर में ही है कि आजकल ठंडी लड़ाई कोल्ड वॉर कहलाती है क्या, उसके नीचे क्या बात है? उसूलों को छोड़िये उसके नीचे है अदावत, शक, डर, एक-दूसरे को बुरा भला कहना, एक दूसरे को। यह दुनिया का हाल है। दुनिया के दो टुकड़े हो गये हैं या दो से ज्यादा और जब तक यह हवा नहीं हटती तब तक दुनिया ख़तरे में है। तो चाहे आप दुनिया के मैदान में देखें या हमारे हिन्दुस्तान को देखें, अलग करने की चीज़ बुरी है, जोड़ने की अच्छी है। जिन दो आदमियों के गुज़र जाने का हम रंज करते हैं आज वो जोड़ने वाले और काम करके जोड़ने वाले थे। इसलिए ख़ास उनकी जरूरत थी, लेकिन ख़ैर वो गुज़र गये और उनसे हम सबक़ सीखें और उस रास्ते पर हम चलें।

जयहिन्द।

[Translation begins:

Mr Mayor,[88] Brothers and Sisters,
Yesterday was a very strange day. At about 10.30 in the morning, we got the news of Shri Tandon's death and then a couple of hours later, at 12.30 came the

88. See fn 87 in this section.

news on the telephone from Calcutta that Dr Bidhan Chandra Roy had passed away at about 12 O'clock.

All of you were acquainted with both of them. My relation with Tandonji dated back to over fifty years. I knew him, in a way, since my childhood. I have known Dr Roy for the last forty-five years. There was a bond of mutual affection between us and we were colleagues too. So you can imagine what the impact of this news has been on me and others too. It was as if a mighty tree had been uprooted. Millions of people have been grieving since yesterday over the passing away of these two stalwarts. There is nothing personal about it. It is a national tragedy.

When I think of Tandonji, I am reminded of the days forty years ago, when we used to tour the villages, especially in Allahabad and the adjoining districts. We did not agree with each other in our views. But there was no lack of respect or affection for him and the fact of the matter is that a man is respected for his honesty and integrity and wisdom whether you agree with him or not. We used to have arguments in and outside the Congress Committee. But inspite of such disagreements, everyone would listen to him very carefully because whatever he said used to come from the heart and was based on real faith.

What can I say about Dr Roy? In everything he did, he showed his greatness. During Partition, when Bengal was divided into two, the brunt of it fell on West Bengal, as you know. Punjab also suffered, but the burden on Bengal was greater. Bengal was passing through an extraordinary time. The entire burden was borne by Dr Roy and he controlled the situation with great courage and wisdom. One thing that comes to mind particularly about Dr Roy is that in spite of his advanced years—he was eighty years old—his ideas and thinking were those of a young man. What is the sign of youth? The number of years do not count, except that they put wrinkles on the face. But the real test is the enthusiasm, the attitude of mind, whether a person looks backward or forward to the future. Old men keep harping on the past and do not look to the future. In that sense, Dr Roy was an extremely youthful person, with his mind constantly on the next thing to be done in Calcutta, Bengal or India. So this was a sign of a youthful mind right till the end, even if his body had grown old.

Just the day before yesterday, some of my colleagues and members of the Cabinet had gone to him and talked about various matters. His mind was full of ideas and plans, little knowing that his end was to come within the next twelve hours. Well, in a sense, he lived up to a ripe old age. We shall feel his loss because he had a great deal more to do in Bengal and India. He has left behind a great void because his very presence and his forceful voice had been reassuring. One would almost go deaf to hear him speak on the telephone—he was so full of fire and spirit.

Well, it is proper that we should respect our elders, revere them and learn from them, particularly the art of fostering unity and cooperation. I would say that a real test of whether something is good or bad is whether it is a binding force or it sunders. Today the Cold War, which grips the whole world, basically arises from fear and suspicion and bitterness. The world is divided into two armed camps and until the atmosphere improves, there will be danger. So anything which brings people together is good, and destructive elements are bad. We mourn the passing away of these two stalwarts today, because they were cementing forces in our lives and we need them particularly at this juncture. But they have gone. So we must try to learn something from their lives and follow the path they showed.

Jai Hind!

Translation ends]

36. To Averell Harriman: On Condolences on B.C. Roy's Death[89]

July 4, 1962

Dear Mr Harriman,

I received your telegram this morning as I was leaving Delhi. Thank you for it. Dr B.C. Roy's death came as a shock to us as, inspite of age, he was apparently keeping well. Only recently he visited Delhi. The day before his death he held a Cabinet meeting and met one of our Central Cabinet Ministers and had a long talk with him. You are quite right in describing him as one of the dynamic personalities of our time. He had the enthusiasm of a youth and was full of plans and projects for the future. His passing away is indeed a very great loss to us. His funeral was an unique event exhibiting the affection of his people for him. Literally millions of people filled the streets of Calcutta.

Thank you again for your kind message.

Yours sincerely,
[Jawaharlal Nehru]

89. Letter to US President's Envoy. Sent from Chashmashahi Guest House, Srinagar.

37. Politics of AICC Appointments[90]

Please reply to this lady, Shrimati Satyabhama Devi, MP.[91] Tell her that I am in Kashmir now. Instead of writing to her, I should like to have a talk with her. Perhaps she could come and see me when I am in Delhi and so is she. You might say that to my knowledge all of us were desirous of having Shri Shyam Nandan Misra[92] as Secretary of the AICC. But as the Working Committee is constituted with various States etc. represented in it, there was no room left for an additional person. Thereupon it was suggested to him to become a permanent invitee to the Working Committee.

2. As for Shri Maqbool Ahmed,[93] I do not know anything about him and I could not very well interfere without personal knowledge.

38. Editing Records of Talks[94]

I have read through all these notes about talks, but I have done so hurriedly. I have not attempted to correct them except at one or two places. (Thus I think I have corrected the date of the starting of the National Congress. This was started in 1885).

2. I have no objection to this being printed and published. That is to say, I do not object to any part of it being left out. But inevitably there is much repetition in what I said in the course of our talks and, as it is, it does not read well in places. A careful revision leaving out these repetitions would improve it greatly.

3. Sometimes at the beginning of a talk, but chiefly at the end, there are necessary passages about time being up and the next meeting, etc. These should be left out.

4. All I can suggest is that in the course of publication, the manuscript should be carefully revised and some parts which are not considered necessary might well be left out. I have no time to do this myself. As it is, I have spent a great deal of time in reading through this.

90. Note, 7 July 1962, for a PS (not identified). Recorded in Pahalgam, Kashmir.
91. Lok Sabha MP, Congress, from Jahanabad, Bihar.
92. Rajya Sabha MP, Congress, from Bihar.
93. Syed Maqbool Ahmed, Congress MLA from Colgong, Bihar.
94. Note, 8 July 1962, not recorded to whom, but presumably a PS. Recorded in Pahalgam, Kashmir.

This is probably a reference to the printed volume of interviews by R.K. Karanjia (London: George Allen & Unwin, 1966), to be reproduced in the last volume of SWJN.

5. In this manuscript, there are sometimes marginal remarks. These are not mine and may be ignored.

39. To Congress MPs: Strengthen the Organisation[95]

July 14, 1962

Dear comrade,

All kinds of criticism are being made about our various policies and Plans. Some people who are proverbially pessimists look at the dark side of everything. Indeed, we have great problems and many difficulties. But these are in the nature of things the result of the progress we are making.

We need, therefore, to be neither pessimistic and despondent nor complacent, but to face our problems with understanding, imagination and courage. Not only we, but our people should understand our problems. For this, it is very necessary for us to strengthen our organisation and to remain in intimate touch with our people.

I suggest, therefore, that you utilise this period of the Parliament's recess to mix with the people in your constituency and maintain intimate contacts with them. At the same time you should endeavour to help our organisation wherever possible and to put an end to the groupings that have unfortunately arisen in some States. If you do this, it will be good for our organisation and work, and you will come back to Parliament invigorated. This is the task before us.

With all good wishes,

Yours sincerely,
Jawaharlal Nehru

40. To Muni Lal: Be Constructive not Factionalist[96]

July 15, 1962

Dear Muni Lalji,

I have your letter of the 11th July.[97] I am interested to learn that you have formed a Congress Socialist Forum. If I may advise you, such a forum must do constructive and positive work and not waste its energy in fighting other groups.

95. Circular letter. Sent from Royal Cottage, Bangalore.

96. Letter to the Convenor of Punjab Congress Socialist Forum, Ludhiana. Sent from Nandi Hills. PMO, File No. 17(502)/62-66-PMS, Sr. No. 7-B.

97. See appendix 58.

What is necessary today is the understanding of our objectives of socialism and the socialist structure of society. Merely fighting other groups reduces one also to a group, and the real objective is missed.

You can see me in Delhi when I am there. But I am not likely to be much in Delhi during this month.

Yours sincerely,
Jawaharlal Nehru

41. To S.N. Swamy: Indira Gandhi Portrait[98]

July 15, 1962

My dear Swamy,[99]
I shall be glad to meet you and see the portrait of Indira Gandhi. I am returning to Bangalore in the late afternoon of the 17th July. I have some engagements after that. If you can bring the portrait to the place where I shall be staying, that is the Royal Cottage, at 8.15 p.m. on the 17th evening that would suit me.

I am leaving Bangalore early in the morning of the 18th July. If, by any chance, it is difficult for you to come on the 17th evening, you can bring the portrait at 8 a.m. on the 18th.

Yours sincerely,
[Jawaharlal Nehru]

42. To C.R. Sreedharan: Decline of Congress[100]

July 18, 1962

Dear Shri Sreedharan,
Thank you for your letter of July 14. I shall gladly see you in Delhi if you come there and I am there at the time.

It is true that many difficulties have arisen in the Congress and in the country, and it is also true that the sense of national service has been much diluted by personal objectives. But I do not understand what you mean by saying that Ministries in States should not be kept up because they cost a lot

98. Letter; address: "Dilkush Cottage", Hyder Ali Road, Nazarabad, Mysore. Sent from Nandi Hills. PMS, File No. 8(226) 62-PMP.
99. (1911-1983); artist based in Mysore.
100. Letter ; address Post Box 77, Baroda. Sent from Rashtrapati Nilayam, Hyderabad.

of money. Democratic working is expensive in every country. But we prefer it to some kind of authoritarian Government.

Yours sincerely,
[Jawaharlal Nehru]

43. To Gulzarilal Nanda: A Job for Mukund Malaviya[101]

July 19, 1962

My dear Gulzarilal,
I enclose a letter from Lal Bahadur. This is about Mukund Malaviya who is a nephew of Pandit Madan Mohan Malaviya.[102] Do you think it is possible from him to do any work in the Bharat Sevak Samaj.

Yours sincerely,
[Jawaharlal Nehru]

(b) Social Groups

44. To C. Rajagopalachari: Malda Riots[103]

June 3, 1962

My dear Rajaji,
I have your letter of the 30th May with its enclosure. The person who has written to you in a highly emotional vein has evidently rather lost his balance. I am not wholly surprised at this because the Calcutta papers have given lurid accounts.

This particular phase of trouble involving killing etc. started in the Malda district of West Bengal.[104] An argument took place between some Muslims there and a Santhal woman who was selling some fruits. The Santhal woman was slapped. Thereafter some Santhal people attached the Muslims. This was in March-April last. Broadly speaking, this conflict was confined to Santhals and Muslims. Altogether fourteen Muslims lost their lives.

101. Letter to the President, Bharat Sevak Samaj, New Delhi. Sent from Rashtrapati Nilayam, Hyderabad.
102. Mukund Malaviya was, in fact, Madan Mohan Malaviya's third son.
103. Letter to the leader of the Swatantra Party.
104. See SWJN/SS/76 items 121-127 and appendix 32.

This was certainly bad, but the accounts that appeared in the Pakistani press were lurid and exaggerated in the extreme. The Governor of East Pakistan[105] also spoke in a manner which incited people there to take revenge. As a result, in Dacca, Rajshahi and Pabna and other districts of East Pakistan, Hindus were attacked by Muslims. It is difficult to know exactly the number of casualties, but, according to our information, many hundreds of people were killed, apart from a great deal of arson. The Pakistani authorities got rather alarmed at the extent of the violence against the Hindus and sent the army to deal with the situation. Subsequently they helped somewhat in the rehabilitation of the Hindus.

Immediately after these attacks on the Hindus, thousands of them wanted to migrate to India. Our people did not encourage them though they did not ban their coming here. Ultimately most of these Hindus went back to their villages.

The actual migration either from West Bengal to East Pakistan or from East Pakistan to West Bengal has not been significant thus far,

Tomorrow I am making a statement in the Lok Sabha on this subject. I enclose a copy of it.[106]

Yours affectionately,
[Jawaharlal Nehru]

45. In the Lok Sabha: Malda Riots[107]

The Prime Minister and Minister of External Affairs and Minister of Atomic Energy (Jawaharlal Nehru): Mr Speaker, Sir, the House will recall that on 12th May I had spoken,[108] at some length, on the unfortunate, disturbances in Malda, in April, in which fourteen people lost their lives, nine on Holi day—this was in March—and five more between 16th and 20th April. There was no trouble whatsoever in Murshidabad district. The grossly exaggerated reports in Pakistan newspapers and some very objectionable statements by high ranking officials in Pakistan, it will be recalled, then led to the very serious disturbances in Dacca, Rajshahi and in several other districts in East Pakistan. We had protested about all this to Pakistan and pressed the Government of Pakistan to take active and immediate steps for the restoration of law and order, the restoration of

105. Ghulam Faruque, Governor of East Pakistan, May-October 1962.
106. Item 45.
107. Statement, 4 June 2017. *Lok Sabha Debates*, Third Series, Vol. IV, May 26 to June 7, 1962, cols 8569-8575.
108. See SWJN/SS/76/item 124.

confidence among the minorities and rehabilitation of those who had suffered in these riots in East Pakistan.

The Government of Pakistan has now replied to our note of protest of 12th May. The Pakistan reply suggests that communal riots never start in Pakistan and whenever there are communal incidents in that country, they take place only as a reaction to the communal troubles in India. The Pakistan reply, however, admits that the trouble in East Pakistan was serious. They have said nothing about the particular incidents in Darsa and other places, to which we had drawn their attention; but they have given a detailed account of the steps taken to restore confidence in the disturbed areas. The House will permit me to read out a part of the Pakistan Government's reply:

> "The latest reports from the district of Rajshahi, as indeed from some other areas, where tension was high owing to the atrocities committed on Muslims across the border, show that the situation is now completely normal throughout East Pakistan and has been so far nearly four weeks. As a matter of fact, troops as well as strong contingents of the East Pakistan Rifles that were posted to the affected areas, are being withdrawn gradually at present. As many as 1908 arrests have been made in the areas where the disturbances took place. Police investigation is being vigorously pursued in order to deal effectively with those responsible for the unfortunate disturbances. Already a large number of persons have been charge-sheeted and further charge-sheets are being filed every day. The local authorities and the Muslims of the affected areas are reconstructing the dwellings of the members of the minority community which were burnt or otherwise damaged. In Rajshahi district, 90 per cent of such dwellings have been reconstructed and more than 50 per cent of the looted properties has also been restored to the respective owners. Instances have not been lacking where Muslims in many places, at great personal risk, provided protection to the Hindu neighbours in distress."

It is clear from all this that there was very serious trouble in East Pakistan. They had to use troops and also strong contingents of East Pakistan Rifles to control the situation. We feared at one time, with ample legitimacy, that there would be substantial migration of the minority community from East Pakistan into India. In the first three weeks of May our Rajshahi office (Assistant High Commission) had interviewed over 4,000 intending migrants. Subsequent reports show that these people had been persuaded, not by us but by Pakistan authorities, to go back to their villages. Our latest reports from Dacca show that, so far, less than 2,000 requests for migration have been received by our

Deputy High Commissioner.[109] (Migration Certificates are issued only by our Deputy High Commissioner at Dacca). He has authority to render them such assistance as may be necessary. But I want the House to understand in all this that there has been no substantial migration from east to west. Our enquiries reveal that about 200 persons belonging to the minority community in Pakistan had come across immediately after the first disturbances in Rajshahi district. Thereafter in May, a little over 600 persons have arrived in West Bengal, about 400 of whom hold Migration Certificates issued to them before the disturbances. The statistics of travelling between East Pakistan and West Bengal actually show that there is reasonable normalcy in the traffic. In the month of April, for instance, 11,664 Hindus had come to West Bengal and 13,015 had left West Bengal for Pakistan. 14,776 Muslims had come into West Bengal in April and 14,264 (i.e. some 500 less) went from West Bengal to East Pakistan, despite the grossly, exaggerated report in the Pakistan Press of the massacres in Malda and the migration of refugees. I do not have with me the full figures for the month of May, but in the first half of May the Hindu arrivals are not high, being 6,464 (which twice over, would be 12,928), though the departure of Hindus is less—2,676 for half the month. The Muslim figures for the first half of May are even more significant. 6,487 Muslims have left West Bengal for East Pakistan in the first half of May; but no less than 5,435 Muslims have come to West Bengal from East Pakistan in the same fortnight. It is perfectly obvious that if Pakistan newspapers reports had any truth in them, over 5,000 Muslims would not be crossing over—as they always do—from East Pakistan into India in the fortnight immediately following the so-called murders in Malda and Murshidabad.

Hem Barua (Gauhati):[110] Sir, may I seek a clarification?

Speaker:[111] Yes.

Hem Barua: May I know whether it is a fact that our High Commission in East Pakistan deliberately slowed down the process of offering facilities to those members of the minority community in Pakistan who wanted to migrate to this country, on the plea that there were no officials working there to cope with this problem? On the other hand, Sir, my information is that Government did it deliberately with a view to check migration as

109. S.K. Chowdhry.
110. PSP.
111. Hukam Singh.

Government feared that this might be an inducement to other members of the minority community in East Pakistan to migrate to this country. If so, why should people be allowed to suffer or face slow death on a big scale like this?

Badrudduja (Murshidabad):[112] May I know....

Speaker: Let us first hear the answer.

Jawaharlal Nehru: Our High Commission in Dacca have issued migration certificates only after due enquiry. They did not offer facilities, or deny them, to anybody. Anyhow, that is a matter to be considered by the authorities in India later. To begin with, it appears that a large number of people came and asked for migration certificates of which some are pending cases. Then, quite a large number went back to their villages, apparently induced by the Pakistan authorities to do so. Whatever the reason may be, the Pakistan authorities took certain steps. As has been stated, after this trouble in Rajshahi, Dacca etc., Pakistan authorities took some effective military steps to put an end to it and endeavoured to rehabilitate the people who have suffered by building their houses etc. Now, whether that was the reason or not, I do not know, but many people went back to their villages and actually did not come. The people who have come here are 400 people who have got their migration certificates before the trouble started there. So, that has nothing to do with the trouble; they came just a little before. Sometime afterwards, about 200 people, I think—I am speaking from memory—came without any certificates because people could cross over. So, I do not think it would be right to say that the people there are stopped from coming by the Indian High Commission. It is true that we have not encouraged them to come by telling them of all the benefits they would derive by coming—I think that is wrong policy anyhow—but they have come, whether with migration certificates or not. Personally speaking, I am really rather surprised to find that in spite of all these troubles, the actual migration from India to Pakistan and Pakistan to India has been remarkably little and not much above the normal traffic. There are plenty of people coming from one place to another between East Pakistan and West Bengal.

Badrudduja: May I know if on the 22nd of March 1962 six Muslims were burnt to death at Malda, three beaten to death and one girl of eight raped and, later on, on the 16th of April, several other persons were beaten to

112. Syed Badrudduja, Independent Democratic Party.

death. This had a demoralising effect upon the entire population of the district resulting in the exodus of Muslims from the town of Malda?

Jawaharlal Nehru: The hon. Member refers to some people being burnt to death. This tragic incident occurred because a burning roof fell on them, which is really unfortunate. They were not actually deliberately burnt to death, but in a burning house the roof fell on them. This, no doubt must have had some effect on the people, but what I am pointing out is that the effect was not such as to make many people to go away. I have given the full figures of migrations on both sides.

Some Hon. Members rose—

Speaker: I cannot allow regular discussion. Shrimati Renuka Ray.[113]

Renuka Ray (Malda): In view of the last question just now put by an hon. Member, I would like to know whether the Government is aware that out of the persons who are killed in Malda there are not only Muslims but also Hindus and the number of the latter is roughly five. Is it not a fact that the figures given by the Prime Minister are only of the Muslims alone?

Badrudduja: May I know...

Speaker: Order, order, Shrimati Renuka Ray says that in the number of persons killed in Malda there were Hindus also and that they were not all Muslims.

Jawaharlal Nehru: No, Sir; as far as I know, 14 persons who lost their lives in Malda were Muslims of which nine lost it on the Holi Day, that is, on the 22nd March, and five more on the 16th to the 20th April. The nine persons included five or six who got burnt by the roof falling on them and killed by that. I do not think in this number there is any Hindu.

Tridib Kumar Chaudhuri (Behrampur):[114] May I ask...

Speaker: No regular discussion can take place.

113. Congress.
114. Revolutionary Socialist Party.

An Hon. Member: But questions can be allowed.

Speaker: Two or three questions are sufficient.

46. To Hafiz Mohammad Ibrahim: Grant to Ajmal Khan[115]

June 5, 1962

My dear Hafizji,

Your letter of June 4th suggesting the grant of Rs 5,000/- to Ajmal Khan[116] for his daughter's wedding. I am afraid I cannot give this money from the National Relief Fund which is meant for specific purposes. I have consistently avoided giving money for marriages. The other funds at my disposal are relatively small. Perhaps, I could give a fairly small sum from them. But it would not be very much.

Yours sincerely,
[Jawaharlal Nehru]

47. To Chief Ministers: Muharram Riots Warning[117]

June 5, 1962

My dear Chief Minister,

We have received information to the effect that efforts will be made to create communal trouble in some parts of India. Muharram, which is on the 13th June, is a day suitable for this. I hope your Government is thoroughly alert and vigilant to avoid any undesirable development.[118]

Yours sincerely,
[Jawaharlal Nehru]

115. Letter to the Minister for Irrigation and Power.
116. Ajmal Khan was Personal Secretary to Maulana Abul Kalam Azad till his death in February 1958, see SWJN/SS/41/pp. 835 and 845.
117. Letter to B.C. Roy, C.B. Gupta, B.A. Mandloi, Binodanand Jha, Chief Ministers of West Bengal, Uttar Pradesh, Madhya Pradesh and Bihar respectively.
118. See also item 171.

48. To Rajeshwar Dayal: Vinoba Bhave to East Pakistan[119]

June 7, 1962

My dear Rajeshwar,

You will remember that Vinoba Bhave expressed a wish to pass through a corner of East Pakistan on his way back from Assam. This was to be, as usual, a walking tour. He is at present in Assam. He had intended coming back earlier, but now he has postponed his return to early in September.[120]

We were informed by you, I think, that the Pakistan Government does not view this walking tour with favour. There the matter ended.

I have now heard from Vinobaji again. He is very anxious to pass through East Pakistan, and he wanted especially to know if the matter had been mentioned to President Ayub Khan or not. I could not give him an answer.

You know that the sole object of Vinobaji wishing to pass through a bit of Pakistan is to create goodwill. He is not a politician and does not wish to talk about political matters. He has made a close study of the Koran in the original and, in fact, has selected a large number (about 800) of the Ayats of the Koran, which he is going to have published. (This fact is not likely to impress President Ayub Khan).

I myself feel that his visit to Pakistan even for a short while will have a good effect on our relations with Pakistan. From that point of view, he is the best ambassador we could send. The fact that there has been trouble in East Pakistan need not come in the way of his going there.[121] In fact, his visit will soothe people and make them look upon these questions in a different light. I should like you, therefore, to mention this matter to President Ayub Khan and find out his wishes in regard to it. If he is at all agreeable to Vinobaji passing through Pakistan, further particulars could be sent to you about his place of entry, his route and where he will leave Pakistan for West Bengal. If he goes there, he is likely to spend about five or six days or a week on his walking tour there. Perhaps, the new Governor of East Pakistan[122] might not object to

119. Letter to the High Commissioner to Pakistan. MEA, File No. P.I/122(9)/62, pp.7-8/Corr. Also available in JN Collection.

120. See SSWN/SS/76/item 468.

121. See items 44 & 45.

122. Ghulam Faruque.

his going. Anyhow, I should like you to find out again about the reaction of Pakistan authorities and let us know.

Yours sincerely,
[Jawaharlal Nehru]

49. To Rajendra Prasad: Malda Riots[123]

June 9, 1962

My dear Rajendra Babu,

Your letter of June 5th with which is enclosed Shri Pravash Chandra Lahiry's letter about occurrences in Rajshahi. It is very difficult to get exact information about what happened at Rajshahi and roundabout. But we have received enough information from our Assistant High Commissioner.[124] The Bengal Press has given a fair amount of publicity to these tragic events. There is no doubt that terrible happenings took place at Rajshahi, more especially in a train at Rajshahi railway station and at Darshyaa village. Possibly the numbers killed have been exaggerated somewhat by Shri Lahiry, but I have little doubt that a large number of people were killed in these two places.

The events that happened in Malda in West Bengal, which resulted in the killing of fourteen Muslims, were grossly exaggerated in the Pakistan press. And the then Governor of East Pakistan delivered very objectionable speeches about them. At Murshidabad, where nothing of note happened, it was said in the Pakistan press that hundreds of Muslims were killed. All this excited the Muslims greatly and I suppose was responsible for large-scale killings in Rajshahi district and to some extent elsewhere. I referred to these in somewhat restrained language in Parliament. But we wrote about them more fully to the Pakistan Government.

You might be interested to learn that the Pakistan High Commissioner expressed his great appreciation of the restraint I had shown in my statement in the Lok Sabha. This itself shows that conditions were pretty bad in Rajshahi.

I made another statement in the Lok Sabha, copy of which I enclose.[125]

The impression I have got is that the Pakistan authorities were rather ashamed of what happened in Rajshahi etc. They took effective steps by sending the Army in considerable numbers and have even helped in rehabilitating some

123. Letter to the former President; address: Sadakat Ashram, Patna.

124. N.K. Ghosh.

125. See item 45. See also other items in section Politics subsection Social Groups.

of the people who had suffered. It is a fact that relatively few persons have come over to India, although a large number intended to do so immediately after these occurrences. This indicates that the Pakistan Government has tried to rehabilitate them as well as discourage them from leaving Pakistan.

We have accepted such as have come. But, naturally, we were anxious to avoid a huge exodus from Pakistan, as that would have resulted in tremendous difficulties to West Bengal and India. But those that have come, we have tried to help.

I think it is wrong to say that Pakistan Government wants to drive out all the Hindus from East Pakistan. After all, there are nearly ten million Hindus still there, and it is no easy matter to dispose of them in this way. The effect on Pakistan itself and on its reputation in other countries will be very great.

East Pakistan is a thorn in the side of the Pakistan Government. There are large numbers of persons there who want to get out of Pakistan. Especially students are out of hand. It was probably because of this that the authorities there wanted to divert attention by creating an intense communal and anti-Hindu feeling. They got a chance by the occurrences at Malda and exaggerated them out of all proportion.

It is manifest that we cannot do anything in Pakistan to give aid to these people. Nor can we encourage a large exodus. We shall be wholly unable to deal with it, and West Bengal will be sunk.

My own information is that the Pakistan authorities want to encourage communal incidents in India to have an excuse for their behaviour in Pakistan.[126]

Yours sincerely,
Jawaharlal Nehru

50. To Rajendra Prasad: Malda Riots[127]

June 10, 1962

My dear Rajendra Babu,

In continuation of the letter I sent you last night about the incidents in East Pakistan,[128] I enclose an extract from a letter from the Governor of West Bengal to the President.[129] It deals with certain deplorable incidents that occurred in

126. See further item 50.
127. Letter to the former President; address: Sadakat Ashram, Patna.
128. Item 49.
129. See appendix 14.

West Bengal where Muslims were killed and harassed and some Muslim houses were destroyed.

This will indicate how any misdeed in one part of Bengal leads immediately to consequences in the other part. If this is not stopped and if newspapers give exaggerated publicity to what occurs, this kind of thing might well increase and lead ultimately to a situation on a large-scale, something approaching the big migrations that occurred soon after the Partition. It is bad for all concerned.

Yours sincerely,
Jawaharlal Nehru

51. To S.C. Samanta: Malda and East Pakistan Riots[130]

June 13, 1962

Dear Samanta,

I have your letter of 12th June.

In the statement I made on the disturbances in East Pakistan, I gave such information as we had received from reliable sources. I could not give the exact number of casualties, killed or wounded, because no exact number has been supplied. So also about the number of women raped or molested, and other matters. I stated that the number of casualties were considerable, more particularly in the railway train near Rajshahi and at Pabna. My own impression is that the casualties amounted to a thousand or so. But, as I have said above, it is impossible to give any accurate figure. There can be no doubt about the seriousness of the occurrence. In the second statement I made in Parliament, I quoted from a letter received from the Pakistan Government which admitted the seriousness of what had happened though it did not give any details.[131]They had to send a large number of troops to deal with the situation.

I have no desire to minimise the seriousness of the situation in East Pakistan, but I do not wish to make any statement which might be proved to be wrong.

I did not know that Shri Badruddujja[132] had made any statement about the rape of a Muslim girl of 8. I have read of this allegation for the first time in your

130. Letter to Congress MP; address: 7 Electric Lane, New Delhi.

131. See item 45.

132. Syed Badrudduja, Lok Sabha MP, Independent Democratic Party, from Murshidabad, West Bengal.

letter. As for what Shrimati Renuka Ray[133] said, on subsequent enquiry I found that some Hindus did die, but it appears that this was not a communal case.

We had informed our officers not to be rigid about migration rules. At the same time, it is true that we have not encouraged large scale migration, but whoever wanted to come could come.

I can assure you that there is no lack of human feeling or sympathy for our unfortunate brothers and sisters who have suffered or are suffering in East Pakistan. Any of those who want to come over can do so. But you must realise that we have to deal with a problem of millions of people. To encourage these large numbers to come over would be doing no good to them. The more they come over, the harder will be the tasks of those who are left behind.

Yours sincerely,
[Jawaharlal Nehru]

52. In the Rajya Sabha: Minority Community Migration from East Pakistan to West Bengal[134]

The Prime Minister and Minister of External Affairs (Jawaharlal Nehru): Sir, on the 11th May, I had made a statement in the Rajya Sabha about certain unfortunate incidents in Malda District in West Bengal, in March and April, and the very serious communal disturbances in East Pakistan in the last week of April.[135] Hon. Members will recall that I had said that on Holi Day, 22nd March, in the trouble between the Santhals and the resident Muslims of Malda, nine people had lost their lives. There was a recrudescence of incidents between the 16th and 20th April and 5 more people died during these 4, 5 days. On 8th April, there was a brutal case of dacoity in Gazole Police Station. Six Hindus were suffocated to death as the only entrance to their room was blocked and the rest of the house was set on fire by miscreants. This was regarded by some as a reprisal by Muslims of the Bilkanchan incident on Holi Day, but local enquiries seem to suggest that this was probably only a case of dacoity.

I have already in my last statement referred to the serious incidents that occurred in Rajshahi and other districts of East Pakistan. We had protested to Pakistan about these happenings and had pressed the Government of Pakistan

133. Lok Sabha MP, Congress, from Malda, West Bengal.

134. Statement, 16 June 1962. *Rajya Sabha Debates*, Vol. XXXIX, No. 3, cols 255-259.

135. For Nehru's statement in the Rajya Sabha on 11 May 1962, see *Rajya Sabha Debates,* Vol. XXXVIII, No. 18, cols 3047-3056. See also SWJN/SS/76/ items 123-124.

to take active steps for the restoration of law and order and the restoration of confidence among the minorities, as also the rehabilitation of those who had suffered as a result of these very serious communal riots in East Pakistan.[136]

The Pakistan Government has replied to our Protest Note of 12th May. They make out that communal riots never start in Pakistan, they always start in India, and if there are any communal incidents in Pakistan, they take place only as a reaction to the communal troubles in India. This is an absurd claim, of course, and something that we do not admit at all to be true. The Pakistan Government, however, in their reply to our protest note have as good as admitted that the trouble in East Pakistan, this time, was very serious indeed. They have admitted that they have had to use troops and strong contingents of East Pakistan Rifles in the affected areas. They had arrested over 1,900 persons and vigorous police investigations were undertaken to deal with those responsible for the disturbances, and a large number of persons had been charge-sheeted and more and more charge-sheets were being filed every day against the miscreants. The Note goes on to say:

> "The local authorities, and the Muslims of the affected areas are reconstructing the dwellings of the members of the minority community, which were burnt or otherwise damaged. In Rajshahi District 90 per cent of such dwellings have been reconstructed and more than 50 per cent of the looted property has also been restored to the respective owners. Instances have not been lacking where Muslims in many places, at great personal risk, provided protection to their Hindu neighbours in distress."

All this proves, if proof was needed, that what I had stated in my earlier statement about happening in East Pakistan was only too true.

There has inevitably been some excitement and a certain amount of tension on our side of the border, mainly in the second week of May, after the stories of the happenings in the East Pakistan districts had trickled through. There have been stray incidents in West Dinajpur, Jalpaiguri and Cooch Behar, but the State authorities had been warned to be vigilant and they have handled the situation with the necessary degree of firmness.

May I once again, appeal for restraint in the discussion of these unfortunate issues, whether here or in Press? We have legitimately accused Pakistan of the grossest exaggeration of incidents on our side of the border. We must not be guilty of the same ourselves. There have been atrocities, but it is wrong for newspapers to give publicity to unverified stories of atrocities. My attention

136. See SWJN/SS/76/items 117-119, and items 52, 55-56, 64, 69 in this volume.

has been drawn to the report of an incident in Natore in Rajshahi district in East Pakistan, of a gentleman by the name of Dr Rabati Bhushan Laihri or Rabati Bhushan Sanyal, as he is otherwise known, having poisoned himself and his wife and two daughters and three sons, because of threats from a certain Muslim resident of the district, who wanted that doctor's daughter to be forcibly married to his—the Muslim's—son. The Pakistan High Commission here has issued a Press release, which says that the story is baseless. There is no person called Rabati Bhushan Laihri in Natore. There is, however, a Dr Rabati Kanta Sanyal, who has been residing in Natore since 1903 and he has been much upset by the number of enquiries regarding his welfare from his relations and friends in India, and he has issued a statement to the effect that he and his wife and his daughters are perfectly safe and hale and hearty. We have verified this with our Dacca Office to be correct.

On the other hand what is important and what I am glad to be able to report to the House is that in the month of May, generally, tension had decreased and the movement of the people between West Bengal and East Pakistan had become almost normal. There was some fear in the earlier stages that there might be large scale migration from East Pakistan to India. Earlier in May, some 4,000 intending migrants had been interviewed by our Rajshahi office—Assistant High Commission. Subsequent reports showed that these people had been persuaded, not by us but by Pakistan authorities, to go back to their villages. The latest figures that we have now received show that the demand for migration certificates to our Deputy High Commission in the month of May was not abnormally high. The number of applications received by our Deputy High Commission in Dacca in May totalled 606, covering 1,793 persons. By way of comparison, 1,312 persons had applied for migration in April and 1,520 had applied in March. Our Dacca office has granted migration certificates to 1,015 persons in May as against 952 in April and 1,080 in March. I am furnishing these figures to show that the statistics for May are not abnormally high.

Apart from the migration certificates, the figures of the normal traffic through the Immigration Check Posts in West Bengal are even more significant. In April, 11,664 Hindus had come into West Bengal and 13,015 had left West Bengal for East Pakistan. That is to say, more had gone to East Pakistan than had come away from there in April. In April again, 14,776 Muslims had come into West Bengal and 14,264 only 500 less, went from West Bengal to East Pakistan. These are the figures for the month of April, when the Pakistan Press was shouting about massacres in Malda and the migration of thousands of Muslims from West Bengal to East Pakistan. The May figures are still more significant. 12,827 Hindus have come from East Pakistan and 8,408 have gone across. The Muslim traffic figures show that 13,053 Muslims have left West

Bengal for East Pakistan in the month of May but as many as 12,720 have come across from East Pakistan to West Bengal. This should amply falsify Pakistan's propaganda that thousands of Muslims had fled across the Indian border because of tension in India.

We have had no reports of any serious trouble in East Pakistan after the last week of April. As I have said, traffic was returning to normal in the month of May. Today, unfortunately, we have had grave news, again, from the Malda border. Hon. Members will have seen reports in the press of Pakistan troops having opened fire on the people trying to cross over from Rajshahi District of East Pakistan into Sarai village in Malda on the border. The report that we have received from the West Bengal Government, on the telephone, says that:

> "While 600 Santhal refugees belonging to those areas of Malda which had gone over to East Pakistan after Partition, were crossing over to Malda from Rajshahi, they were fired at by the East Pakistan Forces."

This was yesterday morning.

> "As a result 2 Santhals died, 8 were seriously injured, subsequently of the 8 injured, 2 more died on the way to the Malda Hospital, bringing the number of dead to 4 and injured 6. Strong action has been taken by the District authorities to ensure that there is no repercussion following these unfortunate events in Malda. The State Government are lodging a strong telegraphic protest with the Government of Pakistan today."

53. In the Lok Sabha: Conflict in Rajshahi District[137]

Speaker:[138] We shall now proceed with the calling attention notice by Shri Hem Barua[139] and others, which had been held over on 16-6-62, for today.

The Prime Minister and Minister of External Affairs and Minister of Atomic Energy (Jawaharlal Nehru): I had made a statement on 4th June on the unfortunate communal incidents in West Bengal and East Pakistan in the months

137. Statement, 18 June 1962. *Lok Sabha Debates*, Third Series, Vol. V, 8 June to 22 June 1962, Ist Session, cols 11391-11403.
138. Hukam Singh.
139. PSP.

of March and April.[140] I had, in this, referred to the Pakistan Government's reply to our protest Note of 12th May, which had as good as admitted that there had been very serious disturbances in East Pakistan.

There has inevitably been some excitement and a certain amount of tension on our side of the border, mainly in the second week of May, after the stories of the happenings in the East Pakistan districts had trickled through. There have been stray incidents in West Dinajpur, Jalpaiguri and Cooch Behar, but the State authorities had been warned to be vigilant and they have handled the situation with the necessary degree of firmness.

We had no reports of any serious trouble in East Pakistan after the last week of April and there was every reason to believe that in the month of May, generally, tension had decreased and the movement of the people between West Bengal and East Pakistan had become almost normal. Unfortunately, there has been a recrudescence of serious trouble again in Rajshahi district in East Pakistan. But before I come to this, I wish to place before the House certain facts and figures for the whole of the month of May which were not available when I made the Statement on June 4.[141]

Earlier in May, some 4,000 intending migrants had been interviewed by our Rajshahi office (Assistant High Commission). The latest figures that we have now received show that the demand for migration certificates in the month of May was not abnormally high. The number of applications received by our Deputy High Commission in Dacca in May totalled 606 covering 1793 persons. By way of comparison, 1312 persons had applied for migration in April and 1530 had applied in March. Our Dacca office has granted migration certificates to 1015 persons in May, as against 952 in April and 1080 in March. I am furnishing these figures to show that the statistics for May are not abnormally high.

Apart from the migration certificates, the figures of the normal traffic through the Immigration Check Posts in West Bengal are even more interesting. In April, 11,664 Hindus had come into West Bengal and 13,015 had left West Bengal for East Pakistan. In April 14,776 Muslims had come into West Bengal and 14,264 (only 500 less) had gone from West Bengal to East Pakistan. These are the figures for the month of April, when the Pakistan Press was shouting about massacres in Malda and the migration of thousands of Muslims from West Bengal to East Pakistan. The May figures are still more significant—12,827 Hindus have come from East Pakistan, and 8,408 have gone across. The Muslim traffic figures show that 13,053 Muslims have left West Bengal for East Pakistan in the month of May, but as many as 12,720 have come across from East Pakistan to West Bengal. This should amply falsify Pakistan's propaganda that thousands

140. Item 45.

141. See also item 52.

of Muslims had fled across the Indian border because of tension in India. This being the position in May, it is all the more regrettable that there should have been trouble again in Rajshahi district of East Pakistan. The reports we have received from West Bengal Government say that on 15th June, at about 03:00 hours in the middle of the night while about 600 Hindus, Pakistan nationals, mostly santhals and Rajbanshis of villages Gopalpur, Joka, Sonamasha, Manchalpara and Ekrampur were about to cross the border at Barabila, Police Station Gomostapur (East Pakistan), withouttravel documents, Pakistan Armed Forces suddenly opened fire on them. As a result of this firing, a one year old female child and another girl of fourteen were killed on the spot and two men and six women were injured. About 300 persons are reported to have crossed over into India. The rest are reported to have been rounded up by the Pakistan forces. Of the eight injured persons, one adult male and a girl of eight years is reported to have died on the way to Malda hospital.

Strong action has been taken by the district authorities to ensure that there are no repercussions following these unfortunate events on our side of the border in Malda district.

On Saturday, June 16, the Commonwealth Secretary has brought all this to the notice of the Pakistan High Commissioner in New Delhi. He has protested against this reported conduct of the Pakistan authorities and has expressed concern on behalf of the Government of India that the East Pakistan authorities should take such strong measures to physically prevent members of the minority community from crossing over into India, when they were doing this in some obvious panic as a result of lack of confidence in the authorities.

The West Bengal Government have already lodged a protest with East Bengal authorities and our Deputy High Commissioner in Dacca[142] is seeing the Governor of East Pakistan[143] today.

I might add that this morning the Pakistan High Commissioner[144] saw the Commonwealth Secretary[145] here in Delhi and he gave the Pakistan Government's version of this incident which amounts to this. The East Pakistan Government's version is that on the 14th/15th night police outpost at Charal Panga got the information that a large mob was proceeding towards the frontier. Police station Gomostapur was alerted and a small police patrol was sent out to investigate. The mob of people would be an unlawful assembly in law as it stands in this region. At 2.30 a.m. the police party contacted the mob and challenged them and were immediately attacked with bows and arrows.

142. S.K. Chowdhry.

143. Ghulam Faruque.

144. Agha Hilaly, Pakistan High Commissioner to India.

145. Y.D. Gundevia.

The police fired 14 rounds in self-defence and one person, an aboriginal, was apparently killed. The police succeeded in rounding up 225 aboriginals. They have no information of any other casualties.

Mr Hilaly said that he had been expressly informed that the communal situation in the area has been completely peaceful after the incidents in the last week of April. There was no communal background to the present incident, in that neither this group of Santhals nor any of their villages had been attacked by anybody. The authorities allege that they do not know why the Santhals were trying to go over the border. Mr Hilaly said that the East Pakistan Government looked upon this as a normal border incident.

I am told that two days ago when this matter came up before this House some concern was expressed [....][146] I have really been quite unable to understand why this criticism is made. The Deputy High Commissioner lives in Dacca. This was at Rajshahi the border to India. There is an Assistant High Commissioner in Rajshahi headquarters. Even he could not know and did not know till much later what has happened. The only persons who could know were the West Bengal Government because they have their border police, etc. and the East Pakistan Government. The West Bengal Government communicated to us immediately and we got...

Hem Barua (Gauhati): That is not so. The Minister of State in the Ministry of External Affairs, Shrimati Lakshmi Menon, pointed out the other day....

Speaker: Order, order.

Jawaharlal Nehru: The West Bengal Government sent us a message almost immediately, the same day, and later, that is, after this, along with the report. What I mean to say is that the Deputy High Commissioner or the Assistant High Commissioner could not possibly get to know. It is physically not possible to

146. Omitted as it is unitelliglble : "and some situation in the area has been comm.-Deputy High Commissioner in East Pakistan was doing when this was happening." This part of the statement was reported in the *Amrita Bazar Patrika* thus: "Shri Nehru then proceeded to state that there was no ground for criticising the other day India's Deputy High Commissioner at Dacca or the Assistant High Commissioner at Rajshahi for not being able to send any report about firing incident." See the *Amrita Bazar Patrika*, 19 June 1962, p. 7 col. 4. On 16 June 1962, Mahavir Tyagi had said "Now there is no information with the hon. Minister and one would like to know as to why our High Commissioner has not sent any information to the hon. Prime Minister." Hem Barua said "...I will request the hon. Minister through you to collect information whether this panicky or large scale flight is indicative of any large scale communal violence in East Pakistan." See *Lok Sabha Debates*, Vol. V, cols 11113 & 11116.

get to know what has happened on the border unless the Pakistan Government inform them. We could not, in the short time, within a day, know it, because the border is rather a remote place and this thing happened in the middle of the night, at 3 a.m.

Renu Chakravartty (Barrackpore):[147] Does the Prime Minister know that for the last three days, from Friday onwards, there have been about a thousand evacuee refugees coming into Malda town from the border area, and may I know whether the Central Government was alerted about this even prior to the firing itself, and if that was so, whether our Deputy or Assistant High Commissioner living in Rajshahi knew nothing as to why these large numbers of people are migrating to India?

Jawaharlal Nehru: I do not think the figure of my hon. friend—1,000—is correct.

Renu Chakravartty: It was admitted by the West Bengal Government itself.

Jawaharlal Nehru: People have been coming in. I think it will be a little less. Some more might have come. But how is the Deputy High Commissioner at Dacca to know....

Some Hon. Members: Rajshahi.

Jawaharlal Nehru: Whether this had been organised at night or not? It is, of course, illegal to come across without papers.

Renu Chakravartty: Are we to take it that there was actually no basic objective or reason for these people to come across? Or, was there really some recrudescence of trouble, because about 600 to 1,000 is the number that is admitted by the West Bengal Government itself.

Jawaharlal Nehru: I have already read the statement in which I said that the only reason could be that there has been a state of panic as to what might happen to them, what might happen there. I do not know. I cannot say exactly what additional thing happened except that there is a general fear in the minds of the minorities about the treatment. That is a different matter. But very recently in Rajshahi district some horrible things happened, about six weeks or a month ago. That is admitted. I do not know what happened exactly just then. My

147. CPI.

information is, the Santhals, chiefly, held meetings, rather secret meetings, deciding that many of them will come over in the middle of the night so as to escape any detection; this is one of them. They started and came away at 3 a.m. What I mean to say is, I cannot understand how the Deputy High Commissioner or the Assistant High Commissioner could have done anything in the matter on this night, when they came over.

Mahavir Tyagi (Dehra Dun):[148] Have they given any information today? It is quite a few days now since all this has happened. Have the Government consulted or contacted them, at least by wireless message, and got confirmation of what has happened?

Some Hon. Members rose …

Speaker: I will allow some questions to be put, one by one.

Mahavir Tyagi: Have they visited those places?

Hem Barua: I would first refer to the Prime Minister's reference. I just remember that the Minister of State in the Ministry of External Affairs, Shrimati Lakshmi Menon, was saying the other day that when she saw this news in the newspapers she contacted that Government for the information. That shows—what a sad commentary—the way our governmental machinery functions. [Interruptions]

Speaker: Order, order.

Jawaharlal Nehru rose …

Hem Barua: Sir, I have not put the question.

Speaker: Order, order.

Jawaharlal Nehru: In this particular matter, the machinery functioned with extraordinary speed and efficiency. Just look at it. The incident happened at 3 a.m. on the 15th March. The matter came up before this House on the 16th morning, that is, roughly about 26 to 27 hours later. We telephoned and we got a message—there was no other way—from West Bengal, which was the only Government to know about it, and it telephoned to us a brief message which

148. Congress.

was read out to the House here. The very next day, they sent us a long report. In answer to Shri Tyagi, the Deputy High Commissioner enquired about it from Dacca and he got a report from the Assistant High Commissioner at Rajshahi about it. And, as I stated, he is going to see the Governor today. He has reported to us. I do not see how there could have been greater speed about it. It is an extraordinary speed, I should say, considering that the thing happened ...

Hem Barua: I discovered this discrepancy in the two statements and I pointed it out.

Jawaharlal Nehru: what is the discrepancy, if I may know?

Hem Barua: The Prime Minister says he got the information immediately, but Shrimati Menon said she got the information first from the newspapers and then she contacted the West Bengal Government. That is the contradiction.

Jawaharlal Nehru: On the 16th morning, there was something in the newspapers which she saw. By that time, we got the information from the West Bengal Government; maybe an hour later, I do not know the exact time. We got it, in fact, if I remember right, on the 16th morning a little later, at about 11 o'clock. Then she came to me and said, "I have just got this from the West Bengal Government." I said, please place it before the Parliament.

[Omitted: exchanges on procedure]

प्रकाशवीर शास्त्री (बिजनौर):[149] अध्यक्ष महोदय, पाकिस्तान के उस भाग में लाखों की संख्या में जो हिन्दू रह रहे हैं और जो पाकिस्तानी व्यवहार से परेशान हो कर भारत की ओर आशा भरी दृष्टि से देख रहे हैं, उन सबको ध्यान में रखते हुए मैं प्रधानमंत्री जी से एक प्रश्न जानना चाहता हूं कि जब नेहरू-लियाकत पैक्ट का इस समय तक कोई सुपरिणाम नहीं निकला और अब भी इस प्रकार के दुर्व्यवहार से तंग आकर हजारों की संख्या में वह भारत आने को उत्सुक हैं तो भारत सरकार इस विषय में क्या अन्तिम निर्णय लेना चाहती है जिससे कि उनको कुछ सन्तोष प्राप्त हो सके?

जवाहरलाल नेहरुः मैंने अभी आपको बताया है कि वाकया यह है कि बहुत कम लोग आये हैं हालांकि उनको पूरा पूरा मौका हमारी तरफ से आने का दिया गया। हमारी तरफ से कोई रूकावट नहीं हुई। मुमकिन है पाकिस्तान की तरफ से कोई रूकावट कहीं-कहीं

149. Independent.

हुई हो मगर वह भी ज्यादा नहीं कर सकते। अब पाकिस्तान में कहा गया कि मुसलमान काफी तादाद में हिन्दुस्तान से भाग कर आये। मैंने आपको पढ़कर सुनाया कि मुसलमान उसी जमाने में यानी मार्च, अप्रैल और मई में कितने पाकिस्तान से हिन्दुस्तान आये और इसी तरीके से हिन्दू कितने वेस्ट बंगाल से पाकिस्तान गये उसी जमाने में। यह तो जाहिर है कि उन नम्बरों में वह लोग शामिल नहीं है जो कि खुफिया तौर से आये हैं उन का अंदाज करना मुश्किल है। खुफिया तौर से कुछ लोग आये हैं इसमें कोई शक नहीं है लेकिन वाकया यह है कि बहुत ज्यादा नहीं आये है।

प्रकाशवीर शास्त्रीः मेरा प्रश्न यह था कि भविष्य के लिये क्या व्यवस्था की जा रही है ताकि......

[Translation begins:

Prakash Vir Shastri (Bijnor): [150] Mr Speaker, all those Hindus, who live in Pakistan and are unhappy with Pakistan's behaviour, are looking to India. Considering their conditions, I want to ask the Prime Minister when no positive results of the Nehru-Liaquat Pact are visible so far and thousands of people feel harassed and eager to come to India in large numbers, what decisions does the Government of India want to take to give them solace?

Jawaharlal Nehru: I have just informed you that very few people have come during this time even though every opportunity was given to them by us. No obstacles were placed by our side. Possibly, some hindrances came from the Pakistan side but they also cannot do much about it. Now, it is being said in Pakistan that a large number of Muslims have gone to Pakistan. Just now I have read out the figures how many Muslims from Pakistan have come to India during this period that is, March, April and May. Similarly, how many Hindus went from West Bengal to Pakistan during this period. Obviously, these numbers do not include those who came clandestinely, it is difficult also. Many came secretly but the fact is that not many have come.

Prakash Vir Shastri: My question was that what arrangements are being made for the future so that……

Translation ends]

Speaker: Order, order.

150. See fn 149 in this section.

H.P. Chatterjee (Nabadwip):[151] Things happened in Rajshahi some time back. I have pointed out that thousands have come over here. I had received information and in my personal visit....

Speaker: He should come to his question.

H.P. Chatterjee: My question is, what arrangement was made by our Government to see that they could get their migration certificates in Rajshahi and not go to Dacca, because there is so much of hindrance in going to Dacca, realising money and all sorts of things? What arrangement was made by the Deputy High Commissioner at Rajshahi to give them migration certificates?

Jawaharlal Nehru: I am sorry I cannot go into that. I do not know the detailed arrangements that had been made by him or might have been made by him. But the Assistant High Commissioner interviewed these people and a large number—about a thousand, as I stated—were given certificates to come over here. The rest did not come. Whether they were asked to go to Dacca, I do not know. But even if they were asked to go to Dacca and they did not come, it shows that they were not terribly keen about coming to India.

H. P. Chatterjee: How ignorant is he. How ignorant is our Prime Minister:

Renu Chakravartty: Sir, the *Amrita Bazar Patrika* points out that late on Friday night Shri K.P. Mukerjee, the Home Minister of West Bengal was contacted to find out exactly the number of people dead but he could not say anything and yet we are now told that nine dead bodies have been brought to Malda on Friday for post mortem examination. It is a statement of fact. May I know whether the Central Government is prepared to find out exactly what the situation is, find out how many have been killed and how many have been injured?

Jawaharlal Nehru: Central Government cannot find out anything there except through the agency of the West Bengal Government. I have read the West Bengal Government's report on it. We sent a man there to find out what happened, two days ago or three days ago. Obviously, things must come through the West Bengal Government who has got the District Magistrate there, the government machinery there.

151. Independent.

Renu Chakravartty: I am saying about his figure of one dead and the figure given here that nine dead bodies have been brought for post mortem examination.

Jawaharlal Nehru: Not "one dead", the figure I have given is I think "four dead".

रामचन्द्र बड़े (खारगोन):[152] क्या माननीय प्रधानमंत्री यह अपना कर्तव्य नहीं समझते कि पाकिस्तान में जो हिन्दू रह गये है उनको प्रोटेक्शन और संरक्षण दिया जाय और जितने हिन्दू वहाँ से इधर भारत में आना चाहते हैं उनको वहाँ से निकल कर आने में प्रोटेक्शन दिया जाय और जब वह बोर्डर पर जाते है तब उनको कुछ मिलिटरी आदि का प्रोटेक्शन दिया जाय ताकि वह सही सलामत यहां पर आ सकें?

अध्यक्ष महोदयः पाकिस्तान के अन्दर ही उनको प्रोटेक्शन दिया जाय?

रामचन्द्र बड़ेः पाकिस्तान के बोर्डर पर प्रोटेक्शन दिया जाय। मेरा कहना है कि हमारी गवर्नमेंट इस तरह से क्यों उन बेचारों को मरवाती है और उनको प्रोटेक्शन क्यों नहीं देती है? By some arrangement they should be escorted to our area.

जवाहरलाल नेहरुः मेरी कुछ समझ में नहीं आता कि उस जमाने में खौफनाक बातें राजशाही वगैरह में हुई और उसी के साथ हौलनाक बातें मालदा में हुई हैं हालाकि उस कदर ज्यादा नहीं हुई। राजशाही के बाद मुझे सब याद नहीं लेकिन कई जिलों में यह साम्प्रदायिक झगड़े हुये जिनमें कि इधर मुसलमान मारे गये। अब यह एक शर्म की बात है कि ऐसी बातें पाकिस्तान में हों या यहां हों। वहाँ ज्यादा होती है मान लिया लेकिन यह चीज महल एक तराजू में नहीं तोली जानी चाहिए कि किसने ज्यादा बदतमीजी या खराब बातें की है और किसने कम की हैं। हम तैयार है। हमने कोई रूकावट नहीं डाली वहां लोगों के आने में। लेकिन माननीय सदस्य कहते हैं कि हमें उनको मदद करनी चाहिए या रक्षा करनी चाहिए तो हम उनकी रक्षा पाकिस्तान में जाकर नहीं जा कर सकते। अब जो वाकये हुए और पाकिस्तान के बयान आप देखे मैंने पढ़ कर सुनाया कि रात को वहां उस जगह बोर्डर पर लोगों का जमा होना गैर कानूनी है। अब रात को वहां बौर्डर पर लोग आये और इस तरह कानून के खिलाफ बात उन्होंने की । उसके ऊपर जब पुलिस का आउट पोस्ट गया तो उन्होंने उन पर कमानों से तीर चलाये जिस पर कि पुलिस ने गोली चलाई और उसमें चार आदमी। मरे। हमारी इत्तिला यह है कि दो आदमी तो उसी वक्त मरे और दो जरा आद में मरे।

152. Ramchandra Vithal Bade, Jan Sangh.

[Translation begins:

Ramchandra Bade (Khargone):[153]Does the honourable Prime Minister not understand that the Hindus left behind in Pakistan should be given protection and all those Hindus who want to come to India should get safe passage and when they reach the border, they should get military protection to arrive here safely?

Speaker: Should they be given protection in Pakistan?

Ramchandra Bade: Protection should be given on Pakistan border. My point is that why does our Government not give them protection and let them be killed. By some arrangement they should be escorted to our area.

Jawaharlal Nehru: I do not understand that at the time terrible incidents took place in Rajshahi etc and at the same in Malda though not on the same scale. After Rajshahi, in some other districts, I do not remember, some Muslims were killed here in communal riots. It is shameful whether it happens here or in Pakistan. Even if we feel that there are more such incidents there, this cannot be weighed in a balance to decide who is worse. We are ready, we have not put any restrictions in the way of people coming here. But the honourable member says that we should help them and provide protection, we cannot go to Pakistan to do so. You have seen what happened and heard Pakistan's statements, I read out that people gathered on the border at night and broke the law. When the police went there those people shot arrows on them; then the police opened fire resulting in the death of four persons. Our information is that two died immediately and two a little later.

Translation ends]

[Interventions by other members have been omitted]

153. See fn 152 in this section.

54. In the Lok Sabha: Tibetan Refugees[154]

Question:[155]Will the Prime Minister be pleased to state:

(a) the total number of Tibetan refugees in India at present;
(b) the efforts and arrangements made by Government for providing them relief, employment and educational facilities; and
(c) the contribution, financial and otherwise made by the Dalai Lama himself towards the rehabilitation of these refugees?

The Deputy Minister in the Ministry of External Affairs (Dinesh Singh):

(a) Approximately 32,300.
(b) Government of India is providing food, clothing, accommodation and other necessities to all Tibetan refugees. About 8,000 persons have been or are in the process of being permanently rehabilitated on land. The majority of the remaining able-bodied workers are employed on road works. Residential and Day Schools have been opened for the children according to requirements.
(c) The Dalai Lama has made some contribution towards some of the welfare activities for Tibetan Refugees.

Hari Vishnu Kamath: How many refugee camps are there all over the country, and could we know the names of the places where they are situated?

The Prime Minister and Minister of External Affairs and Minister of Atomic Energy (Jawaharlal Nehru): I could not give all the names of the camps, but the permanent rehabilitations are in Mysore—a camp of about 3,000 now but it is expected to have more. That is a regular colony of Tibetan refugees established there. It is proposed to have some more colonies, perhaps one in Orissa, perhaps one in Uttar Pradesh. We have to be careful about the climate of the place because a very hot climate will not suit the Tibetans. Then in NEFA there is a camp. The Dalai Lama himself lives in Dalhousie, and a fairly large number of Tibetan children have gathered round him, that is, the parents leave them there feeling rather assured that the Dalai Lama would look after them. The burden is rather heavy. It is now proposed to have a children's village

154. Oral Answers, 19 June 1962. *Lok Sabha Debates*, Third Series, Vol. V, 8 June to 22 June 1962, Ist Session, cols 11577-11582.
155. By Hari Vishnu Kamath of PSP and Krishna Deo Tripathi of Congress.

somewhat after the fashion of the Swiss children's village, which they had after the war, Pestalozzi[156] I think. That is being thought of. And then there are a number of people in Ladakh, and there are people working, young Tibetans working on roads, in various places.

Hari Vishnu Kamath: Have any reports reached Government that in the past some Chinese spies or agents have infiltrated along with the Tibetan refugees into India, and if so, has there been any screening on the part of Government before refugees are admitted into India?

Jawaharlal Nehru: There is some attempted screening. I am not sure it is always wholly successful, but there has been screening and some people have been separated from others.

Hari Vishnu Kamath: On grounds stated by me?

Jawaharlal Nehru: Yes.

Indrajit Gupta:[157] Is it the intention of the Government that these rehabilitation measures should be carried out in such a way that these refugees are to gradually become Indian citizens?

Jawaharlal Nehru: There is no attempt to make them Indian citizens. They may, of course, if they fulfill the qualifications, become Indian citizens, but the main object is to treat them as Tibetans with Tibetan language, Tibetan culture, Tibetan religion etc. In addition, of course, they learn Hindi, and sometimes, maybe, a little English.

M.S. Aney:[158] Are they required to live in specified colonies, or are they permitted to go anywhere they like?

Jawaharlal Nehru: I do not quite know. In a sense, it is open to them to go anywhere they like, but it is very difficult for them to do so because of the difficulty of language and other things. They just cannot do it.

156. The Pestalozzi Children's Village, founded in 1946 in Switzerland for European war orphans, followed the concepts of Johann Heinrich Pestalozzi (1746-1827), Swiss educational reformer.

157. CPI.

158. Independent.

Hem Barua:[159] May I know whether the attention of the Government has been drawn to the fact of China launching a systematic campaign through cinema slides, lectures, and radio broadcasts…

Speaker:[160] He ought to come to the question.

Hem Barua: ...depicting the so-called horrid conditions of life and the hard work to which the Tibetan refugees in this country are supposed to be subjected to and...

Speaker: He should come straight to the question.

Hem Barua: Yes, Sir. If so whether the Government has launched a counter-campaign to nail this Chinese lie to the coffin?

Jawaharlal Nehru: I am sorry it is difficult to grasp the hon. Member's questions; the preamble is too long. We have started no such campaign here.

Hem Barua: My question was whether Government was aware of it.

Speaker: No counter-campaign has been launched; answer has been given.

Ramchandra Bade:[161] Is there any autonomous society by which education is given to the Tibetan students and of which the President is the Education Minister and if so, what is the amount spent by the society for the Tibetan students?

Jawaharlal Nehru: What society?

Ramchandra Bade: It is a non-Government institution. It is said here that an autonomous society registered under the Societies Registration Act has been formed to arrange for the provision of educational facilities for the children of displaced Tibetans. I am asking: what is the amount spent and what is the grant to the society?

Jawaharlal Nehru: I know only of one society: Tibetan Refugees Aid Society, of which, I think, Acharya Kripalani is the Chairman; I do not know of any other.

159. PSP.
160. Hukam Singh.
161. Ramchandra Vithal Bade, Jan Sangh.

Ramchandra Bade: It is written here that the Education Minister[162] is the Chairman of the Society. Dalai Lama is a member.

Speaker: Is any aid given to it.

Jawaharlal Nehru: In regard to students, we have been particularly anxious to provide schools for the children and the Educational Minister is always consulted; in fact, he decides a great deal about it. I do not know if some special or sub-committee is there and where he is a member of that committee for this purpose.

But the Tibetan Refugees Aid Society has nothing to do with Government except that it is in touch with Government.

Nath Pai:[163] Is any aid being received from any country abroad for the rehabilitation of these refugees and, if so, the name of the countries and the amount of aid? Secondly, is it the policy of Government to allow Tibetan children to be adopted by foreign parents?

Jawaharlal Nehru: I cannot give the exact figures of the sum of aid received by the Government. The Government of New Zealand is aiding and the Government of Australia also gave some amount. Switzerland sent some thing, as also, I believe, the United Kingdom Government. From the United States, I believe they have helped the unofficial committee and to some extent, medicines and other things have been sent.

Nath Pai: Is Government encouraging the adoption of Tibetan children by foreign parents and, if so, how many such children have gone so far?

Jawaharlal Nehru: We have not encouraged any such adoption. About twenty or so children were taken away with some of their parents to Switzerland by some organisation in Switzerland. Perhaps they are in the children's village there. I have not heard anything about adoption.

162. K.L. Shrimali.
163. PSP.

55. To B.C. Roy: Malda Refugees for Dandakaranya[164]

June 19, 1962

My dear Bidhan,

Your letter of June 18th about the refugees who have come to Malda from Rajshahi. You suggest that these people should be sent to Dandakaranya directly. I shall discuss this matter with Mehr Chand Khanna[165] and then write to you.

We have to give some relief to such refugees, but there is an obvious danger in our promising some acres of land and other help in Dandakaranya to all the people who may come over from Pakistan. With this great inducement, very large numbers may well come over, creating a problem which neither your Government nor the Government of India nor, indeed, Dandakarnya can solve. The more the people who come over, the harder will be the fate of those who remain behind. The stream will continue till it produces an impossible situation for all concerned.

The point is, therefore, that while we necessarily give some relief to those who come, we should not encourage too many of them to come.

Yours affectionately,
[Jawaharlal Nehru]

56. To B.C. Roy: Rajshahi Refugees[166]

June 21, 1962

My dear Bidhan,

I have had a talk with Mehr Chand Khanna[167] about the refugees coming to Malda from Rajshahi.

It seems clear to us that people who come as refugees must be given relief. But the real question is what has one to do about them in future. For the present I have suggested to Mehr Chand Khanna, and he has agreed, that he should send immediately some representative of his Ministry to Malda to see these refugees and to find out what the exact position is. Each refugee should be given a certificate of identity.

164. Letter to the Chief Minister of West Bengal.

165. Minister of State for Works, Housing and Supply now; Minister of State for Rehabilitation and Minority Affairs till 10 April 1962.

166. Letter to the Chief Minister of West Bengal. Reproduced from Saroj Chakrabarty (ed.), *With Dr.B.C. Roy and other Chief Ministers: A Record upto 1962* (Calcutta: Benson's, 1974), pp. 521-522.

167. See fn 165.

Secondly, we should be prepared to send those who agree to go to Dandakaranya. This requires the agreement of the Orissa and Madhya Pradesh Governments. That can be obtained, at least for those at present likely to be sent. Only those can be sent as agree to go there. I do not know how many of these Santhals who have come over will be prepared to go.

Then there is the question of fishermen. No arrangement can be made for fishing in Dandakaranya; agriculturists can be provided for.

Then also we cannot guarantee seven acres of land to every family. This will have to be looked into as to what we can give them.

The real problem is not of those who have come now. Many may come in the next few days, but large numbers coming over, we should try to avoid this happening. As I wrote to you in my last letter, if the way is opened for a continuous big exodus, then we shall sink under its weight.[168] Therefore, we should not encourage them even though we have necessarily to look after those who have come. It is quite impossible for us to make arrangements for hundreds of thousands or even millions.

I have indicated the first steps that we intend taking. The situation is still somewhat fluid and uncertain and we shall have to give more thought to it later. But, for the present, we have to make scrutiny of those who have come, give them identity cards, select those who are agreeable to be sent to Dandakaranya and make arrangements to send them direct there.[169]

I hope you will agree that this is the most we can do at present.[170]

Yours affectionately
Jawaharlal

57. To A.M. Tariq: Muslims in Congress Party Executive[171]

June 22, 1962

My dear Tariq,

I have your letter of today's date.

I was distressed yesterday at the fact that no Muslim was elected to the Executive of the Congress Party. It might interest you to know that at yesterday's voting I voted for two Muslim candidates, among them Ansar Harvani.[172]

168. Item 55.

169. See also item 432, pp. 720-722.

170. This policy explained again in item 69.

171. Letter to Congress MP; address: 313 Vinay Marg, New Delhi.

172. Lok Sabha MP, Congress, from Bisauli, UP.

While this is unfortunate, I do not think it had anything to do with voting on communal lines. It was really voting on group lines and more particularly on provincial lines which, of course, is equally had.

About housing, you know I have taken some interest in this matter. I do not know what more I can do except to draw the attention of the Housing Committee.

I am surprised to learn from you that you are thinking of leaving the Party. One may be disappointed with the Party but I do not see how one can work more effectively outside the Party. Apart from this, I am not quite sure if it is quite proper for you or for anyone else elected on a certain ticket to discard it. That will work against the persons who function in this way.

Yours sincerely,
[Jawaharlal Nehru]

58. To B.C. Roy: Relief for Malda Victims[173]

June 23, 1962

My dear Bidhan,

Thank you for your letter of the 21st June. In addition to the five thousand, I have already sent you rupees ten thousand more and suggested that this sum or part of it might be given to Renuka Ray's[174] organisation working in Malda.

This morning, I talked to you on the telephone about Malda refugees. It is understood that you are sending one thousand agriculturists to Dandakaranya.

About my going to Rihand Dam, I had not promised to go there because of any pressure on me. I have long wanted to go there and I looked upon this visit as relaxation. Long years ago, I laid foundation-stone or some such thing there,[175] and I am keen on seeing what it looks like now. I know that I cannot go to Rihand straight. It may be possible for me to go by a helicopter.

Yours affectionately,
[Jawaharlal Nehru]

173. Letter to the Chief Minister of West Bengal.

174. Lok Sabha MP, Congress, from Malda, West Bengal.

175. In July 1954, see SWJN/SS/26/p. 570.

59. For the Asprushyata Nivaran Day[176]

I send my good wishes on the occasion of Asprushyata Nivaran Day in Maharashtra. Untouchability is a social evil of the worst kind. If any kind of untouchability prevails, it is absurd for us to talk of democracy and socialism. It surprises me how people who otherwise are democrats and socialists, do not feel the urgent necessity of getting rid of this evil.

Untouchability is a part of our caste system. To remove it completely would give a serious blow to the framework of our caste system and thus give us freedom to develop through democracy to socialism.

60. Transfer of Population with East Pakistan[177]

[Note, 25 June 1962, by Y.D. Gundevia, CS, MEA, begins]

There have been suggestions in some quarters after the recent serious disturbances in East Pakistan that the Government of India should seriously take up with the Government of Pakistan the question of transfer of population. Probably the short notice question placed below which the Ministry of W.H. & S. is faced with, aims at this issue.[178] There is no doubt that any discussion with Pakistan on the lines suggested in (a) of the question would lead to serious trouble with Pakistan. The whole idea is, of course, completely against the policy of the Government of India. I have attempted a draft reply to say that the Government of India would not raise this matter with Pakistan because it can only lead to increase in tension between the two countries. The draft is for the Prime Minister's approval.

Y.D. Gundevia
25-6-1962

CS

[Note, 25 June 1962, by Y.D. Gundevia, CS, MEA, ends]

176. Message, 25 June 1962. PMO, File No. 9/2/62-PMP, Vol. IV, Sr. No. 75-A.
177. Noting, 25 June 1962. MEA, File No. 2(114)/62-P.IV, pp. 4-5/note. Nehru's note is also available in the JN Collection.
178. The question by V.M. Chordia, Jan Sangh Rajya Sabha MP from Madhya Pradesh to be answered in the Rajya Sabha, was: "Will the Minister of Works, Housing and Supply be pleased to state: (a) whether Pakistan Government have been asked to give land and property in proportion to the number of persons who have migrated to India in excess of those who have migrated to Pakistan; and (b) if not, what are the reasons for not making the demand?" See *Rajya Sabha Debates*, 26 June 1962, Vol. XXXIX, No. 11, cols 2180-2181.

[Note, 25 June 1962, by Nehru, begins]

I am surprised that this question was admitted. Obviously our answer is "NO". However, as it is an unstarred question, the following reply is suggested.

a) No.
b) Any question of transfer or exchange of land between India and Pakistan would raise a great deal of controversy and argument and would necessarily lead to an increase of tension between India and Pakistan. The Government of India's firm policy is to do nothing that would increase tension between India and Pakistan. This question, therefore, does not arise.

J. Nehru
25-6-1962

CS

[Note, 25 June 1962, by Nehru, ends]

61. To Morarji Desai: Haj Pilgrimage Funding[179]

June 28, 1962

My dear Morarji,
Your letter of the 28th June about the foreign exchange involved in Haj pilgrimages. I think we should try to limit the sum involved in this. I am glad you have written to Hafizji[180] on this subject.

Yours sincerely,
Jawaharlal Nehru

62. Meeting with Agha Hilaly[181]

India Does Not Want Tension— PM

New Delhi, June 29 – Prime Minister Nehru has told the Pakistan High Commissioner in India, Mr Agha Hilaly, that India was anxious to see that there

179. Letter to the Minister of Finance.
180. Hafiz Mohammed Ibrahim, Minister of Irrigation and Power.
181. PTI report of meeting with the Pakistan High Commissioner, 28 June 1962. *National Herald*, 30 June 1962, p. 1.

was no increase in tension on the Indo-Pakistan border near Tripura according to a spokesman of the External Affairs Ministry.

Pandit Nehru conveyed his views when the Pakistan High Commissioner called on him yesterday to express the concern of Pakistan Government over the reports of large-scale eviction of Pakistani nationals from Tripura.

It is understood that in order to help tension. India is likely to slow down the pace of deportation of Pakistani infiltrators into Tripura.[182]

Recently, India evicted 581 Pakistani nationals who were unlawfully present in Tripura. According to official estimates, about 50,000 Pakistanis had infiltrated into Tripura since partition –PTI

63. To Lal Bahadur Shastri: Ajmer Dargah Committee[183]

June 29, 1962

My dear Lal Bahadur,

Syed Yusuf Maharaj of Ajmer[184] came to see me this morning. I have met him for the last fifteen or sixteen years either at Ajmer or at Delhi. He told me a fairly long story. The present position appears to be that he wishes to be a member of the Dargah Committee of Ajmer. I do not know what is coming in his way as there appears to be a vacancy or rather two vacancies in that committee.[185]

He showed me a number of testimonials and gave me a letter written to you by some MPs two years ago, which I enclose.

Will you kindly have this matter enquired into and dealt with?

Yours affectionately,
[Jawaharlal Nehru]

182. See also item 60.
183. Letter to the Home Minister.
184. Details of Syed Yusuf Maharaj and his family may be found in the following website managed by his family https://chishtiyamaharaj.jimdo.com/, retrieved on 25 July 2018.
185. In accordance with the Dargah Khawaja Saheb Act, 1955, the Dargah Committee is constituted by the Government of India for its management.

64. To B.P. Chaliha: Infiltrators from East Pakistan[186]

June 30, 1962

My dear Chaliha,

You have written to me more than once about the infiltration of Pakistani Muslims into Assam. We are all concerned about it. I hope that effective steps have been taken to stop this process. The question, however, arises about past infiltrations and how to deal with them.

The same question has arisen in Tripura and we asked the Tripura Administration to look into this matter and send out clear cases of infiltration. In the course of the last few days nearly 3,000 persons were thus sent out of Tripura across the Pakistan boundary.[187]

I do not know yet how this selection was made and how far care was taken not to send out old established residents. Reports have reached us from Pakistan about tension there on account of this matter and it has been said that many people who had been resident for several generations have thus been sent out. There are many women and children living in camps in Pakistan. Pakistan newspapers gave a lurid account of this. We have, therefore, for the moment stopped this process and have said that if clear cases of mistake have been made, we are prepared to consider them if adequate evidence is produced.[188]

I am writing to you now as to what should be done in Assam. We do not want anything which might result in acute tension between India and Pakistan. As a counter-move, Pakistan might well pick out a few hundred or more of Hindus living there and turn them out. Thus a vicious process will start which will lead to great tension.

Therefore, care has to be taken as to what should be done and how this should be brought about. The first question is what your definition of infiltration

186. Letter to the Chief Minister of Assam.

187. On Tripura, see also item 68.

188. The Press reported that Pakistan was appreciative:

> "Pak. Immigrants in Tripura
> Nehru's Gesture Praised
>
> Karachi, July 12. The Secretary of the Pakistan Ministry of External Affairs, Mr S.K. Dehlavi, yesterday welcomed the recent gesture of Prime Minister Nehru in stopping the eviction of Pakistani immigrants from Tripura.
>
> He told a press conference it was a step 'in the right direction' and Pakistan appreciated it.
>
> However, Mr Dehlavi said there were some 'reactionay and militant elements' in India who 'are out to defy and embarrass' the Indian Prime Minister." See *The Hindu*, 13 July 1962, p. 1.

is and how you prove it? Do you fix any date for this infiltration into Assam from East Pakistan? The date cannot be before Independence. I understand that after Independence there was no regular check of people coming and a fair number, therefore, came then. It was only some time in 1952 that some checks were applied, though they were not very adequate. Still I imagine that it should be relatively easy to find out cases of infiltration since 1952. Even that is ten years ago. In any event, I would suggest that the more recent arrivals should be dealt with first, that is, since 1952. After having dealt with them, you might consider what other steps you might take.

In choosing people in this way, I hope a simple test of Bengalee-speaking Muslims will be avoided. There are, as you know, many Bengalee-speaking Muslims in Assam and to pick them out would create a great deal of consternation amongst others and lead to increasing tension. The position in East Pakistan during the past few months has not been a satisfactory one and I am anxious that this mutual pushing-out of people should not lead to disastrous results and serious incidents.[189] Also you will appreciate the repercussions of this kind of thing in Kashmir and among the Muslims in other parts of India.

I hope, therefore, that you will proceed with caution in this matter.

Yours sincerely,
Jawaharlal Nehru

65. To Lal Bahadur Shastri: Malerkotla's Nephew wants to return[190]

July 1, 1962

My dear Lal Bahadur,
The Nawab of Malerkotla[191] came to see me this afternoon. He gave me a letter and other papers. I enclose a copy of them.[192]

He has long been asking for his brother to come to India. He is an officer of the Pakistan Army. Now he asks for his nephew, the brother's son, to be allowed to come here for the reasons that he has given. The nephew is just out of college and is about 22 years old. I do not see any particular reason for

189. Referred to also in item 69.
190. Letter to the Home Minister. MHA, File No. 10/40/62-F III, p.1/c. Also available in the JN Collection.
191. Nawab Iftikhar Ali Khan of Malerkotla.
192. See appendix 46 (a), 46 (b) and 46 (c).

preventing him from coming to India. I should like your advice in regard to this matter.[193]

I am writing to Krishna Menon also and sending him a copy of these papers.[194]

Yours affectionately,
Jawaharlal Nehru

66. To V.K. Krishna Menon: Nawab of Malerkotla[195]

July 1, 1962

My dear Krishna,

I am sending you some papers which the Nawab of Malerkotla has given me. He had an interview with me this afternoon. He wants permission for his nephew to come to India and ultimately to be allowed to become an Indian national.

We have refused permission to his brother, the father of the nephew, to come here and I think this was done quite rightly as he is an officer in the Pakistan Army and has otherwise none too good a reputation. How far this refusal should apply to his son, a young man in college or just out of the collage, 22 years of ago, I do not know. Perhaps we might allow him to come here.

The Nawab of Malerkotla is a good man. His wife and sister have just been elected to the Punjab Assembly on Congress ticket.[196]

I have sent these papers to Lal Bahadur also.[197] But I thought your advice might be taken.[198]

Yours affectionately,
[Jawaharlal Nehru]

193. See appendix 46 (d).
194. See item 66; see also SWJN/SS/76/item 149 and SWJN/SS/69/item 167 and appendix 67.
195. Letter to the Defence Minister.
196. For names of various family members, see Malerkotla's letter to Nehru, appendix 46 (a).
197. See item 65.
198. For Krishna Menon's reply, see appendix 59.

67. To Mehr Chand Khanna: Malda Refugees for Dandakaranya[199]

July 2, 1962

My dear Mehr Chand,

Padmaja Naidu[200] has sent me a message that almost the last thought which worried Bidhan Roy[201] was the question of the refugees in Malda. She also says that the amount of relief being given to them according to the rules is woefully small.

I do not know what rules limit the relief. It is up to the West Bengal Government to give what is needed within reason, I have sent Rs 15,000/- from the Prime Minister's Relief Fund already and am prepared to send more.

As for the general problem of the refugees, I suggest that you should or the West Bengal Government should offer to take a few of the Santhal refugees to Dandakaranya to see for themselves what the place is like and to come back and report to their friends. That appears to me the only way of sending a number of them there, which I think should be done.[202]

Yours sincerely,
[Jawaharlal Nehru]

68. To N.C. Chatterjee: Santhals to Dandakaranya[203]

July 6, 1962

My dear Shri Chatterjee,

Thank you for your letter of the 2nd July.

Dr Bidhan Roy's death was a great shock to all of us. It is always difficult to think of replacing a great leader and especially a man like Dr Roy. He was so warm-hearted. I thought of going to Calcutta for his funeral, but then I remembered his last advice to me which was repeated the day before his death. He urged me strongly not to travel about or to accept engagements unless they

199. Letter to the Minister of Works, Housing and Supply, formerly Minister of Rehabilitation.

200. Governor of West Bengal.

201. B.C. Roy, Chief Minister of West Bengal, died 1 July 1962.

202. See item 226.

203. Letter to the President of the Civil Liberties Committee, West Bengal, Calcutta, and former president of Hindu Mahasabha. Sent from Pahalgam, Kashmir.

were quite unavoidable.[204] I have received full accounts of the mighty procession which followed him in his last journey.

About Malda refugees, as you know, we had agreed to take most of the agriculturists to Dandakaranya. Dr Roy decided to send 1000 of them straight from Malda.[205] Unfortunately, some people circulated fantastic and absolutely untrue stories. I did not know that the Santhals had suggested sending some of their leaders to Dandakaranya first. As a matter of fact, after I heard about these fantastic stories being circulated among them I made the same suggestion. I understand that some dozens of Santhals have already gone to Dandakaranya. I am sure they will be satisfied with the arrangements there and this will result in other Santhals going there.

You refer to a directive to "go slow". This was to Tripura because thousands of these people were being sent suddenly to Pakistan which created a difficult situation and we were anxious to avoid any undesirable reactions to it. Besides, we were told that some of the persons sent had been living in Tripura for a long time past and we wanted to make sure that only infiltrators were sent across.[206]

I am asking my Ministry to send you some material on the subject of the Nagas. Mr Roger Baldwin[207] has been supplied with this material from time to time in the past.

Yours sincerely,
[Jawaharlal Nehru]

69. To Arun Chandra Guha: Migrations from East Pakistan[208]

July 8, 1962

My dear Guha,

Your letter of the 30th June.

I am sorry that the letter I wrote to Dr Roy found publication and probably in a distorted way. I do not think I wrote anything, as you have reported, to the effect that I "have sought advice whether it was possible to stop their coming to India completely". As a matter of fact, there is no question at any time for

204. For B.C. Roy's letter, see SWJN/SS/76/appendix 36.
205. See item 432, pp. 719-721.
206. See item 64.
207. American civil rights activist.
208. Letter to Congress MP in Lok Sabha from Barasat, West Bengal; address: 32 Acharya Prafulla Chandra Road, Calcutta-9. Sent from Pahalgam, Kashmir.

us to think in these terms or of sealing the border. Our express instructions were to a contrary effect, that is, that the strict migration rules may be relaxed. But I did point out that we should not otherwise encourage migrations. These have accumulated and growing effect and they create conditions of greater uncertainty and trouble for the people who are left behind. This may even lead to a repetition of the terrible events that happened in Western Pakistan and Northern India after the Partition. Certainly I do not want this to happen.

What I meant by not encouraging them to come over was that if an idea goes out that everyone who comes over gets several acres of land free and other help, then it may well be that large numbers may come over. Those who come over must of course be helped to the best of our ability.[209]

Recently about 3000 or more original migrants from East Pakistan to Tripura were pushed across the border into East Pakistan.[210] This has created a new situation of which much is made by the East Pakistan press and authorities. I do not know what tests they had of finding out who were recent migrants. But it is said in Pakistan that many of them who have been pushed across have been settled in Tripura for generations. Therefore, we asked the Tripura authorities to go slow in this matter and to make quite sure that those whom they were dealing with had recently come over.

Yours sincerely,
[Jawaharlal Nehru]

70. To Y.D. Gundevia: Communal Conflict in Noakhali District[211]

I have rec[eive]d the following telegram from N.C. Chatterjee[212] Calcutta.

> Begins. Extremely shocking report of massacre of leading merchants at Chaukhusani[213] in Naokhali [Noakhali]. Recent migrants report deliberate plan to butcher leading men of Shaha community occupying important positions in commercial life. Please order Deputy High Commissioner

209. See letter to B.C. Roy, item 56.
210. See item 64.
211. Telegram, 9 July 1962, to the CS. MEA, File No. 8(17)/62-P. IV, Part VII, pp. 409-410/corr. Spellings as in original; but the correct spellings are Noakhali and Chaumuhani.
212. President of the Civil Liberties Committee, West Bengal.
213. Choumuhani in Gundevia's note.

> Dacca[214] to proceed Chaumusani[215] and report details in name of oppressed humanity. Urge you to inform President Ayub that you will order diversion of food ships back to India unless he stops oppression and tortures in minorities of Pakistan. Ends.

There is of course no question of diversion of food ships but I hope you are enquiring into these matters.[216]

71. Communal Conflict in Noakhali District[217]

I sent you yesterday a telegram repeating a message I had received from Shri N.C. Chatterjee about the alleged massacre of leading merchants of Chaumuhani. I have received another telegram on this subject today, which I enclose.

2. Whatever the exact facts are, this will create great excitement in West Bengal. I do not know what is meant by firm action to be taken by us with the Pakistan authorities. We should, of course, approach them and send them a strong note. Otherwise what else we can do is not clear to me. It may be that the removal of some Pakistanis who had infiltrated into Tripura might have some connection with these new outbursts in Noakhali District. This shows how careful we must be in any action we take, as this must have inevitable reactions on the other side. I feel that sending over 3000 people in one or two

214. S.K. Chowdhry.

215. Choumuhani in Gundevia's note.

216. Y.D. Gundevia's response, 9 July 1962, seen by Nehru on 10 July 1962:

> "The communal outrages, to which Shri N.C. Chatterjee's telegram refers, took place in Choumuhani in Naokhali District on about 1st July. Our Deputy High Commissioner reported on this in a telegram dated 5th July and more details have been given in his subsequent telegram No.271 dated July 7, received today (placed below for reference), which Prime Minister has seen. I have spoken very strongly to Mr Hilaly about these incidents in Naokhali District— vide paragraph 10 of my note dated 9.7.1962, which is being separately sent to the Prime Minister. Our High Commissioner has spoken to President Ayub about these incidents, as Prime Minister will see from Shri Rajeshwar Dayal's telegram No. 48 dated 8th July, and we have asked our High Commission in Karachi to lodge a formal protest with Pakistan on the subject also. Pakistan maintains that these disturbances in Naokhali and also Comilla, are the result of communal propaganda spread by the recent Muslim evacuees from Tripura in these areas."MEA, File No. 8(17)/62-P. IV, Part VII, p. 408/corr.

217. Note, 10 July 1962, recorded in Pahalgam, Kashmir, for Y.D. Gundevia, the Commonwealth Secretary.

bunches was not a wise move on our part. There is something in the criticism made on the part of Pakistan that we should not take any such step without previously informing the authorities on the other side. Anyhow, we should be definitely cautious about any such further step she might take.

3. I have today written a note to the Foreign Secretary which I should like you to see. I have an idea that the next few months are rather critical in some ways in Pakistan. The great meeting that was held a day or two ago in Dacca is a definite challenge to President Ayub Khan. He can hardly ignore it. If he takes any action to suppress these people who took the lead in this meeting and otherwise, there is bound to be a major reaction in East Pakistan which will be reflected to some extent in West Pakistan also.

4. We must not, therefore, get entangled in local incidents but rather wait for the developments in Pakistan itself. Because of this, I rather doubt if it will be advisable for you to go abroad on a tour in the near future. However, we shall discuss this on my return.

72. To Humayun Kabir: Checking Groups Conflicts[218]

July 10, 1962

My dear Humayun,

I have received your letter of June 28th and the note attached to it on "Measures for checking group conflicts". Having a little more time to read long notes, I have done so at Pahalgam.

I agree broadly with what you have written in your note. To some extent, I have been saying the same thing on several occasions.

Among other things you have recommended the use of punitive police and punitive taxes. I have been of the same opinion but I have been told that this kind of thing cannot be done without some kind of an amendment of the Constitution.

I am glad that you have sent copies of your note to the members of our Cabinet and the Chief Ministers of States.[219]

Yours sincerely,
[Jawaharlal Nehru]

218. Letter to the Minister of Scientific Research and Cultural Affairs. Sent from Pahalgam, Kashmir.

219. See further item 75 and appendix 60.

73. To Lal Bahadur Shastri: Malerkotla's Nephew Returning to India[220]

July 12, 1962

My dear Lal Bahadur,

I sent you some time ago a letter from the Nawab of Malerkotla about his nephew coming to India. As the chief objection had been that his father was a member of the Pakistan Defence Forces, I referred this matter to the Defence Minister. I enclose his letter in reply.[221] I think you might adopt his suggestion, that is, a visa might be issued to the nephew and this could be renewed from time to time. Meanwhile we can watch his conduct here after he comes.

Yours affectionately,
[Jawaharlal Nehru]

74. To B.P. Chaliha: Pakistani Muslims Entering Assam[222]

July 12, 1962

My dear Chaliha,

Your letter of the 9th July about infiltration of Pakistani Muslims into Assam. The procedure you have indicated appears to me to be on the whole right, except that I do not understand how you can deport a person who was in Assam at the time of partition even though he might be considered a security risk.

We have recently had a difficult instance of action and reaction in such matters. From Tripura, about three thousand so-called Pakistani Muslims who were supposed to have entered illegally were deported and sent across the border. The Pakistan Government has raised the question that a large number of these people were not in Pakistan at all, but have been resident in Tripura for generations. Whether that is true or not, the fact remains that a sudden forced expulsion of about three thousand persons across the border has created a strong feeling all over the Eastern Pakistan which was fanned still further by the newspapers there. Apparently, as a result of this, communal troubles took

220. Letter to the Home Minister. MHA, File No. 10/40/62-F.III, p. 8/c. Also available in the JN Collection.

221. See appendix 59.

222. Letter to the Chief Minister of Assam.

place in many areas of Noakhali district and a number of Hindus were killed and many others stabbed.

Now the occurrence in Noakhali has excited the Hindus in West Bengal and the situation has become tense in various places. Thus action produces reaction which again produces its own another reaction and the situation gets worse. This may result in a large number of Hindus themselves wanting to leave Pakistan and come over to West Bengal as refugees. If this kind of thing goes on, the problem of large-scale migration will become terrible to handle.

Therefore we should take steps with great care. I agree with you that we should take up the cases of recent infiltration first. Broadly we should consider the cases of infiltration since 1952. Before that, it would be difficult to find out. Of course, if there is a bad case of infiltration after the partition but before 1952, that might also be taken up subject to adequate proof. You must remember that our facts will be challenged and it would not be quite enough for us to say that we were satisfied of our own position.

There is another aspect of this matter. You are entitled to push across the border a few persons if they have illegally entered. If however the numbers involved are large, then I think it is our duty to our neighbouring State to tell them how many are going to be sent and where and when. In fact, a list of persons should be sent also. Otherwise this creates law and order problem in the other State and all kinds of consequences arise.

Yours sincerely,
Jawaharlal Nehru

75. To Lal Bahadur Shastri: Humayun Kabir on Punitive Tax[223]

July 12, 1962

My dear Lal Bahadur,

I enclose a letter from Humayun Kabir.[224] He sent me a note which I believe you have seen. He suggests that we might discuss this matter at a meeting of the Cabinet. I am prepared to do this if you agree. You might have a note prepared for the Cabinet.

Yours affectionately,
Jawaharlal

223. Letter to the Home Minister. MHA, File No. 7/21/62-Poll. II., Sr. No. 2. See also item 72.

224. Appendix 60.

76. To Meer Noor Hussain: Nationalist Muslims Let Down[225]

July 15, 1962

Dear Meer Noor Hussain,

Your letter of the 11th July has come to my notice only this evening, 15th July at Nandi Hills. I would have been glad to meet you, but I fear it is not possible at Nandi as I am not giving interviews here. Also I shall be leaving Nandi on the 17th evening, and after spending the night at Bangalore, proceeding to Hyderabad.

I am sorry that you have a feeling that nationalist Muslims have been let down. To some extent this feeling is shared by many others who are not Muslims. The world changes, and one has to adapt oneself to changing conditions. A person who was a good fighter for a cause often finds it difficult to adjust himself to new conditions after the fight is over.

If you like, you can send me your poem, so that I can read it.

Yours sincerely,
[Jawaharlal Nehru]

77. To B.L. Jani: School for Adivasis[226]

July 16, 1962

Dear Shri Jani,

I have received your letter of the 9th July[227] and have read with pleasure of the good work done by the Sabarkantha Education Society. In particular, what the Society has done in conducting an Adivasi school under difficult conditions has pleased me. I wish the time would come when every child in India would have proper schools, mid-day meals and suitable uniforms. I am glad that some effort is being made to this end.

225. Letter; address 36 Asoka Road, Mysore. Sent from Nandi Hills.

226. Letter to the President of the Sabarkantha Educational Society, 1st Floor, Bhanabhai Chawl, Bhuleshwar, near Kabutarkhana, Bombay-2. PMO, File No. 9/2/62-PMP, Vol. V, Sr. No. 28-A. Also available in the JN Collection. Sent from Nandi Hills, Mysore State.

227. Appendix 55.

You have all my good wishes for the excellent work you are doing among the Adivasis, and I wish you success. It is good that Shri K.K. Shah[228] is taking personal interest in this school. This ought to go a long way in easing your difficulties.

Yours sincerely,
J. Nehru

78. To J.N. Hazarika: Assuaging Ruffled Feelings[229]

July 17, 1962

My dear Hazarika,

I have your letter of the 13th July.

There is no question of your not pleasing me with the work you did. My difficulty is that having appointed so many Ministers and Deputy Ministers, I cannot go beyond that number. Hence I suggested that you might become Parliamentary Secretary. That was the only reason. Otherwise I would have gladly tried to appoint you as a Deputy Minister.

Yours sincerely,
[Jawaharlal Nehru]

79. To N. Sanjiva Reddy: Reservations in Government Jobs[230]

July 18, 1962

My dear Sanjiva Reddy,

I have received your letter of the 9th July here in Hyderabad.[231] This relates to the reservation of Government posts on communal basis.

You have referred to the correspondence that took place between me and your predecessor, D. Sanjivayya.[232] I am enclosing copies of this correspondence. I am also enclosing a copy of my fortnightly letter to Chief Ministers dated

228. General Secretary, AICC.

229. Letter to Congress MP. Sent from Royal Cottage, Bangalore.

230. Letter to the Chief Minister of Andhra Pradesh. Sent from Hyderabad, Andhra Pradesh. PMO, File No. 33(76)/62-64-PMS, Sr. No. 17-A. Also available in the JN Collection.

231. Appendix 57.

232. See SWJN/SS/70/item 74 and 87, and SWJN/SS/72/item 88.

27th June 1961. Paragraphs 24, 25 and 26 deal with this question, and give my views on this subject.[233]

I find that you have written at length to our Home Minister[234] on the 9th July. You will no doubt have the question examined from the Constitutional or like points of view. But I am quite clear that, constitutional provisions apart, we must not encourage any reservation for castes, but rather give them, where necessary, on the basis of economic backwardness. On no account must we lower the standards in administration.

I should like to help backward classes as much as possible. The best way to do so is by giving them educational privileges.

I can understand some kind of reservation or help given in getting positions in the lower grade where there is likely to be relatively equal competence.

As far as I remember, the principle of helping backward individuals not by caste but by effective economic backwardness has been generally accepted by the Chief Ministers at one of our meetings. Of course, insofar as there are Constitutional provisions, we have to abide by them.

Yours sincerely,
Jawaharlal Nehru

(c) Laws and Administration

80. To Mehr Chand Khanna: A Khanna Nagar[235]

June 4, 1962

My dear Mehr Chand,
I see an advertisement on tops of buses about a new housing colony "Khanna Nagar". I do not know who has named it as such. I am told that the Khanna referred to is someone else and not you. Whoever it may be, it will lead people to think that you have agreed to your own name being used. In any event it is not right for people to give their names in this way. Can you not stop this kind of thing?[236]

Yours sincerely,
Jawaharlal Nehru

233. See SWJN/SS/69/item 5.
234. Lal Bahadur Shastri.
235. Letter to the Minister of Works, Housing and Supply. PMO, File No. 45(12)/59-69-PMS, Sr. No. 7-A.
236. For Khanna's reply, see appendix 18.

81. To Mohammad Habib: A Job for Mushtaque Ahmed[237]

June 8, 1962

My dear Habib,

I have your letter of June 6th. You need not worry about my health. I have got over my indisposition. It has warned me, however, that I have to remember my age now and take matters a little more easily than I have been doing.

I am glad to know that Mushtaque[238] has passed his MA examination. I do not quite know what to advise about the proposal that he might go to the United States or about the offer made by the UP Minister of Education.[239] You will be the best person to advise in regard to these matters.

Appointments in NEFA or Goa are, I believe, given to those who are in the Foreign Service already or in the Army. That is to say, those who have passed difficult tests previously apart from their University examination. NEFA is a peculiarly difficult place and there are not many who fit in there. I shall enquire about this matter, but I doubt if a new person from the University will be accepted. Practically all the appointments made by our Ministry or to my personal staff are through the UPSC.

I am having a cheque for Rs.400/- sent to you for Mushtaque Ahmed.

Yours sincerely,
[Jawaharlal Nehru]

82. To Zakir Husain: Rashtrapati Bhavan Reception[240]

June 9, 1962

My dear Zakir Husain,

Your letter of the 9th June. I think it is a god idea for you to meet the Members of Parliament and others at a reception that you might give at Rashtrapati Bhavan. I shall try to come to it on Friday 22nd June.

237. Letter to the Professor Emeritus of Aligarh Muslim University.

238. In 1960, there is a reference to Mushtaq Ahmad, an AMU student, by Nehru, see SWJN/ SS/64/ item 251 appendix 43.

239. No information of any offer by Jugal Kishore, the UP Minister of Education, is available.

240. Letter to the Vice President.

I agree with you that it is not desirable to mix up Diplomats with a crowd of MPs and others.

Yours sincerely,
[Jawaharlal Nehru]

83. To H.K. Bose: Calcutta High Court Centenary Celebrations[241]

June 10, 1962

My dear Chief Justice,
Thank you for your letter of June 4th and your invitation to attend the centenary of the Calcutta High Court on July 1st. This is indeed a great occasion worthy of celebration. The Calcutta High Court has played a significant part in India's history during the last hundred years and its story is full of eminent men whose names have impressed themselves on generation after generation. I am glad that the President is going to inaugurate the celebrations.

I would have gladly accepted your invitation but, owing to my recent illness, I have been told not to travel about too much, more especially during this season. I hope you will forgive me, therefore, for not coming. But I send you all my good wishes on this occasion and my hopes that the Calcutta High Court will continue to occupy a high place in our country, which it has done in the past, and thus serve the public good.

Yours sincerely,
[Jawaharlal Nehru]

84. To Subhadra Joshi: Inquiring about Gossip[242]

June 10, 1962

My dear Subhadra,
I had your note a few days ago. I had not received any complaint of you from Tarkeshwari Sinha[243] or anyone else. She came to me and was much upset about

241. Letter to the Chief Justice of the Calcutta High Court.
242. Letter to Congress Lok Sabha MP from Balrampur ; address: 14 Rajendra Prasad Road, New Delhi.
243. Deputy Minister in the Ministry of Finance.

talk in the lobbies of Parliament about her. I asked her who was indulging in this talk. She said that she did not know definitely but she mentioned three names of persons who might have talked about this matter. Among the three was your name. But there was no accusation of you in any sense.

I asked Satya Narayan Sinha[244] to find out from you and others about this matter. That was all. I do not think you need worry about it.

Yours sincerely,
[Jawaharlal Nehru]

85. To Swami Harinarayananad: Handling Corruption[245]

जून 10, 1962

प्रिय स्वामी जी,
आपका पत्र 1 जून का मुझे मिला। आप जो भ्रष्टाचार और रिश्वतखोरी का लिखते हैं उसकी हमें बहुत फिकर है, और उसके रोकने के लिये कई बातें की हैं। उन से कुछ सफलता भी मिली हैं लेकिन यह बात सही है कि सरकारी कर्मचारियों के प्रयास काफी नहीं हैं। भारत सेवक समाज और भारत साधु समाज इसमें बहुत कुछ कर सकते हैं। मेरी ठीक समझ में नहीं आता कि एक बोर्ड बनाने से क्या विशेष लाभ होगा।

मैं इस बारे में राज्यों के मुख्य मंत्रियों को लिखता रहता हूं और फिर लिखूंगा।

दूसरी बात जो आपने लिखी है गुटबन्दी की, उसमें भी मैं आपसे सहमत हूं। हमारी कोशिश जारी है उसे कम करने की।

आपका
[जवाहरलाल नेहरु]

[Translation begins:

Dear Swamiji,
I received your letter of 1 June. You have mentioned corruption and bribes, we are really worried about it and have taken measures to prevent it. These efforts have been successful to some extent but it is also correct that only efforts of the Government employees are not enough. Bharat Sevak Samaj and Bharat

244. Minister of Parliamentary Affairs.

245. Letter to the Secretary, Bharat Sadhu Samaj; address: L 26, Connaught Circus, New Delhi.

Sadhu Samaj can do a lot in this. I do not understand how the formation of a board will be helpful in this.

I have been writing to State Chief Ministers about this and shall continue to write.

The second point mentioned by you is about groupism, I agree with that also. Our efforts to reduce it are continiuing.

Yours sincerely,
Jawaharlal Nehru

Translation ends]

86. To Mani Ram Bagri: Birla House[246]

जून 11, 1962

प्रिय मनीरामजी,

आपका 6 जून का पत्र मुझे मिला।

मैंने पहले भी आपको लिखा है कि बिड़लाजी के मकान के बारे में हम लोगों ने बहुत विचार किया था, और हम इस नतीजे पर पहुचे थे कि उसका हमें जबरन लेना या एक्वायर करना उचित नहीं होगा। सरदार पटेल, मौलाना आज़ाद वगैरह सभी की यही राय थी, और यह भी ख्य़ाल हुआ कि गांधीजी इस बात को पंसद न करते। जो कुछ हमें स्मारक के तौर पर बनाना है, हम अलग बनायें। गांधीजी हिन्दुस्तान भर में बहुत मकानों में ठहरे हैं, और हर जगह यह सवाल उठ सकता है। यह सही है कि बिड़लाजी का मकान ख़ास था क्योंकि आखिर में वहीं ठहरे थे वे और वहीं उनका देहान्त हुआ। फिर भी यही राय आपस के मशवरे के बाद हुई थी। मैं समझता हूं कि उस राय को बदलने कीकोई इस समय ज़रूरत नहीं है।

बिड़लाजी के मकान को लेकर इसमें कोई और काम करें, यह भी मुझे पसंद नहीं। एक दफा बिड़लाजी ने मुझ से कहा था कि अगर मैं उसको प्रधान मंत्री के रहने के लिए पसंद करूं, तो उसको देने को तैयार हैं। मैंने उनका शुक्रिया अदा किया और उनसे कहा कि यह बात मुझे पसंद नहीं है। मैं उस मकान में रहना बिल्कुल ठीक नहीं समझता था क्योंकि उसके साथ बंधे हुये विचार और ही थे।

आपने लिखा है कि पुलिस ने आपको वहां जाने से रोक दिया। इसकी वजह यही हो सकती है कि आपकी तरफ से घोषणा हुई थी कि आप वहां जबरन जायेंगे। मुझे मालूम

246. Letter to Lok Sabha MP, Socialist; address: Hisar.

नहीं है लेकिन आम तौर से कोई भी उनके बाग़ के उस हिस्से में जा सकता है जहां उनपर गोली चली थी। मकान में जाने पर शायद रूकावटें हों।[247]

आपका
[जवाहरलाल नेहरु]

[Translation begins:

Dear Mani Ramji,
I received your letter of 6 June.

I had written to you earlier also that we had discussed in detail about Birlaji's house, and had come to the conclusion that it would not be proper to forcibly take it or acquire it. Sardar Patel, Maulana Azad and all others held this view; another consideration was that Gandhiji himself would not have liked it. Whatever memorial we want to make, we should make separately. Gandhiji stayed in so many houses in the whole of India, and everywhere this issue may arise. It is true that Birlaji's house is special because it was here he last stayed and died. Still, this is what was decided after discussion. I feel that there is no need to change that stance now.

Should there be some other activity in Birlaji's house; that also I do not like. Once Birlaji told me, if I were interested in using it as Prime Minister's residence, he was willing to give it. I thanked him and told him that I did not like the idea. I do not think it was proper to live in that house because the thoughts associated with it were different.

You have written that Police stopped you from going in there. The reason for this could be because you had announced you would forcibly enter the place. I am not sure but normally anybody can go to the garden where he was shot. There might be restrictions in going into the house.[248]

Yours sincerely,
Jawaharlal Nehru

Translation ends]

247. See also item 95.
248. See fn 247 in this section.

87. To Raghunath Singh: President's Pension[249]

June 12, 1962

My dear Raghunath Singh,

I have your letter signed by you and some of our colleagues in Parliament. I am afraid I do not agree with you. You suggest withdrawing the President's Pension Bill. This Bill was passed long ago and a slight amendment is being made to it now.[250]

This is to give him Rs 2,000/- a month for secretarial assistance and also free medical treatment. I do not think there is anything derogatory to our President in this. This addition is hardly a pension. It is a convenience for doing some writing work. Any person who is President of India deserves certain facilities.

We are not competing with the USA or any other country. We are trying to do something, which I think is correct and which certainly does not affect in any way the high reputation of Rajendra Babu.

Apart from this, having announced this amendment of the Bill, it would be very improper for us to withdraw it now. The fact that an ex-President might take to political activities against the Government is not a sufficient reason to deny him these facilities, which are after all not much.

Yours sincerely,
[Jawaharlal Nehru]

88. To Rajendra Prasad: No Pensions for Governors[251]

June 13, 1962

My dear Rajendra Babu,

Thank you for your letter of June 10th in which you refer to some provision being made for Governors.[252] As you have been good enough to write to me on this subject, I shall consult some of my senior colleagues.

I must confess, however, that I find it a little difficult to agree to the idea of giving any kind of a pension, or even a provident fund contribution, to Governors after they retire. Governors can take part in political life or even

249. Letter to Congress Lok Sabha MP; address: 15 Canning Lane, New Delhi.

250. This was to amend the President's Pension Act, 1951, and was moved in the Lok Sabha by the Home Minister Lal Bahadur Shastri on 18 June 1962.

251. Letter to the former President; address: Sadaqat Ashram, Patna.

252. Appendix 25.

professional life after retirement. It will, I think, be somewhat unbecoming for ex-Presidents to do so. We have in fact one instance, that of Rajaji, who has taken active part in political life. But normally, I take it, this will not be so.

I feel that any proposal to give a pension to Governors in any form would probably not be popular at all. In fact, I remember discussing this matter once with a number of MPs, and they were strongly opposed to this. It is possible for a Governor to save a part of his salary if he so chooses. But to put him in the category of those having provident fund, seems rather odd.

You refer to one Governor who has come to Parliament. I suppose you mean Ramakrishna Rao. As a matter of fact, he was offered an extension of his term so that he could complete five years in the UP. But he preferred coming to Parliament. We did not do so to make provision for him after retirement.

If Governors are to be pensioned, then some people might argue in favour of Ministers also. As you know, there are a large number of Ministers in India. I do not know that Ministers in any country are given any kind of pension.

Anyhow, I shall consult some of my colleagues and let you have their reactions.[253]

Yours sincerely,
Jawaharlal Nehru

89. To Cabinet Colleagues: Benefits for Presidents and Governors[254]

I enclose a letter from Dr Rajendra Prasad and a copy of my reply to him. I really do not see how we can make any provision for pension, or even provident fund, in the case of Governors. I have no doubt that this will be disliked by large numbers of people both in Parliament and outside.

2. In fact, I have received a letter from some Congress Members of Parliament objecting to the amending Bill we have introduced for some additional payments to the ex-Presidents. I think that Bill is not only right, but desirable, and I have told the objecting Members so.

253. Nehru's next letter, item 98.

254. Note, 13 June 1962, to Morarji Desai, Jagjivan Ram, Gulzarilal Nanda and Lal Bahadur Shastri.

90. To Kashi Ram Gupta: Party Symbols[255]

14th June, 1962

Dear Shri Kashi Ram,

I have your letter of the 13th June.[256] I did not send an answer to your previous letter of the 31st May because I felt that there was nothing worthwhile that I would say.

I am afraid I do not think that your suggestions are feasible. I cannot enter into a long discussion of these subjects.

If you have any practical suggestions for keeping down the election expenses, we shall gladly consider them.

Yours sincerely,
[Jawaharlal Nehru]

91. To Paresh Nath Kayal: Leave Me to do My Job[257]

14th June, 1962

Dear Paresh Nathji,

I have your letter of the 12th June.

I am afraid I cannot carry on an argument with you about persons I appoint and those whom I do not. This involves many issues including personal issues which are not suited for discussion. I have to discharge my duties according to the best of my ability.

Yours sincerely,
[Jawaharlal Nehru]

92. Narmada Valley Authority Date[258]

I am prepared to accept this Short Notice question. It may be answered tomorrow, 19th June, after Question Hour.

255. Letter to Independent MP from Alwar, Rajasthan ; address: 137 Constitution House, New Delhi. PMO, File No. 2(397)/61-70-PM, Vol. II, Sr. No. 106-A.
256. Appendix 33.
257. Letter to Congress MP from Joynagar, West Bengal; address: 28 North Avenue, New Delhi.
258. Note, 18 June 1962.

Proposed Answer:

At a meeting held on the 12th February 1962 with the representatives of the Governments of Maharashtra, Rajasthan, Madhya Pradesh and Gujarat, it was suggested that Narmada Valley Authority should be set up. In order to examine this proposal in all its aspects in consultation with the Governments concerned, Shri H.M. Patel[259] has been appointed Officer on Special Duty. He will work out the details of this scheme and the Authority to be set up and also to suggest necessary lines of legislation that will have to be undertaken to establish the proposed Narmada Development Authority. He will work in an honorary capacity and will only charge travel and other actual expenses incurred by him in preparing the report.[260]

(To be answered by Minister of State)

93. To E. Nageshwar Rao: Free Postage for President[261]

June 18, 1962

Dear Shri Nageshwar Rao,
I have your letter of the 14th June. I do not see the importance of giving the privilege of sending mails of the President of India free of postage. This may save a very small sum to the President. But it is not worthwhile spending a lot of time and energy on legislation etc. over such a trivial matter.

Yours sincerely,
[Jawaharlal Nehru]

259. Former Chairman, LIC, and now Chairman of Charutar Vidya Mandal.
260. See also item 96.
261. Letter; address: Raghavendra Rao's Bungalow, Tilaknagar, Bilaspur.

94. IFAS Appointments and Promotions[262]

[Note, 21 June 1962, by M. J. Desai, FS, begins]

Our Parliamentary Secretaries Sarvshri Ering[263] and Jamir[264] saw me this afternoon. Ering gave me a brief note which I attach. This refers to the case of the IFAS officer who has been reverted after a year's officiating service in Grade I and who has made a representation, copy of which we received yesterday.

2. There is some confusion about the operation of the seniority rules promulgated in 1956 when the first batch of recruits was taken and the rules promulgated in 1959-60 when the second batch of IFAS recruits was taken. On the face of it, it seems absurd that a recruit who joined in 1960 should take seniority over a recruit who joined in 1956. This matter was debated in the Indian Frontier Administrative Service Association, Shillong, and their representation in this matter will be coming to us.

3. In the meanwhile, so far as this particular officer's case is concerned, I want a quick decision so that there may be no general feeling of frustration amongst the IFAS officers, particularly the few officers we have from the tribal areas. Shri Ering mentioned to me that there is a vacancy of a Political Officer at Pasighat in which this particular officer could be posted before his leave expires without causing any dislocation. Will JS (E) please study the case and bring it up quickly?

M.J. Desai
21.6.1962

[Note, 21 June 1962, by M. J. Desai, FS, ends]

262. Noting, 21-23 June 1962, between Foreign Secretary and Nehru, and letter from Parliamentary Secretary in the MEA. MHA, (MEA), File No. 23/27/60, NEFA, p. 38.

263. D. Ering, Nominated MP from NEFA, and Parliamentary Secretary attached to the Minister in the External Affairs.

264. S.C. Jamir, Nominated MP from Naga Hiils-Tuensang Area, and Parliamentary Secretary attached to the Minister in the External Affairs.

[Letter from D. Ering to M.J. Desai][265]

23rd June, 1962

My dear [M.J. Desai],

I am writing this in continuation of my discussion with you on the 21st June, 1962, in your room where my friends, Shri R.K. Sing MP,[266] and Shri S.C. Jamir, MP, Parliamentary Secretary, were also present.

I have heard that Shri Shaiza, our experienced Tribal Officer, who has been serving with distinction and officiating in grade I of the IFAS for over a year has been brought down and the officer out of disgrace has tendered resignation and an officer who has been confirmed only recently in grade II has been promoted in his place. It was because I thought such injustice might be done that I had asked a question in Parliament on 5th May, 1961, unstarred Q. No. 4665. It appears now that some definite injustice has been done and you may like to look into this matter as it is likely to have demoralising effect on all IFAS Officers.

When I asked this question I was aware that the Home Ministry had in December, 1959 laid down a general principle that Officers of an earlier batch would be senior to Officers recruited by later Selection Board. These instructions were disseminated by the Ministry in 1959-60 and also the NEFA Secretariat, Shillong. Therefore IFAS Officers of 1956 batch did not feel it necessary to represent to Government. I believe that another Officer had represented on these lines but his application was not forwarded, presumeably because the authority were satisfied that the Officer concerned would not be adversely affected.

As regards Shri Shaiza, I have learnt that not only the NEFA Administration but also the local Mompas of that area have greatly appreciated the work done by him within the very short period in that area. By abolishing all the evil customs left behind by the Tibetan Government of the old days, he has already won the love and admiration of the people of Tawang and has thereby brought the people of this distant and important border area into further integration with our country. I have also heard that the local people and the Tawang Monastery were much upset to hear the news of Shri Shaiza's sudden transfer from Tawang and that the monasteries have already sent their Representations to the Adviser to the Governor of Assam and also to the Prime Minister at Delhi, requesting for posting Shri Shaiza back to Tawang.

265. MHA, (MEA), File No. 23/27/60. NEFA, Vol. II, pp. 134-135.

266. No such person appears in the official lists. However, the *Lok Sabha Who's Who 1962* (New Delhi: Lok Sabha Secretariat, August 1962) has R. Keishing as an MP. This is probably the R.K. Sing.

I will be grateful therefore if you will kindly respect the request of the people and if possible, post Shri Shaiza back to Tawang.

I am taking this trouble myself and also giving you this trouble, to have a better understanding between our people and the Government of India.

With …

Yours [sincerely]
D. Ering

[Nehru's Note, 23 June 1962, for M. J. Desai, begins][267]

Shri D. Ering, MP, came to see me today and showed me a copy of a letter which he had written to you about an officer in NEFA, Shri Shaiza. You must have the original letter. Nevertheless I am sending you the copy.

2. I gather that Shri D. Ering discussed this matter with and you promised to look into it. From the facts given in Shri Ering's letter, the matter does require examination. General rules are not always applicable to the special circumstances of NEFA and to tribal people.[268]

Jawaharlal Nehru
23.6.1962

FS

[Nehru's Note, 23 June 1962, for M.J. Desai, ends]

95. To Mani Ram Bagri: Use of Birla House[269]

जून 23, 1962

प्रिय मनीरामजी,

आपका 22 जून का पत्र मिला। मैं आपको लिख चुका हूं कि श्री घनश्यामदास बिड़ला ने बिड़ला हाऊस को मुझे एक खास काम के लिये देने को कहा था। वह खास काम था कि

267. MHA, File No. 23/27/60, NEFA, Vol. II, p. 37.

268. R.H.M. D'Silva's note of 25/6 explaining the case of Shaiza is available in NMML. (MHA (MEA), File No. 23/27/60-NEFA, Vol. II, pp. 39-42).

269. Letter to Socialist MP of Lok Sabha from Hisar.

इसको प्रधान मंत्री के रहने का स्थान बनाया जाये। यह बात मुझे पसंद नहीं आई। इस लिये वह तजवीज़ गिर गई।[270]

आपका
[जवाहरलाल नेहरु]

[Translation begins:

June 23, 1962

Dear Mani Ramji,
I received your letter of 22 June. I have written to you that Shri Ghanshyamdas Birla had offered to give Birla House for a particular purpose, which was to make it Prime Minister's House. I did not like it. So the offer fell through.[271]

Yours sincerely,
Jawaharlal Nehru

Translation ends]

96. To H.M. Patel: Questions on Appointment[272]

June 26, 1962

My dear Patel,
I have your letter of the 21st June. The answers to the Questions asked in Parliament were based on a brief that the Ministry concerned had sent us. This brief definitely stated that the four Governments concerned had agreed to your being appointed. They did not say clearly whether they had appointed you or not. After the Questions were over, I asked them to make this point clear, and they told me that the actual appointment was by the Ministry of Irrigation & Power, which was based on the recommendations of the four Governments.[273]

As for the Report of the Union Public Service Commission in connection with the Chagla Enquiry, I was aware of it. But at previous stages, reports were

270. See item 86.
271. See fn 270 in this section.
272. Letter to former Chairman, LIC, and now chairman of Charutar Vidya Mandal; address: Charutar Vidya Mandal, Vallabh Vidyanagar, Gujarat.
273. See also item 92.

somewhat different, and also one of the members of the Union Public Service Commission had attached a minute of dissent, as you must know.[274]

I was anxious to give the exact facts as far as I knew them. I do not think that any fact was incorrectly stated, though it is possible that some additional facts might also have been mentioned. I am sorry if anything was said on our behalf which was not correct. Most of the Questions were supplementary ones, and had to be answered on the spot.

Yours sincerely,
[Jawaharlal Nehru]

97. To Suresh C. Bose: Report Accepted[275]

June 26, 1962

Dear Suresh Babu,

Your letter of the 15th June. As you must know, Shri Shah Nawaz Khan,[276] you and another person were appointed to enquire into this matter. The majority report of this Committee has been placed before Parliament and published. We accepted the majority report. This report gives a number of facts.[277]

Our own information conveyed to us by our Ambassadors has been to confirm the facts stated in that report.

In addition to this, the mere lapse of time goes to confirm the conclusion arrived at.

Yours sincerely,
[Jawaharlal Nehru]

274. After the Chagla Committee report on LIC investment case was submitted in February 1958, charges were framed against H.M. Patel, G.R. Kamath and L.S. Vaidyanathan. The Vivian Bose Enquiry Board was constituted on 5 May 1958 with Justice Vivian Bose and two others to enquire into the charges. The three officers concernced submitted their representations to the Board. As required by service rules, their cases were referred to the UPSC, which exonerated H.M. Patel. However, one member of the Commission, J. Sivashunmugam Pillai, dissented. See SWJN/SS/41/pp. 415-416 and SWJN/SS/42/pp. 312, 318-319. See also https://archive.org/stream/in.gazette.e.1959.196/E-2029-1959-0064-91227_djvu.txt, accessed on 21 June 2018.
275. Letter to the elder brother of Subhash Chandra Bose; address: Garia, P.O. Garia Distt., 24 Parganas.
276. Of the INA and the Deputy Minister in the Ministry of Railways.
277. This refers to the Netaji Enquiry Committee, headed by Shah Nawaz Khan. Its reported in August 1956, see SWJN/SS/34/pp. 459-460.

98. To Rajendra Prasad: Provident Fund for Governors[278]

June 30, 1962

My dear Rajendra Babu,

You will remember writing to me on June 10th about some provision being made for Governors.[279] You suggested that some kind of Provident Fund arrangement should be made to which the Governors might contribute Rs 500/- per month.

I felt some difficulty in agreeing to this proposal, but I decided to consult some of my senior colleagues on this subject. I have now done so. They are all of opinion that the ordinary type of Provdent Fund will not be suitabale for Governors and will raise many difficulties. There may, however, be a non-contributory Provident Fund applicable to those who wish to participate. In effect, this is voluntary saving of an agreed sum per month. As a matter of fact, it is probably simpler for the Governors to save this money themselves instead of going through the rather cumbrous process of having a non-contributory Provident Fund arrangement. In any event, this will have to be a purely voluntary effort. To provide by law a compulsory saving by Governors appears to be insppropriate.

Yours sincerely,
[Jawaharlal Nehru]

99. To Swaran Singh: Appointments in Railways[280]

July 3, 1962

My dear Swaran Singh,

I have just been looking at a file in which it was proposed to appoint two persons as General Managers of Indian Railways. As these appointments involved the supersession of eight officers, the Ministry of Railways was requested to forward the confidential records of all these officers. The Railway Board refused to send them. Thereafter the Cabinet Secretary[281] again asked for them as the matter had to be decided ultimately by the Appointments Committee of the Cabinet. Again the Chairman of the Railway Board refused to send them. Ultimately

278. Letter to the former President.

279. See appendix 25 and for Nehru's response, see item 88.

280. Letter to the Minister of Railways.

281. S.S. Khera.

a long explanation was sent about these supersessions. The Home Minister thereafter agreed to the appointment of the two officers recommended, and I have also passed the file.

I am merely writing to you to express my surprise at the way the Railway Board is treating the Cabinet and consistently refused to send the confidential records of certain officers. It seems to me that this was very improper,

I have given more thought to what you spoke to me about last evening. The more I think of it the less I feel that Karnail Singh[282] should be given a further extension. From the public point of view, the Railways have not done very well for some time past, and the Railway Board and more especially the Chairman of the Board must be considered in some way responsible for this. I do not think, therefore, that an extension to Karnail Singh is desirable. If it is particularly necessary, a very short period of about two or three weeks might be given, but I do not see what purpose will be served by such a short extension.

Yours sincerely,
[Jawaharlal Nehru]

100. To S. Radhakrishnan: B.C. Roy, Pulla Reddy[283]

July 5, 1962

My dear President,

Thank you for your letter of July 4th which has reached me here at Pahalgam today.

Bidhan Roy's death has been a special shock. Among his many virtues, he was large-hearted to an extent which is rare. It was good of him to remember me on the eve of his death. I have been trying to follow his advice and am here for that purpose.

It was largely because of his advice to me that I refrained from going to Calcutta when the news of his death arrived. I should like, however, to go there before long.

If you feel that a small house built in Rashtrapati Bhavan Estate, near the main building, would be more convenient for you, I am sure there can be no objection to it. You will decide as you think best.[284]

282. Chairman, Railway Board, April 1960-August 1962.

283. Letter to the President. Sent from Pahalgam, Kashmir.

284. Further on this point, see appendix 54.

You have mentioned Pulla Reddy[285] in your letter. I take it that this in connection with a Governorship. I hope, to discuss this matter with you when I return to Delhi. I hope to be back on the 11th July.

Indira and her two sons left Pahalgam this afternoon for a visit to the cave of Amar Nath [Amarnath]. She hopes to return in three or four days' time.

Jawaharlal Nehru

101. To K. Ram: MPs' Lodging[286]

Please reply to this letter from some MPs in which they complain about he allotment of houses to MPs. Tell them that I am very sorry that this allotment is not to their liking. I do not normally interfere in these matters as the allotment is in charge of the Housing Committee of Parliament. I am, however, sending their letter to the Chairman of the Housing Committee.

2. Please send the letter to the Chairman of the Housing Committee. You can find out from the Lok Sabha who the Chairman is.

102. Note to Y.D. Gundevia: Rozario's Qualifications[287]

I am unable to express any positive opinion about Dr Rozario's[288] competence for the post. There appear to be two opinions about it. When, however, the recent case against him in the law court came to my notice, I expressed my opinion that, in view of this case particularly, it was not desirable then to send him back to India House.

2. Thereafter Prof. Thacker spoke to me on this subject, and as far as I remember pressed for a short extension of Shri Rozario in his present office. I agreed to this. I do not remember what that short extension was. Probably it was about six months. The reason given I think was that there was no other suitable person to be found immediately to take his place.

3. It is clear that the Scientific Adviser must be a person of scientific eminence. I do not know it Dr Rozario is a scientist or not. These papers might be seen by Prof. Thacker and then referred to the Education Ministry.

285. Secretary, Ministry of Defence.

286. Note, 6 July 1962, to the PPS, from Pahalgam (Kashmir).

287. Note, 10 July 1962, to the Commonwealth Secretary from Pahalgam (Kashmir).

288. A.M. D'Rozario was Joint Secretary (Culture) in 1960 (SWJN/Vol 61); and Joint Secretary (Education) in 1968. See *The Quarterly Review of Historical Studies*, Vol XIV 1974-75, p. 11.

103. To V.K. Krishna Menon: Maneckshaw Case[289]

July 12, 1962

My dear Krishna,

I have had now for quite a long time the file dealing with the Maneckshaw case. I think we should dispose of this.[290] If you are free, could you come and see me at my office at 4 o'clock tomorrow, 13th July?

Yours affectionately,
[Jawaharlal Nehru]

104. Note to Morarji Desai: Officers' Salaries[291]

I sent your letter to me of the 26th June about the pay of Indian Commissioned Officers, to the Defence Minister. He has replied to me and I enclose his letter.

I think the arguments he has advanced are worthy of consideration. In any event, I do not think it will be right to vary the pay in regard to an individual officer who has been promoted, after that promotion. I doubt also that the Pay Code should apply to the heads of the Defence Services.

I suggest therefore that you might accept the recommendations made by the Defence Minister.

105. To Humayun Kabir: M.S. Thacker for Planning Commission[292]

July 13, 1962

My dear Humayun,

As you must know, A.N. Khosla who is a Member of the Planning Commission, has been selected as Governor of Orissa. I propose that Prof. Thacker[293] might

289. Letter to the Defence Minister.

290. Krishna Menon instituted an inquiry to go into the "anti-national" activities of S.H.F.J. Manekshaw, who was Commandant, Defence Services Staff College, Wellington. See also SWJN/SS/75/item 172.

291. Note, 12 July 1962, to the Minister of Finance.

292. Letter to the Minister for Scientific Research and Cultural Affairs. PMO, File No. 17 (189)/60-65-PMS, Sr. No. 32-A. Also available in NMML, Humayun Kabir, File No. 5/1958-62, Auto and the JN Collection.

293. M.S. Thacker, Director-General, CSIR. See also item 351.

be made a Member of the Planning Commission in his place. I think he will be a very suitable person for Planning Commission. Apart from other factors, he is connected in some way or other with the Planning Commission.

Khosla is leaving the Planning Commission at the end of this month. If you agree, Prof. Thacker can join from the beginning of September. I would have spoken to Prof. Thacker myself, but I am going out of Delhi tomorrow morning for a week. Perhaps you can mention this to him and say that I shall see him on my return to Delhi about the 20th or 21st of this month.[294]

Yours sincerely,
Jawaharlal Nehru

106. For Asoke Sen: Merging Posts of Law Minister and Attorney-General[295]

I am sorry for the delay in dealing with this matter. This file has been with me for nearly three months.

2. I agree with you that we should try to remove the anomaly. This should be done before the next Attorney-General is to be appointed.

3. You suggest, as far as I can gather, that the two posts, i.e. of the Law Minister's and the Attorney-General's, should be combined and made into one. I suppose this will involve an amendment of the Constitution. I agree with you that something should be done. I should like you to put up precise proposals for consideration of the Cabinet.

4. I see that the Attorney-General has replied to the letter sent from your Ministry. This is unsatisfactory. It is not clear to me what we can do about it now. But, as you say, the least the Attorney-General can do is to issue a contradiction to the press stating that he has not been correctly reported by *Bharat Jyoti* or *Blitz*.

294. For Kabir's reply, see appendix 63.

295. Note, 13 July 1962, for the Law Minister.

107. To Lal Bahadur Shastri: Awadh Royal Family[296]

July 13, 1962

My dear Lal Bahadur,

I have just had an interview with Yusuf Mirza,[297] who styles himself prince, a descendant of the Avadh royal family. With him came "Prince" Sultan Hassan Mirza who is said to be a grandson of Wajid Ali Shah. I gathered from them that they are going to see you and present a memorandum, about the members of the Avadh family, asking for bigger pensions and allowances. I have not seen this memorandum and do not express any opinion on what they say.

But just before I met them I received a letter from one of the lady members of the Avadh family, Imtiaz Begum. This letter makes a fierce attack on Yusuf Mirza. I thought you might be interested in seeing this letter and, therefore, I am enclosing it.

Yours affectionately,
[Jawaharlal Nehru]

108. To Dewan Mohan Lall: About Wanting a Job[298]

July 15, 1962

Dear Dewan Mohan Lall,

I have your letter of July 10 and have read the various statements to the press, copies of which you have been good enough to send me. I have read them with interest.

I am sorry to learn that you are in difficulties from what you call your protracted inactivity. Inactivity can always be got over by a person with some interests. But as for my finding some work for you, I am afraid this is beyond my capacity. I am strictly limited in appointing anybody to a post by our rules and regulations. Everyone who is appointed by me has to come through the Union Public Service Commission as well as to pass various tests. Then there is the age limit. So you will appreciate how difficult it is for me to help you in finding some suitable work.

Yours sincerely,
[Jawaharlal Nehru]

296. Letter to the Home Minister.

297. Grandson of Wajid Ali Shah. See also SWJN/SS/75/item 66.

298. Letter: address: Lakhan Kotri, Ajmer. Sent from Nandi Hills.

109. To M.J. Khaiser: Management for Diplomats[299]

July 16, 1962

Dear Shri Khaiser,

You wrote a letter to me on June 24. I am sorry for the delay in answering it.

Management Education has attracted a good deal of thought from us. Only recently I was at Srinagar where a high level seminar was being held on this subject.

If you wish, you can send me your draft note on the subject. But I do not see how that will be particularly suitable for Indian Foreign Service people. Anyhow I shall be glad to see it and find out how far it suits the IFS.

Yours sincerely,
[Jawaharlal Nehru]

110. To Mehta Puran Chand: Defence Personnel in Service better than Veterans[300]

July 18, 1962

Dear Shri Puran Chand,

I have your letter of the 14th July. I am afraid I do not agree with you wholly in your analysis of the situation. We are quite alert to meet any danger that might come our way.

Our Defence personnel are competent and well trained. They are more up-to-date than retired officers.

Should you wish to see me, you can see me when I am in Delhi, then I can find some time for an interview.

Yours sincerely,
[Jawaharlal Nehru]

299. Letter; address: 70 Marredpally, Secunderabad. Sent from Nandi Hills, Mysore State.

300. Letter to advocate ; address 1583 Dariba Kalan, Delhi. Sent from Rashtrapati Nilayam, Hyderabad.

(d) States

(i) Andhra Pradesh

111. To S. Radhakrishnan: Visit to Hyderabad[301]

July 10, 1962

My dear President,

Thank you for your letter of July 8th. I am returning to Srinagar tomorrow and the day after I go Delhi. I hope to go to Bangalore on the 14th morning. If all goes well, I shall come to Hyderabad to pay you a visit on the 18th, but I am not quite sure of the date yet.

I shall be happy to meet Rajendra Babu,[302] the Governor[303] and the Chief Minister[304] and any others that you think necessary.

Indira will not be going with me to Bangalore. But probably Vijaya Lakshmi will accompany me.

Yours affectionately,
Jawaharlal Nehru

112. To Bhimsen Sachar: No At Home in Hyderabad[305]

July 11, 1962

My dear Sachar,

Your letter of the 9th July.[306] It is my intention to pay a visit to Hyderabad from the Nandi Hills for a day or two. In effect the visit is to the President who will be there then.

I do not think it will be appropriate for you to give an At Home in my honour on this occasion. When the President is there, others should not be given any

301. Letter to the President. PMS, File No. 8(226)62-PMP. Sent from Pahalgam, Kashmir.
302. Rajendra Prasad, the previous President.
303. Bhimsen Sachar.
304. N. Sanjiva Reddy.
305. Letter to the Governor of Andhra Pradesh. PMS, File No. 8(226)62-PMP. Sent from Chashmashahi Guest House, Srinagar. Also available in the JN Collection.
306. Letter not reproduced. Copy available in the NMML.

prominence. As for my programme in Hyderabad, it will entirely depend on the pleasure of the President.

Yours sincerely,
[Jawaharlal Nehru]

113. To N. Sanjiva Reddy: No Engagements in Hyderabad[307]

July 14, 1952

My dear Sanjiva Reddy,
As you probably know, I am paying a brief visit to Hyderabad to see the President. In fact, my visit is mainly for the purpose of seeing him. I hope to reach Hyderabad on the 18th July morning at about 10.30. I shall presumably stay with the President. Vijaya Lakshmi Pandit will be with me.

I shall leave Hyderabad on the 20th morning at about 9 a.m. (Begumpet).

I am not anxious to have any engagements in Hyderabad, but if you wish me to meet your colleagues in the Ministry and some other workers, I shall gladly do so.

Yours sincerely,
Jawaharlal Nehru

114. To S. Radhakrishnan: Hyderabad Visit[308]

July 14, 1962

My dear President,
This is to confirm that I expect to reach Hyderabad at 10.30 in the morning on the 18th July. I shall be leaving on the 20th morning at 9 a.m. (Begumpet).

Vijaya Lakshmi Pandit will be accompanying me.

Yours affectionately,
Jawaharlal Nehru

307. Letter to the Chief Minister of Andhra Pradesh. Sent from Royal Cottage, Bangalore. PMS, File No. 8(226) 62-PMP. Also available in the JN Collection.

308. Letter to the President. Sent from Royal Cottage, Bangalore. PMS, File No. 8(226) 62-PMP.

(ii) Bihar

115. To Binodanand Jha: Avoid Shyama Prasad Singh[309]

June 2, 1962

My dear Binodanandji,
I enclose a copy of a letter I have received from Ram Vilas Sharma.[310] I think what he says is right and it would not be desirable to offer any post to Sri Shyama Prasad Singh.[311]

Yours sincerely,
Jawaharlal Nehru

116. To Binodanand Jha: Fertiliser Factory at Barauni[312]

June 25, 1962

My dear Binodanandji,
I have your letter of June 20 in which you draw attention to the necessity of setting up a nitrogenous fertiliser factory near the Barauni refinery. I am forwarding it to the Planning Commission who will, no doubt, give your suggestion full consideration.

Yours sincerely,
Jawaharlal Nehru

117. To Binodanand Jha: A New Political Job for Tajamul Husain[313]

25th June, 1962

My dear Binodanandji,
Tajamul Husain, whom you must know, was an MP for many years here.[314] He is now unfortunately no longer in Parliament. He came to say good-bye to me

309. Letter to the Chief Minister of Bihar. MHA, File No. 31/1/64 Public-I.
310. MLC, Bihar.
311. MLC, Bihar.
312. Letter to the Chief Minister of Bihar. PMO, File No. 17(494)/62-66-PMS, Sr. No. 3-A.
313. Letter to the Chief Minister of Bihar.
314. Tajamul Husain, Rajya Sabha MP, Congress, from Bihar, 1952-62.

this morning and wanted me to suggest some kind of work for him. It is not possible for me to suggest any work suitable for him here.

In the course of conversation he said that he would be happy if he could be made President of the Bihar Pradesh Congress Committee. I replied that I would be glad if this could happen, but it was not in my power to make him President. As this was an elected post, much depended on the Bihar PCC, but so far as I was concerned I would be happy to see him chosen.

Tajamul Husain has been a good Member of Parliament. He is an old Congressman and is absolutely not communal. His participation in the debates here was good.

I suggest his name to you to consider what is possible to get good work out of him.

Yours sincerely,
[Jawaharlal Nehru]

(iii) Goa

118. To Sadiq Ali: Goa Congress Committee[315]

June 2, 1962

My dear Sadiq,
Your letter of June 2nd about the Ad Hoc Committee of the Congress in Goa. If Dr Gaitonde[316] takes serious objection to any one name, I would abide by his wishes and leave out that name. It is always easy to add a name later. It is not so easy to take out a name which you have once put in.[317]

Yours sincerely,
Jawaharlal Nehru

315. Letter to a General Secretary of the AICC. NMML, AICC Papers, Box 7, F. No. OD-22/1962.
316. P.D. Gaitonde, Nominated Congress Lok Sabha MP from Goa.
317. See also item 120.

119. For M.J. Desai: Violet Alva on Goa[318]

Shrimati Violet Alva[319] came to see me today. She had just returned after a four day visit to Goa where she had gone in connection with a conference on the Konkani language.

I was surprised to learn from her that some people in Goa had asked her why they were having a Lieutenant Governor instead of a Commissioner as in other places.[320] They would have been able to approach the Commissioner more easily. I told her that the Lieutenant Governor will be accessible to all.

Then she said something which surprised me greatly. She said that the old Portuguese Intelligence Service called, the PIDE is still functioning. This is very extraordinary if it is true.

She said that so long as the present Patriarch[321] remained in Goa, he would be a source of trouble and a centre of anti-Indian activities. If he is there because of the Concordat the sooner the Concordat is changed, the better.

She said that a number of old workers there are without employment. Something might be done for them.

About the Konkani language, she said that as it has no script, the best way would be to encourage the Devanagari script. This is the same practically as the Marathi script.

She also mentioned that the Jesuits were trying to start a college there. She did not approve of this.

120. To Sadiq Ali: Goa Congress Committee[322]

June 7, 1962

My dear Sadiq,

I should like you to expedite the formation of the Ad Hoc Committee for Goa. You have all the material before you, and all that is necessary is to announce it. Kakodkar[323] is staying here just for that purpose. He has to go back soon. I

318. Note, 5 June 1962, for the FS.
319. Elected Deputy Chairman, Rajya Sabha in 1962.
320. Major-General K.P. Candeth was the Military Governor of Goa from 19 December to 6 June 1962 and T. Sivasankar the Lieutenant Governor from 7 June to 1 September 1963.
321. José Vieira Alvernaz.
322. Letter to a General Secretary of the INC. NMML, AICC Papers, F. No. OD-22/1962, Box 7.
323. Purushottam Kakodkar, President, Goa Pradesh Congress Committee.

hope, therefore, that you will get the President to agree to this Committee as soon as possible.[324]

Yours sincerely,
Jawaharlal Nehru

121. For M.J. Desai: Protest Against G.K. Handoo[325]

Dr Laura D'Souza[326] and Professor Rodrigues[327] came to see me today. They referred to a woman who is apparently fasting in front of Shri Handoo's[328] house in Goa, her object being that he should leave Goa. In view of this, Dr Laura D'Souza and her companion asked me to keep Shri Handoo in Goa for some time more so that it might not appear that we have surrendered to this fasting business. The woman has declared that Shri Handoo will go away before the 15th July.

2. I understand that Shri Handoo is supposed to leave Goa by the end of this month. I feel there is some substance in what Dr Laura D'Souza has told me and it might appear that Shri Handoo is being sent away because of the fast. Perhaps, it might be desirable for Shri Handoo to stay on in Goa for another month, say until the end of July. [329]

324. See also item 118.
325. Note, 8 June 1962, for the FS.
326. President, National Congress (Goa) (Dissident Group), 1955.
327. Lucio Rodrigues, Professor of English in colleges in Bombay and Goa.
328. G.K. Handoo, former IGP, Kashmir; now Special Adviser to the Military Governor of Goa.
329. Mrs Savigne da Gama Pinto, a housewife on fast from 21 May demanding that the Special Adviser to the Military Governor be replaced by a Goan, ended it on 1 June 1962 on an assurance that Handoo had applied for leave preparatory for retirement from July. See *The Tribune*, 4 June 1962, p. 10 col. 8. *The Hindu* reported on 15 June 1962 (p. 10 col. 4) that the Military Governor's post was being abolished and Handoo would continue as adviser to the Lieutenant Governor and go on leave on 1 July 1962. However, his term was extended till the end of October, see *The Bharat Jyoti*, 1 July 1962, p. 1 col. 4 and *Free Press Journal*, 2 July 1962, p. 3 col. 6.

122. To Gulzarilal Nanda: Make Bharat Sevak Samaj in Goa Popular[330]

June 8, 1962

My dear Gulzarilal,
I understand that the Bharat Sevak Samaj has started doing some work in Goa, but that it is largely official or controlled by officials. I think that a popular basis should be given to it.

Yours sincerely,
[Jawaharlal Nehru]

123. For M. J. Desai: Public Meetings in Goa[331]

I enclose a letter from Purushottam Kakodkar.[332] He will probably be returning to Goa day after tomorrow after he has finished his meetings with the General Secretary of the AICC[333] here.

2. I entirely agree with him that reference to old Portuguese laws should be wholly avoided especially in regard to restrictions on public activities etc. As regards public meetings, all that is necessary is that intimation of a meeting should be sent in time to the requisite authority. Asking for permission for a meeting is not done anywhere in India, and there is no reason why it should be done in Goa. It may be that some undesirable people want to hold a meeting. That is common enough in other parts of India, and on the whole, I think we should take the risk.

3. Probably also, there are plenty of old Portuguese laws limiting public activities. These should be put an end to. Any new regulations that are considered desirable should be announced. This is especially necessary now that civil rule has been fully established.

4. I do not know if it is your intention to have some kind of an Advisory Council in Goa, made up of local people, which would advise the Lieut.-Governor. The process of election etc, will take some months. It would be desirable for an Advisory Council to be appointed of well-known local people

330. Letter to the Minister of Labour & Employment.

331. Note, 9 June 1962, for the FS.

332. President, Goa Pradesh Congress Committee.

333. Sadiq Ali. See item 120.

who are respected in Goa. Old Portuguese officials need not be appointed to this Council.

5. If you like, you can speak to me about this matter.

124. To Krishna Dev Tripathi: Party Committee for Goa[334]

June 10, 1962

Dear Krishna Devji,

I have your letter of the 8th June in which you suggest that a delegation of the Party visit Goa. There is no objection to anyone going to Goa now, but a delegation going there to study the constitutional, social and economic set-up will probably create difficulties and some confusion there. Just a day or two ago, civil administration has been brought in there and the Military Governor has left.[335] I think the Lieutenant Governor should be left to settle down.[336] Later some people can go. Even so, I do not like the idea of a committee of enquiry going on behalf of the Party.

Yours sincerely,
[Jawaharlal Nehru]

125. To Sooryakant Parikh: Mahesh Kothari in Japan[337]

June 13, 1962

Dear Shri Parikh,

Your letter of June 8th.[338]

There was no question of my appointing Mahesh Kothari as my personal representative to the Peace Conference in Japan. But he went there with my knowledge and carried a message from me.

I did suggest to him to go to Goa, Daman, etc. and let me know as to how things were getting on there. There was no question of his going to Lisbon to see Dr Salazar.[339]

334. Letter to Congress MP; address: 202 North Avenue, New Delhi.

335. Major-General K.P. Candeth left on 6 June.

336. T. Sivasankar took over on 7 June.

337. Letter; address: Patdi Building, Ellisbridge, Ahmedabad. NMML, Sooryakant Parikh Papers, Acc No. 434.

338. Appendix 23.

339. A.O. Salazar, Prime Minister of Portugal.

I do not know anything about expenses.

I might mention that he has done good work both in Japan and in Daman and Goa. His reports were useful to us.[340]

Yours sincerely,
Jawaharlal Nehru

126. In the Lok Sabha: Language in Goa Education[341]

Education System in Goa

Nath Pai:[342] Will the Prime Minister be pleased to refer to the reply given to Starred Question No. 737 on 16 May 1962 and state:

(a) whether the Committee appointed by Government to go into the Educational System in Goa has since submitted its report; and
(b) if so, what are the findings of the Committee and their recommendations?

The Minister of State in the Ministry of External Affairs (Lakshmi Menon):

(a) Yes, Sir.
(b) The report is still under the examination of the Government.[343]

Nath Pai: Has the Commission made any recommendation regarding the setting up of a separate university for Goa, and if so, what is its recommendation regarding the medium of instruction and the place of Marathi in primary, secondary and university education?

Lakshmi Menon: The whole matter is under consideration of Government. The Commission did make a number of recommendations. I do not think it made any recommendations for a separate university.

340. See also item 441.
341. Oral Answers, 19 June 1962. *Lok Sabha Debates*, Third Series, Vol. V, 8 June to 22 June 1962, Ist Session, cols 11599-11603.
342. PSP.
343. In April 1962, the GOI appointed a committee to go into the educational system in Goa under the chairmanship of B.N. Jha with A. Menezies as member and Mrs V. Malay as member-secretary. The committee met in Goa, 5-17 May; wrote its report in Delhi, 24-31 May and submitted to MEA on 31 May 1962. See *The Hindu*, 4 June 1962, p. 7 col. 1.

Nath Pai: If the Government is still examining the report, until they are able to finalise their decision, what are the Government's instruction to the Lieut-Governor of Goa Administration regarding the medium of instruction in the primary schools and what place is Marathi being accorded?

The Prime Minister and Minister of External Affairs and Minister of Atomic Energy (Jawaharlal Nehru): I do not know what special instructions have been sent except the general instruction that the mother tongue should be the medium of instruction at the primary stages. There is an indication that the Konkani language should be encouraged not at the cost of any other language, but that being the general language in Goa it should be encouraged. Although it has no particular script of its own, probably the script adopted for it will be Nagari script.

Hem Barua:[344] May I know, Sir, if Government propose to maintain the status quo in education, so far as university education is concerned and if so whether Government propose to maintain the medium of instruction in the University stage Portuguese?

Jawaharlal Nehru: I do not know what the hon. Member refers to as the status quo until recently was the Portuguese language.

Hem Barua: Since the Portuguese language is the status quo and the medium of instruction at the university stage, do Government propose to maintain that?

Jawaharlal Nehru: I am sorry I am still not clear what the hon. Member is driving at.

Hem Barua: May I explain, Sir?

Speaker:[345] He does not explain in one sentence. That is the difficulty. If he explains in one sentence, it will become very clear. He may put the question now.

Hem Barua: May I know whether Government propose to maintain the status quo so far as higher education in Goa is concerned, which means

344. PSP.
345. Hukam Singh.

whether Government propose to maintain the medium of instruction as it obtained in Goa for higher education?

Jawaharlal Nehru: There were no institutions of higher education in Goa. People used to go either to Bombay or to Portugal. Obviously higher institutions may not have Portuguese as their medium of instruction whatever other language they may have.

प्रकाशवीर शास्त्री:[346] जांच समिति की जिस रिपोर्ट पर अभी विचार किया जा रहा है जोकि उसने गोआ में जो शिक्षा प्रणाली है, उसके संबंध में दी है, उसको मूलभूत सिफारिशें क्या हैं, क्या सरकार यह बतलाने का यत्न करेंगे?

जवाहरलाल नेहरु: "सरकार" मालूम नहीं क्या चीज है। मैंने तो उसे अभी नहीं देखा है, इस वास्ते जबाब नहीं दे सकता इसका।

[Translation begins:

Prakash Vir Shastri: Will the Government tell us the basic recommendations of the Commission on the educational system in Goa which are under consideration?

Jawaharlal Nehru: What the "Government" is, I do not know. I have not seen it [report] yet so I cannot answer this.

Translation ends]

Nath Pai: May I know from the Prime Minister—they had promised on the 16th May to give the details—the number of Marathi schools in Goa, and also whether Government are aware that it was the systematic policy of the Portuguese Government to persecute and destroy Marathi as the one symbol of the people of Goa of their link with India, and whether there is any change in this policy?

Speaker: Order, order.

Nath Pai: Mr Speaker, I am basing my question on the reports, and that is why I raised the question.

346. Independent.

Jawaharlal Nehru: I have not seen the report, as I have just said, and therefore I cannot answer about the report. I do not know what the Portuguese policy was; the Portuguese policy was not to encourage the languages here. Marathi is obviously going to be encouraged there, but at the same time, as I said, the Konkani language is also going to be encouraged.

Nath Pai: May I give information that Goa has a number of Marathi schools. He has not answered that; as he stated, he does not know about it.

Speaker: Order, order.

Hari Vishnu Kamath:[347] In view of the fact that for the last four or five centuries, only Portuguese and Konkani were the major languages, if not the only languages, in Goa, is Government giving any thought to the issue of introducing any of the national languages of India—English is out of the question—so as to subserve the cause of integration of Goa with the rest of India?

Raghunath Singh:[348] That is Hindi.

Jawaharlal Nehru: Obviously Marathi is the language that is spoken by a considerable number of persons, and Marathi will be encouraged. But, broadly speaking, we think that Konkani is the language of Goa, more than any other language —the spoken language. And, therefore, we feel that Konkani should be encouraged. But in these matters we are going to draw no rigid line about it.

Hari Vishnu Kamath: But unfortunately, Konkani is not included in the Eighth Schedule to the Constitution.

Speaker: Order, order. I have requested so many times that hon. Members should not shoot up their questions without looking at me even.

Hari Vishnu Kamath: It is not a question.

Speaker: It is a continuation of the same thing. If it is not a question, then it need not be answered. Dr M.S. Aney. [349]

M.S. Aney: There is some trouble about the script also. The script that was used in the Portuguese time was the Roman Script. And instead of that,

347. PSP.
348. Congress.
349. Independent.

the demand has been made by the people of Goa that the script should be Devanagari. Does Government contemplate to give effect to that?

Speaker: That he has said already, he said that the Devanagari script is going to be adopted.

Jawaharlal Nehru: I said that is the present proposal, that for the Konkani language the Devanagari script was recommended.

Nath Pai: May I ask the Prime Minister if he is aware that there is no such dichotomy between Konkani and Marathi and both the greatest Indian philologists, and also the Portuguese, have held them to be one—Dr Gune[350] and Dr Bhandarkar?[351]

Speaker: Order, order.

Jawaharlal Nehru: I am not prepared to accept that statement.

Nath Pai: But certainly, you respect them?

Jawaharlal Nehru: Not at all, because I have seen that experts disagree about that. I am no expert, but all I can say is that experts, even doctors disagree.

127. To Chandrakant Keni: Goa Visit[352]

June 22, 1962

Dear Chandrakanatji,[353]
I have your letter of the 22nd June. I have been wanting to go to Goa for some time past. But, owing to ill-health and other reasons, I could not manage it. Now I am told that it will not be a good time to go there because of the rains. I might, therefore, go to Goa some time in October.

But I do not wish to tie myself down to any particular date at present. Nor do I promise that I shall particularly go there to attend the Writers' Conference. If I happen to be there at the time the Conference is held, I shall try to attend it.

Yours sincerely,
[Jawaharlal Nehru]

350. Pandurang Damodar Gune.
351. R.G. Bhandarkar.
352. Letter; address: "Sannidhi", Rajghat, New Delhi 1.
353. Konkani writer and journalist, associated with several Gandhian institutions.

128. To K. Ram: Handoo's Extension[354]

Pleas reply to this letter from Mrs Athaide. Say that the extension of Shri Handoo's services in Goa was decided by us after full consideration and because we thought that his services would be helpful in Goa. There is no question of prestige involved in this.

129. To M.J. Desai: No Portuguese Laws for Unions[355]

I enclose a letter from Shri S.A. Dange.[356] I do not think it is proper for us to take shelter under the Portuguese laws in Goa in regard to the activities of a trade union. Those laws have to be changed very soon. But even so we can relax their functioning.

130. To Mahesh Kothari: Land Reform in Daman[357]

July 19, 1962

My dear Mahesh,

I have received your letter of the 15th July here in Hyderabad. I am very happy that the proclamation about land tenure in Daman has been received with joy by the tenants. I hope that they will progress now and will have a sense of satisfaction. There is no particular message that I can give them except to say that I am much interested in their well-being and progress, and I wish them well.

Yours sincerely,
[Jawaharlal Nehru]

354. Note, 5 July 1962, to the PPS from Pahalgam, Kashmir.

355. Note, 9 July 1962, to the Foreign Secretary, sent from Pahalgam, Kashmir.

356. Chairman, CPI.

357. Letter; address: c/o Post Master, Daman. Sent from Rashtrapati Nilayam, Hyderabad.

131. To J.M. D'Souza: Electing MPs from Goa[358]

July 19, 1962

Dear Shri D'Souza

I have received your letter of the 13th July.

Since you wrote that letter, Shri R.S. Fernandez[359] has broken his fast and he has met me in Bangalore. I explained to him that as soon as arrangements were properly made for election, the Members of Parliament from Goa would be elected. The present arrangements were temporary and would last only till then. He was satisfied with this.

Yours sincerely,
[Jawaharlal Nehru]

(iv) Himachal Pradesh

132. To Bajrang Bahadur Singh: Lippa Fire Relief[360]

July 17, 1962

My dear Bhadri,

Your letter of the 13th July. I am sorry to learn of the devastation caused by fire in the village of Lippa. On my return to Delhi I shall send you a cheque for Rs 10,000/- from the Prime Minister's National Relief Fund. The demands on this fund are at present and will be progressively great because of the flood damages. I hope, therefore, that you will appreciate that I am at present unable to send you more than Rs. 10,000/-.

Yours sincerely,
[Jawaharlal Nehru]

358. Letter to the President of the Goan National Union, Altinho, Mapuca [Mapusa], Bordez [Bardez], Goa. Sent from Rashtrapati Nilayam, Hyderabad.
359. Roque Santana Fernandez, Goan nationalist leader, had been fasting against the nomination of Dr Antonio Colaco to the Lok Sabha. See *The Hindu*, 16 July 1962, p.1 col. 3.
360. Letter to Raja of Bhadri, Lieutenant Governor of Himachal Pradesh. Sent from Royal Cottage, Bangalore.

(v) Jammu and Kashmir

133. To Ghulam Mohammed Bakhshi: Declining Support for National Conference[361]

June 8, 1962

My dear Bakhshi,

I gather that in the election held in Srinagar in the vacancy caused by Sham Lal Saraf[362] being chosen for Parliament, the majority of the National Conference candidate was a very small one.[363] Only a month or two before, Sham Lal Saraf won this seat by a very big majority.[364] If the facts given to me are correct, I should like your appraisal of the situation and why this big change has taken place within a month or so.

Yours sincerely,
[Jawaharlal Nehru]

134. In the Lok Sabha: The Jammu and Kashmir Constitution [365]

Application of the Constitution to
Jammu and Kashmir

Hari Vishnu Kamath:[366] Will the Minister of Home Affairs is pleased to state:

(a) whether Government propose to amend the Constitution by repealing Article 370, with a view to applying the Constitution in toto to the

361. Letter to the Prime Minister of Jammu and Kashmir.
362. Saraf, Minister of Commerce and Industry in the Jammu and Kashmir Government, was nominated by the President to the Lok Sabha in 1962.
363. On 31 May 1962, Janki Nath Bhat of the National Conference was elected to Kashmir Assembly from the Amira Kadal constituency in the bye-election following the resignation of Saraf. Bhat defeated Mohammad Shafi Qureshi, Independent, by a margin of 298 votes. See *The Times of India*, 1 June 1962, p. 7 col. 5.
364. Saraf had 10, 313 votes against 1,753 votes for Om Prakash of PSP from Amira Kadal, Srinagar City, in the Third General Elections, held on 15 March 1962. See *RECI*, p. 477.
365. Oral Answers, 8 June 1962. *Lok Sabha Debates*, Third Series, Vol. V, 8 June to 22 June 1962, Ist Session, cols 9661-9664.
366. PSP.

State of Jammu and Kashmir, so as to put it on par with other States of the Indian Union; and

(b) if not, the reasons therefore?

The Minister of State in the Ministry of Home Affairs (B.N. Datar): (a) and (b). The question will be considered at the appropriate time.

Hari Vishnu Kamath: In view of the fact that according to the Constitution, this Article 370 is a temporary and transitional provision, is it going to be indefinitely temporary and transitional, or has the Government set a date for its abrogation or is considering or thinking of setting a date for its abrogation?

B.N. Datar: No such date has been fixed, but may I point out to the hon. Member that after 1950 on four or five occasions changes or modifications have been made so far as the relations with Jammu and Kashmir State are concerned, and the President has, with the concurrence of the State Government, issued orders in that respect.

Hari Vishnu Kamath: Exactly, Sir. Clause 3 of Article 370 of the Constitution says that the President may by public notification declare that this Article shall cease to be operative etc., provided the recommendation in this regard, and if it (sic) Jammu and Kashmir has been obtained.[367] May I know whether the Jammu and Kashmir State Assembly has suo motu, made any specific recommendation in this regard, and if it has not done so, does the Government propose to consult the State Assembly with regard to this, whether the abrogation or modification of this provision can be made in the very near future?

The Minister of Home Affairs (Lal Bahadur Shastri): The Jammu and Kashmir Government have not made a general reference at all. There was a question only four or five days ago relating to the need to have direct elections in respect of which the Prime Minister of Jammu and Kashmir made a statement on the floor of the Assembly. We have told the House that until now we have not received a formal reference from the State government. Therefore, unless the concurrence of the State Government is obtained it would be difficult to deal with Article 370 as far as the modifications that the hon. Member desires are concerned.

367. As in the original.

Nath Pai:[368] The extension of the full Constitution of India to Jammu and Kashmir was withheld because of the peculiar conditions prevailing there and we were told that this was to be of a temporary nature. Recently we have told the Security Council, and I think very rightly, that conditions have materially changed and therefore the promise of plebiscite does not arise. In view of the fact that the Government itself has told the world those conditions have materially changed in Kashmir does it not apply with regard to the promise to extend the full provisions of the Constitution also?

Lal Bahadur Shastri: The hon. Member perhaps knows what progress we have made in this regard, especially since 1950. In the years 1958 to 1960, many provisions of the Constitution have been applied to Jammu and Kashmir, especially in regard to the Indian Administrative Service, the functions of the Comptroller and Auditor-General, in regard to the Census as also in regard to the Supreme Court. They can give special leave to appeal from the decisions of the High Court of Jammu and Kashmir. And several other provisions have been made applicable. I do not want to go into them. As my hon. friend has just now said—about direct elections being held for Parliament from that State—in regard to that, I have myself written to Bakhshi Ghulam Muhammed[369] suggesting to him that in the light of his statement I hope he will be writing to us officially so that we might go in for the amendment of the Constitution. In these matters, we are constantly in touch and in consultation with the State Government. We are in entire agreement with the wishes of the hon. Member, but I hope we should not try to precipitate matters and we have to do it in concurrence with the State Government.

Shri Tyagi:[370] Does the restriction pertaining to the purchase of property and building residential houses still, stand? As far as I remember, there is some provision whereby while Kashmiris can go to the rest of India and build houses and buy properties the non-Kashmiris cannot go to Kashmir and build their houses and buy properties. I want to know whether that restriction still stands, or, whether, the Government propose to remove it now.

368. PSP.
369. Prime Minister of Jammu and Kashmir.
370. Mahavir Tyagi, Congress.

The Prime Minister and Minister of External Affairs and Minister of Atomic Energy (Jawaharlal Nehru): I believe it stands without approval. Of course, it sounds odd that in a part of India Indians should not be allowed to take property, but this inheritance from the past was thoroughly justified. If this had not been so, the whole of the land in Kashmir would have been bought up at relatively cheap terms by the foreigners, the English people and others—because it is a very desirable place—or by a few rich people from Calcutta and Bombay, and the Kashmiris would practically have no place left in Kashmir itself. Therefore, one of the Maharajas made it a rule that nobody from outside can do it. That does not apply to the same extent now, but to some extent, it does. And it would become a playground for a number of rich people from outside who will buy up or build chateaux and such like things, and the opportunity for the growth of Kashmir, to the people of Kashmir, would be limited.

135. To Humayun Kabir: Maps of Jammu and Kashmir State[371]

June 11, 1962

My dear Humayun,

Your letter of the 11th June.[372] Of the valleys you have mentioned, two, namely Gilgit and Hunza are in the part occupied by Pakistan. Part of Hunza territory is occupied by China.

Chang Chenmo, Shyok and Nubra are regions of high altitudes with many glaciers about. The Chinese occupy part of the area now. Normally people who have gone there in the past are experienced mountaineers.

There remain the Jhelum and the Sind. The Jhelum is in the valley of Kashmir itself, most of it, and part of it is in the Pakistan occupied territory. The Jhelum valley is being developed in many ways. To some extent, the Sind valley is also being developed. One of the major electric power stations is situated at the foot of the Sind valley. It is a fairly narrow valley leading up to Sonamarg, Baltal and then Ladakh.

371. Letter to the Minister of Scientific Research and Cultural Affairs. PMO, File No. 17(371)/59-66-PMS, Sr. No. 49-A. Also available in NMML, Humayun Kabir Papers, F.No. 15/1962-64, Auto.

372. This letter has not been reproduced here but is available in the NMML. It lists the valleys, with their areas, and proposes developing them.

I do not quite know what you expect us to do about these valleys. I am returning to you the Survey map you sent me.

Yours sincerely,
Jawaharlal Nehru

136. To Lal Bahadur Shastri: Turkistan Refugees in Kashmir[373]

June 12, 1962

My dear Lal Bahadur,

When I was in Srinagar recently, I received a letter from the Turkistan Refugee Committee, which functions in Srinagar. This Committee represented Turkistan refugees who came to Kashmir many years ago and have been carrying on in some way or other ever since then. They ask to be recognised as Indian nationals.

I referred this matter to Bakhshi Sahib.[374] I have received a letter from him, a copy of which I enclose.[375]I am also enclosing a copy of the memorandum given to me by the Turkistan Refugee Committee.[376]

I think that we should agree to their request and recognise them as Indian nationals. Would you please have this matter considered?

Yours affectionately,
Jawaharlal Nehru

137. To K.L. Shrimali: Political Sufferers in Princely States[377]

June 13, 1962

My dear Shrimali,

I enclose a copy of a letter I have received from G.M. Sadiq, Minister of Education of the J & K Government.[378] I think the point he has made is worthy

373. Letter to the Home Minister.

374. Bakhshi Ghulam Muhammed, Prime Minister of Jammu and Kashmir. See SWJN/SS/76/items 223-224.

375. Appendix 21 (a).

376. Appendix 21 (b).

377. Letter to the Minister of Education.

378. Appendix 22.

of consideration. I do not know why Princely States were excluded from your scheme. This might be justified in regard to some States, but not in regard to Jammu and Kashmir where there was a freedom movement for many years and many people suffered.

I do not quite know what your scheme is. But I should like you to consider what Sadiq has written.

Yours sincerely,
[Jawaharlal Nehru]

138. To Ghulam Mohammed Bakhshi: Kashmir Visit[379]

New Delhi,
June 20, 1962

My dear Bakshi,

I am thinking of coming for a few days to Kashmir again for rest. I am afraid I shall not be able to stay long. I might stay for four or five days, if this is convenient to you.

I intend coming on the morning of the 4th July. Probably Indira and Sanjay will accompany me.

Please let me know if this is convenient.

Yours sincerely
[Jawaharlal Nehru]

139. To Ghulam Mohammed Bakhshi: Keep Airport Reception Simple[380]

June 25, 1962

My dear Bakhshi,

Thank you for your letter about my visit to Srinagar. I am looking forward to this visit. I hope to leave Delhi (Palam airport) at 8.30 a.m. I suppose I shall reach Srinagar airport at about 10.15 a.m. or perhaps 10.30.

379. Letter to the Prime Minister of Jammu and Kashmir.

380. Letter to the Prime Minister of Jammu and Kashmir. PMO, File No. 8(225)62-PMP, Sr. No. 3-A.

I would beg of you not to organise a public reception for me at the airport. I do not want all your officials and others to gather there. Nor do I want large numbers of children to be brought there. It is all very well once in a while to do this. But repeating it often is too much of a good thing.

Yours sincerely,
Jawaharlal Nehru

140. To Ghulam Mohammed Bakhshi: Request from Poonch[381]

July 1, 1962

My dear Bakhshi,
I have received the following telegram:

> "In 1958, we the people of Poonch requested you through ex-Defence Minister Dr Katju[382] and Foreign Secretary Mr Sadat Ali[383] to attend to our pitiable condition now reduced to helplessness. We again request and earnestly desire the inclusion of Poonch in your Kashmir tour programme to see the condition personally and feel your flight. Your presence among us should provide us with a stimulus to be brave in distress.
>
> The people of Poonch through Gulam Qadir Bendey[384] Poonch."

I have replied to them that I am sorry I cannot come to Poonch on this occasion.

Yours sincerely,
[Jawaharlal Nehru]

381. Letter to Ghulam Mohammed Bakshi, Prime Minister of Jammu and Kashmir State.
382. Kailas Nath Katju, Defence Minister, January 1955-January 1957.
383. Sadath Ali Khan, Parliamentary Secretary to Nehru in the Ministry of External Affairs.
384. Khwaja Ghulam Qadir Bandey, a freedom fighter, was also an Independent candidate from Poonch for Jammu and Kashmir Legislative Assembly in the Third General Elections, see *RECI*, p. 475.

141. To A. Krishnaswami: Integrating Kashmir[385]

July 4, 1962

My dear Krishnaswami,[386]

I have your letter of the 30th June. I entirely agree with you that any attempt to amend the Constitution in Kashmir is not desirable. The attitude of the Jan Sangh and other Hindu communal organisations has a contrary effect to the one we desire.

As for emotionally integrating Kashmir, we have tried to do this and will continue to do so. Unfortunately, certain events happening in India produce wrong reactions here.

Yours sincerely,
[Jawaharlal Nehru]

142. To Ghulam Mohammed Bakhshi: Balraj Puri's Letter[387]

July 4, 1962

My dear Bakhshi,

Just before I left Delhi, I received a letter from one Balraj Puri. I have a vague idea that Balraj Puri belongs to the PSP, though I am not sure.[388] I am enclosing this letter as it might interest you.[389]

I am not sending any reply to Balraj Puri and I do not propose to see him here.

Yours sincerely,
[Jawaharlal Nehru]

385. Letter; address: 19 Curzon Road, New Delhi-1. Sent from Chashmashahi Guest House, Srinagar.
386. Probably Arcot Krishnaswami, Special Rapporteur of the UN Subcommission on Prevention of Discrimination and Protection of Minorities, 1959-60.
387. Letter to the Prime Minister of Jammu and Kashmir. Sent from Chashmashahi Guest House, Srinagar.
388. See also SWJN/SS/75/items 105 and 108.
389. Nehru forwarded another letter to Bakhshi on 6 July: "As I was leaving Delhi, I received a long letter from Prem Nath Bazaz. I have just read it here at Pahalgam. I have briefly acknowledged it.

Perhaps you might be interested in reading what he has written to me. I am, therefore, sending this letter to you."

143. To Ghulam Mohammed Bakhshi: Dhirendra's Misdeeds[390]

July 6, 1962

My dear Bakhshi,

I enclose a copy of a telegram which I received today.[391]

Yours sincerely,
[Jawaharlal Nehru]

144. Dredging the Jhelum[392]

I have read these papers. I have shown them to Shri Ghulam Mohammed Bakshi[393] also. We agree broadly with the proposal made in the summary.

2. Bakshi Sahib, however, attaches great importance to his project for a hydro-electric scheme, more so than to the flood control works and the widening of the outlet of the Jhelum river in the Valley. About the hydro-electric project, he pointed out that a scheme for 100,000 Kw will cost only a little more than a scheme for 50,000 Kw. Therefore, he says that while we may only take less water first and just enough for 50,000 Kw, the scheme should be drawn up on the larger basis.

3. It seems to me and to Bakshi Sahib that a reservoir, such as is proposed, will be to the advantage of Pakistan. They will get a controlled water supply according to their needs and will escape sudden floods in one season and possibly a shorter water supply during other seasons. This could easily be regulated if the reservoir was built. There should be no question of lessening the water supply. But, however desirably this may be, the Pakistan Government is bound to raise objections as has already been indicated by the

390. Letter to the Prime Minister of Jammu and Kashmir State. Sent from Pahalgam.

391. The telegram read: "Katra public harassed. Land being procured and fenced forcibly for Vishwaytan Yogashram. Legal rights ignored. High-handedness irregularities jusfified in the names of Prime Minister Nehru and Indiraji. Malpractices and misappropriation of funds by Managing Trustee Dhirendra (d. 1994). For personal aggrandisement. Solicit immediate enquiry and redressal of wrongs. Pray intervene. Action Committee, Public Hanhali, Katra"

392. Note, 7 July 1962, for the CS, MEA. Ministry of Irrigation (I.T. Section), F. 16(13)61-IT, Vol. I, 1961.

393. Prime Minister of Jammu and Kashmir State.

High Commissioner. Therefore, it was desirable not to raise this question with them at present.

4. It is also true that by the time this hydro-electric scheme takes shape, the Mangla Dam will be functioning. But all this is reasonable logic which does not come in when Pakistan is considering its relations with us.

5. I agree that investigations for storage on the tributaries of the Jhelum might immediately be made.[394]

145. To Ghulam Mohammed Bakhshi: Relief for Poonch Muslims[395]

July 7, 1962

My dear Bakhshi,
I have received the following telegram today from Poonch:

> "Hon'ble Jawaharlalji Nehru, Pahalgam
>
> Rupee three lakh sanctioned by Central as relief to Poonchi Muslims and list prepared but relief withheld on recent election grounds. Kindly direct local authority to distribute relief without considering partial colours also requesting to visit Poonch on returning.
>
> President Muslim Kumbajat"

I do not understand it. Perhaps you can understand the meaning.

Yours sincerely,
[Jawaharlal Nehru]

394. In the NMML, there is a lengthy note of 25 June 1962 by H.C. Kalra (designation not mentioned) of the Ministry of Irrigation and Power, for the Secretary of that Department. It deals with the flooding and dredging of the Jhelum and with the Mangla Dam. Owing to its length and technical nature, it is not reproduced here.
395. Letter to the Prime Minister of Jammu and Kashmir State. Sent from Pahalgam, Kashmir.

146. To C.N. Kashkari: Balancing Regional and Indian Culture[396]

July 7, 1962

Dear Shri Kashkari,

I have received your letter of 4th July while I am staying at Pahalgam in Kashmir.[397]

For any attempt to encourage literary and cultural activities, you have my good wishes. But I must confess that such activities confined to separate States or community groups, tend to keep up our divisions and are, perhaps, a slight barrier towards the integration of all peoples in India. Kashmir undoubtedly has something to give to India in the way of culture and literature. While this should be encouraged, I hope that any narrowness of approach will not take place. Our principal aim must be to develop a common culture all over India which will include the separate States cultures and will thus help in the process of integration.

Yours sincerely,
Jawaharlal Nehru

396. Letter to the Editor of the *Kashmir Sabha Annual* for Kashmir Sabha, Calcutta. Sent from Pahalgam, Kashmir. PMO, File No. 9/2/62-PMP, Vol. V, Sr. No. 3-A. Also available in NMML, JN Papers, C.N. Kashkari, JN Supplementary Papers and in the JN Collection.

397. Kashkari's letter from Calcutta : "The Kashmiri Pandit residents of Calcutta, like their other friends, the Maharashtrians, the Tamils, the Gujaratis, the Malayalees and others, have formed a social and cultural association under the name of 'Kashmir Sabha'. The Sabha is functioning for the last six years and caters to the social and cultural needs of the Kashmiris here, not in an exclusive or communal sense but as a distinct part of the All-India community. Since August 1959, we circulate to our members here, a monthly bulletin which, besides giving the news about the affairs that relate to and affect the Kashmiris, also tries to apprise the members of our literary and cultural traditions and history. As in the previous years, the Annual will contain contributions on the various aspects of the Kashmiris's life, his contribution to art, literature, religion, etc.

We have no doubt that being interested in seeing the literary and cultural activities grow in the various parts of India, you will kindly give us your blessings in this venture and favour us with a message of encouragement."

147. To T.T. Krishnamachari: Industrialisation of Jammu and Kashmir[398]

July 8, 1962

My dear T.T.,

D.P. Dhar, the Minister of Jammu & Kashmir Government in charge of Industries etc. gave me a note today for industrialisation of Jammu & Kashmir state. I am sending this to you, as it will give you some idea of the possibilities here. After you have read it, you might pass it on to K.D. Malaviya[399] and Subramaniam.[400]

I have been interested to note that the Jammu & Kashmir Government has arrived at some kind of a tentative agreement with the Punjab Government to supply them with coal.

Yours affectionately,
Jawaharlal Nehru

148. To V.K. Krishna Menon: Misbehaviour by Army Officers[401]

July 9, 1962

My dear Krishna,

I have received a letter in which it is stated that some foreign women tourists who had come to Kashmir were complaining bitterly about the behaviour of Indian Army officers in Kashmir. I do not know how far this allegation is correct. It is said that there is misbehaviour in clubs and hotels. I wonder if anything can be done about this, that is, some kind of advice or direction to be issued. If there is any truth in their behaviour to foreign tourists, this can surely be done to local women even more so. This, as you know, has bad reactions in Kashmir.

Yours affectionately,
[Jawaharlal Nehru]

398. Letter to the Minister without Portfolio. Sent from Pahalgam, Kashmir. PMO, File No. 17(480)/61-66-PMS, Sr. No. 2-A. Also available in NMML, T.T. Krishnamachari Papers, File 1963, Auto and the JN Collection.
399. Minister of Fuel and Fuel.
400. C. Subramaniam, Minister of Steel and Heavy Industries.
401. Letter to the Defence Minister. Sent from Pahalgam, Kashmir.

149. In Srinagar: To the Vidhan Sabha[402]

चेयरमैन साहब,[403] भाइयो और बहनो, साथियो,

मुझसे यह कहा गया था कि आज यहीं आकर मैं कुछ लेजिस्लेचर से या मेम्बरान असेम्बली और कौंसिल से मिलूँगा। मुझे नहीं मालूम था कि यहाँ एक चाय का बड़ा इंतज़ाम है और तरह-तरह के लोग होंगे उसमें। ख़ैर, मुझे कोई एतराज़ नहीं है कि कैसे ही लोग हों, किस रंग के हों लेकिन मालूम नहीं था इसका। [हँसी] मैं तो समझता था कि आपस में हम बैठके कुछ बातचीत करेंगे, हालांकि आपस की बातचीत भी बहुत आपस की नहीं रहती है। पहले तो यह कि मेरा काश्मीर में आना, मुझे ताज्जुब होता है कि क़रीब-क़रीब मैं कुछ भी करता हूँ इसमें कुछ न कुछ माने पहनाये जाते हैं, कोई न कोई दूर का ख़्याल है तब मैं कर रहा हूँ। सीधी सी बात थी, अब्वल तो यूँ भी मैं कभी-कभी काश्मीर आता हूँ, कुछ अपनी आँखों को आराम पहुँचाने इसको देखकर, कुछ इस दफ़े ख़ासतौर से मेरी तबियत ज़रा सी अजीब हो गई और मैं चाहता था कि फिर से पूरीतौर से अच्छा हो जाऊँ।

तो मैं यहाँ आया था सेहत की तलाश में, और कोई मेरा मतलब नहीं था ख़ास। लेकिन मैंने देखा चन्द अख़बारों में ज़िक्र कि बड़े पेचीदा सवाल काश्मीर में पैदा हुए हैं। इसलिए मैं यहाँ आ रहा हूँ मशविरा करने, सलाह देने वग़ैरह। पेचीदा सवाल तो हमारे यहाँ सुबह से शाम तक रहते हैं, सारे हिन्दुस्तान में, हर हिन्दुस्तान के सूबे में और कुछ बढ़ते ही जाते हैं पहले से। क्या माने हैं पेचीदा सवालों के बढ़ने का? वह बुरी बात नहीं है, तरक्की के माने हैं, ज्यों-ज्यों मुल्क एक तरक्की करता है तो उसके सवाल बढ़ते हैं, जो एक मुर्दा मुल्क होता है उसमें सवाल नहीं होते हैं या कम होते हैं। तो इससे तो मैं घबराता नहीं सवालों से।

तो आजकल आप हिन्दुस्तान, सारे हिन्दुस्तान पर निगाह डालिए तो आपको कितने बड़े सवाल नज़र आयेंगे। एक तो ख़ैर जिससे आपको ख़ास ताल्लुक़ है वह हमारे सरहद ही का सवाल है। अब आज ही यहाँ पहुँचकर श्रीनगर में मैंने अख़बारों में पढ़ा, कुछ रेडियो में सुना कि लद्दाख़ के एक हिस्से में कोई चीनी फ़ौजें ऊपर-नीचे टहल रही हैं। इन्हीं सब बातों से ज़ाहिर है कुछ दिमाग़ पर बोझा होती है, परेशानी होती है। और सवाल लीजिए, हिन्दुस्तान में सबसे बड़ा सवाल इस वक़्त है वह हमारे सारे मुल्क का आगे बढ़ना, तरक्की करना, किसी तरह से ग़रीबी के पंजे से निकलना मुश्किल काम है, ख़ासकर जब सैकड़ों बरस का सिलसिला होता है तब इससे निकालना बड़ी आबादी को मुश्किल होता है और यह भी नहीं है कि कुछ ऊपर से कुछ जादू कर दें या ऊपर से कुछ हम कुछ एकाध फैक्टरी बना दें वग़ैरह, यह भी ग़लत है। प्लानिंग हम करते हैं, योजनाएँ बनाते हैं, इसके

402. Speech at a reception held by the Chairman of the Legislative Council, S.N. Fotedar, 11 July 1962. NMML, AIR Tapes, TS No. 8449, 8450, NM No. 1670. See the *National Herald* of 12 July 1962, p. 1, and *The Hindu*, p.7.

403. S.N. Fotedar.

माने नहीं हैं कि हम इधर-उधर फैक्टरी खड़ी कर दें। आख़िर को इसके माने हैं इंसान को बदलना, इंसान को बदलने से मतलब है कि कुछ आजकल की दुनिया को हम समझें, मामूली इंसान समझें और इससे फ़ायदा उठायें, क्योंकि इससे फ़ायदा बहुत हो सकता है जब हम उसको समझ सकें।

आजकल की दुनिया साइंस और विज्ञान की है, और बातें भी जरूरी हैं, मैं नहीं कहता ख़ाली साइंस से हम लोग चलें, हमारी बहुत बातें हममें हैं, हमारे पुराने बुज़ुर्गों ने हमें बताई हैं, हमारे इतिहास में हैं, उनको क़ायम रखना है लेकिन आजकल की दुनिया फिर भी साइंस और विज्ञान की है और जो उसको नहीं समझता है वो पिछड़ जाता है। हमारा मुल्क और और भी एशियाई मुल्क पिछड़ गये थे, इसलिए कि वो इस बात को समझे नहीं थे। यूरोप बढ़ गया और उसको कुंजी मिल गयी फ़ितरत की, दौलत को पाने का। प्रकृति क्या, क्या है, क्या है उनकी ताक़त और क्या है उनकी दौलत? वह सब है जो विज्ञान ने उनको कुंजी दी कि ज़मीन के नीचे और ज़मीन के ऊपर से और बिजली से, इससे, उससे, वो चीज़ें पैदा करें जो फ़ितरत में हैं। वह क्या हैं? एक तलाश है, तलाश है इस दुनिया को समझने की, महज़ आँखें बंद करके बैठने की नहीं जो कुछ है इस, उससे बेहद फ़ायदा हुआ और मुल्कों को, यूरोप को ख़ासकर। और पहली बार दुनिया की तारीख़ में, हज़ारों वर्ष की तारीख़ में पहली बार यह कहा जा सकता है कि ग़रीबी को क़ाबू में ले आयेंगे, क्योंकि पुराने ज़माने में यह अव्वल तो एक माने में आसानी थी क्योंकि आबादी बहुत कम थी आजकल की आबादी के लिहाज़ से। चुनांचे सवाल ऐसी ग़रीबी का नहीं था, लेकिन वाक़िया यह है कि तारीख़ भर में ग़रीबी क़ायम रही है और ज्यादातर लोगों को गिरफ़्तार उसने किया है। पहली बार ग़रीबी हटी है जब डेढ़ सौ बरस हुए, पौने दो सौ बरस हुए यूरोप में नई दुनिया क़ायम होनी शुरु हुई है, यूरोप में, फिर अमेरिका में यानी, यानी नये तरीके, फ़ितरत के, प्रकृति के समझने से नई-नई ताक़तें मिलीं, यह ताक़त है, बिजली की ताक़त एक ज़बरदस्त वह जिससे इंजन चलता है, ऐसी ताक़त क्या चीज़ है? कुछ जादू तो नहीं है, कोई लड़का भी सीख सकता है लेकिन यह किसी ने नहीं सीखा था उस वक़्त तक, और सीखने से एक नई ताक़त इंसान के हाथ में आ गई। मशीन क्या चीज़ है? मशीन है एक आपका नया हाथ, समझो हो गया जिसकी ताक़त बहुत है। तो इस तरह से दुनिया में नई ताक़तें आईं और फ़ितरत के जो ताक़तें हैं वे उस पर क़ाबू आईं। [Recording indistinct]

[बँटवारे का] बुरा असर पड़ा हिन्दुओं पर, मुसलमानों पर, हरेक पर, जो अब तक वहाँ पूर्वी पाकिस्तान में ठीक याद नहीं अस्सी लाख, नब्बे लाख हिन्दू रहते हैं उन पर पड़ा, इधर मुसलमानों पर पड़ा यानी सारी चीज़ उखड़ जाती है, यह गाड़ी चल नहीं सकती किसी मुल्क की भी, किसी तरक़्क़ी-याफ़्ता मुल्क की। इस तरह से कि एक नज़र डालें, हाकिम हो आप समझिए हर बात में। अब दूसरे अपने को दूसरे दरजे के सिटीज़न समझें और इसलिए कश्मीर का मामला ख़ास अहमियत देता है, हमारे कश्मीर के लिए तो देता ही है, सारे हिन्दुस्तान, सारे पाकिस्तान के लिए, ख़ाली जुगराफ़िया में कुछ ज़मीन इधर जोड़ दी जाये, उधर जोड़ दी जाये, यह नहीं है। यह सवाल, हालांकि इस मामले में सभी

आख़िर में जो वहाँ के लोग रहते हैं उन्हीं की मर्ज़ी से वहीं फ़ैसला कर सकते हैं, उन्हीं की मर्ज़ी से लेकिन यह बात कि काश्मीर एक, एक महज़ फ़िरक़ापरस्ती के जज़बात से कोई फ़ैसला हो उसकी निस्बत उसका बहुत बुरा असर हिन्दुस्तान और पाकिस्तान दोनों पर पड़ता है। और एक आप, आपकी कुछ नाइत्तफ़ाक़ी है जो कि मैं उम्मीद करता हूँ हल हो जायेगी, फ़ैसला होगी और एक जड़ गहरी जो आपस के झगड़े की हो जाती है हर हिस्से में हिन्दुस्तान के और हर हिस्से में पाकिस्तान के, यह मज़हबी ख़ाली बात नहीं है। आप देखें इस वक़्त पाकिस्तान में कुछ दिक़्क़तें पेश आई हैं, वहाँ की हुकूमत, यह उनका हक़ है जैसी हुकूमत चाहे करें, मैं तो नहीं उसमें कुछ दख़ल देता लेकिन वाक़िया यह है कि दिक़्क़तें हैं काफी और क्योंकि एक दफ़ा हम इस ढंग से चलते हैं तो उसका असर एक फ़िरक़ापरस्ती वग़ैरह का, उसका सबका असर बहुत तरह होते हैं। ख़ैर, हम तो चाहते हैं पाकिस्तान तरक्की करे, हमसे उसका क़रीब का रिश्ता हो, आख़िर हमारे भाई वहाँ रहते हैं, दुनिया में कोई इत्ता क़रीब नहीं है हमें जितना पाकिस्तान वाले और हम हैं, इसमें कोई शक नहीं और वही होता है जिसके क़रीब हों, जित्ते भाई-भाई हों उत्ती नाइत्तफ़ाक़ी बढ़े, नाराज़गी हो जाती है एक-दूसरे से। यह तो और बात है लेकिन फिर भी वह आदमी तो अपने हैं, और बातें हो सकती हैं और होंगी क्योंकि सारी तारीख़ का तक़ाज़ा यह है हल हों और नहीं हो तो कम हों।

इस वक़्त एक काम है हमें और पाकिस्तान को और और मुल्कों को एशिया के कि वह अपनी तरक्की करें, दुनिया में इस वक़्त तरीका है कहने का [कि] दो क़िस्म के मुल्क हैं। एक तरक़्क़ीयाफ़्ता मुल्क हैं, एक पिछड़े हुए मुल्क हैं, एक जिनको आप चाहें कहें दौलतमंद मुल्क हैं, अमीर मुल्क हैं, एक ग़रीब मुल्क हैं, बीच में बहुत सारे हैं लेकिन हमारी, हमारा शुमार ग़रीबों में, मुल्कों में ही होगा, चाहे देखने की बड़ी-बड़ी बातें, बड़े-बड़े शहर हो जाओ, क्योंकि उसका इम्तिहान होता है देख-देखके आपकी फ़ी-आदमी की हैसियत, मामूली आदमियों की हैसियत क्या है, कैसे रहते हैं, क्या कमाते हैं, ऊँच-नीच ज्यादा तो नहीं, वग़ैरह-वग़ैरह। हमारा काम है, पाकिस्तान का काम है कि मिलके करें, एक-दूसरे की मदद करें तरक्की में, हम बाख़ुशी करें, लेकिन बदक़िस्मती है इसमें फंस गये हैं।

तो हमारा, हिन्दुस्तान का काम है कि किसी तरह से हम इस अपने पाँच बरस के प्रोग्राम को पूरा करें। इसके बाद दूसरे पाँच आयेंगे, ख़त्म थोड़े ही हो जाते हैं और जो हमने अब तक किया है इस बुनियाद व जड़ पर हम और आगे जायें। सबमें बड़ा काम यह है कि हम तो नहीं चाहते हम दुनिया के सवालों में न फंस जायें, और मुल्कों से झगड़ा करें, अपने घर को हमें संभालना है। पढ़ायें-लिखायें, हमारे ख़ूबसूरत बच्चे हैं, देखके मुझे रंज होता है, देखके उनकी हालत देखके, कितने ख़ूबसूरत काश्मीर के बच्चे होते हैं। तो उनको मैं देखता हूँ कैसे गंदे कपड़े पहने हैं, पैर नंगे हैं, हाथ-पैर भी बहुत साफ नहीं हैं और पढ़ाई तो बहुत बढ़ गई है यहाँ, अभी बहुत कुछ गुंजाइश है करने की। अब कुछ वर्दी वग़ैरह पहनते हैं स्कूल के बच्चे, अच्छा लगता है, ज़मीन व आसमान का फ़र्क़ हो जाता है, फिर भी कितना अभी बाक़ी है, उधर तवज्जो हम दें बजाय फ़िज़ूल ज़ाया करने के अपनी ताक़त को। अभी मैंने आपसे बहुत कहा काश्मीर में बहुत गुंजाइश है, यों भी

असल जो चीज़ काश्मीर में है वह यह कि यहाँ के आदमी आमतौर से ज़हीन होते हैं। [Recording indistinct]

तो आप इस सवाल में आपके ज़रा ज्यादा समझ में आये हैं और संभाल सकेंगे आप। अभी मैं यहाँ आया तो मैंने अख़बारों में कुछ देखा, एक तो मैंने आपसे कहा कि मेरा यहाँ आना ही समझा गया कि कोई बड़े इसके पीछे पेंच हैं, कुछ ख़ास यहाँ के, कुछ काश्मीर के सवालों में दख़ल देने आया हूँ। यह तो बिल्कुल ग़लत है। ज़ाहिर है कि मुझे काश्मीर के सवालों में दिलचस्पी है, सभी हिन्दुस्तान के सवालों में दिलचस्पी है। एक माने में काश्मीर में और भी ज्यादा है कुछ थोड़ी बहुत, लेकिन कहा गया कि मैं तो कुल्लू जाने वाला था और बजाय कुल्लू के मैं आख़िर में एकदम से बदल के काश्मीर आ गया दुबारा। कुल्लू जाने का जो चर्चा हुआ था इधर बारिश शुरु हुई, कुल्लू अच्छी जगह नहीं है बारिश में, इसलिए मैंने छोड़ दिया, मैंने कहा कहाँ मैं बारिश में फंस जाऊँ, न निकल सकूँ न कुछ। इधर बामुक़ाबले यहाँ पे ज़रा कम बारिश इस ज़माने में होती है। चुनांचे मैं यहाँ आया, मुझे ख़्याल ही नहीं था कि कोई और कोई वजह है जो मुझे यहाँ खींचती है और मैं यहाँ आया।

ज़ाहिर है आप में से बाज़ लोग मुझसे कभी-कभी मिलें, उनसे बातें हुईं, मुझे दिलचस्पी है, आपकी दिलचस्पी है सवालों में, काश्मीर के सवालों में बातचीत होती है, हमेशा होती है, कुछ और योजनाओं पर बातचीत होती है, वह तो हुई। फिर और कोई ख़ास मेरी नियत यहाँ आने की नहीं थी, कोई ख़ास सवाल के वजह से जैसे मैंने आपसे कहा, मैं यहाँ कुछ सेहत की तलाश में आया हूँ। इस सिलसिले में भी आपसे कह दूँ, मेरी सेहत कोई इतनी ख़राब नहीं हो गई थी जितनी कि धूमधाम हुई [हँसी] लेकिन फिर भी कुछ मैं अपनी दिमाग़ी सेहत और कुछ जिस्मानी सेहत की तलाश में जरूर हूँ। कुछ मुझमें यह ग़लतफ़हमी हो जाती थी अक्सर कि मैं बहुत काम कर सकता हूँ जैसे मैं बीस-तीस बरस का लड़का हूँ। ज़रा मुझे धक्का लगा यह सोच के कि मैं बीस-तीस बरस का अब नहीं हूँ, सही बात है लेकिन अपनी उम्र या अपनी के कुछ क़रीब कभी कम भी लोगों का मुक़ाबला मैं सभों का करने के लिए तैयार हूँ। [हँसी] बहरसूरत अगर कोई अंदाज़ा आप लोग कर सकते हैं चेहरा देखके तो आपने देखा मुझे यहाँ आते और जाते देख रहे हैं, देख सकते हैं, कितना फ़ायदा मुझे हुआ यहाँ आने पर [तालियाँ] और उसका फ़ायदा ख़ाली जिस्म को नहीं दिमाग़ को भी होता है, जगह कुछ ऐसी है और मोहब्बत है इस जगह से। तो यह तो ग़लत बात है कि मैं कोई यहाँ ख़ास बात अख़बारों में छपी थी ग़लत है।

यहाँ आकर मुझे एक बात, मैंने अख़बारों में मैंने देखी, कुछ चर्चा यहाँ हुआ था कि हमने एक दफ़ा हमारी है, कांस्टीट्यूशन की, [370] है शायद काश्मीर के मुतालिक़, उसके निस्बत हमारी पार्लियामेंट में कुछ बहस हुई और कुछ लोगों ने ज़ोर दिया कि इसको हटा देना चाहिए और फिर हमारे होम मिनिस्टर लाल बहादुर शास्त्री जी ने इसका कुछ जवाब दिया। मैं दिल्ली में रहता हूँ, मेरी तवज्जो उधर नहीं, किसी ने मुझसे कहा भी नहीं, क्या हुआ वहाँ, कोई अहमियत ही नहीं उसमें लगाई गई।[404] हाँ, बहुत बहसें होती हैं, वो भी

404. Nehru had, in fact, intervened in the debate, see item 134.

बहस हुई लेकिन यहाँ मैंने सुना कुछ बहुत दूरबीन लगा के देखा गया वहाँ क्या-क्या कहा गया और कुछ शक पैदा हुआ कि क्या इसके माने हैं। उसके माने मेरी समझ में नहीं आता कि इस पेंच के माने क्या हैं। मेरा ख़्याल है, शरअन बात है, और बातें छोड़ दीजिए आप कि इस वक़्त हिन्दुस्तान के दो जो अंदरूनी सवालों को छोड़कर बाहरी सवाल बड़े से बड़े हैं, वो दोनों काश्मीर के हैं। एक तो पाकिस्तान की तरफ से, एक चीन की तरफ से यानी दोनों एक माने में हमलावर हो जाते हैं या पैरवी करते हैं इसकी, काश्मीर का ताल्लुक़ दोनों से है तो काश्मीर की ख़ास हैसियत हो ही जाती है अलावा और बातों के। और यह सब समझ के हमने यहाँ कभी दस बरस हुए, आठ बरस हुए, मुझे याद नहीं दस बरस हुए आठ बरस हुए वो 370 दफ़ा रखा और ठीक रखा था मुझे याद है। आप देखेंगे कि इस ज़माने में हालांकि वह दफ़ा है लेकिन कितनी बातें हुई हैं जिसमें कुछ एक हमारे काग़ज़ों में एक क़ायदे हो गये हैं यानी काश्मीर के जो और मिलाने के लिए, कई बातें हैं हमारी इलेक्शन के सिलसिले में, हमारे और कुछ ...[Recording indistinct]

मुझे याद दिलाया, सुप्रीम कोर्ट वग़ैरह-वग़ैरह है, कुछ बातें जो थोड़ी बहुत हैं जो इसमें नहीं हैं। यह चीज़ें मेरी भी ख़्वाहिश है कि हल्के-हल्के इसमें एकता होती जाये और यही लाल बहादुर जी ने कहा था, लेकिन यह बातें अपने आप बढ़ते-बढ़ते साफ होती हैं, इनको इधर या उधर दबाने से नहीं होती हैं। वाक़िया यह है कि काश्मीर की हैसियत इसलिए मैंने आपको बताया, सरहदी हैसियत एक ख़ास है और हमने यह भी कहा है कहीं मालूम नहीं, आइन में या कहाँ है कि काश्मीर में कोई फ़र्क़ नहीं हो सकता बग़ैर इजाज़त के यहाँ के असेम्बली के। यह सब बातें हम कह चुके हैं, हम क़ायम रहेंगे, तो इस पर कोई, कोई यह सवाल उठता कैसे है मेरी समझ में नहीं आया, कोई इसकी 370 हटाने की जरूरत नहीं, हल्के-हल्के इत्तफ़ाक़न वो घिसता जाये और बात है। [हँसी] जैसे मैंने आपको बताया कि यह कहना कि हो गया, लेकिन हटाने की न उसके ज़ोर देने की, दोनों बातें, एक चीज़ है, तारीख़ ने उसको रंग दिया है एकबात को और ठीक दिया है, वो क़ायम रहे जब तक उसकी जरूरत है, नहीं जरूरत होगा, वह अपने आप ग़ायब हो जायेगा। एक तो इसको हटाना ग़लत बात है, कोशिश करके हटाना, जैसे यह कहा गया हमेशा के लिए यह चीज़ क़ायम रहेगी, वह भी ग़लत बात है मेरी राय में। यह सिचुएशन है एक, एक क्या कहूँ अंग्रेज़ी में फ़्लूइड [fluid] कहते हैं, एक जमी हुई नहीं है बहती हुई ठीक है। [हँसी]

अब बातें तो बहुत आपसे कहनी होती हैं, एक हजूम ख़्यालों का रहता है दिमाग़ में और मैं चाहता हूँ कि अपने साथियों को बताऊँ, वह भी सोचें। ख़ाली वो ज़माना गुज़र गया है नारों का, नारे भी वक़्त पर काम दे देते हैं और बातें जोश दिला दें, बुरी चीज़ नहीं है, लेकिन नारों से दिमाग़ नहीं चलता है, नारों से दिमाग़ कुछ रुक जाता है। तो मैं आपके दिमाग़ को चाहता हूँ कि कुछ आप देखें दुनिया की तरफ क्या हो रहा है, हिन्दुस्तान की, दुनिया, सारी दुनिया, हमारी सरहद ख़ासकर। यह साइंस की दुनिया जो है वह बढ़ती जाती है आजकल, सबकी तरफ तवज्जो करें और किसी तरह से हम अपने को उस गढ़े से निकाल लें, अपने को एक ख़्यालात के गढ़े से निकाल दें, वह गढ़े ख़तरनाक होते हैं, ज़मीन के गढ़े बुरे होते हैं, फंस जायें आदमी, जिस ख़्यालात के गढ़े में दिमाग़ फंस जाता

है वह बहुत ख़तरनाक हो जाता है, जो उसमें फंस जाता है वो निकलता ही नहीं उसमें और हमारे सारे हिन्दुस्तान के लिए एक सबमें बड़ा ख़तरा है कि हम ख़्यालात के गढ़ों में फंस गये हैं, अब निकल रहे हैं। और मेरी भी बातचीत करने का यही मतलब होता है कि आपके सामने कुछ तस्वीर इधर-उधर की रखूँ ताकि आपके दिमाग़ में कुछ न कुछ असर हो, आप भी सोचें उस पर क्योंकि जिधर हमें चलना है हमें साथ चलना है, मिलकर चलना है और कुछ उसूलों को हमें सामने रखना है अपने, और मिलके चलना है। तो एक-दूसरे को समझना चाहिए, कुछ पैर मिला के, कुछ हाथ मिला के चलना चाहिए और यह समझना चाहिए कि जो हमारी ताक़त है इसको हम अगर हम ज़ाया कर दें फ़िज़ूल कामों में तो अच्छे कामों के लिए कम रह जाती है और वाक़िया यह है कि जो काम हमने उठाये हैं इतने बड़े हैं कि सारी ताक़त की हमारी जरूरत है मजमूई। तो बस काफी वक़्त मैंने आपका लिया, आप माफ करें और कल मैं रवाना होता हूँ दिल्ली के लिए। [तालियाँ]

[Translation begins:

Mr Chairman,[405] Brothers and Sisters, Colleagues,
I had been told that I would be meeting the members of the Legislative Assembly and Council. I did not know that a large tea party like this had been arranged, to which all kinds of people must have been invited. Well, I have no objection to people of any kind or shade. But I was not aware of it. [Laughs] I was under the impression that we will talk to one another, though even that does not normally remain intimate. First of all, I am amazed that when I come to Kashmir, almost everything that I do is given a different garb or meaning. The fact is that I come to Kashmir every now and then to refresh myself, and particularly this time, I have been feeling rather unwell and wanted to become fully well.

So, I came here for health reasons and had no other purpose in mind. But I have seen it being mentioned in some newspapers that complex problems have arisen in Kashmir, and so I am here to hold talks and give advice. Complex problems beset us day and night, all over India, in every province in the country and which have now increased in number. What does that imply? It is not a bad thing because progress implies problems and as we march ahead, the problems multiply. It is only a defunct nation that has no problems. So I am not afraid of problems.

If you look at India today, you will find innumerable problems. One of them which concern you particularly is the border problem. On arrival here today, I read in the newspapers, and also heard on the radio, that there is some Chinese troop movement in one corner of Ladakh. These things obviously perturb the mind and cast a burden upon it. Then the other great problem before the country

405. See fn 403 in this section.

is of progress. Somehow it is extremely difficult to extricate oneself from the shackles of poverty, particularly when it has been there for centuries. It is not as if it can be achieved by magic or by putting up a few factories here and there. That is wrong. We need to have planning; which ultimately implies changing human beings, training them to understand the times that we are living in, take advantage of it and we can benefit enormously.

The world today belongs to science and technology—predominantly. I do not say that we should neglect everything else. We must retain and cherish the values of our ancient heritage and at the same time adopt the teachings of modern science and technology; for those who fail to grasp them become backward. This is how India and the other countries of Asia had become backward in the past, because they failed to appreciate the significance of modern science. The West advanced because modern science gave them the key to an enormous treasure trove in the form of hidden sources of natural energy. Today, the West is wealthy and powerful because they have learnt to tap these resources both above and below the ground, like electricity and what not. It is a search for new knowledge, which cannot be acquired by keeping one's eyes closed, and Europe and the United States benefited enormously by it. It may be said that for the first time, in the thousands of years of world history, poverty can be brought under control. In the olden days, there was one advantage that the world population was far less than what it is today. Therefore, there was no question of such dire poverty. But the fact is that throughout history poverty has shackled the majority of the world population. For the first time in history, poverty was eradicated in Europe and then in America about a couple of hundred years ago and a new world began to emerge with the discovery of hidden sources of natural energy. Electricity is one of them, as also steam power, which are being used to do great things. There is no magic in it and even a child can learn it. But it had not been thought of earlier and the moment it was discovered, Man acquired a great source of energy. What is a machine? It adds to the strength of a human being. So, mankind has acquired tremendous sources of energy by bringing under control the resources hidden in nature. [Recording indistinct].

Partition made a bad impression on the Hindus and Muslims alike. The eighty to ninety lakh Hindus, who live in East Pakistan even now and the Muslims on this side, were affected. It uprooted everything. A progress-oriented country cannot carry on like this. You must try to understand this. It is absurd to think of any section of society as second class citizens. That is why the Kashmir issue has special significance, not only for Kashmir but for the whole of India and Pakistan. It is not a question of merely transferring a piece of land geographically to this side or that. Ultimately the matter will have to be decided with the concurrence of everyone who lives there. But to decide this issue merely on the basis of communalist emotions, will affect India and Pakistan alike—adversely. I hope you will be able to solve the problem and come to a decision. The roots of the problem go deep, and it is not merely a religious issue because some fresh problems have arisen in Pakistan at the moment. The Government of Pakistan have every right to do what they wish and I do not wish to interfere. But the fact is that there are great difficulties, and once we adopt a communalist, sectarian approach, it adversely affects various other issues. We want that Pakistan should progress and we must have cordial relations between the two countries. After all, the people of Pakistan are like our own brothers and there is nobody who is closer to us than them. There is no doubt about it, and unfortunately the closer two people are, the more the chances of misunderstandings and anger between them. Anyhow, the people are our own, and the entire process of history demands that the tensions between the two countries must become less and the problem be solved.

At the moment, the task before India, Pakistan and the other countries of Asia is to progress and catch up with the West. The world today consists of the developed countries and the underdeveloped ones, the wealthy countries and the poor. There are many countries which come in between. But India will be counted among the poor countries—inspite of the big projects and the big cities. The real test of affluence is the status of the ordinary man, his per capita income and standard of living, etc. It is the duty of both India and Pakistan to help one another willingly. Unfortunately, we have got involved in a dispute.

We are engaged, at the moment, in completing the Five Year Plans. The moment one plan is over another begins, because the process is unending. What we have done, so far, constitutes the basic foundation on which we can build further. The most important thing is that we do not wish to get involved in international problems or in a dispute with any other nation. We want to put our house in order, educate our beautiful young children, etc. It pains me to see their sad condition. The children in Kashmir are beautiful but they go about in rags and are dirty. Education is spreading but there is scope for much more. It is good to see children in school uniforms. They make a great deal of difference. But there is scope for much more and we should pay attention to that, instead of frittering away our energies. I said just now that there is tremendous scope in Kashmir. The fact of the matter is that the people here are generally brilliant. [Recording indistinct]

Now you will be able to understand this problem, and deal with it better. As I told you just now, my coming here has been misconstrued and the newspapers have been saying that I have come in connection with some complex problems which have arisen in Kashmir. That is absurd. It is obvious that I am interested in the problems of Kashmir and for that matter, the problems of the whole country;

in a sense, the interest is slightly greater in Kashmir. But it has been made out that I was actually supposed to go to Kulu but there was a last minute change and I came here instead. There was talk of my going to Kulu but it started raining there, and Kulu is not very pleasant in the rains. Therefore I dropped the idea and came to Kashmir because there are less rains here in this season. I had no idea whatsoever that any other reason could be attributed to my coming here.

It is obvious that some of you have been meeting me and we have discussed the problems of Kashmir, as we generally do. But I had no special reason for coming here. As I told you, I came here to improve my health, though I would also like to mention that there is nothing greatly the matter with me, certainly nothing to warrant the fuss that has been made. Yet I do stand in need of better mental and physical health. I often labour under the illusion that I can do far more than I actually can and that I am a youth of twenty or thirty. It was a bit of a shock to realise that I am no longer young. But I can take on anybody near my age, or younger and compete with them. [Laughter] Anyhow, perhaps you can judge from my face the difference my visit to this place has made to my health. [Applause] It is not only the body, but the mind too which benefits and somehow I have a particular affection for this place. So what the newspapers said is absolutely wrong.

There has been some talk about deleting Article 370 of the Constitution, which gives a special status to Kashmir. There was a debate in Parliament about it, and our Home Minister, Shri Lal Bahadur Shastri had replied to it.[406] I live in Delhi and yet so little importance was attached to this debate that I was not even told about the reactions to it. There is always some debate or the other on. But I believe everything that was said, has been put under a microscope, and there is a suspicion about the intent. I cannot understand what this is all about. In my opinion, leaving aside the smaller issues, the two great external problems that India faces today are the Kashmir issue where Pakistan is involved; and the other is China. In a sense, both are aggressors. Kashmir is involved in both the issues and so apart from everything else, this in itself gives it a special status. Taking all this into consideration, we had incorporated Article 370 into the Constitution, and rightly so in my view. You will find that inspite of this Article there has been a great deal of effort to merge Kashmir in India [recording indistinct], about elections, etc.

I have been reminded that there is the Supreme Court, etc., etc., and some other things which are not mentioned here. I too want that gradually we should become united, and this is what Lal Bahadurji had also mentioned. But these things become clearer as you go on. There is no need to suppress it. The fact

406. See fn 404 in this section.

is that Kashmir occupies a special position being a border state, and I think it has been laid down in the Constitution, or somewhere else, that the status of Kashmir cannot be changed without the permission of the Kashmir Assembly. We have said all this, and we will stick to it. I cannot understand how there can be any question at all. There is no need to remove Article 370. If it gradually fades into insignificance, that is a different matter. [Laughter] It is a product of a historical exigency and will be maintained as long as it is necessary and will disappear when it is no longer essential. It would be wrong to remove it by design. On the other hand, it is equally wrong to say that it should be a permanent thing. This is a fluid situation, not something which has to be regarded as permanent. [Laughter]

I have a great deal that I could say to you, for there is always a crowd of ideas in my mind. I want to share them with my colleagues, so that they can also ponder over them. The time for shouting slogans has gone; for though they are useful to whip up enthusiasm, they prevent objective thinking. I want you to see what is happening in India and the rest of the world. The boundaries of knowledge are expanding day by day and it is extremely important for us to get out of the mental rut into which we had fallen in the past. Mental ruts are just as dangerous as pits in the ground. It is difficult to get out once you are stuck in it. This is the biggest danger, that we in India have been facing in the past. So my intention is to make an impression upon your minds by talking about various issues. You must also think about the goals we have before us and the need to abide by our principles and of unity and harmony. We must understand clearly, that if we fritter away our energies in futile preoccupations, we will have less energy for worthwhile tasks. The fact is that we have taken on such great tasks that we need all the resources, mental and physical, that we can command to complete them. Please forgive me for taking up so much of your time. I am leaving for Delhi in the morning. [Applause]

Translation ends]

150. To M.J. Desai and B.F.H.B. Tyabji: Kashmir for German Ambassador[407]

I agree wholly with the argument advanced by SS to the German Ambassador.[408] Also with the remarks of FS. I think it would be desirable to write a note on

407. Note, 11 July 1962, to Foreign Secretary and Special Secretary, MEA. Sent from Chashmashahi Guest House, Srinagar.
408. Georg Ferdinand Duckwitz.

this subject both for publication and to be sent to our Missions abroad for their information.

2. I have always laid stress on this aspect of the Kashmir question, apart from legal and constitutional issue involved in it. Even today at a meeting of Kashmir Legislators and others, I laid stress on it. But it is quite true that the argument has greater weight of it comes from an Indian Muslim.

3. I hope, therefore, that a note or article, as suggested, will be prepared.

(vi) Kerala

151. To Pattom A. Thanu Pillai: Release of C.A. Balan[409]

July 5, 1962

My dear Thanu Pillai,

I enclose a copy of a letter I have received from E.M.S. Namboodiripad, General Secretary of the Communist Party of India. 1 do not know all the facts about the case mentioned. But if it is true that he was sentenced in Madras and other prisoners like him have been released by the Madras Government, it appears reasonable that the same test should apply to him[410] and that he should also be released.

Yours sincerely,
[Jawaharlal Nehru]

(vii) Madhya Pradesh

152. To B.A. Mandloi: Be Discreet[411]

June 9, 1962

My dear Mandloi,

I am rather distressed at seeing statements in the press, some of which apparently emanate from you, about the decision of the High Command of the Congress.

409. Letter to the Chief Minister of Kerala, sent from Pahalgam, Kashmir.

410. C.A. Balan.

411. Letter to the Chief Minister of Madhya Pradesh.

There has been no decision except to consider this matter after we have received the report from Shri Ramakrishna Rao.[412] I expect that we shall get this report in the course of the next few days. Immediately after, we shall consider both the report and the general situation in Madhya Pradesh and give our advice in the matter.[413]

[Katju's Delusion]

NO DECISION HAS BEEN TAKEN ON M.P. LEADERSHIP.
KATJU FEELS HE IS STILL THE CHIEF MINISTER.
WHO IS THIS MANDLOI? IS HE FROM U.P. OR MADRAS?

From Left: Lal Bahadur Shastri, K.N. Katju

(From *Shankar's Weekly*, 8 July 1962, p. 12)

It is desirable therefore, that nothing should be said about any decision or views of the so-called High Command of the Congress at this stage.

Yours sincerely,
[Jawaharlal Nehru]

412. B. Ramakrishna Rao, Governor of Uttar Pradesh till 1962 and Rajya Sabha MP from 21 June 1962, was deputed by the CWC to inquire into the Congress electoral reverses in Madhya Pradesh.
413. The report was likely to be strongly condemnatory of Deshlahra and his followers, according to *The Times of India*, 28 June 1962, p. 1 col. 6. See also item 155 and appendix 65.

153. To Lal Bahadur Shastri: Trouble in Madhya Pradesh[414]

June 13, 1962

My dear Lal Bahadur,
I am enclosing a copy of a letter which I am sending to Mandloi.[415]

Pataskar,[416] whom I saw a little while ago, has given me a very dim report of conditions in Madhya Pradesh. These conditions are bad politically, administratively and economically.

On the 25th of this month, their Assembly is meeting. Before that date we must come to some decision about the political aspects. It seems that whatever political decision is taken, will create some difficulties. Anyhow, we have to face the problems and come to some decisions. We have been awaiting the report of Ramakrishna Rao.[417] You promised to telephone to him to expedite it. Do you know when this report is coming? Time is short.

Yours affectionately,
[Jawaharlal Nehru]

154. To B.A. Mandloi: Poor Governance in Madhya Pradesh[418]

June 13, 1962

My dear Mandloi,
I gather that the Administration in Madhya Pradesh is not functioning well. There are very large arrears of revenue, especially from forests and land revenue. Also that the law and order position is not good.

414. Letter to the Home Minister.
415. Chief Minister of Madhya Pradesh.
416. H.V. Pataskar, Governor of Madhya Pradesh.
417. Congress, Rajya Sabha MP from 21 June.
418. Letter to the Chief Minister of Madhya Pradesh. PMO, File No. 17(507)/62-67-PMS, (Vol. I to V), Sr. No. 8-A.

There have been considerable over-drafts from the Reserve Bank. You must be thinking now of additional taxation. But the first thing to do is to collect the arrears.

I should like you to let me know how far my information is correct.

Yours sincerely,
[Jawaharlal Nehru]

155. To Moolchand Deshlahra: Resign as President of PCC[419]

July 19, 1962

My dear Deshlahra,

I have received your letter of the 17th July.[420]

I am not a member of the 7-man committee which was appointed to consider the state of Congress affairs in Madhya Pradesh. I have read Shri Ramakrishna Rao's report.[421] My impression after reading it was that while specific charges against you were not considered to be proved, it was thought desirable for you to resign from the Presidentship of the PCC, as apparently has been suggested by the 7-man committee. Madhya Pradesh has become an arena of intense groupism,[422] and unfortunately you have been connected with one of the groups. For the President of the PCC, this is not a desirable thing. He should command general approval.

419. Letter to the President of the Madhya Pradesh PCC. Sent from Rashtrapati Nilayam, Hyderabad.
420. Appendix 65.
421. Report on Congress electoral reverses in Madhya Pradesh submitted by B. Ramakrishna Rao, Rajya Sabha MP.
422. See also SWJN/SS/75/item 112 and appendices 20 (a) and 20 (b).

[REWARDS OF GROUPISM]

You Said It

By LAXMAN

There you go again—"Eschew Groupism"! I don't know why you've become so critical of groupism now. After all it did help you to become the chief!

(From *The Times of India*, 26 June 1962, p. 1)

As I have said above, I have not taken any part in the discussions of the 7-man committee. But whatever its advice to you should be followed as a matter of discipline. One must not look upon this as a personal issue, but think of the good of the organisation we are privileged to serve. Surely it is possible to serve it even after resigning from its Presidentship.

Yours sincerely,
[Jawaharlal Nehru]

(viii) Madras

156. To H.H.K.M. Bhora: Madras Corporation Elections[423]

July 18, 1962

Dear Shri Bhora,

I have your letter of the 14th July.

From what you say it appears that Shri Sivashanmugam Pillai[424] would help considerably in the Corporation elections. I have no objection to his going there and working to this end. But it would be odd and unusual for me to depute any person to go to Madras for such a purpose. I do not know what you mean by "providing him with all comforts". If the Madras Congress or the Chief Minister of Madras[425] desires his presence there, they can certainly ask him. As I have said above, I shall have no objection.

Yours sincerely,
[Jawaharlal Nehru]

(ix) Mysore

157. To S.R. Kanthi: Marathi Speakers in Belgaum[426]

June 2, 1962

My dear Kanthi,

I enclose a copy of a letter I have received.[427] I am not putting up this matter before the National Integration Council. But I must say that I am concerned at the continuance of this boundary dispute. Apart from where the boundary should be, the complaints of ill-treatment of Marathi-speaking people in the Belgaum area continue. Every effort should be made to avoid any such complaints.

423. Letter; address: 73 Kumarasami Chetty Street, Cantt. Pallavaram, C. R. Dist., South India. Sent from Rashtrapati Nilayam, Hyderabad.
424. J. Sivashanmugam Pillai, Rajya Sabha MP, Congress, from Madras.
425. K. Kamaraj.
426. Letter to the Chief Minister of Mysore State.
427. Appendix 12.

Marathi-speaking people whether they live in Mysore or elsewhere, have the right to expect protection from the State Government of their language etc.

Yours sincerely,
[Jawaharlal Nehru]

158. To S.R. Kanthi: Bangalore Visit[428]

June 4, 1962

My dear Kanthi,

Your letter of May 31st has just reached me. I had promised to go to Bangalore in July for the All India Manufacturers' Organisation's Conference as well as the opening of the Visvesvaraya Museum. I now understand that the conference is taking place in Bombay earlier.[429]

I am prepared, however, to go to Bangalore sometime in July for the Visvesvaraya Museum.[430] I can then inaugurate the Mysore Pradesh Panchayat Raj Parishad.[431] About the second week of July will suit me.

Yours sincerely,
[Jawaharlal Nehru]

159. To S.R. Kanthi: Bangalore Visit[432]

June 13, 1962

My dear Kanthi,

You will remember that I have promised to visit Bangalore to open the Visvesvaraya Industrial Museum and possibly for another engagement. I have not fixed a date yet. Would it suit you and the organisers of the Museum if I went there about the middle of July, say, for two days. Ajit Prasad Jain has

428. Letter to the Chief Minister of Mysore.
429. The conference, held in June, was not attended by Nehru, see his letter to G.V. Puranik, SWJN/SS/76/item 340.
430. See item 165.
431. See item 167.
432. Letter to the Chief Minister of Mysore State. PMS, File No. 8(226) 62-PMP. Also available in the JN Collection.

asked me if possible, to open a Polytechnic at Tumkur[433] which, I believe, is his constituency.[434] I am prepared to do so, if it is convenient.

If and when I go to Bangalore, I should like to take advantage of your kind offer for me to spend a short time in the Nandi Hills. I am afraid I cannot spend much time there. But I might be able to go there for two or three days.

Yours sincerely,
[Jawaharlal Nehru]

160. To S.R. Kanthi: Bangalore Programme[435]

June 19, 1962

My dear Kanthi,

I wrote to you about the date of my visit to Bangalore for the Visvesvaraya Industrial Museum. I have had no reply from you.[436] But the Museum people have intimated to me that the 13th or the 14th July will be suitable for them. I have, therefore, decided to come to Bangalore on the morning of Saturday, the 14th July. The Museum ceremony can be held during the afternoon on that date. I hope this suits you.

As I have already told you, I am prepared to have the other ceremony you want me to attend the next day, 15th July, in Bangalore. I should also like to go to the Polytechnic in Tumkur. I hope this also can be arranged on the 15th in the afternoon or some suitable time.

On the 16th July, if that suits you, I could go to Nandi Hills for three or four days.[437]

Yours sincerely,
[Jawaharlal Nehru]

433. See item 166.
434. Congress, Lok Sabha MP from Tumkur, and President of the UPCC.
435. Letter to the Chief Minister of Mysore State.
436. Item 159.
437. See further item 161.

161. To S. Nijalingappa: Mysore Visit in July[438]

June 21, 1962

My dear Nijalingappa,

I see from the newspapers that you have been elected Leader of the party and, consequently, you will become Chief Minister of Mysore. My congratulations and good wishes.[439]

I had written to Kanthi about my visiting Bangalore in the middle of July principally for the Visvesvaraya Industrial Museum. I had suggested one or two other engagements too, namely, inauguration of the Mysore Pradesh Panchayat Raj Parishad and a visit to Tumkur for the opening ceremony of a Polytechnic. Further I had suggested that I might go to Nandi Hills for two or three days afterwards.[440]

I have received his reply dated 19th June, with which he has sent a draft tour programs. I do not like at all this draft programme as he has put everything in the course of half a day at Bangalore. I should like this to be spread out.

I suggest that I might go to Bangalore on the 14th July arriving there at about 11.30 a.m. The only function that day should be the opening of the Visveswaraya Museum at about 5 p.m. or so.

The next day, I could go to Tumkur in the morning, coming back for lunch to Bangalore, and in the afternoon at about 5 p.m. the inauguration of the Mysore Pradesh Panchayat Raj Parishad.

The next day, that is the 16th July, I could go to Nandi Hills in the morning and spend two or three days there.

If this suits you, you can arrange accordingly.

Yours sincerely,
Jawaharlal Nehru

438. Letter to the Chief Minister to-be of Mysore State. PMS, File No. 8(226)62-PMP. Also available in the JN Collection.

439. On 20 June 1962, S.R. Kanthi resigned as Chief Minister in favour of Nijalingappa, President of the Mysore Pradesh Congress Committee. See *The Times of India*, 21 June 1962, p. 7 cols 1 & 2. Nijalingappa took over as Chief Minister on 21 June, see *The Hindu*, 22 June 1962, p. 1 cols 2-3.

440. See item 160.

162. To S. Nijalingappa: No Ostentation at Bangalore Reception[441]

July 6, 1962

My dear Nijalingappa,

I have received a letter from someone in Bangalore informing me that the Bangalore Corporation has set apart Rs 5,000/- to give me a civic reception.[442] I am rather distressed at this. I do not mind a civic reception being given to me, but why spend Rs 5,000/- over it. I have repeatedly stated that I do not like silver or the like being presented to me. Please inform the Mayor of Bangalore of my views on this subject, and request him to avoid any large sum of money being spent on my reception.

Yours sincerely,
Jawaharlal Nehru

163. To S. Nijalingappa: Meeting with K. Hanumanthaiya[443]

July 10, 1962

My dear Nijalingappa,

K. Hanumanthaiya[444] has written to me that he would like to welcome me on my arrival at the airport at Bangalore. Could you kindly arrange to have a pass sent to him?

441. Letter to the Chief Minister of Mysore State. Sent from Pahalgam, Kashmir. PMO, File No. 8(226) 62-PMP. Also available in the JN Collection.

442. The letter is reproduced below:

"16 Veeranna Gardens, Bangalore-5, 1 July 1962. Your Excellency, I have to inform you that the Bangalore Corporation has set apart Rs. 5000 to give you a civic reception when you come to Bangalore next week. You have on many previous occasions discouraged presentation of caskets and huge garlands touching almost the shoes, out of public funds. I am bringing this to your notice to consider whether the civic authorities are right in spending tax payers'money in this fashion in these hard days. Quite recently, a reception was held to Chief Minister Sri Kanthi, at a cost of Rs 1500, but this gentleman has resigned to make room for Sri Nijalingappa. Most probably a reception will be held to the new chief at some cost.Yours faithfully, Parthasarathy, A Tax payer." PMO, File No. 8(226)62-PMP, Sr. No. 80-A.

443. Letter to the Chief Minister of Andhra Pradesh. Sent from Pahalgam, Kashmir. PMS, File No. 8(226)62-PMP.

444. Lok Sabha MP, Congress, from Bangalore city, Mysore.

He would also like me to visit him in his new house on my way to the Nandi Hills. I should like to do so. Would you kindly arrange accordingly?[445]

Yours sincerely,
Jawaharlal Nehru

164. To K. Hanumanthaiya: Visit to Bangalore[446]

July 10, 1962

My dear Hanumanthaiya,

Your letter of the 5th July has reached me today at Pahalgam in Srinagar.

I am only going to the Nandi Hills for a couple of days. I have never been there and a visit appears worthwhile. A little occasional rain will not matter. Indira will not be coming with me to Bangalore. Probably Vijaya Lakshmi Pandit will accompany me.

Of course you are welcome to come to the aerodrome when I go there. I am sure a pass will be sent to you if you indicate your desire to go to the aerodrome.[447]

I should like to visit you in your new house, but the time when I am going to the Nandi Hills is in the late afternoon or early evening. I am afraid that is hardly suitable for a meal.

Yours sincerely,
Jawaharlal Nehru

445. See item 164.

446. Letter to Congress MP; address "Kengal Krupa", Bellary Road, Bangalore-6. Sent from Pahalgam, Kashmir. PMS, File No. 8(226)62-PMP. Also available in the JN Collection.

447. See item 163.

165. In Bangalore: Science Museums[448]

Mr Governor,[449] Chief Minister[450] and friends,

I am glad to be here today because that means my fulfilling a promise which I made some years ago. Unfortunately, there have been repeated postponements of this celebration, or opening of the museum, partly due to me, and partly perhaps, to other causes. So I am glad that at last I am here and you are here and we are participating in the formal opening of this museum.

The history of a country can be seen in many ways. It is the history of the activities of numerous folk, unknown, whose names are not written down, and forces at play, and yet in a sense the history of a country is the history of the famous men who have lived in that country, famous not because they were kings or rulers or warriors, as usually one finds in records of old times, but because they have helped in building up the nation, in creative activities. To my mind a great sculptor, a really great sculptor, is a much bigger man than a king, or any creative artist, whether he is a writer or an engineer. An engineer is definitely a creative person, he builds, so you judge of a period of history by the fact as to who the leading men were, whom did the public honour. If the public honours merely a king, who is nothing but a king, then the public has not advanced enough in intelligence or civilisation. If a public honours a great artist, it is something, they value the art, not the man but the art, the builder. If the public honours a builder it again means something definite. In the present age, obviously anywhere, but more specially in India, the creative builder is the man whom we have to honour, and Dr Visvesvaraya was a creative builder, not only in the schemes he undertook but in the thinking he gave to it and the impetus he gave to this business during his long life. Therefore, he was one of the men, one of the famous men whom the country must honour in his life, and after he has passed away, and must treat him as an example for others.

We are in the present day busy, occupied with building India, building not in the sense of putting up constructions, building India, building the people of India. It is a tremendous task as we all of us realise, and there are a multitude of our critics who find great solace in running India down, and the people of India down and trying to point out that the task is too big for them, they will not succeed in doing it. Well, it is difficult to prophesy what the future will bring. But speaking about my own conviction, that is the most I can say, it is

448. Speech, 14 July 1962, on opening the Visvesvaraya Industrial and Technological Museum. NMML, AIR Tapes, No.8419, NM, No. 1651.

449. Jayachamaraja Wodeyar.

450. S. Nijalingappa.

this and it is based on my belief, my faith in the people of India as a whole, because I do believe in them even as I have affection for them. I am convinced that the people of India will fulfil the great tasks that they have undertaken, and there is no question of completing the picture because the picture goes on growing, the tasks go on growing, but only of completing every stage as it arises. Oddly enough, the mere existence of problems is a sign not of failure, but of success. Problems come to a growing organisation, to a growing nation, not to the dead, not to the weary and the aged, who cannot move their minds or legs or feet, but only to those who are moving, and India is moving today, and all the problems, the difficult problems, are signs of its growth, not of its weakness. Unfortunately, some people are not growing with India. So they can only think of the problems and the difficulties and bemoan their lot that they have been born at such a period of India's history. But as a matter of fact for every Indian, whoever he may be, this period is one of great, should be a period of great joy, that he or she is living in a period when this great nation, with such a magnificent, past is going to have a great future, and he in his own way, he or she is putting, is doing something to build that present and the future up.

We live in a world, which it is a truism to say, is a changing, dynamic world. It is changing because of many things but changing more specially because of the development of science and technology. The last 150, or 170 years have gradually changed the face of the world. The Western countries, European countries, to some extent American countries a little later, were changed by this impact of science and technology. Now in spite of all our growth in India and in the countries of Asia, we did not profit by science and technology. It is an astonishing thing which I have been unable to understand, how we failed to receive this impact. One thing it may be, that a nation exhausts its reserves for a time being till it renews them. India's reserves being very deep and great, lasted it a long time, did not exhaust them but it prevented it somehow from receiving the impact of science, in the modern sense. Take a simple example, the printing of books. It was taking place for hundreds of years in Europe but it did not reach India, and when it did reach India during the Moghul Empire, and books were presented by the Jesuit priests to the emperor, he was interested in a novel phenomenon and that is all. It did not strike his imagination, as it ought to have done, that this is a mighty thing, the printing of books, the spread of knowledge, the spread of so many things, and even from the strict point of view of the governance of an empire, printing was a great help. It did not strike anybody. Nobody did it. Ultimately the printing of books came when the British established themselves in Bengal, and at Serampore again some missionaries established a press. That amazes me, that lack of grasping a new idea. We were so full of ideas, our minds were not empty, our minds were full, but somehow we had closed the doors to them, and once the mind, however full it may be, closes the doors to new ideas, it tends to become decadent, however rich those ideas may be. The creativeness, the life force, the spirit, lessens, and without the life force you cannot develop either as an individual or as a nation. So we fell back, and the countries of Asia fell back in the race in the world and Europe became, consisting of various countries, the dominant continent in the world and dominant countries in the world. Great colonial empires were built up. America then came into the field and outstripped Europe, some countries of America.

Now there can be little doubt that the countries of Asia are having their resurgence, their renaissance, call it what you will. That can only be by an understanding of the modern world, modern science and modern technology. That does not mean a copying of what other countries have done and losing their own spirit, their own life force, their own methods of thinking, their own past history. That we must preserve. But it does mean that without our understanding the modern world, we perish or just decay, become decadent in spite of all the virtues that we may possess. It is that, when the centenary took place of Dr Visvesvaraya, that I referred, something to which reference has been made today, to the joining together of science and spirituality, spirituality which is something deeper and broader, I take it, than mere religion, which is part of religion, but a deeper and broader part of it. I think these two are essential in the modern world, if the modern world is to survive and progress. Without science you perish, without spirituality you perish also. Because science, you know, will overwhelm this world with these atom bombs and hydrogen bombs. Therefore, we see in Dr Vishvesvaraya a man of vision, a man of creative activity, a man looking ahead and a man who built around himself, and around others, a tradition of looking to science and technology, which was very, very necessary for India. Others were working to that end, but he was pre-eminent in it, and it is right that you have this museum as a memorial, if you like, of him, but more so in the sense of carrying on the work he began. A museum is not and should not be a dead thing, a memorial of somebody but it should be a living thing which evokes pictures to your mind of the past, of the present, of the future.

A reference was made by one of the speakers to this museum seeking to be something like the Deutsches Museum in Munich, and the Chicago Museum. Well, these are noble ambitions. I know, I have been fascinated by museums. Chicago Museum, I certainly was fascinated by that when I went there. South Kensington Museum in London I went to repeatedly, and the Deutsches Museum in Munich was, appeared to me to be, a place where it was difficult to leave. It was so interesting, so fascinating that walking miles upon miles of its corridors and rooms and thoroughly exhausted one could hardly stand, yet one wanted to remain there. That is the type of museum I should like to have, with that tremendous appeal and fascination because it showed the growth of technology and science, it showed the growth of various things that we take for granted, whether it is transport, communications or anything else, and by living examples, not living but by working examples, and if you can achieve anything like it, then you will have surely succeeded. I should like museums, not these big museums, but small museums to be spread out all over India, because museums excite a child's mind and every school boy and school girl should be taken to a museum. That is more important than a lesson in a class, and the things there should be explained.

So I am happy to open this museum in memory of Dr Visvesvaraya and in anticipation of the future that Sir Visvesvaraya looked forward to build and which he did build to some extent.

Thank you. [Applause]

166. In Tumkur: Public Meeting[451]

Separatist Trends
Condemnation by Nehru
Service to Country Biggest Religion

Tumkur, July 15 – Addressing a mammoth public meeting here, Prime Minister Nehru today called on the people to eschew separatist tendencies like provincialism, linguism and casteism and forge a united front in the service of the country. The biggest religion was the service of the motherland he said.

Mr Nehru hailed the recent election of Mr Ajit Prasad Jain to Parliament from Tumkur as a symbol of national integration and congratulated the 50,000 people on this.

451. Report of speech, 15 July 1962, reproduced from *The Hindu*, p.7 cols 5-6. From this report, it appears that Nehru fulfilled four engagements in Tumkur in the forenoon, and inaugurated the Panchayati Raj convention in Bangalore in the afternoon before going to Nandi Hills.

A.P. Jain was elected from Tumkur in a bye-election. He had earlier lost in the general elections from Kairana Parliamentary constituency in UP. See *RECI*, p. 69.

[VICTORY AFTER DEFEAT]

You Said It

By LAXMAN

His great success in this by-election is truly a triumphant victory over the majority of people who defeated him in the General Election!

(From *The Times of India*, 4 June, 1962, p. 1)

The Prime Minister fulfilled four engagements simultaneously from a common platform. He received a citizens' reception given by the town municipality, inaugurated the Government polytechnic building, laid the foundation for the new building of the Aryan High School besides distributing certificates in a Hindi convocation. The arrangement was obviously done with an eye on the Prime Minister's convenience and to save him from strain.

Stressing the importance of Hindi the Prime Minster said he was glad to learn that a large number of people in Mysore were learning Hindi. There was no compulsion about that. That was also a sign of national integration Hindi should be learnt all over India in addition to the great State languages and other regional languages should also be learnt.

The municipal address was read by the President, Mr D.N. Ananthanarayana Setty. The Law Minister, Mr M.V. Rama Rao made a welcome speech on behalf of the other three institutions.

Jain's Election from Tumkur

Addressing the gathering from a high rostrum in front of the local high school's open air theatre, Mr Nehru said he had come to Tumkur for the first time. He was happy at the opportunity to meet the town's people and see its prosperity. He had come chiefly because of the pressure from his friend and colleague, Mr Ajit Prasad Jain, whom they had recently elected to Parliament. He wanted to convey his high appreciation and congratulate them on the election, because it was a symbol of something which he held very dear. For the first time, a person from North India had been elected in an election in the South. Therefore, it was a symbol of national integration. He hoped that kind of thing would take place more and more both in the South and in the North.

Mr Nehru said that at the present moment, when they had so many problems facing them they should always remember that national integration was the first thing and the country's unity should be strengthened. Without that all their efforts were likely to be wasted. They should always remember the unity of India was the first thing, whether they lived in the North or the South. They must not allow anything to increase the feelings of provincialism, casteism, etc. Such separatist feelings would weaken the country. They must get over the barriers of that kind and build up a unified India.

Ever since they obtained Swaraj, Mr Nehru said, they had been engaged in trying to put an end to poverty. That was a great and tremendous task. They had to go step by step and had to work hard for it and on right lines.

They had the example of the Western countries becoming prosperous by taking advantage of science and technology in agriculture and in industry and soon. If India had to progress likewise they had also to modernise their way of thinking. They had to increase the yield on the farm and in the factories by improved techniques.

Raising the condition of 400 million people of the country was a great task. No outsider could raise them. No outside money could help them very much. It was by their own efforts they could raise themselves. It was through education, mass education and hard work that this can be achieved. He was happy to find that primary and secondary education was growing fast all over the country. He was particularly happy to find technical institutions being established in various part of the country. They were the foundation of growth. There was no other way. In their educational system, there should be greater emphasis on science and technology without which they would perish.

Mr Nehru referred to the Five-Year Plans in general and the Third Plan in particular and said they had done well so far inspite of difficulties. He was convinced that the progress India was making would continue and lead them to their aims. He would ask the people to understand the five year plans. They should not be frightened of the difficulties facing them in the implementation of the plans, but work harder to reach the goal. They were working not only for the present but also for the future and more for the latter, since the future represented the children who were the citizens of tomorrow who would inherit whatever they did today. Therefore, they had to consider India as one great nation and not think too much of their difference of religion caste, State etc. Religion was good if it unified the people and bad if it created hatred and separation.

Mr Nehru reminded the people of Mysore that they were living in a "beautiful State." Mysore, he said, was a great State which was already making good progress. Bangalore was one of the great cities of India and was the centre of industry, science, and technology. They were fortunate in that. But they should also bear in mind that all those things about Bangalore did not belong to Bangalore alone but to the whole of India. If India progressed, all of them progressed and if India did not then all of them suffered.

Mr Nehru renewed his call for a united front and said they had to think they were members of a great family that was India. Wherever they lived whatever part of the country they belonged to and whatever religion or caste they professed. In India, he said they had great religions like Hindusim, Islam, Christianity, and Buddhism and other religions. All the religions of India must respect each other and there should be a spirit of friendliness among one another. The biggest religion after all, was service to motherland. If they learnt that lesson, then their religions also helped them. Otherwise they would suffer.

Mr Nehru then pressed the buttons fixed on the rostrum to signify the fulfilment of his engagements.

Mr Nehru's speech in English was rendered into Kannada by Mr Siddavanahalli Krishna Sharma.

Earlier, Mr M.V. Rama Rao, Law Minister, in his welcome speech, referred to the great need for the expansion of technical education in Mysore to provide opportunities for the deserving young men and women and requested the Prime Minister to use his good offices to persuade the Planning Commission to provide for at least four more engineering colleges and six more polytechnics in the State.

Inaugurating the Second Convention of the Mysore Panchayat Raj Parishad in Bangalore today,[452] Mr Nehru explained the difference between the present concept of Panchayat Raj and the former concept of limited panchayats doing

452. For full speech on this occasion, see item 167.

little jobs for the villagers. The new concept was to give the elected bodies full authority over certain matters and resources and to make them responsible not by putting officials at the head, but by entrusting the panchayats with the work. The fact, that some of these bodies behaved foolishly or wrongly, was no reason for denying the vast number of panchayats the opportunity to learn and to grow. Ultimately, it was a question of having faith in the people. Mr Nehru said he believed in Panchayat Raj as in democracy because he had full faith in the people. It was this faith that had given him strength all these years. He was convinced about the great future before India because of his faith in the people and not in individuals.

Duty of Officials

Mr Nehru said that while officials, being trained people were necessary for carrying on the administration, they should not come in the way of the initiative of the people. He found that the old distinction between officials and non-official still persisted to some extent. That distinction came about because of the officials being looked upon in the old sense as masters. But that should not be. Now the officials should be all the more the servants of the people. He commented the idea of the sponsors of the convention to organise training classes and said that the progress of the country depended on training in agriculture and industries, big and small.

Earlier, Mrs Vijaya Lakshmi Pandit, releasing the souvenir number of the Convention, said the one thing which could contribute to the greater progress of India was to make the villages strong. The responsibility given to the panchayats would be the real leadership that would bring about the fruition of their cherished dreams.

Mr R. Dayananda Sagar, Deputy Minister, presented the souvenir to Mrs Pandit.

Mr S. Nijalingappa, Chief Minister, who presided, said the participants should not hesitate to tell the Government frankly the difficulties that were met in the working of Panchayat Raj. At the same time, they should also consider how best they could contribute to the success of the scheme. He said that they should profit by the suggestions made by the Prime Minister and make sincere efforts to achieve the results expected of them.

Earlier, Mr H.S. Linga Reddy welcoming the gathering on behalf of the Reception Committee, said about 2,000 representatives of local bodies and legislators were attending the Convention.

Mr S.K. Dey, Union Minister for Community Development was among those present.

Before leaving Lalbagh, the Prime Minister cheerfully allowed an old man to garland him with a Tulsi mala. The old man hailed Mr Nehru as the "Kaliyuga Krishna Paramatma".

Arrival in Nandi Hills

Mr Nehru and Mrs Vijayalakshmi Pandit reached the Cubbon House atop the Nandi Hills late this evening, where the Prime Minister will have a quiet holday. On his way, Mr Nehru dropped in at the residence of Mr K. Hanumanthaiah, MP, and had tea with him and the members of his family.

Mr Nehru will return to Bangalore on the evening of July 17 and will be accorded a civic reception by the Municipal Corporation at the Banquet Hall of the Vidhana Soudha.

167. In Bangalore: To the Panchayati Raj Parishad Convention[453]

Mr Governor,[454] Chief Minister,[455] Friends and Comrades,

When I was asked during my visit to Bangalore to inaugurate this Panchayati Raj Convention, I gladly accepted it because I attach the greatest importance to this movement of Panchayati Raj in this country. People discuss it and often criticise it and find fault with it and there are many faults even here in Mysore: but you must understand the concept lying behind it. In the address, just read, it said it will train future Parliamentarians. True. I shall tell you something more about it. Panchayati Raj is meant to produce Prime Ministers of India.

Some people having nothing better to do are often asking the question: what after Nehru? And my answer to them: get awake, wide awake and look round you and you will find large numbers of people, thousands and tens of thousands who are being trained to run this country after Nehru is no more.

But people are so accustomed either to the old British Raj with its viceroys and governors, or to the State rajas with their maharajas and nawabs, that they cannot think in any other terms but some big boss sitting on top. We don't want a big boss in India. They are, of course, in every country great men and everybody cannot become great. But everybody can attain a certain measure of

453. Inaugural Address, 15 July 1962, to the Second Convention, held at the Lalbagh. NMML, AIR Tapes, TS No. 8420, 8423, NM No. 1654.

454. Jayachamaraja Wodeyar.

455. S. Nijalingappa.

greatness and out of that large number, individuals rise up to positions of great responsibility. So the training one gives is not for an individual prince who will become a maharaja, or somebody else who will become the viceroy, but one trains hundreds of thousands of persons to a higher degree of competence, self-reliance and to look after the affairs of the modern world and out of those hundreds of thousands and millions, individuals rise higher and take to these positions of responsibility.

So, we must be clear as to what we are aiming at in India. We want competent men, well trained men, because nothing worthwhile, nothing that is great, can be done with untrained men. We want competent administrators, we want good engineers, we want good scientists, we want good farmers—all these are essential and so many other people, all trained people, are essential if a country is to run properly. And we want particularly all people whoever they are to understand the modern world—the modern world which is based on science and technology. Unless we understand that, all of us, we cannot make good progress or solve our problems. Therefore, we have to train hundreds of thousands and millions of people, in fact, we hope to train everybody in the country, not all of them to be Prime Ministers—we do not require quite so many Prime Ministers—but there are other people who do work even more important than Prime Ministers do. The scientists may raise the level of your country greatly, an engineer may do great things, a medical man may be fine, may be a great person, a farmer who raises the amount that he produces from the land, does good to millions of people. So each person is trained for his own particular job. But all are trained, I hope they will be, and out of them, many people are competent enough to run the country as Prime Ministers and Ministers.

So you must remember that every child in India, whether boy or girl, is potentially a President of India or a Prime Minister of India. Take the case of our ex-President, Dr Rajendra Prasad. He was a small farmer. He is still a small farmer in Bihar. But by his ability, by his great service to the country, he rose to the highest rank in India. Our present President, he does not belong to a family of aristocrats, but by his great ability and sacrifice, he has won a name for us all over the world and he is now adorning the highest office in India.

So, I believe, and if I may say so with all respect, that given the opportunity there are many Rajendra Prasads and Radhakrishnans in India—given the opportunity. Today we left, most of our young people, left that opportunity. It is not their fault. But given the opportunity any number of them can rise to the highest positions in this land. Therefore, I am anxious that whenever I see children and I see plenty of them and I like them, children in the villages, I think of them as potential, great leaders of this country, either great leaders in the political field or some other scientific or technical or agricultural, but great leaders I look upon them—potentially speaking. And it hurts me to see that they are not well looked after, not well fed, not well clothed or well housed or well educated. They do not get those opportunities. Therefore, it is our first business to provide these opportunities to all our children and to grown-ups too. But above all to our children who are to represent the India of tomorrow.

I have mentioned various types of training. You must have good education, you must have good living conditions, but above all you should have training in, shall I say, training in self-reliance, training in leadership, so that it is only when you have that training that you can assume places of responsibility. If we can afford all these types of training to our people, boys and girls, men and women, then we shall build up a true and indestructible democracy, because that democracy will not depend upon Rajendra Prasad or Dr Radhakrishnan or Jawaharlal Nehru or anybody else. It will depend on four hundred million people, each one of whom is capable of being a President or the Prime Minister of this country.

This takes some time, as all great things take time. You cannot change the face of the nation by magic or by some jugglery, or by looking at the stars and praying for something to happen. It takes time and it takes hard work and sacrifice. Now I have said that self-reliance and the capacity to do things is most important. How does one learn it? One does not learn it entirely from books, a little he can. One learns it by doing the job. One learns it by shouldering the burden of responsibility. When the British were here, they used to tell us that they train us in self-government. Gradually, step by step, generation after generation, they give us some little thing, some local self-government or something, and said we are training you for self-government. Apart from the fact that India had just a few thousand years of experience of this, it is absurd to train anybody in self-government by sitting upon him. You train him in self-government by allowing him to govern himself. That is the only way of training that is real. You do not learn how to swim in water by being taught motions in the air in a school. You have to jump into the water and swim and swallow a lot of water perhaps also. That is how you learn how to swim.

So, Panchayati Raj is the mighty school of the nation to train millions of people in the exercise of responsibility, of administration and so many other things. Therefore, that is the basic school of the country and if you want to profit by it, you must give them real responsibility, real authority, now give these to them in name only.

What is the difference between the conception of Panchayati Raj and the previous conception of limited panchayats, doing some little jobs in their villages. The Panchayati Raj conception was to give those elected bodies full authority over certain matters, and resources and make them responsible, not by putting officials at their heads, not by making officials responsible, but making the panchayats themselves responsible for it.

It may be that those to whom you give this authority will make mistakes. It may be that some of them will behave foolishly and wrongly. We take the risk. The risk has to be taken. It is better that a few persons behave wrongly—and if you catch them you deal with them—than not to give them authority for fear that they might behave wrongly. Ultimately it is a question of having faith in the people of India and I speak to you not merely because, not merely because in theory I believe in the Panchayati Raj business and in democracy, but because I have full faith in the people of India. It is the faith that has carried me for all those years and has given me strength and I am convinced of the future of India, because I have faith in the people of India, not because of one individual or two, not of somebody who will come after me, after Nehru—that would be a poor substitute for the leadership of the people of India.

Nehrus come and go, that is the way of the world. But the people of India continue and will if we raise strong foundations, they will produce enough people to lead them and to march forward hand in hand. Now I am telling you all this because I find that in some parts of India the concept of Panchayati Raj is not fully understood. I believe that even in Mysore it has not been fully given effect to. There is far too much official interference, there is far too little real transfer of power and authority and resources. The policy is too cautions. Now, I am not blaming anybody. One has to be cautious in doing big thing, but the bigger the thing, the more you have to, when you have to take a leap, you have to take a leap. You cannot take half a leap and fall down in the middle of the water you are trying to cross. So, it is important that this great experiment which is more than an experiment today in India should be given the full opportunity to grow, and that growth will only come if people are trusted, people are given authority and resources.

I am not criticising officials. Officials are trained people, more trained than many of you or me. They have been trained to do certain jobs, to do them well. No administration of any country can be carried on without trained and experienced officials. Therefore, officials are necessary and essential. But officials should not come in the way of the initiative of the people, the authority of the people, but help them and serve them and raise them, but not direct them to do this or that.

In the old days there was a great distinction between officials and non-officials. That distinction still persists in the minds of people to some extent, although it should not persist. There should be no difference between officials and non-officials. Officials are trained persons, administrators who are given some service to perform for the nation. Non-officials may or may not be so trained, may be more trained or may be little trained. But that old distinction came into being because officials in the old days were in the sense of being masters, administrators as masters. That sense has gone because they are not, and should not be bosses or masters. They should be all the more servers of the people. Therefore, this distinction between officials and non-officials is fading out and rightly fading out.

I hope your convention will think about the problems I have mentioned to you, and build up a strong Panchayati Raj movement in Mysore State and I hope you will always keep high ideals before you; not only do you have to keep to build up a good movement here, but you must remember you have to shoulder a big burden of carrying India—not only Mysore State, but India, because all of you inherit the whole of India, not only your taluk or district of Mysore, but you inherit the whole of this great country from the Himalayas down to the Southern Seas, which is one—and it is important that you and your children should always realise, feel the unity and oneness of India, and at the same time the great diversity of this mighty country. This country has many religions, many provinces and states, many castes, groups and communities, many climates, but overall it is India. It is the oneness and unity of India that you must remember and teach your children because in the past we have suffered by our disunity. We must never again allow ourselves to be made the playthings of narrowness.

We meet here in this great city of Bangalore which is perhaps the symbol of modern forces at work in India—the symbol in science, in technology, in industry, representing the modern world. From this you can learn much; you can learn much from this. And I hope you will imbibe this atmosphere of the modern world from Bangalore as well as from the rest of India. It is essential, but we must get out of our grooves and think on these broad lines that are affecting the world today. That does not mean that we should uproot ourselves from our ancient culture, old ideals—that would be fatal. We have to keep to our ancient culture and keep our roots and water them; at the same time we have to keep pace with this modern world of science and technology.

You have great scientists here and great scientific institutions in Bangalore and great industries, but remember that the greatest industry of all in India is agriculture, and it is our growth in agriculture by modern methods that the country will ultimately progress. In that particular matter all of you who come from the distant parts and villages of Mysore can help, first by understanding it and then by carrying your message to others.

Officials who work with you perform very important tasks because they can help in training you and advising you. I understand that you are going to have training classes for your panchayats. That is good because without training no man can do good work, whatever work he may undertake. You can be a carpenter or blacksmith or a tailor—you require training for it—or a teacher. Therefore, attach importance to training and thus grow up, trained people, trained in various things, trained above all in modern agriculture and in industry, small and big. So I wish you well. You have all my good wishes in the work you are doing and I hope you will give a good answer, a good and strong answer to all those who talk about after Nehru who?

168. In Bangalore: Reply to Civic Address[456]

Mr Mayor,[457] Councillors of the Corporation, Mr Governor,[458] Mr Chief Minister[459] and Friends,

I am very grateful to you for your words of welcome though I wondered why you have chosen this special occasion of my visit to Bangalore for a civic address, because it is not the first time I have come here. I come here fairly frequently. However, I am very grateful to you for all the kind words you have said.

You have referred to this great city of which you are the guardians. Yours is a highly important and responsible task. To look after a great city and all those who live in it, to beautify it at the same time, to provide all the amenities that are necessary for the citizens is a tremendous task. In the case of Bangalore, which has grown phenomenally during the last few years, the burden of those who look after it must be heavy indeed.

Bangalore, in many ways, is unlike the other great cities of India. Most of the other great cities of India remind one certainly of the present, certainly a bit of the future but essentially of the past. Bangalore, more, as I said, than any other great city of India, gives one a picture of the future of India, more specially because of the concentration of science, technology and industry, especially in the public sector here. Therefore, to build for the future and to keep in view the kind of future that is coming is very important for you here, more so than the old cities representing the past of India. They represent the history; you represent the future that you are moulding, and I can imagine no greater and more fascinating task than to be in charge of a city like this which, in addition to representing the future, is one of the most beautiful cities in India.

456. Speech, 17 July 1962. NMML, AIR Tapes, TS No. 8418, NM No. 1650.
457. V.S. Krishna Iyer.
458. Jayachamaraja Wodeyar.
459. S. Nijalingappa.

I am afraid you are going to have a hard task to maintain this beauty with this growing population, because too rapid growth of the population will probably come in the way of your taking care of the beauty of the place. But I do hope that you will pay adequate attention to it.

Beauty in a city is not so much a question of spending money but of forethought and careful planning and an essential love of the city. It is not merely a matter of the Corporation, it is a matter of all the residents of the city. In many cities in Europe they have, apart from the official municipality, they have what is called an organisation called "Friends of the City,"— certainly in Switzerland, and I think in Germany—to which citizens belong and who are interested in seeing that their city is beautiful and grows and prospers. They have no official status but they are respected and they do a lot of good. I do not suggest that you should start a "Friends of Bangalore" society here but I should like the people who live in Bangalore to have an active, vivid, civic sense and a love of Bangalore so that they can help in beautifying the city and improving it in any way they can and keeping the Corporation up to the mark, if I may say so with all respect to you, Mr Mayor. It is that civic sense ultimately that pays dividends, whether it is in a city or in a country. I am afraid we do not have it as much as we ought to have. I do not know about Bangalore, but in most cities some have it, but it is not one of our inherited virtues. We have to build it up and build up not only the beauty of the city but the way people should behave to each other in the city, the way people should walk on the roads or drive on the roads. I find that neither the people who drive on the roads nor those who walk on the roads have any civic sense about them, jaywalkers and jay drivers mostly. Again, I am not talking of Bangalore. I do not know, I am generally saying something.

Bangalore, anyhow, should have very careful planning. It is a city which was planned, to begin with and I suppose you plan continuously, but more specially, because it is growing so fast it becomes very necessary to have careful plans for its development in the present and in the future. To have a plan as to what Bangalore City will be like, say, twenty years hence, and having got a plan like that, then all your immediate programmes and plans of the city should fit in with the twenty year plan. It is not enough to plan every year for something or to carry on a scheme of improvement or removal of slums. It is a scandal that a city like Bangalore should have slums, and I would advise you strongly not to allow them to grow up here. Root them out. Because once they grow up they have a tendency to stay. But what I was suggesting was, and it may be you have done it, I do not know, is to have a very competent team to examine every aspect of Bangalore City and plan for the next twenty years, what Bangalore should be like twenty years later. Because if you have that in view, your permanent plan, then everything that the Corporation does in between will fit in with that. Otherwise you might do something now which five years later may not fit in, or ten years later.

I think it is very important that all cities should have plans like this, all big cities, more particularly, a city like Bangalore which is both beautiful and is growing very fast. The lack of a plan creates great difficulties. You cannot uproot a city and build a new city, you cannot do that. Therefore, when the city is growing, if you plan, to begin with, you will be keeping within the picture you have of the future city. Take a small matter, roads. You have good roads here and, I do not know, again, I am not speaking of Bangalore but rather of some other cities I know, great cities of India, even of Bombay which is one of our fine cities and which is the city with a great deal of civic pride. In the suburbs of Bombay roads are made, a suburb grows up. There is, for instance, a part of Bombay which leads to the Atomic Energy establishment, Trombay. There was no house or anything there. The Atomic Energy establishment was made there and then a narrow road led to it. No care was taken about that road because people said it is in the suburbs, there are no houses here, why bother. Now I find that that narrow road has got all manner of broken down shanties on both sides, houses are growing up and without any planning, without any room for the road to grow; and the result is, if you want to make a broad road there now, you have to buy up all those houses and break them down altogether, inconvenience many people and spend a lot of money. The point I am laying stress on is this, that even in the outskirts of a city the roads that are built should always be broad because when houses are built you cannot broaden them. At any rate, even if the roads are not broad, there should be room for their expansion, the space allotted for the road on either side should be enough, no houses should be allowed. You need not build a road a hundred feet wide but there should be room for a one hundred and twenty feet wide road always. In Europe, if you go to the ancient and old cities it is a great nuisance because all the roads were built long ago, cities grew up and in the days of motor traffic, extreme motor traffic today, the quickest means of locomotion is walking in those cities. A car does not take you anywhere because it moves at the rate of about half a mile an hour because it is so crowded, the road is so narrow. Take Rome, take London. You just cannot move because the roads are narrow. It is very difficult to broaden the roads and break down thousands of huge buildings. Therefore, you have to take care, and before the buildings are put up, to make a broad road, usually in the suburbs, or the environs, leave room for growth. The road may be narrow, it does not matter, because broad roads are not required now. Broaden it as the need for it arises.

So I am venturing, Mr Mayor, to offer some suggestions to you. I hope you will forgive me for my temerity in doing so. But I am interested in cities and the city beautiful. Now the test of a city, of course, is buildings, gardens, etc., but the ultimate test is not the few fine buildings like this magnificent structure that you have got here, but the test of a city is what kind of slums do you have. Palaces are no test. Anybody can put up a palace if he has enough money. Slums require a lot of imagination—to remove them, I mean not to have them, constant effort, and a city is to be judged by the absence of slums. A city is to be judged, above all, by what it does to its children, the future citizens. I am very anxious about this matter, about children, and I attach the greatest importance to it because I think the future of India will depend on the kind of care we take of our little children and bigger children today. I should like to have not only competent schooling or every child in India but also midday meals for every child in the schools, also some kind of a proper uniform for them, clothing for them. I attach value to the uniform idea; sometimes it is necessary in India where they have not got enough clothes to wear, has a psychological effect, it disciplines, it makes one cleaner, neater, more upright. Therefore, I should like the Corporation specially to pay attention to the children.

One more suggestion I would put to you which I have been whispering to the Mayor while sitting here. Long ago, that is very long ago, when I was chairman of the Allahabad Municipality, I put it to the Municipality; but then I left the chairmanship for various other reasons, not because of this, and my proposal lapsed. And I do not know if anywhere in India any corporation or municipality has paid much attention to it. The proposal is about taxation of land values. At the present moment the taxation in most cities is of a house and sometimes of the site on which the house is built, both or only of the house. Often, if the site is left vacant, the person does not choose to build on it, there is no tax on it because he is not utilising it. If the house is left vacant there is no tax on it. The result is that there is a premium on the owner of the site to leave the site unbuilt on, he does not pay any tax. Therefore, the development of the city is hampered by this type of taxation when an empty piece of land can be kept empty and the owner speculating on it to sell it at a higher price. Why at a higher price? Because the price of the land is rising; not because of any effort of his, but because of the efforts of thousands and thousands of persons who are raising the level of the city, because amenities are coming in, because the corporation spends money on roads, on lighting, on water supply, on so many things on schools, this, that, the land values rise. Why are land values higher in Bangalore than outside Bangalore? Well, simply because there are all kinds of amenities in Bangalore. The owner of the land does not do anything; he merely profits by the additional price that he gets. There does not seem to me to be any reason why he should not pay for the value of the land becoming greater. It is true, to some extent that is done now. When you reassess the land after every five years or ten years you can reassess it at a higher figure. But the principle is important, and in some big cities like New York, values of land double and treble year after year sometimes. One piece, one area becomes fashionable, values go up. Nothing has happened; it is simply considered fashionable to live there. And the result is, there is an assessment commission in New York City which functions from day to day, month to month, year to year, it never stops functioning. But I do not quite know what the position is in New York. But anyhow, I suggest that the principle governing the assessment should be the land values. If a land has become greater in value because not of the owner doing anything but because of the neighbours, the corporation and the government doing something, well, the owner, it is only right, should pay for the increase in the value. There is a famous book on this subject which created some stir, by an American, I forget, written, I should say, oh! I do not know, maybe a hundred years ago or eighty years ago, towards the end of the nineteenth century or beginning of the twentieth, I do not quite know, a man called Henry George, and I forget the name of the book, I cannot, I am sorry I am getting forgetful, but "Poverty and" something.[460] Anyhow, the main burden of the book is taxation of land values. He thought, just one tax on land values was quite enough. He did not quite realise the complexities that have arisen since, in the last hundred years, but he argued this out very ably and so far as land values are concerned I have been a convert to him ever since I read that book, in prison of course. Yours is a growing city, but land values must be changing here rapidly. A five year assessment is one thing, but the principle laid down is another, that it should be according to the land values, and therefore, an empty piece of land, if anybody has got it and wants to speculate on it, he must pay tax and not be allowed to speculate so much; he must help in the development of the city. Development should not be taxed so heavily as the accretion to the land value.

I am afraid I have spoken to you about serious matters and not merely thanked you for your gracious address to me and the welcome that you and the citizens of Bangalore have given me during the last two or three days. I am just coming back, as you know perhaps, from Nandi Hills where we spent, my sister and I, two days. It is a lovely place and the air there is particularity delightful and invigorating. I am rather surprised that it is not patronised as

460. Henry George, *Progress and Poverty*, published in 1879, a bestseller, which proposed a land value tax of the kind Nehru is speaking about.

I thought it would be. I am told, people go there for an afternoon or maybe sometimes for a night, and that is all. It surprises me. I should have thought a place about an hour and a quarter from here by car would have more residents, permanent residents there or residents who spend a month or so there and not go there for an hour or two, look round and come back. Why it is looked upon as a place where VIPs should go, should be taken by the Mysore Government, and others, less important mortals should not be encouraged to go, I do not understand. Of course there is no prohibition to non-VIPs going. I mean to say, if there are no places to live in, how can anybody else go? There is Mr Cubbon's[461] bungalow there which is a remarkable piece of architecture, if I may say so, which could have only emerged in the middle of the nineteenth century, not twentieth century. It is a very solid piece of work. Nevertheless it is not the type of work which one fancies in the twentieth century. However, it is there; no doubt it represents the mentality of Mr Cubbon or Mr Cubbin, whatever the name is, I do not know. (What is the name exactly? Cubbon! all right Mr Cubbon). There is that solid structure, there are one or two other structures. There is another house which is called the Gandhi Nilaya where Gandhiji stayed, very good place. But as far as I can see, there is no place where any normal mortal can stay. I being just like an abnormal person, stayed in Cubbon's bungalow and a host of people looked after me. It is surprising, it surprises me when I go abroad, how many people are required to look after me. It astonishes me really. That acts as a check on my going anywhere, a new place, and I know that I will upset it and so many people will be put in to look after me, even quite apart from the security and the police. Merely personal looking after seems to require quite a crowd. When I go to some hill station really, in North India by myself, I insist on the Government being unaware of my going there, almost. I take one or two men, a cook and one or two other men and we go there and we live quite comfortably, not being crowded out by the other people who are looking after us. But however that may be, it is a sign of the extreme courtesy and affection which surrounds me wherever I go and which is a very strength-giving thing. All along the road to Bangalore and from Bangalore to Nandi, the crowds along the streets and the villages—not the streets, the villages, affectionate people; and it always pleases me, strengthens

461. Mark Cubbon (1775-1861), an army officer under the East India Company and Commissioner of Mysore State, 1834-1860, after whom the Cubbon Park in the heart of Bangalore was named.

me and troubles me when I see so much affection because I wonder what we are doing for them, for these people who have so much faith and affection. I feel that it may be because circumstances are not very propitious always, that what we are doing is not anywhere near the affection that we give and what they deserve. I hope we are moving along the right lines and we shall bring some measure of security and happiness to these masses of people. That is the only test, ultimately, of a nation, as of a municipality, a corporation; how much good you are doing to the masses of people and not what you are doing to a few selected and rather privileged people. I hope the Bangalore Corporation will remember that always and test every step it takes by the effect it has on the ordinary people who live in Bangalore.

Thank you Mr Mayor. [Applause]

Mr Mayor reminds me of one of the biggest problems of Bangalore, that is the inadequacy of the water supply. I entirely agree with him that a city like Bangalore, anywhere, Bangalore or a village, town, city or any other place, one the elementary things which have to be supplied is water. It shocks me that there are many many villages in India—I do not know if they are here—where there is no water or very little water and where people have to go, women chiefly have to go distances to fetch water. I think, I am not for the moment talking about Bangalore, but the question of water supply, it is one of the most important things which should be given the highest priority, that good water, good drinking water, should be available in every village in India without having to go some distance to fetch it. I think, I hope, that by the end of this Third Plan that will be so. Now, coming to Bangalore, in a growing city like this, I might tell you, even in Delhi we are constantly facing trouble about water and there are huge schemes to fetch water from the Yamuna many many miles out from the city, just like you are thinking of getting water from the Cauvery. I cannot, obviously, say anything definite as to what the Central Government will do but I am quite sure that Bangalore City requires an adequate water supply and in your efforts to get it, so far as I am concerned, I feel you deserve every help.

(x) Northeast

169. In the Lok Sabha: Phizo's Cable to Prime Minister[462]

Question :[463] Will the Prime Minister be pleased to state:

(a) whether it is a fact that Mr Phizo[464] has sent a cable to him appealing to settle the case of Nagas by personal conversation and has desired to see him;[465]
(b) if so, the details of the cable;
(c) whether any reply has been sent; and
(d) if so, the details thereof?

The Parliamentary Secretary to the Minister of External Affairs (D. Ering):

(a) Yes.
(b) The cable reads "Killing Nagas brings both sorrow and disgrace to us all let us talk and settle our affairs as a truly civilised people."
(c) No.
(d) Does not arise.

D.C. Sharma: May I know why the Prime Minister did not have any negotiation or talks with Mr Phizo? He could have brought about the stoppage of hostilities.

The Prime Minister and Minister of External Affairs and Minister of Atomic Energy (Jawaharlal Nehru): I am not quite clear as to what the hon. Member said. Apparently he asked me why I did not have talks with Mr Phizo. I did not have talks because I did not think it proper to do so.

Hari Vishnu Kamath:[466] Is it not a fact that the Government's policy is not to have any talks with Mr Phizo unless and until he disbands the hostile Naga organisation?

462. Oral Answers, 1 June 1962. *Lok Sabha Debates*, Third Series, Vol. 4, May 26 to June 7, 1962, cols 8259-8261.
463. By D.C. Sharma of Congress.
464. A.Z. Phizo, Chairman, Naga National Council, now in exile in London.
465. This was disclosed by S.C. Jamir, Parliamentary Secretary in the External Affairs Ministry, during the question hour on 1 June 1962. See *The Hindu*, 2 June 1962, p. 1.
466. PSP.

Jawaharlal Nehru: There is no such rigid policy. But where it is obvious that Mr Phizo wants to take propaganda advantage of this matter, we do not wish to encourage him.

Hem Barua:[467] May I know whether the attention of the Government is drawn to a letter written recently by Mr Shilo Ao[468] to Mr Phizo which reads as follows:

> "Our Naga brothers who still are underground are always welcome to come overground and join with us in building up this new State of Nagaland."

If so, may I know whether Government visualises a political settlement with the hostile Nagas?

Jawaharlal Nehru: Government always want a political settlement with all its opponents, whoever they may be and wherever they may be. Governments do not take a rigid attitude. But the point is the political settlement should be a right settlement and should fit in with the circumstances. In Nagaland we have already gone as far as we can go as the House knows, a Bill will be coming up here presently to make them a full State. So, it is open to the hostile people to come up and participate in the scheme of things.

C.K. Bhattacharyya:[469] May I know whether the cable has come from East Pakistan?

Jawaharlal Nehru: This cable came from London, I think.

467. PSP.

468. P. Shilu Ao, leader of the Naga People's Convention, and chief executive councilor, Nagaland Interim Body, 1961-63.

469. Congress.

170. To David Astor: Conor Cruise O'Brien's Visit to Nagaland[470]

June 3, 1962

Dear Mr Astor,

Thank you for your letter of the 19th May.[471] I am sorry for the little delay in answering it. I have not been well and I went to Kashmir for some rest.

T.N. Kaul[472] has sent me a report of the discussions you and Guy Wint[473] had with him, to which you refer in your letter. He has also communicated to me your message that you would like to publish your letter of the 19th May and any reply that I may send you.

There is nothing very secret about your letter to me or my reply. But I confess that I do not like the idea of publishing any correspondence between us on this subject. This may involve me and the Government of India in a press controversy. I would like to write to you freely and frankly. But if I feel that the letters are meant for publication, then I would probably hesitate to write in the same manner.

As I wrote to you previously, a visit by Dr O'Brien[474] or any other distinguished representative of *The Observer* in the near future will be very inconvenient. The rains are going to start very soon and it is difficult to move about Nagaland during the rainy season. Dr O'Brien may be used to discomfort and hard travel, but we cannot rule out security considerations. Apart from this, as you perhaps know, Phizo[475] has reached East Pakistan and is apparently conferring with some of the Naga hostiles who escaped into East Pakistan last month. The visit of any correspondent to Nagaland now or in the near future is bound to be exploited for propaganda purposes by Phizo and the Naga hostiles.

In view of these considerations, I would suggest that if you want to send a representative, whether it is Dr O'Brien or anybody else, he should come early in the cold weather and not during the next few months.

470. Letter to the Editor of *The Observer*, 22 Tudor Street, London, EC4.

471. See previous correspondence in SWJN/SS/76 appendix 33 and item 261.

472. Deputy High Commissioner in London.

473. British journalist and author.

474. Conor Cruise O'Brien, former UN Representative in Katanga.

475. A.Z. Phizo.

You will appreciate that we would not like your name or the names of *The Observer* to be exploited in any way by Phizo and the Naga hostiles for their own purposes.[476]

With kind regards,

Yours sincerely,
[Jawaharlal Nehru]

171. To B.P. Chaliha: Communal Riots and Phizo Return Possible[477]

June 5, 1962

My dear Chaliha,

I have received information, which is presumed to be reliable, that the Assistant High Commissioner of Pakistan in Shillong[478] has been advised by his Government to fan communal trouble in Assam. Partly the idea appears to be to create conditions in Assam which would enable the Naga hostiles, including Phizo, to slip back from East Pakistan to Nagaland.

I hope your Government will be vigilant about the activities of the Pakistan Assistant High Commissioner in Shillong.

Further, as Muharram is on the 13th June, your Government should be particularly alert and vigilant on that occasion.[479]

Yours sincerely,
[Jawaharlal Nehru]

172. For M.J. Desai: Rehabilitating Nagas[480]

I agree with you that we should make some constructive approach to the problem of rehabilitating hostile Nagas who surrender. Some such statement might well be made when the Nagaland Bill comes up before Parliament. You

476. See also item 176.
477. Letter to the Chief Minister of Assam.
478. S.A. Moid.
479. See also item 47.
480. Note, 8 June 1962, for the FS.

may discuss this matter with Shilu Ao[481] when he comes here. I should also like to meet Shilu Ao when he comes.

2. We cannot obviously think of keeping any detenus as the British kept some Kikuyus in the first category that is, keeping them in chains etc.

3. There is a possibility of more Nagas going to East Pakistan as well as another possibility of the Nagas in East Pakistan now trying to get back to Nagaland. Our security forces must be on the alert to prevent either movement.

4. I rather doubt if Phizo[482] will go to Nagaland. Probably he will go back to Europe or, perhaps, to New York for some approach to the United Nations.

5. Meanwhile Patterson[483] is doing some mischief. I understand he has said in his reports that the Nagas have shown him good evidence to justify their charges of atrocities by the Indian Army. In support of this, he quotes some intelligence report as well as some statement made by one of the Indian airmen kept in detention by the Nagas.[484] Patterson met Mrs Pandit[485] in Karachi a little while ago and pleaded the cause of the Nagas with her. He mentioned this new evidence that he had seen and which had impressed him greatly.

173. To M.J. Desai: *The Observer* on Nagaland[486]

I am sending you a letter I have received from Mr David Astor. He now wants to state in *The Observer* that Dr O'Brien was willing to come to India and Nagaland but the Indian Government would not give permission. I can hardly tell him not to do so. What do you advise? I do not propose to send a reply to him, but to ask T.N. Kaul to give him my message.

481. P. Shilu Ao, chief executive councilor, Nagaland Interim Body.
482. A.Z. Phizo, Naga leader in emigration.
483. George Neilson Patterson, journalist.
484. For previous references to captured Indian airmen, see SWJN/SS/68/items 95, 96, 98 and appendices 10 (a) and (b).
485. Vijaya Lakshmi Pandit, Nehru's sister and former High Commissioner in London.
486. Note, 11 June 1962, to the Foreign Secretary.

174. In the Lok Sabha: Admonition of Army Officers in NEFA[487]

(II) REPORTED ADMONITION OF SOME SENIOR ARMY OFFICERS POSTED IN NEFA

F.H. Mohsin (Dharwar South):[488] Under Rule 197, I call the attention of the Minister of Defence to the following matter of urgent public importance and I request that he may make a statement thereon:-

> The reported admonition of some senior army officers posted in NEFA for their failure to prevent hostile Nagas from escaping into East Pakistan.

Krishna Menon:[489] The notice under rule 197 mentions a "reported admonition of some senior Army officers posted in NEFA for their failure to prevent hostile Nagas from escaping into East Pakistan." As the House is aware, about 150 Nagas crossed the river Surma into East Pakistan near Pirnagar in Cachar District of Assam in the early hours of 1st May, 1962. At no stage these Nagas went into NEFA. Army officers posted in NEFA are, therefore, in no way concerned with this incident.

These Nagas started from Tamenlong area of Manipur and followed a route which went through the forest area of Cachar hills. During the period of about three weeks which they took to reach the border, they came into inhabited areas only at intervals to collect food etc. They disappeared into thick forests as soon as they had obtained what they required. Whenever any report about their presence in any area came to the Security Forces, patrols were sent, but no contact could be made with them. The area through which the Nagas passed is thickly forested providing effective cover to the

487. Calling Attention, 13 June 1962. *Lok Sabha Debates*, Thirs Series, Vol. V, 8 June to 22 June, 1962, Ist Session, cols 10576-10585.

Three issues were discussed in this meeting (i) Reported Movement of Chinese Tanks and Armoured Vehicles in Occupied Indian Territory in Northern Ladakh, (ii) Reported Admonition of some senior Army officers posted in NEFA, (iii) Scarcity of Filtered Water in West Vinay Nagar, Delhi. This item covers the second part, the first issue is included in the section on External Affairs sub-section China, the third one does not have any intervention by Nehru.

488. Congress.

489. Minister of Defence.

escapees on the one hand and difficulties of movement and communication for our patrols on the other.

The only occasion on which the Security forces sighted the Nagas was when they were actually crossing the Surma river in the early hours on 1st May 1962. The Police outpost at Pirnagar opened fire against them, but the fire was returned from across the river, and even though some of the Nagas were wounded or killed, most of them escaped.

A conference was held in Shillong under the presidency of the Governor of Assam[490] on 7th May 1962 to consider this matter. Among those who attended the conference were representatives of the Ministry of Defence, Ministry of External Affairs and Army Headquarters. The object of this conference was to review the problem as a whole and also to consider this incident from all aspects and to render our efforts in relation to hostile Nagas more effective, it will not be in the public interest to disclose details of these discussions or their results or inferences drawn. The hon. The Prime Minister has already stated in this House on the 11th May 1962 that there appears to have been a certain lack of adequate coordination of various efforts and that information regarding the incursions of Nagas into inhabited areas did not always reach the appropriate quarters in time. All practical steps that are possible have since been taken by way of remedial measures.

The House is aware that we are not at war with the Nagas in Nagaland. The overwhelming majority of Nagas are cooperating with the Administration and the new arrangements about Nagaland. A relatively small proportion of Nagas are living in well covered forests and jungles. The people in Nagaland as a whole live normal lives as in the rest of India and move about in the normal way and are not subject to surveillance or punitive precautions. It will, therefore, be appreciated by the House that action can and should be taken in this context only against those found or apprehended in offences against law and order. We may deal with them only when they are seen carrying unauthorised fire-arms orare caught in hostile actions against the civilian population or are preparing to do so.

If errors are made by Army personnel or lapses occur in relation to the arrangements or efforts for the maintenance of law and order in assistance to civil authority, corrective action is always taken. If any officers are concerned in any such lapses, they aresuitably advised. This is the normal procedure. The Army has a very unusual and difficult task in Nagaland. Nagas are Indian nationals. In dealing with a recalcitrant minority, Government and local authority have to be careful that the innocent do not

490. S.M. Shrinagesh.

suffer and that there is as little interference as possible with normal life in that area. Our patrols have, therefore, to work at all times with considerable discretion and quite often have to refrain from action even at some risk to themselves. There are, as the house will appreciate, several factors and difficulties inherent in the situation. Problems of terrain, topography and communications present great hazards. I feel sure that the House will agree with the Government that the Armed Forces and the personnel under Army's command are performing their very onerous duties and functions with energy as well as patience and restraint. The pressure which the Army and the Assam Rifles and other civil forces under operational control of the Army are exerting and the general public opinion in Nagaland itself is creating great difficulties for hostile Nagas locally and also affecting their own morale. Hence escape and not resistance has become their tactics. Life of banditry and crimein Nagaland is becoming increasingly difficult for those lawless element.

F.H. Mohsin: Are the Government aware of the recent statement of the Assam Chief Minister Shri Chaliha on the floor of the Assam Assembly in reply to a Calling Attention notice, in which he has said that the Army officers knew of this escape, knew of Naga hostiles going into Pakistan area four days in advance, that this was intimated to the Army officials and the Army officials said that they would take all precautions and even then they have failed. What explanation would the Defence Minister give to this statement of the Chief Minister?

Krishna Menon: Explanation I have given. That is what the Prime Minister referred to. We have information. But, that does not mean that the information is adequate or in time; may or may not be. Secondly, the fact that we know that Nagas are escaping does not mean where they are escaping. We have to take into account the terrain where regular Army information cannot do anything. The Army has instructions not to use force any more than necessary and even to take risks to their own lives to prevent any action against the innocent.

मनीराम बागडी:[491] क्या आप हिन्दी में भी कुछ कहला सकेंगे?

अध्यक्ष महोदय:[492] यह बहुत लम्बा स्टेटमेंट है, और आप इतना समझ सकते हैं।

491. Socialist.
492. Hukam Singh.

मनीराम बागड़ीः सवाल तो मैं करूंगा लेकिन लोग समझेंगे कि गलत सवाल कर रहा हूं। क्या डिफेंन्स मिनिस्टर साहब यह बतलाने की कृपा करेंगे कि जब चार या पांच दिन पहले उन को यह इत्तला हो चुकी थी कि नागा होस्टाइल्स जा रहे हैं पाकिस्तान को, और मि० फीजो से मिलने जा रहे हैं, जो उन्होंने उसके वास्ते एहतियाती तदबीर करने के लिये, जो फौज वहां पर थी वह तो थी, लेकिन क्या खास तौर पर कोई मजीद फौज भेजने का इन्तजाम किया? और कितनी तादाद में वहां पर मजीद फौज लगाई गई जो कि उन्हें रोके। आप कहते हैं कि मुठभेड़ हुई और उस में कुछ मरे है। क्या मैं पूछ सकता हूँ कि कितने लोग मरे हैं?

इसके बाद सवाल जो पूछना चाहता हूं वह यह है कि वह लोग वापस आना चाहते हैं, बगावत करने के लिये। तो क्या उन को रोक थाम के लिये कोई प्रबन्ध किया गया है ताकि वह वापस न आ सकें?

जवाहरलाल नेहरुः शायद माननीय समझे नहीं जो अभी डिफेन्स मिनिस्टर ने कहा। इसलिये मैं उस को दोहराता हूँ। अभी चार पांच रोज पहले मालूम होने की बात कही गई। उन को ठीक मालूम नहीं था। मालूम था कि कुछ लोग जाने को कोशिश कर रहे हैं, बल्कि कई दफा मालूम हुआ, लेकिन यह तो मालूम नहीं था कि ये किस तरफ से जा रहे है, किस जंगल में से हो कर जा रहे है, और उस का इन्तजाम जाहिर है कि कम हुआ हमारी तरफ से, कोआर्डिनेशन का, खबर को चारों तरफ फैलाने का। यह नहीं मालूम था आखिरी दम तक कि किस तरफ से आयेंगे। आखिर में मणिपुर से आये। नागालैंड से नहीं बल्कि मणिपुर हो कर आये। इसलिये उन को रोका नहीं जा सकता।

आपने इस के बाद क्या कहा, मुझे याद नहीं।

अध्यक्ष महोदयः जब खबर आ गई थी तो कोई ऐडीशनल फोर्स लगाई गई ताकि वे आखीर में वापस न आ सकें।

जवाहरलाल नेहरुः ऐडोशनल फोर्स का सवाल नहीं हैं। सवाल यह है कि मौका हम को ठीक मालूम होना चाहिये था कि कहां हैं। 100,150 आदमी आसानी से जंगल में छिप सकते हैं, जा सकते हैं तरह तरह के रास्तों से। हर कदम पर तो फौज खड़ी नहीं होती। इस की इत्तला आई कि वह जा रहे हैं। लेकिन कहां से जा रहे हैं 100 मील के अन्दर, यह पता नहीं था। तो यह बात हुई और उस वक्त कमजोरी हमारी साबित हुई उस की इत्तला करने की रोकने की नहीं। हमें ठीक ठीक इत्तला नहीं मालूम हुई कि किस तरफ से जा रहे हैं। जब मालूम हुई तो हम ने रोकने को कोशिश की, लेकिन वह उस तरफ पहुँच गये। जहां तक उनके लौटने का सवाल है, इस बात पर भी गौर करना चाहिये कि उन का वहां जाना किस लिये हुआ। फीजो साहब से मिलने के लिये हो सकता है, यह भी हो सकता है कि वह इतने परेशान हो गये थे कि चले गये वहां। और अगर मेरी राय लीजिये तो वहां जा कर वहीं पर रहने लगें तो ज्यादा अच्छा है।

मनीराम बागडीः मैंने यह भी पूछा था कि सूचना किस ने दी थी। कहा गया कि मुठभेड़ हुई थी, उस में कुछ मरे भी थे। तो कितने मरे थे?

अध्यक्ष महोदयः यह तो पहले बतलाया जा चुका है कि कितने मरे थे, जो मुठभेड़ हुई थी उसमें मरने वालों की तादाद।

जवाहरलाल नेहरुः मुझे याद नहीं ठीक से। लेकिन देखा था कि कुछ मरे थे, कुछ जख्मी हुए थे, और उनके जो हथियार थे वे वह भी गिरफतार हुये थे लेकिन जो मरे थे उन की लाशें वे घसीट ले गये थे।

मैं एक बात और अर्ज करना चाहता हूँ हमारे कोई भी सदस्य हाथ से लोगों की तरफ इशारे न करें, नहीं तो हाथ पैर बहुत हिलने लगेंगे यहां। मैं किसी की शिकायत नहीं करता, लेकिन माननीय सदस्य अक्सर हाथ पैर हिलाते हैं। अगर यह आदत हो जाय तो हाथ पैर बहुत हिलने लगेंगे।

मनीराम बागडीः उम्र का तकाजा है। बूढ़ा हो जाऊंगा तो हाथ नहीं हिलेंगे।

अध्यक्ष महोदयः मैंने माननीय सदस्य से पहले भी कहा था, लेकिन वे अपनी आदत से मजबूर हैं।

[Translation begins:

Maniram Bagri:[493] Can you get them to speak in Hindi?

Speaker:[494] This is a long statement, and you can understand this much.

Maniram Bagri: Questions, I will ask questions but people will think I am asking wrong questions. Will the Defence Minister be pleased to inform that did he arrange to send reinforcements when he got this information four-five days back that the Naga hostiles were going to Pakistan and meet Mr Phizo. How much extra force was sent there to stop them? You say some persons were killed there in encounter. May I ask how many?

Jawaharlal Nehru: Perhaps, the honourable Member has not understood what the Defence Minister has said just now. So I am repeating it. It was said that information was available four-five days before. He was not properly informed. It was known that some persons were trying to cross, known several times but

493. See fn 491 in this section.
494. See fn 492 in this section.

it was not known from which side they were going, which jungle they were crossing. Obviously, coordination of information network from our side was less than enough. It was not known till the end which way they would come. Ultimately, they came through Manipur, not Nagaland but through Manipur. That is why they could not be killed.

What did you say after that ! I don't remember.

Speaker: When information was received, some additional force was deputed so that they could not come back.

Jawaharlal Nehru: This is not an issue of additional force. The issue is that we have to know which is the right way. 100, 150 people can easily hide in the jungle and cross it at several points. Army cannot be present everywhere. Information came, they were coming, but where were they going within 100 miles, it was not known. So this happened and it proved to be our weakness, we did not get proper information about their movements. When we got to know, we tried to stop, then they went to the other side. So far as the question of their return is concerned, it should be a matter of concern that why they have gone there. Maybe, they went to meet Phizo, it is also possible that they were so troubled that they went there. And in my opinion, it would be very good if they continue to live there.

Mani Ram Bagri: I had also asked who provided the information. It was said there was encounter and some of them died. So, how many were killed?

Speaker: The number of those killed in the encounter has already been given.

Jawaharlal Nehru: I do not remember correctly. But some were killed, some injured, and their arms were confiscated. But they dragged the bodies of those killed.

I also want to mention that our Members should not hint towards other Members, otherwise many limbs [hands and feet] will start moving. I am not complaining, but honoroubale Member often shakes his arms and feet. If it becomes a habit, then many would start shaking.

Mani Ram Bagri: My age is such, in old age, hands will shake.

Speaker: I had told the honorable Member about this earlier also but he has become a slave of this habit.

Translation ends]

Hem Barua:[495] Apart from the allegations made by the Chief Minister of Assam to the effect that the military got the information about the movement of those hostile Nagas to East Pakistan, may I draw the attention of the hon. Prime Minister and the Defence Minister to those articles published in the London *Observer* by Mr George Patterson, on 3rd June and 10th June,[496] wherein definite things have been spoken out by Gen. Kaito[497] who is in East Pakistan? He has said two things. He has said first that "We traversed 500 miles of Indian territory, and it took us four months to do it; the military authorities knew about our whereabouts, but they could do nothing; they were inept"; they have said like that, and in fact, they have used that word.

They have also said, on the other hand, that "We have come here not for what the Prime Minister thinks we have come here, that is, for asylum or something like that," but he says that they want to go to the UNO to present their case.

May I draw the attention of Government to these facts as revealed in these articles, and ask them to say what their reactions are?

Jawaharlal Nehru: The hon. Member wants to know our reactions to those articles. I have not read all the articles.

Hem Barua: I have them here with me.

Jawaharlal Nehru: But as regards those that I have read—I have read one full article, and a little summary of the other one—it seems to me that they are full of false statements from the beginning to the end. I am surprised that any responsible newspaperman of a responsible newspaper should give publicity to this kind of one-sided statement, without enquiry and without anything.

Hem Barua: That man, George Patterson, was in India.

Hari Vishnu Kamath:[498] He was in Darjeeling.

Nath Pai:[499] One of the accusations is almost of genocide, that we have already killed one lakh persons and about 4,00,000 are in concentration camps.

495. PSP.

496. Articles in *Observor* by George Patterson on 3 and 10 June 1962.

497. Gen Kaito Sema, commander of the Naga rebel army.

498. PSP.

499. PSP.

Hem Barua: The accusation is that one man out of every ten has been killed.

Jawaharlal Nehru: The whole thing is so fantastic and absurd which no person reasonably could even believe in without enquiry, but he has not enquired and he gives publicity to it.

Renu Chakravartty (Barrackpore):[500] In Europe it has come out in big headlines. In the whole Europe it has been flashed.

Nath Pai: This is what they say "Nagas—Indians kill, one in ten". What is the External Publicity Division doing about it? Are we trying to react in some way? We are accused of genocide.

Jawaharlal Nehru: If a newspaper publishes it, we deny it. We place the real facts about this. We have done it about Mr Phizo's statement fully; I think, last year he made more or less this statement. Now the *Observer* newspaper has come out with another bunch of the same story adding to it that this is not old but still occurring. I am really surprised at any person being taken in by this kind of thing.

Hem Barua: What are the Government doing to counter it?

Hari Vishnu Kamath rose—

Speaker: Shri Kamath.

Hari Vishnu Kamath: Do the statements made by the Prime Minister in the House earlier in this session and that made by the Chief Minister of Assam in the State Legislature the other day indicate that the Army and security forces are competent and strong enough, but they are unwilling to deal vigorously with the matter because of Government's policy, and consequent directive to the Army not to queer the pitch for a political settlement of the Naga problem?

Jawaharlal Nehru: I do not know; the hon. Member has put the question in a curious way. There is no question of queering the pitch for the Army.

500. CPI.

Hari Vishnu Kamath: Not for the Army—queering the pitch for Government for a political settlement of the Naga problem.

Jawaharlal Nehru: Naturally, we have always to pay attention to the political aspect or the aspect of not going against those who are loyal citizens of India. It is difficult to distinguish. We have issued instructions in this connection. For instance, the great majority of the Nagas do not want all this trouble. They are harassed by it; they want to live a peaceful life. So care has to be taken that these people are not mistaken for the hostiles. In fact, once or twice, unfortunately mistakes had been made in the past which had bad consequences. That was not proper. So this is done. Otherwise, what would be the position? I do not wish to compare it with other places where very large armies and air forces have functioned, as in the jungles in Malaya and elsewhere. Year after year greater and greater air and land forces were in occupation and they took a very long time to deal with them. It is the terrain that is difficult.

Till recently, they used to hop in and out of Burma. We could not follow them there. That would not have been proper for us to do. Now such pressure is being exercised that it is becoming obviously difficult for them to continue their old tactics. That does not mean that the situation is completely satisfactory. But it is becoming much more satisfactory than it was.

175. To B.P. Chaliha: Nagaland State[501]

13th June, 1962

My dear Chaliha,

Your letter of June 12th about the Draft Bills in regard to Nagaland. The principle of these Bills was agreed to long ago when we made the announcement in Parliament.[502] We cannot go back on the statements we have made and the assurances we have given. Therefore, the question of a separate State has necessarily to be agreed to on terms and conditions which we stated last year. If this is agreed to then it naturally follows that representation in the Rajya Sabha and the Lok Sabha has to be given, just as we are giving to Goa etc. The fact that each representative in the Nagaland Assembly will represent six thousand population does not affect any other State or interest. As it is, they are different in different States.

501. Letter to the Chief Minister of Assam.

502. For NNC's proposals, see SWJN/SS/61/item 150 and for Nehru's statement in the Lok Sabha on 1 August 1960, see SWJN/SS/62/item 85.

The whole question of Nagaland being a State has not only been decided upon, but sufficiently publicised in India and abroad. Everyone knows about it. It is impossible for us to go behind this clear pledge that we have given.

Yours sincerely,
Jawaharlal Nehru

176. To David Astor: *The Observer* on Nagaland[503]

14th June, 1962

Dear Mr Astor,

I have your letter of June 8th. You can, if you so wish, publish the broad facts in *The Observer*. I take it that you will state that *The Observer* was willing to send Dr O'Brien to the Naga areas and that he was willing to go there, but the Government of India asked that the visit should take place in the autumn because of the difficulties in making security arrangements and because of the rains which make travel in Nagaland extremely difficult during this season.[504]

I have been astonished and somewhat distressed to read reports in *The Observer* from your correspondent Mr Patterson. His reports are largely untrue. I should have thought that even without further inquiry these reports would not have been accepted as true. No attempt was made by your correspondent to inquire into this matter. I deeply regret that *The Observer* is giving publicity to such reports which come from sources which cannot be said to be models of truth.

With kind regards,

Yours sincerely
[Jawaharlal Nehru]

503. Letter to the Editor of *The Observer*, 22 Tudor Street, London, E.C.4.

504. See item 170 and item 173.

177. In the Rajya Sabha: Whereabouts of A.Z. Phizo[505]

Whereabouts of Phizo

Nawab Singh Chauhan:[506] Will the Prime Minister be pleased to state:

(a) whether it is a fact that the leader of Naga hostiles, Phizo, has arrived in Pakistan and is organising Naga hostiles from there and instigating them to create trouble in the Indian territory;
(b) whether it is a fact that the Pakistan Government is giving assistance to the Naga hostiles in the shape of arms and money; and
(c) whether the source of arms and explosives found in possession of the Nagas has been detected?

The Deputy Minister in the Ministry of External Affairs (Dinesh Singh):

(a) Official spokesmen of the Pakistan Government have already confirmed that Phizo is in Pakistan and this information has been given in the Lok Sabha already on 29th May, 1962.
(b) The Government have no information suggesting that Pakistan is giving assistance to the Naga hostiles in the shape of either arms or money.
(c) Of the arms recovered from the hostiles many are Japanese rifles and ammunition from the wartime dumps located in the Naga jungles during World War II. Some others are weapons lost by the security forces. The hostiles are also known to have some artisans who can manufacture country-made muzzle-loading guns.

नवाबसिंह चौहानः जैसा कि समाचारपत्रों में प्रकाशित हुआ है कि नागा विद्रोही फिजो पूर्वी पाकिस्तान से पश्चिमी पाकिस्तान चला गया है और अपने साथ कुछ नागाओं को ले जा रहा है ताकि यू० एन० ओ० में हिन्दुस्तान के खिलाफ प्रचार कर सके। क्या सरकार बतलाने की कृपा करेगी कि इस समाचार में कोई तत्व है?

जवाहरलाल नेहरुः हमने यह खबर अखबारों में पढ़ी है। हमें मालूम नहीं कि उनका क्या इरादा है। शायद कुछ नागा विद्रोही पश्चिमी पाकिस्तान में फिजो के साथ गये हों। वहां से कहाँ गये, यह मैं नहीं कह सकता हूँ।

505. Oral Answers, 16 June 1962. *Rajya Sabha Debates*, Vol. XXXIX, No. 3, cols 147-151.
506. Congress.

ए० एम० तारिक:[507] क्या मैं वजीरे आजम साहब से यह जान सकता हूं कि क्या इस बात में हकीकत है कि जब पिछले दिनों मि० फिजो पश्चिमी पाकिस्तान आये थे तो उन्हें पाकिस्तान के अफसर हवाई अडडे से किसी नामालूम मुकाम पर ले गये और क्या यह भी दुरूस्त है कि मि० फिजो को मशरिकी पाकिस्तान में प्रेसिडेंट अयूब के हवाई जहाज में उड़ा कर पहुंचाया गया। अगर यह दुरूस्त है तो हुकूमत हिन्दुस्तान ने इस सिलसिले में क्या कार्रवाई की है?

जवाहरलाल नेहरुः माननीय सदस्य को मालूम होना चाहिये कि हर एक बात में हिन्दुस्तान कूदकर कार्यवाही नहीं करता हैं, कभी कभी ऐसी कार्यवाही नामुनासिब होती है और नुकसानदेह होती है। इस तरह से पूछना कि क्या कार्यवाही की गई है, मुझे बड़ा अजीब मालूम देता है। यह बात सही है कि जब फिजो साहब पाकिस्तान पहुचे तो उन्हें एक नामालूम जगह ले जाया गया, कहां ले जाया गया, यह मैं नहीं जानता।

ए० बी० वाजपेयी:[508] क्या सच है कि जब 150 नागा विद्रोही पूर्वी पाकिस्तान में प्रवेश कर रहे थे तो पाकिस्तान की फौजों ने गोली चलाकर उनकी रक्षा की और हमें वहां जाने से रोका। यदि यह सच है तो फिर प्रश्न के उत्तर में यह क्यों कहा गया है कि नागा विद्रोहियों को पाकिस्तान से मदद नहीं मिल रही है?

जवाहरलाल नेहरुः प्रश्न के उत्तर में यह कहा गया है कि सरकार को इसकी कोई खबर नहीं है कि पाकिस्तान उनको हथियार या रूपया दे रहा है। उन्होंने खाली दरिया के पार से गोली चलाई -- कभी गोली चलाया करते हैं -- दरिया के पार से लेकिन यह ग़ालिबन सही है कि इस वक्त जो गोली चलाई गई वह नागा विद्रोहियों की हिफ़ाज़त करने के लिए चलाई गई थी।

[Translation begins:

Nawab Singh Chauhan: As has been reported in the newspapers, the Naga rebel Phizo has gone to West Pakistan from East Pakistan and has taken some Naga hostiles also so that he can indulge in propaganda against India in the UN. Will the Government be pleased to state if there is any truth in this news?

Jawaharlal Nehru: We have read this news in the newspapers. We do not know what their intentions are. Perhaps some Naga hostiles may have gone to West Pakistan with Phizo. From there, where they have gone, I cannot say.

507. Congress.
508. Jan Sangh.

A.M. Tariq:[509] May I ask the Prime Minister if it is true that when Mr Phizo came to West Pakistan, Pakistani officials took to him to some unknown destination? And is it also correct that Mr Phizo was flown into West Pakistan in President Ayub's aeroplane? If it is correct, what steps the Government of India has taken in this matter?

Jawaharlal Nehru: The honorable member should know that India does not take action on everything. Sometimes such actions are improper and harmful. I find it strange someone asking what steps were taken. It is correct that when Phizo Saheb arrived in Pakistan he was taken to an unknown destination, but I do not know where.

A.B. Vajpayee: [510] Is it true that when 150 Naga hostiles were entering East Pakistan, their forces resorted to firing in order to save them and prevent us from going there? If it is true, why was it said that Naga hostiles are not getting help from Pakistan in reply to a question?

Jawaharlal Nehru: The answer to the question is that the Government has no information about Pakistan giving them arms or money. They only fired from across the river—sometimes they fire from across the river but probably at that time firing was resorted to to protect the Naga hostiles.

Translation ends]

Bhupesh Gupta:[511] What exactly is the position? When Phizo came to Karachi, he made it known that he was going there to meet the Naga rebels or rather hostiles who would be coming or who had come to Pakistan. Then afterwards the Pakistan Government made it known that they did not know where he was after having reached Pakistan, and we know that the Nagas are going, slipping through the fingers of the Government of India into East Pakistan. May I know whether in view of all these facts the Government have made any—I do not know what it is called—representation, or whatever it is, to find out the exact position as to where the Pakistan Government stands in regard to this matter, whether Phizo has absconded in Pakistan—he is becoming an elusive Pimpernel—or

509. See fn 507 in this section.
510. See fn 508 in this section.
511. CPI.

whether he is available? These things are important because Nagas are going through Assam into East Pakistan?

Jawaharlal Nehru: I am not aware of the fact that more Nagas are going to Pakistan. I do not think there is much chance of their going, and if I may say so, express my private opinion, the more Nagas go there the better—that is neither here nor there—because there are difficulties in Nagaland. They have become rather unpopular, the hostile people there, and they have been pressed greatly, under the pressure of our Army. That may be one reason among others why a few have gone to Pakistan. As for Mr Phizo's movements, we have not addressed the Pakistan Government, we did not think it proper, but to some extent we are kept informed of them through other sources.

N. Sri Rama Reddy:[512] May I know if the hon. Prime Minister is aware of the activities of the hostile Nagas who have escaped into Pakistan? I would like to know whether they are engaged in any anti-Indian activities.

Jawaharlal Nehru: No, Sir. To our knowledge they are not engaged in any worthwhile activities.

178. In the Rajya Sabha: Phizo's Visit to Geneva[513]

A.D. Mani:[514] Will the Prime Minister be pleased to state:

(a) whether Phizo, the Naga rebel leader, visited Geneva, and
(b) whether he tried to contact the International Commission of Jurists in order to have his charges against India investigated?

The Prime Minister and Minister of External Affairs (Jawaharlal Nehru):
(a) and (b). Mr Phizo reached Geneva on 9th May 1962 and met the Administrative Secretary of International Commission of Jurists on 10th May 1962. He is reported to have repeated his charges of atrocities by our security forces. The Government of India have received no communication from the International Commission of Jurists. It appears that the Commission has taken no notice of allegations made by Phizo.

512. Congress.
513. Written Answers, 20 June 1962. *Rajya Sabha Debates*, Vol. XXXIX, No. 6, col. 1013.
514. Independent.

179. To S. Radhakrishnan: The Name of Nagaland[515]

June 21, 1962

My dear Mr President,

Thank you for sending me Dr Suniti Kumar Chatterji's[516] letter. I am returning this to you. The matter he has suggested was carefully considered by us and we decided on the name "Nagaland". I do not think this convey the impression of an independent State. In any event, the Nagas were very keen on this name and we did not wish to go against their wish in this matter.

Yours sincerely,
[Jawaharlal Nehru]

180. To Lal Bahadur Shastri: Letter from Nichols-Roy[517]

June 21, 1962

My dear Lal Bahadur,

I enclose a copy of a letter I have received from the General Secretary of the Council of Action of the All Party Hill Leaders' Conference.[518]

I am not sure if this letter needs any reply from me.

Yours affectionately,
Jawaharlal

181. To K.D. Malaviya: Assam Oil Royalties[519]

June 21, 1962

My dear Keshava,

I have received a letter from Chaliha, Chief Minister of Assam, a copy of which I enclose.[520]

515. Letter to the President.
516. Chairman of the Legislative Council of West Bengal.
517. Letter to the Home Minister. MHA, File No. 4/1/62-SR(R)-A., p. 49/c.
518. See appendix 30.
519. Letter to the Minister of Mines and Fuel. PMO, File No. 17(490)/62-70-PMS, Sr. No. 20-A.
520. Of 18 June 1962, see appendix 37.

Apart from the other important questions raised in this dispute, I think any decision made by us which reduces the amount earned by the Assam Government from royalties from oil, etc, will be bad. I can quite understand the Assam Government objecting to any such decision which will put them in a great difficulty. If they have been getting certain royalties for a considerable time past, surely we cannot suddenly reduce it in this way.[521]

Yours affectionately,
Jawaharlal Nehru

182. To Lal Bahadur Shastri: Proposal for Assam Committee[522]

June 26, 1962

My dear Lal Bahadur,

I am sending you a copy of a letter from Chaliha[523] to me in which he suggests the appointment of a high powered committee to consider the problems of Assam. There is no doubt that Assam's problems require consideration, but I rather doubt if all these mixed problems, including the development programmes in the Hill areas, can be profitably considered by a committee. Anyhow, I should like you to let me know what you think of the proposal.

Yours affectionately,
[Jawaharlal Nehru]

521. For previous correspondence on this subject, see SWJN/SS/75/section Politics subsection Assam.
522. Letter to the Home Minister.
523. B.P. Chaliha, Chief Minister of Assam.

183. For V.K. Krishna Menon: Mizo Hills Roads and Airfields[524]

I enclose a note given to me by the Governor of Assam about the Mizo Hills District. The situation there is gradually worsening.[525] Unfortunately, communications are almost wholly lacking there. We have decided to take up some major roads, which the Border Roads Organisation is dealing with, but this will take some time. Meanwhile, it seems desirable that some small landing strips for Otter aircraft etc. might be made.

184. To B.P. Chaliha: Oil Royalty Issue for Supreme Court[526]

June 27, 1962

My dear Chaliha,

I received your letter of the 18th June a few days ago. This relates to the question of oil royalty. I have discussed this matter with our Minister, Keshava Deva Malaviya.[527] It seems to me that the best course would be to refer it, through our President, to one of the judges of the Supreme Court. You have raised certain legal points which should be decided at the highest level. This question may well come up in other States also.[528]

Yours sincerely,
Jawaharlal Nehru

524. Note, 26 June 1962, for the Defence Minister.

525. An extract from a secret letter from the Governor of Assam S.M. Shrinagesh dated 23 June 1962 to the President read: " 3. The Mizo National Front has been further extending its activities. Its leader, Pu Laldenga, is reported to have stated at a public meeting that there was an agreement with the British Government that the Mizo people could choose to opt out of India 10 years after the date of Independence. If the approach to an international forum failed to achieve Mizo Independence, he suggested that Mizos should adopt the line of action taken by Nagas and establish an exile Government in Pakistan. Latest reports indicate that, at a recent close door meeting at Aizawl, a decision has been taken that Pu Laldenga or his Vice-President, John Manliana, should proceed to Pakistan and Burma in order to enlist support for their independence movement." See MHA, File No. 15/1/62-SR (R)-A.

526. Letter to the Chief Minister of Assam. PMO, File No. 17(490)/62-70-PMS, Sr. No. 23-A.

527. Minister of Mines and Fuel.

528. See further item 185.

185. To B.P. Chaliha: Oil Royalty Issue for Arbitration[529]

June 27, 1962

My dear Chaliha,

I wrote to you a day or two ago about the Oil Royalty matter and said that as there was no agreement and it raised substantial questions of law, we would be agreeable, if you so wished, to refer the matter to the Supreme Court through the President.[530]

This afternoon I raised this subject at our Cabinet meeting. We did not discuss the merits of the question. But it was felt that it would be rather unfortunate for us to go through this rather complicated process of reference to the Supreme Court. It would be far better if, in the event of an agreement, the matter was referred to an arbitrator whose decision be accepted by the parties concerned.

The arbitrator necessarily must be a top ranking person who would apply a fresh mind to the subject. It was generally recognised that the calculated resources for the Third Five Year Plan should on no account be lessened whatever the result of the arbitration might be.

The name of our Finance Minister Shri Morarji Desai was suggested as an arbitrator. It was felt that he would be particularly suitable as he would have the full financial picture before him. I hope you will agree to this proposal.[531]

Shri Morarji Desai is leaving Delhi tomorrow and will be going very soon to Europe for three weeks. He will return about the 23th July. If you agree, as I hope you will, then this matter can be referred to him and he can take it up soon after his return.

He could also consider the questio of the sales tax.

Yours sincerely,
Jawaharlal Nehru

529. Letter to the Chief Minister of Assam. PMO, File No. 17(490)/62-70-PMS, Sr. No. 25-A.
530. This seems to refer to his letter of 27 June, item 184.
531. Extract from the minutes of the Cabinet meeting of 27 June 1962:"The Prime Minister referred to the dispute which has been going on for some time between the Ministry of Mines & Fuel and the Government of Assam, regarding royalties and sales tax on oil. The Prime Minister suggested, and the Cabinet agreed, that, if the Government of Assam was agreeable, the dispute might be referred to the Union Minister of Finance for arbitration. The State's Third Plan resources would not be allowed to suffer." PMO, File No. 17(490)/62-70-PMS, Sr. No. 24-A.

186. To Arjun Arora: Arbitration on Assam Royalty Problem[532]

July 2, 1962

Dear Shri Arjun Arora,

Your letter of the 1st July.[533] I agree with you that it is better to decide this amongst ourselves or by reference to an arbitrator than to have a reference made to the Supreme Court.[534]

Yours sincerely,
Jawaharlal Nehru

187. To Liladhar Kotoki: Development Plans in General[535]

July 10, 1962

Dear Liladharji,

I have received your letter of June 27th. Having a little more leisure here at Pahalgam, I have read your long letter carefully.

You refer to Pakistani infiltration. This is perfectly true. But you will appreciate that this infiltration from Bengal to Assam has been taking place for a very long time past. I remember reading about it in the census reports of half a century ago. Therefore, we should not look upon it as essentially a political move. Nevertheless, it is true that this infiltration should be stopped and effectively dealt with. I believe that much of this infiltration took place in the first five years after Independence when the border was not adequately guarded. After that, it has been limited greatly. Therefore, steps have been taken recently to stop such infiltration. We may take further steps to remove illegal immigrants. In doing so, however, great care has to be taken, as you yourself say, so as not to cause injury and harassment to innocent people. Probably it will be difficult now to deal with illegal immigrants who came before 1952. We might, therefore, fix 1952 as the date of our enquiry.

532. Letter to a Rajya Sabha MP, Congress; PMO, File No. 17(490)/62-70-PMS, Sr. No. 29-A.

533. See appendix 48.

534. See item 185.

535. Letter to Lok Sabha MP, Congress, from Nowgong, Assam ; address: 50 South Avenue, New Delhi. Sent from Pahalgam, Kashmir.

You then refer to the Assam-East Pakistan border and the Naga hostiles. These matters are constantly being considered by us and I believe there has been considerable improvement in recent months. It is impossible, however, to prevent depredations from time to time in some of our States like Rajasthan and Madhya Pradesh where there is the very serious dacoit problem. There is no international border there. Nevertheless, the dacoits can create a lot of mischief.

You refer to transport and communications and suggest the building of railways in some places and roads in others. All this as well as the control of floods and power shortages are essentially problems of development which are considered by the Planning Commission and incorporated in the Five Year Plan. The Third Five Year Plan was drawn up after a great deal of thought. It now appears that it might be difficult because of the lack of foreign exchange as well as other reasons to give full effect to it. It is manifest, therefore, that we cannot add to it as this would be entirely beyond our capacity.

At present each State should try to implement fully the present Third Five Year Plan. If we succeed fully in that, this in itself will mean progress for that State and for the whole of India and the laying of the base for further progress in the next phase.

Yours sincerely,
[Jawaharlal Nehru]

188. To B.P. Chaliha: Assam Legislative Assembly on Nagaland Bill[536]

13th July, 1962

My dear Chaliha,
Your letter of July 9th asking of an extension of time to give the views of the Assam Legislative Assembly in regard to the Nagaland Bill, 1962. I appreciate the difficulty of dates.

In accordance with your wishes we are extending the period of time to the 12th August.

We have advised the President accordingly and I have no doubt that his consent will be forthcoming.

Yours sincerely,
[Jawaharlal Nehru]

536. Letter to the Chief Minister of Assam.

189. To S.M. Shrinagesh: Northeast Problems[537]

July 13, 1962

My dear Shrinagesh,
In one of your letters, you referred to a number of matters. I sent your letter to the Defence Minister who has sent me a note on the subjects dealt with in your letter. I enclose a copy of that note.[538]

Yours sincerely,
[Jawaharlal Nehru]

190. To Lal Bahadur Shastri: All Party Hill Leaders' Conference[539]

July 13, 1962

My dear Lal Bahadur,
Your letter of the 13th July about the activities of the All Party Hill Leaders' Conference.[540] I think I have explained the position quite adequately to them and there is no misunderstanding. If you like, you can write to the Governor[541] explaining the matter and he can convey the substance of your letter to them. As I am leaving early tomorrow morning, I cannot do this myself as I have not got their letter with me at present.[542]

Yours affectionately,
Jawaharlal

537. Letter to the Governor of Assam; address: Assam Governor's Camp.
538. See appendix 56.
539. Letter to the Home Minister. MHA, File No. 4/1/62-SR(R)-A., p. 57/c. Also available in the JN Collection.
540. Appendix 61.
541. S.M. Shrinagesh, Governor of Assam till 7 September 1962.
542. For earlier correspondence, see item 180 and appendix 30.

(xi) Orissa

191. To K.D. Malaviya: Paradip Port Development[543]

June 24, 1962

My dear Keshava,

I have your letter of the 24th June.[544] Some little time ago, about two or three months, when Patnaik[545] was here, a meeting was held at which, besides Patnaik and myself, Morarji Desai,[546] Gulzarilal Nanda[547] and A.N. Khosla[548] were present. Even before this meeting, this matter had been discussed on several occasions by some of us with Patnaik, and he had been given the assurance that he could go ahead with building a highway to Paradip. At this meeting where we went into various proposals made by Patnaik with some thoroughness, he was told that he could certainly proceed with this highway and also that he could obtain two dredgers to deepen the approach to Paradip.

This question of building the highway was practically agreed to even before this meeting. The other schemes that he put forward, were appreciated by us, but we told him that they would have to be examined thoroughly from various points of view. The impression I have got from these examinations that we made, was that essentially the schemes were good subject to their being examined and our resources. We had asked Patnaik then to speak to the Japanese Ambassador[549] and find out what help we would get from Japan. I suppose it was in furtherance of this direction that Manubhai[550] and Patnaik met the Japanese Ambassador.

I do not think, therefore, that anything has been done which was wrong.

543. Letter to the Minister of Mines and Fuel. PMO, File No. 17(43)/56-64-PMS, Sr. No. 108-A.
544. Appendix 43.
545. Bijoyananda (Biju) Patnaik, Chief Minister of Orissa.
546. Finance Minister.
547. Deputy Chairman of the Planning Commission.
548. Member, Planning Commission.
549. Koto Matsudaira.
550. Manubhai Shah, Minister of State for International Trade in the Ministry of Commerce and Industry.

The matter should certainly be put up before the Cabinet for their consideration.[551]

Yours affectionately,
Jawaharlal Nehru

(xii) Punjab

192. To Ajit Singh Bhatinda: Restoring Political Career[552]

June 13, 1962

Dear Ajit Singhji,
I have your letter of June 11th.[553] I remember receiving your previous letter also. I am writing to Sardar Partap Singh Kairon about what you have said in your letter. Perhaps, you can see him and explain the situation more fully to him or to Sardar Darbara Singh.

Yours sincerely,
[Jawaharlal Nehru]

193. To Partap Singh Kairon: Restoring Ajit Singh's Career[554]

June 13, 1962

My dear Partap Singh,
I enclose a copy of a letter from Ajit Singh Bhatinda. Perhaps, you can see him and get him some work to do in the Congress Organisation, if not elsewhere.

Yours sincerely,
[Jawaharlal Nehru]

551. On Orissa development plans, see SWJN/SS/76/items 264-279.
552. Letter to former Congress MP; address: Civil Station, Bhatinda.
553. See appendix 27.
554. Letter to the Chief Minister of Punjab.

194. To Partap Singh Kairon: Farmers' Misery[555]

14th June, 1962

My dear Partap Singh,

I enclose a copy of a letter received from Mani Ram Bagri, MP. He is a troublesome person belonging to the Socialist Party, but, according to my custom, I would like to reply to him giving him the facts. Could you please advise me as to what I should write to him?[556]

Yours sincerely,
[Jawaharlal Nehru]

195. To Mani Ram Bagri: Farmers' Misery[557]

14 जून 1962

प्रिय मनीराम जी,

आपका 12 जून का ख़त मिला।[558]

मैं ने उस को मुख्य मंत्री, पंजाब को भेज दिया है।

आपका
[जवाहरलाल नेहरु]

[Translation begins:

14 June 1962

Dear Mani Ramji,

I have received your letter of 12 June.[559] I have sent it to the Chief Minister, Punjab.

Yours sincerely,
Jawaharlal Nehru

Translation ends]

555. Letter to the Chief Minister of Punjab.
556. See item 195 and appendix 31.
557. Letter to Socialist Lok Sabha MP; address: 75, South Avenue, New Delhi.
558. See appendix 31.
559. See fn 558 in this section.

196. To Partap Singh Kairon: Industrial Projects for Punjab[560]

June 23, 1962

My dear Partap Singh,

Your letter of June 21st. I am afraid I am unable to promise any particular major industry for the Punjab or for any other place. We are very hard up at the present moment regarding our resources and the aid we expected from outside is becoming more and more doubtful.

Every big project is located keeping in view the economics of the location. Experts go into it and then recommend it. As for the Small Car Project, it is rather doubtful if it will go through at all.

Yours sincerely,
Jawaharlal Nehru

197. To Partap Singh Kairon: Sumitra Devi's Frustration with Politics[561]

25th June, 1962

My dear Partap Singh,

Sumitra Devi, MLA of the Punjab,[562] came to see me today. She told me that she was feeling very unhappy in the new political atmosphere in which she had entered after the elections. She had obviously been concerned with social work and not with this kind of thing. So, she wanted my advice as to what to do.

She complained that the SDO in her constituency was himself asking people to vote for certain candidates in the Samiti[563] elections which took place a week or so ago and was taking shelter under your name. He was now doing the same thing for the Zila[564] elections.

I told her that this was not proper for the SDO to do or for any Government official. I advised her not to enter into any groups in the Assembly, but try to interest herself even there in social and like work.

560. Letter to the Chief Minister of Punjab. PMO, File No. 17(407)/60-67-PMS, Vol. II, Sr. No. 60-A.
561. Letter to the Chief Minister of Punjab.
562. Congress MLA from Rewari.
563. Panchayat Samiti.
564. Zila Parishad.

This lady is, I believe, the sister of Rao Birender Singh.[565] She produced a favourable impression upon me. I told her that her brother had struck me as a quarrelsome person.

Yours sincerely,
[Jawaharlal Nehru]

198. To Partap Singh Kairon: Construct Road to Jaito[566]

June 25, 1962

My dear Partap Singh,

This morning, some members of the Panchayats of Mallan and Kauni in district Ferozepore came to see me. Among them were one or two persons who had accompanied me to Jaito in the twenties, that is, nearly forty years ago.[567] They gave me a paper which I enclose.

They are very anxious to have a pucca road constructed on the route of our march to Jaito. This distance is about twenty-six miles of which ten miles are already covered by a pucca road. All that is necessary, therefore, is to make a kutcha road pucca for sixteen miles. This does not seem to me very much and appears worth doing. It is for you to decide.

Yours sincerely,
[Jawaharlal Nehru]

(xiii) Rajasthan

199. To S.K. Dey: Misuse of Cooperatives[568]

June 4, 1962

My dear Dey,

In a confidential report which Khandubhai Desai[569] has made to the AICC about Congress activities in Rajasthan, the following paragraph occurs:

565. Former Minister in Punjab.
566. Letter to the Chief Minister of Punjab.
567. On September 21, 1923, Nehru and other freedom fighters were arrested at Jaito for taking part in the morcha undertaken for gurdwara reforms. For his message from Nabha jail where he was then lodged, see SWJN/FS/2/pp. 31-32.
568. Letter to the Minister of Community Development, Panchayati Raj and Cooperation.
569. Rajya Sabha MP, Congress, from Gujarat.

"A very significant development which has come to my notice is that the whole cooperative movement in Rajasthan, because of these pressure tactics and weakness of Mohanlal Sukhadia[570] was passing into the hands of Kumbha Ram who is the Chairman of the Cooperative Union[571] and Nathuram Mirdha[572] who is in charge of Cooperation. Through this state wide cooperation and its employees, Nathuram and Kumbharam began to strengthen their hold throughout Rajasthan by undesirable practices. This was naturally resented by the public at large. I was almost shocked to hear this utilisation of cooperative movement for personal ends and aggrandisement. It would be worthwhile to institute an impartial inquiry into the working of cooperative institutions in the State before the whole movement comes into disrepute—but Mohanlal Sukhadia could not give any relief to the injustice done to non-Jat Congressmen or even to Jats who did not conform to the views and behests of Kumbharam and his associates like Nathuram Mirdha and Mathuradas Mathur[573]."[574]

Yours sincerely,
[Jawaharlal Nehru]

200. To Mohanlal Sukhadia: Misuse of Cooperative Union[575]

June 4, 1962

My dear Sukhadia,

A report has come to us about the cooperative movement in Rajasthan which says that this movement has been utilised for personal ends and aggrandisement by Kumbharam who is Chairman of the Cooperative Union, and Nathuram Mirdha who is in charge of Cooperation. It is suggested that an impartial

570. Chief Minister of Rajasthan.
571. Kumbha Ram Arya, also Congress Member of Rajya Sabha from Rajasthan.
572. Nathu Ram Mirdha, Minister of Agriculture, Animal Husbandry, Community Development, Panchayats and Cooperation, Rajasthan.
573. Minister of Home, Law, Judiciary, Legislative Asembly, Elections and Publicity, Rajasthan.
574. See also item 200.
575. Letter to the Chief Minister of Rajasthan.

inquiry should be held into the working of the cooperative institutions in the State before the whole movement comes into disrepute.[576]

I pass this on to you for your consideration.

Yours sincerely,
[Jawaharlal Nehru]

201. To Lal Bahadur Shastri: Man Singh's Letter to MLAs[577]

June 29, 1962

My dear Lal Bahadur,

I enclose a cutting from the *Blitz*. In this reference is made to the Maharaja of Jaipur[578] writing a letter to the MLAs. I think it would be worthwhile your writing to the Maharaja drawing attention to this report and asking him for a copy of that letter.

Yours affectionately,
[Jawaharlal Nehru]

(xiv) Uttar Pradesh

202. To C.B. Gupta: Poverty in East Uttar Pradesh[579]

June 11, 1962

My dear Chandra Bhanu,

I had a talk with G.D. Birla two or three days ago about going to Rihand. I suggested that I might go there towards the end of July. Are you agreeable to some such date?

This afternoon in the Lok Sabha, a Congress Member, presumably coming from Balia or Ghazipur,[580] spoke in rather moving terms about the terrible

576. Suggested by Khandubhai Desai. See item 199.
577. Letter to the Minister of Home Affairs.
578. Maharaja of Jaipur Sawai Man Singh II was Rajya Sabha MP, Independent, from Rajasthan, 3 April 1962-8 November 1965, thereafter appointed Ambassador to Spain.
579. Letter to the Chief Minister of Uttar Pradesh.
580. Viswanath Singh Gahmari from Ghazipur. See also item 203.

condition of the districts of Balia, Ghazipur and Azamgarh. He said that during the last fifteen years, ever since Independence, no good has come to these districts, which are the poorest in the UP and probably in India. Eighty percent of the inhabitants there have only one meal a day and the daily wage for agricultural labourers is two annas.[581]

I know that these districts are poor, but I was nevertheless shocked to hear a [the] speech. Surely, it cannot be that the daily wage of large numbers of people there is two annas. I should like you to let me know how far these allegations are correct.

Yours sincerely,
[Jawaharlal Nehru]

None To Blame

The Planning Commission disclosed that East U.P., among other 'backward' areas, has received special allocations for development.

(From *Shankar's Weekly*, 24 June 1962, p. 19)

581. For Gahmari's speech, see *Lok Sabha Debates*, Third Series, Vol. V, June 8 to 22, 1962, cols 10089-10094.

203. To Gulzarilal Nanda: Poverty in East Uttar Pradesh[582]

June 12, 1962

My dear Gulzarilal,

Yesterday a moving speech was delivered in the Lok Sabha by Viswanath Singh Gahmari, a Member from Ghazipur. He said that in the districts of Ghazipur, Ballia and Azamgarh nothing had been done for the benefit of the people ever since Independence. They were frightfully poor and because of the increasing population, they were becoming poorer. Eighty percent of them had only one meal a day because they could not afford another. The daily agricultural wages were two annas per head. Possibly, he exaggerated, but there is no doubt that he felt all this as tears trickled down his face when he was speaking. It is better, he said, for people to die of epidemics and diseases than to endure this slow death by starvation. Why then should efforts be made to improve their health by combating diseases? And so on. Viswanath Singh is a Congress Member and his speech had considerable effect on those who listened to it. I happened to be there myself.

I suppose there are other areas in India too that are as bad as the eastern districts of UP which include not only Ghazipur, Ballia and Azamgarh, but also Basti, Deoria, Gorakhpur and Gonda. All these districts suffered from the big zamindari system and they have not recovered from it. Apparently, nothing substantial has been done to help them to get out of their miserable condition. I suppose the State Government is partly responsible for somewhat ignoring them. But whoever may be responsible for this, the fact remains that these districts are a disgrace to our administration. Cannot something special be done to them as indeed to other poverty-stricken districts in India? Our big schemes do not touch them. I do not know if Community Development has done them any good. Apparently not.

I think, it is our duty that all such regions, not only Eastern UP but other places too, should be treated rather separately because the problems they face are enormous. I should like you to give thought to this. The Planning Commission should consider the case of all these districts and suggest some steps to be taken.[583]

Yours sincerely,
[Jawaharlal Nehru]

582. Letter to the Deputy Chairman of the Planning Commission.

583. See reply by G.L. Nanda, appendix 34; item 204; also item 202.

204. To Gulzarilal Nanda: Backward Areas[584]

June 14, 1962

My dear Gulzarilal,

Thank you for your letter of June 14th. I shall certainly come to the meeting of the Planning Commission when you discuss these matters relating to particularly backward areas.[585] I think it would be worthwhile inviting Keshava Deva Malaviya[586] to it too as he represents these areas in Eastern UP.

I am afraid the UP Government cannot be relied upon to produce any kind of useful information. If we want any further information we shall have to take steps to get it.[587]

Yours sincerely,
[Jawaharlal Nehru]

205. To Mahendra: Nepal Bund on the Great Gandak[588]

June 17, 1962

My dear friend,

Last month you wrote to me a letter dated 14th May about constructing the Nepal Bund on the river Narayani. Your Majesty said that no detailed papers were available about this.

I was in Kashmir then. I wrote to the Chief Minister of Uttar Pradesh on the subject and asked him to send the necessary information to our Ambassador in Nepal.[589] I understand from him that he has sent this information to our Ambassador in Kathmandu. I hope that the Ambassador will place this information before Your Majesty.[590]

With kind regards,

Yours sincerely,
J. Nehru

584. Letter to the Minister of Planning, Labour and Emplyment.
585. See appendix 34; item 203.
586. Minister of Mines and fuel.
587. See further item 207.
588. Letter to the King of Nepal.
589. Harishwar Dayal.
590. See item 206.

206. To Harishwar Dayal: Nepal Bund on the Great Gandak[591]

June 17, 1962

My dear Harish,

You will remember that when the King of Nepal[592] was here,[593] I mentioned to him a matter to which the Chief Minister of UP[594] had drawn my attention. This was the necessity and urgency of constructing the Nepal Bund on the river Narayani or the Great Gandak. The King had said that he would look into this immediately. Last month he wrote to me that he could not find any papers or information on this subject. Thereafter I wrote to the Chief Minister of UP who has sent me a reply now. With this reply he has sent me a note on this subject together with a map. He says that he has already sent you a copy of these papers. I am therefore not sending his note to you unless you want it specially.

Please give this information to the King. I enclose a copy of a brief reply I have written to the King today.[595]

Yours sincerely,
J. Nehru

207. To C.B. Gupta: East UP Poverty and Rihand Visit[596]

June 22, 1962

My dear Chandra Bhanu,

I have written to you two letters in recent weeks. So far as I know no answer has come to me to these letters.

One of these was about a speech delivered by a Member from Ghazipur in the Lok Sabha where he gave some startling facts, or alleged facts, about the extreme poverty of certain parts of Ghazipur district and indeed of all the eastern districts. It was quite shocking for us to hear these facts because, poor as India is, nobody has ever stated before that the average wage in these pockets is two annas a day or even less.

591. Letter to the Ambassador in Kathmandu.

592. Mahendra Bir Bikram Shah Deva.

593. Mahendra arrived on 18 April on a four-day visit, see SWJN/SS/76/items 471-472.

594. C.B. Gupta.

595. Item 205.

596. Letter to the Chief Minister of Uttar Pradesh.

My object in writing to you about this speech was to draw your particular attention to the very bad state of the eastern districts. We all know that they are in a bad way and something has got to be done about them. That something is not starting a big factory, but immediate attempts to improve agriculture and start village and small industries. I have referred the matter to our Planning Commission who, I hope, will take some action by sending someone to enquire personally into the matter. But I want the UP Government to take personal and urgent interest into all these eastern districts of Ghazipur, Ballia, Gorakhpur, Deoria and Azamgarh. They are pulling down the whole of the UP and, unless this is remedied, it will be difficult for the UP to make progress.[597]

Separately I am writing to you about my programme for going to Rihand.[598]

Yours sincerely,
[Jawaharlal Nehru]

208. To C.B. Gupta: Rihand Visit[599]

June 22, 1962

My dear Chandra Bhanu,

I wrote to you some time ago suggesting that I might visit Rihand Project during the last week of July. I have not received any reply from you to that letter.

I now suggest the following programme for your consideration:

25th July - Go to Lucknow for the day.
Meet Ministers, MLAs etc.
26th July - Go to Allahabad and stay there till the 27th, touring in the villages of the Phulpur constituency.
28th July - Go to Rihand from Allahabad.

It is not quite clear how I go to Rihand. I suppose I can go by air to Mirzapur and thence by car. Or, perhaps, a smaller plane might take me to a nearer place. This matter can be fixed up later if you broadly agree with my suggested programme. This will be the rainy season, and one has to keep that in mind. Public meetings in the open will hardly be possible.

Yours sincerely,
[Jawaharlal Nehru]

597. See items 202-204, and appendix 34.

598. See item 208.

599. Letter to the Chief Minister of Uttar Pradesh.

209. To C.B. Gupta: Developing UP Mountain Regions[600]

June 24, 1962

My dear Chandra Bhanu,

Bhakt Darshan, MP,[601] has sent me a note on the development of the mountain regions of Uttar Pradesh. I understand that he has sent you a copy of this note.[602]

Some of his suggestions seem to me good. I hope you will have them all examined and let me know what you propose to do about them. These mountain regions have been neglected for a long time past and we should do all we can to develop them. As a matter of fact, even our border troubles with China necessitate the development of these regions.

Yours sincerely,
Jawaharlal Nehru

210. To Ajit Prasad Jain: UP Tour Programme[603]

June 26, 1962

My dear Ajit,

My present intention is to go to Lucknow on the 25th July and spend the day there. On the 26th and 27th, I am going to Allahabad. On the 28th I go from Allahabad to the Rihand Dam in Mirzapur District. This dam is rather difficult of access and involves a long road journey from Mirzapur. I am trying to arrange for a helicopter to take me there. I am not yet sure if that is possible.[604]

If the 25th does not suit you, I might be able to go to Lucknow on the 26th and postpone the remaining part of my programme by a day. Please let me know.

Yours sincerely,
[Jawaharlal Nehru]

600. Letter to the Chief Minister of UP. PMO, File No. 2(242)/58-64-PMS, Vol. I, Sr. No. 66-A.
601. Lok Sabha MP, Congress, from Garhwal.
602. See summary of note, by M.L. Bazaz, Nehru's PS, appendix 42.
603. Letter to the President of the Uttar Pradesh PCC.
604. On the Rihand Dam visit, see also items 207-208, 211-212.

211. To Ajit Prasad Jain: UP Programme without Rihand[605]

June 26, 1962

My dear Ajit,

I met Chandra Bhanu Gupta[606] today and had a talk with him about my programme. He was not at all keen on my going to the Rihand Dam at the end of July. He pointed out that apart from certain difficulties in my journey to that place, it would be difficult to make proper arrangements in the middle of the rainy season for the crowds that might gather there.

After my talk with him I decided to give up my visit to Rihand on the 28th of July. I shall now probably go there early in October, provided I do not go out of India them.[607]

I shall now go to Allahabad on the 26th and 27th July and to Lucknow on the 28th. I had agreed to go to Lucknow on the 28th to suit MLAs etc. who would be coming for the Assembly meeting.

I suppose we can have a joint meeting of the MLAs and PCC. It will be an informal affair. Whatever I have to say to one will be much the same as to the other.

My programme to go to Bangalore remains as fixed.[608]

Yours sincerely,
Jawaharlal Nehru

212. To G.D. Birla: Postpone Rihand Dam Visit[609]

June 26, 1962

My dear Ghanshyamdas Ji,

I have yet been unable to find out if a helicopter could take me to the Rihand Dam on the 28th of July. Meanwhile I have seen Chandra Bhanu Gupta, the Chief Minister of UP. He did not like the idea of my going to Rihand at that time. Because of the rainy season it would be difficult to make arrangements for large numbers of people.

605. Letter to the President of the Uttar Pradesh PCC. PMO, File No. 8(227)-62-PMP, Sr. No. 5-A.

606. Chief Minister of Uttar Pradesh.

607. See items 207-208, 210-211 on Rihand.

608. See items 165-168.

609. Letter to industrialist; address: 3 India Exchange Place, Calcutta.

Because of C.B. Gupta's feelings in the matter and other peoples' opinion also, I have decided to postpone my visit to Rihand to a later date. Probably I might be able to go early in October when the rains are over. This is subject to my not going out of India then.

I hope you agree with this change of plan.[610]

Yours sincerely,
[Jawaharlal Nehru]

213. To Ajit Prasad Jain: Must Attend Cooperation Function[611]

July 1, 1962

My dear Ajit,
When I go to Lucknow on the 28th July, I should like to attend a Cooperative function which Chaturbhuj Sharma[612] is organising.[613] Please, therefore, put it in the programme. You can find out more about it from Chaturbhuj Sharma.

Yours sincerely,
Jawaharlal Nehru

214. To Baldeo Prasad Gupta: Feroze Gandhi Memorial Meeting and Nature Cure Institute[614]

July 6, 1962

Dear Baldeo Prasadji,
I have received your letter of the 2nd July. I am afraid I shall not be able to attend any special memorial meeting for Feroze Gandhi during my brief visit to Allahabad.

610. The Hindustan Aluminum Corporation Limited, a Birla firm, commissioned its unit in 1962 at Renukoot near Rihand dam, 160 kilometers from Banaras.
611. Letter to the President of the Uttar Pradesh PCC. PMO, File No. 8(227)-62-P.M.P., Sr. No. 12-A.
612. Minister of Cooperation in UP.
613. Nehru addressed a convention of 4000 representatives of cooperative societies. See SWJN/SS/78/item 308.
614. Letter to an Advocate, Kurwi, Banda, Uttar Pradesh. Sent from Pahalgam, Kashmir.

I do not myself see the appropriateness of having a nature cure institute in Feroze Gandhi's memory. Such an institute is good but it has no relation to Feroze Gandhi.

Yours sincerely,
[Jawaharlal Nehru]

215. To C.B. Gupta: Subhadra Joshi on Balrampur[615]

Pahalgam (Kashmir)
July 6, 1962

My dear Chandra Bhanu,
Subhadra Joshi has written a letter to me about her constituency, Balrampur. I am enclosing her letter in original. You will no doubt pay attention to what she has said.

Yours sincerely,
[Jawaharlal Nehru]

216. To Narain Prasad Asthana: Visit to Nehru Gram Bharti[616]

July 7, 1962

My dear Narain Prasad,
I have your letter of 3rd July. It is true that I am going to Allahabad for two days, 26th and 27th of this month. If it is possible to include the inauguration of the Gram Bharti in my programme, I shall be glad.

Yours sincerely,
Jawaharlal Nehru

615. Letter to the Chief Minister of Uttar Pradesh.

616. Letter to lawyer; address: Nehru Gram Bharti, Panchshila, Triveni Road, Allahabad-3. PMO, File No. 8(227)-62-PMP, Sr. No. 19-A. Sent from Pahalgam, Kashmir.

217. To C.B. Gupta: Madan Upadhyaya[617]

July 7, 1962

My dear Chandra Bhanu,

I have received your long letter of July 1st and have read it. It is good of you to take all this trouble to write to me. I had sent you the Hindi letter as it is my usual practice to forward such letters. But I did not certainly want to trouble you on this matter and to induce you to write at such length.

You may be right in thinking that Madan Upadhyaya[618] is at the back of this letter. Personally, I have not heard any complaint about you from Madan Upadhyaya.

Yours sincerely,
[Jawaharlal Nehru]

218. To Biswanath Das: Forthcoming Visit to Uttar Pradesh[619]

July 9, 1962

My dear Biswanath Das,

I have just received your letter of the 4th July. It is true that I intend to go to Allahabad for two days, 26th and 27th July, and then to Lucknow for one day, the 28th.

In Allahabad I shall of course stay in my own house. You need not take any trouble about sending any servants or the people there.

In Lucknow, I have been hoping to stay with you chiefly because this is the first time I am going to Lucknow since you became Governor. I still hope that this will be fixed up. I am writing to your Chief Minister, Chandra Bhanu Gupta, on the subject and I hope he will agree to this.

I am on rather strict diet now, chiefly vegetarian. On the whole, I avoid anything cooked in ghee. Normally my food is cooked in safflower oil. But I do not want to give you any special trouble about my stay. So long as the food is simple and not spiced or richly cooked, that will do.

I shall, of course, have talks with you when we meet.

Yours sincerely,
Jawaharlal Nehru

617. Letter to the Chief Minister of Uttar Pradesh. Sent from Pahalgam, Kashmir.
618. Probably, Madan Mohan Upadhyaya, PSP MLA from Ranikhet, UP, 1952-1957.
619. Letter to the Governor of Uttar Pradesh. Sent from Pahalgam, Kashmir. PMO, File No. 8(227)-62-P.M.P., Sr. No. 16-A. Also available in the JN Collection.

219. To C.B. Gupta: Forthcoming Visit to Uttar Pradesh[620]

July 9, 1962

My dear Chandra Bhanu,

Your Governor has written to me about my stay in Allahabad and Lucknow. In Allahabad of course I shall stay in my house. In Lucknow, I had thought of staying with the Governor chiefly because this is my first visit to Lucknow since he took charge and it would give him pleasure if I stayed with him, I still think that it will be better.

I would, of course, be happy to stay with you but, on this occasion, I do think it more desirable for me to stay at Raj Bhavan. Anyhow, you can have a talk with the Governor and fix this up.

I am on rather strict diet now. My food is usually cooked in a cooker without any spices or chillies. It is light food and I avoid ghee as far as possible. My meal is cooked in safflower oil. All this is rather troublesome and it is not necessary for very special arrangements to be made for me for a day or two. But anyhow it has to be light and simple.

Yours sincerely,
Jawaharlal Nehru

220. To Lal Bahadur Shastri: Officers' Training School in Allahabad[621]

July 14, 1962

My dear Lal Bahadur,

I enclose a letter I have received from the Mayor of Allahabad.[622] I do not know what this Officers' Training School, to which he refers, is. Does this mean civil officers or military officers? If it has anything to do with the military, you can send this letter on to the Defence Ministry. If it has something to do with Civil Aviation, this can be sent on to Jagjivan Ram.[623]

Yours affectionately,
[Jawaharlal Nehru]

620. Letter to the Chief Minister of Uttar Pradesh. Sent from Pahalgam, Kashmir.
621. Letter to the Home Minister. Sent from Royal Cottage, Bangalore.
622. Zulfiquarullah. For Nehru's reply to Zulfiquarullah, see item 221 and letter to C. B. Gupta, item 222.
623. Minister of Transport and Communications.

221. To Zulfiquarullah: Officers' Training School in Allahabad[624]

July 19, 1962

Dear Shri Zulfiquarullah,

You wrote to me on the 12th July about a certain proposal to transfer the Officers' Training School from Allahabad to Lucknow. I did not know about this school or about the proposal to transfer it. On enquiry I find that this institution of the UP Government gives training to the officers of the State Civil Services.[625] The matter is thus entirely in the hands of the UP Government. I am, therefore, sending your letter to the Chief Minister.

Yours sincerely,
[Jawaharlal Nehru]

222. To C.B. Gupta: Shifting Officers' Training School from Allahabad[626]

July 19, 1962

My dear Chandra Bhanu,

The Mayor of Allahabad wrote to me a few days ago expressing the concern of the Corporation of the city at the report that the Officers' Training School would be shifted from Allahabad to Lucknow. I did not know anything about this, and so I enquired from Lal Bahadur Shastri. He has replied to me. I enclose the Mayor's letter as well as Lal Bahadur's reply.

I do not know of the circumstances before you. But Allahabad has got a great grievance of being neglected. I hope you will keep this in mind.[627]

Yours sincerely,
[Jawaharlal Nehru]

624. Letter to the Nagar Mahapalika (Mayor) of Allahabad. Sent from Rashtrapati Nilayam, Hyderabad.
625. See item 220.
626. Letter to the Chief Minister of Uttar Pradesh. Sent from Rashtrapati Nilayam, Hyderabad.
627. See also items 220 and 221.

(xv) West Bengal

223. For B.C. Roy: On Completing Eighty Years[628]

I have known Dr Bidhan Chandra Roy for nearly forty years. I have known him as a dear friend and colleague, as a physician of eminence and as a statesman of high standing. I am, therefore, very partial to him. But, apart from the personal equation, I am convinced that he has been a towering figure in Bengal and has steered that State with wisdom through enormous difficulties, indeed, his position is not confined to Bengal, but is an All India one, and his advice has always been helpful in consideration of All India problems. He has been a giant figure in our public life, dominating Bengal and influencing our national life. On his completing eighty years of age, I gladly contribute my affection and tribute to him and hope that he will live many long years yet to carry on the good work he has been doing.

224. To Gulzarilal Nanda: Plight of the Sunderbans[629]

June 29, 1962

My dear Gulzarilal,

I had a small deputation today from the Sundarbans area of West Bengal. These people have often come to me in the past and told me of the woeful state of that area and pressed me to see for muself. I should like to go and perhaps I might do so after the rains are over.

I do not know if the Planning Commission or the West Bengal Government has paid any special attention to this area. I think it deserves such special attention. We may not be able to take up major schemes there in the near future, but surely something should be done.

The deputation left with me a number of copies of a memorandum. I am sending you six copies in case they might be of use to you.[630]

Yours sincerely,
Jawaharlal Nehru

628. Message, 21 June 1962, sent to the editor of *New India*. PMO, File No. 9/2/62-PMP, Vol. IV, Sr. No. 64-B. Also available in NMML, Iswara Dutt Papers, Subject File No. 48.

629. Letter to the Minister of Planning. PMO, File No. 7(181)/59-66-PM, Volume I, Sr. No. 97-A.

630. See also item 225.

225. To C.D. Deshmukh: Student's Application for Admission[631]

June 30, 1962

My dear Deshmukh,

Yesterday I had a visit from some people of the Sundarbans area of West Bengal. They spoke to me about the very bad conditions of that area and wanted special help to be given. Among other things they handed to me a letter and an application from a young student from Sundarbans seeking admission to the M. Library Science course of the Delhi University. I enclose these papers.

It is entirely for you to decide what can or should be done in this matter. All I know is that Sundarbans is a very neglected area and deserves encouragement.[632]

Yours sincerely,
Jawaharlal Nehru

226. To Padmaja Naidu: B.C. Roy's Successor and Malda Refugees[633]

July 2, 1962

My dear Padmaja,

I have just had a report from Krishna Menon[634] and from Khera[635] about what happened in Calcutta today. I suppose you must feel worn out, and now you will have to face the struggle for succession. Immediately, I suppose, there is no difficulty as the senior Cabinet Minister should function as the Chief Minister. I presume Prafulla Sen is the senior Minister. In fact, he functioned as Chief Minister during Bidhan Roy's absence from India whenever this took place.

Then comes the more ticklish problem of the permanent successor. This can only be decided by the Party. My own impression is that Bidhan Roy wanted P.C. Sen[636] to succeed him. But Atulya Ghosh[637] is a formidable rival, even though he is not a member of the Assembly.

631. Letter to the Vice-Chancellor of Delhi University. Prime Minister's Office, File No. 7(181)/59-66-PM, Volume I, Sr. No. 98-A.
632. See item 224.
633. Letter to the Governor of West Bengal. NMML, Padmaja Naidu Papers.
634. V.K. Krishna Menon, the Defence Minister.
635. S.S. Khera, the Cabinet Secretary.
636. Prafulla Chandra Sen, Minister for Food, Agriculture and Supplies in B.C. Roy's Ministry.
637. President, West Bengal Pradesh Congress Committee.

Khera told me that one of the worries which troubled Bidhan was that of the refugees at Malda. Also your saying that the amount of relief being given to them according to the rules was wholly inadequate. I do not know under what rules relief is given. Normally relief is given according to needs. I have sent Rs 15,000/- from the Prime Minister's Relief Fund to Bidhan for relief in Malda. I am prepared to send some more money.

As for a more permanent solution for this problem, we had agreed to send these refugees direct to Dandakaranya, A special train for one thousand had already been arranged. When the Santhal refugees refused to come because somebody had told them that the place was full of snakes, scorpions and wild beasts, the proposal fell through.

It seems to me obvious that we should send four or five of these Santhal refugees to Dandakaranya to see the place for themselves and when they come back assure their fellow refugees about it. Then others could be sent. I am suggesting this to Mehr Chand Khanna,[638] but really it is the West Bengal Government who should arrange to send these few persons, preferably accompanied by a Bengal officer.[639]

Yours affectionately,
Jawaharlal Nehru

227. To Suniti Kumar Chatterji: New Job and Tours Abroad[640]

July 7, 1962

Dear Suniti Kumarji,

Your letter of July 4th has reached me here at Pahalgam in Kashmir.

I hope you will be elected to the Chairmanship of the West Bengal Legislative Council. I do not know how far your tours abroad come in the way of this. I should like you to go abroad for the various functions you have mentioned. I am sure your visits to foreign countries are good for India as well as for scholarship. The question of foreign exchange is indeed a very difficult

638. Minister of Works, Housing and Supply, previously Minister of Rehabilitation. See item 67.
639. See section Politics subsection Social Groups.
640. Letter to the Chairman of the Legislative Council of West Bengal, Calcutta. Sent from Pahalgam, Kashmir.

He was elected to the West Bengal Legislative Council from the Graduates constituency and remained its Chairman from 1952 to 1965.

one and we have been forced to become rather strict about it. I hope, however, that a little foreign exchange for your personal expenses may be possible.

I shall be glad to have your two new books both of which deal with subjects which interest me greatly.

Yours sincerely,
[Jawaharlal Nehru]

228. To Atulya Ghosh: Appreciating Smooth Succession in West Bengal[641]

May I congratulate you on the worthy part you have played in ensuring unanimity in the election of the new leader and Chief Minister.[642] I greatly appreciate this and trust that there will continue to be united working in trying to solve the great problems of West Bengal. The great heritage of Doctor Bidhan Chandra Roy has to be preserved and improved upon.

Jawaharlal Nehru

229. To Prafulla Chandra Sen: Congratulations on Election[643]

I am happy to learn about your unanimous election and congratulate you upon it. Nothing is more important today than our Party to hold together without groups and to work together in order to solve the great problems that we have. Bengal especially requires this cooperative approach. I know that Doctor Bidhan Roy has set a great example which it is not easy to follow. But I feel sure that you and your colleagues will together carry on the good work in West Bengal. You have all my good wishes.

Jawaharlal Nehru

641. Telegram, 9 July 1962, to the President of the West Bengal PCC. NMML, JN Supplementary Papers. Also available in the JN Collection.
642. Prafulla Chandra Sen.
643. Telegram, 9 July 1962, to the Chief Minister of West Bengal. Sent from Pahalgam, Kashmir.

230. To J.M. Majumdar: Development of Sunderbans[644]

July 11, 1962

Dear Shri Majumdar,

I have received your letter of the 7th July.[645] I am greatly interested in the development of the Sunderbans area. I am glad you are starting some industry there for this purpose. Obviously, I am not in a position to give you any opinion about the industry in question. But you will have all my good wishes in anything that you do for Sunderbans.

Yours sincerely,
[Jawaharlal Nehru]

231. To Atulya Ghosh: Visit to Calcutta[646]

July 13, 1962

My dear Atulya Babu,

I am thinking of coming to Calcutta for a day on the 29th July,[647] returning to Delhi on the 30th morning. I have no particular work to do in Calcutta and my visit is just by way of paying my homage to Dr Bidhan Roy.[648]

644. Letter to the General Manager, Calcutta Ceramic Industries, and President, Sunderbon Proja Mongal Samity, Former Special Officer, Sunderban ; address: Raj Kumari Villa, 5/1 Moore Avenue, Calcutta-40. Sent from Chashmashahi Guest House, Srinagar. PMO, File No. 7(181)/59-66-PM, Volume I, Sr. No. 102-A. Also available in the JN Collection.

645. Extract from Majumdar's letter: "Subsequently I sent a scheme prepared with my resources to you and Nandaji for the development of industries in the Sunderbans so that its materials, which now run to waste, may be properly utilised and provide employment. The Planning Commission did not think it worthwhile to give effect to or consider the scheme. It were a waste of my time and energy.

Hence I have taken up utilisation of raw materials which are in abundance in the DVC area of West Bengal and Bihar and in Orissa for the manufacture of electrical porcelain insulators of low tension and other ceramic articles. West Bengal is specially suited for this industry because of the availability of qualified technical staff and cheap unskilled labour from amongst the refugee women. Service facilities from the Bengal Ceramic Institute and also proximity to a large market and distribution centre are added advantage." PMO, File No. 7(181)/59-66-PM, Volume I, Sr. No. 102-A.

646. Letter to the President of the West Bengal PCC. PMO, File No. 8(227)-62-PMP, Sr. No. 23-A. Also available in the JN Collection.

A similar letter was sent the same day to Prafulla Sen, the Chief Minister of West Bengal. PMO, File No. 8(227)-62-PMP, Sr. No. 24-A.

647. See SWJN/SS/78.

648. The previous Chief Minister of West Bengal.

I have written to Prafulla Sen also. If he wants me to address the members of the Legislature, I shall gladly do so. Perhaps, if you approve, some Congress workers might also be addressed. A public meeting is not indicated during the monsoon.

Yours sincerely,
Jawaharlal Nehru

232. To Atulya Ghosh: Memorial to B.C. Roy[649]

July 15, 1962

My dear Atulya Babu,

I have your letter of the 11th July about the memorial to Dr Bidhan Roy. I think it is eminently desirable that a suitable memorial should be set up to him in a manner which will serve the ideals and objectives that appealed to him. The people of West Bengal will, no doubt, be specially concerned with this memorial, but the appeal should be to the whole of India and should not be confined to the people of West Bengal. A children's hospital, as suggested, appears to me a suitable memorial.

On my return to Delhi, I hope to send you my personal contribution to this memorial.[650]

Yours sincerely,
[Jawaharlal Nehru]

233. To P.C. Sen: Calcutta Programme[651]

July 17, 1962

My dear Prafulla Sen,

I have received your two letters of July 13 and 14. As for your suggestions made in your July 13 letter, I agree.

As for a public meeting, I have no objection, but this will depend so much on the weather that it seems to me rather unwise to fix it. However, I leave it to you.

649. Letter to the President of the West Bengal PCC.

650. Tushar Kanti Ghosh, President of Dr B.C. Roy Memorial Committee, had issued an appeal for contributions on 6 July 1962.

651. Letter to the Chief Minister of West Bengal. Sent from Royal Cottage, Bangalore. NMML, Padmaja Naidu Papers.

As I have already written to you, I hope to reach Calcutta on the 29th July morning. I shall be coming from Lucknow and will probably get there about 11 or so. I do not know by what plane I shall travel.

Yours sincerely,
Jawaharlal Nehru

(e) Media

234. To N.D. Prabhu: Press Trust of India[652]

June 10, 1962

Dear Shri Prabhu,

I received your letter of the 1st June some days ago.[653] I am naturally interested in the proper management and success of the Press Trust of India. But it is difficult for me to go into details and make recommendations. You have informed me that you have already sent a detailed letter to Shri Gopala Reddi, Minister for Information & Broadcasting. That is right. I am sure he will pay attention to it.

Yours sincerely,
Jawaharlal Nehru

235. To K.C. Reddy: Fraud by Modern India Press[654]

June 21, 1962

My dear Reddy,

I am informed that the Modern India Press of Calcutta applied for an import licence of glassed newsprint as printers of *Betar Jagat*.[655] The Press got a licence for 160 tons worth about rupees two lakhs.

I am told that the persons who applied are not the printers of *Betar Jagat*. If that is so, then the statement made by them was untrue. I should like you

652. Letter to the General Secretary of the Federation of the Press Trust of India Employees' Unions; address: 357 Dr Dadabhoy Naoroji Road, Bombay. PMO, File No. 43(180)/62-71-PMS, Sr. No. 11-A.
653. Copy available in the NMML. PMO, File No. 43(180)/62-71-PMS, Sr. No. 10-A.
654. Letter to the Minister of Commerce and Industry.
655. A Bengali fornightly, published by AIR, Calcutta.

to enquire into this matter, who recommended them for this and who was the officer who sponsored the application based on untruth.

Yours sincerely,
Jawaharlal Nehru

236. To B. Gopala Reddi: Fraud by Modern India Press[656]

New Delhi,
June 21, 1962

My dear Gopala Reddi,

I enclose copy of a letter I have sent to K.C. Reddy about the licence for 160 tons having been given to the Modern India Press for importing glazed newsprint. This was asked for as printers of *Betar Jagat* which, I am told, is not a fact. Will you also please enquire.

Yours sincerely,
[Jawaharlal Nehru]

237. To A.C. Guha: Newsprint for Modern India Press[657]

June 23, 1962

My dear Guha

We have taken some action already and an enquiry is being made about the grant of an import licence for glazed newsprint to the Modern India Press of Calcutta. It is understood that the present printers of *Betar Jagat* are Shri Saraswati Press Ltd. and not Modern India Press Ltd.

Yours sincerely,
[Jawaharlal Nehru]

656. Letter to the Minister of Information and Broadcasting.
657. Letter to Congress MP.

238. To Jai Narain Vyas: Answer G.D. Birla in the Press[658]

June 26, 1962

My dear Jai Narainji,

I have received a copy of your letter dated 26th June addressed to the Chairman of the Rajya Sabha. I did not know anything about the Questions previously, nor have I read the report of Shri G.D. Birla's speech. I imagine that if any proper answer is to be given to Shri G.D. Birla, it should be done publicly in the press, etc. The disallowance of the Question by the Chairman, under the rules, was probably correct.

Yours sincerely,
[Jawaharlal Nehru]

239. To B. Gopala Reddi: Role of Press Council[659]

July 9, 1962

My dear Gopala Reddi,

Your letter of the 7th July.[660]

The Press Council which you are forming will of course cover a wider area and not be confined to the problems of integration. As for your other proposal about having a sub-committee of the Consultative Press Committee, you will decide as you think best.

Yours sincerely,
Jawaharlal Nehru

658. Letter to Congress Rajya Sabha MP; address: 83 South Avenue, New Delhi.
659. Letter to the Minister of Information and Broadcasting. PMO, File No. 43(186)/62-63-PMS, Sr. No. 2-A. Sent from Pahalgam, Kashmir.
660. Appendix 53.

240. To B. Gopala Reddi: Simplifying Hindi in AIR[661]

July 10, 1962

My dear Gopala Reddi,

Dr Keskar has written to me a letter and has sent me a note about simple Hindi in AIR bulletins. He is distressed at the fact that his efforts of simplifying Hindi while he was Minister have been ignored and he is criticised for the somewhat stilted language that is often used now. I know that his constant effort was to simplify the language and it is not his fault that this continues to be difficult and often not understood by the public.[662]

I enclose a note he has sent me. You will see that he is somewhat distressed at your not mentioning his work for simplifying Hindi. I think it would be worthwhile if on some future occasion you refer to it.

I am writing a letter to Dr Shrimali, the Education Minister. I enclose a copy of this.[663]

Yours sincerely,
Jawaharlal Nehru

241. To B.V. Keskar: Hindi[664]

July 10, 1962

My dear Balkrishna,

I have received your letter of July 5th here in Pahalgam in Kashmir. I have read it as well as the note attached to it.

I am sorry if any impression has gone abroad that I criticised your attitude on the language issue. I had no such intention and, indeed, I know that you have been trying to evolve simple Hindi

Sometimes I have heard the Hindi bulletins and I have found them rather difficult to understand. That is partly my fault. In the main, I listen to Hindi replies to questions in Parliament. Generally, these are stilted and not at all

661. Letter to the Minister of Information and Broadcasting. PMO, File No. 43(117)/58-63-PMS, Sr. No. 26-A. Also available in the JN Collection. Sent from Pahalgam, Kashmir.
662. See item 241.
663. Item 242.
664. Letter to former Minister of State for Information and Broadcasting ; address 3 Kushak Road, New Delhi. Sent from Pahalgam, Kashmir. PMO, File No. 43(117)/58-63-PMS, Sr No. 25-A. Also available in the JN Collection.

happy. That is not your fault or the fault of the I & B Ministry. It is, as you say, the fault of the education as well as some of the dictionaries that we have produced.

[SIMPLE AS HINDI COMES]

You Said It

By LAXMAN

That announcer is very clever, I must say!
He's taking an interpreter along!

(From *The Times of India*, 16 June 1962, p. 1)

I agree largely with the note you have sent me. So far as its technical words are concerned, we cannot easily lay down any single method of approach. Broadly we have laid down that the scientific and technical words in ordinary use in English to which we have got largely accustomed should be used with possibly some variations.

Secondly, we have to adopt words which have gradually come into use among the common people, regardless of purity of language.

Thirdly, we have to coin words, but I hope the coining process will be limited to the two above factors.

I think that these technical and scientific words will not give us much trouble though the choice will often be difficult. I feel that it is the simpler words which create trouble. I would suggest, and I am writing to this effect to the Education Minister, that a Hindi dictionary consisting of not more than 5,000 words in common use should be prepared. We have special dictionaries dealing with technical words. Where necessary they can be revised. But what seems to me especially necessary is that the basis of the language consisting of about 5,000 or so common words, should be definitely laid down. It does not matter if the Hindi and Urdu equivalents are both given. Thus, for "water", we can give "jal" and "pani". The preparation of such a dictionary would be a great advantage.

I am sending the note you have sent me to Gopala Reddi, Minister of I & B. I hope you do not mind my doing so.[665]

Yours sincerely,
Jawaharlal Nehru

242. To K.L. Shrimali: Simple Hindi[666]

July 10, 1962

My dear Shrimali,

In the controversy between Hindi and Urdu, or rather simpler Hindi, I think it would be helpful if we could produce a small Hindi dictionary of say 5,000 common words in constant use. We have concentrated on big dictionaries and less of technical words. That was essential, although in making those lists, perhaps we have not been very happy.

In regard to scientific and technical words, we have given the direction that they should approximate to the words in use in English and other European languages. Sometimes this is not possible and we have to coin words. In doing so we have to be careful not to coin stilted or rather unnatural words which are neither in accordance with Hindi usage nor approximate to modern English usage.

However, what I am writing to you about is a small dictionary of 5,000 words or so. This list will not contain scientific or technical words, except perhaps some very commonly used ones, but will be the ordinary words used in common parlance. They will form the basic structure of the language. If we

665. See also item 240.

666. Letter to the Minister of Education. Sent from Pahalgam, Kashmir.

are clear in our minds about this basic structure, and everybody knows this, then the specialised words will not be much cause for argument.

In giving the common words we should give the actual words in use in Urdu and Hindi equivalent. Thus "water" will be "jal" and "pani", both being common. I think you will be doing a real service to this controversy by producing some such dictionary of common words. In selecting common words or even some technical words in common use, I think it would be advisable to find out what are the words which mistris or industrial workers use.[667]

Yours sincerely,
Jawaharlal Nehru

243. To B.V. Warerkar: AIR Hindi[668]

July 15, 1962

My dear Mama Warerkar,

I have your letter of the 13th July. I have not been able to follow the Hindi bulletins of the AIR, but I have noted with regret the controversy that has been started. The kind of Hindi that I sometimes heard in the bulletins and in Answers to Questions in Parliament appeared to me to be stilted, and sometimes not easy to understand. But I do not want any change to take place which will err on the other side.

I am sending your letter to Minister Gopala Reddi.[669]

Yours sincerely,
[Jawaharlal Nehru]

667. See also items 240-241.

668. Letter to Marathi writer and translator, Nominated Rajya Sabha MP, 1956-62; address: 191 South Avenue, New Delhi. Sent from Royal Cottage, Bangalore.

669. Minister of Information and Broadcasting.

244. To V.P. Nayar: Starting a Weekly Newspaper[670]

July 18, 1962

Dear Shri Nayar,

I have your letter of the 14th July. I am interested to know that you are going to issue a weekly paper. I can hardly express an opinion about a paper before I have seen it. But from what you say about encouraging University and High School students to write about constructive work, the idea appears to be good, and I send you my good wishes.

Yours sincerely,

[Jawaharlal Nehru]

670. Letter to the Chief Editor, *Keralasabdam*, P.B. 88, Quilon. Sent from Rashtrapati Nilayam, Hyderabad.

IV. DEVELOPMENT

(a) Economy

245. To Morarji Desai: Foreign Exchange Crisis[1]

June 2, 1962

My dear Morarji,

I have your letter of the 2nd June about the foreign exchange position.[2] As you say, the situation is a difficult one and we must take necessary steps to meet it. If it is necessary, a notification will have to be issued to enable the Reserve Bank to allow the Sterling Balances to fall below the legal minimum. Is it necessary to issue that straight away, or to wait [for] a short time to find out if we can get some aid from other countries in the near future?

Yours sincerely,
Jawaharlal Nehru

246. To K.C. Neogy: Transport Committee[3]

June 4, 1962

My dear Neogy,

I have your letter of June 4th which I have read together with the enclosures that you have sent. So far as I am concerned, I think that the thorough way in which you are studying this problem is the right way. Having given so much time and thought to this subject, I think that you should continue and complete it in the manner you think right.[4]

I am sending your letter to Jagjivan Ram.[5]

Yours sincerely,
Jawaharlal Nehru

1. Letter to the Finance Minister. PMO, File No. 37(35)/56-63-PMS, Volume III, Sr No. 157-A.
2. Appendix 15.
3. Letter to the Chairman of the Committee on Transport Policy and Coordination, Planning Commission. PMO, File No. 27(51)/59-70-PMS, Sr. No. 81-A.
4. The Committee on Transport Policy & Coordination under K.C. Neogy was appointed in July 1959, see also SWJN/SS/66/item 221.
5. Minister of Transport and Communications. See item 247.

247. To Jagjivan Ram: Neogy's Transport Committee[6]

June 4, 1962

My dear Jagjivan Ram,

I enclose a letter received today from K.C. Neogy about his Committee on Transport Policy and Coordination.[7] He appears to be rather irritated by some remarks about him or his Committee in the Lok Sabha. He is rather sensitive. I think that he has been studying this subject very thoroughly and we should encourage him to do so that we may have a really useful report which looks to the future as well as the present. I hope your Ministry will give him every assistance.

Yours sincerely,
Jawaharlal Nehru

248. To K.L. Shrimali: W.B. Reddaway's Book[8]

June 11, 1962

My dear Shrimali,

I enclose a letter from Mr W.B. Reddaway of the University of Cambridge, Department of Applied Economics.[9] He came here about two years ago and spent many months here with the Planning Commission and especially with Pitambar Pant, studying our economy and our Plans. I remember reading a note of his, which I rather liked and had circulated among Ministers. I have not read his present book, but I think it is a useful one for people to read.[10]

His idea is that the book might be included in the series in which special editions are brought out according to certain conditions. I do not exactly know what is to be done about it, but I would recommend this book for that series. As he has stated, there is no question of profit, as the royalty coming out of it will be paid to the Prime Minister's Fund.

I enclose also a copy of my reply to Mr Reddaway.

6. Letter to the Minister of Transport and Communications. PMO, File No. 27(51)/59-70-PMS, Sr. No. 82-A.
7. See item 246.
8. Letter to the Minister of Education.
9. British economist; Director of the Department of Applied Economics, 1955-70.
10. *Development of Indian Economy* by W.B. Reddaway (London: George Allen & Unwin, 1962).

When he was here, he gave me a cheque for 1,000 dollars for the Prime Minister's National Relief Fund. This was apparently the sum he had received for his work here. This will also indicate that he is not a person who was after making money. He is genuinely interested in India and the work we are doing here.

Yours sincerely,
[Jawaharlal Nehru]

249. To Humayun Kabir: Saving Foreign Exchange[11]

June 13, 1962

My dear Humayun,

Your letter of June 12th.[12] As a matter of fact, constant attention has been given to utilising our capacities in India for the making of machinery, equipment, etc. In Ordnance factories in the last three or four years, the output has increased from rupees eight crores to rupees eighteen crores I think and it is still increasing. Every effort is being made to use our capacity to the best advantage.

As for labour-management relations, it is obvious that we should try our best to increase the efficiency and productivity of management and labour. I think that our Labour Ministry is doing its utmost to this end, and we have achieved substantial results.

A small unit such as you suggest to survey the position of machinery as well as scientific apparatus in India will be helpful. We have in the last few years increased our production of machine tools and machinery very greatly. We have been particularly successful in machine tools. We are now building

11. Letter to the Minister of Scientific Research and Cultural Affairs. PMO, File No. 17(453)/61-63-PMS, Sr. No. 7-B. Also available in the JN Collection.
12. Humayun Kabir's letter of 12 June 1962: "I am sending for your consideration a note on certain measures for improving our foreign exchange position. They relate to the construction as far as possible of machinery within the country by preparing our own designs and utlising the capacity in private and State-owned factories including Ordnance factories. If the scheme proves successful, it will not only save foreign exchange but reduce cost of plants.

    The other measure relates to improvement of productivity of labour and management by linking earnings with quantum of production. This would in fact be a kind of combination of a basic fixed wage and piece rates rising sharply with rise in production." PMO, File No. 17(453)/61-63-PMS, Sr. No. 6-A.

a plant for the biggest type of machinery, including steel plants. Once we do that, we shall almost be free of dependence on outside assistance.

Yours sincerely,
[Jawaharlal Nehru]

250. To S.S. Khera: Capital Goods Committee[13]

I enclose a letter from Shri T.T. Krishnamachari.[14] In this he refers to the Capital Goods Committee. I had forgotten about this committee and I do not know who its members are. I should like to know who they are and what they are doing at present. Thereafter, I think the point raised by Shri T.T. Krishnamachari should be put before them.

2. We are trying hard to save small sums of money in foreign exchange. But the major sums somehow slip past us.

251. To Swaran Singh: Late Trains[15]

June 22, 1962

My dear Swaran Singh,
I enclose a letter from K. Hanumanthaiya[16] together with its enclosure. I think what the lady says deserves attention. Something should be done to make our trains punctual. There is absolutely no reason for these local trains to be late.

An old incident comes to my mind. Sometime in the thirties, I was travelling by train from Calicut to some place. I waited and waited at the station and there was no train. Ultimately it came very late. Although I had nothing to do with the Government in those days, I created a big row at the Calicut station and told the Station Master and all concerned that it was scandalous for the trains to come so late without any apparent reason. My shouting at them had, I believe, some effect in the near future.[17]

Yours sincerely,
[Jawaharlal Nehru]

13. Note to the Cabinet Secretary, 14 June 1962.
14. Minister without Portfolio.
15. Letter to the Minister of Railways.
16. Congress, Lok Sabha MP from Bangalore City, Mysore State.
17. Nehru visited Calicut on 31 May 1931, see SWJN/FS/4/pp. 543-544.

252. To Jagjivan Ram: Night Airmail Service via Nagpur[18]

June 26, 1962

My dear Jagjivan Ram,

Some Nagpur people have been coming to me and protesting against the stoppage of the night airmail service via Nagpur. If you have decided about this, I am sure you must have taken all facts into consideration and I do not wish to interfere. But I should like to know what your decision is and how the mails will be sent speedily now to various important cities as they have been going via the night mail.

Yours sincerely,
Jawaharlal Nehru

253. To Chief Ministers: Coordination of Rail and Road[19]

June 27, 1962

My dear Chief Minister,

You are aware that the problem of rail-road coordination is one which has given headaches to many countries. We have not been free from these troubles. Ultimately we appointed a Committee on Transport Policy & Coordination to consider this matter and make recommendations. This Committee, under the Chairmanship of Shri K.C. Neogy, has worked hard and is still making a thorough study of the subject. Shri Neogy intends sending some of his officers to visit various States on behalf of the Committee so as to expedite the necessary discussions on the spot.[20]

I should like you to give all help to Shri Neogy and his officers. While you are all interested in road transport, perhaps you are not so much interested in transport by rail. But the two questions are intimately interlinked.

18. Letter to the Minister of Transport and Communications. PMO, File No. 27/72/60-71-PMS, Sr. No. 17-A.
19. Letter to Chief Ministers of all States and the Prime Minister of Jammu and Kashmir State. PMO, File No. 27(51)/59-70-PMS, Sr. No. 85-A.
20. See also SWJN/SS/50/item 85, SWJN/SS/61/items 210 & 342 and appendix 48, SWJN/SS/66/item 221.

I am afraid that some States have not taken much interest in this Committee, and a questionnaire issued by them elicited replies only from very few States.[21] I hope, therefore, that you will kindly pay attention to this matter.

Yours sincerely,
Jawaharlal Nehru

254. To P.C. Mahalanobis: Circulating Scientific Papers to MPs[22]

July 15, 1962

My dear Mahalanobis

You will remember giving me a paper which you wrote on the scientific base of economic development. I sent this to various Chief Ministers in India as well as to one or two Ministers at Delhi. Subsequently you have sent me another paper on "Problems of Internal Transformation".

It has just struck me that the members of our Party in the Lok Sabha and the Rajya Sabha would profit by reading your two papers. That will mean a fairly large number as there are 500 members of our Party alone.

How am I to get all these numbers? I do not suppose you have them. Could you yourself get them printed? Also it might be desirable to have them translated into Hindi. I could have that done if you agree.

Yours sincerely,
[Jawaharlal Nehru]

21. Excerpt from Neogy's letter of 27 June 1962 to Nehru: "I am making this suggestion because the State Governments have been rather apathetic towards our enquiry, though they are vitally interested at least in road transport which is their special responsibility. A questionnaire was issued by the Committee to the States in June 1961, and West Bengal was reasonably prompt in replying to it. Kerala, however, took 7 months and Rajasthan about a year to send their replies. Repeated reminders sent through the Transport Ministry here, and also directly by us, have not been heeded by the rest as yet. The issues are undoubtedly complicated, but there is no excuse for deferring their examination."PMO, File No. 27(51)/59-70-PMS, Sr. No. 83-A.
22. Letter to Honorary Statistical Adviser to the Cabinet, and Director, Indian Statistical Institute, Calcutta. Sent from Nandi Hills, Mysore State.

255. To S. Chandrasekhar: Good Work at Population Studies Institute[23]

July 16, 1962

Dear Dr Chandrasekhar,

I send you my good wishes and congratulations for the Twelfth Anniversary of the Indian Institute for Population Studies. The question of population growth is highly important all over the world. In India it is a vital problem for us. I have welcomed, therefore, the good work done by your Institute.

I think that the importance of the subject of population control is generally realised in India, and there has been some definite progress, even though this appears to be very small in the context of India. We have one advantage. There is no organised opposition to it.

In any event, a scientific approach to the problem of population is very necessary, and the *Population Review* which is the journal of your Institute, is helping in popularising this approach.

Yours sincerely,
J. Nehru

(b) Industry and Labour

256. To Mir Mushtaq Ahmed: Labour Deputation[24]

June 3, 1962

Dear Mushtaq Ahmed,

I have your letter of the 2nd June. I have sent it on to the Labour Minister, Shri Jaisukhlal Hathi.[25] I am sorry I have no time to receive a deputation. In any event, the matter will have to be dealt with by the Labour Minister to whom I have sent your papers.

Yours sincerely,
Jawaharlal Nehru

23. Letter to the Director of the Indian Institute of Population Studies, Gandhinagar, Madras-20. Sent from Nandi Hills, Mysore State. PMO, File No. 9/2/62-PMP, Vol. V, Sr. No. 26-A. Aslo available in the JN Collection.
24. Letter to the Organiser, INTUC Ad Hoc Committee, 22 Theatre Communication Building, New Delhi. NMML, Mir Mushtaq Ahmed Papers.
25. This seems to be related to the Rourkela incident, see items 257, 260-261.

257. To Jaisukhlal Hathi: Labour Dispute[26]

June 3, 1962

My dear Hathi,

I enclose a letter from Mir Mushtaq Ahmed which will speak for itself.[27] I presume you are acquainted with this matter. I hope you will look into it. The kind of charge that has been brought against the Manager is the sort of thing which excites people greatly. Anyhow, if the great majority of the workers feel that there is some truth in it, that itself is a fact to be borne in mind.[28]

Yours sincerely,
[Jawaharlal Nehru]

258. To Lalit Narayan Mishra: National Projects Construction Corporation[29]

June 3, 1962

My dear Lalit Narayan,

Thank you for your letter of May 27th with your note on the National Projects Construction Corporation.[30] I confess I did not know much about

26. Letter to the Minister of Labour.
27. See item 256.
28. This seems to be related to the Rourkela incident, see items 260-261.
29. Letter to the Chairman of the National Projects Construction Corporation; address: 7 York Road, New Delhi. PMO, File No. 17(506)/62-66-PMS, Sr. No. 2-A.
30. Extract from Mishra's note of 27 May 1962, as available in the NMML: "The National Projects' Construction Corporation under the Ministry of Irrigation & Power came into being nearly five years ago broadly with a view to provide for scope and avenue of employment to trained technical personnel, to use machinery found surplus in completed river valley projects, to prevent exploitation by private contractors employed in the construction of these projects, to reduce construction costs and make savings for the public exchequer. During this period, although this Corporation has done some good work and has, even in the eyes of the Estimates Committee of Parliament, fulfilled in some measure its aim to prevent exploitation by contractors by forcing them by its example not to quote high rates, it must be said that the start so far made points only to much bigger tasks ahead. We have a huge construction programme in the Third Five Year Plan and will have much bigger programme in the successive plans. It would be wrong to allow private contractor to earn inflated profits out of public constructional works. The Corporation has to prepare itself to meet the needs of the time and expand its activities." PMO, File No. 17(506)/62-66-PMS, Sr. No. 1-B.

this Corporation and when it was started. But it seems to me a good idea and I wish you success in the work you are doing. Your note gives some idea of the comprehensiveness of the work that has to be done. I would suggest to you to be a little careful in building up a big organisation as is often done by Government. The result often is that it becomes top heavy. I would suggest that it should grow as work requires it to do so. I have no doubt that it can be of great advantage to our construction programme which forms such a big part of our Five Year Plan.

Yours sincerely,
[Jawaharlal Nehru]

259. For INTUC: Handling Labour Disputes[31]

I gladly send my greetings and good wishes to the annual session of the INTUC. Industrial labour has always an important part to fulfill in the country. But this part is growing in importance because of rapid industrialisation of our country.

Labour unions have necessarily to look after the interest of their members and to see to it that they do not suffer. But, in doing so, they have also to remember the larger interest of the country of which they are a part. Ultimately, it is this larger interest which will govern the living conditions and the advancement of the people generally, including labour. It is short-sightedness to forget the larger interest in order to gain some advantage for a group at the cost of the country.

On the other hand, the country as a whole should remember the importance of labour and be just to them and to their demands. We must remember that the vast majority of our people are agriculturists and however much industry may progress, as it undoubtedly will, industrial workers will remain a relatively small part of the total population. We have to raise the total population and to give everyone of them a certain decent minimum standard of life. This can only be done by greater production of wealth for the country. Anything that lessens this production, therefore, comes in the way of our progress.

Stike is an important weapon in the hands of labour. But I believe that the days of strikes and lock-outs are, broadly speaking, over. They represent a condition of affairs which is the result of continuous conflict. We should evolve a system where disputes are settled without such strikes and lock-outs, and with justice to the people concerned.

31. Message for the thirteenth annual session of the INTUC. Reproduced from report of 9 June 1962 from *The Hindu* of 10 June 1962, p. 1.

260. To C.H.M. Koya: Death during Labour Dispute[32]

June 22, 1962

Dear Shri Koya

I have your letter of 21st June. I have learnt with great regret of the incident which resulted in the death of the Electrical Foreman, M.A. Narayanaswami.[33] I am forwarding your letter to Shri Subramaniam, Minister in charge.[34]

The incident was highly regrettable, but it is a little difficult to trace a man who has thrown a stone from a crowd. Shri Raja,[35] General Manager, is a very competent man and looks after his employees. Anyhow, I hope that adequate precautions will be taken in the future.[36]

Yours sincerely,
Jawaharlal Nehru

261. To B. Patnaik: Narayanaswami's Death in Rourkela[37]

June 23, 1962

My deer Patnaik,

I enclose a copy of a letter from our Minister of Steel, C. Subramaniam.[38] This was in answer to what I wrote to him about the death of Narayanaswami, a foreman at the Rourkela Plant. Subramaniam has sent me a copy of the letter he has written to you.[39] Nevertheless I am sending you his letter to me as I think this kind of thing requires quick and stern action.[40]

I understand that the Orissa Police have been delaying in this and raising what seem to me rather absurd pleas.[41]

Yours sincerely,
Jawaharlal Nehru

32. Letter to Muslim League MP in Lok Sabha from Kozhikode, Kerala, 5 Western Court, New Delhi. PMO, File No. 17(12)/61-65-PMS, Sr. No. 28-A.
33. This is about the conflict at Hindustan Steel Ltd, Rourkela, in May, see appendix, 41(a).
34. C. Subramaniam, Minister of Steel and Heavy Industries.
35. S.T. Raja.
36. See further item 261.
37. Letter to the Chief Minister of Orissa. PMO, File No. 17(12)/61-65-PMS, Sr. No. 32-A.
38. Appendix 41 (a).
39. Reproduced as footnote no. 100 to appendix 41 (a).
40. See also item 260.
41. For Patnaik's reply, see appendix 41 (b).

262. To S.R. Vasavada: Indian Railwaymen's Federation[42]

June 26, 1962

My dear Vasavada,

I must apologise to you for the delay in sending my good wishes for the Annual Convention of the National Federation of Indian Railwaymen. I had put your letter aside for an answer not realising that the Convention was taking place so soon. Anyhow, you know that you have my good wishes.

Yours sincerely,
[Jawaharlal Nehru]

263. To B. Patnaik: Rourkela Conflict[43]

July 1, 1962

My dear Biju,

Your letter of the 26th June.[44] Certainly we should take effective measures. I do not know what the Goonda Act or Security Act in Bengal is and can give you no opinion about it. Probably some such measure may be useful, if carefully applied.

Yours sincerely,
Jawaharlal Nehru

264. To K.C. Reddy: Malerkotla's Plans for Industry[45]

July 1, 1962

My dear Reddy,

The Nawab of Malerkotla, Punjab, came to see me this afternoon. He is anxious to start some industry to give employment to a large number of weavers in his State. Apparently some people in Ludhiana are prepared to do so if they get some facilities.

42. Letter to the President of the National Federation of Indian Railwaymen, 17 Janpath, New Delhi.
43. Letter to the Chief Minister of Orissa. PMO, File No. 17(12)/61-65-PMS, Sr. No. 34-A.
44. See appendix 41 (b).
45. Letter to the Minister of Commerce and Industry.

He gave me a paper, a copy of which I enclose. I have made it perfectly clear to him that no foreign exchange could be sanctioned. In the paper he gave me, there is one scheme, No. 2, which does not require any foreign exchange.[46]

I should like to know what your Ministry advises.[47]

Yours sincerely,
[Jawaharlal Nehru]

265. To Muhammad Iftikhar Ali Khan: Malerkotla's Nephew[48]

July 4, 1962

My Dear Nawab Sahib,

Thank you for sending me the two bottles of honey.

I have written to the Home Minister about your nephew. As soon as I hear from him I shall let you know.[49]

46. The Paper given by Nawab Muhammad Iftikhar Ali Khan read:

"The Malerkotla Woolen Mills

(1) Industrial licence for 3000 worsted spindles.

(a) No foreign exchange will be asked for the import of machinery. The entire plant and machinery will be processed from within the country.

(b) Foreign Exchange to the extent of about 15 lakhs of rupees will be required P.A. for the import of raw material to feed the machines.

Gradually the import of raw materials will be curtailed and use of Indian wool will be made.

Or

(2) One hundred power looms for the manufacture of worsted fabrics should be sanctioned. No foreign exchange for either the machinery or for raw material will be asked for. Only the supply of worsted yarn from the Indian Mills should be ensured.

Or

(3) Industrial licence and import licence for 2000 shoddy spindles. Foreign Exchange for the import of machinery to the tune of Rs 15 lakhs will be required. Raw material will also be imported.

Or

(4) Industrial licence and import licence for a wool tops combing plant with a capacity of 2½ million lbs per annum. Foreign exchange expenditure will be Rs 30 lakhs."

47. See appendix 50.

48. Letter to Nawab of Malerkotla. Sent from Chashmashahi Guest House, Srinagar.

49. See items 65-66, 73 and appendices 46(a)-(d) & 59.

As for the proposal to start some industry in Malerkotla, I sent a copy of your note to the Minister of Commerce and Industry. I enclose a copy of his reply to me.[50]

Yours sincerely,
[Jawaharlal Nehru]

266. To C. Subramaniam: Reorganisation at Rourkela[51]

July 6, 1962

My dear Subramaniam,
Your letter of the 1st July with your note on decentralisation of work and authority in Hindustan Steel Limited.[52] So far as your broad approach to decentralisation is concerned, I entirely agree with you. As for the details, you are in the best position to judge.

Yours sincerely,
Jawaharlal Nehru

267. For Jaisukh Lal Hathi: Ghaziabad Workers[53]

A large number of workers from Ghaziabad have come to my house and I saw two of their representatives who handed over to me the attached memorandum.

2. I do not know the facts. Perhaps, you are better acquainted with this matter because this has been going on for some weeks past and I understand they have addressed you on the subject. The UP Government or their Labour Department has not been able to help them.

3. I should like you to look into this matter immediately and give them such help as is possible. These people remaining here in a dissatisfied state is not good for the factory or for the administration. I think the least that the factory could do was to enable them to go back.

4. Anyhow, I should like you to enquire into this matter and do what is possible.

50. See appendix 50.
51. Letter to the Minister of Steel and Heavy Industries. Sent from Pahalgam, Kashmir. PMO, File No. 17(12)/61-65-PMS, Sr. No. 36-A.
52. Appendix 47.
53. Note, 12 July 1962, for the Minister of Labour.

268. For the Khadi and Village Industries Commission[54]

I send my good wishes on the occasion of the University of Delhi and the Khadi and Village Industries Commission having a "Khadi in Indian Economy" Exhibition. Such an exhibition will, I feel sure, bring out many aspects of village industries which are not normally before the public, and will make people realise the importance of these industries in present-day India.

269. To M.K. Mathulla: Congratulations on Award[55]

From Nandi Hills, Mysore State
July 15, 1962

My dear Mathulla,
Thank you for your letter of the 13th July with which you have sent the Annual Report of Hindustan Machine Tools Ltd. for 1961-62. I have read this report with great interest and appreciation, and I congratulate you and all those who are working in Hindustan Machine Tools Ltd. for a very successful year. I am glad you have received the Presidential Award for the best managed Public Sector undertaking. HMT is a credit to the nation.[56]

Yours sincerely,
Jawaharlal Nehru

270. To Biju Patnaik: Lawlessness in Rourkela[57]

July 17, 1962

My dear Biju,
Your letter of the 13th July has reached me here at Bangalore. I am worried at the situation in Rourkela, more especially in regard to the fear complexes that you mention. I suppose the only thing is to have a proper Security Force there.

54. Message, 12 July 1962, forwarded to K.T. Potdar, Officer on Special Duty, Khadi and Village Industries Commission, Pataudi House, Canning Road, New Delhi.
55. Letter to the Managing Director of Hindustan Machine Tools Ltd, Bangalaore. Sent from Nandi Hills. Prime Minister's Office, File No. 17(21)/59-64-PMS, Vol. I., Sr. No. 41-A.
56. For Nehru's earlier appreciative comments on Mathulla, see SWJN/SS/42/p. 152.
57. Letter to the Chief Minister of Orissa. Sent from Royal Cottage, Bangalore. PMO, File No. 17(12)/61-65-PMS, Sr. No. 37-A.

You mention that you are taking necessary steps at the request of Subramaniam.[58]

As for having some legislation on the lines of the Goonda Act of West Bengal, the matter should be examined. I am not quite clear in my mind if this would meet the situation.[59]

I am sending your letter to our Home Minister, Lal Bahadur Shastri.

Yours sincerely,
Jawaharlal Nehru

(c) Agriculture

271. To Hafiz Mohammad Ibrahim: Reorganising the DVC[60]

June 2, 1962

My dear Hafizji,

I have your letter of May 31st, with the long note on the DVC. I have read this note.

It seems to me clear that the existing organisation of the DVC is not adequate and requires a charge. It is difficult for me, even after reading the long note of your Secretary, to be quite clear as to what this change should be. I suggest that you should have this matter examined by the Planning Commission and the CW & PC. Also, by the DVC and our Ministry of Finance.

I would gladly see you if you so wish, about this matter. But I do not think it will be worthwhile to discuss this matter more fully with me till it has been considered carefully by the Planning Commission and the others concerned.

Yours sincerely,
Jawaharlal Nehru

58. C. Subramaniam, Minister of Steel and Heavy Industries.
59. For earlier correspondence on this matter, see items 260-261, 263, 266.
60. Letter to the Minister for Irrigation and Power. PMO, File No. 17(13)/56-68-PMS, (Vol. III), Sr. No. 118-A.

272. To Krishna Dev Tripathi: Farmers' Cooperatives[61]

June 3, 1962

Dear Krishna Dev,

I have your letter of the 30th May about Cooperative Farming.[62] As a matter of fact, cooperative farming has made progress in the country, though not as much as we would have hoped. We have laid first stress on service cooperatives because we felt this was an initial step to cooperative farming. The latter requires a good deal of training and only trained persons can organise it and run it.

I have an idea that a fairly large number of selected cooperative farms are included in our programme. I agree with you that it is necessary to explain this thoroughly to the people, but I do not think any subsidy is necessary or desirable.

I suggest that you talk about this matter to our Minister of Cooperation, Shri S.K. Dey.

Yours sincerely,
Jawaharlal Nehru

273. To Gulzarilal Nanda: M.S. Sivaraman[63]

June 14, 1962

My dear Gulzarilal,

Shri M.S. Sivaraman[64] came to see me this morning and gave me a memorandum. He is a good man and has done excellent work in agriculture. I told him that I was not interested in questions of promotions and status. All I was interested in was opportunities being given for good work to be done.

I am enclosing the memorandum he gave.

Yours sincerely,
[Jawaharlal Nehru]

61. Letter to Lok Sabha MP, Congress, address: 202 North Avenue, New Delhi. PMO, File No. 31(93)/59-70-PMS, Sr. No. 55-A.
62. Appendix 11.
63. Letter to the Minister of Planning, Labour and Employment.
64. ICS, Adviser, Planning Commission.

274. To S.K. Patil: Pamphlets on Plan Projects[65]

June 18, 1962

My dear S.K.,

Thank you for your letter of June 15th and the various pamphlets you sent with it. I am afraid I have no time to read through these pamphlets, interesting as they appear to be. But I have glanced through their titles and some other particulars in them. Further, your letter tells me of the useful work that the Committee on Plan Projects has done in this matter. I congratulate you and the Committee.

I am sending back these pamphlets as they might be of use to you. I would suggest your sending the pamphlets, if you can spare them, to all the Chief Ministers with covering letters.

Yours sincerely,
[Jawaharlal Nehru]

275. To S.K. Patil: An Agriculture Commission[66]

June 25, 1962

My dear S.K.,

I enclose a copy of a letter from Bibhuti Mishra, MP, suggesting the appointment of a "Royal (?) Agriculture Commission" to consider all aspects of agriculture in India.[67] I am personally rather averse to the appointment of big commissions which roam about the country and spend a lot of money and then produce a fat report. But you might give this proposal consideration and, if you like, we can discuss it in the Cabinet.[68]

Yours sincerely,
Jawaharlal Nehru

65. Letter to the Minister of Food and Agriculture.
66. Letter to the Minister of Food and Agriculture. PMO, File No. 31/111/60-64-65/PMS, Vol. II. Sr. No. 45-A.
67. See item 276.
68. Extract from Patil's letter of 18 July 1962: "I, therefore, feel that at least during the Third Plan we should not entertain the idea of appointing any Agricultural Commission of this kind. Instead of collecting facts and assisting Government in the formulation of policies, such a Commission is likely to waste the time of the administrative and technical officers in the states and detract considerably from the implementation of the schemes included in the Third Plan."

276. To Bibhuti Mishra: Agriculture Commission[69]

नई दिल्ली,
जून 26, 1962

प्रिय मिश्रा जी,
आपका 25 तारीख का पत्र मिला। इसमें आपने लिखा कि रायल एग्रीकलचर कमीशन की नियुक्ति हो। "रायल" तो खैर हो नहीं सकता, शाही ज़माना हिन्दुस्तान में खत्म हो गया।

मैने आपके पत्र को श्री एस० के० पाटिल को भेज दिया है कि वे इस पर विचार करें। मुमकिन है कि ऐसा कमीशन कुछ फायदा करे, लेकिन ऐसे बड़े कमीशन वर्षों तक घूमते हैं, बडा खर्चा होता है और फिर कमोबेश ऐसी बातें कहते है जो कि ज्यादातर मालूम है। इसीलिये यह ख्याल मुझे बहुत पसन्द नहीं है, लेकिन फिर भी आपकी तजवीज़ पर ग़ौर किया जायेगा।

आपका,
जवाहरलाल नेहरु

[Translation begins:

Dear Mishraji,
Received your letter of the 25th. You have written that a Royal Agriculture Commission should be appointed. It cannot be "Royal" in any case, royal times are over in India.

I have sent your letter to Shri S.K. Patil to consider the suggestion. It is possible that such a commission may be useful, but such big commissions tour for years, involving huge expenditure and then say more or less what is already known. So, I do not much like this idea, but still your suggestion will be considered.

Yours sincerely,
Jawaharlal Nehru

Translation ends]

69. Letter to Lok Sabha MP, Congress; address: Village Manguraha, Post Office Radhia, District Champaran, Bihar.

277. To Mohanlal Sukhadia: K.N. Kaul's Irrigation Experiments[70]

July 4, 1962

My dear Sukhadia,

Professor Kailas Nath Kaul, the Director-General of the National Botanical Gardens in Lucknow, has sent me a letter which he has received.[71] This gentleman helped Kailas Nath Kaul greatly in his work in organising an Underground Water Board in western Jodhpur in 1949-50 and in constructing a well near Dundara Railway Station for the villagers for the supply of drinking water. I thought you might be interested in reading this letter. I am, therefore, sending it to you.

Yours sincerely,
[Jawaharlal Nehru]

278. To Harekrushna Mahtab: Foodgrain Import[72]

July 17, 1962

My dear Mahtab,

Your letter of the 13th July has reached me today. Thank you for it.

I myself do not like our importing foodgrains from abroad unless there is a serious emergency. This must necessarily have a somewhat demoralising effect or, at any rate, produce complacency. Basically nothing is more important than our relying on ourselves for agricultural products.

As for the Congress Constitution, I should be glad to discuss your ideas with you when we meet in Delhi.

Yours sincerely,
[Jawaharlal Nehru]

70. Letter to the Chief Minister of Rajasthan. Sent from Chashmashahi Guest House, Srinagar.
71. Letter, dated 4 July 1962 from R.N. Joshi, Retired Station Master, not reproduced here but copy available at the NMML.
72. Letter to Lok Sabha MP, Congress, from Angul, Orissa; address: Ekamra Nivas, Bhubaneswar 2. Sent from Royal Cottage, Bangalore.

279. To S.K. Patil: An Agriculture Commission Unnecessary[73]

July 19, 1962

My dear S.K.,

Thank you for your letter of July 19 about the proposal to appoint an Agricultural Commission.[74] You have dealt with this matter fully, and I agree with you that the appointment of such a Commission is not likely to do any good. It might only waste time and energy and money, and leads to most people sitting down and waiting for its report instead of implementing the policies and programmes already accepted.

I do not think it is necessary to discuss this matter in the Cabinet.

Yours sincerely,
Jawaharlal Nehru

(d) Health

280. To Sushila Nayar: Examinations of the Royal College of Surgeons[75]

June 1, 1962

My dear Sushila,

I have now received a letter from Dr B.C. Roy[76] about the proposal to hold Primary Fellowship Examinations of the Royal College of Surgeons in England. You spoke to me about this matter. I should like you to see all the papers and then advise me.[77]

Yours sincerely,
J. Nehru

73. Letter to the Minister of Food and Agriculture. Sent from Rashtrapati Nilayam, Hyderabad. PMO, File No. 31/111/60-64-65-PMS, Vol. II, Sr. No. 48-A. Also available in the JN Collection.
74. In fact, Patil replied on 18 July, see footnote 68 in item 275.
75. Letter to the Minister of Health. PMO, File No. 40(230)/61-70-PMS, Sr. No. 6-A.
76. Chief Minister of West Bengal.
77. See appendix 17, also item 281.

281. To B.C. Roy: Examinations of the Royal College of Surgeons[78]

June 5, 1962

My dear Bidhan,

Your letter to me suggesting that the primary FRCS examination of the UK should be held in India was sent by me to our Health Minister.[79] I enclose a copy of her reply to me.[80]

Yours affectionately,
J. Nehru

282. To Chief Ministers: Eradicate Smallpox[81]

June 8, 1962

My dear Chief Minister,

I am writing to you about a matter, which may perhaps appear to you unimportant, as it is not political, but which is I think of essential importance. This is the eradication of smallpox, a perfectly preventable disease. It has indeed been eradicated from many countries of the world. Unfortunately, our country as well as Pakistan is considered important foci in the world from which there is danger of importation of disease to other countries.

Our Ministry of Health is making an effort to put an end to this disease in India and to remove this national stigma. They have formulated a National Smallpox Eradication Programme for covering the entire country with mass smallpox vaccination. The Planning Commission has provided a sum of Rs 688.98 lakhs during the Third Five Year Plan for this Scheme.

The Government of the USSR has made a gift of 250 million doses of this vaccine to us. It is highly desirable and indeed essential for us to take advantage of this gift and of the resources that are now available to carry through this

78. Letter to the Chief Minister of West Bengal. PMO, File No. 40(230)/61-70-PMS, Sr. No. 8-A.
79. See item 280.
80. Appendix 17.
81. Letter to Chief Ministers of all States and to the Prime Minister of the Jammu and Kashmir State, with copies to the Lieutenant Governors of Himachal Pradesh and Goa, and to the Chief Commissioners of Delhi, Manipur, Tripura, and the Andaman and Nicobar Islands. PMO, File No. 28 (94)/62-71-PMS, Sr. No. 2-A.

campaign. I hope that not only your Health Department but also all other Departments in the State will extend their cooperation to this campaign. I trust also that you will take a personal interest in this matter. It will be a great thing for us to rid our country of this scourge, which has caused so much sorrow and suffering to our people.

Yours sincerely,
Jawaharlal Nehru

283. To Sushila Nayar: Army Medical College in Poona[82]

June 10, 1962

My dear Sushila,

Your letter of the 7th June about the Defence Ministry's proposal to start an undergraduate Medical Collage at Poona.[83]

This matter was raised nearly four years ago and was discussed at some length then. The proposal was based on the fact that there is a short supply of qualified medical men, in the Army especially. At the same time, there are a large number of very qualified teachers stationed at Poona and there were very big medical hospitals there. In fact, some kind of post-graduate teaching was being done there. We should thus take advantage of the available talent and the big hospitals at Poona, which, in a sense, were not being fully utilised at present. This meant some fresh arrangement being made for undergraduate medical students. If the normal civil arrangements were made for these, this would cost a far larger sum and it would involve a great deal of building etc. In Poona, much of this would be cut out and all that would be necessary would be some relatively small buildings or hostels, etc. I should imagine that the standard would be higher than in an average medical college because Army medical standards are generally high.

We discussed this in our Defence Committee meeting and I think the Health Ministry was also brought in. Ultimately, the matter was postponed for the time being. I do not know why it was not brought up again.

Personally, I was attracted to the scheme because we want to use all available talent, especially such as is not utilised now. Also, the cost was far less than is normally required. The actual turnout of qualified students would be as many as in a full-fledged medical college. At that time, I think the number of

82. Letter to the Minister of Health. PMO, File No. 23(84)/62-71-PMS, Sr. No. 2-A.
83. Appendix 20.

students suggested was probably under one hundred, and the extra sum involved was about Rs 20 lakhs. Now it is proposed to raise the number of students to 150 and the cost of structures etc. has gone up also. Even so, it is far less than a new medical college would require.

It is true that running of medical colleges is not a function of the Defence Ministry. But the Defence Services require a large number of doctors and we should use whatever resources we have to produce them, both for the Defence Services and for civil purposes. It should be a matter of arrangement between Defence and the Ministry of Health. I would imagine that as regards efficiency and competence, the Defence Services will give a better account than the average civil medical colleges and hospitals.

I think that it would be best if you discussed this with the Defence Minister. I do not know if you will find the opportunity as he is going away soon to New York again for the Security Council meeting. Anyhow, you could do so on his return.

Yours affectionately
Jawaharlal Nehru

284. To B.N. Datar: Prohibition[84]

June 18, 1962

My dear Datar,
I have your letter of June 18th about prohibition.[85] I am all in favour of prohibition. But the reports I receive about illicit distillation and the increase of crime in prohibition areas, especially in large cities, disturbs me very much. I think the whole question has to be fully examined. I can hardly write on

84. Letter to the Minister of State in the MHA. PMO, File No. 2(428)/62-65-PMS, Vol. I, Sr. No. 9-A.
85. Extract as available in the NMML:

> "My dear Jawaharlalji, I am writing this letter to you for the purpose of securing your help and guidance with a view to give an immediate impetus to the problem of prohibition on which discordant views are being expressed though the Central Prohibition Committee has taken a decision in principle to have total prohibition in the whole of India before the expiry of the Third Five Year Plan period.
>
> In short, I am seeking your good offices for the purpose of inducing the Chief Ministers in all the States except three to consider actively the advisability of introducing total prohibition in their respective areas by a phased programme during the Third Plan period." PMO,File No.2(428)/62-65-PMS, Vol. I, Sr. No. 8-A.

this subject without dealing with every aspect of it and the necessity of its examination.

Yours sincerely,
Jawaharlal Nehru

285. To Sushila Nayar: Council of Medicine[86]

June 18, 1962

My dear Sushila,
I enclose a letter from the General Secretary of the Council of State Boards and Faculties of Indian Medicine. I do not know anything about this organisation. They want to see you and me separately. I suppose I shall have to see them. But, before I fix any date, I should like your advice in this matter.

Yours affectionately,
[Jawaharlal Nehru]

286. To Sushila Nayar: State Boards for Indian Medicine[87]

June 19, 1962

My dear Sushila,
Thank you for your letter of June 19th about the Council of State Boards and Faculties of Indian Medicine. I am asking them to see me on the 29th June at 10.00 a.m. If you have any further information to give me about this subject, you can write to me before that date. I shall of course, not commit myself to anything in my interview with them. I shall say that I am all for the examination and development of Indian medicine on modern scientific lines. As for the Unani Tibbia College, I shall say that the matter will be examined.[88]

Yours affectionately,
[Jawaharlal Nehru]

86. Letter to the Minister of Health.
87. Letter to the Minister of Health.
88. He wrote to Sushila Nayar after he met them on 29 June, see item 290.

287. To Swami Dayananda: Shishumangal Pratishthan[89]

June 23, 1962

Dear Swami Dayanandaji,

I have your letter of June 21st. I am glad to learn that the Shishumangal Pratishthan has grown and has now become a large fully equipped general hospital.[90] This is good news.

You have asked me to open the extension of the Hospital and have suggested a date between September 1st and December 31st. In September, I shall be going to England. It is very difficult for me to promise at this stage what time will suit me in October or later. You know that I am happy to do anything for the Ramakrishna Mission. But at present I cannot promise. Perhaps, later, I might be able to say more definitely.

Yours sincerely,
[Jawaharlal Nehru]

288. To Mehr Chand Khanna: AIIMS Building Extension[91]

June 25, 1962

My dear Mehr Chand,

I enclose a copy of a letter from Rajkumari Amrit Kaur.[92] I think we should permit the All India Institute of Medical Sciences to go ahead with their building programme and not only on the CPWD for it. Some one of your engineers can be nominated to their Building Committee. This will probably speed up things and the cost may be less. Anyway, it is worth trying the experiment.

Yours sincerely,
Jawaharlal Nehru

89. Letter to the Secretary of the Ramakrishna Mission Seva Pratishthan, 99 Sarat Bose Road, Calcutta 26.
90. At 99 Sarat Bose Road, Kolkata 700026.
91. Letter to the Minister of Works, Housing and Supply. PMO, File No. 40(134)/59-64-PMS, Sr. No. 160-A.
92. Former Health Minister, Chairman of the Governing Body of AIIMS, and Member, Rajya Sabha.

289. To Sushila Nayar: Prize for Family Planning Clinics[93]

June 28, 1962

My dear Sushila,

Your letter of the 27th June.[94] It seems to be rather odd for me to give a prize for family planning clinics to the Chief Minister of Maharashtra. Also, no date has been fixed yet for the National Development Council. We may consider this matter further later.

Yours affectionately,
Jawaharlal Nehru

290. To Sushila Nayar: Indian Medicine[95]

June 29, 1962

My dear Sushila,

The Deputation of the Council of State Board and Faculties of Indian Medicine came to see me today. They gave me a memorandum which I enclose. I understand they have seen you recently and so you know their viewpoint.

In referring them to you, I told them that I would be glad to encourage Indian Medicine provided always that work in it is based on the scientific outlook and approach. Apparently they agreed with me in this matter.[96]

Yours affectionately,
[Jawaharlal Nehru]

93. Letter to the Minister of Health. PMO, File No. 28(50)/61-65-PMS, Sr. No. 70-A.

94. Only two paragraphs from Sushila Nayar's letter are available in the NMML: "The Ministry of Health had instituted prizes for the best rural and urban family planning clinics and also an award to the State in India doing the most outstanding work in family planning. A Selection Committee has recommended the award to Maharashtra State for outstanding work in the family planning during 1960. The information for 1961 is being collected.

I shall feel most grateful if you could consider making the presentation of this award to the Chief Minister, Maharashtra, on a suitable occasion." PMO, File No. 28(50)/61-65-PMS, Sr. No. 69-A.

95. Letter to the Minister of Health.

96. See also item 286.

291. To Amrit Kaur: Scholarly Exchanges with New Zealand[97]

July 5, 1962

My dear Amrit,

I have your letter of July 3rd.[98] I imagine that there will be no difficulty in exchanging Fellowships as suggested by Sir Douglas Robb.[99] I shall refer this matter to the Health Minister.[100]

As for using the Red Fort at Delhi, as suggested by Sir Douglas Robb, this would require consultations with many persons and it would involve many changes and upsets. It would mean our finding accommodation for a large number of people who live in the Red Fort, chiefly soldiers.

The "Le son et lumière" technique is, I am told by many persons, very attractive and fascinating. Perhaps the Taj at Agra or Fatehpur Sikri would be specially suited for this.[101]

[Yours affectionately]
Jawaharlal Nehru

97. Letter to the President of the AIIMS. Sent from Pahalgam, Kashmir. PMO, File No. 40(134)/59-64-PMS, Sr. No. 166-A. Also available in the JN Collection.
98. Not reproduced, available at the NMML.
99. Cardiac surgeon from New Zealand.
100. See item 292.
101. Douglas Robb's suggestion, in his letter of 25 June 1962 to Amrit Kaur, was as follows: "I had another, doubtless 'crazier' thought, this morning after going over your wonderful Red Fort at Agra. I am sure there are many other similar buildings at least partially useful even as they are. Could an occasional one be withdrawn from 'public' enjoyment and turned into a retreat for scholars—a collegiate university? The setting and atmosphere is wonderful already—outshining some Oxford and Cambridge Colleges. History would be in the air—quietness—courtyards—and a lot else." PMO, File No. 40(134)/59-64-PMS, Sr. No. 165-B.

292. To Sushila Nayar: Scholarly Exchanges with New Zealand[102]

July 5, 1962

My dear Sushila,
I enclose a copy of a letter from Sir Douglas Robb of New Zealand,[103] which he has sent to Rajkumari Amrit Kaur. I do not see any difficulty about our exchanging scholars with New Zealand, as suggested by him. I hope you agree.[104]

Yours affectionately,
Jawaharlal Nehru

293. To G. Samboo: Soviet Medication[105]

July 7, 1962

Dear Dr Samboo,[106]
Your letter of the 3rd July has reached here in Kashmir where I have come for a few days. You need not worry at all about my health. I am in fairly good condition and there is no reason whatever for any anxiety on that score.

I am glad to learn that you went to the Soviet Union and found that Indians were welcome there.

We have repeatedly received various vaccines from the Soviet Union. We know well that they are willing to supply more of these when needed.

Yours sincerely,
[Jawaharlal Nehru]

102. Letter to the Minister of Health. Sent from Pahalgam, Kashmir.PMO, File No. 40(134)/59-64-PMS, Sr. No. 167-A.
103. Cardiac surgeon from Auckland, New Zealand. The copy of his letter, dated 25 June 1962, and sent from Palam Airport, New Delhi, in the NMML, is itself an extract and has not been reproduced here. However, he proposed as follows: "When I get back I plan to suggest to the NZ [New Zealand] Government that it might consider establishing a regular Fellowship to be held in NZ by a nominee of the AIIMS. The converse would be a regular place in the AIIMS which could be filled from NZ nominees in turn."
104. See item 291.
105. Letter ; address 177 Avenue Elisée Reclus, Pierrefitte (Seine), France. Sent from Pahalgam, Kashmir.
106. Dr Gopaljee Samboo, Chairman, France-India Committee.

(e) Education

294. To A.A.A. Fyzee: Middle Eastern Studies[107]

June 9, 1962

My dear Fyzee,

Your letter of the 6th June with your note on Middle Eastern Studies.[108] As I told you, I entirely agree with you in your proposal to have a diploma course in Modern Arabic and Persian. I am sending a copy of your note to the Chairman of the University Grants Commission.[109]

So far as the External Affairs Ministry is concerned, they will fully support your proposal.

You can certainly send your note to the press. I would suggest that it might be sent as an article by you and not as an open letter to me.

Yours sincerely,
[Jawaharlal Nehru]

295. To D.S. Kothari: Fyzee's Note on Middle Eastern Studies[110]

June 9, 1962

My dear Kothari,

I am sending you a note by Shri A.A.A. Fyzee on the Middle Eastern Studies. He particularly recommends a diploma course in the study of Modern Persian and Arabic. He includes Turkish also and proposes that it may be taken up later.

I entirely agree with his opinion. I think it is important that these languages in their modern shape should be studied.[111] I hope the University Grants Commission will take up the matter especially for Delhi and Bombay.

107. Letter to the former Ambassador to Egypt and former Vice-Chancellor of Jammu and Kashmir University ; address: 102 Bhulabhai Desai Road, Bombay 26.
108. The copy of the note by Fyzee is not reproduced here but is available in the NMML along with this letter.
109. D.S. Kothari.
110. Letter to the Chairman of the UGC.
111. See item 294.

I am not sending you the annexure to Shri Fyzee's article, which consists of figures of imports and exports.

Yours sincerely,
[Jawaharlal Nehru]

296. In New Delhi: To the National Foundation for Teachers' Welfare[112]

I welcome the formation of the National Foundation for Teachers Welfare.[113] The idea is a good one but more important than even the financial benefits that might come of this foundation, although they are important, is the idea of the community looking after the teachers more, thinking of their needs, and trying to fulfil them. For the teacher ultimately is, I think, perhaps, plays the most important part in the community. It has always struck me that all of the pleasing aspects of old Indian culture was the respect given to the teacher. A teacher was almost at the top of the social ladder because the teacher represented the giving of learned wisdom to the pupil and what more important gift there can be? Nowadays learning and wisdom whisper while money shouts. It is unfortunate that this change in standards has come about and money plays such an important part in our lives. Still I suppose in India something of the old values still remain and I should like them to be emphasised and to be respected. So this National Foundation for Teachers' Welfare is not only a scheme for helping teachers—there are none more worthy of receiving help from the community—but also a method of giving them higher status in life. It is important that this should be so and status should not go by the position of money only, or indeed by money at all, and I welcome this scheme for both the reasons. The community being made to think of the teacher as the most vital part of itself and of giving it a certain status and giving it help. Therefore, I hope that this scheme would succeed in both ways and will raise the status of our teachers much more than it is today and will give them certain facilities which they so richly deserve.

112. Speech, 22 June 1962, at Teen Murti House, New Delhi. NMML, NM No. 1671, TS No. 8451. This message was to Radio Newsreel broadcast by All India Radio on 23 June on the National Foundation for Teachers' Welfare. Education (PIB) Shastri Bhawan.

113. Set up in 1962 with an initial contribution of Rs 1,00,000 from the Central Government, the foundation looks after the school teachers' welfare through various schemes.

297. To K.L. Shrimali: School Meals for Children[114]

June 24, 1962

My dear Shrimali,

I am sorry for the delay in acknowledging your letter of June 15th. In this you refer to providing school meals to children at the primary stage of education.

I am anxious that this should be done and I am glad to know that already four million children in the country are receiving such meals. I agree with you that it may not be possible to cover all the children going to primary schools now. This will become too much of a burden for us. But substantial progress can be made as you suggest. It will be a good thing if we reach the figure of fifteen million in the next two or three years.

I agree with you also that external aid should not be refused and should be taken advantage of, but I am quite sure that we should not entirely depend upon this. Any scheme that we make should depend on our internal arrangements plus what external aid we might be able to get. We must be prepared for external aid to be reduced or to be cut off even, and yet be able to carry on.

Yours sincerely,
[Jawaharlal Nehru]

298. To K.M. Munshi: Inaugurating Sardar Patel College of Engineering[115]

July 1, 1962

My dear Munshi,

Your letter of June 27th.[116] I am afraid I cannot come to Bombay in July as I am pretty well occupied throughout the month. In September I have to go abroad for the Prime Ministers' Conference in London.[117] The only time therefore that

114. Letter to the Minister of Education.

115. Letter to the Chairman of Bharatiya Vidya Bhavan. PMS, File No. 8(228)62 PMP.

116. Excerpts from K.M. Munshi's letter of 27 June 1962: "I refer to the conversation we had on 12th June 1962, and write to thank you for accepting our invitation to inaugurate the Bhavan's Sardar Patel College of Engineering, Andheri, Bombay. [...]I had also mentioned to you about declaring open at the same function the new building of the Hansraj Morarji Public School, an allied Trust, of which I am the Chairman. The said school is also situated in the same campus and is hardly a few hundred yards away from the Engineering College building.[...]" PMS, File No. 8(228)62 PMP.

117. See SWJN/SS/78 items 362-363.

might be possibly convenient would be in August. Parliament will be meeting then, but perhaps I could find a day to visit Bombay.

Yours sincerely,
Jawaharlal Nehru

299. To C.B. Gupta: Urdu in Three-Language Formula[118]

July 1, 1962

My dear Chandra Bhanu,

Hifzur Rahman[119] has sent me a copy of a letter dated 25th June that he has written to you. This is about the three-language formula and he pleads for Urdu to be included in it.

So far as the formula is concerned, which we have accepted, there is no doubt that Urdu can be inducted in it. The three-language formula is: (1) Hindi, (2) English, or possibly any European language, and (3) any modern Indian language other than Hindi. Thus, in No. 3, Urdu certainly can come in. It is a language mentioned in our Constitution.

Some doubt arose about this matter and I referred it to our Education Minister[120] who has cleared it up. Sanskrit or any classical language would be a special subject which anyone can take up, but it does not affect the three-language formula.

Yours sincerely,
[Jawaharlal Nehru]

118. Letter to the Chief Minister of Uttar Pradesh.
119. Lok Sabha MP, Congress, till 1962, Member, Anjuman Taraqqi-e-Urdu Hind, All India Muslim Educational Conference, and general secretary of the Jamiat-ul-Ulema-i-Hind.
120. K.L. Shrimali.

300. To Hifzur Rahman: Urdu in Three-Language Formula[121]

July 1, 1962

My dear Maulana,

I have received a copy of your letter dated 25th which you have sent to Shri C.B. Gupta.

I think you are under a misapprehension. The formula agreed upon at the Chief Ministers' Conference[122] as well as at the Integration Conference[123] was the three-language one, namely, (1) Hindi, (2) English or possibly any other foreign language and (3) any modern Indian language other than Hindi.

You will see that this obviously includes Urdu. As there was some doubt about this matter, I wrote to the Education Minister and he has cleared it as stated above by me.

I hope that your treatment is doing you good and that you will be fit again before long.

Yours sincerely,
[Jawaharlal Nehru]

301. To Virendra: Indian Migration to UK[124]

July 2, 1962

Dear Virendra,

I have your letter of June 30. I am sending the paragraph about the teaching of Modern Indian Languages at Cambridge to our Education Minister.[125]

We have been discouraging for some time Indians, that is specially Punjabis, from going in large numbers to the United Kingdom, We have not wholly succeeded. Anyhow no question of this arises now as a restriction is coming into force at the other end.

121. Letter to former Congress MP, Member, Anjuman Taraqqi-e-Urdu Hind, All India Muslim Educational Conference, and general secretary of the Jamiat-ul-Ulema-i-Hind.
122. SWJN/SS/70/item 63.
123. SWJN/SS/71/item 68.
124. Letter to MLC, Punjab, Secretary, Hindi Raksha Samiti, and editor of *Daily Pratap*, Jullunder.
125. Item 302.

I think that not many are interested to know about our case on Kashmir. Their attitude is not governed by facts but their likes and dislikes as well as the cold war.

Yours sincerely,
[Jawaharlal Nehru]

302. To K.L. Shrimali: Indian Languages in Cambridge[126]

July 2, 1962

My dear Shrimali

I have received a letter from Virendra, MLC, Punjab, who has just come back from abroad. I give an extract from his letter which might interest you.[127]

> "In Cambridge, I had a meeting with Sir Harold Bailey, Professor of Indology.[128] While discussing the future prospectus of any of the Modern Indian Languages in Cambridge, Sir Harold Bailey told me that there is no arrangement for the teaching of any of the Modern Indian Languages in Cambridge at present. He also told me that the Pakistan Government has recently offered to bear all the expenses if a chair is set up in Cambridge for the development of Urdu Language. Sir Harold Bailey was of the view that if this materialises, it will give set-back to India's prestige in Cambridge. In his opinion the Government of India should also be prepared to help the Cambridge University in making arrangements for the teaching of Modern Indian Languages. At present, a number of students are coming forward to take up Chinese and Arabic for special studies. One of the reasons given by Sir Harold Bailey for this was that there is a general impression amongst students that in India they can do without acquiring any knowledge of any of the Modern Indian Languages as English is still the medium of communication in India. This is again a point which needs your special attention."

Yours sincerely,
[Jawaharlal Nehru]

126. Letter to the Minister of Education.
127. See item 301.
128. Harold Walter Bailey.

303. To Sampurnanand: The Shri Har Prasad Shiksha Nidhi[129]

July 2, 1962

My dear Sampurnanand,

Your letter of the 29th June. As you may have already heard, the meeting of the Shri Har Prasad Shiksha Nidhi[130] could not be held yesterday. Another date has been fixed for it—21st July.

It seemed to me that the proposals made by the Vice-Chancellor Shri Birbal Singh[131] were reasonable. But I found there was some objection to them on the ground that the Vidyapith was not being conducted properly. The argument seemed to me not very reasonable.

Yours sincerely,
[Jawaharlal Nehru]

304. To Bishanchander Seth: Hindi[132]

नई दिल्ली,
दिनांक 3 जुलाई, 1962

प्रिय श्री बिशनचन्द्र जी,

आपका 17 जून का पत्र मुझे कुछ दिन हुये मिला था। जवाब में देर हुई, इस के लिये माफ़ी चाहता हूं। आपका ख़त कुछ और काग़जों में मिल कर अलग सा हो गया था फिर जवाब की याददहानी आई तो फिर उसको ढूँढ कर निकाला।

हिन्दी के बारे में जो आप ने लिखा है वह बहुत कुछ ठीक है, लेकिन भाषाओं का मामला ऐसा पेचीदा हमारे देश में है कि अगर हम ज़रा भी ज़बरदस्ती करें तो उसका असर उलटा जो जाता है। मेरा ख़्याल है कि हिन्दी काफी तेज़ी से फैल रही है और फैलेगी। यह ज़्यादा अच्छा है कि वह अपनी शक्ति और हमारी मदद से फैले, उस के ऊपर आपसी झगड़े न हों। आप जानते हैं कि मद्रास में और किसी कदर बंगाल में उसका काफ़ी विरोध है। मद्रास में एक बड़ी संस्था उसकी विरोधी है। बावजूद इस के मद्रास में थी वह तेज़ी से फैल रही है, क्योंकि लोग जानते हैं कि इस के बगैर भविष्य में काम ठीक नहीं चलेगा।

129. Letter to the Governor of Rajasthan.
130. Har Prasad Smarak Nidhi, the Board of Management of Kashi Vidyapith.
131. Birbal Singh was Congress MP in the Lok Sabha from Jaunpur, UP, 1952-62; the official website of Mahatma Gandhi Kashi Vidyapith lists Birbal Singh as Vice Chancellor from August (no date) 1962 to 13 August 1967.
132. Letter to Lok Sabha MP, Hindu Mahasabha ; address: 28, South Avenue New Delhi.

मैं समझता हूं कि इस तरह हिन्दी को बढ़ने देना अच्छा है। अगर कुछ जबरदस्ती की तो बढ़ना रूक जायेगा। और जो बात आप चाहते हैं उस के होने में और देर लग जायेगी।

हमारे देश में सभी भाषायें हमारे राष्ट्र की भाषायें हैं। केवल फ़र्क यह है कि हिन्दी अधिकतर बोली जाती है। सब भाषाओं को हम ने अपनाया हैं। अंग्रेज़ी को भी हम ने किसी कदर अपनाया हैं, इस लिये कि वह एक दरवाज़ा हैं आजकल के विज्ञान के लिये और अगर हम इस दरवाज़े को बन्द करें तो हमारी हानि होगी, क्योंकि आजकल की दुनिया विज्ञान की है। हर वैज्ञानिक आदमी को आजकल दो तीन विदेशी भाषायें सीख़नी पडती हैं।

आप ने चीनी इतिहास की मिसाल दी है। चीन में काफ़ी कठिनाई आजकल की भाषा से वहां के अधिकारियों को महसूस हुई है और कोशिश है कि उस की लिपि और कुछ बातें बदली जायें।

संयुक्त राष्ट्र की भाषाओं का जो लिखा है वह निश्चय ही था जब संयुक्त राष्ट्र बनाई गई। स्पैनिश स्पेन की वजह से स्वीकार नहीं हुई बल्कि इस लिये कि 20, 25 देश लैटिन अमरिका के, स्पैनिश का प्रयोग करते हैं। फ्रैंच एक अर्न्तराष्ट्रीय बोली है जो बहुत दिन से समझी जाती है और अबतक बहुत देशों में इस में काम होता है। चीनी भाषा का होना एक अजीब बात है, चूंकि यह पिछली लड़ाई का नतीजा है। समय आयेगा जब शायद हिन्दी भी अर्न्तराष्ट्रीय भाषायों में शामिल कर ली जायेगी। इस समय इस विषय में कुछ करना सफल नहीं होगा।

आप ने गोरक्षा का लिखा है, जितना इस पर मैं ने विचार किया है मैं इसी नतीजा पर पहुँचा हूँ कि उस की रक्षा एक तरह हो सकती है और वह है आर्थिक और वैज्ञानिक ढंग से। ख़ाली कहना कि उसकी रक्षा होनी चाहिए, उसका नतीजा उलटा होता है। अजीब बात है कि और देशों में जहां गाय की कोई पूजा नहीं होती उस की हालत बहुत अच्छी है। क्योंकि उसकी देख भाल ठीक होती हैं। भारत ही में उस की हालत ख़राब है। हमारे देश के लिये गाय का ठीक होना बहुत आवश्यक है, उस की पूरी कोशिश होनी चाहिये।

आपने जो प्रश्न अपने पत्र में उठाये हैं वे काफ़ी गंभीर हैं। उसका जवाब मैं आपको छोटा सा दे रहा हूं।

आपका
[जवाहरलाल नेहरु]

[Translation begins:

Dear Shri Bishanchanderji,

I received your letter your letter of 17 June a few days ago. I am sorry for the delay in reply. Your letter got mixed up with other papers. When I remembered to send a reply, it was searched and found.

Whatever you have written about Hindi is more or less correct, but the language issue is so complex in our country that if something is done forcefully it has a reverse affect. In my opinion Hindi is spreading pretty fast and will spread. It is better if it spreads on its own strength and with our efforts. You know well that in Madras and to some extent in Bengal, there is opposition to it. In Madras, one big organisation opposes it. In spite of that, Hindi is spreading fast because people understand that it will be difficult to work without its knowledge in future. I consider this the best way for Hindi to spread. If Hindi is forced its spread with stop. And what you want, will take longer to fulfill.

All languages of our country are our national languages. The only difference is that Hindi is widely spoken. We have adopted all our languages, English too, to an extent, because it is a door to modern science and closing this door will be harmful for us because the present world is the world of science. Every scientist has to learn two, three foreign languages.

You have given the example of Chinese history. These days the officials in China are facing many difficulties and efforts are being made to make some changes in it and its script.

You have mentioned United Nations languages, it was because when the United Nations was formed, Spanish was accepted not because of Spain but because twenty to twenty-five countries of Latin America use Spanish. French is an international language which has been in use for a long time and even now it is used in many countries. It is strange to have the Chinese language since this is the outcome of the last War. A time will come when Hindi will also be included in the international languages. Making any efforts on these lines now will not succeed.

You have written about cow protection, I have thought about it a lot and have come to the conclusion that the only way to protect the cow is by economic and scientific way. Only paying lip service that it should be protected, may have the reverse effect. It is indeed strange that in other countries, where the cow is not worshipped, it is in a better condition and well looked after. Only in India it is in bad shape. It is very important for cows to be looked after well and every effort should be made for this.

You have raised very serious questions in your letter. I am sending you a brief reply.

Yours sincerely,
Jawaharlal Nehru

Translation ends]

305. For the Bharat Scouts and Guides[133]

I send my good wishes to the Bharat Scouts & Guides. I have always felt that the Bharat Scouts & Guides are doing very good work in India in training our younger generation. Among other things, their work must help in the integration of India which is so important.

306. To B.F.H.B. Tyabji: Becoming Vice-Chancellor at Aligarh[134]

July 7, 1962

My dear Badr,

I enclose a copy of a letter from the Education Minister, Dr Shrimali.[135] I casually mentioned this subject to you in Delhi. I should like to discuss this with you on my return.

The request of the Education Minister puts me in some difficulty. I fully realise the great importance of the Aligarh University. It is something more than a University. It is the intellectual centre of the growing generation among Muslims in India. It has thus inevitably to play a vital part in our future. Most people who have spoken to me about it, including Dr Zakir Husain,[136] have strongly recommended you for the Vice-Chancellorship. I, therefore, think that your going there will be a good thing.

On the other hand, I would regret your leaving the External Affairs Ministry, even for a limited period, which is likely to be at least three years. Still, in the balance, I am inclined to think that it will be desirable for you to go to Aligarh if you are at all attracted to it. Certainly I do not wish to come in the way.

We can discuss this matter when I return.

Yours sincerely,
[Jawaharlal Nehru]

133. Message, 6 July 1962, forwarded to A.N. Gupta, Joint Editor and Publisher, Bharat Scouts and Guides, Regal Building, Parliament Street, New Delhi-1. PMO, File No. 9/2/62-PMP, Vol. V, Sr. No. 1-A.
134. Letter to the Special Secretary at the MEA. Sent from Pahalgam, Kashmir.
135. Appendix 51.
136. Vice-President.

307. To K.L. Shrimali: B.F.H.B. Tyabji for Vice-Chancellor at Aligarh[137]

July 7, 1962

My dear Shrimali,
I have your letter of July 4th about the Vice-Chancellorship of the Aligarh University.[138] I would regret Badruddin Tyabji leaving the External Affairs Ministry. But I fully realise the importance of Vice-Chancellorship in moulding this very important University and the young people who go there. I feel, therefore, that in the balance I should not come in the way of Tyabji going there if he is willing to do so. I shall speak to him about it on my return to Delhi. I expect to be back on the 11th of this month.

Yours sincerely,
[Jawaharlal Nehru]

(f) Culture

308. To Humayun Kabir: Science versus Culture[139]

June 3, 1962

My dear Humayun,
You spoke to me the other day about your Ministry and the heavy load which Professor Thacker[140] was carrying. I agreed with you about lightening his burden. I sent you a note to this effect which apparently you returned to me.

Your proposal appears to be that Thacker should be Director-General, CSIR, with the status of a Secretary, and that another Secretary should look after the cultural and like activities.

I rather doubt if a full-fledged Secretary is needed to look after the cultural wing. As for Scientific services, societies and scientific literature etc., I think it should come under Thacker. In fact, the CSIR, Technical Education and all scientific activities should be put under Thacker.

137. Letter to the Education Minister. Sent from Pahalgam, Kashmir.

138. Appendix 51.

139. Letter to the Minister of Scientific Research and Cultural Affairs.

140. M.S. Thacker, Secretary and Educational Adviser in the Ministry of Scientific Research and Cultural Affairs, and Director-General of CSIR.

As for the cultural wing, this will hardly require a full Secretary. A Joint Secretary can look after this.[141]

Yours sincerely,
[Jawaharlal Nehru]

309. To Humayun Kabir: A Secretary for Culture[142]

June 5, 1962

My dear Humayun,

Your letter of the 5th June.

I quite understand that Thacker[143] is over-burdened with work and that some arrangement should be made to lighten his load. I imagine, however, that Technical Education or any subject dealing with Science, should be dealt with by a scientist and preferably by Thacker, who can be assisted by another person.

There is strong objection now to adding to our list of Secretaries. But if you think this is absolutely necessary to have a Secretary or Additional Secretary, you may try to get Finance to agree to it.[144]

Yours sincerely,
[Jawaharlal Nehru]

310. In the Cabinet: Viceregal Lodge in Shimla[145]

The President's letter to the Prime Minister regarding the Viceregal Lodge and attached Buildings at Simla.

The Prime Minister read out to the Members of the Cabinet a letter received by him from the President in which the President had observed that the Viceregal Lodge at Simla had not been put to much use in the last fifteen years and that he would, therefore, like to transfer the Viceregal Lodge and an

141. See also item 309.

142. Letter to the Minister for Scientific Research and Cultural Affairs.

143. M.S. Thacker, Secretary and Educational Adviser in the Ministry of Scientific Research and Cultural Affairs, and Director-General of CSIR.

144. See also item 308.

145. Meeting of the Cabinet held on June 7, 1962. Case No. 145/16/62. GOI, Cabinet Secretariat, Rashtrapati Bhawan, File No. 70/6/CF/62, p. 3.

attached buildings, known as Armsdell, to the Government, who might utilise them for such purpose, as holiday homes for workers or lower middle class officials, as might be decided by them. The Prime Minister also read out the reply he had sent to the President thanking him for the generous offer. The Cabinet asked the Prime Minister to convey their gratitude to the President.[146] The Prime Minister observed that thought should be given as to how best to utilise these buildings.[147]

311. To S. Radhakrishnan: Using the Viceregal Lodge in Shimla[148]

June 8, 1962

My dear Mr President,

Yesterday I mentioned at a Cabinet meeting that you had been good enough to make an offer of Rashtrapati Niwas (previously called Viceregal Lodge) in Simla to the Government for such public purpose, as it might consider desirable.[149] The Cabinet asked me to convey their thanks to you for this offer, which they gladly accept.

Before coming to a final decision as to what use this building as well as the other building referred to by you can be put to, I have asked the Cabinet Secretary to pay a visit to Simla and personally inspect them. On his return, we shall consider his suggestions. I shall keep you informed.

Yours sincerely,
[Jawaharlal Nehru]

312. To Humayun Kabir: State of the Akademies[150]

June 10, 1962

My dear Humayun,

How are the Akademis functioning now? I keep in touch more or less with the Sahitya Akademi. But I do not know anything about the Sangeet Natak or the Lalit Kala. I gather that many of the old members of the Sangeet Natak

146. See item 311.
147. See also SWJN/SS/76/item 394.
148. Letter to the President.
149. See item 310. See also SWJN/SS/76/item 394.
150. Letter to the Minister of Scientific Research and Cultural Affairs.

Akademi are no longer there, and it is said that it is not running well.[151] I shall be glad to know how things are. Who is the Secretary of it?

Yours sincerely,
[Jawaharlal Nehru]

313. To Swami Vijoyananda: Science and Spirituality[152]

June 19, 1962

Dear Swami Vijoyananda,
I am glad to know that the Bharat Sevashram Sangha is going to publish a book entitled *Ideals of Indian Education and Culture*.[153] I have also noted that this book will contain articles from a large number of eminent men and educationists. The book should prove useful to all those who are interested in education.

Indeed everyone is to some extent interested in this vital subject. This question was considered by the National Integration Conference and some suggestions were made.[154] These suggestions did not lay any stress on moral education. But education, if it is to be worthwhile, has to deal with moral and ethical standards even though it does not teach any specific religion as such. Life cannot be divorced from these ethical problems and from its spiritual aspect, or else, it becomes lopsided.

We have seen tremendous advances made by science and technology. Indeed the emblem of the modern world can well be said to be the mushroom cloud, which is the product of the atomic bomb explosion. Unless this advance is balanced by progress in the spirit of man, the world, which is near disaster already, may well succumb to it.

We cannot do without science, for that is the essential aspect of truth and represents the modern world. At the same time, we cannot do without spirituality in our education and make up. The only way, therefore, is, as Vinoba Bhave has put it, to combine science and spirituality.

151. For an earlier reference, see SWJN/SS/67/item 178.

152. Letter to Vijoyananda of Bharat Sevashram Sangha ; address: Bharat Sevashram Sangha, 211 Rash Behari Avenue, Calcutta 19. PMO, File No. 9/2/62-PMP, Vol. IV, Sr. No. 60-A.

This letter has been reproduced without a date as the foreword to the book mentioned.

153. *Ideals of Indian Education and Culture: Acharya Swami Pranavananda Memorial Volume* edited by Swami Vijoyananda (Calcutta: Bharat Sevashram Sangha, 1962).

154. See items 6-8.

I do not know how this can be done satisfactorily, avoiding the narrowness of many religious beliefs. But I am sure that this is the only way. I hope that your book will throw some light on this subject.

Yours sincerely,
J. Nehru

314. To W.D. Tucker: Women for International Cooperation[155]

June 19, 1962

Dear Mrs Tucker,
Thank you for your letter of June 13, 1962. I am interested to learn of the Conference of Women for International Cooperation Year, which is to be held in September next in Montreal. I do not know if Mrs Pandit[156] will be able to attend it. She is holidaying in Kashmir at present and I am not in touch with her. As you have written to her directly, I suppose she will let you know herself.

Yours sincerely,
[Jawaharlal Nehru]

315. To Humayun Kabir: Sangeet Natak and Lalit Kala Akademis[157]

June 23, 1962

My dear Humayun,
You wrote to me on the 11th June about the two Akademis, Sangeet Natak and the Lalit Kala. I am glad that progress has been made in regard to these Akademis, especially the Sangeet Natak. It is important, I think, that none of

155. Letter to the Chairman of the Initiating Committee, Conference of Women for International Cooperation Year, Toronto 5, Canada.
156. Vijaya Lakshmi Pandit.
157. Letter to the Minister of Scientific Research and Cultural Affairs. PMO, File No. 40(213)/60-74-PMS, Sr. No. 14-A. Also available in NMML, Humayun Kabir Papers, File No. 16/1962-64, Auto.

these Akademis should be officialised too much. Artistes do not function in an official atmosphere.[158]

I showed your letter to Indiraji. She has sent me a note which I attach.[159]

Yours sincerely,
Jawaharlal Nehru

316. To Y.S. Parmar: Using Rashtrapati Niwas in Shimla[160]

June 23, 1962

My dear Parmar,

Your letter of the 22nd June.

I am afraid I do not agree with you about the use of Rashtrapati Niwas[161] in Simla. I entirely agree with the President's suggestion that it should be used for a public purpose. There is absolutely no point in keeping a huge building like this vacant merely to maintain some supposed dignity of the President.[162]

What it will be used for we have not decided. We shall consider that in the course of the next few weeks. Personally I am inclined to use it for children

158. Kabir replied on 25 June:

> "Thank You for your confidential letter No. 929-PMH/62 of June 23, 1962.
>
> I entirely agree with you that the Akademies should not be officialised too much. In fact, we have only two representatives, one from this Ministry and one from the Ministry of Finance, who function as other members of the Committees and whose advice is accepted by the others only when they agree. The only subject where our representatives put their points of view strongly is in matters of finance.
>
> I am writing separately to Shrimati Indira Gandhi."

NMML, Humayun Kabir Papers, File No. 16/1962-64, copy.

159. Indira Gandhi's note: "I have seen this letter. I am afraid the reference to Shri Baldoon Dhingra is not quite accurate. The Sangeet Natak Akademi is completely under the Ministry now and this is not a desirable state of affairs, all well-known connoisseurs of music & dance are being alienated.
Indira Nehru Gandhi"
NMML, Humayun Kabir papers, File No. 16/1962-64, Holo.

160. Letter to the President of the Himachal Pradesh PCC. PMO, File No. 45(21)/62-70-PMS, Sr. No. 6-A. Also available in the JN Collection.

161. Previously the Viceregal Lodge.

162. See items 310-311 in this volume and SWJN/SS/76/item 394.

or for Government employees of the lower grades. However, your suggestion will also be borne in mind.[163]

Yours sincerely,
[Jawaharlal Nehru]

317. To Dietmar Rothermund: No Time to Read *The Philosophy of Restraint*[164]

June 23, 1962

Dear Mr Rothermund,

I have your letter of June 14th. I am afraid it has not been possible for me to read the manuscript of the book by your wife called *The Philosophy of Restraint*.[165] Nor am I likely to have time to do so in the foreseeable future. I should like to read it because the subject interests me. If I can keep the manuscript, I shall read it at my leisure.

I can see you on Thursday, the 28th June, at 10.00 a.m. at my office in External Affairs Ministry.

Yours sincerely,
[Jawaharlal Nehru]

318. To K.R. Kripalani: Grant for PEN Conference[166]

June 24, 1962

My dear Krishna,

I enclose a letter from Madame Sophia Wadia.[167] In this she refers to the Writers' Conference which the PEN is organising in Mysore. She wants some financial help from the Sahitya Akademi.

163. Extract from Parmar's reply of 28 July 1962: "I am indeed grateful to you for your kind letter of June 23, 1962, No. 937-PMH/62. I am glad the matter of the use of the Rashtrapati Niwas, Simla, for the Himachal Pradesh Medical College and State Hospital will receive your due consideration at the proper time..." PMO, File No. 45(21)/62-70-PMS, Sr. No. 8-A.

    On another suggestion, see item 326.

164. Letter to German historian of India; address: A-334 Defence Colony, New Delhi-3.
165. *The Philosophy of Restraint: Mahatma Gandhi's Strategy and Indian Politics* by Indira Rothermund (Bombay: Popular Prakashan, 1963).
166. Letter to the Secretary of the Sahitya Akademi. Sahitya Akademi Records, File No. S.A. 2, Part V, Executive Board, 1962. Also available in the JN Collection.
167. Founder-Organiser of PEN All India Centre (1901-1986). See appendix 39.

I do not know what your rules are about giving financial help on such occasions. If rules permit it, perhaps some help might be given. You might consult the President[168] about it.[169]

Please return to me Madame Wadia's letter.

Yours sincerely,
Jawaharlal Nehru

319. To B.C. Nanjundaiya: Convocation of Hindi Prachar Samiti[170]

June 24, 1962

Dear Shri Nanjundaih,

I have your letter of Jane 23rd.[171] It is true that I intend going to Bangalore probably on the 14th of July. It may be that on the 15th I might visit Tumkur.[172] I do not wish to over-burden myself with engagements. But if it does not add too much to my programme, I shall gladly preside over your Annual Convocation. Please find out from the Chief Minister of Mysore what the exact dates of my

168. The President of India, S. Radhakrishnan was the Vice President of the Sahitya Akademi; Nehru was the President of the Sahitya Akademi, and in the internal correspondence of that body, Nehru is referred to as "President."
169. Kripalani's note of 28 June 1962 to Nehru: "As desired by him [Nehru], I had referred the note to the President of India whose comment is noted in the margin. He has suggested that Madame Sophia's request should be referred to the Ministry of SR & CA. Madame Sophia's letter and the President's note thereon are kept below."

    Nehru responded on 28 June 1962: "I agree. This should be forwarded to the Ministry of SR and CA. You might write to Madame Sophia Wadia that her request to me has been forwarded to the Ministry." Sahitya Akademi Records, File No. S.A. 2, Part. V, Executive Board, 1962.
170. Letter to Congress Rajya Sabha MP; address: 14 D Ferozeshah Road, New Delhi. PMS, File No. 8(226)62-PMP. Also available in the JN Collection.
171. Excerpt from Nanjudaiya's letter of 23 June 1962:

    "On behalf of the Distict Hindi Prachar Samiti I extend you this invitation to preside over the Annual Convocation of the Prachar Samiti. The Samiti was founded in 1945 to propagate Hindi, and it has so far given education to 35 thousand people. The previous convocations were presided among others by Dr Rajendra Prasad, B.G. Kher, Morarji Desai, G.V. Mavlankar, and Acharya Vinoba Bhave." PMS, File No. 8 (226) 62-PMP.
172. See item 166.

visits to Bangalore and Tumkur are likely to be and how far it is possible to include this in the programme.

Yours sincerely,
Jawaharlal Nehru

320. To B. Gopala Reddi: B.N. Sanyal's Grievance[173]

June 24, 1962

My dear Gopala Reddi,

A very old colleague of mine, B.N. Sanyal, came to see me a day or two ago. He was sentenced in the Kakori Conspiracy Case long ago and spent many years in prison. After that, he did some writing in journalistic work.

I have found out from him that he has been employed by the AIR as a staff artiste at Jaipur. Apparently he has a grievance. I am forwarding an extract from a note he gave me.[174] It is for you to judge what is possible to be done for him. I believe he is a competent Hindi writer.

Yours sincerely,
[Jawaharlal Nehru]

173. Letter to the Minister of Information and Broadcasting.

174. Extract (22 June 1962) forwarded by Nehru:

> "I feel most reluctant to relate to you a tale of personal worries but I can assure you that I would not have bothered you if it all I could help it. Mine has been a political career and perforce I must appeal to a political leader gifted with generous human sympathy. Even so I desire no nepotistic favour but only a little accommodation.
>
> 1. As you are aware, Sir, after the closing down of *Amrita Patrika*, I fell into the job of a staff artiste in the All India Radio, as a sub-editor, Regional News Unit, at Jaipur on a meagre salary. Now it so happens that the post is being converted into a class IV service in the cadre of the Information Services. I am already 56 years of age and cannot hope to be included on a regular service. But there are still a few Staff Artistes posts in the News Division of the AIR and all I request is that I may be accommodated in one of these.
> 2. Alternatively, there is a vacant post of Assistant Editor or Research Assistant in the Section of *Collected Works of Mahatma Gandhi* under the Publications Division. There is no age bar there and I could continue till the age of 60 or even more. I am prepared for a test if it be so desired."

321. To Amar Nath Sehgal: Your Sculptures Are Good[175]

June 26, 1962

Dear Amar Nathji,

Your letter of June 16th.[176] What I wrote to Shri Mani Ram Bagri,[177] of course, did not apply to all Indian sculptors.[178] Unfortunately, those who patronise statues seldom go to good sculptors and get some very third-rate stuff made.

Anyhow, I know that your works have been very good. I have no desire whatever to discourage our sculptors.

Yours sincerely,
Jawaharlal Nehru

322. In New Delhi: Van Mahotsav[179]

श्री पाटिल जी,[180] डॉ. राम सुभग सिंह[181] और दोस्तो,

आपने सुना कि बारह-तेरह बरस हुए जब यह वनमहोत्सव शुरु हुआ था और इसमें कोई संदेह नहीं कि एक जरूरी काम शुरु किया गया था। क्योंकि हमारे देश में वनों की बहुत आवश्यकता है, आबादी बढ़ने से वो कम होते गये हैं, लेकिन यह आबादी के लिए भी अच्छी नहीं है और देश के लिए अच्छा नहीं है। ये सब बातें ज़रा भी सोचें, सब जानते हैं, ख़ाली ख़ुदग़र्ज़ी करके काटते जाते हैं दरख़्तों को। मुझे तो कोई बड़ा अच्छा पेड़ काटा जाये तो बड़ा दुख होता है जैसे किसी आदमी का सिर काट लिया, और मेरी राय में यह तो मैं नहीं कह सकता उतनी सज़ा होनी चाहिए लेकिन कुछ सज़ा होनी चाहिए उसकी जो काटे। मुझे ठीक मालूम नहीं कि इस समय यहाँ क़ानून क्या है इस बारे में, चर्चा तो बहुत होता है लेकिन कुछ क़ानून को मदद नहीं मिलती इसमें। अगर हो सके तो मैं समझता हूँ अच्छा हो अगर क़ानून बने कि बग़ैर इजाज़त के मज़बूत पेड़ न काटे जायें, चाहे वो, चाहे वो अपने हों या किसी और के हों। रामसुभग सिंह जी ने आपसे कहा, मैंने कहा था एक दफ़ा कि एक काटने के बजाय दो लगाने चाहिये। दो लगें या तीन लगें वह और बात है

175. Letter to sculptor; address: 303, Vinay Marg, Diplomatic Enclave, New Delhi. PMO, File No. 2(433)/62-70-PMS, Sr. No. 19-A.
176. See appendix 35.
177. Mani Ram Bagri, Lok Sabha MP, Socialist, from Hissar, Punjab.
178. For Nehru's note to K. Ram on Bagdi's letter asking for these statues, see SWJN/SS/76/ item 383.
179. Speech, I July, at the Zoological Park. NMML, AIR, TS No. 8444, 8445, NM No. 1666.
180. S.K. Patil, Minister for Food and Agriculture.
181. Minister of State in the Ministry of Food and Agriculture.

लेकिन पहले काटने ही नहीं चाहिये अच्छा दरख़्त को, वो ज़रा बूढ़ा हो गया, सूख गया, वो और बात है और वनों में तो ख़ैर कोशिश करनी चाहिए बढ़ाने की। मैं देखता हूँ बहुत सारी हमारी सड़कें हैं, उनके दोनों तरफ दरख़्त लगे थे वो सूख गये, गिर रहे हैं और नये दरख़्त नहीं लगे, काफी वक़्त के पहले लगने चाहिये ताकि वो बढ़ जायें, जब उनकी जरूरत हो, यह नहीं कि जब वो मुरझा के गिर जायें तब लगाये जायें, बहुत दिन तक उनका साया भी नहीं मिले, बढ़ने में लगे। यह सारे हिन्दुस्तान में हज़ारों सड़कें हैं, उनके दरख़्त हैं उनका ख़्याल करना चाहिए।

तो बारह बरस हुए आपको इसको करते हुए। यह विचार करने की बात है कि इन बारह बरस में कितनी हमारी उन्नति हुई, कितनी तरक्की हमने की इसमें, महज़ एक ज़ाब्ते से कुछ पौधों को लगा देना और लगाते हुए तस्वीर भी खींच जायेगी और अख़बारों में भी छप जायेगी, वो तो कोई एक बहुत कारामद बात नहीं है। असल में देश में कितनी तरक्की हुई, इसकी कितने लोगों में उत्साह हुआ, जज़बात हुए, इसके बारे में वो देखने की बात है। मैं पसंद करता अगर आज वनमहोत्सव के दिन कोई तेरह बरस की रिपोर्ट छपती और विशेषकर यह सुनने में आया है कि जो लोग बहुत वनमहोत्सव के दिन तो बहुत पेड़ लगाते हैं, पौधे लगाते हैं लेकिन फिर उनकी देखभाल नहीं करते या कम करते हैं देखभाल और नतीजा यह होता है जो लाखों लगते हैं उनमें से आधे से ज्यादा सूख जाते हैं। यह बहुत ही ग़लत बात है और बेफ़िकरी, दो तरह से ग़लत है—एक तो अपना काम किया हुआ ख़राब होता है और बेफ़िकरी जो इससे ज़ाहिर होती है, वो जो शख़्स करता है ज़ाहिर हो जाता है वो निकम्मा आदमी है या औरत जो कोई हो। यह बेफ़िकरी बड़ी ग़लत चीज़ है मुल्क में और एक काम का आधा करके उसको ख़त्म कर देना, उसको ख़राब कर देना यह भी एक अक़्ल की बात नहीं है बल्कि यह भी एक गुनाह सा है। तो इसका क्या हो? मैं जानता हूँ इधर तवज्जो दी गई है और कुछ न कुछ तरक्की हुई है, लेकिन मैं आशा करता हूँ कि इस पर पूरा ध्यान दिया जायेगा, चाहे कुछ कम दरख़्त लगाये जायें, लेकिन एक-एक दरख़्त जो लगेगा उसका ख़्याल रखना है, उसको देखना कितना बढ़ा, नहीं बढ़ा तो किसकी वजह से नहीं बढ़ा, किसका उसमें क़सूर है उसको सज़ा देनी है। इस तरह से इसको करना है, लेकिन इन सब बातों के पीछे एक और बात है—कोई काम भी आप करें अगर उस काम में आपको दिलचस्पी हो, उससे कुछ मोहब्बत हो तो काम चलता है, अगर एक चालू काम हो, फ़र्ज़ अदा करने को और फ़िकर न हो तो वो नहीं चलता, हर बात में जाने, वो बात उसूल अस्पष्ट जाने, पेड़ों में, जानवरों में, इन सभों में।

हम जो यहाँ जुलोजीकल गार्डन देख रहे हैं अब अच्छा जरूर बना है, लेकिन कुछ पिछले दिनों से इसकी शिकायतें सुनी। शिकायतों की मैं कोई तफ़सील नहीं देता, लेकिन मैं आपको बताऊँ मेरा नवासा है, संजय, कभी-कभी यहाँ आता है, उसने मुझसे कहा अब मैं नहीं जाऊँगा उसमें, क्यों भई, वहाँ के लोग जानवरों से प्यार नहीं करते उसमें, काफी प्यार नहीं करते, हाँ, अपना काम करते हैं, खिलाते हैं, पिलाते हैं लेकिन प्यार नहीं करते, यह उसने एतराज़ किया। अब मैं नहीं कह सकता कहाँ तक यह सही है कहाँ तक ग़लत है लेकिन यह असर पैदा करना एक लड़के के दिमाग़ पर, जिसको मोहब्बत है जानवरों

से, यह अच्छा नहीं है। क्यों असर पैदा हुआ ग़ौरतलब बात है, अगर उसको हुआ तो दस-बीस-पचास-सौ को और होगा और अगर ऐसे लोग यहाँ जुलोजीकल गार्डन में रहते हैं, जो जानवरों से असल में मोहब्बत नहीं करते, तो यहाँ उनका रहना ग़लत है, उनको कुछ और पेशा ढूँढना चाहिए। ऐसे लोगों को यहाँ रखना चाहिए, जिनको असली मोहब्बत है जानवरों से। यही बात है पेड़ों की, फूलों की, कि उनसे मोहब्बत होनी चाहिए, ख़ाली फ़र्ज़ अदा नहीं करना चाहिए और कोई आर्थिक नीति से कहना कि मुल्क को फ़ायदा होगा वो तो होगा, लेकिन जो एक पौधा लगाया गया उससे मोहब्बत होनी चाहिए जैसे बच्चे से, उसकी सेवा करनी चाहिए, उसके बढ़ने में ख़ुशी होनी चाहिए। इस तरह से अगर वनमहोत्सव का काम हो तो आप देखिए इसका क्या ज़बरदस्त नतीजा निकलता है।

एक बात से मुझे आश्चर्य होता है कि हमारे यहाँ देहात में कुछ लोग थोड़े बहुत देहाती नाम जानते हैं, फूलों के तो कम, दरख़्तों के तो जानते हैं ही, लेकिन आमतौर से इतने कम लोग हैं जो न यहाँ के दरख़्तों के नाम जानते हैं, जानवरों के जानते हैं, चिड़ियाओं के जानते हैं, तारों के जानते हैं। जो रोज़मर्रा की चीज़, जिनको हम रोज़ देखते हैं न वो पहचानते हैं न बच्चे न बड़े।

मुझे याद आता है एक दफ़ा अल्मोड़ा जेल में था, तो वहाँ अच्छी-अच्छी चिड़ियाएँ आती थी दूर-दूर से। तो मैंने वहाँ के हैड वार्डन से पूछा क्यों भई तुम कुछ नाम जानते हो इन चिड़ियाओं के, उसने कहा जी हाँ मैं कौवा को पहचानता हूँ। अब यह बड़ी ख़ुशी की बात है। तो क़रीब-क़रीब वो जवाब अक्सर लोगों का हो दिल्ली के शहर वालों का भी, वो कौवे को पहचान लें, शायद एकाध को और पहचान लें, शायद बाज़ शहरी भी हों, शहरी भी बहुत बुलबुल वग़ैरह की चर्चा करें, पहचानेंगे नहीं क्या चिड़िया है, पहचानेंगे नहीं। यह अजीब हालत है। और मुल्कों में छोटे बच्चों को ख़ास सिखाया जाता है कि दिलचस्पी हो, पेड़ों के नाम जानें, फूलों के जानें, तारों के जानें, चिड़ियाओं के जानें, और नाम जानना कोई महज़ कोई एक सबक़ पढ़ना नहीं, जानने से हमारे दोस्त बहुत बढ़ जाते हैं, हम अकेलापन नहीं कहीं इस दुनिया में हमें मालूम होता, एक मज़बूत चीज़, ज़बरदस्त चीज़ उससे दोस्ती करना। इन सब बातों से एक तर्ज़ होता है प्रकृति के सामयिक चीज़ों से दोस्ती करना, प्रकृति को उससे अपनाना अपने को, वो यहाँ कुछ कोशिश नहीं होती, अब शायद हो रही है मैं नहीं जानता स्कूलों वग़ैरह में सिखाने की, लम्बे-लम्बे शास्त्रार्थ होते हैं यहाँ, हमारा दस्तूर है शास्त्रार्थ करने का, लेकिन मोटी से मोटी बातें जो नाक के सामने हैं वो पहचानते नहीं हैं, यहाँ उसको समझते नहीं।

विज्ञान है, क्या है विज्ञान? जिससे दुनिया ने तरक्की इतनी की है, विज्ञान है प्रकृति को समझना, प्रकृति में जो बातें होती हैं उनको देखना और समझना और उससे फ़ायदा उठाना। बिजली आप चारों तरफ दुनिया में देखते हैं। कहाँ से आयी बिजली? बिजली को सब लोग जानते थे हज़ारों बरस से, कड़कती थी, ऊपर से कभी गिर के मारती थी, डरते थे उससे, पूजन करते थे उसका, पूजन करना अच्छा हो बुरा हो यह मैं नहीं जानता, लेकिन समझना उससे ज्यादा अच्छा है कि, क्या चीज़ है, और लोगों ने उसको समझने की [कोशिश] की, एक अमेरिका में एक बड़े आदमी थे उन्होंने पतंगें उड़ाई थी बादलों

में, जिनमें बिजली पैदा होती है, पतंग उड़ाई कि पतंग के धागे के ज़रिये से बिजली आ जाये, देखें क्या चीज़ है। इस तरह से हल्के-हल्के बरसों गुज़रे, सौ-पचास बरस गुज़रे इसको पहचानने में, पहचाना उसे क्या है, उसको अपने लेबोरेटरी में या दफ़्तर में पैदा किया, उसको फिर तार पे इधर-उधर भेजा, उससे हज़ार काम भी ले लेते हैं, एक दुनिया में नई शक्ति आ गई ज़बरदस्त क्या है प्रकृति को पहचाना। एटम बम्ब का आप चर्चा सुनते हैं, एटोमिक एनर्जी, वो क्या चीज़ है? प्रकृति को समझना और उससे लाभ उठाना, ख़ैर वो तो अलग चीज़ है समझना, लेकिन चीज़ है। प्रकृति को समझना, उसको दोस्त बनाना अपना, यह तो एक बड़ी भारी बात है जिससे हमारे दोस्त ही दोस्त होते हैं जिधर देखें, एक फूल है वो हमारा एक मित्र है, जिधर देखते हैं मित्र है, चिड़िया है मित्र है, तारें हैं मित्र हैं सारे और हमारा दिमाग़ का तर्ज़ बदल जाता है मित्रों को देखके, अच्छा हो जाता है। इंसानों में भी मित्र हमें ज्यादा मिलने लगते हैं ऐसी हालत में, बजाय इसके कि हम रूठ कर, कुढ़ कर कोने में खड़े रहें, हरेक से नाराज़ रहें, वो नहीं बात रहती, दूसरा दिमाग़ हो जाता है। तो मैं तो चाहता हूँ इस ढंग की हमारी पढ़ाई हो, माँ बाप करें, माँ बाप ख़ुद नहीं जानते किसी चीज़ के नाम तो बच्चों को क्या बतायें या बहुत कम जानते हैं, कौवा वग़ैरह को जानते हैं लेकिन और कम जानते हैं।

तो इसलिए प्रकृति से हमें दोस्ती करनी है और प्रकृति का एक बहुत ज़बरदस्त निशानी दरख़्त हैं, पेड़ हैं, उनसे करनी है, उनको लगाना है, उनकी रक्षा करनी है, क्योंकि रक्षा करना तो यह दो तरफ की बात है। हम उनकी ज़रा सी बचपन में करते हैं वो हमारी करते हैं। अगर हम ज़रा सी बचपन में उनकी हिफ़ाज़त करें, सेवा करें, तो वो पचास-साठ-सत्तर बरस तक, सौ तक इंसानों की सेवा करते हैं आइन्दा के लिए। इसलिए बहुत जरूरी है कि मुल्क की तरक्की के लिए, वन होना और शहरों में भी सड़क के इधर-इधर, और जगह जहाँ हो सके दरख़्त लगें। लेकिन दरख़्त ऐसे ही लगाने चाहियें जिनकी देखभाल ठीकतौर से हो, रक्षा हो और यह आम ख़्याल फैलना चाहिए कि जो दरख़्त काटता है वो एक जुर्म करता है, जब तक कि वो दरख़्त काटने के क़ाबिल न हो।

तो आज का दिन इसीलिए मुक़र्रर हुआ है, वनमहोत्सव तेरहवाँ है। तो इस ढंग से काम हो, तो मैं समझता हूँ इसका नतीजा और फल बहुत अच्छा हो बजाय इसके कि ज़ाब्ते को हम दो-चार या दो-चार सौ या दो-चार लाख दरख़्त लगा दें, फिर उनकी फ़िकर न करें और वो सूखें और मुरझा जायें, मर जायें क़ब्ल इसके दूसरा महोत्सव मनायें। तो मैं आशा करता हूँ कि इस दफ़ा जो दरख़्त लगाये जायेंगे उनकी देखभाल काफी होगी और ज़ोरों से बढ़ेंगे, ताक़तवर होंगे और फिर वो इंसानों की ख़िदमत करेंगे।

जयहिन्द!

[Translation begins:

Shri Patilji,[182] Dr Ram Subhag Singh,[183] Friends,
As you heard just now, we started the tradition of Van Mahotsav, twelve to thirteen years ago and there is no doubt about it, that it is an essential task. We need more and more forests in the country for they are being cut down because of the growing population. But it is not a good thing for the population, or the country. People cut trees for selfish purposes, fully aware of the consequences. I feel terrible almost as if a man's head has been cut off when a good tree is felled and I think the punishment for such acts should be severe. I do not know what the law is on this at the moment. It is always talked about, but the law is not supported by the people. If possible, I think some stringent laws should be passed against the illegal felling of trees without permission. Ram Subhagji mentioned just now that I had once said that instead of cutting one tree, two should be planted. Trees should not be cut down in the first place except when they become too old or dry. An effort should be made to increase the forest cover. I often see that the trees planted along roadsides are dried up, or have fallen down, and new ones are not planted in their place. This should be done well in advance, so that they replace the old trees in time. Otherwise, if trees are planted when the old ones have fallen, they will take years to grow and provide shade. Proper attention should be paid to the trees along the thousands of roads in India.

So twelve years have gone by since we started this. It is worth considering what our progress has been. It is not enough to plant trees for the sake of an occasion and have yourselves photographed doing so, which are then published in newspapers. The real test is the enthusiasm which has been created among the people, and their feelings in this matter. I would have liked to have had a report put out on the progress made during the last thirteen years, particularly because I have heard that the trees which are planted on the day of Van Mahotsav are not looked after properly later, with the result that of the millions of trees which are planted, more than half wither. Such neglect is criminal, because for one thing, a good act goes waste and it shows the general attitude of the people. Negligence is very bad in a nation, as also the tendency to leave something half done. It is criminal. What is the solution? I am aware that attention has been paid to this, and some progress is visible. But I hope there will be whole-hearted attention to this. Even if the number of trees planted is not large, those that are planted should be well looked after and those who fail to do so, must

182. See fn 180 in this section.
183. See fn 181 in this section.

be punished. But there is something else behind all this. It is only when you do something wholeheartedly with genuine interest and love that it works. If something is done as mere duty, and there is no proper care after that, nothing can come of it, whether it concerns trees, animals or something else.

The zoological garden that we see here, is a good one, but I have been hearing complaints about it during the last few days. I will not go into the details but I would like to mention that my grandson, Sanjay, who used to come here, refuses to do so now. When asked for the reason, he said that the animals are not loved, though they are given enough to eat and what not. This was his objection. Now I do not know how far this is true, but it is not a good thing that such an impression should be created in the mind of a young boy who loves animals. So I felt this is worth looking into. The same impression would be created in the minds of hundreds of children, and if there are people in charge of the zoological gardens who do not really love animals, then they should not be allowed to remain here. They must look for something else to do. Only those who have a real love of animals must be allowed to look after the zoological garden. The same thing applies to trees and flowers. The people in charge must have a genuine love of them and not do their work as mere duty. To look at trees merely as an economic proposition which will benefit the country is all very well. But each tree that is planted should be loved like a child and must be nurtured and looked after, and there should be real joy in watching it grow. If this is the spirit behind Van Mahotsav, you will see what excellent results are obtained.

One thing that amazes me is that though in the rural areas people know the names at least of the common trees, if not all the flowers, by and large most urban people can identify neither trees nor animals, or birds. Neither children nor adults can recognise even the common things that we see around us in our daily lives.

I remember that once when I was in the Almora Jail, all kinds of beautiful migratory birds would come there. When I asked the Head Warden if he could recognise any of those birds, he replied, "Yes, Sir, I can recognise the crow". It is indeed amazing. This would probably be the answer given by most of the urban folk. They may be able to recognise the crow, and perhaps talk about the bulbul, but whether they would recognise it is doubtful. In other countries, special effort is made to teach little children the names of trees, flowers, birds and stars, to identify them, and to make friends with them. All this is not done merely as text book learning. Once we begin to recognise and make friends with the living beings abound us, we will no longer be lonely in this world. A love of nature and friendship with things of nature paves the way to identifying oneself with Nature. Here in India, no such effort is made and even in the few places that there is some effort, it degenerates into lengthy lectures. This is one of our failings that immersed in lengthy arguments and debates, we fail to see what is right under our nose.

What is science which has enabled the world to progress so far? It is an understanding of nature and taking advantage of its various forces. What is electricity? People have been seeing lightning for thousands of years and were sometimes struck by it. But they were afraid of it and so they worshipped it. I do not know whether that is good or bad, but I think it is far better to understand something well. An intelligent young man in the United States recognised what electricity is while flying a kite, and harnessed it to man's use. Now within a hundred years, electricity has become a great source of energy in the world. Now we are on the threshold of acquiring atomic energy. All this is merely recognising the hidden mysteries of nature and nurturing them. It is a great thing to be able to befriend nature for then our friends would be legion, surrounded as we are by birds and flowers and stars. Our entire thinking changes, and we will find more friends among human beings too, instead of isolating ourselves, the entire attitude of mind changes. I want that our education should be geared to this. Parents must themselves do this, but then how can they teach their children, when they themselves know so little?

Therefore we must befriend Nature, and one of its greatest symbols is the tree, which must be planted in large numbers and protected and looked after. Protection is a two way affair. If we look after them when they are young, they will look after us for the next hundred years. Therefore it is essential for the progress of the nation to have forests and tree-lined avenues in cities, etc. Trees should be planted wherever it is possible and looked after and cared for properly. The feeling should be fostered that felling trees is a crime.

Today is the thirteeenth Van Mahotsav. If the work is done properly, I think we will get excellent results, instead of treating this entire thing as a formality or routine, and letting the trees die for lack of proper care before the next Van Mahotsav comes around. I hope that the trees, which are being planted today, will be very well looked after, and that they will grow well and strong and be able to serve human beings later.

Jai Hind!

Translation ends]

323. For Amar Nath Seth: Roman or Nagari Script for Indian Languages[184]

Please send a reply in Hindi to the enclosed letter from Shri Amar Nath Seth. Tell him that I do not think it is practical, inspite of some advantages, to have a common Roman script for all our languages. I think an attempt might be made gradually for the Nagari script to be accepted by other languages in India. This is not an easy matter at present. We have been suggesting that Nagari script should be used in addition to the existing scripts so as to make it easier for many people to read books in the other languages in India.

2. This is not a question of simplifying the Nagari script, though that might be attempted where necessary. It is a question of deep psychological and emotional feelings.

324. To Prafulla Chandra Das: Romain Rolland's Biography of Vivekananda[185]

July 10, 1962

Dear Shri Das,

I have received your letter of the 6th July. I am glad to learn that you are bringing out an Oriya translation of Romain Rolland's life of Vivekananda.[186] This book is a notable one and deserves wider publicity in India than it has thus far been given. Your work, therefore, is commendable and I wish it success.[187]

Yours sincerely,
[Jawaharlal Nehru]

184. Note, 4 July 1962, for Kesho Ram, the PPS.
185. Letter to Oriya translator ; address "Mohan Mahal", Chandnichouk, Cuttack-2. Sent from Pahalgam, Kashmir.
186. *The Life of Vivekananda and the Universal Gospel* by Romain Rolland (publisher: Advaita Asrama Mayavati Almora Himalayas, 1931).
187. An Oriya translation of this book by Lakshmi Narayan Mahanty appeared in 1962, see *Indian Literature*, Vol. 6 No. 2, p. 111. It is not clear if this book is being discussed here.

325. To Uday Chandra Naval: Hindi Book on Work Study[188]

July 10, 1962

Dear Professor Uday Chandra Naval,

I have received your letter of July 5th with attached papers. I am glad that you have written a book in Hindi on Work Study.[189] I am unable to find time to read this book but I have glanced through it and it seems to me a very useful work, which ought to do good. I hope many people will read it.

For the last few years I have been much interested in the subject of Work Study. We have been utilising this method in some of our Embassies as well as our Ministries in Delhi and it has produced good results. I am sure that this approach is profitable and, if generally adopted, will produce good results.

Yours sincerely
[Jawaharlal Nehru]

326. To S.N. Sen: Rashtrapati Niwas in Shimla[190]

July 11, 1962

Dear Dr Sen

The President has forwarded to me your letter of the 3rd July. I am afraid at present all I can do is to acknowledge it. The question of the future of Rashtrapati Niwas in Simla is being considered from all points of view. I am forwarding your letter, therefore, to the Cabinet Secretary who is dealing with this matter.

188. Letter ; address: Amritsar Productivity Council, Hall Bazar, Amritsar. Sent from Pahalgam, Kashmir.

189. The following is published on the blurb of another book *Striped Zebra: The Immigrant Psyche* by Uday C. Naval and Soofia K. Hussain (New Delhi: Rupa & Co, 2008): "Dr Uday C. Naval, retired professor of English from the City University of New York, has taught generations of immigrant students from all over the world. Earlier in India, his Hindi book *Kaarya Jaanch Kyoon Aur Kaise* won Prime Minister Nehru's commendation in a personal 'Dear Professor Naval' letter, of July 10, 1962, as the first-ever Asian publication on the management technique of 'work study'. And Professor Naval's earning his Ph.D. at age sixty-five bespeaks his profound dedication to scholarship. Author of numerous articles on literature, art criticism, aesthetic theory and linguists, he was also a regular broadcaster from All India Radio before settling in the USA in 1970."

190. Letter; address: P404/5 Gariahat Road Calcutta-19. Sent from Chashmashahi Guest House, Srinagar.

He will subsequently present a report of his recommendations to us for the consideration of the President.[191]

If you so wish, you can send some details of your proposal. But please leave me out of the picture. It will be very undesirable for my name to be associated with it.

Yours sincerely,
[Jawaharlal Nehru]

327. To Lal Bahadur Shastri: Loss of Wild Life in Indore[192]

July 13, 1962

My dear Lal Bahadur,
Someone told me today that Usha Raje of Indore[193] has been very lavish in opening out her game preserves for shooting. Large numbers of Americans and others are going there and putting an end to our wild life. I think it would be desirable for you to have a letter sent to her from the Home Ministry expressing our concern at this.

Yours affectionately,
[Jawaharlal Nehru]

328. To Atulananda Chakrabarti: Symposium on India since 1947[194]

July 14, 1962

Dear Chakrabarti,
I have your letter of the 12th July. I am sorry I could not see you in Delhi as I was only there for one busy day, the 13th of July. I have now come to Bangalore not to return till the 20th.

191. See earlier items 310-311, 316.
192. Letter to the Home Minister.
193. Usha Devi Raje Holkar, Maharani of Indore, succeeded Yeshwantrao II Holkar, on 5 December 1961 and formally recognised by the President of India on 2 May 1962.
194. Letter ; address: Bangabhavan, 3 Hailey Road, New Delhi. Sent from Royal Cottage, Bangalore.

Your idea of having an international symposium on India since 1947 is an interesting one, and to some extent it appeals to me. But the subject is a vast one and has innumerable facets. I rather doubt if all these aspects can be dealt with in one symposium. Who will attend it? If the purely cultural side is stressed, then there will be one type of persons; if the Planning side or the scientific and technical side, then there will be a completely different type of persons.

It is thus not clear to me that the ultimate shape of this might be and how it can help here.[195]

Yours sincerely,
[Jawaharlal Nehru]

329. To Narsingh Narain: Humanist Ideas should Spread[196]

July 15, 1962

Dear Shri Narsingh Narain

I have your letter of July 12 and have read it as well as its enclosures with interest. Whether I am a perfect type of humanist I doubt very much, but I certainly sympathise greatly with the broad humanist position, and wish that its ideas may spread.

I may be in Delhi on the 30th and 31st of this month. I shall probably return to Delhi on the 30th forenoon. If you wish to see me just before you leave for Oslo, I shall try to fix some time for it, if that is possible.

Yours sincerely,
[Jawaharlal Nehru]

195. Atulananda Chakrabarti ed., (n.p. : India Since 1947 (An International Symposium), 1967).

196. Letter to the Honorary Secretary of the Humanist Union, New Blyth Cottage, Nainital, Uttar Pradesh. Sent from Nandi Hills.

330. To Gurmukh Nihal Singh: Send Book to Sahitya Akademi[197]

July 15, 1962

My dear Sardar Gurmukh Nihal Singh,

Thank you for your letter of the 11th July. It is very good of you to express your sentiments about me in such a kind manner. We were all very happy with your tenure as Governor of Rajasthan, and I should like to express my high appreciation of it.

You need not worry about my health. I am fairly well, and practically normal in my health. I am at present here at Nandi Hills for two days.

About your book, I would suggest that you might send it to the Secretary of the Sahitya Akademi, Shri Krishna Kripalani. He will have to place it before the Council of the Akademi.

Yours sincerely,
[Jawaharlal Nehru]

331. To Gopal Singh: Publishing Journal[198]

July 15, 1962

Dear Dr Gopal Singh,

I have your letter of July 13. I think it will be a good thing if you could issue a quarterly journal of high class. But I am afraid I cannot undertake to write articles for it. I find it exceedingly difficult to find time for articles, and I have not written any for a long time. But I send you my good wishes for it, and I am sure that it will do good.

Yours sincerely,
[Jawaharlal Nehru]

197. Letter to the former Governor of Rajasthan; address: D 312, Defence Colony, New Delhi 3. Sent from Nandi Hills.

198. Letter to Nominated Rajya Sabha MP; address: 62 South Avenue, New Delhi. Sent from Royal Cottage, Bangalore.

332. To Harry W. Laidler: Upton Sinclair and Nobel Prize[199]

July 16, 1962

Dear Mr Laidler,[200]

Thank you for your letter of July 3. I have been an admirer of Upton Sinclair[201] as a man and as a writer for many years. I think he deserves the highest prizes for his work.

But it has been our practice not to make any recommendations for the award of the Nobel Prize. During the past years we were asked on many occasions to make such recommendations, but we refrained from doing so. I hope you will appreciate our difficulty.

I would, of course, be happy if Upton Sinclair is chosen for the award.

Yours sincerely,
[Jawaharlal Nehru]

333. For E.N. Mangat Rai: Allow Children to Meet Nehru[202]

July 18, 1962

My dear Mangat Rai,

During the Prime Minister's visit to Amritsar in January last,[203] he was presented a petition by the Secretary, Civil Aerodrome, Amritsar, complaining that the families and children of Airport staff were denied permission to go to the Aerodrome for paying respects to the Prime Minister. As the complaint made pertained to Amritsar Aerodrome which is controlled by the Directorate-General of Civil Aviation, it was referred to the Secretary, Department of Communications, Ministry of Transport & Communications, and he has in reply intimated that the Aerodrome Officer, Amritsar made endeavours to get this permission for the families and the children of the Airport staff but the police authorities in charge of the security arrangements at the Aerodrome did

199. Letter; address: 292 Garfield Place, Brooklyn 15, New York. Sent from Nandi Hills, Mysore State.

200. American economist and author, (d. 1970).

201. American novelist.

202. Letter to the Chief Secretary, Government of Punjab, Chandigrah, from Nehru's PPS. PMS, File No. 8(211)62-PMP.

203. See SWJN/SS/74/item 78.

not agree. Thereupon the Secretary of the Civil Aviation Employees' Union approached Shri Surjit Singh Majithia, the then Deputy Defence Minister and he asked the Deputy Inspector General of Police to allow the children of the Airport Colony to meet the Prime Minister but as there was very little time left for his arrival, nothing further could be done. He has in this connection further mentioned that the Aerodrome authorities have no jurisdiction to interfere in the security arrangements made by the police on such occasions. The Prime Minister desires that the attention of the Punjab Government should be drawn to this matter and they should be asked to ensure that children are allowed to see him on such occasions.

Yours sincerely,
K. Ram

334. To Prataprai G. Mehta: Children's Encyclopedia[204]

Undated
[19 July 1962][205]

Dear Shri Prataprai,[206]
I was happy to meet you at Nandi Hills and to listen to your enthusiastic talk about the children's museum and the children's encyclopedia. I am greatly interested in your ideas. I do not quite know how you expect me to help you. If you will indicate this, I shall try to do so within the limits of my capacity.

I am returning to Delhi tomorrow.

Yours sincerely,
Jawaharlal Nehru

204. Letter ; address: 112, 4th Cross Road, Gandhi Nagar, Bangalore 9. PMS, File No. 8(226)62-PMP.
205. It should be 19 July 1962, from Hyderabad, since Nehru says he is returning to Delhi the next day, and he returned on 20 July.
206. One of the pioneers of museum activities in India, President of All India Children's Museum Association, see *Gujarat State Gazetters*, (Ahmedabad: Amreli District, 1972), p. 555-556; founder of Shri Girdharibhai Children's Museum in 1955 in Amreli, Gujarat, see *Directory of Museums in India*, (New Delhi: Ministry of Scientific Research and Cultural Affairs, 1959), p. 22.

(g) Sports

335. For Major John D. Dias: Spirited Attempt at Everest[207]

I send you my congratulations and high appreciation at the courageous way in which the summit team and, indeed, your whole party fought against tremendous odds and bad weather to reach the summit of the Everest. In view of the great difficulties encountered by your party, your achievement was remarkable.[208] We naturally are disappointed that all this did not lead to final success. But your gallant attempt is in itself a great success and significant in the annals of mountaineering. Please covey my congratulations and good wishes to all members of your team.[209]

336. For the Olympic Team[210]

I send my good wishes to the Indian Olympic Team which is going to the Fourth Asian Games to be held at Djakarta. I hope they will do well at these games and increase the standard of games and athletics in India. Above all, I hope that they will play their games in the spirit of the game. It is more important that we maintain this spirit and high standards than merely aiming at success.

207. Message, 2 June 1962, for Major John D. Dias. PMO, File No. 40(202)/60-74-PMS, Sr. No. 43-A.
208. For a team member's account of the expedition, see Suman Dubey's "Everest; 1962" in *The Himalayan Journal*, Vol. 24, 1963. For the web version, see https://www.himalayanclub.org/hj/24/4/everest-1962/ accessed on 30 November 2017. See also M.S. Kohli's *Miracles of Ardaas: Incredible Adventures and Survivals* (New Delhi: Indus Publishing Company, 2003) pp. 84-89.
209. Nehru had met the team in Delhi before they left for the expedition, see SWJN/SS/75/item 15 fn 41.
210. Message, 15 July 1962, sent from Nandi Hills, Mysore State.

(h) Welfare

337. To Ramnarayan Chaudhary: Gram Sahyog Samaj[211]

जून 10, 1962

प्रिय रामनारायणजी,
आपका पत्र मुझे कुछ दिन हुए मिला था। मैं आपसे नाराज़ नहीं हूं। मालूम नहीं क्यों आप ऐसा समझते हैं। लेकिन यह सही है कि मैंने मुख्य मंत्रियों से ग्राम सहयोग समाज के बारे में नहीं कहा। मुझे इस तरह की सिफारिश करना एक संस्था के लिए कुछ अच्छा नहीं लगता। कोई मुझ से पूछे तो मैं अपनी राय दे दूंगा।

आपका
[जवाहरलाल नेहरु]

[Translation begins:

Dear Ramnarayanji,
I received your letter a few days back. I am not angry with you. I do not know why you think so. But it is true that I have not spoken to the Chief Ministers about Gram Sahyog Samaj. I do not consider it proper to endorse an institution. If someone enquires about it, I will give my opinion.

Yours sincerely,
Jawaharlal Nehru

Translation ends]

338. To Sudhavati Narayan: Help for Chikitsalaya[212]

June 26, 1962

My dear Sudhavati,
I got your letter of the 13th June some days ago.[213] I am glad that you got some help in Maharashtra for your Chikitasalaya.[214]

211. Letter to the founder of Akhil Bharatiya Gram Sahyog Samaj; address: Lakshman Bagh, Faridabad.
212. Letter to the daughter of Sri Prakasa, former Governor of Maharashtra. PMO, File No. 8/217/62-PMP.
213. Appendix 32. Nehru's letter item 338 refers to her letter of 13 June; but her letter, appendix 32 has the date 12 June.
214. Tapovardhan Prakritik Chikitsa Kendra, Bhagalpur.

I am keeping very well. I hope that the Chikitsalaya is flourishing.[215]

Yours affectionately,
Jawaharlal Nehru

339. In New Delhi: To the Missionaries of Charity[216]

Mother Teresa,[217] Your Excellency[218] and friends,
When I was invited a little while ago to come to this function,[219] I gladly and if I may say so, unhesitatingly accepted because I knew something, not very much but something, of the excellent work that has been done in Calcutta, in Bengal and here by Mother Teresa and her colleagues. And I wanted to show, I am interested of course in children, but apart from that I wanted to show my high appreciation of the love in service that had gone into this work. And so, I am here, not only because it is a function, because it is a work that is worthwhile, but it is made doubly worthwhile by the love and service that lies behind it and of which Mother Teresa is a living example and I have no doubt her many colleagues will work with her. So when the Swiss Ambassador said that is embarrassing to Mother Teresa who is vowed to humility to hear too much about her, I don't say much, therefore; but this kind of work is in many ways uplifting work for others, those who work have their reward in the work, those who see that work are themselves lifted up a little by these examples of this type of work. So all of us are lifted up somewhat by it and of course the children who are looked after, benefit from it. So I thank you Mother Teresa and your Missionaries of Charity who are doing this good work here and elsewhere. [Applause]

215. See an earlier letter and message in SWJN/SS/76/items 401 and 402.
216. Speech, 3 July 1962, at the Nirmala Shishu Bhavan. NMML, AIR Tapes, TS No. 8719, NM No. 1702.
217. Founder of the Order of the Missionaries of Charity.
218. Jacques Albert Cuttat, the Swiss Ambassador.
219. Nehru opened the Nirmala Shishu Bhawan, a home for crippled and unwanted children, run by the Missionaries of Charity, in Commissioner Lane in Delhi. The home, gifted by "Swiss Aid Abroad", a charitable institution, was built at a cost of Rs 125, 000. See *The Statesman*, 4 July 1962, p. 5 cols 3 and 4.

340. To Durgabai Deshmukh: Fixing Appointment[220]

July 9, 1962

My dear Durgabai,

I have just received your letter of the 7th July. I shall, of course, gladly meet you but it is difficult to find time immediately after my return. I am returning to Delhi on the 12th midday and leaving again on the 14th morning. The 12th and 13th are all full up for me with Cabinet and other Committee meetings. Perhaps 1 could see you for a few minutes in the afternoon of the 13th.

Yours sincerely,
Jawaharlal Nehru

(i) Urban Development

341. To Mehr Chand Khanna: Rents and Housing in Delhi[221]

June 10, 1962

My dear Mehr Chand,

It has become a perfect scandal as to how people who have built houses here let them out at exorbitant rents. For a relatively small house, rents of five thousand rupees a month are charged and for big houses rupees ten thousand a month. This is perfectly scandalous. Some of our officers have built houses and are charging these exorbitant rents.

Can we not do something about it and have some control over these rents? Some of the diplomatic personnel of the small foreign missions are very hard hit and complain bitterly to us.

Apart from the question of rent control, which should be looked into, I think Government should build some houses, or better still some apartments or flats. The old style houses with compounds are becoming less and less feasible in Delhi. If we could put up a building, which would contain a number of large flats, this would be welcomed greatly. In fact, many of our officers would like it too. It would be an investment because adequate rent can be charged on it.

220. Letter to the Chairman of the Central Social Welfare Board, New Delhi. NMML, Durgabai Deshmukh Papers (Minor Collections) Acc. No. 87. Sent from Pahalgam, Kashmir.

221. Letter to the Minister of Works, Housing and Supply.

The apartments should be quite up-to-date and naturally with air-conditioning, etc. It is much easier in a flat than in a house.

Yours sincerely,
Jawaharlal Nehru

342. Defence Headquarters Near Central Vista[222]

There is apparently some confusion about this matter. The Cabinet definitely wanted an independent opinion of the Town Planning Authority in regard to the proposals made. It appears that the Town Planning Authority was told that the Cabinet had already made the decision and hence they could not go into it.

2. I think that the matter should be referred to the Town Planning Authority for their opinion about the complex roundabout Central Vista. Their first proposal about this complex, which involved some very high structures was not approved by the Cabinet.

3. Prima facie, I do not like the idea that a building similar to Parliament building should be built behind the South Block of the Secretariat. The Parliament building should remain unique and should not be duplicated. If the Defence building is to be erected there, it should be of a different design and should not overshadow the Parliament building in any way.

4. Anyway I should like the Town Planning Authority to consider this matter fully and to give us their frank and independent opinion. The matter may have to be considered afresh by the Cabinet.

343. To Mehr Chand Khanna: Delhi Rents[223]

June 10, 1962

My dear Mehr Chand,

I wrote to you only today about the fantastic rents that are being charged for houses in New Delhi. Since writing, I have received a note from our Secretary-General R.K. Nehru. I am sending you a copy of this note. That does not mean that I agree with every one of his proposals. But I feel strongly that something has to be done to put an end to this scandal.[224]

222. Note, 10 June 1962, for Kesho Ram, the PPS.
223. Letter to the Minister of Works, Housing and Supply.
224. For R.K. Nehru's note, see appendix 24.

Apart from other aspects of this question, I think there should be a taxation on land values so that people who keep land vacant for speculative purposes should have to pay heavily for it.

Yours sincerely,
[Jawaharlal Nehru]

344. To Lal Bahadur Shastri: Rents and Housing in Delhi[225]

June 10, 1962

My dear Lal Bahadur,

It has become a scandal and a racket in New Delhi to possess land and houses. Speculators control the situation and very heavy rents are charged. Sometimes these houses in New Delhi are rented out for as much as Rs 5000/- to Rs 10,000/- a month. We have constantly to face this problem with foreign diplomats who are very hard hit, quite apart from our own officers. Some of our officers who were fortunate enough to put up buildings are charging heavy rents.

I think something must be done about this and that urgently. Why should there not be rent control and why should speculators keep their land vacant. I think we should have a tax on land values so that it is not worthwhile for anyone to keep his land not built upon.

Our Secretary-General R.K. Nehru has sent me a note. I do not agree with all that he has said in this note. But I thought it might interest you to read it, so I enclose a copy.[226]

I have written on this subject to Mehr Chand Khanna[227] and to Chief Commissioner Bhagwan Sahay also.

Yours affectionately,
[Jawaharlal Nehru]

225. Letter to the Home Minister.
226. Appendix 24.
227. Item 341.

345. To Bhagwan Sahay: Land Speculation in Delhi[228]

June 10, 1962

My dear Bhagwan Sahay,

I wrote to you this morning about the fantastic position in New Delhi about houses and the extraordinary rents charged for them. I have now received a note from our Secretary-General R.K. Nehru in which he makes various suggestions.[229] I do not agree with every one of his suggestions. But I do feel that something has got to be done about this matter. It is a terrible racket and some people are making a lot of money while others suffer and we get a bad name.

I have long been in favour of taxation on land values. Apart from other steps that might be taken, could not such tax be introduced in Delhi to prevent speculators keeping vacant pieces of land?

Yours sincerely,
[Jawaharlal Nehru]

346. To Hafiz Mohammed Ibrahim: Najafgarh Drain[230]

July 16, 1962

My dear Hafizji,

I have your letter of the 15th July, with a note on the progress of work done on the Najafgarh Drain. Thank you for sending me the note.

As far as I understand, phase I has been completed, and phase II is also on the way to completion. It is phase III that will take much more time. In all such work, the rapidity with which it is done not only is economical in the end, but otherwise beneficial also.

I do not know what you would like me to do in this matter. I should be glad to help.

Yours sincerely,
[Jawaharlal Nehru]

228. Letter to the Chief Commissioner of Delhi. A similar letter, dated 10 June 1962, was sent to Mehr Chand Khanna, the Minister of Works, Housing and Supply. This letter was sent after item 341.

229. Appendix 24.

230. Letter to the Minister of Irrigation and Power. Sent from Nandi Hills, Mysore State.

347. To C.B. Gupta: Cars in Nainital and Mussoorie[231]

July 16, 1962

My dear Chandra Bhanu,

I enclose a cutting from the *Statesman* newspaper. This is about the use of motor cars in Mussoorie and Naini Tal.

I remember some years ago my taking strong exception to cars being allowed to move about freely in Naini Tal. Later I felt the same in Mussoorie. I do feel that, apart from the occasional danger to foot traffic involved, this rather spoils the attractions of Naini Tal and Mussoorie for the average person going there. A car does not really fit in. Also I do not see why diplomats should have free run of the places in cars.

Perhaps it may be a little difficult to put an end completely to the use of cars in these two places. But I think that it might be possible to restrict their use very greatly to certain roads and certain times. Thus, in Naini Tal, I think they might well be restricted to the Mall Road. In Mussoorie they might probably be allowed to go towards Happy Valley and Camel's Back, although I feel they would rather spoil the Camel's Back for pedestrians. On no account should cars be allowed to go up Kulri in Mussoorie and near about.

But this is a matter for examination. On principle it is a bad thing for Ministers or even a Governor to have special privileges of this kind. If it is not possible to permit everyone to use a car there and it is obviously not possible, then Ministers and Governors should also do without them. I used to go to Mussoorie frequently in past years I never felt the need of a car. I rode on horseback usually or walked.

Yours sincerely,
[Jawaharlal Nehru]

231. Letter to the Chief Minister of Uttar Pradesh. Sent from Nandi Hills, Mysore State.

(j) Science

348. To Humayun Kabir: An Academy of Sciences for India[232]

June 1, 1962

My dear Humayun,

Your letter of May 27th[233] about building up a scientific society in India on the lines of the Royal Society in London or the Soviet Academy.[234] It would certainly be desirable to have some such organisation here, but I rather doubt if you can evolve such a society through a conference. I imagine that there will be no agreement at the conference, however limited the conference might be.

I think that an attempt should be made, to begin with, to get a dozen or so topmost scientists in India to agree to something. The approach should be informal to begin with. Once they agree to this, it would be easier to proceed more formally. The idea is that the new organisation should be definitely a very select one, membership of which should be considered a privilege and an honour.

I discussed this matter some time ago with Mahalanobis,[235] Bhabha[236] and probably Kothari[237] and Thacker[238] also. I think it will be advisable to proceed rather cautiously and informally in this matter and later to think of a conference. I do not myself see how a conference can yield results.

Yours sincerely,
J. Nehru

232. Letter to the Minister for Scientific Research and Cultural Affairs.PMO, File No. 17(504)/62-66-PMS, Sr. No. 2-A. Also available in the NMML, Humayun Kabir Papers, F. No. 5/1958-62 Auto.
233. See appendix 6.
234. USSR Academy of Sciences.
235. P.C. Mahalanobis, Honorary Statistical Adviser to the Cabinet, and Director, Indian Statistical Institute, Calcutta.
236. H.J. Bhabha, Secretary in the Department of Atomic Energy.
237. D.S. Kothari, Chairman of the UGC.
238. M.S. Thacker, Director-General, CSIR.

349. To Humayun Kabir: Meeting of Directors of the National Laboratories[239]

July 13, 1962

My dear Humayun,
Your letter of the 13th July about the meeting of Directors of the National Laboratories at Hyderabad. I shall be glad to meet the Directors if I have the chance. But it is difficult for me to say where I shall be in November or December. Probably in December I shall be in Delhi. But it would hardly be worthwhile to convene a special meeting just for me to meet them.

Yours sincerely,
Jawaharlal Nehru

350. International Equatorial Sounding Rocket Launching Facility[240]

Ministry of External Affairs
(Disarmament Unit)

Subject: Proposal to set up an International Equatorial Sounding Rocket Launching Facility in India

[Note, 3 July 1962, by Deputy Secretary, MEA, to FS begins]

Spoken to FS

2. The previous letter referred to by Dr Bhabha in F.R. has been submitted to the Defence Minister directly by the Secretary-General.[241] It deals with Project Transit, the American proposal for establishing a satellite tracking station in India and the new proposal for an International Equatorial Sounding Rocket Launching Facility is mentioned only incidentally in it. The present papers are self-contained in so far as this new Project is concerned.

239. Letter to the Minister of Scientific Research and Cultural Affairs. PMO, File No. 17(213)/56-64-PMS, Sr. No. 10-A. Also available in NMML, H. Kabir Papers, File No. 5/1958-62 "Auto".
240. Noting, 3-13 July 1962, for the M. J. Desai, the FS, and V. K. Krishna Menon, the Defence Minister. MEA, File No. E (405)/DISARM/1962, pp. 1-3/Note. Nehru's Note of 13 July is also available in JN Collection.
241. R.K. Nehru.

3. Two sub-committees of the UN Committee on the Peaceful Uses of Outer Space met last month in Geneva, one to consider the scientific and technical problems and the other the legal problems involved. The Legal Sub-Committee broke up without being able to agree even on a formal report to the UN Committee, but the Scientific Sub-Committee agreed on certain measures of cooperation which are listed in Annexure 'A' to Dr Bhabha's Note forwarded with F.R. The establishment of the International Equatorial Sounding Rocket Launching Facility is one of these agreed items. We do not know whether it was approved unanimously or by a division of votes but in para 6 of his note Dr Bhabha explained that the establishment of this rocket facility in India aroused the active interest not only of the Western Powers but of the USSR, which should thus free the proposal from any cold-war controversy. The facility would also obtain UN sponsorship if it complies with a set of principles approved at the Geneva meeting and listed in para 34 of Annexure 'A'.

These would require the facility to be

(a) used for peaceful for peaceful Scientific experiment only, the results of the experiments being made available openly to all;
(b) available for use by other States through direct agreements, inter alia, covering the supply of funds or equipment;
(c) open for inspection of its facilities by scientists and technicians of all participating States; and
(d) managed and operated by the host State, who would, however, have to reports periodically on the operations and use of the facilities to the UN Committee on Outer Space, and would have an Advisory Panel of scientific representatives of user States to advise on the implementation of the projects that may be proposed.

4. For the Indian facility, the Department of Atomic Energy propose obtaining assistance from the USA, France, UK and USSR. The Department was already negotiating an agreement with the United States National Aeronautic & Space Administration for the establishment of such a facility on a bilateral basis, and now propose to conclude that a agreement and begin negotiations with the other three countries for other types of assistance.

5. This proposal has already been submitted by the Department of Atomic Energy directly to the Prime Minister, who has agreed to it. Dr Bhabha now wants us to inform the UN that we agree to be a host State. He has also suggested in the earlier letter which is under submission to the Defence Minister that we explain our decision on the launching facility to the USSR and use the occasion to explain also our agreement to the more controversial Project Transit and our desire to cooperate with the USSR in that field. Before we speak to the Russians,

however, we have to obtain a final decision on Project Transit (of linked files below). FS may also care to submit the present case to Defence Minister before we take any action to inform the UN.

(K.S. Bajpai)
3.7.62
Deputy Secretary

FS

[Note, 3 July 1962, by Deputy Secretary, MEA, to FS ends]

M.J. Desai
4.7.62
[Signed and marked to the Defence Minister]

Defence Minister

[Note, undated, by the Defence Minister to FS, begins]

I regret I do not agree to our becoming involved in this matter except through the UN and with both the US and USSR cooperating with us on equal terms. I have mentioned this matter to the PM. Since then I have discussed this with the Scientific Adviser who has also stated his views. It may be placed on record that the Defence Minister and the Ministry were never consulted or even informed. In fact it will be seen in the note of the SG that he has mentioned other Ministries as concerned Ministries but not Defence.

It is my considered view that both politically and militarily it is unwise and undesirable to enter into collaboration with the US on this matter.

I know I will be referred to 'A' on reverse. It leaves me unconvinced. I cannot agree in any circumstances to the US setting up or participating in the setting up of launching sites in India on their initiative and without the UN and the USSR. I think this is a dangerous step and contrary to our professed view and should not be pursued.

Itd. K.M.

[Note, undated, by the Defence Minister to FS, ends]

Recd on 12/7 [Noted and initialled by M.J. Desai in the margin]

M.J. Desai
12.7.62
[Signed and marked to the Prime Minister]

PM

[Note, 13 July 1962, by Prime Minister to FS and the Defence Minister, begins]

I have not wholly understood where the difference of opinion lies in this matter. This is a UN Project and it is stated that the US, the USSR, UK and France are cooperating in it. If that is so, then there can be no objection or difficulty in our joining it. It was on this basis that I said that I agreed with the Project.

2. The only thing I should like to point out is that it would not be right for us to conclude a bilateral agreement with the NASA of USA to begin with and before we have had our negotiations with the Governments of France, UK, and the USSR. All these negotiations should go together. It should always be understood that we are accepting this Project for India because it is a UN Project and the USA, the USSR, UK and France are cooperating in it and will be prepared to give facilities.

3. Defence Minister refers to his Ministry not being consulted. I am unable to find SG's note to which he refers. At the time this matter came up before me, the Defence Minister was away from India.

4. Our Permanent Representative at UN[242] might be informed of this and he may make use of such information as he thinks necessary. It should be made clear to him that it is on the basis of the Project being a UN one with the cooperation of the Principal Powers that we are prepared to go on with it.

(J. Nehru)
13.7.62

[Note, 13 July 1962, by Prime Minister to FS and the Defence Minister, ends]

FS
Defence Minister

242. C.S. Jha.

351. To Humayun Kabir: Finding a Director-General of the CSIR[243]

July 15 1962

My dear Humayun,

Your letter of 14th July.[244] I agree that a small committee, as suggested by you, might be appointed to suggest two or three names for appointment as Director-General of the CSIR.

I saw Prof. Thacker yesterday and told him about his being invited to join the Planning Commission.[245] He said that while he would welcome this, his sudden departure from the CSIR might create some difficulties. I told him that there was no need for him to cut himself off from the CSIR. He could well remain a member of it, and for some time possibly a small informal committee may be formed to help the new Director-General.

Yours sincerely,
[Jawaharlal Nehru]

243. Letter to the Minister of Scientific Research and Cultural Affairs. Sent from Royal Cottage, Bangalore. NMML, Humayun Kabir Papers, File No. 5/1958-62. Also available in the JN Collection.
244. Appendix 63.
245. See item 105.

V. EXTERNAL AFFAIRS

(a) Disarmament

352. In the Lok Sabha: Disarmament Conference[1]

P.C. Borooah:[2] Will the Prime Minister be pleased to state:

(a) whether India has recently suggested a plan for an International Disarmament Treaty at a meeting of the 17-Power Disarmament Conference;
(b) if so, the broad outlines of the plan; and
(c) the reaction of the Conference thereto?

The Prime Minister and Minister of External Affairs and Minister of Atomic Energy (Jawaharlal Nehru): (a) to (c). Draft programmes covering the different stages of complete and general disarmament have so far been submitted to the 18-Nation Disarmament Committee[3] only by the Delegates of the Soviet Union and the United States of America. Other delegates have in the course of discussion put forward ideas or proposals designed to assist in achieving an agreed disarmament treaty and Indian representatives have also made such suggestions, both procedural and substantive, which have proved helpful. They have not, however, proposed any draft of International Disarmament Treaty.[4]

1. Written Answers, 6 June 1962. *Lok Sabha Debates*, Third Series, Vol. IV, May 26 to June 7, 1962, cols 9145-9146.
2. Congress.
3. Meeting of the Eighteen-Nation Committee on Disarmament Committee started in Geneva on 14 March 1962 but France did not participate.
4. For verbatim record of the Conference of the Eighteen-Nation Committee on Disarmament (United Nations), see the UN website https://quod.lib.umich.edu/e/endc/4918260.0001.001?view=toc, accessed on 5 July 2018.

353. Sharp Exchanges in Geneva[5]

[Note, 17 June 1962, by M.J. Desai, the FS, for Nehru, begins]

Please see World Press Review No. 5896 of 11th June.[6]

2. I have gone through the record. There were rather sharp exchanges between Godber[7] and Lall.[8] Lall did mention A (page 2) though this was partly to illustrate his point. He could have been more tactful and could have avoided the temptation to score a point.

M.J. Desai
17-6-1962

PM

[Note, 17 June 1962, by M.J. Desai, for Nehru, ends]

[Note, 17 June 1962, by Nehru for M.J. Desai, the FS, MEA, begins]

Mr Duncan Sandys[9] referred to the part Mr Lall had played at the Disarmament Conference in Geneva and said that he had been patently supporting the Russian case and had not been impartial or helpful. He gave an instance, that on one occasion Mr Arthur Lall supported the Russian viewpoint even when later the Americans and the Russian came to an agreement on the American basis.

I do not know what the exact point was unless it was the one referred to in the attached *Daily Telegraph* report.

I think you might inform Mr Arthur Lall of this and especially say that we are not there to make points in argument but to help in creating an atmosphere

5. Noting, 17 June 1962. MEA, File No. B (104)-DISARM/62 Vol-II, p.18/ note. Nehru's note also available in JN Collection.
6. See appendix 28.
7. Joseph B. Godber, British Minister of State for Foreign Affairs and Chairman of the British Delegation to the Eighteen-Nation Disarmament Committee.
8. Arthur S. Lall, member of Indian delegation to the Disarmament Conference, March 1962-August 1963, and Ambassador to Austria.
9. British Secretary of State for Commonwealth Relations.

of agreement. It is desirable not to create an impression that we are siding with any party.

J. Nehru
17-6-1962

FS

[Note, 17 June 1962, by Nehru for M.J. Desai, ends]

I have written to Shri Arthur Lall.

M.J. Desai
18-6-62

354. To Henry H. Oelbaum: Only General Disarmament Meaningful[10]

June 23, 1962

Dear Mr Oelbaum,

I thank you for your letter of June 18th which I have read with much interest. To some extent I agree with you. But you will no doubt realise that, in a democratic country, no leader can impose his will if this is entirely against the wishes of the people. I am afraid it is beyond my capacity to disarm my country completely when it is threatened both by Pakistan and China. Very few people out of millions of this country will agree to it.

But I agree with you that we must do everything in our power to bring about general and complete disarmament all over the world.

Yours sincerely,
[Jawaharlal Nehru]

10. Letter; address: American Fuel Company, 215 East 149th Street, New York 51, NY.

355. To Albert Schweitzer: Danger of Nuclear Warfare[11]

June 24, 1962

Dear Dr Schweitzer,

Thank you for your letter of June 1962. I shall gladly meet your Alsatian[12] compatriot, Mr Jean Marc Meyer when he comes to Delhi. I hope you will let me know in good time.

I have read your letter with great interest. You know how I admire the good work you have been doing in Africa,[13] as also your work for peace. I do believe that the most important thing in the world today is this quest for peace and peace cannot come by some artificial arrangement but, as you say, by development of the human spirit. We have arrived at a crisis in human destiny and the decision that is taken will govern our entire future, if there is a future left for humanity. The spirit of power dominates most thinking today and that spirit has led us to nuclear bombs.

I believe, however, that there is an increasing realisation of the dangers that come from nuclear warfare. But I fear that only a limited number of people think of a basic change in our thinking so that the power of the human spirit may prevail. Yet, at the back of my mind, I believe that it will prevail.

With all good wishes to you and in admiration for your work, I am,

Sincerely yours,
J. Nehru

356. For Kaoru Yasui: Conference against Atomic and Hydrogen Bombs[14]

The modern world is supposed to be based on science and logic. Yet the most extraordinary thing about this world today is the continuance of the arms race and more especially the oiling up of nuclear and thermonuclear bombs when it is admitted all round that a nuclear war might well mean the extinction of humanity. When there may be no victory in such a war and the result will be

11. Letter to the philosopher ; address: Lambaréné, Gabon, West Equatorial Africa.
12. "alsacien" in original.
13. Schweitzer had set up a hospital at Lambaréné in 1913.
14. Message, 12 July 1962, for Kaoru Yasui, Chairman of the Japan Council against Atomic and Hydrogen Bombs. PMO, File No. 9/2/62-PMP, Vol. V, Sr. No. 13-A. Also available in the JN Collection.

defeat and disaster for all, it is amazing that great countries should continue to prepare for it. This is not a scientific approach nor is it a question of logic.

I hope, however, that people all over the world and their Governments will increasingly realise that the only way to save humanity is to put an end to war itself. We cannot limit the war to conventional weapons. Once a country fights for its life it will surely have recourse to nuclear weapons. It is war itself that should be ended and thus create a world where nuclear and like weapons cannot be used.

I send my good wishes to the conference that is being held in Tokyo.[15]

(b) Anti-Nuclear Arms Convention

357. To M.C. Davar: Anti-Nuclear Conference[16]

June 2, 1962

My dear Dr Davar,

Your letter of June 2nd.

The persons invited to the anti-nuclear conference,[17] have been invited because of their particular connection with this business and not because they are men of goodwill or nationalists. The choice has been made by a committee and I am afraid I am unable to add to it. It was decided that very few persons should be invited from outside India.

Yours sincerely,
Jawaharlal Nehru

15. See appendix 52.
16. Letter to a homeopath and Congressman; address: 32 B Block, Connaught Place, New Delhi. NMML, M.C. Davar Papers.
17. The three-day Anti-Nuclear Arms Convention, held in New Delhi (16-18 June 1962) under the auspices of Gandhi Peace Foundation, was attended by about 100 delegates including foreign delegates. Inaugurated by Rajendra Prasad, the first session was also attended by Nehru and addressed by S. Radhakrishnan and C. Rajagopalchari. See the *Amrita Bazar Patrika*, 17 June 1962, p.1 col. 1, and *National Herald*, 17 June 1962, p. 1 cols 6 & 7. For Nehru's address to the session, see item 360.

358. To C. Rajagopalachari: Anti-Nuclear Conference[18]

June 7, 1962

My dear Rajaji,

As you know, the Gandhi Peace Foundation has decided to convene an Anti-Nuclear Arms Conference on the 16th of this month. I agreed with this proposal even though I was not quite sure what the Conference could do about it. I felt that even holding such a conference would have some good effect.

I hope you will attend this Conference. Your presence will certainly be very helpful.

The proposal to send a ship is no longer feasible. A ship going from India would take many weeks to reach that place. Apart from this, it is now proposed to have a nuclear test in the upper atmosphere. Nobody can reach there to lodge a protest.

I do hope you will be able to come here for this Conference.[19]

Yours affectionately,
Jawaharlal Nehru

359. In the Lok Sabha: China Delegates to Anti-Nuclear Conference[20]

Hem Barua (Gauhati):[21] Sir, under rule 197, I call the attention of the Prime Minister to the following matter of urgent public importance and I request that he may make a statement thereon:

"The invitation accorded to People's Republic of China to send delegates to the proposed Anti-nuclear bomb Convention at Delhi."

The Prime Minister and Minister of External Affairs and Minister of Atomic Energy (Jawaharlal Nehru): Sir, I find after enquiry that an invitation has been sent on behalf of the Gandhi Peace Foundation not to the people of the Republic of China but to a gentleman Mr Ko-Mu Jo. The Gandhi Peace Foundation is a

18. Letter to leader of the Swatantra Party. A copy was sent to G. Ramachandran, Secretary of the Gandhi Peace Foundation, Rajghat, New Delhi.
19. See also SWJN/SS/76/items 406-422.
20. Calling Attention, 8 June 1962. *Lok Sabha Debates*, Third Series, Vol. V, 8 June to 22 June 1962, Ist Session, cols 9728-9729.
21. PSP.

non-official private organisation not connected with Government, except that some government people are also members of it. They decided to hold an Anti-Nuclear Arms Convention in the middle of this month and they appointed a sub-committee to send invitations. It is a limited convention. I think it is limited to one hundred persons from India, and, maybe, about 15 or 20 persons might come from abroad. They have appointed a sub-committee to make a list of persons to be invited and, I presume, that the name of this gentleman, Mr Ko-Mu Ju was included in the list of people to be invited by that sub-committee. That is all I know of. I heard of this very lately and later from newspaper reports. I do not know anything more.

Hem Barua: May I put a supplementary question? In view of our strained relations with China and in view of the experience that we have gained from the behaviour of the Chinese Delegation to the World Peace Conference at New Delhi,[22] may I know what guarantee is there that Mr Ko-Mu Ju, who is the Vice-Chairman of the Chinese Peoples' Political Conference and who is a full-blooded apologist of Mao Tse-tung's regime may not behave in the same odd way?

Jawaharlal Nehru: I take it that most people, most prominent people, in China will be presumed to be in favour of the regime there. So, to say that this gentleman is a full-blooded apologist does not make any difference. The fact that he has been invited to this Conference, I do not think it should necessarily have a bad effect on our strained relations with China. I am not saying anything in favour of the invitation or against it, but it need not affect our relations, if he has been invited as an individual and in the hope that he will be helpful. I cannot say whether he will be helpful or not.

Hem Barua: That is the trouble.

Jawaharlal Nehru: Anyhow, Government has nothing to do with the invitation or with the Anti-Nuclear Conference that is being held.

22. For a discussion in the Lok Sabha on the World Peace Council session on 27 March 1961, see SWJN/SS/67/item 260.

360. In New Delhi: The Anti-Nuclear Arms Convention[23]

Mr Chairman,[24] Delegates and friends,

We are on the point of concluding our three days' session and I have been thinking what we have achieved during these three days. Presently, the statement will be placed before you which you have already approved. I am in the happy position of not knowing what their statement in its final form is. Happy I say, because I have not got to speak on that statement, not to praise it or to criticise it. I did see an early draft of it, but what changes have been made, I do not know. That is really a matter of wording, because all those who are gathered here in this Convention did not require to be converted. We have previously been converted or held broadly one opinion, apart from minor differences. How did we represent? People have talked about non-violence. Do we all believe fully in non-violence, taking it to its utmost conclusion? I suppose not. We are not all pacifists. The word "Gandhian" is used more and more frequently and by frequent use it has lost all meaning. So the most violent of men call themselves Gandhian. We all of us have had the privilege of serving Gandhiji, but I think, it is a little presumptious on the part of myself for instance, to call myself a Gandhian. We are powerfully influenced by what he said, by what he taught us, but he was too big. Let us recognise it that we live in his glory, the glory of his name. We in India take the name of the Buddha and Gandhi and think that we have done our duty. We assume vicariously the virtues of Buddha and Gandhi, to some extent. Just as to some extent, in the West fierce and brutal wars are fought in the name of Christ.

So, I have been wondering whether it was only a tournament of talk for three days or whether we have achieved anything worthwhile. I do not know. But, I have a feeling that we have achieved something worthwhile, and without attaching too much importance to it. It will help in the solution of this tremendous problem which faces the world today. The problem can, put it as you like, be one of survival, one of not being gradually reduced to brute beasts, one of the increase of civilisation, of moral values and all that. I think that what we have done in the last three days, the mere fact of meeting, has helped us somewhat in the solution of this problem. Certainly, I think, that in India it will help to draw the attention of people and make them feel a little more consciously, a little more intensely about this problem; and from feeling about it, they will first perhaps be led to doing something. And therefore, I would

23. Speech in the concluding session of the Convention, 18 June 1962. NMML, AIR Tapes, T.S. No. 8238.

24. R.R. Diwakar presided over the Convention.

like to congratulate the Gandhi Peace Foundation for this idea and for giving effect to this idea of holding this Convention.

Now, all of us know, it does not require any argument from me, that a nuclear war, not only does it mean the end, the destruction of humanity, but it is something infinitely degrading to our sense of all values that we have had. It surprises me that the practical aspect is bad enough, but the normal aspect, the standards we presume we have, how they can be even thought of in connection with a nuclear war? Well, we agree about that. And I take it that vast numbers of people agree in the world. Nobody can like being liquidated, or joining in this or being part of this widespread destruction. But nevertheless, large numbers of people also are prepared to put up with this idea, because presumably they think that something worse may take place unless they are ready for nuclear war. They are afraid, afraid of defeat by another country, and therefore this arms race may continue, even facing the possibility of nuclear war, or else they satisfy themselves by saying, that nobody wants nuclear war, but we must have nuclear bombs as deterrents to prevent the other party having, using them.

All this is curious logic. And meanwhile, as the eminent Russian delegate said, we go nearer to an explosion because all this, all the bombs that are being collected, made, and all the tests and everything, gradually brings the probability of an explosion nearer, and time is limited. If you do not put an end to it soon enough, it may be beyond the capacity of human beings or nations to stop this rot. At the present moment, we have three powers or four powers essentially, two and two others who have these nuclear arms and who have already collected vast numbers of them. If and when we decide on this complete disarmament, it will be a terrible problem, what to do with these bombs that we have collected? How to dispose of them, without injury to somebody? You cannot throw them into the sea. The sea would be contaminated. I do not know, what they will do? Well, that is a matter for scientists. Anyhow, where there is this vast collection, even without any future addition to it. Time is limited and it is really a question of a race between the good sense of humanity and the fear of humanity.

Now fear I think is a terrible thing. Fear and cowardice are the most degrading things that anybody can have and any nation can have. They make one brutal. Now, that is why, if I may say something different, when people talk about non-violence in theory, speaking for myself, I completely agree, but I am horrified at the idea of the coward and the weak and the person who is afraid living in the shade of non-violence. Of course, Gandhiji's non-violence was of the brave, and he said so: I'd rather you took out the sword which you have in your heart and used it than through fear kept it hidden in your hearts. There is nothing, nothing to do with fear, in his mind, in his idea of non-violence; but I am afraid that the non-violence of many people in this country—and I say so quite frankly—is a non-violence of the timid. They are afraid and are fearful and from that nothing good can come. Nothing good can come from people who are afraid, who are cowards, and if they lived under some kind of non-violence, they will condemn even non-violence as such.

But of course, that has to be separated from the idea of non-violence. We are not all here addicted to non-violence, but speaking for myself, I accept completely the theory of non-violence. But—there is a but—an individual may accept it, if he be strong enough to live up to it. But when you come up, you have to deal with large numbers of people, a population, the people of a country, and ask them to be non-violent. First of all, you require a Gandhi to deal with the situation, and secondly, even Gandhi may not wholly succeed. Even while Mahatma Gandhi was here—he had won this great battle of Indian Independence through non-violence—we saw terrible things happen here in this city of Delhi and in Pakistan and in Northern India as the result of Partition. Non-violence did not help us. That was sheer cowardice and brutality of the worst type. Speaking for myself, I prefer any amount of violence to that type of thing. [Applause] So the difficulty arises, that when you ask masses of human beings to follow a policy, they must be trained to it as Gandhiji, indeed, tried to train and succeeded in large measure, in a limited field. But, they must morally, spiritually—call it what you like—have to realise the significance of their action. If not, then they fall between two stools. They are neither here nor there, and only fearfully look on to what might happen. That is a bad thing. That is my difficulty, when I think of applying non-violence to large numbers not to make them cowards. If they are really non-violent, well and good, let us go ahead. And I am quite sure, if we went ahead in courage, I am quite sure that non-violence would win, not cowards. And in India especially we talk, we have a habit of talking in the highest terms, but not acting up to it, and in action not coming anywhere near the ideals we profess. I am quite frank, because I am speaking largely to Indian friends. I have the greatest pride in India and in the many things that India has given to humanity, and I think those are things of the greatest value to humanity and humanity will yet profit by them. I do believe, I know my people to some extent, liking them enormously. I do know their failings too, and I do not want to make them profess one thing and do something entirely opposite to it. That is hypocrisy and cowardice. There is a grave danger. So while I am convinced of the virtue of non-violence and its power, I am not sure that people in this country, or for that matter of any other country, at the present moment are capable of carrying the burden of non-violence. And if they fail, they fail utterly. That is one difficulty.

To put it differently, one has to face the problem of a leader of a country. Well, I am talking of a good leader because bad leaders, of course, are bad;

but an honest and good leader, compare him to another type of human being, who might be called the prophet, like Gandhiji. Now, Gandhiji had the supreme virtue of joining the role of the prophet and the role of the leader. It seldom happens, that kind of thing and training the people while never losing sight of his methods, of his standards, and training them and performing wonders in this country. Yet even he did not wholly succeed in changing all of us. We are weak mortals, still making enormous numbers of mistakes all the time. Now the prophet declares the truth in him regardless of consequences. It is the truth which has to be declared and as a result the prophet is usually stoned to death, and later his name will resound through the ages. That is true, But for the moment he suffers martyrdom. He will not temporise, he will not qualify his statements or qualify truth as he sees it. The leader, the good leader and especially in a democratic age, he is limited and inhibited by what, how far, he can get those whom he leads, to understand what he says. He is strong enough to act up to what he says. Their receptiveness to truth is limited. Presumably he cannot go too far beyond the receptiveness of his followers to truth, presuming that he wants, he believes in, the truth, and if he did go far beyond, he ceases to be leader. There is that essential difference between the prophet and the leader, however great the leader might be. And in a democratic age, which is an age of levelling, differences come out even more. However, these are considerations, thoughts, which I have placed before you. But difficulties one has to face all the time. The leaders presumably, a good leader, if he does not let go of the truth but he is always in danger of compromising, in temporising, because politics and the like is always a matter of compromise and in compromising there is a danger of slipping and falling lower and lower. There is no hard and fast rule left. Because all this, in these matters of adopting the rule of non-violence, of unilateral disarmament, I am absolutely convinced that any country which adopted unilateral disarmament through strength, nobody can injure it and it would win. But what is the good of my saying so when I feel that those who adopted, do not adopt it through strength, will not adopt at all in fact probably, but will be fearful of the consequences and indulge in violence of all types. Vinobaji, a man of the present day, in the great tradition of India, Vinobaji has said in his message to us, that he is a little more afraid. He is less afraid of nuclear bombs, he is more afraid of the dagger and the sword. What does that mean? That is, he is referring to the evil in our hearts, to the violence in our hearts, which comes out, whichever little thing that we may do. We will commit murder. That is true. That nuclear bombs increase the danger tremendously. But, the fact remains that we have come [to this point].

I am sorry to repeat something which has become too common, that a crisis in human affairs, where either humanity survives or it does not; and this crisis can only be resolved, I think finally, not by some nuclear tests being stopped but by something deeper, by the minds of men and the hearts of men and the spirits of men, rising to somewhat higher levels. I believe they will do that, I believe humanity will rise. I have firm faith. Because there is no other way, otherwise it will perish. But, we cannot bring about that change. I might still say that we talk about nuclear bombs etc. These are parts of the larger things, abolishing war, putting an end to war absolutely. I am quite clear, before war goes, we must have full disarmament and so on, these things connect one to the other, and lead to the next step. But if we talk about the final step all the time, we never take any step at all. Therefore, for the present we concentrate at this convention, on the stoppage of nuclear tests. I do not know, what has been done or suggested. I do not mind, of course, I do not mind, but I shall be very happy to subscribe to something against the whole manufacture of nuclear bomb etc. That is an evil thing. But remember this, all your desire to put an end to it will not lead you far, because nuclear bombs in an advanced scientific age, in a country which is advanced scientifically and technologically, can be manufactured with ease. You put an end to all the nuclear bombs today and human beings want to make them later, they will make them in a year or two, they will make them. They are advanced enough and may be technology will advance still further and make it easier to make them. I remember, a very eminent nuclear physicist telling me once that one of these days they will manufacture nuclear bombs in your backyard, in a small laboratory. Well, that may be a slight exaggeration, a manner of speaking, but the fact is, nuclear bombs are all the time planted in our minds and hearts and unless we can get rid of that, how can we be certain? We can never be certain. They can be produced. If war comes, if there is no nuclear bomb, if war comes, nuclear bombs will be made by the countries fighting, while war is progressing and will be used too. So, in the ultimate analysis, war must be abolished. War will not be abolished till there is a change in human beings. That is a big question. I do not feel competent to argue it. But, there is no alternative left. So, we must have disarmament, we must have a world without war, as it is said, but a present step is an urgent step to put an end to nuclear tests, not only because of the horror and the abomination of these tests being carried on. When we are told that every test, every series of tests means, I do not know how many hundred thousands of children born and unborn are being affected and that already millions have been affected. The horrors of it! The continuing of nuclear tests does bring the possibility of war nearer. It creates an atmosphere of an arms race, of fear and of the possibility of those accidents happening to which reference was made, because it is recognised today that no country is deliberately going in for a nuclear war, but it is equally recognised, that accidents are likely to happen. And if accidents happen, well, the result is the same, whether it is deliberate or accidental. War starts and once it starts, it brings all its terrible consequences in its train, nuclear war.

So, one thing also personally I should like, not as a solution, but as a step to lessen these tensions, and that is having areas, atom free areas, or areas in Asia, in Africa, Europe which are recognised to be, to have known nuclear secrets and which will not be used for nuclear weapons. All this does not mean much, because ultimate thing is the abolition of the thing, ultimate thing is having no war, full disarmament. But all these are steps which help. Today, the worst thing is this terrible tension and fear behind it. Imagine thousands of aircraft with nuclear bombs are always in the air, day and night. It is a horrible thought, and in order to protect one's country for fear of somebody invading it and imagine also those thousands of aircraft are piloted by young men, brave young men. Any person may lose his nerve, and losing his nerve or losing his head or whatever may be, may do something which will be, which may lead to a war. It is a horrible thought, and still it goes on, this mad race.

So, I feel that merely putting an end to these tests, and I would say, we talk about unilateral disarmament, unilateral putting an end to tests, is a little easier, much easier. That surely can be done. This idea, that one country does it, another must do it, necessarily or else it will lose in the race is odd. So, I hope and I think, that this convention has done some good, I will not put it higher than that. Every little step that we take towards the goal is a good one and I hope. We do not know what effect it will have in other countries, but in India at any rate I hope it will draw the attention of our people to these problems. So, we are a curious mixture of exceedingly mild people, who turn terribly violent occasionally and misbehave. We are mild, there is no doubt and an average Indian will deliberately avoid stepping on any little insect, will go round it. But the same average Indian may not be so kind to human beings. And war which has devastated humanity so much has not in that form descended upon India. We have no idea. Most people have no idea what nuclear war or any war means? So, I hope that this convention will bring some education and throw some light on these problems, on our own people. Because after all, all of us are rather small men grappling with enormous problems, grappling with the future of humanity, and small as we are, we can do something to it, if we can work together, if we understand it, and do our little bit to that end. So if a little step counts and I think this Convention has been a good step to that end, and therefore, I congratulate the Gandhi Peace Foundation and all of you delegates because you have taken, are finally going to take presently, that step. Thank you.[25]

25. See further items 361-362.

361. For R.K. Nehru: Anti-Nuclear Convention Resolution for UN[26]

I enclose a letter from Shri R.R. Diwakar[27] who recently presided over the Anti-Nuclear-Arms Convention.[28] He has sent me a statement issued by that Convention which is enclosed.

2. In para 3 of this statement, the Government of India is requested to take steps in the General Assembly of the UN to secure an immediate and permanent ban on all nuclear tests as also a ban on the transfer of and traffic in nuclear weapons of any kind whatsoever.

3. We should endeavour to take these steps and, for this purpose, we should inform our Permanent Representative at the United Nations as well as the Leader of our Delegation to the General Assembly about this matter.

362. To R.R. Diwakar: Anti-Nuclear Arms Convention[29]

June 23, 1962

My dear Diwakar,

Thank you for your letter of the 22nd June. I do not think it is necessary to send the statement of the Anti-Nuclear Arms Convention direct to the Secretary-General of the UNO. It will do more harm if it is so sent. Probably it will not attract much attention.

I do not think that it should be sent by post to the Heads of Governments concerned.

I rather doubt if it will be feasible for members of the delegation sent on behalf of the Convention to be included in the Indian Delegation to the United Nations. The UN delegation is especially chosen for the subjects discussed there. Apart from this, the UN delegation will go about three months later. That will be too late for your delegation. Further, your delegation will go to Russia, France, England, Washington, etc.

26. Note, 21 June 1962, for the SG, MEA. MEA, File No. D (310)-DISARM/1962, p. 1/Note. Both the letter from R.R. Diwakar, and the text of the Convention's Resolution, not reproduced here, are available at the NMML, along with Nehru's Note of 21 June to the SG.
27. Chairman of the Executive Committee, Gandhi Peace Foundation, Rajghat, New Delhi.
28. For Nehru's speech at the convention, see item 360 and further item 362.
29. Letter to the Chairman of the Gandhi Smarak Nidhi.

Appointment of a Committee to carry on the work of the Convention seems to me a good idea.[30]

Yours sincerely,
[Jawaharlal Nehru]

363. To N.C. Zamindar: Creating Opinion Against Nuclear Tests[31]

July 5, 1962

Dear Shri Zamindar,
I have your letter of the 29th June. I can suggest nothing special about creating public opinion against nuclear arms. Normal methods are through public meetings and the press. As you know, public opinion in India is almost unanimously against nuclear tests and the use of nuclear weapons. Different parties are of the same opinion about it.

Yours sincerely,
[Jawaharlal Nehru]

(c) Moscow Peace Congress

364. To J.D. Bernal: World Congress in Moscow[32]

June 1, 1962

Dear Professor Bernal,
I have your letter of the 25th May about the International Preparatory Committee for the World Congress for General Disarmament and Peace.[33]

Our Government's views in regard to disarmament are, I believe, well known. We are in favour of giving effect to the UN General Assembly's resolution asking for general and complete disarmament. But it is clear that this is a matter intimately connected with the fears and apprehensions of countries and cannot be dealt with purely on the logical level. There is far too much of

30. See also items 360-362 & 431 pp. 699-701.
31. Letter; address Bada Rawla, Juni Indore, Indore City. Sent from Pahalgam, Kashmir.
32. Letter to the Chairman of the International Preparatory Committee for the World Congress for General Disarmament and Peace, 94 Charlotte Street, London, W.1.
33. Appendix 9.

threats from one country or the other and boastfulness of its strength. It is this attitude that has to be changed. Any one country blaming another leads to a stiffening of the other's attitude.

I have no doubt that disarmament is not only essential but is feasible, keeping in view the apprehensions of different countries. Thus complete disarmament should take place, as has been generally agreed to, in a phased manner so that no one country can gain any temporary advantage over the other in the course of disarmament. The subject has been argued at great length in all its aspects and I do not think we can add anything to it. Even if we could, it would be better to put forward our viewpoint informally so as not to appear to preach to others, which is normally objected to.

But I am quite sure that the whole approach to it should be based on a firm determination to achieve it and in a friendly way. There should be no war propaganda or any action which leads to fear. I realise that it is very easy to say so and difficult in existing circumstances to bring it about. But there is no other way when we have to succeed in our objective.

I am afraid I shall not be able to send officially any representative to the World Congress to be held in Moscow. I am not clear in my mind that it will be helpful for us to associate formally with a conference of this kind which is likely to have political implications which may well come in the way of any actual progress which might be made. At present the Disarmament Committee is meeting in Geneva and trying to find a way out. We are trying to help there to the best of our ability. Any pressures exercised from other directions might well result in stiffening of attitudes.

Yours sincerely,
Jawaharlal Nehru

365. To Diwan Chaman Lall: Too Many for Moscow Peace Congress[34]

June 13, 1962

My dear Chaman,

Your letter of June 11th.[35] I am astonished and somewhat alarmed at the idea of a delegation of 125 persons going to the conference in Moscow from India or from any country. Is it going to be a mass meeting or a deliberative

34. Letter to Rajya Sabha MP, Congress; address: 30 Prithviraj Road, New Delhi.
35. Appendix 26.

assembly? I am not attracted to these mass gatherings calling themselves Peace Congresses.[36] They are obviously meant for propaganda purposes and not for any deliberation.

Who pays their fares and other expenses? I gather that the Soviet Government or some organisation there pays a lump sum to them. I confess I do not like the idea at all, though I can understand inviting a few persons and paying their fares.

It was first agreed, I think, to allow about thirty or so to go, although I thought that much too large a number. If you like, this number can be increased somewhat, but not too much.

I gather that you are also thinking of going to a conference at Accra. I do not know how all this fits in. But I have been rather concerned to find that there is some argument going on between the Ghana authorities and some of their invitees here about the payment of travelling expenses. They have apparently suggested Economy Class fares, but this has not been accepted and insistence has been made on First Class passage being provided. The Ghana authorities are finding it a little difficult to meet all these expenses and anyhow it seems odd that there should be this kind of wrangling with them.[37]

Yours affectionately,
Jawaharlal Nehru

366. To Mulk Raj Anand: Moscow Peace Jamboree[38]

June 25, 1962

My dear Mulk Raj,
I have your letter of the 21st June. I must confess to you that I am a little tired of these jamborees taking place from time to time. They may have some value. I think they help in young people meeting each other. But in effect they afford free trips abroad, and who will not accept these if they are offered?

So there is going to be a mass gathering in Moscow I think for peace and disarmament, a very praiseworthy objective.[39] But I do not understand why this should be also on a mass scale. I rather doubt if the cause of peace is advanced

36. See also item 366.
37. See also item 364.
38. Letter to the writer; address: Department of Fine Arts, Univesity of Punjab, Chandigarh-3.
39. To be held 9-14 July 1962.

in this way except, to some extent, in the country where such gatherings take place. Inevitably, as things are, they have a political tinge in them.[40]

I fear it will be very difficult in these hard times for Government to give any kind of financial help.

If you wish to see me, you can do so on the 2nd July at 12 o' clock, in my office in the External Affairs Ministry.

Yours sincerely,
Jawaharlal Nehru

367. For the USSR Embassy Information Department[41]

Please inform this gentleman that I am sorry I cannot find time for an interview. After two days I am going to Kashmir. But I am giving brief answers to the two questions they have put to me:[42]

(1) I think that full disarmament cannot adequately take place so long as there is an atmosphere of fear and suspicion and distrust all round. It is not possible suddenly as if by magic to get rid of this fear and distrust. Yet it must be realised that war should be out of the question and should be ruled out. It is better to take a risk than to drift inevitably towards a human catastrophe which may put an end to civilisation as we know it. It is a question of survival.

While fear and distrust cannot be ended suddenly, there might be an approach to this problem by step by step lessening the element

40. See items 364-365.
41. Note, I July 1962, for a Private Secretary [unnamed]. MEA, File No. A(3)-DISARM/1962, p.32/Corr.
42. The two questions were: "The International Congress for General Disarmament and Peace is going to take place in Moscow from July 9, 1962. Nearly 2,000 delegates from different parts of the world, and following different ideologies and schools of thoughts, will meet on a common platform to discuss the problem of general disarmament and peace. On the eve of this Congress we would like to present to you, Sir, the following questions: 1. What in your opinion are the first essentials for paving the way for an agreement on general disarmament? 2. What do you think about the Moscow Congress; how do such meetings help to create an atmosphere for an agreement leading to general disarmament?"
Extract from letter of 22 June 1962 from D. Surov, Acting Head of the Information Department of the Soviet Embassy, asking for an interview on behalf of the Novosti Press Agency of the USSR and posing these two questions. MEA, File No. A(3)-DISARM/1962, p.33/Corr.

of fear. This can be done by positive steps of disarmament, aiming ultimately at complete disarmament. Every step that is taken, if it is a real one, will reduce the element of fear.

(2) The Moscow Congress will, I suppose, like many other such meetings, help a little in creating an atmosphere which might lead to disarmament. But it cannot take one very far. In the country where it is held, it might create a stronger atmosphere. But its effect will be limited to that country. If the approach is a friendly one to other countries, it might do some good even there. Otherwise, if the approach is not sufficiently good, it may add to the fear and distrust.

368. To Partap Singh Kairon: Moscow Peace Congress[43]

July 2, 1962

My dear Partap Singh,

Your letter of June 29th with the correspondence you have had about the World Congress for General Disarmament. I entirely agree with you that you should not have accepted the invitation to go to Moscow for this conference. These conferences may do some good some time, but I do not understand why they want to make them some kind of mass meetings inviting hundreds and thousands of persons to them.

Yours sincerely,
[Jawaharlal Nehru]

(d) USA

369. US Military Aircraft Transit to Thailand[44]

[Note, 2 June 1962, from Mohammad Yunus, Director S, MEA, for Y.D. Gundevia, CS, MEA, begins]

We have been receiving requests from the US Embassy for transit facilities of their military aircraft, both MATS and other military aircraft. Papers regarding later aircraft are placed below at flag 'A'.

43. Letter to the Chief Minister of Punjab.

44. Noting, 2 June 1962. MEA, File No. SII/113/25/62, pp. 4-5/Note.

The Ministry of External Affairs considers the political aspect of these flights, and clearance has been refused in some cases in the past—notably to Netherlands. In one instance permission was refused recently even to a US aircraft. These papers are placed below at flags 'B' & 'C'.

CS is aware that British fighter aircraft are ferried to Singapore through India, where the British have a big base for operations in the South-East Asia. Recently, we have also allowed 8 French military aircraft to transit through Indian territory to Bangkok to participate in SEATO exercises.

The Defence Minister[45] wishes to know the level at which this matter was considered. Attaché (UK) had seen the papers and considered the request in a routine manner. The US Embassy had given the particulars of these flights. They have stated, very clearly that no troops or ammunition are being carried. According to our rules, the aircraft can be and will be checked when they transit through India on the specified dates, namely, 12th June, 13th June and 23rd June, 1962.

CS may kindly see.

Mohammad Yunus
2-6-962

CS

[Note, 2 June 1962, from Mohammad Yunus, Director S, MEA, for Y.D. Gundevia, CS, MEA, ends]

[Note, 2 June 1962, by Y.D. Gundevia, CS, MEA, for Nehru, begins]

The US Embassy has asked for flight clearance for 16 US Army (Beechcraft Seminole) aircraft to transit through India in three batches. The aircraft are on a ferry flight from USA to Bangkok (Thailand). Granting the US Embassy's request is an important matter and should have been referred to the Defence Ministry after taking the Prime Minister's concurrence. It is regretted that this was not done. As the Defence Minister has pointed out, these aircraft are presumably parts of US operations in Thailand connected with the crisis in Laos.

2. We have allowed military aircraft to transit across India, in the past, provided they do not carry arms and ammunition nor any military personnel in uniform. In the past we have permitted, inter alia, French military aircraft to transit across India to take part in SEATO exercises; and we have also allowed British aircraft to go to Singapore. We are not particularly happy at the

45. V.K. Krishna Menon.

American build up in Thailand; but there is no doubt whatever that Thailand has asked for more and more military aid because of their nervousness in regard to the situation in Laos. We have no quarrel with Thailand and I feel that we should allow the transit of these 16 American planes under the usual stipulated conditions.

3. This is submitted to the Prime Minister for his approval.

Y.D. Gundevia)
2-6-1962

[Note, 2 June 1962, by Y.D. Gundevia, CS, MEA, for Nehru, ends]

[Note 2 June 1962, by Nehru, for Y.D. Gundevia, CS, MEA, begins]

There can be little doubt that the aircraft are part of the US build up in Thailand. On the other hand, they have no arms or ammunition or military personnel. In fact, there are no passengers at all. There is at present no military operation on the Thai-Laos border. We have, as has been pointed out, allowed military aircraft to pass through India if they have no arms or ammunition or military personnel. This is by no means a clear matter to decide upon. But in view of our past practice and keeping all the circumstances in view, I think we should allow transit of these sixteen American planes across India under the usual stipulated conditions.

J. Nehru
2-6-1962

[Note 2 June 1962, by Nehru, for Y.D. Gundevia, CS, MEA, ends]

370. For B.K. Nehru: MIG Purchase and American Reactions[46]

Your telegram 417 June 14th. We have not come to any understanding with the Soviet about MIG deal. In fact, no proposal has been made by us to them or by them to us. When some of our Air Force technicians went to Russia some months ago for some engines, they examined MIGs from every aspect and approved of them greatly. They have experience of similar foreign planes and

46. Telegram, No. 35026, 15 June 1962, to the Ambassador in Washington D.C.

I believe have even flown British Lightenings. They were strongly of opinion that MIGs were more suited for us.

2. Since then, nothing more has transpired except the great deal of noise in American and British papers about MIG transaction. Naturally this has reached Russia and they must be interested in it, though they have not said anything. It is our intention some time later to send some of our Air Force people to look into the MIGs further and report about possible terms. Only then will question arise for us to decide finally.

3. In Parliament during discussion on Defence estimates, there was widespread approval of our buying MIGs. We have obviously considered this matter purely as a commercial one and no other question would have arisen but for the reactions in America and, to some extent, Britain, which have made any decision on our part against purchase and manufacture of MIGs very difficult. In any event, we would not like to receive aircraft from Britain or America as a gift.

4. I understand Lightnings are gradually being given up by British Air Force and Australia has not approved of them.

5. I am seeing Duncan Sandys[47]tomorrow.[48]

371. In the Rajya Sabha: C.S. Jha and the *New York Times*[49]

Shri C.S. Jha's Reported Statement in the "*New York Times*"

Niren Ghosh:[50] Will the Prime Minister be pleased to state:

(a) whether his attention has been drawn to a news item published in the "*New York Times*" that Shri C.S. Jha, India's Permanent Representative to the United Nations, is reported to have said, "the United States of America lost China 12 years ago by sheer folly and they may lose India the same way. If India goes, all of Asia goes."; and

(b) whether it is a fact that Shri C.S. Jha made such a statement?

47. British Secretary of State for Commonwealth Relations.

48. On MIGs, see Press Conference of 13 June, item 1 pp. 7-13, items 373 and 432 p.p 708-710.

49. Oral Answers, 16 June 1962. *Rajya Sabha Debates*, Vol. XXXIX, No. 3, cols 136-139.

50. CPI.

The Minister of State in the Ministry of External Affairs (Lakshmi Menon):

(a) Yes, Sir.
(b) No, Sir.

Niren Ghosh: There is a press report dated May 13, that in New York he made such a statement and afterwards he said that it was an unauthorised, garbled and tendentious version of a private conversation. May I know what is the actual text of the speech or conversation he made to that representative of the newspaper?

Lakshmi Menon: It was not a speech, it was supposed to be the report of a lobby conversation and it was not cleared with our Permanent Representative and as the hon. Member has pointed out, Mr Jha repudiated it entirely and said that the report was an unauthorised, garbled and tendentious version of a private conversation which is quite common in the lobbies of the UN between delegations and members of the press.

Niren Ghosh: I wanted to know what is the actual report of the conversation. From the report it appears that he says that it is tendentious or garbled but what is the actual text of the conversation?

Jawaharlal Nehru: Actual reports are not kept of casual conversations in the lobbies.

Niren Ghosh: Whether our Ambassadors or representatives are allowed to make such comments …

Jawaharlal Nehru: Yes, they are encouraged to do so.

Bhupesh Gupta:[51] The hon. Minister has been pleased to state that there was a conversation and the report is a garbled version of the conversation. In view of the fact that the matter has been reported in such a widely circulated paper as the *New York Times* and also in view of the fact that the *New York Times* has published no contradiction in regard to this matter, may I know whether the Government enquired of the particular officer exactly what transpired or not in that conversation and, if so, whether the Government instructed that particular officer to write a letter to the Editor contradicting the report that had appeared?

51. CPI.

Jawaharlal Nehru: I am not sure whether our Ambassador wrote any letter, but he did mention it to the correspondent, who as far as I remember, expressed his regret for it. He did not think worth while pursuing it still further.

Niren Ghosh: May I know, Sir, whether there is any standing instruction from the Government of India not to indulge in such sorts of private conversation contrary to the policy of the Government of India and whether the Government of India will consider the question of recalling the person concerned?

Jawaharlal Nehru: It is not our rule to keep our Ambassadors in purdah.

Bhupesh Gupta: What I want to know from the Prime Minister is this. Our friends in Western Europe and especially in the United States also, it seems quote some of the Ministers and officers and always they want to make out that this and that officer of the Government has sought aid and should be given or else India would go the China way. I take it that it is not the policy of the Government to seek aid in this matter by saying that unless you give aid, India will go the China way. If so, may I know whether the Government have given any general instructions to their officers so that they are careful, since such conversations are liable to be abused in this manner in the American press? Even the Prime Minister is not spared on that score.

Jawaharlal Nehru: I do not know whether it is worthwhile my answering this question. The same thing is repeated again and again. Our policy is supposed to be well known to our Ambassadors and far from stopping them from talking, it is their business to talk to members of the press and others. Of course, if they talk wrongly, it is their responsibility, but very often the talk is somewhat garbled in any kind of report that issues. One has to put up with that when one deals with the press. If it is worthwhile, it is corrected orally and in writing. As for India going the way of China, personally I may give the assurance to the hon. Member opposite that it is not likely to happen at all, whatever happens or not.

Niren Ghosh: History will tell.

Bhupesh Gupta: I have listened to the assurance. Now, we go our Indian way. The point is I find many such reports in the Western press that this and that officer, Mr B.K. Nehru, Mr Jha or somebody there, had been pleading for economic aid on the ground that unless you give aid India might go the

China way or some other way. And this they quote in the American Senate also. I think these are material factors which the Government of India should take into account when they deal with their diplomatic personnel in other countries, especially in a country where their words are liable to be distorted in this particular manner.

Chairman:[52] It seems to me that the Prime Minister has made it clear that nothing of the kind is going to happen.

372. In the Rajya Sabha: B.K. Nehru's Television Interview in USA[53]

Bhupesh Gupta:[54] Will the Prime Minister be pleased to state:

(a) whether the Indian Ambassador in the United States of America gave any television interview there on May 23 last;
(b) if so, what is the full text of that interview;
(c) the circumstances under which and the reasons for which this television interview was given; and
(d) the reaction in the United States press to this interview?

The Minister of State in the Ministry of External Affairs (Lakshmi Menon):

(a) Yes, Sir.
(b) The full text of the interview is placed on the Table of the House.
(c) The NBC television network invited the Ambassador to appear in a television interview. It is a normal and established practice amongst diplomats working in the USA to accept such invitations.
(d) The press in the USA did not take any special notice of this interview.

52. Zakir Husain.
53. Oral Answers, 20 June 1962. *Rajya Sabha Debates*, Vol. XXXIX, No. 6, cols 886-895.
54. CPI.

[Text of Interview, as tabled, begins]

Text of Television interview given by Ambassador B.K. Nehru on May 23rd in Washington on NBC Network

Program Moderator:

On Monday, Senate Foreign Relations Committee cut $ 90 million from Administration's request for $ 815 million for aid to India. Now Missouri's Senator Symington[55] usually supporter—down the line supporter—of Administration's Foreign policy led fight for this reduction. As a matter of fact Senator Symington tried to induce Committee colleagues to cut India off without a cent of American aid money. He argued that India was using our aid to arm itself against our SEATO ally Pakistan, that India was anti-American in United Nations, and that India's Defence Minister, Krishna Menon, was pro-communist. Well, India is reportedly deeply disturbed by this act and it raises some significant questions we think about the United States foreign aid. These questions, some of them, revolve around central issue of whether United States should or should not try to influence foreign policy of recipient countries through money we give them. Our Washington correspondent, Martin Agronsky, has invited Indian Ambassador to this Country to talk with us about these things and I have asked Welles Hangen who is NBC correspondent, New Delhi, to sit in with me on this end in New York. He knows B.K. Nehru who is Ambassador and I believe they are in Washington now. Good Morning, Ambassador. Martin (another panel member) would you like to begin?

Correspondent: Yes, Ambassador, I think we will begin with simplest and most obvious question. How does your Government feel about this $ 90 million cut if it is sustained in Senate?

B.K. Nehru: Well, I suppose, I have not a reaction from my Government but I suppose my Government will feel badly about it, because you are aware that Indian development program requires great deal of foreign aid and foreign aid put into American proposals—Administration proposals—was short of what is required for us—by us—for next year. So if you cut that further, it is obviously going to have some effect—it will have an effect on our developmental program.

55. Stuart Symington.

Correspondent: In view perhaps of industrialisation of India was there any specific aim of money—had you set aside the money for any specific purpose?

B.K. Nehru: No, as you know we have an integrated development plan, which includes industry, agriculture, transport, power and everything. So when you run short of money you have to cut across board which means in effect slowing down of general development.

Correspondent: I wonder if Welles Hangen who has been in India recently would like to come in.

Correspondent: Ambassador, I would like to know—it is often said in India that purchase of MIGs, which I believe Russians have offered against rupee payment, would not involve any foreign exchange. Of course, this would be charged against your exports—exportable Indian goods. I wonder if you could comment on that. Do you think this will take place; and second, will MIGs be paid for in goods that could otherwise be earning foreign exchange?

B.K. Nehru: I would estimate—I do not know whether deal will finally take place or not. We are in need of reequipping Indian defence forces for obvious reasons, not quite reasons Senator Symington has given, but for reasons I think much more fundamental.

Correspondent: I wish you would clarify that. I do not think that everyone would know the reasons Senator Symington has given. Senator Symington contended actually that American economic aid to your country was being converted into military armament, which threatens our SEATO ally Pakistan. How would you answer that particular criticism?

B.K. Nehru: [The] number of Indian defence forces in spite of impressions to contrary is certainly insufficient for protection and security of country because they are badly equipped. We have never been able to equip them properly because we have been short of money. Now, India is a large country and India—as you know the only neighbour India has got is not Pakistan, India has much more important neighbours and much more dangerous neighbours than Pakistan. It is true that Pakistan has been threatening us and making noises about second era (sic), (other methods)[56] and that is

56. Same in original, probably should be "secondary methods".

certainly something that we can never completely forget. But we have also as you are aware China at our border, we have a really substantial dispute with China and you never know what China's intentions are and China of course is a much more powerful country than Pakistan and it will be necessary for us to be able to defend ourselves against—certainly against China and incidentally against Pakistan. And if we can defend ourselves against China which we must, we can—the forces that we have obviously will also be enough and more than enough to defend ourselves against Pakistan. This equation between India and Pakistan is something that does not appeal to us at all—we are five times the size of Pakistan and we have five times its problems, so that it is ridiculous to say that what Pakistan has we should have, or what we have Pakistan should have. Now coming back to question of purchase of MIGs, our procedures in these matters are—unfortunately we cannot manufacture our own equipment today—our procedures are that we go around all over world looking for equipment and we buy it wherever it is best, wherever it is cheapest, and wherever the cost of it in terms of foreign exchange is to our benefit. Furthermore we have been linking up our purchases recently with programs for manufacture of equipment in India so that we are not—we should eventually cease to be dependent on imports from abroad. One of the difficulties we have had apart from fact that we need foreign exchange to purchase equipment from abroad is that we do not seem to be able to get service and maintenance equipment in time. Now MIGs, our trading with Soviets is carried out in terms of rupees, that is to say, it involves no foreign exchange directly. The rupees are used by Soviets for purchase of Indian goods and whether or not these goods are committed to foreign exchange depends on whether or not we can send these goods elsewhere for foreign exchange. Now, so far, under Trade Plan we have unsaleable matters that Soviets buy, what in effect are surplus unsaleable commodities, unsaleable in the sense of—unsaleable in terms of foreign exchange abroad. So that in effect we have not had to pay in terms of foreign exchange.

Correspondent: American aid then to some extent makes it possible for you to make the best of both possible worlds—that is both Eastern and Western?

B.K. Nehru: No, no no. You seem under an illusion that non-aligned or neutrals as you call them make the best of both possible worlds. We get aid from the Eastern world and the Western world but we get less aid per capita on a combined basis from both sides than your allies—all of your allies—get from one source. The fact that we get aid from two sources does not make it bigger than aid other people get.

Correspondent: I did not advance that as criticism—it was a question primarily Mr Nehru. Let me ask you the criticism that has been raised as a matter of fact. Committee Chairman Senator Fulbright[57] who has through the years certainly been a friend of India …?

B.K. Nehru: Certainly.

Correspondent: In announcing the cut Fulbright said this that there was strong feeling among members on the Committee that the attitude of Krishna Menon who is India's Defence Minister, especially his uncooperative attitude in the United Nations and otherwise perhaps influenced the cut. Now do you think that this is true and do you think that the Committee by this action will induce Krishna Menon to change his ways?

B.K. Nehru: You know that is a very difficult question to answer. You ask me as Indian Ambassador—I know very well that Krishna Menon is not popular in this country and the manner in which he often speaks at the United Nations irritates the American people. Yes, we are aware of that. And I suppose this is one of the reasons for the Senate Committee being a trifle displeased with us. But as regards our policies in the United Nations, I wish people would be a little more specific what they complain about. We have had to refute—look at the last twelve months or so—one major thing that has been done in United Nations is the Congo operations and I think you will recall—many people have forgotten—that there was a period when nobody was willing to send their troops to Congo for the United Nations. We came in at that time and by coming in, I think we saved more American lives and more American money than not cut but whole aid program.

Correspondent: You think that nullifies Krishna Menon's attitude in other—

B.K. Nehru: What other things—example.

Correspondent: Like Goa for example.

B.K. Nehru: Well, Goa—Krishna Menon has got nothing to do with Goa at all. Goa is a matter of national policy, which I explained on this very

57. J.W. Fullbright.

programme before and it seems to me this is an area in which we still have not been able to convince Americans about unfortunately.

Correspondent: What we come right down to really is: do you think this action by the Committee will influence change in Indian policy and is this the way to do it?

B.K. Nehru: No, this is not the way to do it at all. I do not think that foreign aid should be used to influence foreign policy and if it does what in effect are you doing? You are putting this country which would accept this proposition—selling itself to highest bidder.

Correspondent: Well Ambassador, I wish we could pursue this further but we have run out of time. Thank you so much.

Correspondent from New York Studio: Thank you very much both of you. Now there was a demonstration I think of ambassadorial expertise at about its highest level. We asked him, as you know, some very tough ones to field and I think Ambassador Nehru fielded them about as expertly as he could.

Correspondent: He is one of the best.

Another Correspondent: He is and I think we are lucky to have him despite the fact that his Defence Minister Krishna Menon really genuinely is not very popular here. Thank you, Welles.

[End of B. K. Nehru's interview in USA as tabled]

Bhupesh Gupta: Sir, please refer to the Statement, which has been placed on the Table of the House, containing the text of the television interview. Now, just seek information with regard to one particular question, to begin with. The question is about Mr Krishna Menon and it contains about 62 words. The answer contains 176 words.

An Hon. Member: So what?

Bhupesh Gupta: The question was short and the answer was very long. Now, the last part of the question was: "Now do you think that this is true and do you think that the Committee by this action will induce Krishna Menon to change his ways?"

The question was to this effect: Do you think, Mr Nehru, that is to say, Mr B.K. Nehru, not Prime Minister Nehru, that the Foreign Relations Committee, by cutting the allocations to India, would induce Mr Krishna Menon to change his ways? There could have been a simpler answer to it—"No"—unless Mr B.K. Nehru thinks there is the possibility of inducing somebody or the other.

Chairman:[58] What is the question?

Bhupesh Gupta: Therefore, I would ask the Prime Minister whether he has asked Mr B.K. Nehru, particularly with regard to this question, why he gave such a long answer in which he admitted that Mr Krishna Menon was unpopular in the country, in the USA? May I know, Sir, in this connection, whether Mr B.K. Nehru had made enquiries from all sections of the American public to find out whether Mr Krishna Menon was unpopular and why he had to accept it at the television interview? Did he say that Mr Krishna Menon was unpopular in America, after making enquiries from all sections of the American public opinion?

Jawaharlal Nehru: I do not know whether the hon. Member would like me to follow his advice with regard to the length of questions and answers. It is obvious that his questions are very long if the answer is much longer, it would take up the rest of the Question Hour.

As I stated in another place, these questions asked at these conferences are very loaded questions. They are impromptu questions, questions, put just to have the answers immediately. And at this conference, I think our Ambassador was not very happy in the choice of some of his words. But I appreciate his difficulties in answering such questions. He has himself said it in the first part, that is was difficult for him to answer these questions. Obviously, it is difficult for him to answer questions about a member of the Government. It is embarrassing. Well, we have told him that the expressions were not very happy. As for the rest, the length of the answer and so on, I had not counted the words in the answer or the question. No doubt, if the hon. Member had been answering them, he would have been possibly more precise, though it is very difficult for me to believe that he can be precise.

58. Zakir Husain.

Bhupesh Gupta: Well, Sir, when I deal with America, I will be precise.

A.B. Vajpayee:[59] And about Russia?

Chairman: Do you want to put question?

Bhupesh Gupta: Yes, I want to put a question, and also give some background of the question, because the Prime Minister also gave it. You sometimes remind the Prime Minister also. Now, what I want to know is this. Why was it necessary at all for Mr B.K. Nehru to embark on such a lengthy answer with these remarks, when the question simply was whether he thought that by what the Americans were doing in the Senate, Mr Krishna Menon could be changed? It is a very simple question. At the end of the question you have the operative part of it and the answer could have been a simple one.

(No reply)

A.D. Mani:[60] The Ambassador must have tendered some explanation for the things that he said at the television interview. If he has tendered an explanation, would the Prime Minister give us an idea of this explanation?

Jawaharlal Nehru: I do not think that any explanation was needed or called for, because the thing is obvious that he was suddenly put these questions and he answered them to the best of his ability. Anyway, we must remember that he had an audience before him, an audience of a few million people, whom he had to satisfy. He should not satisfy them at the cost of our policy or our beliefs in this matter, no. He answered at the spur of the moment and there is nothing to explain in it. He did it to the best of his ability. He might not have done it as well, perhaps, as the hon. Member, if he had been asked the questions, might have done. But our view about this report is this.

Bhupesh Gupta: In another part of the reply that Mr Nehru gave, he seems to have played on the American prejudice and their anti-communism. Needlessly he brought in many countries in order, perhaps, to humour the Americans. May I know whether it is the policy of the Government to allow its Heads of Missions to go to television interviews and instead of

59. Jan Sangh.
60. Independent.

answering charges like these, that are made against India, try to be on the right side of the listener—in this case the American audience—by playing on their prejudices against another system or another country?

Sudhir Ghosh:[61] What is the sin that the Ambassador has committed when he says, "You say Mr Krishna Menon is unpopular? So what? Why don't you say what is wrong with our policy"?

Chairman: Please sit down.

Bhupesh Gupta: Is he not answering my question?

Chairman: Would the Prime Minister like to say something?

Jawaharlal Nehru: I find it very difficult to answer these questions just as he would no doubt like me to do. He wanders about; the questions are so vague and fluid. Obviously it is not proper for any ambassador to criticise another country, any country in fact, and if he does that, it creates embarrassing situations. That is obvious.

Bhupesh Gupta: Sir, the Ambassador further said that India was badly equipped as far as defence things were concerned. Here today in the Press we find Mr Duncan Sandys saying that India was equipped with the most modern weapons. May I know who is telling the truth?

Chairman: It is our Ambassador against Mr Duncan Sandys.

Jawaharlal Nehru: These are odd questions. Neither may be telling the truth or both may be telling partial truths.

373. In the Rajya Sabha: US Reactions to MIG Purchase from USSR[62]

Bhupesh Gupta:[63] Will the Prime Minister be pleased to state:

(a) whether his attention has been drawn to the reactions in the United States official circles and otherwise in the United States Press to the

61. Independent.
62. Oral Answers, 20 June 1962. *Rajya Sabha Debates*, Vol. XXXIX, No. 6, cols 896-900.
63. CPI.

reported negotiations by India with the Soviet Union for the purchase of Supersonic Jet Planes;

(b) whether his attention has been drawn to *The New York Times* report that the United States of America would not consider such transaction as commercial but would deem it as military aid; and

(c) whether in connection with the above reported negotiations the Ambassador of the United States[64] and the High Commissioner for the United Kingdom[65] in New Delhi met the Secretary or any other officer of the Ministry of External Affairs towards the middle of May, 1962?

The Ministry of State in the Ministry of External Affairs (Lakshmi Menon): (a) to (c). Yes, Sir.

Bhupesh Gupta: The answer is only yes. Very terse. With regard to the last part of my question, may I know whether it is customary in diplomatic relations that when one country seeks to buy certain things from another country a third country comes into the picture and lodges protests to the Government that they should or should not buy. Are such things common in international practices? If not, how were the Ambassador of the United States of America and the High Commissioner of Britain concerned over this matter?

Jawaharlal Nehru: Nobody to my knowledge has said that India has no right to buy where it wants. That is not the question at all. So the answer to it is, yes; it is not right for any country to say that.

Bhupesh Gupta: Here in today's newspaper again we find the British Commonwealth Minister, Mr Sandys, saying it has been a regular practice for me to be in close consultation between the two countries regarding any new requirements. "From my talks with Mr Nehru I am satisfied that before any decision is reached, the Indian Government intends, in accordance with the practice, to discuss with the British Government its requirement of fighter aircraft." In the light of what the Prime Minister has said may I know whether this statement is correct that there is a practice in this country for the Indian Government to consult the British Government and discuss matters which relate to Indian Defence and may I know whether in pursuance of that kind of practice the High Commissioner for the UK saw the External Affairs Minister here over the MIG affair?

64. John Kenneth Galbraith.

65. Paul Gore-Booth.

Jawaharlal Nehru: There is no question of consulting people about our defence but it has been the practice in the past to buy our defence apparatus and equipment largely from the United Kingdom, partly from the USA and partly from France and other countries. That has been the practice. We do not consult them about our defence but we have bought things from them largely because of the continuation of our old methods, but that does not mean that they can come in the way. They are sellers; they want to sell their goods and no doubt they sell at a profit. It is quite understandable that they would like that practice to continue so that they can dispose of their goods to us.

Bhupesh Gupta: Is it not a fact that only when the Soviet Union offered to sell MIG jet aircraft the British Government came into the picture and started doing something by way of making offers in order that the negotiations with the Soviet Union could not materialise? Why did they not appear earlier before the Government of India entered into negotiation with the Soviet Government?

Jawaharlal Nehru: I do not know how the hon. Member got to know that the Soviet Government made an offer. I know of no such offer. No such offer has been made by the Soviet Government. No doubt the Soviet Government is a wide-awake Government; they know what is happening but that is a different matter. A team of ours went to the Soviet Union some three months ago or thereabouts to deal with another matter, the purchase of an engine for our supersonic aircraft. They went there because the engine which we hoped would be supplied by the British manufacturers could not be supplied by them because they had given it up for various reasons. So our team went there and discussed this with them. The Soviet Union had the engine but it did not quite fit in with our frame. They said, "You change your frame", and we said, "You change your engine" and ultimately it was decided that the engine should be adapted. That is why our team of engineers went there. They were for some weeks; they were interested in the MIG and they enquired about it and I believe they piloted it and made various engineering enquiries. It was a very high class engineer who had gone there. When they came back they told us about it and they gave us a report. No offer was made by us or by the Soviet Government to purchase or to sell, but certain preliminary enquiries were made by our engineers. In fact I did not know till they came back and reported about it and it was then that this matter came up in the Press and a lot of shouting is taking place since then about it.

Bhupesh Gupta: From what the Prime Minister has said even when there was no formal offer or tender for offer, it seems the Americans and the

Britishers are raising such a big noise over it. May I know how Mr Sandys was discussing this matter? Did the Prime Minister tell him that there was no offer or no request for an offer and that this was an irrelevant subject for him to discuss with the Government of India?

Jawaharlal Nehru: I did not say so because it was not irrelevant. There was an intention—it would have become obvious—and he was anxious to sell his own goods.

A.B. Vajpayee:[66] May I know if India would be allowed to use the Soviet MIGs against China if at all we decide to purchase them?

Jawaharlal Nehru: I do not see how that question arises. India uses her planes wherever she is endangered and India is going to manufacture the planes herself.

A.B. Vajpayee: I am referring to the planes that we are going to purchase from Soviet Russia.

Jawaharlal Nehru: When we purchase them they become our property and we use them when needed.

Bhupesh Gupta: Do I understand from the Prime Minister's last reply that the position today is that there is no suggestion—do not call it by the technical term—from the Soviet side that should India not make jet planes these planes could be available to India and also further assistance to construct aircraft factories to produce similar planes in our country?

Jawaharlal Nehru: I cannot go on discussing a matter which should not be discussed but as the hon. Member has asked me, there has been no Government-to-Government negotiation. Our engineers talked to them and they reported to us.

374. For MEA Officials: Publicity in USA[67]

I continue to receive criticisms from all manner of people about our publicity abroad. I do not know if we have continued to send by morse code the kind of

66. Jan Sangh.
67. Note, 25 June 1962, to the SG, FS, CS, and SS at the MEA.

publicity material that we used to send every day. Whenever I have seen it, I have found it to be singularly profitless.

2. We must do something about this and take up this work imaginatively. Shri S.K. Dey, our Minister for Community Development and Cooperation, recently visited America. I shall send you the report he has given to me.[68] He went to an old University there and to various places, including New York and Washington. He addressed large numbers of gatherings and people, and created a minor sensation wherever he went; sensation meaning thereby that what he told the people interested them greatly. He told them of how we are building democracy from the village upwards, of our programmes of development, of Panchayati Raj, etc. No one had made this approach before to them and they were vastly interested, much more so than being told that we were making a steel mill. He found that even in our Embassy at Washington, there was none of the literature that we were issuing in some abundance on our programmes here. Indeed, our Embassy staff people knew practically nothing about them. He is arranging to send some of his own literature to our Washington Embassy.

3. I think that we must get some experienced people who are interested in publicity, to advise us and to be kept in intimate touch with our publicity work. We can form an Advisory Committee of some such persons.

4. The saddest part of it is that the thousands of students who are studying in America and elsewhere, know practically nothing of what is happening in India. It should be our first duty to inform them and orientate them and make them some kind of Ambassadors of India wherever they might be. One can well imagine what good this would do if carried through by these thousands of young Indian men and women.

375. To James W. King: India and US have much in common[69]

June 29, 1962

Dear Mr King,

Thank you for your letter of June 25th.

I must have expressed myself badly in our Parliament if I gave the impression that I doubted the goodwill of the United States to India. I have never doubted the goodwill of the people and, indeed, I am very grateful for

68. Appendix 40 (a) and appendix 40 (b).

69. Letter; address: First Baptist Church, 111 W. Monument Ave., Dayton 2, Ohio, USA.

what has been done to India by the Administration of the US. More particularly, I am grateful to the President.

What I laid stress on was that there were some matters like Goa and Kashmir which had a powerful impact on the masses of our people.[70] Unfortunately, the American representative at the Security Council[71] has functioned in a way to create strong reaction in India.

I realise that we have to live together and that there is a very great deal in common between the United States and India. It is desirable to lay stress on the common features and not so much on the few points of difference.

Yours sincerely,
[Jawaharlal Nehru]

376. To J.K. Galbraith: Health[72]

July 7, 1962

My dear Ambassador,

Thank you for your latter of July 6th which has just reached me at Pahalgam in Kashmir. I am grateful to Mr Harriman[73] for his kind thought. If at any time I stand in need of medical advice from the United States, I shall not hesitate to avail myself of it.

But, as a matter of fact, there is nothing seriously wrong with me and what little trouble I had is almost past history now. There is nothing to worry about. I am not yet hundred percent fit, who is at my age, but I am in good trim. My doctors are insistent on my having more rest. I am trying to oblige them in this matter. Also they have put me on diet and have almost made me a vegetarian which is not a great burden on me.

Thanking you again,

Yours sincerely,
[Jawaharlal Nehru]

70. Items 126, 431-432, pp. 703-708.
71. Adlai Stevenson.
72. Letter to the US Ambassador. Sent from Pahalgam, Kashmir.
73. Averell Harriman, US diplomat and President Kennedy's roving Ambassador.

377. To V.K. Krishna Menon: Soviet Aircraft Purchase and Non-Alignment[74]

July 18, 1962

My dear Krishna,

Your letter of the 17th July. I think that the record of the last meeting of the DCC was more or less correct. The discussion at the DCC touched upon the question of our spending a large amount on aircraft now or not. But the general opinion was that if this was considered necessary, there was no escape from it. It was further felt that of all the proposals made to us, we could not accept the proposals other than the Soviet one. This was in view of the opinions and recommendations of our experts. We were thus driven to the conclusion that we should consider the question of the Soviet purchase and manufacture of aircraft in India.

But we decided not to come to a final decision then and to have a talk with our team on its return.

While we have driven to the conclusion to proceed with negotiations about the Soviet aircraft, we also felt that this should be done in a manner which did not show any excessive anxiety or panic; nor did it indicate that all that we had done in sending a team to the United Kingdom was for the sake of show although we had come to a decision previously.

I was not thinking of the so-called Aid India Club and Consortium. I did not even know when the next meeting would take place. In fact I do not think our decision should depend on the Aid India Club. We should decide quite independently of that. It might even be considered rather undesirable for us to wait for the Aid India Club people to come to their decision and immediately after to take up the Soviet purchase. I am quite clear in my mind that we should not allow this aid to India to influence our decision.

While I should be glad if we get the aid we have been trying for some time past, it will not upset me if that aid is denied to us or is drastically cut down. There should be no question of timidity in our proceeding with our decision because of the possibility of aid coming to us.

But I do wish to do things in what appears to me to be a proper and straightforward way and one which does not lead anyone to think that we have not been straightforward. I am anxious not for aid, but for the goodwill of other countries. To some extent, I realise that this is no fault of ours. Nevertheless, to some extent, I feel that the failure must be ours. Anyhow, it is unfortunate that

74. Letter to the Defence Minister. Sent from Rashtrapati Ṅilayam, Hyderabad.

we should lose the goodwill of any country. I would dislike greatly to lose the goodwill of Russia or of the United States; apart from any question of aid or help, to lose this appears to me to be a lack of something on our part. The whole essence of non-alignment is watered down if we lose goodwill. Inevitably we are driven into an aligned position.

It is, therefore, not a question of aid at all, but of our taking a firm decision in a manner which avoids, as far as possible, reactions of ill-will.

Yours affectionately,
[Jawaharlal Nehru]

(e) UK

378. To T.N. Kaul: Meeting Indian Delegation in UK[75]

June 7, 1962

My dear Tikki,

I enclose a copy of a letter I have received from the Indian Workers' Association, Great Britain. Almost every time I have been to England, I have been asked to address a public meeting by them. I am reluctant to address public meetings in London. At the same time, I do not like this repeated refusal. Is it possible for me to meet these people, even though I do not address a public meeting as such?

I certainly do not wish to go to a dinner party, as suggested.

As for my receiving a delegation of the Executive, please let me know what you advise. On the whole, I am prepared to receive such a delegation.[76]

Yours sincerely,
[Jawaharlal Nehru]

75. Letter to the Deputy High Commissioner in London.

76. For a previous meeting of the deputation of Indian Workers' Association, London, on 13 May 1960, see SWJN/SS/60/item 185 and appendices 20 (a) & 20 (b).

379. To Louis Mountbatten: Health and Personal[77]

June 11, 1962

[My dear Dickie,]

I have just received your letter of the 7th June. I wish I could visit you at your Irish home[78] about which I heard so much from Edwina. I am afraid I cannot manage it or even go to England for rest. I have already had a two weeks' holiday in Kashmir which did me much good.[79] Probably I shall go for a week next month to Kulu.[80]

I am as a matter of fact, feeling ever so much better. I have got over the indisposition I suffered from. The main thing is now that I take some rest in the afternoons and regulate my diet. I am doing this now and feel all the better for it. You can rest assured that I shall look after myself. But I cannot run away from my responsibilities.

I was much distressed to learn of John's illness.[81] I hope he is much better now and is on the way to health. My love to you and to the rest of the family.

Yours sincerely,
[Jawaharlal Nehru]

380. To Manendra Mohan: Little Time in England[82]

June 29, 1962

Dear Shri Manendra Mohan,

Thank you for your letter of the 26th June and for your invitation to visit Manchester. I would gladly welcome an opportunity to meet the Indian students, but I am afraid I cannot at present give any assurance on this subject. My visit to England for the Prime Ministers' Conference is fixed at rather a bad time to

77. Letter to the British Chief of the Defence Staff.
78. Classiebawn Castle, Mullaghmore, County Sligo.
79. 16 to 28 May 1962, see SWJN/SS/76.
80. Instead he again went to Kashmir on 4 July and returned on 12 July.
81. John Knatchbull, also known as Lord Brabourne, husband of Mountbatten's elder daughter, Patricia.
82. Letter to the President of the Indian Students' Association, Oxford Road, Manchester 13, England.

accept other engagements.[83] All my time is taken up by engagements in London and it is difficult to leave London. However, I shall keep your invitation in mind.

Yours sincerely,
[Jawaharlal Nehru]

381. To Harold Macmillan: MIGs[84]

June 30, 1962

My dear Prime Minister,

Some two weeks ago when Duncan Sandys was here to discuss the consequences of the United Kingdom joining the European Common Market, he spoke to me about the proposal of India buying Russian MIG aircraft. I am writing to you on this subject.

A little over six years ago, we were much concerned about the supply of military equipment and aircraft from the United States to Pakistan. This equipment was in many ways superior to India's, and we felt that we could not face this risk especially in view of the constant talk of war against India that was going on in Pakistan. We, therefore, decided to buy some modern aircraft. We found that the UK was not in a position then to supply us with suitable aircraft. After considering the matter fully and examining the various possibilities, we thought of buying the Russian IL-28 which appeared to us to be suited to our requirements and was easily available. The price was also relatively moderate. We realised that questions of security would arise, and we decided, in case we bought the Russian aircraft, to take the fullest security precautions.

Subsequently, I had a letter from Anthony Eden, who was then Prime Minister of the UK, on this subject. I discussed this matter also with Dickie Mountbatten who happened to be here then. As a result of these talks and the fresh offer made to us about Canberras, we decided to buy the Canberras offered, and not the Russian IL-28.

In the letter I wrote to Anthony Eden on the 23rd March 1956,[85] I made it clear that the Government of India could not give any undertaking for the future. I added, however, that if at some future date we should wish to reconsider this matter, we would give the United Kingdom Government adequate warning and

83. For Commonwealth Prime Ministers' Conference, see SWJN/SS/78.

84. Letter to the British Prime Minister.

85. Nehru sent a cable to Eden, see SWJN/SS/32/pp. 290-291 paragraph 8.

consult with them with every desire to reach an agreement on the subject. We would only take a decision after these consultations.

Much has happened since I wrote that letter six and a quarter years ago. Again, a situation arose for us vis-à-vis Pakistan which was a matter of grave concern. Pakistan was supplied by the United States with some supersonic aircraft which were far superior to anything that we had and, as previously, there was loud talk in Pakistan of military measures against India. Border incidents and raids took place in an ever-increasing measure. We decided, therefore, to purchase some suitable aircraft. In particular, we came to the conclusion that it was far better to manufacture them here, and it was from the point of view of manufacture that we considered this question. This was a difficult decision for us to make as we have to strain every nerve to fulfil our Third Five Year Plan. But we felt that we could not take any risk.

We considered the various supersonic aircraft that might be available for us. These were the British Lightnings, the American F-104s and the French Mirage. In particular, we considered them from the point of view of speedy manufacture in India under licence. Our Air Force experts who had some experience of all three of these makes, went into this matter very thoroughly. Subsequently, they had to go to the Soviet Union for another purchase, namely, to get an engine suitable for an aircraft that we were making. While they were there, they profited by the occasion to examine the MIG and discussed this with the Soviet experts.

On their return, they gave us their own appraisal of these four types of aircraft. They told us that the British Lightning, though eminently suitable for the United Kingdom, would not fulfil our requirements in the conditions in India. The American and the French aircraft were also good in so far as performance was concerned, but the three of these were much more complicated and sophisticated, and their manufacture in India would be difficult. They were also much more expensive than the Soviet MIG. According to the view of our experts, the MIG was a simpler aircraft and more easily capable of speedy manufacture in India. They, therefore, recommended to us to buy a few MIGs-21 and to arrange for their manufacture in India. This was, of course, to be done in an entirely separate place so that there could be no risk of security being endangered.

No proposal was made by us to the Soviet Union about such a purchase, and no offer was made by the Soviet to us. But undoubtedly we were giving a good deal of thought to the matter and were proposing to send an expert team to Russia to find out more particulars about the MIG. Somehow, the foreign press got wind of this matter and immediately a loud outcry arose. I was surprised at this because the whole transaction was thought of purely as a commercial one and there were no politics involved in it insofar as we were concerned.

I have pointed out to you the situation that arose here vis-à-vis Pakistan, and you will appreciate that we have had to face recently a dangerous situation on all our North-East frontier where a large portion of our territory in Ladakh has been occupied by Chinese forces. All this made it important and necessary for us to take some steps to increase our Air strength. Indeed, because of this frontier development, we had to purchase from the Soviet some big transport planes and helicopters which have been of great use to us on the frontier.

When Duncan Sandys was here, I pointed all this out to him. He laid stress, however, on the letter I had written to Anthony Eden in March 1956, in which I had said that I could give no undertaking for the future, but I had also given an assurance that we would give the United Kingdom Government adequate warning and consult with them if at a future occasion we wished to reconsider our decision. It is in pursuance of this that I am now writing to you frankly on this subject.

It is our experts' view that the British Lightning, though suited to the United Kingdom, is not suited to our requirements here, and the price also is comparatively a very heavy one. But what we are concerned with chiefly is not the purchase of a few aircraft, but their manufacture in India, including weaponry, electronics and raw materials for their manufacture. The question, therefore, is how far it would be possible for us to manufacture the Lightning or any other aircraft in India and how speedily this could be done.

In order to save time, we are arranging to send a team of high level experts to England in about a week. We had previously decided to send a team of senior officers to the United Kingdom in connection with the Avro and its further development in India. We are instructing them to examine any other British aircraft, including fighters, which might be suitable for us, especially from the point of view of manufacture. They will report to us, and we shall consider their relative suitability. Meanwhile, we may make further investigations in regard to the MIG aircraft.[86]

With kind regards,

Yours sincerely,
Jawaharlal Nehru

86. For Nehru's most recent statement on the subject of MIGs, see item 432 pp. 708-710. See also item 3 paragraphs 13-16.

382. To M.C. Chagla: MIGs[87]

June 30, 1962

My dear Chagla,

You must have followed the controversy and the shouting about the proposal for us to buy the Russian MIG aircraft. I had a talk about this with Duncan Sandys when he came here. I have now written to Prime Minister Macmillan on this subject. I enclose this letter which kindly have delivered to him by safe hand. The letter is sealed, but I enclose a copy of it for your information.[88]

You will observe that in about a week's time, we shall be sending a team of senior officers connected with our Defence Ministry and the Air Headquarters to England. Originally this was to discuss problems connected with the Avro. Now they will, in addition, discuss the other matter I have referred to in my letter to Mr Macmillan.

I hope these officers will complete their work fairly soon and not keep us waiting.

Yours sincerely,
[Jawaharlal Nehru]

383. To Louis Mountbatten: Visit to Delhi[89]

July 9, 1962

[My dear Dickie,]

Your letter of the 3rd July reached me here at Pahalgam in Kashmir today. Apparently you forgot to enclose your reply to the President in it.

I think it would be best for you to stay with the President at Rashtrapati Bhavan. I shall, of course, see a good deal of you wherever you might stay.

I have come to Kashmir for about a week. Srinagar was very warm and so I came up to Pahalgam which is much higher up. The weather here has been good and I feel the better for it. I shall be returning to Delhi in two or three days' time.

Bidhan Roy's death has been a great shock to us. Although he was just eighty on the day of his death, he was essentially young and enthusiastic in

87. Letter to the High Commissioner to the UK.
88. Item 381.
89. Letter to the Chief of the Defence Staff, UK. Sent from Pahalgam. Kashmir. Salutation not available.

mind and full of future schemes and plans. Only the day before his death, he insisted on presiding over a Cabinet meeting, although he was not quite well.

The West Bengal, as you know, has been full of problems ever since the Partition. Fortunately, we had Bidhan Roy as Chief Minister there who dealt with these problems and kept the State together.

[Yours sincerely,]
Jawaharlal Nehru

(f) USSR

384. To Subimal Dutt: Condolences[90]

I am deeply grieved to learn of your son's death.[91] You have all our sympathy and affection. You can certainly take leave.

(g) China

385. To Chintamani Panigrahi: Vinoba and Border Dispute[92]

June 2, 1962

Dear Shri Panigrahi,
I have your letter of the 30th May. I do not think it will be right or really helpful to burden Vinobaji with the task of trying to settle our border dispute with China.

Yours sincerely,
[Jawaharlal Nehru]

90. Telegram to the Ambassador in Moscow, 16 June 1962.
91. Nineteen-year old Sujit Dutt on 16 June 1962 in Moscow.
92. Letter to former Lok Sabha MP, CPI; address: Ganesh Kuteer, Cuttack 2, Orissa.

386. In the Lok Sabha: China on Longju[93]

Question: [94]Will the Prime Minister be pleased to state:

(a) whether it is a fact that China has recently lodged a protest with the Government of India alleging violation of Chinese territorial integrity at Longju in NEFA; and
(b) if so, how far this allegation is corroborated by facts?

The Deputy Minister in the Ministry of External Affairs (Dinesh Singh):

(a) Yes, Sir.
(b) The Chinese allegation is entirely without foundation. The Chinese note of 19th May, 1962[95] and our reply thereto dated 28th May, 1962[96] are placed on the table of the House.

Hem Barua: May I know whether the Chinese allegations about Longju in NEFA are a part of the calculated design on the part of China to dislodge the McMahon Line, which she proposed to do during November 1961 and which she has been repeating now? If so, has this position been examined by our Government?

The Prime Minister and Minister of External Affairs and Minister of Atomic Energy (Jawaharlal Nehru): Whether it is design or not is a matter of opinion.

Hem Barua: I could not follow, Sir.

Speaker:[97] It is a matter of opinion whether it is a calculated design or not.

Hem Barua: I have linked it with the Chinese threat held out during November 1961 to dislodge the McMahon Line. Therefore, I want to know …

Speaker: He should put some question.

93. Oral Answyers, 6 June 1962. *Lok Sabha Debates*, Third Series, Vol. IV, May 26 to June 7, 1962, cols 9100-9106.
94. By PSP MP Hem Barua and Congress MP P.C. Borooah.
95. See *White Paper VI*, p. 46 and in this volume appendix 5(a).
96. See *White Paper VI*, pp. 52-53 and in this volume appendix 5(b).
97. Hukam Singh.

Hem Barua: Some other question, Sir?

Speaker: Yes.

Hem Barua: May I know whether it is a fact that China has built up or installed a network of transmission centres, at least 15 in number, along the McMahon Line and has been carrying on regular slanderous propaganda against India which could be heard even at places like Digboi and Naharkatiya in distant Assam? If so, may I know what steps Government have taken to counteract this?

Speaker: That also is not allowed. Has he any other question?

Hem Barua: I do not understand why it is not allowed.

Speaker: It covers such a wide range that the question does not warrant that.

Hem Barua: It is in connection with NEFA.

Speaker: There are so many connections between one and the other that sometimes we have to travel a long distance to have that connection.

Hem Barua: It has been a very serious matter of late; and they are indulging in hostile propaganda.

Speaker: A discussion can be raised on it, questions are there to elicit information. He may put a question if he wants.

Hem Barua: May I know whether it is a fact that when Shri Chou En-lai met our Prime Minister last time he gave an impression that the eastern sector of our Sino-Indian border would be left severely alone and if so, whether these actions do not show a tendency on the part of China to go back on her assurance?[98]

Speaker: Then again, tendency has to be interpreted.

98. For Nehru-Chou meeting in April 1960, see SWJN/SS/60/items 9-10, 14, 16, 24, 27 and 30.

Jawaharlal Nehru: Hon. Member is introducing questions on the whole border on the eastern side.

Hem Barua: I come from there.

Speaker: Therefore, the whole border should also come here?

Jawaharlal Nehru: We cannot answer these questions. They have been dealt with in the course of the numerous debates as to what happened and what impressions one gathered two years ago or six years ago when Shri Chou En-lai came or somebody else came.

P.K. Deo:[99] Even though we know that our troops have withdrawn from Longju since 1959 from this correspondence we find that false allegations are made against our Government. May I know if these allegations are linked with our defensive action in the western sector, that is, Ladakh?

Jawaharlal Nehru: They are linked not in the minds of somebody else. So far as Longju is concerned it is verging on the border and according to us it is on this side of the McMahon Line. The Chinese have said, quite apart from their refusal to recognise the McMahon Line, that it is on their side of the McMahon Line. That is a factual difference of opinion. Whether their agitation or their propaganda is due to something that happens in the west, I do not know. It is all part of the same thing and the propaganda goes up and down.

S.N. Chaturvedi:[100] Have the Chinese taken up any position south of Longju in a village called Rouya or in any other place?

Jawaharlal Nehru: I do not know, Sir. I cannot give more information than stating that the posts are within a short distance of the border?

D.C. Sharma:[101] In the note that our Government sent to the Chinese Government, it is said:

> "If the Chinese Government have any doubt about the precise alignment of the border in this area, the Government of India would be glad to discuss the matter with them and clarify their doubt."

99. Swatantra Party.
100. Congress.
101. Congress.

Jawaharlal Nehru: At Longju?

Speaker: In the note sent to them it is said that if they have any doubts about it the Government of India would clarify it.

Jawaharlal Nehru: Is it about Longju?

D.C. Sharma: Yes; the last few lines of the last but one paragraph of our note to China. May I know if they have shown any desire to discuss this matter so that the doubts may be clarified?

Jawaharlal Nehru: Not yet; not to my knowledge.

Hari Vishnu Kamath:[102] In the words used by the Government in one of their notes to China, is it the Government's policy to merely pile protests on protests while China mounts aggression on aggression? Has the Government administered so far a warning, apart from protests to China against aggression?

Jawaharlal Nehru: I do not think that requires any reply. This is a wider question which has been dealt with.

Speaker: They want to know whether any warning has been given.

Jawaharlal Nehru: On what?

Hari Vishnu Kamath: Against the Chinese aggression on India.

Hem Barua: China has warned us already.

Jawaharlal Nehru: Well, hon. Members have heard many times the statements on the subject. [Interruption]

Hari Vishnu Kamath: There is a difference between warning and protest. China has not been warned yet.

Speaker: Order, order. He may frame a question if he wants to put one.

102. PSP.

Hari Vishnu Kamath: Has the Government administered, up to this day, a warning to China against any aggressive or subversive activity against India? That is the question; it is a simple question.

Jawaharlal Nehru: The hon. Member must have taken the trouble to read what he calls protest after protest that we have made. I do not know what he considers a warning to be, unless the warning is that we shall go to war with China.

Hari Vishnu Kamath: Not at all. He has misunderstood the question.

Hem Harua: rose—

Speaker: Order, order, Hon. Members should not stand all at one time. Warning to do what? If that is not given, how can any answer be given?

Hari Vishnu Kamath: The warning is just this—I had quoted an example, in the House, a few days ago, namely, a warning was administered by President Nasser to the Chinese Mission in Cairo two years ago, against subversive activity, on pain of the Mission being closed down. I mean some such step, not that very step.

Speaker: Then it come to this: a warning must have something that would follow.

Hari Vishnu Kamath: A warning to desist from the activity on pain of something happening. [Interruption]

Surendranath Dwivedy: Not necessarily war.

Jawaharlal Nehru: The question appears to be a suggestion that we should warn them, that we should cut off diplomatic relations.

Hari Vishnu Kamath: No, not quite.

Some Hon. Members: rose—

Speaker: Order, order. Unless a warning has been issued, that is, if this is not conceded, then another thing, namely, breaking, I should say, of diplomatic intercourse or other steps should be taken. That is what he means.

Jawaharlal Nehru: That is what I said.

Speaker: We have not given any warning.

Jawaharlal Nehru: Certainly not. We do not propose to, till we decide on breaking or other steps.

Hem Barua: The question has been misunderstood. The point is this.

Speaker: He might put a question.

Hem Barua: In view of the fact that China has mounted up her allegations against India during recent days, and, at the same time, she has bolstered up her claims by slow and steady military occupation also, may I know whether our Government consider that to be a step towards further aggression or a total war on us by China?

Speaker: That goes too far. Is there any answer to be given to it?

Jawaharlal Nehru: This is a question of opinion; I do not think any total war is a prospect in view.

387. In the Lok Sabha: Expiry of Indo-Tibetan Agreement[103]

Mohsin (Dharwar South):[104] Sir, under rule 197, I beg to call the attention of the hon. Prime Minister to the following matter of urgent public importance and I request that he may make a statement thereon:

> "The expiry of the Indo-Tibetan Agreement 1954 with China and the closing of Chinese trade missions in India."

The Prime Minister and Minister of External Affairs and Minister of Atomic Energy (Jawaharlal Nehru): As the House is aware, we have, since the beginning of December 1961, been in correspondence with the Government of People's

103. Calling Attention, 6 June 1962. *Lok Sabha Debates*, Third Series, Vol. IV, May 26 to June 7, 1962, cols 9165-9168.
    Nehru's statement is also available in [MEA], Agreement between India and China on Trade and Intercourse between India and Tibet region of China 1954—Decision against Renewal 1962, (File No. F. 12/458/NGO/61) pp. 19-20.
104. F.H. Mohsin, Congress.

Republic of China to find a dependable basis for negotiations between the two Governments in order to reach a new agreement in place of the Sino-Indian Agreement of 1954 which was due to expire on the 3rd June 1962. In our correspondence we urged upon the Chinese Government the necessity of laying a proper foundation and creating a favourable atmosphere for fresh negotiations between the two countries and suggested that, as a first step, the Chinese Government should, with a view to creating the proper atmosphere, withdraw their forces from Indian territory and restore the territorial status quo as it existed at the time of the signing of the 1954 Agreement. While these exchanges were continuing, the Chinese Government informed us on the 23rd May, through their Chargé d'Affaires in Delhi, of their decision to recall their Trade Agencies in Calcutta and Kalimpong and asked for requisite facilities for the withdrawal of these Agencies. The Foreign Secretary[105] assured the Chinese Chargé d'Affaires that necessary facilities will be accorded. Foreign Secretary also added that the Government of India will be taking a decision on the winding up of Indian Trade Agencies in Tibet on a reciprocal basis and will request the Chinese Government to give necessary facilities.

We received a report that the Chinese Trade Agency at Kalimpong had started moving out on the 27th May. A later report indicated that the official of the Chinese Trade Agencies at Calcutta and Kalimpong had left India on the 1st June. The Chinese Embassy had informed us some time back that they had only two Trade Agencies at Kalimpong and Calcutta and there was no Trade Agency in New Delhi. The Chinese Embassy informed us after the withdrawal of the Agency at Kalimpong that the property and buildings of the Trade Agency at Kalimpong have been placed in charge of their Consul-General at Calcutta.

We informed the Chinese Chargé d'Affaires on the 30th May, of our decision on withdrawing our Trade Agency at Gyantse by 10th June and our Trade Agency at Yatung by the 15th June, and asked for facilities for the Trade Agencies to pack, crate and transfer records and stores. As regards the third Trade Agent who used to visit Gartok, we asked for facilities for him to visit Western Tibet as soon as the Lipulekh Pass was open so that he could wind up his Mission. We told the Chargé d'Affaires that none of our Trade Agents will be functioning as such with effect from the 3rd June, but they will take some time to move out with their records and stores and asked that certain administrative facilities be given to the Trade Agents till the date of withdrawal. We also informed the Chinese Chargé d'Affaires that we intended to place our property and buildings at Yatung in charge of our Consul General at Lhasa who

105. M.J. Desai.

would keep a small maintenance staff there and convert the place into a hostel for the use of our countries and officials proceeding to or returning from Lhasa. The Chinese Government have asked that the withdrawal of the Indian Trade Agencies in Tibet should be completed within a month. They have also stated that reasonable facilities will be guaranteed for such withdrawal. They have, however, regretted their inability to grant certain administrative facilities, like communications in cypher, with the Government of India until the date of the withdrawal of the Trade Agencies.

Apart from the withdrawal of the Trade Agencies of the two countries provided in the 1954 Agreement, the immediate consequence of the termination of the 1954 Agreement will be the termination of the facilities provided in the Agreement for trade and intercourse between India and the Tibet region of China. Such trade and intercourse in future will, to the extent permitted by each side, be regulated by national laws and regulations of the countries concerned.

Mohsin: What will be the effect of the closure of these trade agencies in both the countries on our trade and commerce specially in regard to exports and imports of our country?

Jawaharlal Nehru: Obviously, the effect will be that such small trade as was carried on will be reduced still further.

P.K. Deo (Kalahandi):[106] Consequent upon the expiry of the Indo-Tibetan Agreement of 1954, it is learnt, Indian traders in Tibet are winding up their business. May I know if the Governments are taking steps for the transfer of their assets to this country?

Jawaharlal Nehru: There has been some correspondence about that. The House would have noticed, when I read out, certain facilities for withdrawal etc. That will be part of those facilities that we have asked for.

S.N. Chaturvedi (Firozabad):[107] Will our other Trade Missions in China continue to function?

Speaker: No, the statement makes that clear.

106. Swantatra Party.
107. Congress.

Hari Vishnu Kamath (Hoshangabad):[108] In view of the fact that the 1954 Agreement had an Appendix embodying what has since come to be known as the doctrine of Panchsheel in international relations, it having been enunciated for the first time in that context in modern history, may I ask whether the scrapping of this 1954 Trade Agreement will entail, as a regrettable consequence thereof, the snapping of the Panchsheel tie between India and China as well?

Jawaharlal Nehru: Those principles embodied in what is called the Panchsheel agreement are basic principles which remain, whether anybody breaks them or not. So far as we are concerned, we shall try to abide by them in the changed circumstances. I do not know how far it will be possible altogether to act up to them. But we do not propose to contravene them unless we are compelled to do so.

388. In the Lok Sabha: China Border[109]

Settlement of Sino-Indian Border Dispute

Question:[110] Will the Prime Minister be pleased to state:

(a) the details of the latest offer made to China for settlement of the border dispute;
(b) whether in the event of its acceptance by China, India will have to withdraw from a much larger area than the other party will have to; and
(c) the area of "No man's land" which will be another consequence thereof?

The Minister of State in the Ministry of External Affairs (Lakshmi Menon):

(a) In our Note dated l4th May 1962[111] we have repeated the offer made in the Prime Minister's letter of 16th November 1959 to Premier Chou En-lai.[112] There it had been proposed, as an interim measure, so as to

108. PSP.
109. Oral Answers, 11 June 1962. *Lok Sabha Debates*, 3rd Series, Vol. V, 8 June to 22 June 1962, Ist Session, cols 9924-9927.
110. By one PSP MP, one Swatantra Party MP and two Congress MPs.
111. See *White Paper VI*, pp. 41-43 and in this volume appendix 4.
112. See SWJN/SS/54/item 154.

relax tensions and to avoid possible clashes, that in the Ladakh region the Government of India should withdraw their personnel to the west of the line shown in the 1956 Chinese map and the Government of China should withdraw their personnel to the east of the international boundary shown in the Indian official maps. This withdrawal would apply not only to armed but also to unarmed and administrative personnel and the entire area between the boundaries claimed by the two sides would be left unoccupied.

In the same Note, we had also expressed our willingness, in the interest of a peaceful settlement of the boundary question, to permit the continued use of the Aksai Chin Road for Chinese civilian traffic, pending negotiations.

Copies of the relevant correspondence are placed on the Table of the House. (Placed in Library. See No. LT-188/62)

(b) No, Sir,

(c) The area of No-man's land envisaged in our note would be approximately 11,300 square miles.

Hari Vishnu Kamath:[113] How can this latest offer be reconciled with the earlier stand of the Government to which they have adhered consistently over many months to the effect that there can be no talks or negotiations with the Chinese unless and until they vacate their aggression completely or is it now the stand of the Government that they desire only a token vacation of aggression?

The Prime Minister and Minister of External Affairs and Minister of Atomic Energy (Jawaharlal Nehru): This is not only completely, in keeping with what has been said, but it has been the consistent line adopted throughout. The hon. Member must have misunderstood some statement if he thinks otherwise. This offer was made in 1959 November, and although we have not repeated the exact offer several times, the general statements made are in line with it. In accordance with this offer, the Chinese Government would actually vacate the aggression from the past. The only difference is, we do not occupy that area for the time being and that creates conditions for us to negotiate after they have vacated. That is what we have said.

Hari Vishnu Kamath: With regard to the No-man's, land which will be as large as 11,330 square miles, if I heard her aright....

113. PSP.

[Mahavir] Tyagi:[114] It is ours.

Hari Vishnu Kamath: May I know whether India will exercise any kind of jurisdiction or authority over that area at all or it is completely no-man's and godforsaken also?

Jawaharlal Nehru: This offer is made for a temporary period while negotiations take place about these matters. During that temporary period, the idea is that no country—neither of the countries would exercise any administrative authority there apart from military.

Hari Vishnu Kamath: Who will look after the people?

Speaker:[115] Shri Hem Barua.[116]

Hem Barua: In view of the fact that recently Chinese allegations are mounting up and even China has held out threat of consequences, bloody conflicts and all that and charged the Government with chauvinism, may I know whether the Government propose to take drastic action which does not naturally mean war but might mean severance of diplomatic connection with China?

Jawaharlal Nehru: The hon. Member suggests that we should live up to the charges made by China against us.

Hem Barua: No. I do not mean that. China has been making these charges and of late, as the notes exhibit, the charges have mounted up in their intensity. What does the Government propose to do in the face of the charges? Sending notes only?

Jawaharlal Nehru: As far as I can see, he wants us to do something, which will justify the charges made against us.

S.M. Banerjee:[117] I want to know whether it is the intention of the Government, when we withdraw and when the Chinese also withdraw, that

114. Mahavir Tyagi, Congress.
115. Hukam Singh.
116. PSP.
117. Independent.

the further negotiations will be at the official level only or at the ministerial level. I want to know what will be the sort of negotiations.

Jawaharlal Nehru: It is a matter, which, when the question arises, will be decided. If that takes place and the road is open for negotiation, whether it should be at the official level first and at the ministerial level afterwards or straight off at the ministerial level, is a matter, which can be easily decided.[118]

P.K. Deo:[119] This offer may be a fine piece of diplomacy. May I know if this creation or a No-man's land does not virtually amount to surrender of Indian Territory?

Jawaharlal Nehru: I would suggest to the hon. Member reading the letters and then concluding in his own mind.

389. For Y.D. Gundevia: Foreign Governments Publishing Statements[120]

The attention of the Speaker[121] might be drawn to this matter. It should be pointed out that our policy is that official statements of Government are allowed to be published in the bulletin which they may issue in Delhi. This was the case in regard to the document circulated by the Consul General of the DRV[122] in New Delhi.

In the case of China, objection was taken by us because they did not give the official statement as a whole, but gave parts of it and comments.[123]

It might be pointed out further that the reports made by the Chairman of the International Commission have not been given publicity yet.

118. For China's reply to the Indian Government's note, see *White Paper VI*, pp. 56-58 and in this volume appendix 3 (b).
119. Swantantra Party.
120. Note, 13 June 1962, for the Commonwealth Secretary, regarding Calling Attention Notice of 13 June 1962 by Ramchander Bade (Jan Sangh), Brij Raj Singh (Jan Sangh), and Brahmajit Singh (Jan Sangh).
121. Hukam Singh.
122. Democratic Republic of Vietnam.
123. See Nehru's intervention in the Lok Sabha on 15 June 1962, item 391.

390. In the Lok Sabha: Chinese in North Ladakh[124]

(i) Reported Movement of Chinese Tanks and Armoured Vehicles in Occupied Indian Territory in Northern Ladakh

P.C. Borooah (Sibsagar):[125] Sir, under Rule 197, I beg to call the attention of the Minister of Defence to the following matter of urgent public importance and I request that he may make a statement thereon:

> "The reported movement of Chinese tanks and armoured vehicles in occupied Indian territory in Northern Ladakh and sighting of long convoys of Chinese Military vehicles in Southern Sinkiang and Quizil Jilga in occupied Aksai Chin."[126]

The Minister of Defence (Krishna Menon): Mr Speaker, Sir, Government have no information regarding the reported—that is, in the Press—movement of Chinese tanks and armoured vehicles in the Indian territory in Northern Ladakh, parts of which are under the occupation of the Chinese. Vehicles belonging to the Chinese have, however, been plying in Quizil Jilga area for some time. The terrain also lends itself to easy construction of tracks in this area on which vehicles can ply. These tracks have been used by vehicles for some of the posts which have been illegally set up by the Chinese.

P.C. Borooah: May I know whether it is construed that the storm of allegations and charges of provocation launched by China against India in recent months was to cover their sinister design of further aggression against India?

Krishna Menon: I could not follow the question.

124. Calling Attention, 13 June 1962. *Lok Sabha Debates*, Third Series, Vol. V, 8 June to 22 June, 1962, Ist Session, cols 10563-10576.

Three issues were discussed in this meeting (i) Reported Movement of Chinese Tanks and Armoured Vehicles in Occupied Indian Territory in Northern Ladakh, (ii) Reported Admonition of some senior Army officers posted in NEFA, (iii) Scarcity of Filtered Water in West Vinay Nagar, Delhi. This item covers the first part, the second part is covered in item 174, and the third one does not have any intervention by Nehru.

125. Congress.

126. This refers to a news item in *The Times of India*, 10 June 1962, p. 1 cols 6, 7, 8 with the heading "China brings tanks and armoured vans in Ladakh."

Speaker:[127] He wants to know whether these aggressive acts construed as a design for further aggression into the Indian territory. Is that the question?

P.C. Borooah: Yes, Sir.

Krishna Menon: We know nothing about these tanks or anything.

Hari Vishnu Kamath (Hoshangabad):[128] Sir, the Minister has been pleased to say that the Government has no information about this particular matter, that is to say, the movement of convoys, tanks and vehicles in occupied Ladakh area. But may I ask Sir, whether Government has received reports that China has moved not merely such convoys and vehicles to western Tibet on the edge of the occupied Ladakh area but has also flown Soviet MIG planes and jet fighters as well as Ilyushin bombers and other transport planes to western Tibet from Sinkiang on the edge of the boundary of Ladakh; and, if so, when China alongside a lying propaganda offensive is also preparing or threatening to launch a military operation....

Speaker: How long is the question?

Hari Vishnu Kamath: My question further is, is it, Sir, in the defence interests of the country that the Minister for Defence should prepare to fly to New York at this moment of near crisis and thereby....

Speaker : Order, order. It is not relevant here.

Hari Vishnu Kamath: Why not here? At this moment of near crisis the Defence Minister is flying to New York.

Speaker: What has his flying to New York to do with this?

Hari Vishnu Kamath: He should be a whole-time Defence Minister and he should be in the country at the time of crisis.

Speaker: That is a wider question and cannot be discussed here. Has he any question to put or not?

127. Hukam Singh.
128. PSP.

Hari Vishnu Kamath: My first question may be answered, my question about MIG fighters in western Tibet on the edge of Ladakh border.

The Prime Minister and Minister of External Affairs and Minister of Atomic Energy (Jawaharlal Nehru): We have no information about these various statements that the hon. Member has made, about MIG fighters and tanks in western Tibet. Naturally, it is not easy to get information from there. Anyhow, I think much of this information that sometimes appears in the Press, we have found, has little justification or basis.

Nath Pai (Rajapur):[129] Is it a fact that the Chinese defence forces or, rather, aggressive forces are logistically so placed that they have a definite advantage over us and they are in a position to haul their lighter weapons from their bases in Sinkiang through the Aksai Chin road; and, if so, do we take note of the fact which is emerging from their latest note, an increasingly menacing note which has appeared, where they accuse "India is determined to encroach on Chinese territory and to this end does not scruple to provoke even if bloody conflict...." In the face of the combination of these two facts – their superior advantage over us and their new menacing tone, what do we propose to do?

Speaker: Order, order. There is one thing that I must bring to the notice of hon. Members. Calling Attention Notice is on a matter of urgent public importance. There is one thing to which the whole attention is to be directed. But hon. Members open out the whole controversy of the border.

Nath Pai: It is strictly relevant. With the increasing forces that they have got whether they can bring equipment with ease....

Speaker: The matter that we have before us is:

> "The reported movement of Chinese tanks and armoured vehicles in occupied Indian territory in Northern Ladakh and sighting of long convoys of Chinese military vehicles in Southern Sinkiang and Quizil Jilga in occupied Aksai Chin."

Nath Pai: May I ask in all humility; is it not most logical if we ask that if they are not already placed there whether they can place them there with considerable speed?

129. PSP.

Speaker: Logic would certainly take us too far. [Interruptions] Order, order.

Nath Pai: Let us see what the reply is.

Hari Vishnu Kamath: No reply.

Krishna Menon: I can only answer for military equipment on the Indian territory. As the Prime Minister has already stated, we have no such information, as most of these reports, particularly about military equipments on the Himalayas, are not based on facts.

Nath Pai: He did not answer the question. We want to be assured on this question, and that is why we have raised it; we have refrained from raising it in any other form following your guidance in this matter. If they have any advantage over us in logistics, then they can bring their dangerous weapons so quickly to that area, which is a matter of great concern to us. We would like to be assured by the Defence Minister, before he leaves the country, or the Prime Minister, that they do not enjoy any such advantage and were being prepared for any such eventuality. That particular report may be false, but this fact cannot be ignored lightly that we are not in possession of information. Certainly, we are in possession of information of what you are doing. Do not disclose your military secrets, but what about the points which I am repeatedly seeking clarification of?

Jawaharlal Nehru: The hon. Member should realise that even if we have some idea about the logistic position, it is not desirable to disclose it; it does not help us. We know the fact and it may help the other party. It is well known that, to some extent, logistically, it is easier to transport things from the plateau of Tibet and then go forward into Ladakh than to transport things across the Himalayas. It is a well-known fact. But to draw inferences from that may not be justified.

Hem Barua (Gauhati):[130] The way that China has been shifting up her position about the border since 1959 shows that China might not have any qualms of conscience in yielding up....

Speaker: Order, order. Again I have to request that some attention at least be paid to my rulings. I have suggested only just now that direct and relevant questions should be put.

130. PSP.

Hem Barua : I am just now coming to that.

Speaker: He will come after travelling long distances.

Hem Barua: No, Sir. The whole thought layer....

Speaker: Some relevant question should be put, and that too precisely.

Hem Barua: I will do so.

Mahavir Tyagi (Dehra Dun):[131] He is in Chinese strategy.

Hem Barua: I will be quite relevant. This is very positive. China has been shifting her position along the border....

Speaker: What is the question?

Hem Barua: I am coming to that. Since 1949 China has been shifting...

Speaker: I wish he came to that question directly.

Hem Barua: I will come to that directly. To be very straight, whether the implementation, the unilateral implementation, of Panchsheel ethics as the Prime Minister stated the other day, is possible against background of this sort. That is what I want to know from the Prime Minister.

Jawaharlal Nehru: Panchsheel is like, well, King Charles's head. It comes up again and again. Panchsheel is civilised behaviour. Does he want us to say that we will not follow civilised behaviour because somebody else does not do so?

Hem Barua: I said "unilateral implementation". Is it possible?

Jawaharlal Nehru: What does implementation of civilised behaviour mean? To the extent implementation of civilised behaviour is possible, we will do it, whether the other party does it or not. It has nothing to do with the defence or non-defence. Defence is looked upon from the point of view of defence.

Hem Barua: It is ethically all right, but, in practice, it does not yield results.

131. Congress.

Jawaharlal Nehru: I am afraid, the hon. Member has not understood what, Panchsheel means.

Hem Barua: I have.

Jawaharlal Nehru: Then I would like to advise him to read it again a little more carefully. I would like to know what part of it he wants to object to. Which part does he want us not to accept?

Hem Barua: What about peaceful coexistence with China? A lamb cannot coexist with a lion until it is in the lion's belly.

Speaker: It is becoming difficult for me. Coexistence is becoming difficult even inside the House. How can I coexist with all these things? There ought to be some limit, but I find the discussion is going on.

रामचन्द्र बड़े:[132] हर एक अखबार में यह समाचार प्रकाशित हुआ है कि चाइना ने छिपछाप नदी के उस पार ट्रक्स और मिलिटरी फोर्सिज इकट्ठी की है। इस के अतिरिक्त यह हिन्दुस्तान के क्षेत्र में नई नई पोस्ट्स भी स्थापित कर रहा है। चाइना का यह एटीटूयड देखने से क्या शासन यह नहीं समझता है कि वह इस देश पर नया आक्रमण करना चाहता है?

अध्यक्ष महोदयः इस का जवाब तो दे दिया गया है।

रामचन्द्र बड़ेः इस का जवाब नहीं दिया गया है।

अध्यक्ष महोदयः अभी मिनिस्टर साहब ने कहा है कि हमारे पास इस बारे में इत्तिला नहीं है। माननीय सदस्य उसे बात को दोहरा रहे है कि अखबारों में यह छपा है।

लहरी सिंह (रोहतक):[133] इस विषय में अखबारों में जो, खबर छपी है, क्या गवर्नमेंट ने उस का सोर्स मालूम किया है कि वह कहां से आई है, कैसे आई है?

जवाहरलाल नेहरुः माननीय सदस्य यह तो अखबार वालों को पूछें। उन के अजीब अजीब जरिये होते हैं।

132. Jan Sangh.
133. Jan Sangh.

[Translation begins:

Ramchandra Bade:[134] Every newspaper has published a report that China has collected trucks and military forces on the other side of the Chip Chap river. Besides, she is establishing new posts in the Indian territory. Is it not clear to the administration by this attitude of China that she is getting ready for fresh aggression on this country.

Speaker: Answer to this has been given.

Ramchandra Bade: This has not been answered.

Speaker : Just now the Minister has said that we don't have information about it. Honourable Member is repeating that it is published in newspapers.

Lahri Singh (Rohtak): [135]Has the Government tried to find out the source of the news published in the newspapers.

Jawaharlal Nehru: Honourable Member should ask the newspapermen. They have strange ways.

Translation ends]

Speaker: The hon. Member's question is whether Government have cared to find out the sources of the paper from which they published that news.

Jawaharlal Nehru: It will not be proper if we have to use our intelligence operations. It will not perhaps be liked to put the intelligence on newspapers to find out what their sources are.

Speaker: Does Shri Harish Chandra Mathur[136] want to ask any question?

Harish Chandra Mathur (Jalore): No, Sir.

Surendranath Dwivedy (Kendrapara):[137] The hon. Defence Minister says that he has no information about this reported movement, but he does not

134. See fn 132 in this section.
135. See fn 133 in this section.
136. Congress.
137. PSP.

deny that the Chinese vehicles may be moving in that area. Since China in its note of the 2nd June[138] has already hinted that there may be a border clash at any moment....

An Hon. Member: Bloody clash.

Hem Barua: Bloody conflict.

Surendranath Dwivedy: They have said....

Speaker: Quotations need not be read.

Surendranath Dwivedy: They have accused India and have said that India is carrying on intrusion so that a border clash may be touched off at any moment which indicates that most probably China is preparing for some eventuality. In view of this, may I know whether the Government is thinking of any emergency measures not only at Defence level but at the popular level also to build up the morale of the country to meet any emergency?

Jawaharlal Nehru: To build up the morale of the country?

Krishna Menon: At civil level also.

Jawaharlal Nehru: I suppose the hon. Members are helping in not building it up. [Interruption]

Surendranath Dwivedy: I said at popular level. [Interruption]

Speaker: Order, order,

Jawaharlal Nehru: I do maintain, Sir, that the kind of questions that have been asked are not helpful in building up the morale of the country.... [Interruption]

Hari Vishnu Kamath rose-

Hem Barua: On a point of order, Sir.... [Interruption]

Nath Pai rose -

138. See *White Paper VI*, pp. 56-58 and in this volume appendix 3 (b).

Hem Barua: On a point of order, Sir.... [Interruption]

Surendranath Dwivedy rose -

Speaker: Order, order.

Ramchandra Bade rose-

Speaker: Order, order. Will he kindly resume his seat? Let them say one by one what they have to say. Shri Nath Pai.

Nath Pai: Mr Speaker, Sir. [Interruption]

Speaker: Order, order. Can we proceed in this manner?

Nath Pai: It is indeed a great pity that every time we try to exercise our legitimate elementary duty which alone justifies our presence in this House, that is, of calling attention to what we regard as a matter of concern, the hon. Prime Minister instead of trying to guide and tell the facts is irritated. I must say this. The two recent accusations are firstly, that we are indulging in war-mongering when all we say is, "Are we from the defence point of view fully prepared?" And, secondly, now comes this even worse allegation. I ask whether it is fair for him when we ask for simple information to level such a serious charge that we are interested in weakening the morale of the country. Does it lie well in the mouth of the hon. Prime Minister?.... [Interruption]

Hari Vishnu Kamath: It is unworthy of the hon. Prime Minister, the good democrat that he is.... [Interruption]

Surendranath Dwivedy: He should not take advantage of his position.... [Interruption]

Speaker: Order, order,

Ramchandra Bade: He should take those words back.... [Interruption]

Speaker: Order, order. Can we go on in this manner? Even if one is provoked and agitated, at least there must be some method in our proceedings.

Surendranath Dwivedy: It is a serious matter, Sir, if the hon. Prime Minister says like that. [Interruption]

Speaker: How can I deal with it unless hon. Members allow me to do so? They do not allow anybody to speak. How can I deal with it if all of them stand up simultaneously and speak?

Nath Pai: It pains....[Interruption]

An Hon. Member: They are standing up in fours and fives.

Nath Pai: I will not be bowed down like this. May I say in conclusion that it pains us to see the Hon. Prime Minister losing his temper every time we try to raise a matter in the House which we regard as a legitimate one.... [Interruption]

Ansar Harvani[139] rose-

Nath Pai: These tactics will not bow me down.... [Interruption]

Speaker: Order, order. All hon. Members should help me in maintaining discipline and decorum in the House. It is very regrettable.

Hari Vishnu Kamath: We are at your service, Sir.

Nath Pai: Let not Shri Harvani be more loyal than the king.... [Interruption]

Speaker: Order, order. I will request that hon. Members to remain silent unless I require their assistance. I would ask for that assistance if I require it. They should just keep silent and listen. One hon. Member is on his legs; let us hear him.

Nath Pai rose –[Interruptions]

Speaker: Order, order.

Nath Pai: This is a very serious charge, Sir. Here is a responsible journal, a national journal. Either the journals are indulging in panic-mongering, or they are discharging their duties.

Speaker: What is the journal?

139. Congress.

Nath Pai: This is the *Times of India* of Sunday.[140] We think they are doing a very vital national service. We can only know such information as the national papers give and ask Government which have better sources for clarification. When we ask such a question if a danger is looming large on the horizon are we doing something wrong. Is it betraying the country, or helping the Prime Minister? How does he combine the two, Sir?

Jawaharlal Nehru: May I repeat, Sir, that I do not wish to hurt anybody. But I am surprised at the kind of questions hon. Members ask. When the Hon. Member talked about the lion and the lamb, it does not increase the morale of the country.

Hem Barua: Since the reference is to me, may I say....[Interruptions]

An Hon. Member: Sit down!

Speaker: Order, order.

Hem Barua: You cannot cow me down. I will not be cowed down like this. [Interruptions]

Speaker: I would ask Mr Hem Barua to address the Chair.

Hem Barua: Why should they shout like this? They are howling. [Interruption]

Speaker: Order, order. Would he resume his seat? If someone shouts he can draw my attention to it. I will ask him to keep silent. Not that he should enter into a duel with him directly and settle the matter. Shall I be a silent witness to all this? Can we carry on the proceedings of the House in this manner? I have appealed to hon. Members again and again that they should maintain at least some minimum decorum. Let us hear the hon. Member.

Surendranath Dwivedy: The Prime Minister while replying to my question said that by putting such questions we are not building the morale of the country. It may be his opinion. He is surrendering the country to the Chinese and others. But I want to know what his answer is to the first part of my question. I asked whether they are thinking of any emergency measures at the Defence level. Is there any reply to that question, I want to know.

140. Sunday, 10 June 1962, datelined 9 June.

Jawaharlal Nehru: May I Know, Sir, if this is the proper way of putting it –that I am surrendering the country to China. I think it is a scandalous charge to make. [Interruptions]

Speaker: Order, order. No more questions I would allow. Perhaps, hon. Members who felt agitated have satisfied themselves with these charges.

Surendranath Dwivedy: He cannot accuse us of betrayal of this country – it is too much.

Speaker: I cannot allow every hon. Member to go on like this. I have allowed so many questions. Only one is permitted; but so many questions have been put.

Hem Barua: Will you let me clarify my position? I had not completed my idea, when I was interrupted by hon. Members.

Speaker: Order, order. His leader asked him to sit down, because he wanted to put a question himself. How can I help that?

Hem Barua: The reference with regard to the lion and the lamb was to me....

Speaker: Order, order, now.

Hem Barua: This will have a bad effect.

Speaker: What more does he want now?

Hem Barua: I have to vindicate my position. When I referred to the lion and the lamb, I had my own arguments to offer.

Speaker: He may have his arguments; others also have their own arguments. The Treasury Benches have their arguments. They have expressed their opinion; he has expressed his. Where is the trouble now?

Hem Barua: The Prime Minister has made certain remarks.

Speaker: Order, order. He has said that reference to these things does not improve the morale of the country. Can't he hold that opinion? Why should there be a quarrel about it – calling one country as a lion and the other as a lamb, he says does not improve the morale of the country. Should I give the hon. Member opportunity to go on making a lecture?

Hem Barua: I did not say one country is a lion and the other country is a lamb. May I submit that I had never completed my statement? My statement has been completely distorted.

I would be the last man to call my country a lamb, we are interested in defending the morale of this country, defending the boundaries of our country and the frontiers of this country and if a call comes tomorrow, we shall be the first to go to the battlefield with guns in our hands. But what pains us is this, that the Prime Minister has tried to distort our statement. I said that by the very policy of weakness that the Prime Minister or the Government is following towards China we are made to look like lambs....

Speaker: Order, order. I would ask the hon. Member to resume his seat.

Hari Vishnu Kamath: One question.

Speaker: I have allowed them so many questions. There have been more than enough.

Nath Pai: Sir, just one word.

Speaker: If they want to raise a discussion they might do it in some other manner. I have always allowed it.

Nath Pai: May I say just one sentence regarding this lion and lamb? Vivekananda told the whole of India, "Ye lions, shed off the delusion that you are lambs". And there was no insult meant to India when he said so.

Hem Barua: I did not want to mean any insult.

Jawaharlal Nehru: When he said that we are surrendering to the Chinese, that was of course a mild statement to make!

Hem Barua: But you provoked us.

Jawaharlal Nehru: Yes, yes, we have had enough of this kind of things.

Hari Vishnu Kamath: When he talked of our not helping to build up the morale of the country, do his statements....[Interruptions]

Speaker: Order, order, would there be an end to it? Shri Mohsin.[141]

Mahavir Tyagi: I move, Sir, that the question may now be closed and we take up the next item.

391. In the Lok Sabha: China Protests Confiscation of *China Today*[142]

Protest Note from China Re: Confiscation of "*China Today*"

D.C. Sharma:[143] will the Prime Minister be pleased to state:

(a) whether China has protested to India against the confiscation of issues of the news bulletin *China Today* which its Embassy published in New Delhi;
(b) whether China has also counter-charged India with reprinting in its Embassy's news bulletin "materials from unofficial sources slandering the Chinese Government,"and
(c) if so, the details of the reply sent to the Chinese Government, if any?

The Minister of State in the Ministry of External Affairs (Lakshmi Menon):

(a) Yes, Sir.
(b) The Government of China have charged that Indian Embassy bulletins published in Peking have reproduced documents and statements attacking China, including a summary of the *Officials' Report*[144] and the AICC Resolution on National Integrity (published in *India News* of 1-1-1961). Our Embassy's fortnightly bulletin is by and large innocuous. It has a limited circulation in the diplomatic corps of Peking. Moreover our Embassy has been very careful in observing international norms as well as the laws and regulations of the People's Republic of China in putting out this bulletin. There is, therefore, not much substance in the Chinese Government's counter allegations.

141. F.H. Mohsin, Congress.
142. Oral Answers, 15 June 1962. *Lok Sabha Debates*, Third Series, Vol. V, 8 June to 22 June 1962, Ist Session, cols 10768-10773.
143. Congress.
144. Republished as SWJN/SS/66/Supplement.

(c) The Chinese note has just been received and is under study.

D.C. Sharma: May I know whether there are unofficial sources prevailing in China? I think all the sources in China are official. If there are unofficial sources, do they refer to the Indian sources or the sources which are available in China?

The Prime Minister and Minister of External Affairs and Minister of Atomic Energy (Jawaharlal Nehru): Undoubtedly there must be many unofficial sources but they are not known.

Hem Barua:[145] In the Chinese note of May 11,[146] published in *China Today*, it is said that "the Aksai-Chin area has always been Chinese territory", and subsequently in the Chinese note of 2nd June,[147] the Prime Minister's offer to allow the Aksai-Chin road to be used for civilian traffic by China is described as an absurdity. In the context of it, may I know whether the Prime Minister's offer still holds any validity?

Jawaharlal Nehru: The offer is very good, very reasonable, very logical and very valid. The fact that it is not admitted does not make it unreasonable.

Hem Barua: Then why did they point out in the reply that it is not accepted.

Speaker:[148] Order, order.

Jawaharlal Nehru: If it is not accepted, it is not accepted. There the matter ends.

Nath Pai:[149] The charges and counter-charges, the allegations and counter-allegations, do not seem to get abated in anyway. May we, therefore, know from the Prime Minister, what makes him think, as he said the other day, that China is unhappy with her relations with us and would like settlement?

Jawaharlal Nehru: It is rather difficult to analyse certain feelings that are derived from a multitude of sources, and it may not be wholly justified. I do not know;

145. PSP.
146. See *White Paper VI*, p. 40 and in this volume appendix 3 (a).
147. See *White Paper VI*, pp. 56-58 and in this volume appendix 3 (b).
148. Hukam Singh.
149. PSP.

but I did say so. That does not mean that anything special is in view at the present moment. I did say that various factors led me to it.

Nath Pai: No grounds on which it may be based ...

Speaker: Order, order.

Hari Vishnu Kamath:[150] Is it not a fact that the Chinese Stalinists who are in power have mastered the Nazi Goebbelsian technique of repeating lies ad nauseam …

Speaker: Why go so far?

Hari Vishnu Kamath: It is about China.

Speaker: He is saying so many things and making imputations.

Hari Vishnu Kamath: It is a fact; it is against China and not against India.

Speaker: Against China also we should be careful.

Hari Vishnu Kamath: It is about the lying propaganda; it is admitted by the Government also. In view of this and together with the corollary—the bigger the lie, the better for Chou En-lai—may I know what is the attitude of the Government to the New Age Press owned, so far as I know, by the Communist Party of India, which is abetting this anti-national propaganda in this country? *China Today* is printed at the New Age Press –

Speaker: He should confine himself to the question instead of saying so many things.

Hari Vishnu Kamath: The question is concerned with *China Today*.

Speaker: The Communist Party of India does not come here. If he wants to put any question about the charges or counter-charges made in that publication, he might put it.

150. PSP.

Hari Vishnu Kamath: All right, Sir. Is it not a fact that the charges contained in *China Today* against India and in the other documents referred to by my friend, Shri Hem Barua, have been made in this country since the last six months or more or even longer than that, and is it a fact that the New Age Press has had a hand in propagating these charges, the lying propaganda, inside India—the New Age Press is owned by the Communist Party of India—and what action has been taken by the Government in this connection?

Jawaharlal Nehru: The hon. Member has such an abundance of things in his mind that he is wholly confusing. I am confused what he is after. I remember a string of words and phrases, but I do not quite follow his logical arguments. He said something about the Stalinists in China. I do not understand. [Interruptions]

Speaker: Order, order.

Jawaharlal Nehru: These are emotional and evocative phrases.

Renu Chakravartty:[151] Please ask him to repeat what he said he should withdraw it.

Hari Vishnu Kamath: You provoked me.

Speaker: These private conversations should not continue. A supplementary has been asked and the Prime Minister is answering that. Meanwhile, private conversations are going on and the same charges and countercharges are being levelled there.

Hari Vishnu Kamath: She started the game.

Speaker: Whoever might have done it, both were unauthorised. I do not allow that.

Jawaharlal Nehru: I do not quite know what is the question. He ended by asking what action has been taken against the Communist Party of India or the *New Age*.

Hari Vishnu Kamath: New Age Press.

151. CPI.

Jawaharlal Nehru: All the rest was a confusing preamble which has nothing to do with this.

The position is, according to the international practice, any official documents are allowed to be circulated in another country. That is, if we send a message to the Chinese authorities, we have the right to publish that in any paper that we may issue in Peking or elsewhere. If *China Today* publishes Chinese messages, they have a right to do it. We are not going to object to it, even though it may be highly offensive to us.

Hari Vishnu Kamath: Anti-Indian; it has been confiscated.

Jawaharlal Nehru: Let him try to understand a little and not be confused in his own circles of thought. If an official message or a statement of a Government is published, whether a speech or a letter to us, it is perfectly right, even though it might be offensive to us. We allow such things to be printed. But where selections from it giving a particular point are brought out and comments are made, then it is different. Then it becomes difficult. In *China Today*, something of this kind was done. It was not purely an official statement. If it had been their official statement, we would have taken no action, however offensive it might have been, because that is a statement that is sent by one Government to our Government. If a statement is sent by our Government to China, we claim the same right of publicity for that. But where it is changed and one-sided extracts are printed, then it becomes pure propaganda and not an official statement being reproduced. The hon. Member referred to the *New Age* and said that the *New Age* have been the publishers of it.[152]

Hari Vishnu Kamath: Printers.

Surendranath Dwivedy:[153] They are the printers of *China Today* which has been proscribed.

Jawaharlal Nehru: Being printers—somewhat less than being publishers. [Interruption] If they do anything against the law, then we do proceed against them. They naturally will suffer if they go against the law, but from the mere fact that they are printing a document which occasionally offends us for some reason and which we forfeit, it does not necessarily follow that we proceed against them on this basis; otherwise we might.

152. See item 389.
153. PSP.

392. To M.J. Desai: On a Draft[154]

I have glanced through these papers. As far as I have seen after hurried view, there is no reference in them to the talks we had with the Chinese authorities in Delhi and probably in Peking also about Barahoti or some other places in UP. The Chinese representative was in Delhi for many weeks then. I think this should be included.

I think also that the date of the Dalai Lama entering India to seek refuge should also be given.

393. In the Lok Sabha: India in Chinese Territory[155]

Alleged Indian Intrusion into
Chinese Territory

Question:[156] will the Prime Minister be pleased to state:

(a) Whether the Chinese Government in their protest note dated the 28th May, 1962[157] have accused India with further intrusions and provocations in the western sector of the Sino-Indian border; and
(b) If so, the reaction of the Government thereto?

The Prime Minister and Minister of External Affairs and Minister of Atomic Energy (Jawaharlal Nehru): (a) Yes, Sir. The Chinese Government in their note have baselessly alleged that India has set up a military post 35 18′ North 78 05′ 30" East, 8 kilometres west by south of the Chinese post at 35° 19′ N 78 12′ E. The Chinese Government have named this place Hongshantou. There is no such place as Hongshantou on the map and the area referred to is Indian territory.

(c) The Chinese note dated 28th May, 1962 has just been received and is under study.[158]

154. Note to FS, 18 June 1962.
155. Written Answers, 19 June 1962. *Lok Sabha Debates*, Third Series, Vol. V, 8 June to 22 June 1962, Ist Session, col. 11650.
156. By two Congress MPs D.C. Sharma and P.C. Borooah.
157. See *White Paper VI*, pp. 54-55 and in this volume appendix 7 (a).
158. For India's reply of 22 June 1962, see *White Paper VI*, pp. 68-70 and in this volume appendix 7 (b).

394. In the Lok Sabha: Development in NEFA[159]

P.C. Borooah: [160] Will the Prime Minister be pleased to state:

(a) whether the Foreign Secretary[161] visited Shillong to discuss various problems relating to the development of NEFA region with the Governor of Assam and Senior Officers of NEFA in the 1st week of June, 1962;

(a) If so, what particular matters were discussed during his visit; and
(b) what decisions, if any, were taken in consultation with the Foreign Secretary for the development of the NEFA region?

The Prime Minister and Minister of External Affairs and Minister of Atomic Energy (Jawaharlal Nehru): (a) The Foreign Secretary paid a visit to Shillong from 31st May to 2nd June. A conference of senior officers of the NEFA commenced at Shillong on 1st June and the Foreign Secretary sat in at one or two sessions of this conference to acquaint himself with the administrative and other problems which the NEFA Administration has to deal with and give necessary guidance and assistance in dealing with these problems.

(b) The Foreign Secretary took advantage of this visit to discuss logistic and other problems facing the NEFA Administration and the Assam Rifles, with the Governor[162] and also met some of the Assam Ministers and Chief Secretary of Assam.[163] He also met a number of officers of the Indian Frontier Administrative Service serving in NEFA to acquaint himself with the conditions in the various regions of NEFA and discuss the difficulties experienced by these officers in their day to day work. Besides, the Foreign Secretary presided over a meeting of the Association of Indian Frontier Administrative Service Officers, where certain proposals regarding improvement of the service conditions were discussed.

(c) No decisions were taken on any major questions. As a result of the consultations, which took place however, some of the difficulties and problems were adjusted by internal re-arrangements and guidance was given as to the lines on which other problems including development proposals should be processed and sent up to the Government of India.

159. Written answer, 19 June 1962. *Lok Sabha Debates*, Third Series, Vol. V, 8 June to 22 June 1962, Ist Session, cols 11665-66.
160. Congress.
161. M.J. Desai.
162. S.M. Shrinagesh.
163. A.N. Kidwai.

It might be added that such consultations between the Governor and the officers of the NEFA Administration go on continuously when the Governor or Senior NEFA Officers visit Delhi and occasionally when the Foreign Secretary visits Shillong.

395. In the Lok Sabha: Chinese Incursions into Indian Territory[164]

Speaker:[165] I have received notice of an adjournment motion by Shri Hem Barua. This is based on the correspondence that was placed on the Table of the House yesterday. The news that has appeared in the papers rather confuses the reader. Will the hon. Prime Minister like to say anything about it?

The Prime Minister, Minister of External Affairs and Minister of Atomic Energy (Jawaharlal Nehru): We have placed, as usual, the full correspondence on the Table of the House. The reports appearing in the press give rather a wrong impression by picking out a phrase here and there.

The fact of the matter is that in this area all kinds of movements are taking place by us as well as by the Chinese authorities. Because of our movements, sometimes going behind the Chinese posts, some apprehension has been created in the minds of the Chinese, and they have also moved. These movements are confined to a small area. To call them fresh incursions is hardly correct, though it may be in an area of half a mile or two miles or something like that that has taken place.

It is not very proper for me to discuss these matters publicly. But I can assure the House that the position, as it is, is more advantageous to India than it was previously, and the advantage is growing as our roads are being made and other facilities of communication are being established. That is the chief drawback. Our Army is good enough, but that is not enough. The Army has to get there and has to be fed and supplied. That is the chief drawback, and we are making good that lack. I do not say that the position is 100 per cent satisfactory. It is not. But it is getting better and better.

164. Motion for Adjournment, 20 June 1962. *Lok Sabha Debates*, Third Series, Vol. V, 8 June to 22 June 1962, Ist Session, cols 11934-36.

165. Hukam Singh.

Hem Barua (Gauhati)[166] rose …

Speaker: If I need it, I will certainly request him to give me some information. I just requested the Prime Minister to make a statement, seeing that the headlines given in the papers create an impression that there have been some recent incursions and fresh encroachments. The House only needs to be assured on this point.

Jawaharlal Nehru: The recent encroachments are referred to in the notes. The headlines have taken extracts of some phrases here and there from the notes. There have been movements, patrols coming, our movements and theirs. Naturally, our movements are not referred to. Theirs are referred to in our notes to the Chinese Government. But broadly speaking, there has been no real advance. They may have moved a few hundred yards this way or that. This is manoeuvring for better positions.

Speaker: In view of the statement made by the Prime Minister ...

Hem Barua: I want to congratulate the Prime Minister ...

Speaker: I will make this request to the hon. Member. In view of what has been stated, probably he would be better advised in not pursuing it further.

Hem Barua: I just want to congratulate the Prime Minister on giving us the information that the situation is improving. This is a great thing for the country.

Speaker: In view of the statement made by the Prime Minister, I do not feel called upon to give my consent to the adjournment motion.

166. PSP.

396. In the Rajya Sabha: Chinese Incursions in the North[167]

A.B. Vajpayee:[168] Will the Prime Minister be pleased to state:

(a) whether there have been any fresh Chinese incursions on the Northern border; and
(b) if so, whether a statement giving the details of these incursions will be laid on the Table of the House?

The Minister of State in the Ministry of External Affairs (Lakshmi Menon):

(a) Yes, Sir. Subsequent to our protest note dated 15th April, 1962[169] regarding the Chinese post established at a point 6 miles west of Sumdo, Chinese troops have set up another post on Indian territory at 78. 52.30′ East 33.30′ North, approximately 8 to 10 miles South-East of Spanggur. This new post set up on Indian Territory has been fortuitously admitted by the Chinese in their note dated the 11th May 1962.[170]
(b) Copies of the Chinese note and our reply[171] thereto; are placed on the Table of the House.

[Though China's Note of 11 May and India's Note of 21 May form part of the Debates, these are given in appendices in this volume.]

A.B. Vajpayee: Am I to understand that no fresh Chinese incursions have taken place apart from what has been stated by the Minister?

Lakshmi Menon: It is obvious from the admission by the Chinese themselves.

A.B. Vajpayee: Sir, May I draw your attention to part (b) of the question? I asked for a statement giving the details of fresh Chinese incursions but what we have been supplied with are copies of the Notes that have been exchanged between India and China, and there is no mention about the

167. Oral Answers, 20 June 1962. *Rajya Sabha Debates*, Vol. XXXIX, No. 6, cols 862-871.
168. Jan Sangh MP from Uttar Pradesh.
169. See *White Paper VI*, p. 26 and in this volume appendix 1(a).
170. See *White Paper VI*, p. 40 and in this volume appendix 1(b).
171. See *White Paper VI*, pp. 49-50 and in this volume appendix 1(c).

entry of the Chinese personnel into the village Roi, half a mile south of Longju. Am I to understand that it is not a case of Chinese incursion?

Jawaharlal Nehru: This question deals with Ladakh. It does not deal with Longju because it has nothing to deal with there. Longju is of the least relevance to this question. Longju is situated actually on the border and there is an argument as to which part of Longju is on this side or that side of the so-called McMahon line. I do not think that there has been any movement on this side of that line. The argument is as to which part of Longju is on that side of the border or on this side of the border. But still, apart from it, the Chinese had occupied Longju long ago. It is that part that is discussed, not any other village to the south of Longju.

As for the other matters about Ladakh about which the answer has been given, the correspondence itself states the position. It should be realised that there is a peculiar position where we are making certain advances, small advances—patrol posts and others and the Chinese are advancing. It is a game of military chess that is going on in the wide expanses and a few persons, about a dozen or so, come and make a patrol post as it is called or our people go and make a post endangering their positions. In fact, this is largely due to the movements on our side, which have induced the Chinese to make some movements on their side to protect themselves. Not all these things are said in public but since the hon. Member is going on asking me, I cannot go on saying "No". These things are never given out in public, when there is a delicate situation as to what we are doing to inconvenience them. It is well known in knowledgeable circles in the world who follow this that the position in these areas has changed to our advantage somewhat. That does not mean any final thing. That is a continual thing to our advantage and the Chinese themselves are rather concerned about it and are trying to protect their posts because the new posts are to their disadvantage.

A.B. Vajpayee: On a point of personal explanation, may I submit that I did not ask for any information that might go to help the Chinese? But it is surprising indeed that when it is a question of sending protest notes to the Chinese, the Government takes one position and when it is a question of replying to supplementary put by hon. Members, the position taken by the Government is quite different. I fail to understand how these two positions can be reconciled.

Jawaharlal Nehru: I have not understood where the difference is.

A.B. Vajpayee: I put a specific question whether the entry of the Chinese troops in the village Roi, half a mile south of Longju, is a case of Chinese incursion or not.

Jawaharlal Nehru: If it is not south of Longju, how can it be an incursion because north of Longju is Chinese territory?

A.B. Vajpayee: Longju is not Chinese territory.

Chairman: [172]Half a mile north of Longju is Chinese territory, he said.

A.B. Vajpayee: In our protest note, we have said that this village is situated well within Indian Territory and that is what we have protested against. Now the Prime Minister says that it is not Indian Territory.

Jawaharlal Nehru: I am sorry I do not know anything about the village. I have forgotten the names. There are plenty of small villages.

A.B. Vajpayee: Sir, he should come here prepared.

Jawaharlal Nehru: Territory north of Longju is Chinese territory.

A.B. Vajpayee: I have a copy of the protest note, which says that the Chinese have made a fresh incursion in this village. This is well within our territory.

Lakshmi Menon: This village Roi or Ruyu, as the Chinese call it, is a place with two households, one and a half miles south of Longju. There was no incursion at all. It was discovered that two officers, a patrol leader and some other Chinese, strayed into the village and went back. You would not call this intrusion or invasion.

A.B. Vajpayee: I have never called it invasion or intrusion, but it is incursion. There may be no dispute about it and we have protested against this.

Lakshmi Menon: Certainly.

Chairman: You have got the replies.

172. Zakir Husain.

Jawaharlal Nehru: Sir, the point is that it is a most trivial occurrence and there is nothing to get excited about it.

A.B. Vajpayee: May I put a supplementary, Sir? In our note sent on the 6th of June,[173] we have protested against the setting up of five military bases by the Chinese on our territory. But, on the 13th June at a New Delhi Press Conference, the Prime Minister was pleased to state that China is eager for a settlement.[174] May I know, Sir, how China can be eager for a settlement when military preparations are being made like this?

Jawaharlal Nehru: We are making military preparations too but we would like a settlement.

A.B. Vajpayee: Not on Chinese territory. We are not making military preparations on Chinese territory.

Jawaharlal Nehru: That is what the Chinese say, that we are making military preparations on Chinese territory.

A.B. Vajpayee: Are we to go by what the Chinese say?

Jawaharlal Nehru: We say something and the Chinese say something else. They say it is Sinkiang territory. It may be immaterial. But they are wrong. The two are mutually contradictory. In fact, one helps the other in order to make a settlement. But one wants to make one's position as strong as possible. However, what I said there was not based on any precise fact but an impression I had got that the Chinese would like a settlement. That does not help very much because the kind of settlement that they may like maybe completely objectionable to us. That is a different matter. But I guessed that the mood of the Chinese was in favour of a settlement, which would not involve too considerable a loss of face to them.

Niranjan Singh:[175] Yesterday it had been published that about five posts have been set up by the Chinese and they are constructing new roads in the south. May I know, Sir how far they are away from the Indian Army posts or near about or whether they have entered the Indian area, which has Indian posts.

173. See *White Paper VI*, pp. 60-61 and in this volume appendix 1(d).
174. See item 1.
175. PSP.

Syed Ahmad:[176] My friend's supplementary does not arise out of this question.

Jawaharlal Nehru: I do not know what the hon. Member means by the Indian border. The Chinese are far inside the Indian border.

Niranjan Singh: If they are far inside the Indian border, may I know, Sir, whether they have crossed the Indian bases.

Jawaharlal Nehru: I suppose the straight answer would be to say "No". But the whole thing is so crooked not straight, because in some places we are behind the Chinese posts, in some places they are in front. It is a zigzag thing, which has developed. Therefore, to say whether they are beyond or not is not very accurate.

Chairman: It is not a static situation; it is a moving situation. We are moving and they are moving. It is very difficult to state the position at a certain point of time.

Bhupesh Gupta:[177] PSP and Jan Sangh are also moving.

397. In the Lok Sabha: China's Note of 31 May 1962[178]

Question:[179] Will the Prime Minister be pleased to state:

(a) whether the attention of Government has been drawn to the reference to Nepal, Sikkim and Bhutan in Chinese note dated the 31st May, 1962[180] replying to India's note regarding proposed Sino-Pak border talks dated the 10th May, 1962;[181] and
(b) the reaction of Government thereto?

176. Congress.
177. CPI.
178. Oral Answers, 22 June 1962. *Lok Sabha Debates*, Third Series, Vol. V, 8 June to 22 June 1962, Ist Session, pp. 12407-12.
179. By PSP MPs Hari Vishnu Kamath, Hem Barua and Congress MPs Shree Narayan Das, Bhakt Darshan.
180. See *White Paper VI*, pp. 99-102 and in this volume appendix 8 (a).
181. See *White Paper VI*, pp. 96-97 and in this volume appendix 8 (b).

The Deputy Minister in the Ministry of External Affairs (Dinesh Singh):

(a) Yes, Sir.
(b) In our protest note of 10th May 1962, we drew the attention of the Government of China to the fact that China had no common border with Pakistan whether in the West or in the East, and cited the two terminal points of our border to prove it. It was not meant to be a complete description but enough to show that China and Pakistan had no common border. The Government of China in their reply gave this description a meaning which our note did not seek to convey, and drew certain conclusions there from which are calculated to affect our relations with Nepal, Sikkim and Bhutan.

It is needless to reiterate that we have close and enduring relations with Nepal based on mutual respect for each other's territorial integrity and sovereignty.

In regard to Bhutan, we have special treaty obligations and, at the request of the Government of Bhutan, we have at various times taken up with the Government of China matters such as Chinese cartographic aggression on Bhutan, the violation of Bhutan's air space by Chinese aircraft and the protection of Bhutan's interests in Tibet.

As to Sikkim, our position is clear. The Government of India are entirely responsible for the defence and external relations of Sikkim and no foreign power has any right to interfere in Sikkim.

Hari Vishnu Kamath: China in its note replying to India's note of the 10th May says that Nepal does not exist, Sikkim does not exist and Bhutan does not exist. Is it clear evidence of China's mala fides and has Government got any other information in its possession to show that these expressions are an outward sign of an inward design to liberate these territories in the Chinese meaning of the word "liberation" and, if so, what is Government's reaction to that?

The Prime Minister and Minister of External Affairs and Minister of Atomic Energy (Jawaharlal Nehru): Government's immediate reaction is that the question is too complicated to be understood, further all the inferences the hon. Member has drawn have no justification. I do not know or remember where this phrase occurs in the Chinese note that there is no Nepal, no Bhutan and no Sikkim.

Speaker:[182] Some newspapers gave this report and put the interpretation that Bhutan etc. do not exist according to China.

Jawaharlal Nehru: I do not know where this occurs. In some newspapers? I do not read all the newspapers. It is patently absurd for anybody to say either for China, or for the newspapers or the hon. Member opposite, whoever it may be. It is quite absurd. They have come to a treaty with Nepal.[183] Did they have a treaty with something that does not exist?

Hari Vishnu Kamath: The Prime Minister has misunderstood my question. May I make it clear that the Chinese in their reply to India's note say, according to press reports, that it, Nepal, does not exist, Bhutan does not exist and Sikkim does not exist. Is it not clear evidence of intention on their part to liberate these territories in the Chinese meaning of the word "liberation" and then incorporate them into the vast Chinese Communist empire?

Speaker: How can our Government say about that?

Hari Vishnu Kamath: Is there any information in their possession to show….

Speaker: Order, order. Whether China had that design or not, how could the Prime Minister say that?

Hari Vishnu Kamath: Have they any information or reports in their possession to show that?

Jawaharlal Nehru: What China has stated in its note is that, according to India, because India has only stated the nodal points and not the middle, therefore, India apparently thinks that Nepal does not exist. They have negatively accused us of forgetting the existence of Nepal, Bhutan and Sikkim. Of course, it has no meaning. I do not know who drafted the note of China.

Speaker: Shri Hem Barua.

Hari Vishnu Kamath: I have put only one question.

182. Hukam Singh.
183. In 1960.

Hem Barua: In view of the fact that China used or inserted the word "proper" before "relations" in the Chinese official version of Mr Chou En-lai's press conference on 25th April, 1960 at Delhi,[184] may I know whether Government would not proceed on the assumption that here was China bent upon introducing new dimensions to the problem of Sikkim and Bhutan?

Jawaharlal Nehru: The Chinese language is a difficult language to translate. I do not know what word he used in Chinese.

Hera Barua: But this was made clear from the tape recorder.

Jawaharlal Nehru: But anyhow our experience of the Chinese statements is that they usually are very carefully drafted which may mean more than one thing. They are not precise. It may mean something else. What the word "proper" means I do not know. So far as our relations are concerned, they are patent, that is, with Bhutan and Sikkim, and on other occasions the Chinese Government have assured us that the authority recognised our relations with Bhutan and Sikkim.

Hem Barua: In this latest note they have described our relations with Sikkim and Bhutan as power chauvinism.

Jawaharlal Nehru: I do not know.

Hari Vishnu Kamath: Does Government still stand by the hon. Prime Minister's declaration which he made a couple of years ago that any aggression against Bhutan or Nepal, or Sikkim also included perhaps, will be regarded as aggression against India and dealt with as such?

Jawaharlal Nehru: Yes, Sir; the position in regard to Nepal and Bhutan is different. Obviously, we would regard any aggression in Nepal, if not directly, indirectly against India. But it is for the Nepal Government to decide what should be done in the circumstances. We cannot take action against the wishes of the Nepal Government. But Bhutan, as I stated in reply to this question, has constantly asked us to state their case to China, They recognise our great interest in the defence of Bhutan.

184. See SWJN/SS/60/item 34.

Hari Vishnu Kamath: Sikkim?

Shivaji Rao S. Deshmukh:[185] May I know whether it is a fact that the recent mention of Nepal, Bhutan and Sikkim in the latest Chinese note arises from the Chinese anxiety to recognise Indo-Chinese border dispute as a border dispute between China on the one hand and Nepal, Bhutan and Sikkim on the other?

Jawaharlal Nehru: The question is not clear to me. What does Indo-China mean? Does it mean the region in South-East Asia?

Hem Barua: India-China.

Jawaharlal Nehru: I do not understand the question.

Speaker: Will he kindly repeat the question?

Shivaji Rao S. Deshmukh: May I know whether this latest reference to Nepal, Bhutan and Sikkim in the Chinese note arises out of the Chinese anxiety to refer to the Indo-Chinese border dispute and the border dispute between China and Nepal, Bhutan and Sikkim?

Jawaharlal Nehru: Please do not call it Indo-China. Indo-China is an area in South-East Asia.

Shivaji Rao S. Deshmukh: India and China.

Some Hon. Members: Sino-Indian.

Speaker: What he wants to know is rather an opinion on that and how it arises. It is not a direct attempt to elicit information.

185. Congress.

398. In the Lok Sabha: India's Offer to China[186]

Hari Vishnu Kamath:[187] Will the Prime Minister be pleased to refer to the reply given to Starred Question No. 1401 on the 11th June, 1962[188] and state:

(a) who actually exercises administrative authority at present over the area of "no man's land" envisaged in the latest offer made to China for settlement of the border dispute; and
(b) the Chinese Government's reaction to the offer?

The Deputy Minister in the Ministry of External Affairs (Dinesh Singh):

(a) The area in the western sector from which the two sides should withdraw, as proposed in our note of the l4th May 1962,[189] is for the most part under the military occupation of the Chinese except for certain portions in the south which are under our jurisdiction and control.

    There is no administration as such in this area as it is largely uninhabited.
(b) In their reply dated 2nd June 1962[190] the Chinese Government have stated that our offer is as unacceptable to them now as it was before (in 1959). They would consider our proposal only if it is applied equally to the eastern sector of the border as well. In other words, they want India to withdraw simultaneously from the area south of the Macmahon [McMahon] Line up to the foothills, which are claimed by China.

Hari Vishnu Kamath: When the Government in its offer made to China for settlement of the border dispute offers to withdraw to the western line in Ladakh shown in the Chinese maps, is it not tantamount to admission on the Government's part of the Chinese charge against India that India has committed aggression on Chinese territory?

186. Oral Answers, 22 June 1962. *Lok Sabha Debates*. Third Series, Vol. V, 8 June to 22 June 1962, Ist Session, cols 12426-12428.
187. PSP.
188. See item 388.
189. See *White Paper VI*, pp. 41-43 and in this volume appendix 4.
190. See *White Paper VI*, pp. 56-58 and in this volume appendix 3 (b).

Dinesh Singh: No, Sir.

The Prime Minister and Minister of External Affairs and Minister of Atomic Energy (Jawaharlal Nehru): If it is Chinese territory then it is an admission. But when we do not admit that it is Chinese territory, it ceases to be an admission.

Hari Vishnu Kamath: Now that the Chinese Government has rejected the offer and has not accepted the offer made by the Government, does the offer still stand or has it been withdrawn?

Jawaharlal Nehru: The offer is there; it stands.

Hari Vishnu Kamath: Still it is there?

Jawaharlal Nehru: Yes.

U.M. Trivedi:[191] In view of one fact that we have ourselves admitted the existence of no man's land will it not make a sort of an estoppel against us because this land rightfully belongs to us?

Jawaharlal Nehru: No, Sir.

Hem Barua:[192] In view of the fact that China has unilaterally fixed the extent of her territory on our northern border on the basis of which she is threatening action against India, may I know what is the sense in pursuing this policy of making offers?

Jawaharlal Nehru: Because the offers are to our advantage.

399. In the Lok Sabha: Reported Chinese Occupation of Indian Territory in NEFA[193]

Ramchandra Bade (Kharagone):[194] Sir, under rule 197, I beg to call the attention of the hon. Prime Minister to the following matter of urgent public importance and I request that he may make a statement thereon:

191. Jan Sangh.
192. PSP.
193. Calling attention to matters of urgent Public importance, 22 June 1962. *Lok Sabha Debates*, Third Series, Vol. 5, 8 June to 22 June 1962, Ist Session, cols 12494-98.
194. Ramchandra Vithal Bade, Jan Sangh.

The reported occupation by China of about 500 square mile of Indian territory in NEFA.

The Deputy Minister in the Ministry of External Affairs (Dinesh Singh): Although the Chinese have maintained that they do not recognise the MacMahon [McMahon] Line they have not committed any serious intrusions or attempted to set up check-posts in this sector except in the case of Longju which they occupied in August 1959 and then vacated sometime in 1961.[195] The last minor intrusion which occurred in the NEFA area related to some Chinese officers who visited the village Roi, half a mile south of Longju, about which we protested to the Chinese in our note dated 18th April, 1962.[196]

The statement made in the *Free Press Journal* report datelined New Delhi June 17th,[197] that the Chinese soldiers have advanced in the NEFA area is not correct nor is it true to say that the Government of India have lodged a protest with Peking in respect of any such advance, other than the minor incident I have already referred to in respect of village Roi, half a mile south of Longju. The press report refers to the Chinese army having traversed an area of about 500 square miles between the Indian territory and Tibet, hitherto unoccupied by them. We have no definite information about Chinese activities in areas of Tibet to the north of the MacMahon [McMahon] Line but some 50 Tibetan refugees have arrived at one of our border check-posts in the NEFA on June 17th, from the Pemako area of Tibet. This area is to the north of the MacMahon [McMahon] Line on the eastern extremity of Siang Frontier Division of NEFA.

रामचन्द्र बड़े: 19 जून के अखबार में निकला है कि प्रधान मंत्री ने लोक सभा में बयान दिया था कि अन्डर सेक्रटरी[198] श्री देसाई और आसाम के चीफ मिनिस्टर नेफा गये थे। और यह भी बतलाया था कि वे आसाम राइफल्स के झगड़े के सम्बन्ध में वहां गये थे।[199] क्या यह बात सत्य है कि चूंकि चाइना ने इन्सपैक्शन करने के लिये वहां नये चैक पोस्ट कायम किये हैं इस वास्ते अन्डर सेक्रटरी श्री देसाई और चीफ मिनिस्टर आसाम वहां गये थे?

195. See SWJN/SS/51/item 193 and SWJN/SS/65/items 210, 216 and appendix 5.
196. See *White Paper VI*, p. 27 and in this volume appendix 2.
197. In *Free Press Journal* on 18 June 1962, p.1 cols 1 & 2.
198. In fact, Foreign Secretary.
199. See item 394.

प्रधान मंत्री तथा वैदेशिक कार्य मंत्री तथा अणुशक्ति मंत्री (जवाहरलाल नेहरु): सवाल जो शुरू में था उसमें यह इशारा था कि गोया चीनी फौजें आ गई है मैकमोहन लाइन के नीचे। उसका जबाब यह है कि कोई नहीं यह सब बिल्कुल गलत है। अगर तिब्बत में अपनी फौजें वे इधर उधर करे तो मैं ठीक जबाब नहीं दे सकता। लेकिन मैकमोहन लाइन के नीचे कोई नहीं आया। यह जबाब हो गया। अब आप कहते हैं अन्डर सेक्रेटरी गये। शायद आप का मतलब फौरेन सेक्रेटरी से होगा, फौरेन सेक्रेटरी वहां गये थे। वह गये थे इसलिये कि बहुत सारे काम थे। सोचा कि बजाय कुछ खत व किताबत होने कि बातचीत हो जाये। उन्हें बातचीत करनी थी।

अध्यक्ष महोदय:[200] उन का ऐक्यूज़ेशन है कि वह इस सम्बन्ध में वहां गये थे कि चीन की फौजों ने कब्जा कर लिया था।

जवाहरलाल नेहरुः चीनियों ने कब्ज़ा ही नहीं किया है तो सम्बन्ध कैसे हो सकता है उस से?

रामचन्द्र बड़ेः सवाल है कि वहां आसाम राइफल्स में असन्तोष होने के कारण नहीं बल्कि इन्स्पेक्शन के लिये वहां पर चाइना ने चैक पोस्ट कायम कर लिया है इसलिये वे गये थे।

जवाहरलाल नेहरुः आपने सवाल किया है कि वहां पर कब्ज़ा किया है या नहीं। उसका जबाब है "नहीं"। कब्जा किसी ने नहीं किया कोई इशारा इस का नहीं हुआ, कोई ज़िक्र नहीं हुआ गरज़ ख्बाब में भी यह नहीं हुआ।

Priya Gupta (Katihar):[201] Simply took possession.

जवाहरलाल नेहरुः फौरेन सेक्रेटरी वहां बहुत से कामों से गये थे। वहां पर नागालैंड के सिलसिले में फ्रंटियर सरविसेज़ को एक मीटिंग होने थी, उन लोगों से मिलने और बातचीत करने गए थे। गवर्नर से भी मिलना था। इस तरह से उनको बहुत से काम थे।

[Translation begins:

Ramchandra Bade: It is reported in the newspapers of 19 June that the Prime Minister had stated in the Lok Sabha that Under Secretary[202]Shri Desai and Chief Minister of Assam had gone to NEFA.[203] And it was also

200. Hukam Singh.
201. PSP.
202. See fn 198 in this section.
203. See fn 199 in this section.

stated that they went there in regard to the problems of Assam Rifles. It is true that China has set up new checkposts there for inspection and for this reason Under Secretary Shri Desai and Chief Minister, Assam had gone there?

Prime Minister and Minister of External Affairs and Minister of Atomic Energy (Jawaharlal Nehru): The question initially hinted that the Chinese forces had come and crossed the McMahon Line. The answer to this is no, all this is wrong. If they move their forces in Tibet, I cannot answer that correctly. But nobody crossed McMahon Line. This is the answer. Now you say Under Secretary went. Probably you mean Foreign Secretary, Foreign Secretary went there. He went there because he had to clear a few things. So instead of corresponding with them, he thought of talking to them.

Speaker:[204] His accusation is that he went there because the Chinese forces had occupied the area.

Jawaharlal Nehru: The Chinese have not occupied it so how can it be related to that?

Ramchandra Bade: The question is that he went there not because of discontent in Assam Rifles but because China has established check posts for inspection.

Jawaharlal Nehru: Your question is whether that was occupied or not. The answer is "no". Nobody has occupied it, there is no indication of that, no mention of that, not even in dreams.

Priya Gupta (Katihar): Simply took possession.

Jawaharlal Nehru: Foreign Secretary had gone there to attend a number of issues. There was a meeting of the Frontier Services in connection with Nagaland, he had gone to meet and discuss with them. He had to meet the Governor. So, there were a number of things to address like these.

Translation ends]

Speaker: Any question by any of the Members who have sponsored this?

204. See fn 200 in this section.

Jashwant Mehta (Bhavnagar):[205] The Deputy Minister has stated that some portion of our land was taken by them in 1959 in the NEFA area. May I know what was the position in 1961, what was the land taken into possession by the Chinese in 1961?

Speaker: The hon. Member wants to know what was the position in 1961 and whether some of our territory was taken into their possession by the Chinese in 1961.

Dinesh Singh: No, Sir. I read out a statement just now saying that apart from Longju itself there was no other territory taken by them.

Hari Vishnu Kamath (Hoshangabad):[206] The statement said "no serious intrusion". Minor things might have been there?

Hem Barua (Gauhati):[207] They came to the village Roi.

Hari Vishnu Kamath: What is the difference between serious intrusion and ordinary intrusion. That may be explained.

Jawaharlal Nehru: Four or five of them speak at time. It is difficult to distinguish. [Interruptions] Again two of them are speaking.

Nath Pai (Rajapur):[208] Sir, if we have not been heard we will make it clear.

Speaker: If four Members stand up and speak at the same time....

Nath Pai: Now only one is standing, Sir.

Speaker: I am referring to the difficulty that is always experienced by me as well as by any Minster when four Members stand up and at once start speaking.

Nath Pai: We are sorry for any inconvenience caused in hearing. The hon. the Deputy Minister stated that no serious type of event has taken place.

205. Jaswantraj Mehta, Congress.
206. PSP.
207. PSP.
208. PSP.

It implied by its very nature that there was something which was not very serious. May we, therefore, know what it meant?

Jawaharlal Nehru: The answer is perfectly clear. In the NEFA area there has not been a single incursion etc., except for the fact that two years ago or three years ago there was this Longju incident, and except for the fact that two officers – not a force – came down half a mile to that village Roi. Except for these two there has been no attempt, to our knowledge, of any incursion anywhere on the whole MacMahon [McMahon] line.

400. To Chintamani Panigrahi: Vinoba Bhave Invitation to China[209]

June 26, 1962

Dear Shri Panigrahi,
I have your letter of the 20th June. In this you ask me if I have any objection if any organisation of China invites Vinobaji. That is a question which should be addressed to Vinobaji himself. If he wishes to go anywhere, he is free to do so. We will not raise any difficulties. I rather doubt, however, if he will agree to do so.

Yours sincerely,
[Jawaharlal Nehru]

401. In New Delhi: To Presspersons[210]

PM: Chinese will have to end Encirclement
Only way to avoid Armed clash

New Delhi, July 12.

Prime Minister Nehru said here today that no conflict had occurred so far between the Indian and Chinese personnel at the Galwan outpost in Ladakh.[211]

209. Letter to former Lok Sabha MP, CPI; address: Ganesh Kuteer, Cuttack 2.

210. At Palam airport on arrival from Srinagar, 12 July 1962. Report from the *National Herald*, 13 July 1962, p.1.

211. According to a spokesman of the MEA on 11 July, "There has been no change in the situation caused by encircled Indian post in the Galwan river valley in Ladakh by Chinese intruders since morning." See the *National Herald*, 12 July 1962, p. 1 cols 1 & 2.

He told pressmen at the Palam airport that some time or the other the Chinese would have to end their encirclement of the Indian outpost to avoid an armed clash.

Pandit Nehru returned here by a special plane from Kashmir after a week's holiday. He was accompanied by Mrs Indira Gandhi, Mrs Vijaya Lakshmi Pandit and his two grandsons. The Prime Minister was looking better after the rest. He was cheerful and in good humour.

When correspondents surrounded him after he had alighted from the plane to inquire about the latest situation in regard to the Chinese encirclement, Pandit Nehru laughingly asked: "Are you now encircling me?"

"ENCIRCLEMENT"

(From *The Times of India*, 13 July 1962)

A correspondent: "There is no hostile intention".

Pandit Nehru said that he had just come back and he wanted to find out the position. "I have had some information and I want to know more", he said.

Asked whether the situation was serious Pandit Nehru replied: "I do not know".

A correspondent pointed out that the Indian note made it appear that the situation was serious.

Pandit Nehru: "Yes. The notes on both sides are serious.[212] They are pitched in a high key. Anyhow, so far as I know nothing has happened: no conflict has occurred."

Asked whether he would say that the Chinese would have to end the encirclement to avoid a clash, Pandit Nehru replied: "Some time or the other they will have to."

Asked whether in view of the Chinese action he proposed to cancel his holiday at Nandi Hills (Mysore) Pandit Nehru said that he was not going to Bangalore for holiday. "I have got business to do there", he said.

The Prime Minister was received at the airport by his Cabinet colleagues, including Mr Lal Bahadur Shastri and Mr Krishna Menon, the Congress President Mr D. Sanjivayya, and others.

Asked by correspondents how he had enjoyed his holiday, Pandit Nehru said: "I enjoyed it thorougly". PTI

402. In New Delhi: To Presspersons[213]

India must be ready
Nehru admits risk of clash

New Delhi, July 14 – Mr Nehru expressed the view this morning that, while there was a risk of clash between Indian and Chinese forces at Galwan post in Ladakh, he did not think there would be any major clash.[214]

Mr Nehru was speaking to Pressmen at Palam airport before he left for Bangalore by the IAF plane *Raj Hunsa*.

> Question: What do you expect will happen now in Ladakh? The Chinese are now accusing us of never having been there and the tone of the notes is steadily getting worse.

212. Perhaps this refers to the Indian and Chinese notes, both dated 10 July 1962, published in *White Paper VI*, pp. 79-82.

213. At Palam airport before departure for Bangalore, 14 July 1962. Report from *The Hindu*, July 15, 1962, p.1.
"Mr Nehru" has been replaced by "Jawaharlal Nehru".

214. The Chinese forces, who had come up to fifteen yards of the Indian post in Galwan, withdrew by about two hundred yards from the post on 14 July, reported the *National Herald* on 15 July 1962, p. 1 cols 1 & 2.

Jawaharlal Nehru: Well, they accuse us and we accuse them. It is very difficult to say what will happen. But we have to be prepared.

Question: Will there be a major clash in Ladakh?

Jawaharlal Nehru: There is a risk of a clash but not a major one.

The Prime Minister said that there was no significance in his lunch to the retiring Chinese Ambassador in New Delhi Mr Pan Tzu-li. The engagement had been fixed a long way back.

Chinese Red Carpet

From Left: Chou En-lai, V.K. Krishna Menon

(From *Shankar's Weekly*, 15 July 1962, p. 12)

403. To V.K. Krishna Menon: Cabinet Defence Committee Meeting[215]

July 16, 1962

My dear Krishna,

I have just received your letter of the 15th July. I suppose you have to go to Geneva for the Laos Conference, although the Ladakh situation would indicate

215. Letter to the Defence Minister. Sent from Nandi Hills, Mysore State.

your staying on here.[216] I see that the Chinese Foreign Minister[217] is also going to Geneva.

I suppose you will come back soon from Geneva as the meeting is not likely to last long after the signature. You will thus be away from Delhi about four or five days. The sooner you come back, the better.

As for the meeting of the DCC,[218] I do not like the idea of our showing any kind of panic. I do not think a few days' delay should make any difference. We are all responsible. I should like to meet the delegation that has come back from London before the Defence Committee meeting.[219] That means, at the earliest, on the 20th late afternoon. The delegation that it is proposed to send to Moscow might also meet me then. If it is possible for you to be present then, I shall be glad.

It will thus be difficult to hold the Defence Committee meeting on the 20th. If you like, the meeting fixed for the 21st may be postponed by a few days pending your return from Geneva. Or it may be held so that the members of the Defence Committee might hear the report of the delegation that had gone to London.

As you will be leaving Delhi on the 20th evening, we might meet and also see the delegation at 5 p.m. that day.

Yours affectionately,
[Jawaharlal Nehru]

216. See items 401-402.
217. Chen Yi.
218. Defence Committee of Cabinet.
219. This was regarding purchase of MIG.

(h) Tibet

404. In the Lok Sabha: Indian Trade Agency Employees[220]

Employees of the Indian Trade Agency
at Yatung

Hari Vishnu Kamath:[221] Will the Prime Minister be pleased to state:

(a) Whether the Chinese authorities in Tibet have arrested some persons employed in the Indian Trade Agency at Yatung;
(b) If so, how many; and
(c) The reasons therefor?

The Minister of State in the Ministry of External Affairs (Lakshmi Menon):

(a) Yes, Sir.
(b) The following arrests were made by the Chinese at Yatung on the night of 4th June 1962:
    (1) 2 local employees of our Trade Agency at Yatung and 4 members of their families;
    (2) Wives of 2 other local employees at Yatung;
    (3) Tibetan wife of an India protected person (Sikkimese) employed at Yatung.
(d) It seems that the persons mentioned were arrested as they were trying to escape to India.

Hari Vishnu Kamath: Have all the three trade agencies of India, at Yatung, Gyantse and Gartok, had been closed since the 1954 trade agreement lapsed?

Lakshmi Menon: Yes.

Hari Vishnu Kamath: is it a fact that there was a large number of Tibetan employees in the three Indian trade agencies at Yatung, Gyantse and

220. Oral Answers, 19 June 1962. *Lok Sabha Debates*, Third Series, Vol. 5, 8 June to 22 June 1962, Ist Session, cols 11611-15.
221. PSP.

Gartok? If so, is it a fact that most of the Tibetan employees have been arrested and deported to unknown destinations and Indians among the employees have been insulted and humiliated beyond measures by the Chinese authorities in Tibet?

The Prime Minister, Minister of External Affairs and Minister of Atomic Energy (Jawaharlal Nehru): I have not heard of any particular insult being offered to Indian employees....

Hari Vishnu Kamath: It was in the papers.

Jawaharlal Nehru: As the Tibetan employees were being considered as Chinese citizens, possibly pressure was brought to bear upon them, a number of them disappeared from the Indian Missions at Gyantse and....

Hari Vishnu kamath: Gartok.

Jawaharlal Nehru: Not Gartok, but Yatung. In Gartok, there was no permanent Mission. It was wandering.

Nath Pai:[222] Disappeared or kidnapped?

Jawaharlal Nehru: A number of them disappeared. The Chinese authorities demanded an explanation from the Indian Mission as to where they had gone. It is evident, or one can presume, that they had disappeared because they wanted to escape possibly to India or any other place. We know nothing about it. They simply disappeared. One, I am reminded by my hon. colleague, committed suicide. That is what happened.

In regard to the wives of the other employees, they also, according to Chinese law, are Chinese citizens. It is possible that they might be allowed to come to India with their husbands, but, according to Chinese again, only after they have admitted that they are Chinese, and had got the requisite papers etc. and taken permission. They do not automatically accompany their husbands.

Nath Pai: Is it not a well-established international convention that when such missions— are closed, their staff, whatever the nationality, are accorded safe conduct to destinations of their choice? If so, has not China violated that convention in arresting these personnel?

222. PSP.

Jawaharlal Nehru: I do not know who they have arrested yet, but I am not sure about the international convention about people of same nationality. I am not sure of that at all. Of course, people ought to be accorded every facility to go away, but where the people belong to the country where the mission is situated, they are of that nationality, then it is doubtful what the rights and wrongs are.

Hem Barua: [223] May I know whether Government have lodged any protest with China over these unhappy incidents; if so, whether the Government expect a reply from China calling us liars.

Speakers: Order, order.

Hem Barua: They will call us liars.

Speaker: They may call that, but this is not the question.

Hem barua: In "*China Today*" in the 24th issue they have done so.

Speaker: Unnecessarily, he is putting in some adjectives and making inferences that are not warranted. During the question Hour at least that should not be done.

Nath Pai: May I ask one thing, arising out of the reply he gave? It is quite true that a country has the right to arrest its own nationals, but it is customary to hand over a list of persons whom we regard as part of the staff and in that case they are covered by immunity too. May I know from the Prime Minister whether these persons were covered by such immunity or not?

Jawaharlal Nehru: I do not think all of them were covered. Usually there are two or three lists. One is that of diplomatic immunity. In any country, all our staff is not covered by immunity. Out of the Indian staff, some have diplomatic immunity, the others are just staff, they do not have diplomatic immunity. Thirdly, local people who are engaged are not covered at all by any immunity.

Hari Vishnu Kamath: Has Government received any report, or is there any evidence to show, that the action taken by the Chinese authorities in Tibet is part of a set policy on their part to liquidate Tibetan friends of India and squeeze the last Indian out of Tibet?

223. PSP.

Jawaharlal Nehru: Which action does the hon. member refer to?

Hari Vishnu Kamath: These arrests made.

Jawaharlal Nehru: I do not know if a single arrest has been made. I do not know if any arrests have been made.

Hari Vishnu Kamath: That is what I had asked in the previous question, whether there had been any arrests.

Jawaharlal Nehru: The hon. member repeatedly refers to arrests. I do not know of any arrests in this connection.

Hem Barua: On a point of personal explanation, Sir.

Speaker: I am sorry.[224]

405. In the Lok Sabha: Tibetan Refugee Camps[225]

Hari Vishnu Kamath:[226] Will the Prime Minister be pleased to state:

(a) whether the Tibetan refugee camps at Buxa and Dalhousie are the exclusive responsibility of Government;
(b) whether any person has suggested through medium of the International Buddhist News Forum, Rangoon, that those camps are centres of the Tibetan Friendships Group, New Delhi, and appealed in the name of that Group, and funds; and
(c) if so, the action taken by Government in the matter in order to check such undesirable and fraudulent activity?

The Prime Minister and Minister and Minister of External Affairs and Minister of Atomic Energy (Jawaharlal Nehru):

(a) Yes, Sir.
(b) The Government have seen the article referred to, which gives a misleading impression about the control of these camps.

224. See also item 406.
225. Written Answers, 22 June 1962. Lok Sabha *Debates*, Third Series, Vol. 5, 8 June to 22 June 1962, Ist Session, col. 12491.
226. PSP.

(c) The writer of the article in question was warned not to send out such misleading reports in future.[227]

406. In the Lok Sabha: Tibetan Wives of Agency Employees[228]

Tibetan Wives of the Employees of
Indian Trade Agencies in Tibet

P.C. Borooah:[229] Will the Prime Minister be pleased to state:

(a) whether it is a fact that Chinese authorities in Tibet have refused to permit the Tibetan wives and children of several Indian and Sikkimese employees of the Indian Trade Agencies to accompany their husbands and fathers to India;
(b) if so, how many persons have been so denied permission; and
(c) what action has been taken by Government in the matter?

The Deputy Minister in the Ministry of External Affairs (Dinesh Singh):

(a) No, Sir. The Chinese authorities insist that the Tibetan wives of Indian and Sikkimese employees of our Trade Agencies in Tibet are Chinese citizens. As such they should hold Chinese passports and observe formalities required under Chinese immigration laws before they are permitted to accompany their husbands who are returning to India. There is no clear indication yet whether these Tibetan wives will be permitted to leave for India.
(b) Six Tibetan women are involved.
(c) We had requested the Chinese Government to permit these women to accompany their husbands to India on compassionate grounds. A further approach to the Chinese Government will be made in this behalf if necessary.

P.C. Borooah: How many total families have been affected by this decision of the Chinese authorities and how many have returned to India without their wives?

227. This seems to refer to George Patterson, see item 176.
228. Oral Answers, 22 June 1962. *Lok Sabha Debates*, Third Series, Vol. 5, 8 June to 22 June 1962, Ist Session, cols 12422-25.
229. Congress.

Speaker:[230] It has been answered. None has returned.

L.M. Singhvi:[231] Are Government in agreement with the view that this constitutes a violation of the human rights of these husbands whose wives have been denied to them? If so, what do they intend to do to establish these human rights for these husbands?

Prime Minister, Minister of External Affairs and Minister of Atomic Energy (Jawaharlal Nehru): I am not aware that this is mentioned in the Human Rights Charter specifically.

Hari Vishnu Kamath:[232] the Prime Minister answering a question in the House on the 19th of this month – I am reading from the transcript – said that he does not know of any arrests of Tibetan employees in these trade agencies, while earlier on the same day his colleague, the Minister of State, Shrimati Lakshmi Menon, detailed five arrests of Tibetan employees including one of the wives of the employees.[233] Which would be correct?

Speaker: About this question?

Hari Vishnu Kamath: Because they refer to Tibetan employees.

Speaker: Only the wives are not allowed to accompany their husbands.

Hari Vishnu Kamath: Because they have been arrested, they cannot accompany their husbands.

Speaker: He wants to know whether the wives have been arrested?

Hari Vishnu Kamath: Yes.

Speaker: That is not answered.

Hari Vishnu Kamath: Because she was arrested, therefore, she could not accompany her husband.

230. Hukam Singh.
231. Independent.
232. PSP.
233. See item 404.

Jawaharlal Nehru: I am not aware of the wives being arrested, nor have the Chinese definitely said that they cannot accompany their husbands. All that they have said is that they are Chinese nationals, that they must abide by Chinese regulations. It may be that after they have got their passports etc. they may be permitted to come, or it may be that they may not be allowed to come. It cannot be definitely said either way.

As to who has been arrested and when, I confess I cannot straightway say anything about that. But my impression is that in this particular case, very few arrests have been made.

Priya Gupta:[234] Will the hon. Prime Minster kindly state if in such stations or before marriage the credentials of the brides will be obtained from the Governments of the countries where they are posted?

Speaker: It is a suggestion.

P.C. Borooah: Have Government a proposal to assure the Chinese Government that these wives when they are brought here would be allowed to continue their Chinese nationality.

Dinesh Singh: That question does not arise. The Chinese treat them as their citizens and they will continue to be so treated till they change their nationality.

(i) Pakistan

407. In the Rajya Sabha: Lt-Col.Bhattacharya's Appeal in Pakistan[235]

Disposal of Lt.-Col. Bhattacharya's
Appeal by Pakistan

A.B. Vajpayee:[236] Will the Prime Minister be pleased to state whether the appeal filed by Lt-Col. Bhattacharya against his conviction by the Pakistan Special Military Tribunal has since been disposed of?

234. PSP.
235. Oral Answers, 16 June 1962. *Rajya Sabha Debates*, Vol. XXXIX, No. 6, cols 162-165.
236. Jan Sangh.

The Deputy Minister in The Ministry of External Affairs (Dinesh Singh): No, Sir, but we hope that the President of Pakistan, to whom Lt-Col. Bhattacharya has addressed his appeal, will accord it his special attention and remove the serious injustice done to Lt-Col. Bhattacharya.

A.B. Vajpayee: May I know, Sir, what assistance the Government of India has offered in this case?

Dinesh Singh: Sir, as the hon. Member knows, this matter was discussed in the Lok Sabha when he was a Member there, and the Law Minister[237] had given details of all the assistance that was given by us. We have given him the necessary legal assistance and his family financial assistance in that connection.[238]

A.B. Vajpayee: Is it not a fact that his case is not being dealt with at the Governmental level, and that Col. Bhattacharya has been left to the tender mercies of Pakistan?

Dinesh Singh: No. But it is a matter that cannot be discussed at Governmental level.

Bhupesh Gupta:[239] How?

A.B. Vajpayee: Why not?

Dinesh Singh: It is because we do not recognise it was a legal act since he had been dragged away from our territory.

Jawaharlal Nehru: In all the circumstances we considered it undesirable for Government to become a kind of agent to Col. Bhattacharya, but in actual fact we helped his family to get legal assistance, gave them financial help, etc., but the formal representation was not done by Government because it was not considered right and proper in a case of this kind for us to acknowledge that court which was trying him.

237. Asoke Sen.

238. Lt-Col. G.L. Bhattacharya, abducted on 4 April 1961 and sentenced to eight years' rigourous imprisonment by Pakistan Tribunal, was released after four years. See SWJN/SS/72/items 278 & 280.

239. CPI.

A.B. Vajpayee: Is it not a fact that Col. Bhattacharya was kidnapped from Indian territory, that too when he had gone on official duty and, if so, why the Government should hesitate to make a formal representation to the Government of Pakistan?

Jawaharlal Nehru: That was the matter at issue—the trial.

Bhupesh Gupta: I understood the Prime Minister or his deputy saying that the Government does not recognise this particular act, the trial, but, assuming, Sir, that it is an illegal act, even so, what prevents the Government from taking up this matter with the Pakistan authorities saying that without prejudice to the legality or otherwise of this act they want to discuss this matter? It is open to this Government. Now, in view of the fact that martial law has been lifted there, may I know, Sir, whether, taking that into account, the Government has considered the advisability of ensuring that the matter is now taken up in the civil court and the appeal is heard on the basis of the civil law, as now there is no martial law? And this cannot happen unless the Government steps into the picture and makes its weight felt in this matter.

Jawaharlal Nehru: Sir, Col. Bhattacharya's case did not suffer in any way because it was conducted by an able lawyer and the Government helped in getting the services of that lawyer.[240] I still maintain, Sir, that in the nature of the case it was not desirable for Government to take any official part in it, and whatever had been done previously under the martial law, I do not know the legal significance of it but I suppose that it still holds the field even though martial law may not be in force today.

Bhupesh Gupta: Is it not then possible for the Government to initiate action? I do not understand why the Government cannot come into the picture. Of course, Government have made it known that they do not recognise this act, that they consider it an illegal act. Even so, when it is a question of Col. Bhattacharya, Government can certainly come in. However, Sir, now it is important; martial law has been lifted; he was tried under the Martial Law Administration when the normal processes of law were denied to him. Today, I would like to know whether the Government have found out in what manner his appeal could be heard. Would it go to any Military Tribunal or come under certain Ordinances that they have promulgated in

240. Guru Ghatak, engaged by Bhattacharya's wife.

Pakistan or would it be heard under the ordinary law of the land of Pakistan and not under the Ordinances they have issued?

Jawaharlal Nehru: I am sorry I am unable to add to what I have said.

408. To Lal Bahadur Shastri: Intelligence on Badruddoza[241]

June 19, 1962

My dear Lal Bahadur,

I wonder if you have seen some old Intelligence reports about the activities of Badrudduja.[242] These show that he is in constant touch with the Pakistan High Commission in Calcutta and has even received some money from them. I enclose a bunch of these reports, which the Commonwealth Secretary has given me.

Yours affectionately,
[Jawaharlal Nehru]

409. To V.K. Krishna Menon: UN Debate on Kashmir[243]

Your telegram No. 272 dated June 20.[244] There was no expectation really that USA and UK would not support Pakistan and we also knew that USA was interested in the original little five resolution. Speeches have referred changed conditions after old UNCIP resolutions[245] since debate has not completely gone in favour of Pakistan, this may have led to Pakistan Ambassador seeing Kennedy[246] in attempt to gain more active support. It would be best if Council

241. Letter to the Home Minister.

242. Syed Badrudduja, Lok Sabha MP, Independent Democratic Party, from Murshidabad, West Bengal.

243. Telegram no. Primin 21097, 21 June 1962 to the Defence Minister, then at the UN. NMML, V. K. Krishna Menon Papers (Official), File No. 4. Also available in the JN Collection.

244. See appendix 38.

245. Resolutions of 13 August 1948 and 5 January 1949 adopted by the United Nations Commission for India and Pakistan.

246. This refers to US Ambassador to Pakistan, Walter P. McConaughty, see appendix 38 paragraph 8.

could adjourn sine die without any resolution but if non-permanent members are being pressured by the Western you may decide whether time has not come for us to put forward unobtrusively if you like an innocuous and harmless resolution on the lines suggested by you vide telegram No. 24776 to Jha.

410. To Y.D. Gundevia: No Land Exchange with Pakistan[247]

I am surprised that this question was admitted. Obviously our answer is "No". However, as it is an unstarred question, the following reply is suggested:

(a) No.
(b) Any question of transfer or exchange of land between India and Pakistan would raise a great deal of controversy and argument and would necessarily lead to an increase of tension between India and Pakistan. The Government of India's firm policy is to do nothing that would increase tension between India and Pakistan. This question, therefore, does not arise.

411. To Y.D. Gundevia: Hydroelectric Project[248]

I have read these papers. I have shown them to Shri Ghulam Mohammed Bakhshi also. We agree broadly with the proposal made in the summary.

2. Bakhshi Sahib, however, attaches great importance to his project for a hydro-electric scheme, more so than to the flood control works and the widening of the outlet of the Jhelum river in the Valley. About the hydro-electric project, he pointed out that a scheme for 100,000 kW will cost only a little more than a scheme for 50,000 kW. Therefore, he says that while we may only take less water first and just enough for 50,000 kW, the scheme should be drawn up on the larger basis.

3. It seems to me and to Bakhshi Sahib that a reservoir, such as is proposed, will be to the advantage of Pakistan. They will get a controlled water supply according to their needs and will escape sudden floods in one season and possibly a shorter water supply during other seasons. This could

247. Note to the CS, 25 June 1962, for reply suggested for the unstarred question No. 368 by V.M. Chordia, for 26 June 1962, in the Rajya Sabha.

248. Note, 7 July 1962, to the Commonwealth Secretary, sent from Pahalgam (Kashmir).

easily be regulated if the reservoir was built. There should be no question of lessening the water supply. But, however desirable this may be, the Pakistan Government is bound to raise objections as has already been indicated by the High Commissioner. Therefore, it was desirable not to raise this question with them at present.

4. It is also true that by the time this hydro-electric scheme takes shape, the Mangla Dam will be functioning. But all this is reasonable logic which does not come in when Pakistan is considering its relations with us.

5. I agree that investigation for storage on the tributaries of the Jhelum might immediately be made.

(j) Africa

412. In the Lok Sabha: Indian Troops in Congo[249]

Question :[250] Will the Prime Minister be pleased to state:

(a) whether it is a fact that situation in Congo has of late considerably improved; and
(b) if so, whether Government have fixed any date by which it is proposed to completely withdraw our troops from there?

The Minister of State in the Ministry of External Affairs (Lakshmi Menon):

(a) No, Sir. The situation in the Congo cannot be said to have definitely improved until there is a settlement between Mr Tshombe[251] of Katanga and Mr Adoula,[252] Premier of the Congolese Central Government. No progress has been made on the question of ending the secession of Katanga, which is the main problem remaining unsolved in the Congo. Renewed talks are now going on between Mr Tshombe and Mr Adoula and much will depend on their outcome.
(b) Does not arise.

249. Oral Answers, 1 June 1962. *Lok Sabha Debates*, Third Series, Vol. 4, May 26 to June 7, 1962, cols 8248-8251.
250. By two Congress MPs Rameshwar Tantia, Shree Narayan Das and one PSP MP Hem Barua.
251. Moise Tshombe, President of Katanga.
252. Cyrille Adoula.

Hem Barua:[253] In view of the recent decision of Mr Adoula and Mr Tshombe to integrate their armed forces into the Congolese Army as also to take steps for the complete integration of the Katanga province into the Congo,[254] may I know if the situation is not ripe enough for us to withdraw our troops?

Lakshmi Menon: No. The situation is not ripe enough for us to withdraw our troops. I would like to bring to the notice of the hon. Member the news that appeared this morning.

Hem Barua: I have seen that.

Lakshmi Menon: Mr Tshombe says that he will not continue discussions unless the movement of the Congolese army is stopped and it does not endanger the Katangese gendarmerie.[255]

Hem Barua: I have also read that news. The position is that the movement of Congolese troops is supposed to take place into the Katanga province. On the other hand, they have already appointed a committee or commission to go into the question of complete integration of Katanga into the Congo.

Speaker: [256] He is arguing. Has he a question in a definite form to ask?

Hem Barua: Yes. In view of our pressing needs on the frontier because of the new situation arising out of disturbed conditions with neighbours like Pakistan and China, is it not worthwhile for us…

Speaker: He is arguing, drawing inferences, using adjectives and so on. What is the straight question?

Hem Barua: Is it not worthwhile for us to withdraw our troops?

Speaker: The hon. Minister has said that.

Hari Vishnu Kamath:[257] The Prime Minister can reply.

253. PSP.
254. On 30 May 1962, see the *National Herald*, 31 May 1962, p. 1 col. 8.
255. On 31 May, Tshombe threatened to suspend the negotiations with Adoula, see also *The Statesman*, 1 June 1962, p. 12 cols 4 & 5.
256. Hukam Singh.
257. PSP.

The Prime Minister and the Minister of External Affairs and. Minister of Atomic Energy (Jawaharlal Nehru): We do not wish to keep our troops in the Congo a day more than is necessary. We have given these troops to the United Nations. And, it is, finally, for the United Nations to judge whether they have finished their work or not. At the present moment, although there are some slightly hopeful signs—the talks between Tshombe and Adoula—our past experience is that they tend to break up at the right moment or the wrong moment; and Mr Tshombe is not a peculiarly reliable individual in such matters. So, it would be doing no service at all for us to do something now which would upset all the work that has been done and upset the further talks that these people may be having.

Hari Vishnu Kamath: To what extent has the despatch of combat troops to the Congo and their participation in the Congolese affairs been consistent or compatible with Government's oft repeated emphasis on the peaceful settlement of disputes, internal as well as international and also compatible or consistent with the tenets of *Panchsheel*.

Speaker: It is a matter of opinion.

Jawaharlal Nehru: It is compatible completely with both.

Hari Vishnu Kamath: I could not hear.

Speaker: It is compatible completely with both.

H.N. Mukerjee:[258] May I know if the attention of Government has been drawn to Press reports that Gizenga[259] is very likely in danger of his life; and, if that is so, if Government has any ideas in regard to this matter? I ask this because the first part of the answer says that the situation in Congo has considerably improved.

Jawaharlal Nehru: We have read news about Mr Gizenga in danger. But I should think not, because we would have heard about it otherwise.

258. CPI.

259. Antoine Gizenga, an associate of Patrice Lumumba and deputy prime minister to Adoula Government, was exiled to the Bulabemba island in January 1962. See *The New York Times*, 18 July 1964, accessed on 17 July 2018.

Vasudevan Nair:[260] One of the main aims of the presence of the UN Troops was to expel the foreign mercenaries working in Katanga. May I know whether the UN Army has achieved that aim or whether it has miserably failed in that aim?

Jawaharlal Nehru: I cannot say whether it has achieved it absolutely. But, if the whole Katanga Army is put under the unified control of the Congolese Army, it is clear that the mercenaries will either be under the control of that Army against whom they have been functioning or will go.

Brajeshwar Prasad:[261] Are we to understand that the UN Troops will not be withdrawn from the Congo till Katanga is integrated with the Congo?

Speaker: A hypothetical question. Next question, Shri Yajnik.[262]

413. To Shriyans Prasad Jain: Training Africans[263]

June 8, 1962

Dear Shri Shriyans Prasadji,

Thank you for your letter of the 8th June and report of the meeting of the Council of the Afro-Asian Organisation for Economic Cooperation, which was held last month in Cairo. I shall have your report carefully considered by my Ministry.

I agree with you that we should give opportunities for the training of African young men at mechanical level. As a matter of fact, we give a large number of scholarships to young men and women from Africa for studies in India. It should not be difficult to make some of these scholarships applicable to mechanical training, or, if necessary, some additional scholarships might be added.

Yours sincerely,
[Jawaharlal Nehru]

260. P.K. Vasudevan Nair, CPI.
261. Congress.
262. Indulal K. Yajnik, MGJP.
263. Letter to the President of FICCI.

414. To Antoine Kiwewa: Good Wishes for Congo[264]

25th June, 1962

My dear Senator,

I have received your letter of the 17th May, 1962.

I need hardly say that I was touched by your references to me and to Mahatma Gandhi and his teachings. I am sure that these teachings have a particular value for Africa where he first evolved and employed them.

As you know, we have been taking a great deal of interest in the Congo and we are trying our best to do what we can to help it in emerging as a truly independent, united, National State. I assure you that this sympathy and interest will continue. The Congo has experienced more than its fair share of trouble, but I hope that soon it will become what all of us have looked forward to seeing it—a strong bastion of freedom in the heart of Africa.

We can best remain in touch with the Congo through our Embassy at Leopoldville and I would request you to utilise it for our mutual benefit and for exchange of views.

With best wishes,

Yours sincerely,
Jawaharlal Nehru

264. Letter to Senateur and Secretaire-Général, Mouvement National Congolais, Aile Lumumba, Leopoldville, Congo.

415. To Morarji Desai: World Peace Brigade Wants Funds[265]

June 29, 1962

My dear Morarji,

Your letter of the 27th June about the World Peace Brigade, London.[266] I agree with you that we cannot be over-generous in this respect. Perhaps we might give them a little more but I think we should deal with Jayaprakash Narayan in this matter.[267] If he has any suggestions to make, you might consider them, So far as I know, he has not make any request for additional funds.[268]

Yours sincerely,
[Jawaharlal Nehru]

416. For the Kenya Students Scholarships Fund[269]

Please reply to this letter and say that I appreciate and welcome the Kenya Students Scholarships Fund which they have started. It has my good wishes, but I do not quite know what purpose will be served by my becoming one of its patrons. If, however, importance is attached to this matter, I have no objection.

265. Letter to the Finance Minister. MEA, File No. A-IV/102/13/62, p. 43/corr.

266. Morarji Desai's letter: "Kindly refer to your letter No. 161-PMO/62 dated 17th March 1962 and my reply of 20th March 1962 [see SWJN/SS/74/item 479 and appendix 13] regarding the release of some foreign exchange for the delegates to participate in the World Peace Brigade movement and for a contribution of Rs 5,000 which was then agreed to. The Reserve Bank have now received a proposal for another Rs 10,000 to be remitted to the World Peace Brigade, London, to be followed by a further demand of Rs 20,000 in the course of the year. It has been explained that the budget of the organisation is to be met 1/3rd from India and the rest from USA and UK. In view of our very difficult foreign exchange position, I feel that we could ill afford to permit these remittances. If you also agree, the proposal will be turned down explaining our difficult position." MEA, File No. A-IV/102/13/62, p. 42/corr.

267. On 23 May 1962, World Peace Brigade prepared a report of the Chairmen, signed by A.J. Muste, Jayaprakash Narayan and Michael Scott. At the end of the report was noted, present at meetings and concurring in this report: Bayard Rustin, Suresh Ram, Randhir Thaker, Bill Sutherland. Another of their report submitted to the UN Committee on Colonialism on 5 June 1962 was from Dar es Salaam.

268. For the earlier correspondence, see SWJN/SS/76/item 479 appendix 13.

269. Note, I July 1962, for the PPS, Kesho Ram. PMO, File No. 9/5/62-63-PMP, Sr. No. Minute-33.

The Government of India is already giving a considerable number of scholarships to young men and women from Africa for studies in India. I understand that an Africa Council, which has been formed non-officially here, is arranging for further scholarships. I am afraid, therefore, that we will not be able to contribute to the Fund which has been started in London. But I entirely agree with their objective.[270]

417. For B.F.H.B. Tyabji: Visit to Morocco Not Possible[271]

The situation in India and abroad is by no means satisfactory. We are chiefly concerned with China and Pakistan, apart from the important question of our Five Year Plan and the economic situation generally. In view of all this, I cannot remain away from India for long. I am a little doubtful even of my capacity to visit Ghana and Nigeria. However, since we have asked them about it, we had better wait for their reply.

2. But, in any event, I do not see how I can visit the North African countries after Ghana and Nigeria. It will be difficult for me to go to any one of them, just like Morocco, and not to others. I feel, therefore, that a visit to the North African countries should be taken separately. I would have very much liked to go there.

3. The troubles in Algeria also are not over and it may not be advisable to go there till the country is a little more settled.

4. I think, therefore, that for the present our answer to Morocco will be that I would much like to thank them for the invitation and say that I would have much liked to go there, but it is very difficult for me at present to take a decision owing to very difficult problems arising in India which require my presence.

270. The appeal, apparently without a date, was sent by J. Karuga Koinage, Chairman of the Kenya Students Scholarship Fund, set up in London, and due to be registered under the Charities Act of 1960. He claimed that Vijaya Lakshmi Pandit, the Prime Minister of Nigeria, and the President of Ghana, had already agreed to be Patrons. A copy of the full text is available at the NMML, attached to Nehru's Note above. PMO, File No. 9/5/62-63-PMP, Sr. No.32-A.

271. Note, 9 July 1962, for SS, MEA. Recorded in Pahalgam, Kashmir.

418. To Jayaprakash Narayan: Badshah Khan, African Students, Health[272]

July 19, 1962

My dear Jayaprakash,

Thank you for your letter of July 15.[273] I have read the papers you have sent with it and found them very interesting and informative. I am forwarding them to the Ministry of External Affairs and am pointing out to them the desirability of providing more scholarships for African students.[274]

I have for the first time read Khan Abdul Ghaffar Khan's[275] statement which you have sent me. I think it would be a good thing if you had it published through the Sarva Seva Sangh.

I am keeping quite well. I shall be returning to Delhi tomorrow morning.

Yours affectionately,
Jawaharlal

272. Letter to Sarvodaya leader; address: Kadam Kuan, Patna-3. Sent from Rashtrapati Nilayam, Hyderabad. NMML, Jayaprakash Narayan Papers.
273. Appendix 64.
274. Nehru's note, 19 July 1962, for Y.D. Gundevia, the Commonwealth Secretary, MEA:

> "I am sending you a bunch of papers given to me by Shri Jayaprakash Narayan. These papers are informative.
>
> 2. In these papers is a statement of Khan Abdul Ghaffar Khan before the High Court of East Pakistan. This was made in September 1956. This is a good statement, and the Sarva Seva Sangh will publish it.
>
> 3. The question of providing more scholarships to African students might be considered."
>
> Sent from Hyderabad. MEA, File No. A-IV/102/13/62, p.8/Note.

275. Also known as Badshah Khan.

(k) Nepal

419. In the Lok Sabha: Nepal's Claim over Bihar Forest[276]

Question: [277] Will the Prime Minister be pleased to state:

(a) Whether it is a fact that the Government of Nepal have advanced some claim over a portion of Narsahi forest in Champaran district of Bihar; and
(b) If so, what reply has been sent to the Government of Nepal in this regard?

The Minister of State in the Ministry of External Affairs (Lakshmi Menon): (a) and (b). It is true that the Government of Nepal lays claim to a small portion of Narsahi forest in Champaran district of Bihar. But this is not a new claim. This matter has been under correspondence between the Government of India and Bihar on the one side and the Government of Nepal on the other for the past several years. No final reply has been sent to the Government of Nepal.

Surendra Pal Singh:[278] Has Nepal advanced similar claims elsewhere also?

Lakshmi Menon: No, Sir.

विभूति मिश्रः[279] क्या यह सही नहीं है कि यह जंगल अभी हम लोगों के कब्जे में है और हमारे कागज पत्तर से भी मालूम होता है कि वह हिन्दुस्तान का है तो क्या भारत सरकार ने नेपाल सरकार को ऐसी सूचना दी है कि कागज पत्तर में हमारा भी भाग है और हमारे कब्जे में है?

जवाहरलाल नेहरुः यह सवाल बहुत वर्षों से चला आ रहा है। आजादी के पहले से सवाल चला आ रहा है काफी पुराना सवाल है। हमारे कागज पत्तर में जो कुछ है वह हमारे हक में है उनके कागज पत्तर में कुछ और ही लिखा हुआ है। अब इसी बात पर बहस हुआ

276. Oral Answers, 19 June 1962. *Lok Sabha Debates*, Third Series, Vol. V, 8 June to 22 June 1962, Ist Session, cols 11591-94.
277. By eleven MPs—six Congress, three PSP, one Socialist and one Independent.
278. Congress.
279. Congress.

करती है पुराना झगड़ा है, जरा से जंगल के हिस्से का सवाल है। वह इतनी अहमियत नहीं रखता है और हमें मिल कर तय कर लेना चाहिये कि वह इधर रहे या उधर।

भक्त दर्शनः[280] अभी सरकार की ओर से बताया गया हे कि नरशाही फारेस्ट पर नेपाल सरकार का कब्जा नहीं है, केवल दावा है, अब कि बिहार की विधान परिषद् में वहां के मंत्री महोदय की ओर से कहा गया था कि उस पर दो साल से नेपाल का कब्जा है। इस सम्बन्ध में वास्तविक स्थिति क्या है, क्या इस पर प्रकाश डाला जायेगा?

जवाहरलाल नेहरुः मेरा ख्याल है -- ठीक मालूम नहीं है -- कि कब्जा उन का नहीं है, लेकिन नेपाली लोगों ने आ कर उस जंगल से दरख्त काट लिये थे और इस पर बिहार सरकार ने ऐतराज किया था।

[Translation begins:

Bibhuti Mishra:[281] Is it not true that this jungle is in our possession and there are papers to this effect that it is a part of India. Has our Government informed the Nepal Government about it?

Jawaharlal Nehru: This question is being debated for a long time even before Independence. Whatever is written in our papers is in our favour. In their papers something else is written. On this issue the discussion goes on. It is an old issue of a small part of the jungle. It is not so important and we should mutually decide whether it should remain here or there.

Bhakt Darshan:[282] the Government of India has informed that Narsahi forest is not under Nepal Government's possession, it is only a claim. Now in Bihar Legislative Council, a Minister has said that it is in Nepal's possession for two years. Could we get the facts of the real situation?

Jawaharlal Nehru: I think—I am not sure—that is not in their possession, but Nepali people came and felled some trees and the Bihar Government objected to it.

Translation ends]

280. Congress.
281. See fn 279 in this section.
282. See fn 280 in this section.

Hem Barua:[283] In view of the fact that the border between Nepal and our country is an intangible frontier, like US-Canada border, may I know whether Government propose to define this border so that Nepal cannot make this kind of claims anymore?

Lakshmi Menon: The border has been demarcated except in this portion of about fifteen miles of territory where it is a riverine border. There is negotiation going on between the two countries and there is likelihood of the problem being solved very soon.

Nath Pai:[284] Partially what she has stated towards the end has covered my question. Because of the impression that one country is trying to spread abroad that India can never solve her border disputes with any country and also in view of the fact that our relations with Nepal are very cordial, may I know what the Government is going to do to settle this, not through correspondence alone but perhaps by offering negotiations at a higher level?

Jawaharlal Nehru: It is well known that we expect to solve it peacefully to the satisfaction of both parties. It is not quite correct to say that we have not solved any border disputes. We have solved any number of disputes with Pakistan.

योगेन्द्र झा:[285] कोसी योजना के अन्तर्गत जहां बैराज बन रहा है, वहां भी नेपाल और भारत के बीच मे कुछ जमीन के सम्बंध में झगड़ा शुरू हुआ था कि वह नेपाल में है या भारत में। जैसा कि बिहार विधान सभा में बताया गया है, अभी नेपाल ने नरशाही बन पर दो वर्षों से कब्जा कर लिया है। मैं यह जानना चाहता हूं क्या नेपाल और भारत के बीच सीमा पर जमीन को ले कर इस तरह के और झगड़े हैं और अगर हैं, तो कितने हैं।

जवाहरलाल नेहरुः मुझे मालूम नहीं कि सीमा पर कहीं कोई और झगड़ा हमारा नेपाल से है। यह भी कोई लम्बा चौड़ा झगड़ा नहीं है। कुछ बहस है थोडी बहुत।

[Translation begins:

Yogendra Jha:[286] There was some dispute about land between Nepal and India where barrage is being built under the Kosi Project. Just like Bihar

283. PSP.
284. PSP.
285. PSP.
286. See fn 285 in this section.

Legislative Assembly has been informed about Nepal having occupied the Narsahi forest for the last two years. I want to know if there are other territorial disputes like this between India and Nepal, and if there are, how many.

Jawaharlal Nehru: I do not know if we have any other boundary dispute with Nepal. Even this not a big issue.

Translation ends]

Mahavir Tyagi:[287] The hon. Minister has just now stated that the Government of India has not sent any reply to Nepal. I want to know the reason for this delay in sending a final reply when this quarrel or dispute has been going on for so many years in the past.

Jawaharlal Nehru: The very fact that the dispute has been going on for generations shows that there is something complicated about it. It requires surveys and other things and, I believe, some efforts are being made for a proper survey.

Mahavir Tyagi: Are we quite definite that the territory is ours? If so, why have we not communicated that?

Jawaharlal Nehru: The hon. Member should know that sometimes it is not very easy to do that. We think that it is our territory, a little bit here or a little bit there. It will depend upon surveys, revenue records and other things.

287. Congress.

(I) South East Asia

420. In the Lok Sabha: North Vietnam Accuses India[288]

Question:[289] Will the Prime Minister be pleased to state:

(a) whether the North Vietnamese Consulate General in New Delhi has circulated a note criticising India and accusing her of partiality towards USA; and
(b) if so, the reaction of Government thereto?

The Deputy Minister in the Ministry of External Affairs (Dinesh Singh):

(a) In its publicity bulletin dated the 8th June, 1962, the Consulate General in New Delhi of the Democratic Republic of Vietnam has published the text of a declaration stated to have been made by the Government of the Democratic Republic of Vietnam, criticising the conclusions presumed to have been arrived at by the Indian and Canadian Delegates to the International Commission for Supervision & Control, in a Report which has been submitted by the Commission to the Co-Chairman of the 1954 Geneva Conference.
(b) The Consulate General in New Delhi of the DRVN has published the text of an official statement of their Government and as such the Government of India do not propose to take any action in the matter.

Ramchandra Vithal Bade: Is it a fact that the Consul General of North Vietnam in a press conference in Delhi last year also criticised the Indian stand on the Communist activities in South Vietnam?

The Prime Minister and Minister of External Affairs and Minister of Atomic Energy (Jawaharlal Nehru): Whether last year the Consul General criticised India or the Indian stand? I have no recollection of that.

Ramchandra Vithal Bade: Is it a fact that because of the Indian stand on Communist activities in South Vietnam, almost all Indians in North Vietnam have permanently migrated to South Vietnam?

288. Oral Answers, *Lok Sabha Debates*, Third Series, Vol. V, 8 June to 22 June 1962, Ist Session, cols 12412-12415.
289. By Ram Harkh Yadav of Congress and Ramchandra Vithal Bade, Brij Raj Singh and B.J. Singh of Jan Sangh.

Jawaharlal Nehru: There are very few Indians anyhow in North Vietnam. It may be that a few have come over. There is no large migration.

Hem Barua:[290] So long as the International Control Commission spread out its criticism "evenly on all", to use the words of our Prime Minister, everything was all right. But why is it that it has chosen to reverse the process and apportion the blame? What is the special significance of it?

Jawaharlal Nehru: Significance of what?

Hem Barua: You were pleased to say on a previous occasion that so long the International Control Commission spread out its criticism "evenly on all". They are your own words. Why is it that this process is being reversed and blame is apportioned? Because, that is the trouble spot.

Jawaharlal Nehru: No process is being reversed. The later National Commission, after such enquiry as they could make, have given their opinion that in certain respects the North Vietnam Government has not adhered to the Geneva Agreement and in other respects the South Vietnam Government has not adhered to that Agreement. There is no reversing of any process. They have given their opinion about these things, giving some detailed fact in regard to them.

Indrajit Gupta:[291] Is it not a fact that the Indian and Canadian Members of the Armistice Commission have made certain condemnatory remarks about the alleged activities of the North Vietnam people in South Vietnam, while completely ignoring the other complaints to the effect that a full-scale United States military command has been set up in South Vietnam in contravention of the Geneva Agreement of 1954, and is it not a fact that this is the basis of the North Vietnam Government's objection in that statement which they have circulated? And what is the Government's reaction to this?

Jawaharlal Nehru: I do not think—if that is the basis—that that basis is a correct one. Because—I have not carefully read the document, it has not been published yet—but my own recollection of such parts as I have read is that they are fairly strong in their condemnation of intervention on behalf of South Vietnam by the United Nations and United States forces.

290. PSP.
291. CPI.

Hari Vishnu Kamath:[292] Does the Prime Minister still adhere to and reiterate the statement he is reported to have made some days ago about the peaceful reunification of North and South Vietnam; and does he think, does he believe that these mutual recriminations come in the way of such peaceful reunification?

Speaker:[293] The second part may be answered.

Jawaharlal Nehru: That these things come in the way of reunification of Vietnam? Well, all these things come in the way, all this fighting and what lies behind the fighting comes in the way.

Hari Vishnu Kamath: Does the Prime Minister stand by the declaration he made some days ago about reunification of Vietnam?

Speaker: Next question.

(m) Middle East

421. To B.F.H.B. Tyabji: Ambassador to Algeria[294]

Yesterday we spoke about Shri S. Sen and the fact that it was not particularly desirable to send him to Brazil. In this connection Algeria was mentioned. I think it does require thinking for us as to where best Shri S. Sen should be sent.

2. For the present I agree to Shri B.K. Acharya being chosen for the post of our Ambassador in Algeria. I do not particularly fancy the idea of his going to Algeria during the referendum. He can go there immediately after the declaration of independence and present his credentials.

3. The First Secretary can be sent earlier to get suitable premises. I doubt, however, if in the present conditions there he will be able to do much.

4. You might enquire from our Ambassador in Paris as to how best to recognise independent Algeria and to whom to communicate.

5. You can also inform the Algerian representative here about our intention to Government as soon as it is formed after the declaration of independence.

292. PSP.
293. Hukam Singh.
294. Note to SS, 25 June 1962.

422. Independence of Algeria[295]

Success of an Epic Struggle

New Delhi, July 3 – Prime Minister Nehru today congratulated the Algerian people on the achievement of freedom.

He was speaking at a reception given by the representative of the Arab League in India, Mr Clovis Maksoud,[296] to celebrate the independence of Algeria.

"I express great happiness on this occasion", Pandit Nehru said, "and congratulate the people of Algeria. But who am I to congratulate them when they won freedom through struggle. I do congratulate them nevertheless, because I feel happy that our brothers and comrades in Algeria got freedom."

Pandit Nehru said that today marked the end of a struggle, an epic struggle which would be remembered for very long in the anals not only of Algeria and Arab countries but of the world.

Stating that India's cooperative with the freedom movement in Algeria and other African countries had sprung from the deep root of the past, Pandit Nehru said that for this reason the successful termination of the magnificent struggle of the Algerian people was peculiarly and deeply satisfying.

Pandit Nehru said that the suffering of the Algerian people in their struggle for independence hardly had any parallel. "Freedom gained through sufferings and sacrifices is much more worthwhile than freedom which comes through any other way", he added.

Earlier, Mr Maksoud expressed the hope that India would continue to give her help to Algeria in the social and economic reconstruction of the country.

The gathering, which included Vice-President Zakir Husain, Defence Minister Krishna Menon, and Irrigation Minister Hafiz Mohamed Ibrahim, observed one minute's silence in memory of the martyrs of the Algeria's freedom struggle. PTI

295. PTI report of speech, New Delhi, 3 July 1962. *National Herald*, 4 July 1962, p. 1.
296. Clovis Maksoud (1926-2016); representative of Arab League in India, 1961-1966.

423. Independence of Algeria[297]

"The almost unanimous vote of the Algerian people in the referendum for independence and the French Government's formal acceptance of the independence of Algeria, bring to a happy end the epic story of Algeria's struggle for freedom. Surely history gives us few examples of such a valiant struggle against great odds and involving tremendous suffering and sacrifice. In a world, where almost every day brings some news which distresses us, the news from Algeria has come as a blessing and a tonic.

"Everyone who believes in freedom will rejoice at this happy consummation of a long struggle. We in the Government of India and the people of India are particularly happy and would like to convey our warm and fraternal greetings to the people of Algeria and their brave leaders, more especially the Provisional Government which has for so long guided and inspired her heroic struggle. We rejoice to find that the ideals which they have set before them, of social justice, secularism and non-discrimination on the basis of race, religion or creed are ones which we have ourselves enshrined in our Constitution. We look upon them therefore, as partners in a common endeavour.

"We should also like to congratulate President de Gaulle and his Government on bringing to an end this long-drawn out struggle in a manner befitting the best traditions of France in the cause of human liberty, equality and fraternity.

'We intend to establish diplomatic relations with free Algeria as soon as possible, and to do it in a manner most acceptable to its representatives". PTI.

424. To Dinesh Singh: Visit to Middle East[298]

July 6, 1962

My dear Dinesh,

Your letter of the 5th July. You can certainly go to Lebanon if you are invited to go there by the Government.

297. Statement, 4 July 1962. *The Hindu*, 5 July 1962, p.1.

A PTI report said: "The Prime Minister, Mr Nehru, in a statement on Algeria today conveyed India's warm and fraternal greeting to the people of free Algeria and their 'brave leaders'.

The Government of India, Mr Nehru said, intended to establish diplomatic relations with Algeria as soon as possible, adding that the Government proposed to do it in a manner most acceptable to its representatives."

298. Letter to the Deputy Minister, MEA. Sent from Pahalgam, Kashmir.

As for your visits to Beirut and Cairo, I think that you should inform the Ambassadors of those places that you have been invited by the Arab League and are agreeable to accepting the invitation. If, however, the Governments of those places insist on your being their guest, then I think you should give preference to the Government. In any country, the Government's invitation should have precedence. If, however, the Government agrees to your being the guest of the Arab League, then it is a different matter and you can accept the invitation of the Arab League.

Yours sincerely,
[Jawaharlal Nehru]

(n) Ceylon

425. To V. Velayutham: Highland Welfare Youth League[299]

July 16, 1962

Deer Shri Velayutham,
I have received your letter of the 19th June. I am sorry for the delay in answering it.

I thank you for inviting me to address your Highland Welfare Youth League when I go to Ceylon next. I am afraid I can give no such promise. My visit to Ceylon is for a special purpose,[300] and I do not know if I shall have much time to spare for any other activities. Nor do I know at present how many days I shall be able to stay in Ceylon, as there are many pressures on my time in India and I may not be able to remain there for long.

I am interested to learn of the Highland Welfare Youth League formed mainly by the youth of the recent settlers of Indian origin in Ceylon with the aim of integrating them with the indigenous population in the spirit of national unity and progress. That is an objective with which I entirely agree, and I wish you success in it.

Yours sincerely,
[Jawaharlal Nehru]

299. Letter to the Honorary General Secretary of The Highland Welfare Youth League, 12 Lady Gordon's Road, Kandy, Ceylon. Sent from Nandi Hills, Mysore State.
300. For Nehru's visit to Ceylon, 13-15 October 1962, see SWJN/SS/79.

(o) Burma

426. In the Lok Sabha: Indian Doctors in Burma[301]

Question: [302] Will the Prime Minister be pleased to state:

(a) whether Government of Burma have dispensed with the services of Indian doctors employed in that country; and
(b) if so, reasons therefor?

The Deputy Minister in the Ministry of External Affairs (Dinesh Singh):

(a) Yes, Sir.
(b) According to information available, three months' notices were served on Indian doctors on the 5th of May by the Burmese Government. The notices are in conformity with the terms of contract entered into when the Indian doctors were recruited by the Government of Burma. The reason for such action on the part of the Burmese Government appears to be their desire to Burmanise their services.

Hari Vishnu Kamath:[303] What is the number of Indian doctors affected by this move of that Government.

Dinesh Singh: I have just now read out the number. It is 24.

Hari Vishnu Kamath: May I know whether this is a fact that these doctors were sent to Burma at the express request of the then Burma Government for assistance in different sectors or activities?

Dinesh Singh: They were not sent by us. The Burmese Government recruited them here.

Hari Vishnu Kamath: How many doctors, of those affected by this order, have already returned to India?

301. Oral Answers, 1 June 1962. *Lok Sabha Debates*, Third Series, Vol. 4, May 26 to June 7, 1962, cols 8268-8270.
302. by two PSP MPs, two Congress MPs and two Independents.
303. PSP.

Dinesh Singh: It is rather difficult to say. These doctors have been recruited over a period of ten years for different periods of contract. When the contracts have expired they have come back.

Hem Barua:[304] Since the services of these doctors are being dispensed with, may I know whether it is because of the self-sufficiency so far as doctors are concerned in Burma or it is because of a calculated move to dislodge as many Indians as possible?

The Prime Minister and Minister of External Affairs and Minister of Atomic Energy (Jawaharlal Nehru): It is clear that the present Government wants its own nationals to serve as doctors. It is not a move against India or Indian doctors as such, but the move is, as has been said, to Burmanise—it is an awful word to use; I do not know—its medical services. There the matter ends. They are acting according to the contracts made with those doctors who were engaged by them directly.

A. Nambiar:[305] In view of the fact that there is already a shortage of doctors in India may I know whether the Government proposes to absorb these doctors in Government services as and when they come?

Jawaharlal Nehru: I cannot say that. I do not know who these doctors are. They may have been doctors on the retired list or whatever it may be. Anyhow, if it is possible to utilise the services of trained doctors, that should be looked into.

C.K. Bhattacharyya:[306] May I know whether these doctors were recruited with the consent of the Government of India and whether the Government of India laid down any conditions for their recruitment?

Dinesh Singh: There was no special condition laid down by the Government of India. They were recruited by the Burmese Government with our knowledge and the terms were laid down by the Burmese Government.

P.C. Borooah:[307] May I know whether these doctors have since been repatriated and, if so, their number?

304. PSP.
305. CPI.
306. Congress.
307. Congress.

Speaker:[308] That has been answered. They have been coming from time to time.

(p) General

427. For MEA Officials: Indians in Trinidad[309]

I am sending a letter from our High Commissioner in London[310] about Trinidad and my reply to him.[311] I am perfectly clear that Indians in Trinidad should not take up a separatist attitude.

428. To M.C. Chagla: Indians in Trinidad[312]

June 4, 1962

My dear Chagla,

Your letter of May 29th about your talk with Sir Leary Constantine about Trinidad.[313] You are quite right in informing him that we are entirely opposed to these minority claims, separation, etc.[314] My recollection is that we had informed the Indian representatives of Trinidad that we did not approve of the minority claims in the least.

I am afraid, I shall not be able to go to Trinidad in September or December. I have to slow down to some extent in my activities and I cannot easily leave India for any length of time. I doubt also if our President can go there then.

Yours sincerely,
[Jawaharlal Nehru]

308. Hukam Singh.
309. Note, 4 June 1962, for R.K. Nehru, the SG, and Y.D. Gundevia, the CS. MEA, File No. SII/104-5/62, p. 8/N.
310. M.C. Chagla. See appendix 10.
311. Item 428.
312. Letter to the High Commissioner in London.
313. Appendix 10.
314. See item 427.

429. To U. Thant: C.S. Jha's New Posting[315]

June 7, 1962

My dear Secretary-General,

Thank you for your letter of 9th April, in connection with Ambassador Jha's[316] next posting. I regret very much that I could not reply earlier as I had been unwell for some time. It also took some time to decide where Ambassador Jha should be posted so as to meet the point regarding the work of the seventeen-member Special Committee on the Granting of Independence to Colonial Countries and Peoples, of which Ambassador Jha is the Chairman, to which you had referred in your letter.

It has now been decided that Ambassador Jha and Ambassador Chakravarty[317] should change places. Ambassador Chakravarty will take over as our Permanent Representative at New York some time towards the end of July and Ambassador Jha will take over as our High Commissioner at Ottawa. This arrangement would make it easy for Ambassador Jha to go to New York whenever he is required in connection with the work of the Committee.

With kind regards,

Yours sincerely,
[Jawaharlal Nehru]

430. In the Lok Sabha: Establishing Diplomatic Relations[318]

Diplomatic Relations with
Countries Abroad

Hari Vishnu Kamath:[319] Will the Prime Minister be pleased to state:

(a) the names of countries with which India has no diplomatic relation whatever; and

315. Letter to the Secretary-General of the UN.
316. C.S. Jha, India's Permanent Representative at the UN.
317. B.N. Chakravarty, India's High Commissioner to Canada.
318. Oral Answers, 15 June 1962. *Lok Sabha Debates*, Third Series, Vol. V, 8 June to 22 June 1962, 1st Session, cols 10773-77.
319. PSP.

(b) the factors and criteria which govern Government's decision in each case?

The Minister of State in the Ministry of External Affairs (Lakshmi Menon):

(a) we have no diplomatic or other missions accredited to Cameroons (Republic of), Central African Republic, Chad, Congo (Brazzaville) (Republic of), Costa Rica, Dahomey, Dominican Republic, Ecuador, EL Salvador, Gabon, Guatemala, Haiti, Honduras, Iceland, Israel, Mauretania, Nicaragua, Niger, Panama, Portugal, Peru and Togo.
(b) There are various types of diplomatic contacts, political, commercial, cultural and consular. Generally speaking, diplomatic, consular and commercial missions are accredited to various countries on the basis of our political and other interests subject to availability of trained personnel and funds and on the basis of mutual convenience.

Hari Vishnu Kamath: I would have been grateful, Sir, if a note had been laid on the Table giving the names of the countries. I could not catch the names of all the countries; I could catch only one or two names. However....

Is it a fact that ever since 1949, in the Constituent Assembly of India (Legislative),—neither the Minister of State nor the Deputy Minister was here then—whenever the question of diplomatic relations with Israel was raised on the floor of the House, the Prime Minister told the House, every time and on every occasion that the time was not opportune, and may I know whether the position is the same today and the time is not opportune; if so, is India's attitude to Israel conditioned by an oversensitivity to Arab susceptibilities in the matter?

The Prime Minister and Minister of External Affairs and Minister of Atomic Energy (Jawaharlal Nehru): It is true, the position is more or less the same. Israel was recognised very soon after it came into existence. But we have not exchanged diplomatic personnel because we did not think in the balance of things advantages lay in that.

Hari Vishnu Kamath: I could not hear.

Speaker:[320] The Government did not think that balance of advantage lay in that.

320. Hukam Singh.

Hari Vishnu Kamath: The second part of my question has not been answered properly. I will put it differently. Is it a fact that several European and Asian countries have cordial diplomatic relations with both Arab countries and Israel; if so, may I know what difficulties stand in the way of our having such relations with both Israel and the Arab countries?

Speaker: The hon. Member can also know from other sources. So many European countries have diplomatic relations with both.

Jawaharlal Nehru: We try to have friendly relations with every country. Even with countries who may be hostile to us we want to remove the hostility. We have no enmity towards Israel. We think that Israel's activities have been unfortunate, have been aggressive—in the past, I am not talking of the immediate present. But, apart from that, we feel that our exchanging diplomatic personnel at the present moment will be, in the balance, not advantageous to the causes we pursue there in that area.

Hem Barua:[321] Sir, in view of the fact that recognition is given to China and maintained in spite of the insults and humiliations we meet, may I know it straight from the Prime Minister as to why it is that Israel is not recognised?

Speaker: That answer has been given.

Hem Barua: May I know whether it is the Arab countries that have stood in the way?

Jawaharlal Nehru: It is clear that in the Middle East there is acute friction. Relations between Israel and other Middle-Eastern countries are not only strained but they are very bitter, and any action taken in regard to any of those countries affecting the other country is resented by the others. One has to feel the balance and see what is advantageous to us and to the settlement of these disputes peacefully there.

Nath Pai:[322] Among the criteria for extending recognition to any country, the hon. Minister stated our political interests and availability of suitable personnel. Are these criteria satisfied in the case of Algeria? If so, what is still withholding the recognition of that country?

321. PSP.
322. PSP.

Jawaharlal Nehru: I do not know what he is referring to. I understand.

Nath Pai: The Provisional Government of Algeria of Ben Khedda.[323]

Jawaharlal Nehru: Algeria, at the present moment, is governed by condominium, by joint executives half French and half Algerian representatives. There is going to be a referendum there within, I think, three weeks.[324] After three weeks, Algeria would be formally independent and recognised by everybody and, no doubt, it will be recognised by us and we shall exchange our representatives etc. But, at the present moment, under international law, the position is different and there is no purpose in doing it; only showing off by doing something a month earlier.

Nath Pai: It should have been done many months earlier.

Jawaharlal Nehru: I do not think it would have helped Algeria at all. The whole purpose would be a gesture to show our sympathy to Algeria and nothing else.

Nath Pai: Exactly.

Jawaharlal Nehru: We have shown many many gestures; much more than gestures to show our solidarity with Algerian freedom, which they have recognised, and this would have done no good, we felt then. Anyhow, the question does not arise now. After three weeks, or even before, elections will take place in Algeria. The immediate issue in Algeria is not Algeria versus France or the French Government. That matter has been settled. It is an issue of how to meet the OAS,[325] the secret army of the French colonists there which is committing murder, rapine and arson. Therefore, that is the main question and that question is not affected by this at all.

Hari Vishnu Kamath: Is there any proposal before Government to have at least consular relations with Israel on a bilateral basis, not unilateral as at present, if not relations at the Legation level or Embassy level?

323. Benyoussef Ben Khedda had replaced Ferhat Abbas as head of the Provisional Government of Algeria in August 1961.

324. Referendum was held on 1 July and France formally handed over power to Algeria on 3 July 1962.

325. Organisation de l'Armée Secrète (OAS), a secret army organisation under Raoul Salan was opposing Algerian independence.

Jawaharlal Nehru: There is no such proposal before government at present.

Renu Chakravartty:[326] Has the Prime Minister's attention been drawn to the statement by Mr Ben Khedda that there are attempts of great pressure exerted to change the Evian Agreement? In view of that, may I know whether our support to the Provisional Algerian Government would not actually help them to fight out those who now want to change the Evian Agreement?

Jawaharlal Nehru: I do not think it will make any difference. If the Evian Agreement is upset, in any way it will create a very serious situation. Only yesterday or the day before President de Gaulle spoke very strongly in favour of the Evian Agreement and said that in 24 or 25 days Algeria would be free.

431. In the Rajya Sabha: The International Situation – I[327]

The Prime Minister and Minister of External Affairs (Jawaharlal Nehru): Sir, I beg to move:

"that the present international situation and the policy of the Government of India in relation thereto be taken into consideration."

It is not my intention at this stage to take much time of the House. I shall briefly refer to some matters and then perhaps, with your permission, I shall deal with the comments in the House at the end of the debate.

[Anti-Nuclear Arms Convention]

Recently, an event took place in India which has certain importance from the international point of view. That was the Anti-Nuclear Arms Convention held in Delhi.[328] I think that this was an important Convention and it dealt with a vital matter. Indeed if one looks at the world today and the arms that have been accumulated and that go on being accumulated and the danger of war almost every other question, national or international, sinks into the background compared to this ever-present danger of a war and a war which will be so

326. CPI.

327. Motion, 23 June 1962. *Rajya Sabha Debates*, Vol. XXXIX, No. 9, cols 1624-1631.

328. See items 357-362.

terribly destructive that it might put an end to civilisation and humanity as we know them. I hope that what was done at this Anti-Nuclear Arms Convention will attract enough attention elsewhere in the world—I believe it has attracted a good deal of attention. It was essentially an Indian Convention but we had the advantage of the presence of some eminent people from outside, from the USA, from the Soviet Union, from England and from some other countries.

At the present moment I was wondering if some symbol could be found for the modern world. Every age might be designated by a symbol, just as a country might also be. The present age probably would be designated best by the symbol of mushroom cloud which comes out of an atom bomb. It has become the recognised symbol of the atom bomb and of nuclear warfare and to live under the shadow of this cloud—the possibility of such a cloud arising—is to live a life which is not civilised.

This leads me to the question of these nuclear tests because ultimately it is not merely the avoidance of nuclear tests that will put an end to this danger because there are vast numbers of nuclear bombs accumulated in various countries, notably in the USA and in the Soviet Union, but ultimately there has to be an assurance of a world without war. Some people may say that it is an idealistic concept. The world has never been without war but the world has also never lived with nuclear bombs as its bed-fellow almost. You have to meet this situation and there is no way out. There is no doubt that a war will lead to the use of nuclear weapons and the nuclear weapons will largely destroy the world, as we know it. It is true that even if we stop the tests, the war may occur. Even if we stop the manufacture of nuclear weapons and destroy those that we have got, there is a chance, if war occurs, of those weapons being manufactured again by industrialised communities. Ultimately we have to aim at a world without war. There is no choice left—either survival or extinction. But to aim at that as a far-off thing is logical but to aim at that as the first step is difficult. So we work for disarmament. Even in the matter of disarmament, although some progress has been made at Geneva, it is still rather far-off. The immediate change that we have to face is this question of nuclear tests. Nuclear tests make disarmament more difficult, make it more dangerous and the possibility of conflict increases because a conflict depends more on fear and distrust as well as preparation for war than on anything else. I do not know how many hon. Members present here saw the two films which were exhibited to the members of the Anti-Nuclear Arms Convention. One was a Japanese film and the other I am not sure whether it was American or British. Both dealt with nuclear war and they were horrible films—not horrible in the sense of horrible things that were shown there, that is true—but the whole possibility that it might occur was a horrible idea and all our arguments and ideologies sink into insignificance before this possibility. So far as nuclear tests are concerned, we are arriving probably, I imagine, at the end of the present series of American tests. I do not know if the Soviet Union, as it is said, will have a series of tests now. It is difficult for me to say. But even if they have those tests, I imagine, and experts tell me that this series of tests by the US and by the Soviet Union will probably end for a long time to come this testing business because they have achieved their purposes. They have got such scientific and technical knowledge as was possible by these tests. But either very soon or after some tests have been undertaken by the Soviets, there will be a stoppage of them. Thus, virtue will come out of necessity but it is a very painful truth that we have arrived at a stage in the world when Powers, Great Powers, can play about with these weapons and simply because they are afraid of the other Power, they take the risk of the annihilation of mankind.

[Algeria]

Now, Sir, during these past months two pleasant developments have taken place. One is the agreement about Algeria between President de Gaulle and the Algerian Nationalist Movement. No country that I can think of even in history has suffered quite so much, offered so much sacrifice for its freedom as Algeria. It is said that one million of them died in this struggle apart from the millions who have been injured or who have suffered by being driven out of their country. In a country with a population of ten million, this is a tremendous average and all our heart goes out to these brave people who have suffered so much. I hope that within a few days, possibly early in July, the referendum or plebiscite will take place in Algeria, and there can be no doubt about the result of that, and that it will be followed by the establishment of the independent State of Algeria. The great problem in Algeria now is how to meet the terrorism of the OAS, the secret army there. I do not know how far it is true but it is said that some kind of agreement has been reached between the Algerian Nationalists and this secret army of Frenchmen. Now, there have been fewer outrages by the Secret Army Organisation in the last few days. It is obvious that by these terroristic tactics they are not going to frighten the Algerians or the French authorities. Having gone thus far, no government in France, and certainly no government presided over by President de Gaulle, is going to surrender to some terrorists. We must realise this. Well, we have criticised many of the French activities in Algeria. This gives us a picture of the reality and the difficulties President de Gaulle had to face among his own people, not amongst the Algerians, in coming to an agreement with the Algerian Nationalists and I think we must extend to him our congratulations that he adhered to his decision and ultimately came to an agreement with the Algerians. This is the first thing we welcome.

[Laos]

The second is the settlement in Laos between the three Princes. Now, I speak without full assurance because we have had settlements before and they have broken down when somebody objected to them, but I hope that this settlement will lead to a national government in Laos in the next few days and that will at least end the conflict in Laos and this will no doubt have some effect over the whole Indo-China area including Vietnam which is in a state of high tension. Recently, the Commission there, the International Commission of which India is the Chairman, presented a Report. I cannot say much on the Report because it has not yet been published—it has been sent to the two Co-Chairmen in the United Kingdom and Russia—but this I shall mention that they have pointed out infringements of the Geneva Agreement by both sides and the result is that both sides are annoyed at this Report.

> Niren Ghosh (West Bengal):[329] The Prime Minister has said that violations by both sides have been alleged in the Report. Would he please give us some details or some idea of those violations?

Jawaharlal Nehru: I cannot because, as I said, it is a confidential document. I gave you this idea but I cannot read out portions of the document. On the one side, it is well known that American troops have landed there which is patent, nothing to hide and, on the other side, things there are not so patent but have been held to be violations of the Agreement.

The development in Laos resulted in the American authorities sending troops to Thailand. The SEATO suddenly came into action. All this time, the SEATO has been in existence for some years, it has not functioned at all. Suddenly it functioned. It chose a moment for functioning when it was least necessary to function. However, various countries sent their armies or air forces to Thailand to protect their border with Laos. As far as I know, there was no danger to that border and now that the people in Laos have arrived at a settlement among themselves, there can be no danger to the border and I hope that these forces in Thailand from other countries will be removed.

329. CPI.

[Congo]

In the Congo, the position is one of stalemate. In December last a settlement was arrived at between Prime Minister Adoula and Mr Tshombe at Kitona. During this settlement a declaration was made by Mr Tshombe. It was a good declaration but very soon after he followed his own practice of going back on his declaration and there the matter stands now in stalemate. Mr Tshombe only believes in adequate pressure with some sanctions behind them. He made that declaration because there was great pressure on him. The moment the pressure was lessened he withdrew from it. It is obvious that the United Nations can only succeed in making Mr Tshombe act up to his declarations by making it clear to him that they will take action against him, action including the use of force, if necessary. Unfortunately, he has got into the habit of getting some support from various quarters outside the Congo, I mean in other countries, who piously declare that there must be no force used against him and thereby they allow him to carry on in his peculiar ways.

[Disarmament Conference]

Now, in regard to the Disarmament Conference in Geneva, there has been an adjournment for a month. Their only positive achievement has been an agreement of a draft preamble to the Treaty, an agreement between the United States and the Soviet Union. It is a good preamble but other difficulties remain. It is difficult to say what the result of this Conference on Disarmament will be but it is making some progress however slowly.

[Nepal]

Indo-Nepalese relations are more or less satisfactory. I would not say that they are cent per cent as we would like them to be but the visit of the King of Nepal here on the whole improved those relations. Recently we had a request from the Nepalese Government that in accordance with what we decided in our joint enquiry into some events in the border. We have agreed to that.

[Kashmir at the UN]

Then, there is a matter which must be in the minds of many Members here and that is the discussion going on on Kashmir in the Security Council. Hon. Members will remember that this matter was brought up a little while ago before the Security Council as an urgent and immediate issue because according to Pakistan India was thinking of an armed attack on Pakistan. It was a fantastic notion. Yet that was made the reason for going there because there is no other apparent reason why they should hurry this. For five years the matter has not been there and suddenly it has come because of this alleged reason and this alleged reason has of course no basis. Then that discussion took place there for a few days. Nothing happened; now it has again been revived there and I do not know what the result will be today or tomorrow but I must say that the course of events there thus far has been unsatisfactory, rather unpleasing. It is very difficult for all of us, I believe, and certainly for me, to realise how any country, any representative of any country can fail to understand the basic issues involved in Kashmir; not only the legal issues, not only the constitutional issues which are quite clear and admitted that the Pakistanis or those who came under their shelter, the tribals, invaded Kashmir and committed loot and rape there after Kashmir had acceded to India—that is the legal and constitutional issue—but the practical issue which is raised in Kashmir, which is of vital consequence to us and I believe indirectly to Pakistan also, is whether we should adhere to our policy of a secular State or we should not. Pakistan of course is not a secular State. It is a conflict between these two ideologies and I do not pretend to say that all of us are secular-minded or that all the Pakistanis are anti-secular-minded. Both are incorrect but there is such a thing as policy. We have followed a policy for a long time and gradually it is becoming a part of the texture of Indian life in spite of the difficulties; in spite of breaches of that occasionally, it is the basic fundamental policy of India and I do submit that there can be no other policy for India constituted as India is. Even in theory in the modern age there can be no other policy because any other policy would mean the reversion to some medieval concept but apart from that, India being constituted as it is, any reversion to that would mean India remaining backward and instead of devoting her energies to progress, spending her time in internal conflict. Indirectly—not directly but indirectly—this question comes up when we consider Kashmir because the whole argument for Kashmir on behalf of Pakistan is that Kashmir being a Muslim majority area must necessarily go to Pakistan. We have never accepted that argument even for the partition of India—although it was raised, we never accepted it. We accepted a certain geographical argument and therefore practically speaking anything that we do which hurts that argument hurts the whole concept of India we have had and brings about enormous trouble in India and Pakistan. That is why we have strongly said that we cannot possibly agree to any such thing. I greatly regret that other countries, not perhaps realising the ultimate issues involved, are taking up lines which I think are quite wrong.[330]

330. See appendix 44.

[China]

On our border with China the position is broadly speaking more or less the same as it has been except that, as I have said previously in answer to questions in this House, we made some considerable improvement in our position. That improvement does not justify any complacency but whether any action is contemplated or whether even apart from any action any operations, they can only come from an improved position. The building of roads has gone on apace in those mountain areas and we have opened a number of new check-posts which give us a certain advantage. But whether it is China or whether it is Pakistan or any other country, we do not wish to have war unless it is forced down upon us. In regard to Pakistan we have repeatedly stated that we are prepared to have a no-war declaration; that is to say, that every question between Pakistan and India must be settled or even remain unsettled but we will not go to war. It is Pakistan that has not accepted this. The India-China frontier raises far more difficult problems for us. However we may solve them ultimately—and I have still not given hope of being able to solve them in a peaceful way—we have to be ready for all emergencies and that is what we have been doing all these years.

For myself, Sir, I shall confine myself to these remarks and I shall endeavour to reply to such comments or criticisms, as hon. Members might make, at the close of the debate.

432. In the Rajya Sabha: The International Situation – II[331]

[Kashmir]

Jawaharlal Nehru: Mr Chairman, since I spoke this morning, news has come to us about the fate of the discussion about Kashmir in the Security Council.[332] It appears that a resolution was introduced in the name of Ireland; the Irish delegate who introduced it. It was supported by the permanent delegates, that is, the United States, the United Kingdom, France, Formosan China and two of the South American states, Venezuela and Chile, and it was opposed by two neutrals, Ghana and the UAR and opposed also by the Soviet Union and

331. Motion, 23 June 1962. *Rajya Sabha Debates*, Vol. XXXIX, Nos. 1-11, 14-26 June 1962, cols 1765-1788.

332. See item 409 and appendix 38. But evidently Nehru is referring to later reports. See appendix 44.

Rumania. Now the opposition action of the Soviet Union that has voted against is called loosely a veto. What the Charter of the United Nations desires is that the five permanent Members of the Security Council should vote together in a Resolution. If one votes against, it is called a veto—it is non-voting or voting against. Anyhow the Soviet Union voted against it. As a result, as it is called, it was a veto by the Soviet Union, and it is supposed to be the 100th veto that the Soviet Union has exercised in the last fifteen years. A long discussion has taken place about this matter in the Security Council, and our representative, our Defence Minister,[333] spoke at some length expressing his deep sorrow that this Resolution should have been brought forward and, more especially, that Ireland should have brought it forward. And others also spoke.

Now the resolution is over and the proceedings are over. But it is a matter for deep regret to me that repeatedly, when matters concerning subjects which concern us greatly, about which we feel rather passionately almost, subjects like Goa and subjects like Kashmir crop up, it should be our misfortune that two great powers, the United States and the United Kingdom, should almost invariably be against us. In a matter like Goa every Member of this House knows how strongly we felt about it and how, in spite of our feeling, we delayed any action till it was almost thrust upon us by circumstances. Yet, this was made an occasion for reading to us homilies and lecturing to us as to why we should behave properly in international matters. In regard to Kashmir also, I suppose in the course of the last fourteen or fifteen years, the facts relating to Kashmir have been so often stated that they must be known, at any rate, to responsible people, men who speak in the Security Council and yet, the patent fact that it was India that brought this matter before the Security Council and brought it complaining of aggression by or through Pakistan has not yet received the full-blooded attention of the Security Council. Always India and Pakistan have been placed, notably by those two powers, on the same level. “It is a dispute,” they say, “between two quarrelling people, that they should sit down and settle it.” We are prepared to sit down at any time with anybody, even with people who have done wrong. But this approach has been extraordinary. The United Nations’ Commissions have come here, individuals have come here; we have got about ten fat printed volumes of papers connected with Kashmir. In spite of this, these patent facts have not been realised by them in the Security Council as one would have hoped for. So the only other conclusion one could come to is, having realised them they do not like them, because they have made up their minds to go in a certain way, to decide something in a particular way, and facts are not important, the fact of aggression, the fact of accession, the constitutional

333. V.K. Krishna Menon.

aspects, the legal aspect about which I said something, and, quite apart from all these aspects, also the fact of the consequences of any actions that they suggest. Now we are reminded of the resolutions passed in 1948 and 1949 by the United Nations Security Council and by the commissions they sent, which we accepted, and the very first thing in that resolution was that Pakistan should vacate. Then other questions arose. Now it does not strike the distinguished representative of the United States or the distinguished representative of the United Kingdom to lay stress on the fact that Pakistan has not vacated and has not carried out the Security Council resolution for these fourteen years, and they always go on saying that India has refused to have a plebiscite. We agreed to a plebiscite, and I have no doubt we would have had the plebiscite then and there if Pakistan had withdrawn its forces, and in the normal course steps would have been taken. But they never withdrew their forces—that was an essential part.

Now I am not going into the Kashmir issue here, but I express my deep sorrow that this should be so. As an hon. Member just said, the United States, in addition to this fact, or, may be, as a consequence of it—I do not know which—gives military aid to Pakistan, which leads to all kinds of consequences. It leads to an aggressive attitude on the part of Pakistan, constantly speaking in terms of war. Almost every day or every other day, in the Pakistan newspapers there is something about some kind of aggression on India being thought of, if not by regular armies, by tribal hordes which, consequently, produces reaction on Indian opinion when India feels so strongly over this issue. Well, any person would realise that giving this arms aid to Pakistan is likely to hurt India, not only to hurt us mentally but physically hurt us and drive us into spending more and more. We are getting aid for civil work and we are very grateful for that aid. But at the same time other steps are taken, like the military aid to Pakistan which compel us, out of our slender resources, to spend more money on defence.

All this is very illogical and I really do not understand how these great statesmen of the United States and the United Kingdom fit in all this in their thinking. They are democratic societies and they are pushed hither and thither by the pressure of public opinion or by lobbies or by their Parliament as we are. I wish they would realise that there is such a thing as public opinion in India, there is such thing that no Government in India can ignore—it is only to some extent that it can press the public to go this way or that way—and that things are done in regard to matters to which we are passionately devoted, which hurt and injure that public opinion. It is very much so and which, unfortunately, create a result which we do not want, that is, creates doubt in our minds about the goodwill of these countries towards India, and unfortunately the work done for years, the work of creating that goodwill which we value so much, is washed out by a stroke of pen or a vote given, or by a speech given. The speech given on the occasion in the Security Council by the distinguished representative of the United States about Goa hurt us, annoyed us, irritated us, angered us.[334] It had nothing to do with the facts. It was based simply on certain assumptions and, I regret to say probably, to the dislike of India and all that India stands for. And now the same distinguished representative tells us what to do about Kashmir not realising that Kahsmir is flesh of our flesh and bone of our bone and all that we know about the facts and about the law are in our favour. However, there it is. Unfortunately, much of the good that we have done in regard to relations with countries—I would not say it is washed out because good work always remains and brings its own result—the immediate effect of it is lessened. And I have no doubt that we shall now have a plethora of good advice from newspapers in America as to how we are not behaving properly in Kashmir and how the Soviet Union has misbehaved by voting against the matter.[335]

[MIGs Purchase]

In this connection I might deal with the issue of the so-called MIGs. Now, the facts are quite simple. At no time did I think that this matter would become the major international issue. Our defence forces, perhaps rightly or perhaps not—I do not know—were agitated ever since the United States gave these sabre jets to Pakistan. No defence force is ever satisfied with what it has. It wanted to make its position more assured. So, they were pointing out that in certain respects Pakistan was stronger in the air than we were and they wanted, naturally, the latest type. For my part I believe, as a practical proposition, it is better to have a second rate thing made in our own country than to rely on the first rate thing which we have to import and which may stop functioning for lack of spare parts of anything. Therefore, our policy has been to make things and we have succeeded very largely. The Defence Minister has particularly laid stress on this and our manufactures in our ordnance factories have grown up tremendously.

Apart from that, we have made right from scratch a very fine supersonic aircraft in Bangalore with the help of a very eminent German engineer.[336] But to reproduce it, to make more of it, takes time. It will take two or three years before any numbers are available. If we have them, we would not require anything else. We have made the Avro almost from scratch. We got the blueprint from England and we have made such a good transport plane that some of our

334. Adlai Stevenson, see SWJN/SS/73/item18, p. 259 fn 95.
335. The Kashmir question was discussed again later on in the speech.
336. See SWJN/SS/69/items 360-361and SWJN/SS/70/items 247-248.

nearby foreign countries want to buy off even before we have made it. So, we are concentrating.

So, when our defence people felt anxious, we thought immediately of the manufacture of a plane rather than merely buying it. It is getting terribly expensive, buying these goods and we have to buy to begin with. But we do not want to continue this process. Fortunately, we have got the most excellent engineers and mechanics in our Air Force, those who are in charge of the Avro being made at the Hindustan Aircraft Factory. They are first class men. And what is more to the point, they are men with enthusiasm for their job, not merely as a professional job, but they like building up things for India. So, this was the position. We examined various other plans. We had plenty of information about supersonic aircraft, American, British, French. Some of them were flown by our people too, and they gave us their report in regard to them.

Meanwhile some of our first class engineers were sent by us to the Soviet Union to enquire whether they could make an engine or supply us with an engine for our supersonic aircraft made at Bangalore because the engine we had got from England for it had ceased—not that engine—they had stopped making that type of engine for various reasons. It had nothing to do with us. We were suddenly hard put to it. So, these people were sent out to find out about the engines and they remained there for some weeks, carefully examined the engines, talking, discussing. The engine that the Soviet offered us was excellent but it did not fit into our aircraft. They said, "Change the aircraft". We said, "No. We cannot change the aircraft. You change the engine." There was a long argument as to which was to be changed. Ultimately they agreed to change the engine to fit in with the aircraft. That is the present position.

Only about four or five days ago another team of officers has gone to Moscow about the engine, to decide about small matters as to how that engine is to be fitted in. While this team was previously there, they were interested as experts in the MIG. There was no offer from us, no suggestion from us to my knowledge—certainly I do not know anything about it—but they enquired about the MIG. They saw it. They wanted to offer it. They discussed with the engineers. And it may interest you, Sir, to know about the new language that is growing up, the language of science and technology. To our surprise, our engineer, who does not know a word of Russian but who was a very good engineer discussed with a Russian engineers without any interpreter in some technical language, which I do not understand, for quite a long time. This language is developing, technical language, words, etc. So, these people when they come back, they reported to us. About the MIG they said that for variety of reasons they thought that the MIG was a good proposition for us. So far as the performance is concerned, they said the performance is about the same as the American or the French Mirage but it was probably more suitable for us. It was meant for rougher work. It could land on not very special airfields but ordinary fields, ordinary airstrips. And it was easier to manufacture. It was not so sophisticated and so complicated as the American or the Mirage was. That is important because although we have developed a great deal in our technology and in our manufacture of aircraft and others, still obviously we cannot compare ourselves with experienced technicians in America or in Russia or in England when it is a sophisticated thing. And they said that from the ease of manufacture also the MIG was desirable, apart from other reasons. Their performance was the same and the price was much less. That is the first we heard of it. Well, we discussed it amongst ourselves. And just then somehow—I forget how—it got out into the press, not only in the press here, but in the press of England, American, and may be in other places, and then to our great surprise there was a tremendous noise elsewhere. We had not looked upon it in this way. We thought it was relatively a simple operation of our buying anything that we chose to.[337]

[Arms and Aid]

Now, may I go back a little and tell another story about the purchase of aircraft from the Soviet Union? About six years ago we were again confronted with the fact that Pakistan had got some aircraft from America and was ahead of us and we were worried about it and we wanted some aircraft, not to manufacture them—we did not think of it—but just to buy them.[338] And among the things proposed to us was some Ilyushin aircraft, fighter aircraft, which we might buy from the Soviet Union. Now, till then we had not bought any aircraft except from England or America or France. We had not gone outside that charmed circle. Now, it so happened that a Minister of the United Kingdom was here then—I forgot who he was. Anyhow, he was here and we discussed it with him. He said, "You are going out and if you buy these Russian aircraft"— there was no question of aid, mind you, this is a new question which has arisen—"It will hurt us very much. We have dealt with each other all this time and now you go outside and buy abroad." So he pleaded against it.[339] We had in fact, thought of Russia only because the British people had refused us delivery. They could not supply us with that type of aircraft. Then he said, "No, we shall go and see to

337. For further correspondence on MIGs, see appendix 44; for earlier items, on MIG purchase, see item p. 1, items 370, 373.
338. See SWJN/SS/30/pp. 351-353 and SWJN/SS/31/p. 239.
339. Selwyn Lloyd, British Foreign Secretary. For Nehru's talks with Lloyd, see SWJN/SS/32/pp. 372-374.

it that you get it," although previously, to our enquiry, they had said they could not, now they said they would get it. Well, rightly or wrongly, we decided to buy English aircraft then, when they promised to give us these in quick time.

Bhupesh Gupta:[340] When was this, in point of time?

Jawaharlal Nehru: About six years back, I think. And at that time, I wrote a letter to the Prime Minister of the United Kingdom—not the present Prime Minister,[341] but his predecessor[342]—saying something about this, because he had written to me, I think, and I replied to it, and we said that we would not give up the freedom to buy anything from where we like and when we like and that should be admitted. In the present case we said, "as you are prepared to supply what we want—previously you were not—we will buy it." I added that because of our relations, if we want to buy anywhere else, we shall previously let you know and consult you and then decide, the decision being ours.[343]

This happened some six or seven years ago and I had practically forgotten it, because there was nothing very important about it. But I am mentioning it now because when this question arose in this case, I was reminded of this letter and told that I had promised to consult them and to give them a chance before we came to a final decision. I told them that we had consulted our experts and they had considered various aircraft in England, America, France and Russia. They are good aircraft—it is not for me to say—but some are a little more complicated, some are a little more sophisticated, and some are simpler. That is the position. Now, it is patent that no independent country and certainly not India, can agree to the proposition that our purchases of aircraft or anything can be vetoed by another country. It is an impossible thing to agree to. And nobody has said that to us, I must say that no one has mentioned this. They have all agreed that we can buy where we like and what we like. Nevertheless they expressed their regret and sorrow that we should go and buy elsewhere, other than from their own markets. And behind it all, although it is not said as a threat, behind it all is the question of aid. "Aid will be given", they say, "We shall try our best it will come" and so on. Nevertheless as someone said, although there are no strings attached, something happens that is in its very nature, some kind of a thread, it may be a thin thread, but something which may

340. CPI.
341. Harold Macmillan.
342. Anthony Eden, Prime Minister of UK 1955-1957.
343. Nehru sent a cable to Eden on 23 March 1956, see SWJN/SS/32/pp. 290-291 paragraph 8.

have a certain psychological effect. We are quite clear in our mind. We have not considered the matter sufficiently. We considered it then and we postponed it then, partly because I was going away and because the Defence Minister was going away. I was going to Kashmir.[344] We shall consider it again from every point of view. But speaking for myself, I have a tendency to resist large sums of money being spent on aircraft or any machines which are very costly and which are out of date after two or three years. It is extraordinary that these aircraft that we are talking about supersonic aircraft, are in fact, out of date in big countries. They send us something out of date, because they have moved to the next stage of unmanned missiles. These are manned aircraft, dangerous things for the man inside. A number of accidents occur. You see frequently in the newspapers a small item of news on the Indian Air Force, something about an accident. It may look a small thing, but it is a serious thing, for whenever an accident occurs we lose one of our bright pilots, whom we have trained for years. It is bad enough to lose the plane, but it is much worse to lose the pilot of it who is a precious person. These things occur in every country—I am not talking of India alone—and when you enter the jet age, the accidents mount up. If we buy a dozen aircraft, we shall have to be prepared to see a number of them go under, plus the pilot who flies them. So I don't like these. I would much rather have, although it is the next stage, the unmanned missile. There is no pilot there, at any rate. It is more expensive and it is the next development. Now, most of the modern weapons used by the great powers have gone beyond the old style manned aircraft. These are now meant for petty work. Even these latest type of aircraft are out of date, because now they use unmanned missiles, ballistics and what not, with no man put there but simply electronic devices and so forth. So, it is matter for us to consider how far it is worthwhile for us to spend a large sum of money on things which will be out of date soon. One has to consider the element of risk in not having it during the period, two or three years by which time, I hope, our supersonic thing will be ready. I am taking the House into my confidence and telling things which are really not mentioned in public but I think we should know what the position is. Apart from this, our coming to a decision on the other facts, one thing is certain, that is, in coming to a decision we are not going to be governed or influenced by either pressure tactics from outside or hopes that aid will come if we did not do it. We want badly aid for our civil, economic programmes. All our Five Year Plans, etc., depend on that aid but we are not going to take that aid or ask for that aid if it means giving up our independence in any respect. Now, I was glad, therefore, that in this matter of MIGs, to observe that those hon. Members who referred

344. Nehru was in Kashmir, 4-12 July 1962.

to it, although there were differing opinions in many ways, different groups, parties, opinions and almost as the poles as under in other matters,[345] did agree about this, that it is improper for any country to put pressure on us to buy or not buy a particular type of aircraft that we want. Mr Bhupesh Gupta, I can understand, for various reasons would say that but Mr Vajpayee[346] also said that and that was a peculiar combination.

Bhupesh Gupta: But I might as well add that he is combining with you in this matter. That is also a peculiar combination.

Jawaharlal Nehru: Mr Ganga Sharan Sinha[347] also said it. In this matter there is a certain unanimity which is as it should be. We shall consider this entirely from the point of view of what is necessary and right for India and not be influenced by these pressure tactics and hints, almost threats, that aid will be lessened or will not come. It is not that we do not want aid but this is not a matter to be decided this way or that way now. It is a recurring matter. If we surrender our basic position in this now, we shall have to surrender tomorrow, next year and all the time. It will be said that we create a precedent which is bad for ourselves as well as for others. So much for that but I would remind the House that all this business of our buying these MIGs or any aircraft arose because the United States has supplied sabre jet aircraft to Pakistan. In a sense, in that sense, the responsibility is theirs for taking a step which creates these far-reaching repercussions.

Now, Sir, I should like to come to another subject.

N. Sri Rama Reddy (Mysore):[348] Have they been told that the responsibility is theirs?

Jawaharlal Nehru: Talks? It is patent and it is a fact. I might tell you that it is a fact. Mr Bhupesh Gupta seemed to doubt my statement and, therefore, I repeat. We have not made any offer to the Soviet Government nor has the Soviet Government made any offer but it is so.

Bhupesh Gupta: I accept that. I never questioned that. I only pointed out from the Prime Minister's speech that it was a negotiation. It may not be technically an offer or a request for supply.

345. This phrase as in the original.
346. Jan Sangh.
347. Independent.
348. Congress.

Jawaharlal Nehru: The fact is that we have not even negotiated with them but these original enquiries were made by a team. You might call this a negotiation but it is not. We shall have to send another team to negotiate. Negotiations will come then but obviously one can understand that all this shouting in the world's press must have reached the acute ears of the Soviet Government too. It is obvious. They must know and they must have heeded to it.

[Ideology in Foreign Policy]

Now, I should like to refer to something which I consider rather odd, the hon. Professor Ruthnaswamy's[349] speech. He said that there should be no ideology in foreign policy. That statement may or may not be true but I do not understand what he means by ideology. For instance, he said that ideology means our policy of non-alignment. That itself is an ideology. That, if you permit me to say so, borders on nonsense saying that. I am sorry that he is wasting perhaps…

M. Ruthnaswamy: Not fantastic nonsense, I hope.

Jawaharlal Nehru: … because for a variety of reasons, broadly speaking, I entirely accept that a foreign policy is there to protect the country's interests. What the country's interests are is another matter. A foreign policy has often to change, not the basis of it but the expression of it, the details of it, if the position changes in the world. Non-alignment means independence of one's foreign policy. That is all it means, not trying yourself up in a military way with other countries which ties you up in your foreign policy and in every case, even in war and peace, you are tied up. Therefore, you should keep your independence to that extent. I am not prepared to say that every country should do that. It may be situated in such a way that some small countries cannot afford that. That is a different matter although I think, in the conditions as they are in the world today, it is far better for the small countries as well as for the big ones not to be aligned to any power bloc. When we talk about alignment we talk about alignment with military power blocs, military alliances. I am not again talking about the Arthashastra or the Mahabharata or the Ramayana, of alliances then but in the circumstances of the world today where there are two big military blocs carrying on a cold war, I say it is utterly wrong and dangerous and futile for a country to be part of a military bloc, most dangerous. Of course, it is going to cost your independence. If you are a strong country, then two strong countries having an alliance affect each other may be, but a weak country and

349. Swatantra Party.

a strong country having alliances simply means that you are dragged by the coat tails by the strong country and today it means in the world joining in this present game of the cold war, that hateful, abominable thing, I think it is, and a thing which if not stopped fairly soon will take the world to uttermost disaster.

M. Ruthnaswamy: May I ask the Prime Minister if Pakistan is suffering horribly from the military alliance with USA?

Jawaharlal Nehru: I do not wish to say much about Pakistan, but Pakistan has suffered very greatly and will suffer more if this thing goes on because Pakistan depends so much on its military, because they are there, that if this is withdrawn, Pakistan will be helpless. It is difficult for me to discuss Pakistan. I have rather clear views but they are our neighbours and I do not wish to say much about them. I think they have adopted a policy not only about this but about other matters also, the sworn ideology of which is hatred of India. They have exhibited it to the United States, even to their SEATO partners and to other partners, and their emphasis, their thinking, ultimately is, call it fear of India or hatred of India. And this recent flirtation they are having with China shows what lack of principle there is. One cannot discuss the inner conditions of Pakistan of course. They have received plenty of money but that has not made Pakistan much stronger.

The hon. Member also said something about Commonwealth membership. The essentials of policy should be that it should be ever changing, he said. It is very extraordinary; in fact we should have no policy at all and should hop about from one thing to another. That is what it comes to.

M. Ruthnaswamy: As the interests of India dictate.

Jawaharlal Nehru: The interests do not change from day to day. Non-alignment means that the policy would be governed by the interests of India at every stage and not by pressures from abroad.

[Disarmament, Vietnam]

Now, I shall refer to the other matters Mr Mani[350] said that we should withdraw from the Disarmament Committee unless nuclear tests were abandoned. I entirely disagree with this. It is a bad policy, this kind of boycotting because people do not agree with you. We should remain there. President de

350. A.D. Mani, Independent.

Gaulle has boycotted the Disarmament Conference because something which is not to his liking took place there or is taking place. I think it is completely wrong. The Disarmament Conference will not suffer by our withdrawal very much. It will go on but the good influence that we exercise at the conference will be no more.

About the Report on Vietnam. I do not know how Mr Bhupesh Gupta or someone else disapproves of it. I suppose he has not read it. He may have read the criticism of it; that is possible. Certainly the people we have sent there, who have written the report, are some of our ablest ambassadors and they have done it after personal enquiry and personal knowledge, I for my part accept their report. I may not be personally responsible for it but I do accept it.

Bhupesh Gupta: Have you read that? You said you had not read it also.

Jawaharlal Nehru: I have not read the final report but I have read the proposals they made and which have been incorporated in this. I have not read the actual last thing; I have read the draft etc.

[Kashmir]

Again, may I say about this idea that we should withdraw the Kashmir issue from the Security Council, I do not know if the Defence Minister said it. I suppose we could withdraw it but we may be dragged in there by the other party. We cannot refuse to go if the Security Council takes up the subject at the instance of the other party. We are the complainant, therefore we withdraw but somebody else will be the complainant and we will have to go.

Bhupesh Gupta: On what basis can Pakistan complain?

Jawaharlal Nehru: The hon. Member and I may agree that they have no basis but they are strong enough to induce various great powers and small powers to vote for them. That is the basis.

Bhupesh Gupta: Mr Chairman, I would like to get a little clarification. When we went to the United Nations we referred to certain articles of the Charter and on the strength of that we filled an application. Now if we withdraw I cannot for one see on what ground Pakistan can accuse us. Under what clause of the Charter of the United Nations?

Jawaharlal Nehru: I am not going to argue that matter with the hon. Member but it seems to me, we go there as accusers. We withdraw; that is, we withdraw our accusation, our complaint, against Pakistan. In effect we withdraw it but we leave it to Pakistan to frame such complaints as they like against us. However, we need no entry into that.

[Nepal]

Shri Ganga Sharan asked about certain joint enquiry on the Nepal border. In the joint statement issued by the King and myself it was stated that where any necessity arose, where there was any doubt as to what happened because our facts differed—they said some people have done something from India and we said, "no"—we can have a local joint enquiry, not a complicated thing, an officer of theirs and an officer of ours go to a particular place, where it is alleged, to find out and report to either Government. A little while ago they referred two specific incidents to us and asked us for this enquiry and we promised to send them an officer to do it.

[China]

Mr Mani said something about the officials of the External Affairs Ministry letting us down by not getting China to accept our sovereignty over Kashmir.

I do not quite know how the officials could make the Chinese Government accept something or not accept it. From the very beginning—we have repeatedly referred this to them—the Chinese Government have used a language which can be interpreted in various ways. We interpreted it to begin with in a way which seemed to us natural that they recognised our sovereignty but later when the matter was put to them, they were less clear about it and said something that has made their position a little doubtful. I do not know how the officials could make other countries function in a way we like. If that is so, we have had quite a large number of our ablest officers in the United States and in the United Kingdom but they have no succeeded in making any change because neither Government is prepared to change its mind.

> A.D. Mani: May I clarify the point? What I said was, there has been a let-down in the External Affairs Ministry; in 1956 Mr Chou En-lai told our Ambassador that the people of Kashmir had expressed their will unmistakably on the question of accession. In July 1961 when the Secretary-General visited Peking he reported to the Government that the impression was left on his mind that China supported our stand on Kashmir.[351]

351. See SWJN/SS/70/item 373.

Why should we leave it to a matter of impression? When the matter was mentioned when he went on a tour to which many of us had taken objection, he should have really pinned down the Chinese Government and asked it to clarify its views unmistakably whether it accepted our stand on Kashmir.

Jawaharlal Nehru: The unmistakable clarification would have been against us. He would have insisted on something being said against us. The hon. Member is saying something as if our officials or our Ministers or anybody can go and order about Mr Chou En-lai, who is a very clever person, to accept something that we say although he does not want to say it. Obviously he did not want to say it. Repeatedly I know if they say something which appears to be in our favour there is a qualifying clause afterward.

[Other Matters]

Somebody asked me about Mr Gizenga.[352] So far as I know, he is kept in an island there.

About the Immigration Bill in the United Kingdom, I think Mr Mani asked for quota. I think that would be entirely wrong and rather beneath our dignity. I disapprove of the Immigration Bill, yet I do not like immigration into the United Kingdom from India. And we have tried to stop it—not students and other people who go there. But large numbers of people have gone there in search of employment, especially from the Punjab, and they go there without knowing a word of the language there, without knowing a word of any language except Gurmukhi and Punjabi. And with their habits and customs, they create social problems there. I do not want our people to be looked down upon anywhere, wherever they go. Therefore we have been discouraging it. Because they could earn so much there, these passport scandals took place, where bogus passports were sold for as much as Rs 5000. That is the draw there. But asking for a quota is to accept their scheme of immigration and ask for some people to go there. What for?

A.D. Mani: May I just raise on a point of clarification? The Immigration Act, as it stands now, is an affront to all coloured people. That is what Mr Gaitskell[353] himself has said and under the quota system which the United States have, there is no question of a colour bar. It is a matter of self-respect of the members of the Commonwealth that they should have the right of

352. Antoine Gizenga, was exiled to Bulabemba island.

353. Hugh Gaitskell, Labour leader and Leader of the Opposition in British Parliament.

admission under a quota system, because I quite agree that every country has a right to control its immigration and we realise Britain has special difficulties in this matter.

Jawaharlal Nehru: The quota system applies to places where large numbers of immigrants go like Australia, like Canada, like New Zealand. I can understand that. Some years back, Australia, New Zealand and Canada agreed to have a quota system, because they have a quota for every country. Whatever the quota was—100,200 or 500—I do not remember, but the British have no such quota system for anybody. It is a well-populated country. They do not want people from outside to come and live there. It is rather extraordinary for us to ask for a quota system. We are not going to ask for it. Quota applies to persons who have got to become nationals there. So to ask them for a quota, so that Indian might go and become British subjects is extraordinary to me.

[East Pakistan Migrants]

Now, one thing more and I have done. This is about the migrants from East Pakistan to India. Some reference was made to it. Originally, the story started by some relatively small incident in Malda, about the Holi time in India. This was grossly exaggerated by newspapers there. They said thousands had died and so on. This led to very serious occurrences in Rajshahi district and some other districts, especially Rajshahi, and the casualties were very large. Thereafter, some thousands of people, Hindus, they wanted and expressed their wish to come over to India. They asked for migration certificates. But for some reason they did not pursue this matter further, some hundreds came and they went back. We did not refuse them facilities to come. I think the Pakistan Government tried to induce them and succeeded in keeping them back. They did some rehabilitation there too. Many of their huts that had been burnt were rebuilt and some help was given to them. Anyhow, they did not come, except a few hundreds that came. There is always some traffic coming and going. I gave here too, I think, and in the other House figures of people coming from East Bengal to West Bengal and from West Bengal to East Bengal. It was extraordinary that during all this period of high tension, the traffic was more or less normal. I forget what the figures were, 5,000 or 6,000 either way. It may vary by a few hundreds. Now, when the Muslims were supposed to be, according to the Pakistan press, leaving India in their thousands to go to Pakistan, actually according to our figures, thousands of Muslims in the ordinary course, were coming to India from there. In the same way, thousands of Hindus were going actually to Pakistan at the time these occurrences took place or after. Since then, a new development has taken place and that is what occurred in Rajshahi district. I do not know what happened there, but one night a large number, five hundred or six hundred Santhals at 3 a.m. tried to come across the river into the Malda district. That is the Pakistan version and they saw this crowd going at night. The police were naturally concerned and alarmed. They came up, they challenged them, whereupon these people shot the arrows from their bows, and spears they had. And the police fired at them, with the result—the accounts vary—that one or two persons or seven persons were killed. About a number come across, may be, 100 or 150, and the others went back. Now, the present position is—I heard it today—that about five thousand of these Santhals have come to Malda district from Rajshahi. Apparently, they are coming without any obstruction from the Pakistani authorities. They have come this time with their animals too. They have come with their animals, bulls, cows, etc. and the Pakistanis have allowed them. Five thousand have come. We do not know how many more may come. It has affected especially the Santhals and there are round about 20,000 Santhals on the other side. More may come. Now, this raises difficult questions for us. For the moment, naturally, we have to give relief to those who come over, but permanent settlement is a difficult question. It was suggested that we should send them to Dandakaranya. Well, we can send some to Dandakaranya. We cannot send any unlimited number. For the moment, it has been decided by the Chief Minister, Dr Roy—he has informed us of this—in consultation with our Government here to send a special train carrying about 1,000 of these Santhal refugees to Dandakaranya and to choose agriculturists from them to go there, because there are many fishermen. Fishermen have no particular place there. There is no fish to be had in Dandakaranya.

A.B. Vajpayee:[354] Have you made any enquiries as to why the Santhals are coming in such number? Does it mean that everything is not quite peaceful in East Pakistan?

Jawaharlal Nehru: I have said that originally the difficulties arose because of some conflict between Santhals and Muslims. The very first thing was that a Santhal woman was selling some fruit and they had an argument about the price. The woman was slapped on the face. This was in Malda district. This resulted in the Santhals there too later attacking the Muslims, burning some of their huts and killing two or three persons. Then, on the Holi day, which came soon after, there was another attack by Santhals on Muslims. The Santhals were roused by this incident. On the other side in the major incidents that happened

354. Jan Sangh.

in Rajshahi district Santhals were also sufferers. But I cannot make out one thing, because nothing has been reported to us for the last month or more or six weeks. We thought that was over and we saw this traffic becoming normal.

Bhupesh Gupta: How is it that it has not been reported, because in the Bengal papers—also some Pakistan papers come to West Bengal—we did not see reports appearing. How is it that Government has not received reports from its Mission in Dacca?

Jawaharlal Nehru: About what?

Bhupesh Gupta: What we are saying now.

Jawaharlal Nehru: We have received full reports. I am saying that in the last month or six weeks nothing has happened not only to our knowledge but apparently to Pakistan Government's knowledge or Bengal Government's knowledge. I do not understand why this time particularly Santhals had come out. They had reason to come six weeks ago. May be they were thinking about it and they came to a decision, because they function in more or less a tribal fashion, in a group fashion.[355]

[Conclusion]

I am sorry to have taken so much time. I commend this motion to the House. There is a large number of amendments for which Mr Bhupesh Gupta is responsible, I understand, for 54, I must congratulate him on the hard work he has put in.

Bhupesh Gupta: I can tell you, Sir, that it is not much hard work. It does not take much work from me. One point I want to clarify because it might give a wrong impression. I never meant that we should withdraw the complaint from the Security Council. In fact I never said that. Probably he misunderstood me because how it can be withdrawn; it is there. What I said in my speech at the beginning was that it should be frozen. I said that we should tell them that since the Security Council has failed to discharge its responsibility and since the other parts of the resolutions are not carried out, the matter now ends, lapses. That is my approach.

355. On the East Pakistan migration problem, see items 52, 56, 64, 68-69.

Chairman:[356] That is what he intended.

Bhupesh Gupta: One other question. Why has the Prime Minister not informed us where Mr Gizenga is, the Congolese patriot? We wanted to hear a little more from him on this. Since we are participating in the UN operations there in the Congo, is it not necessary for the Government to find its way to intervening in the situation and seeing that Mr Gizenga is released? At least it should do its part. That is what I wanted to make out.

Jawaharlal Nehru: I am afraid that any action taken by us would create more difficulties. Privately of course I suppose some suggestions can be made, have been made.

Now many of Mr Bhupesh Gupta's amendments are such that I do not object to them, but the whole concept of it is objectionable.

Bhupesh Gupta: Since the Prime Minister agrees with the substance of the amendments, but not the concept which is an intangible term, in deference to him I withdraw all of them. I gave these amendments in order to inform the Prime Minster of the points that he should bear in mind. I thought I would be cooperating with him in this manner.

Jawaharlal Nehru: I regret I am unable to accept the amendments of Shri Vajpayee. Therefore, the first one in the names of Shri Patil Puttappa[357] and Dr Nihar Ranjan Ray[358] I accept.

433. To Humayun Kabir: ECOSOC Delegation[359]

June 25, 1962

My dear Humayun,

Your letter of the 25th June about the delegation to ECOSOC.[360]

This is highly technical matter and the delegation has been very carefully selected. The Finance Minister[361] will head it. The others, I believe, are all

356. Zakir Husain.

357. Congress.

358. Congress.

359. Letter to the Minister of Scientific Research and Cultural Affairs. NMML, Humayun Kabir Papers, File No. 16/1962-64. Also available in the JN Collection.

360. Appendix 45.

361. Morarji Desai.

experts in this. We are not sending any non-expert. Many of the people selected are actually functioning in Europe.

This delegation is on a different basis from that of the United Nations, where we add sometimes some Members of Parliament. Even there, on account of the exchange difficulty, we are reducing numbers. In the ECOSOC delegation, for us to select anyone not fully acquainted with the complicated questions that will come up there, would be a waste of money and foreign exchange when we badly need this.

Yours sincerely,
Jawaharlal Nehru

434. To Bertram Stevens: Appreciating Help in Australia[362]

June 25, 1962

Dear Sir Bertram,

Shri Samar Sen, who was till recently our High Commissioner in Australia, has told me of your valuable work as President of the India League at Sydney, as also of your generous and sympathetic understanding of India and Indian affairs. From time to time, others have given me the same opinion. I am particularly pleased to know of the assistance which you have on all occasions extended to the Indians who live in or visit Australia.

May I, through this letter, convey my sincere appreciation and thanks for all your help and sympathy for our country and countrymen? I have every hope that you will continue in your efforts to stimulate greater understanding of India and Indian affairs in Australia for many years to come.

We shall be happy to have you and Lady Stevens as our guests in India if you can manage to come here. The best time to do so is in our winter season, from October to March.

I wish both you and Lady Stevens well.

With kind regards,

Yours sincerely,
Jawaharlal Nehru

362. Letter to the former Premier of New South Wales, Australia.

435. For the Indian Federation of United Nations Associations[363]

I send my good wishes to the Indian Federation of United Nations Associations on the occasion of their observing the Charter Day. Many of us often criticise the United Nations when we feel it is being exploited for wrong ends. But we must remember that it has a great deal to its credit and, in any event, some such organisation is essential if the world is not to break up into petty fragments. The charter of the United Nations is a noble document. The procedures and some other matters laid down for the United Nations are somewhat out of date because of the large number of new States that have joined it which are not properly represented in the special bodies of the UN. I hope it will be possible to give them proper representation.

436. To P. Kodanda Rao: No Military Alliances[364]

July 6, 1962

Deer Shri Kodanda Rao,

Thank you for your letter of June 29th and for the note which you have sent me. I have read the note. I am afraid I do not agree with your proposal for India to have military alliances. This will mean giving up our policy of non-alignment. I think this would actually weaken India's position in regard to defence. Also such little influences India might possess for helping the forces of peace would largely disappear.

Yours sincerely,
Jawaharlal Nehru

363. Message, 25 June 1962, forwarded to Rajan Nehru, 1 Clive Road, New Delhi. PMO, File No. 9/2/62-PMP, Vol. IV, Sr. No. 78-A.

364. Letter to former editor of *Servants of India* ; address: 4 Sir Krishna Rao Road, Basavangudi, Bangalore-4. Sent from Pahalgam, Kashmir. NMML, P. Kodanda Rao Papers. Also available in the JN Collection.

437. To T.N. Kaul: Argument for Non-Alignment[365]

July 6, 1962

My dear Tikki,

I have received your letter of the 25th June and your paper on "The Philosophy of Non-Alignment".[366] I have read this paper as well as the other one that you have sent.

Broadly I agree with what you have said. Non-alignment in its narrower sense means keeping away from military blocs. It also means having the freedom to follow our own policy and not be compelled by military allies to follow some other policy of their choice. It means, therefore, not following a policy which may entangle us in a war.

Military alliances are necessarily against some actual potential enemy. To join them means practically naming the enemy and thus, in a sense, weakening ourselves. Even from the strictly narrow point of view of defence, it does not add to our strength but rather weakens it. Perhaps this may not apply to all countries but it certainly applies to India.

Military alliances mean thinking and planning of war. They are opposed fundamentally to the search for peace. They add to the dangers of war and create an atmosphere opposed to peace. In fact, anything but non-alignment would be basically opposed to the policy we have followed and all our thinking on this subject. It would create bitter conflicts in India.

I am writing to you from Pahalgam in Kashmir where I have come for a few days' rest.

Yours sincerely,
Jawaharlal Nehru

438. For M.J. Desai: Tours of Missions Abroad[367]

I think that the idea that our Secretaries should undertake tours of inspection and orientation of our Missions in their respective areas is a very good one. From that point of view, I have welcomed your arranging a tour of yourself to some Missions in Europe and also perhaps of having a meeting of our Heads of Missions in different parts of Europe. In particular, I think that our public

365. Letter to the Deputy High Commissioner, London. Sent from Pahalgam, Kashmir.
366. See appendix 67.
367. Note, 10 July 1962, for M.J. Desai, the Foreign Secretary.

relations activities have to be gone into rather thoroughly. In some places, like the Middle Eastern countries, we might consider some non-officials, singly or in a small team, to go there.

2. While I agree with you in the general proposition, I am a little anxious about the developments that are taking place internationally. Apart from world questions which affect us of course, there are the immediate issues of China and Pakistan. So far as China is concerned, the latest note we have received is quite truculent. Whether it is merely wordy warfare or it indicates some possible action by them in the Ladakh area, it is difficult to decide.[368] But anyhow we have to be prepared for all consequences. I suppose that with the coming of winter, say from November onwards, it will be difficult for any effective action to be taken in those Ladakh areas, either by the Chinese or by us. The immediate risks that arise might, therefore, be confined from now onwards to October.

3. It is also possible, though perhaps unlikely, that the NEFA border might see some trouble.

4. Because of all these possibilities, I would hesitate to advise you to go abroad during this period unless the situation vis-à-vis China improves.

5. So far as the Commonwealth Secretary[369] is concerned, he has had his hands full in recent months because of developments in Pakistan and in India in relation thereto. The repeated communal troubles there are partly the reaction of something that happens on one side and partly perhaps a deliberate attempt to create some trouble in order to divert attention from the internal happenings, especially in East Pakistan. In any event, the position in East Pakistan especially is dynamic and, to some extent, all over Pakistan. This is more important for us than the events happening in Southeast Asia. For this reason, I would suggest that the Commonwealth Secretary should not finalise his programme for Southeast Asia before we are clear in our minds about the immediate future in Pakistan.

6. But I see no harm at all in your issuing a detailed questionnaire to our Missions so that necessary information and statistics might anyhow be collected.

7. I hope to discuss these matters with you and the other Secretaries on my return from Kashmir.

8. I have referred above to the desirability of some small teams or individuals going to the Middle Eastern countries. I was specially thinking of some persons from Kashmir going to these more or less Muslim countries. The Kashmir issue is by no means over in the United Nations. It may come before

368. For Memorandum given by the Ministry of Foreign Affairs, Peking, to the Embassy of India in China on 8 July 1962, see *White Paper VI*, p. 78.

369. Y.D. Gundevia.

the General Assembly or otherwise. Shri Ghulam Mohamed Bakhshi, Prime Minister of Jammu & Kashmir, has discussed this matter with me. He feels that such a visit would be helpful to us. He is thinking of sending one or two of his Ministers, led by Shri G.M. Sadiq, to these Middle Eastern countries. Later, he wants to follow this up by going himself to these countries. I think there is something in this which might help us in explaining our position. Our Missions there can be of help but obviously Ministers of the Kashmir Government would carry more weight and explain the situation in all its aspects more fully.

9. I should like you to share this note with Commonwealth Secretary and Special Secretary.[370]

439. To Shaikh Abdulla Al-Salim Al-Sabah: Kuwait Admission to the UN[371]

July 12, 1962

Your Highness,

I thank you for your letter of 28th June 1962.

You have been good enough to write to me frankly about your efforts, and that of your Government, to lead your people on the path of a better life and increased opportunities for self-development, and to establish Kuwait as a peace-loving, non-aligned nation with friendly relations with all others.

I need hardly tell you that we welcome this; and to assure you of our support in this endeavour, especially when it is in regard to a neighbouring country like Kuwait, with which we have an old established friendship and interests, which we wish to develop to our mutual benefit.

We greatly regret the unfortunate dispute that has arisen between Kuwait and Iraq, with the latter of which also we have an old established friendship. In line with our general policy of non-interference we do not believe in taking sides in matters in dispute between the Arab people. We believe that such differences can best be settled by mutual agreement amongst themselves; and we hope that this will soon take place.

So far as the Soviet attitude against the admission of Kuwait to the UN is concerned, we can obviously do little as this is a question which relates to a Great Power whose decisions are presumably based on what it considers its own best interests in the light of the prevailing world situation.

370. B.F.H.B. Tyabji.

371. Letter to the Amir of the State of Kuwait.

We shall however speak to the Soviet representative here in the matter, as desired by Your Highness, and try to represent to them your point of view which, we agree, deserves sympathy and support.

Please accept Your Highness the expression of my highest consideration.

[Jawaharlal Nehru]

VI. MISCELLANEOUS

440. To Horace Evans: Health Advice[1]

June 2, 1962

Dear Lord Evans,

Thank you for your letter of the 30th May. I am also grateful to you for the advice you sent us after seeing some reports about my recent illness.

I am glad to say that I have recovered and am well now. I spent about twelve days in Srinagar in Kashmir and this rest did me a lot of good.[2] Even here in Delhi I am taking things easily and resting a good deal. Our Parliament session will be over by the end of this month and then I shall take another chance of visiting the hills here.[3] You can rest assured that I shall follow your advice to the best of my ability.

Yours sincerely,
[Jawaharlal Nehru]

441. To Sooryakant Parikh: Peace Movement and Buddhist Bodies[4]

June 2, 1962

Dear Shri Parikh,

I have your letter of the 31st May.[5]

Mahesh Kothari is, I think, a good person. He has been to Japan on one or two occasions and has carried messages from me to the Peace Movement there and also to some Buddhist organisations. He has been to Goa and to Daman and Diu, and I believe has done good work there.

1. Letter to the royal physician ; 26 Weymouth Street, London W.1.
2. 16-28 May 1962.
3. 4-12 July 1962.
4. Letter; address: Patdi Building, Ellisbridge, Ahmedabad-6. NMML, Sooryakant Parikh Papers, Acc No. 434.
5. Appendix 13.

But I am not aware of the fact that he is going to Europe, and I have no present intention of asking him to do so.[6]

Yours sincerely,
Jawaharlal Nehru

442. To Arun Gandhi: Cannot Advise[7]

June 7, 1962

My dear Arun,
I have your letter of June 6th. I do not know what to advise you. Although you have written to me on the subject, all the facts are not before me. In any event, this is obviously a question that you must yourself decide.

Yours affectionately,
[Jawaharlal Nehru]

443. To T.R. Deogirikar: G.K. Gokhale after Bankipore Congress[8]

June 9, 1962

My dear Deogirikar,
Your letter of June 7th.[9]

I wrote about the incident in which Gokhale was concerned from my memory. I do not think I was myself present at the station. But I learnt of it from someone who was present. I have no doubt that the account given to me in the main was correct. I have no means of verifying it now. I cannot give you any further details.

6. See also item 125.
7. Letter to Mahatma Gandhi's grandson; address: c/o *The Times of India*, Bombay.
8. Letter to the biographer of G.K. Gokhale; also Marathi journalist, Samyukta Maharashtra leader and Congress Rajya Sabha MP from Maharashtra, 1952-62. NMML, T.R. Deogirikar Papers, ACC No. 411 (A).
9. Appendix 19.

It is quite possible that Gokhale returned before the end of the session of the Congress[10] and Bhupendranath Basu[11] might also have returned at the same time.

I suppose the most convenient way to go to Madras from Bankipore was via Calcutta. Bankipore was the old name of the new part of Patna. Hence, the Congress was called the Bankipore Congress. The name is no longer used now except in the sense of this being a suburb of Patna. Probably, if you can find the old timetable, you will find the name of Bankipore.

Yours sincerely,
Jawaharlal Nehru

444. To Rajendra Prasad: Health[12]

June 9, 1962

My dear Rajendra Babu,

Thank you for your two letters dated June 5. As far as I am concerned, I am keeping well. I have not followed the extreme advice of Maurice Frydman[13] about my diet. But I have approximated to it to some extent. I continue taking wheat and rice and, to a slight extent, fish and eggs. Meat I have reduced greatly and milk I take very little anyhow. I find that milk does not agree with me. In the main, my diet now is fruit and vegetables.

I am writing to you separately about your second letter.

Yours sincerely,
[Jawaharlal Nehru]

10. Held in Bankipore, 26-28 December 1912.
11. A lawyer from Bengal, President of the 29th session of the Indian National Congress held in Madras in 1914.
12. Letter to the former President.
13. Known as Swami Bharatananda, a Polish engineer and an associate of Ramana Maharshi and Mahatma Gandhi.

445. To Rani Tandon: Good Wishes for Election[14]

जून 10, 1962

प्रिय रानी,[15]
तुम्हारा पत्र मुझे मिला और उस से मालूम हुआ कि तुम उतर प्रदेश की विधान परिषद् के लिये खड़ी हुई हो[16] मैं आशा करता हूं कि तुम उसमें सफल होगी। मेरा आर्शीवाद हमेशा तुम्हारे साथ है।

तुम्हारा
[जवाहरलाल नेहरू]

[Translation begins:

Dear Rani,[17]
I received your letter and learnt that you are standing for Uttar Pradesh Legislative Council.[18] I hope you will be successful. My blessings are always with you.

Yours,
[Jawaharlal Nehru]

Translation ends]

446. For the Association for the Advancement of Coloured People[19]

I send my good wishes to the annual convention of the National Association for the Advancement of Colored People. This Association had done good work in the past and achieved substantial results. The progress that has been made

14. Letter to the daughter-in-law of Purushottamdas Tandon.
15. Wife of Sant Prasad Tandon, son of P.D. Tandon, was running a school in Allahabad. After the 1969 split in the Congress, she joined the Congress (O). See Sahitya Akademi, *Who's Who of Indian Writers*, p. 364; and B.N. Tandon, *PMO Diary: Prelude to the Emergency* (Delhi: Konark Publishers, 2003), p. 354-355.
16. She won the UP MLC seat from the Local Authorities constituency.
17. See fn 15 in this section.
18. See fn 16 in this section.
19. Message, 10 June 1962, to John A. Morsell, Assistant to the Executive Secretary, National Association for the Advancement of Colored People (NAACP), 20 West 40th Street, New York 18, NY, USA. PMO, File No. 9/2/62-PMP, Vol. IV, Sr. No. 52-A.

in recent years holds promise of further advancement of racial justice. In the good work, you are doing, you have all our good wishes.

447. To S.C. Das Gupta: On Article "Why Should We be Pessimistic?"[20]

June 10, 1962

Dear Shri Das Gupta,

I have received your letter of the 2nd June together with the article "Why Should We Be Pessimistic?" I have read the article in spite of its length. It is interesting, but I confess that it is rather confusing in many parts. I do not venture to criticise it because to endeavour to do so would mean writing at great length about subjects, which are by no means clear.

Yours sincerely,
[Jawaharlal Nehru]

448. Mian Iftikharuddin's Death[21]

I am deeply sorry at Mian Iftikharuddin's death.[22] He was an old friend and colleague and though circumstances cut us off from each other ever since Independence and the partition of India, he remained dear to me.[23] His death has come has a personal sorrow. His last few years were spent in struggle against illness and authority which no doubt shortened his life.

449. To Padampat Singhania: No Pearl Bhasm Yet[24]

June 13, 1962

My dear Padampatji,

Thank you for your letter of the 11th June. It is very good of you to offer to send me some Pearl Bhasm for me to take. I am at present taking some allopathic

20. Letter to the Dean of Students, Banaras Hindu University, Varanasi 5.
21. Message, 11 June 1962.
22. Mian Mohammed Iftikharuddin, 58, died on 6 June 1962 in Lahore after a heart attack.
23. An old Congressman, he was president of the Punjab Provincial Congress and CWC member before joining Muslim League in 1946. See also http://www.thefridaytimes.com/18022011/page22.shtml, retrieved on 20 July 2018.
24. Letter to the industrialist; address: Kamla Tower, Kanpur.

medicines and they have done me much good. Indeed, I feel quite normal and healthy now. In these circumstances, I think it would not be right for me to add some other medicine of another type. That may well be too much of a good thing. I therefore think that I should leave it well alone. If necessity arises in future, I shall take advantage of your kind offer.

Yours sincerely,
[Jawaharlal Nehru]

450. To Zulaikha Sobani: Personal and Family Matters[25]

June 14, 1962

My dear Zulaikha,

Thank you for your letter. Your information about me was correct in so far as it went. In fact I am quite well.

I am sorry to learn of Fatima's husband's death. Please convey my condolences to her.

My sister, Vijay Lakshmi, was recently in Karachi visiting her daughter. She is now in Kashmir.

Thank you for your offer of your services as a Physiotherapist. But as I have told you, I am quite well and do not require any kind of special treatment.

I hope you will recover completely from your operation for appendicitis.

Yours affectionately,
[Jawaharlal Nehru]

451. To B.K. Bhattacharyya: Kamala's Patriotism[26]

June 18, 1962

Dear Shri Bhattacharyya,

Your letter of the 8th June. When I referred to Kamala Nehru and the fire inside her, I did not refer to her illness. It referred to her blazing wish to serve her country and the causes she had stood for.

Yours sincerely,
[Jawaharlal Nehru]

25. Letter; address: c/o St Elizabeth's Nursing Home, Harkness Road, Malabar Hill, Bombay-6.

26. Letter; address: Karimganj College, Assam.

452. To D.G. Tendulkar: Gandhi's Last Letter to Nehru[27]

June 22, 1962

My dear Tendulkar,

I have your letter of June 15th.

I would certainly like to read *Einstein on Peace*.[28] But you need not send it to me partly because I have no time to read books just at present, and partly I suppose I can get it here.

I am not likely to visit Goa before October next, that is after the monsoon. You can come with me then.

You need not be alarmed about the state of my health. I am fairly well. I had some indisposition and they dosed me a great deal with antibiotic pills. It takes longer to get rid of the after effects of the antibiotics than the indisposition itself.

I am enclosing, as desired by you, a copy of the photostat of Gandhiji's last letter to me.[29] Also, two photographs of the Japanese engraving on stone of Gandhi. One is of the back of the stone. I do not know the name of the artist. I shall try to find out. Also, two photographs of mine.

Yours sincerely,
Jawaharlal Nehru

27. Letter to Mahatma Gandhi's biographer; address: "Ekanta", Rocky Hill, Narayan Dabholkar Road, Bombay 6. NMML, D.G. Tendulkar Papers. Also available in PMO, File No. 2(427)/62-64-PMS, Volume I, Sr. No. Nil.
28. Editors, Otto Nathan and Heinz Norden (New York: Simon and Schuster,1960).
29. Dated 18 January 1948. The translation as published:

" January 18, 1948

CHI. Jawaharlal,

Give up your fast.

I am sending herewith a copy of the telegram received from the Speaker of West Punjab. Zaheed Hussain had said exactly what I had told you.

May you live long and continue to be the jewel of India.

Blessings from
Bapu "

See Government of India, Ministry of Information and Broadcasting, Publications Division, CWMG, Vol. XG, p. 449; and Government of India, Ministry of Information and Broadcasting, Publications Division, D.G. Tendulkar, *Mahatma, Life of Mohandas Karamchand Gandhi*, Vol. Eight.

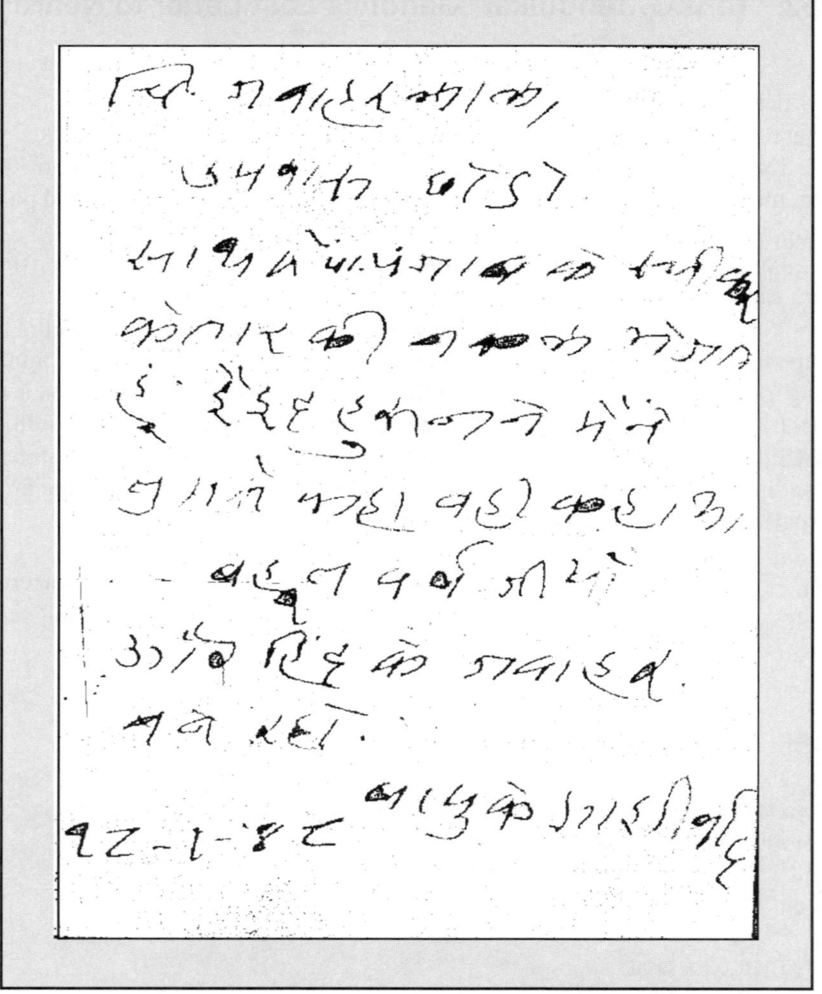

Gandhi sent a note to Nehru, dated January 18, 1948, asking him to end his sympathetic fast, adding: "May you long remain Jawahar, the Jewel of India."

(From D.G. Tendulkar, Life of Mohandas Karamchand Gandhi, Volume Eight)

453. To Robert Barron Nemiroff: Play on German Wartime Experiences[30]

June 28, 1962

Dear Mr Nemiroff,

I have received today your letter of June 23rd and typescript of "Postmark Zero".[31] I am afraid I am very heavily occupied at present and for some little time. But I certainly hope to read your play. After reading it, I hope to write to you again.

Yours sincerely,
[Jawaharlal Nehru]

454. For *The Gandhi Story*[32]

This pictorial representation of the Gandhi Story must appeal to children in India. The Gandhi Story has become an essential part of our rich heritage from the past and is still moulding our present. I am sure that generations to come will wonder at this great story. It is well, therefore, that our children should get acquainted with it before they read more about it in books.

455. To K. Ram: Prince Peter's Book[33]

Please send a reply to this letter from the Prince of Greece and Denmark. Prince Peter who has written the letter is the gentleman who use to live in Kalimpong and who attracted somewhat unfavourable attention from the Government because of his activities here.[34]

30. Letter to Broadway producer; address: 337 Bleecker Street, New York 14, N.Y.
31. A Broadway play, produced in 1965, based on letters from German soldiers in Stalingrad during World War II.
32. Foreword, 30 June 1962, to *The Gandhi Story*, sent to S.D. Sawant, Raj Bhavan, Malabar Hill, Bombay-6. PMO, File No. 9/2/62-PMP, Vol. IV, Sr. No. 93-B.

    Written by S.D. Sawant and illustrated by S.D. Badalkar in a comic book format, it was published in New Delhi by the Government of India, Ministry of Information and Broadcasting, Publications Division in 1966.
33. Note, 4 July1962, to the PPS from Chashmashahi Guest House, Srinagar.
34. For previous references to Prince Peter, see SWJN/SS/48/items 16, 132 and appendix 11 (pp. 224, 472-475, 588).

2. Tell him that I am interested in the subject he is dealing with and shall be glad to have the book he has written.

456. To Rani Maharaj Singh: In Good Health[35]

July 6, 1962

Thank you for your letter of the 3rd July which has reached here at Pahalgam in Kashmir. I am afraid you must have seen the wrong pictures of me. I am feeling well and there is no need for you or anyone to be concerned about my health.

I have come here to Pahalgam for a few days' rest. Indu is with me. Indu and her children have left us and gone on a hurried trip to the cave of Amar Nath [Amarnath].

I hope you are keeping well.

Jawaharlal Nehru

457. To Padmaja Naidu: Immediate Travel Plans[36]

July 10, 1962

Bebee dear,

I am sorry that our attempt at the telephone conversation failed. As a matter of fact, soon after I heard the news of Prafulla Sen's uncontested election on the radio and felt very glad that things took place in the way they did. I sent telegrams to Prafulla Sen[37] and Atulya Ghosh[38] congratulating them.

I have received your letter of the 8th July. Tomorrow morning I am returning to Srinagar and the day after to Delhi. On the 14th July, I shall go to Bangalore and the Nandi Hills for three or four days. Indu will not be going with me but Nan[39] hopes to accompany me. It is taken for granted now that I require looking after. The President, who is in Hyderabad now, wants me to pay him a visit. I shall, therefore, probably go there for a couple of days from Bangalore.

35. Letter to the wife of Raja Maharaj Singh, Governor of Bombay, 1948-52, and elder brother of Rajkumari Amrit Kaur ; address: Prem Niwas, Fyzabad Road, Lucknow, Uttar Pradesh. Salutation not available. Sent from Pahalgam, Kashmir.
36. Letter to the Governor of West Bengal. Sent from Pahalgam, Kashmir. NMML, Padmaja Naidu Papers. Also available in the JN Collection.
37. Chief Minister of West Bengal.
38. President, West Bengal PCC.
39. Vijaya Lakshmi Pandit.

I expect to be in Delhi for a few days on my return from Hyderabad. On the 26th I have to go to Allahabad and then to Lucknow. I have been thinking of paying a day's visit to Calcutta about the 24th or 25th July, if that suits you. I have no particular engagement there. It is only meant as a homage to Bidhan.

I have kept very well here and the weather has been very kind to us. In Srinagar, I am told, it has been hot. Here it has been just pleasant, though it might have been colder.

Love from

Jawahar

458. To B.K. Nehru: Tracing Bipan C. Awasthi[40]

July 10, 1962

My dear Bijju,

You will remember my writing to you some months ago about a young man, Bipan C. Awasthi. His father had not heard from him for a long time and was anxious about him. You replied, I think, that the boy was doing well.

I have now received another letter from his father enclosing some letters from his son. I enclose them. I wish you would find out again how this young man is doing and induce him to write directly to his father.

I am writing to you from Pahalgam in Kashmir. I came here six days ago and will be leaving tomorrow for Srinagar and then Delhi. It has been pleasant here and I have profited by my stay.

Yours affectionately,
[Jawaharlal Nehru]

459. To Joginder Nath Joshi: Good Deeds[41]

10th July 1962

Dear Shri Joshi,

I have received your letter of the 5th July and read it with interest. The three proposals you have made are all worth consideration.

40. Letter to Ambassador to USA. Sent from Pahalgam, Kashmir.

41. Letter ; address: Goraya, District Jullundur. Sent from Pahalgam, Kashmir.

So far as the first one is concerned, that is, the organisation of village industrial cum agricultural centres, this is in fact what we have been doing in establishing our industrial estates.

As for a press, while I agree with you, it is not clear to me how an official press can be of help. A non-official press which agrees with our policies and puts them forward boldly and clearly would certainly be helpful.

As for taking advantage of old and veteran Congress workers, we should always endeavour to take advantage of their experience. It. is not, however, clear how this can be done in a democratic organisation. To some extent attempts are being made to do this. But some of our old workers are out of touch with realities today. However, I agree that we should take advantage of them.

Yours sincerely,
Jawaharlal Nehru

460. To K.G. Saiyidain: Translation of *Letters from a Father to his Daughter*[42]

July 11, 1962

My dear Saiyidain,

Thank you for your letter of July 10 in which you refer to the Kashmiri translation of my *Letters from a Father to his Daughter*.[43] I think the suggestion you have made is a good one, that is, that the translator should be asked to revise his translation carefully. I shall then be glad to give him permission.

Yours sincerely,
[Jawaharlal Nehru]

42. Letter to the Education Adviser, Jammu and Kashmir Government. Sent from Chashmashahi Guest House, Srinagar. JNMF, "Letters from a Father to his Daughter"–Kashmiri. Also available in the JN Collection.

43. First published by Allahabad Law Journal Press in 1929.

461. To Nargis Captain: Personal News[44]

July 11, 1962

Your letter of the 5th July reached me yesterday at Pahalgam in Kashmir. I have come to Srinagar today and tomorrow morning I shall be returning to Delhi. I am very sorry to learn of Bul's[45] ill-health. I hope this is temporary and will pass off. I am glad you are taking her out to Vellore.

I have just spent a week at Pahalgam and this has done me a great deal of good. Even before I went there, I had recovered adequately. In fact, there was nothing much the matter with me at any time and there was needless news about my health. However, I am pretty well now. I have to keep to some kind of a fairly strict diet and have to take regular rest.

I am going to Bangalore in two-three days' time. I do not know when I shall be going to Bombay. If and when I go there, I would certainly like to meet you and Psyche.[46]

Indu has been with me and will be returning to Delhi tomorrow.

Yours sincerely,
[Jawaharlal Nehru]

462. For the World Festival of Youth[47]

I send my good wishes to the Eighth World Festival of Youth and Students for Peace and Friendship which is going to be held in Helsinki. It is becoming increasingly clear that if this world is to continue the relationship of nations and individuals should be based on peace and friendship as well as tolerance of each other's ways. It is particularly important that the youth of the world should increasingly believe in this approach. I hope the Helsinki festival will lay stress on our tolerance of each other even when we differ.

44. Letter to the granddaughter of Dadabhai Naoroji; address 78 Napean Sea Road, Bombay-6. Salutation not available. Sent from Chashmashahi Guest House, Srinagar.
45. Khurshed A.D. Naoroji, granddaughter of Dadabhai Naoroji, a trained musician, worked for Gandhiji, served under the INA Defence Committee appointed by the AICC, 1945. Nirmal Kumar Bose, *My Days with Gandhi* (Hyderabad: Orient Longman, 1974), pp. 17-20.
46. Goshiben Captain, granddaughter of Dadabhai Naoroji, associated with Hindustani Prachar Sabha, died, 1976.
47. Message, 12 July 1962. Forwarded to Jagdesh Kodesia, Secretary, Delhi PCC. PMO, File No. 9/2/62-PMP, Vol. V, Sr. No. 7-A. Also available in the JN Collection.

463. To Onkarnath Sharma: Don't Worry about the Future[48]

July 15, 1962

Dear Onkarnathji,

I have your letter of the 10th July. I would suggest to you not to worry too much about the future. If we do our duty in the present, the future will look after itself.

If you as wish to see me, you can come to Delhi for the purpose when I am there. I am not likely to be in Delhi much during this month.

Yours sincerely,
[Jawaharlal Nehru]

48. Letter to the Proprietor of the Rajkumar Foundry and Engineering Works, Batala. Sent from Nandi Hills.

VII. APPENDICES

1. (a) From MEA[1]

[Refer to item 396]

Note given by the Ministry of External Affairs, New Delhi, to the Embassy of China in India, 15 April 1962

The Ministry of External Affairs present their complements to the Embassy of the People's Republic of China and have the honour to draw the attention of the Embassy to yet another instance of Chinese violation of India's territorial integrity resulting from the setting up of a new Chinese Military post at MR 7834 E 3501 N, 6 miles west of Sumdo. This Chinese post has obviously been developed recently and constitutes, needless to say, a flagrant breach of the repeated assurances extended by the Chinese Government regarding maintenance of the status quo in the area.

The Government of India, in their note dated 31st October 1961, have already drawn the attention of the Government of the People's Republic of China to three new Chinese Military checkposts established on Indian territory between 1960 and 1961 and to the numerous other instances of intrusion by Chinese Military patrols and survey parties into Indian territory. The Government of China, however, have continued to make the untenable claim that these posts so set up are within Chinese territory although such an assertion cannot be sustained for a moment when examined on the basis of available facts.

It is a matter of deep concern to the Government of India that the Government of the People's Republic of China should continue in this manner to persist in their systematic and deliberate encroachments into Indian territory without proper regard to the grave consequences that these may entail.

While lodging a strong protest against the establishment of this latest Chinese post on Indian territory at MR 7834 E 3501 N the Government of India express the hope that the Chinese Government will take immediate action to withdraw from this new position that they have occupied.

The Ministry of External Affairs avail themselves of this opportunity to renew to the Embassy of the People's Republic of China, the assurances of their highest consideration.

1. Note, 15 April 1962. *White Paper No. VI*, p. 26.

1. (b) From the Ministry of Foreign Affairs, China[2]

[Refer to item 396]

Note given by the Ministry of Foreign Affairs, Peking, to the Embassy of India in China, 11 May 1962

Ministry of Foreign Affairs of the People's Republic of China presents its compliments to the Indian Embassy in China and, with reference to another recent case of intrusion and provocation by Indian troops in the western sector of the Sino-Indian boundary, has the honour to state as follows:

Recently, Indian troops, about twenty in number, again intruded into Chinese territory in the area south of the Spanggur Lake in Western Tibet, China. On May 2, 1962, they pressed forward to a place (approximately 33° 28' 30" N, 78° 50'30"E) only about four kilometers from the Chinese outpost at Jechiung, and there they set up a military post and constructed fortifications in preparation for prolonged entrenchment. Moreover, on May 5, 1962, two of the above-mentioned Indian military men continued to sneak deeper into Chinese territory for about 600 meters and from there fired three shots at the Chinese outpost, (two shots were fired at 1211 hours and the third at 1223 hours). If the Chinese frontier guards had not put themselves on the alert in time and firmly maintained an attitude of cool headedness and self-restraint, the aforesaid unwarranted provocative firing by the Indian troops would have led to very serious consequences.

The Chinese Government hereby lodges a serious protest with the Indian Government against the abovementioned intrusion and provocative activities of the Indian troops and demands that India immediately withdraws its aggressive post and puts an end to all its intrusions and provocations. As the Chinese Government pointed out in its note of April 30, 1962, India's encroachment on

2. Note, 11 May 1962. *White Paper No. VI*, p. 40. This and appendix (c) formed part of the Rajya Sabha debate but for the sake of convenience have been placed as appendices.

The following was prefixed to the note from China tabled in the Rajya Sabha on 20 June 1962.

"Correspondence Exchanged Between the Governments of India and China Regarding a Military Post Near Spanggur

20 June 1962

Copy of English translation of the Note from the Ministry of Foreign Affairs of the People's Republic of China handed over to Dr P.K. Banerjee, Chargé d'Affaires of India in China, on 11th May, 1962 by Deputy Director Chang Tung of the Asian Department regarding alleged intrusion into Chinese territory by Indian troops.

(62) Pu Yi Tzu No. 406."

the border of Sinkiang and its provocations against a Chinese post there have already created a very grave situation on the border between the two countries. And now the Indian Government, in disregard of the warning of the Chinese Government, has furthermore stepped up its encroaching and provocative activities in Western Tibet, threatening the security of another Chinese outpost. This shows that the Indian Government has set its mind on aggravating tension in the entire western sector of the Sino-Indian boundary and does not scruple to create incidents of bloodshed. The Chinese Government hereby reiterates, if India does not withdraw its aggressive posts and intruding troops from Chinese territory and continues to carry out provocative activities, the Chinese frontier guards will have to defend themselves, and the Indian side will be held wholly responsible for all the consequences arising therefrom.

The Ministry of Foreign Affairs of the People's Republic of China avails itself of this opportunity to renew to the Indian Embassy the assurances of its highest consideration.

1. (c) From MEA[3]

[Refer to item 396]

Note given by the Ministry of External Affairs, New Delhi, to the Embassy of China in India, 21 May 1962

The Ministry of External Affairs present their compliments to the Embassy of the People's Republic of China and have the honour to refer to the note handed over by the Chinese Ministry of Foreign Affairs to the Indian Embassy in Peking on May 11, 1961.

The note, under reference, contains certain totally unjustified and baseless allegations.

These are:

a) That on 2nd May, 20 Indian troops intruded into a place at 33° 28:30' N, 78° 50:30' E about 4 kms from a new Chinese military post set up at Jechitung;
b) That intruding Indian troops have set up a military outpost in the area; and

3. Note, 21 May 1962. *White Paper No. VI*, pp. 49-50.

c) That on 5th May, 2 Indian soldiers advanced 600 meters deeper into the area and fired three rounds at a Chinese post.

The Government of India firmly repudiates these allegations. Indian troops did not enter the area on 2nd and 5th May as alleged in the Chinese note. Nor have they established any fresh post. On the contrary, Chinese troops moved down south from their post at Spanggur and established a new post at 78° 52:30' E 33° 30' N approximately 8/10 miles southeast of Spanggur on Indian Territory. This has been fortuitously admitted in the Chinese note. Furthermore, as the Government of China are aware, Chinese troops are digging in at this new post and are constructing fortifications. As to the allegation that intruding Indian troops resorted to firing on Chinese troops on 5th May, this again is untrue. A similar allegation about firing by Indian troops made in the Chinese note of August 12, 1961, was categorically repudiated in the Government of India's reply dated October 31, 1961 (vide under Allegation I) fortuitously admitted in the Chinese note. Furthermore, as the Government of China is aware, Chinese troops are constructing for fortifications. As to the allegation that intruding Indian troops resorted to firing on Chinese troops on 5th May, this again is untrue. A similar allocation about firing by Indian troops made in the Chinese note of August 12, 1961, was categorically repudiated in the Government of India's reply dated October 31, 1961 (vide under Allegation I).

In the face of the aggressive activities being systematically pursued by Chinese Forces on Indian territory, it is incongruous for the Government of China to bring up charges against India of "aggravating tension" and "creating incidents of bloodshed." There can be no doubt in any quarter that the Government of China are resorting to these allegations as they had done in the past in order to cover up their fresh sets of aggression on Indian Territory.

As the Government of China is aware, the international boundary in this sector of the border cuts across the eastern part of Spanggur Lake and follows the northern and eastern watershed of the Indus. The setting up of the new Chinese military post at 78° 52:30' E 33° 30 N about 8/10 miles southeast of Spanggur constitutes a further serious violation of Indian territory and an act of grave provocation.

The Government of India lodge an emphatic protest with the Government of China for thus continuing their aggressive activities and establishing fresh posts on Indian territory and accusing the Government of India of sending troops to intrude into what is indisputably Indian territory. If the Government of China were at all interested in maintaining the status quo and the peace on the border, they would be well advised to restrain their forces and desist from constantly pushing forward and setting up new military posts on Indian Territory.

If any breach of the peace results from the unabated pursuit of aggressive ends by China, the responsibility rests solely with the Government of the People's Republic of China. Allegations against the Government of India, totally devoid of any substance whatever, only add to the mischief of aggression, which China, conducts continually.

The Ministry External Affairs renew to the Embassy of the People's Republic of China the assurances of their highest consideration.

1. (d) From MEA[4]

[Refer to item 396]

Note given by the Ministry of External Affairs, New Delhi to the Embassy of China in India, 6 June 1962

The Ministry of External Affairs present their compliments to the Embassy of the People's Republic of China and have the honour to refer to the Note dated the 21st April 1962 from the Chinese Ministry of Foreign Affairs.

The Note makes two entirely unwarranted allegations: (1) That on 11th April 1962 at about 1200 hours, about 25 Indian soldiers penetrated 10 Kms into Chinese territory, reached a point approximately 35° 22′ North 78° 00′ East and carried out prolonged reconnaissance; and (2) That on 13th April 1962 at 1300 hours and 1500 hours two parties of Indian soldiers "intruded into the same area and sneaked to a point approximately 35° 20′ North, 78° 07′ East for reconnaissance".

Indian troops are in certain areas of Ladakh to defend Indian territory. Of these Indian troops move about inside Indian territory, it should not be a matter of any concern to the Government of China.

However since the Government of China made certain specific allegations, these were carefully investigated and it was found that no Indian soldiers had been at either of the places at the time cited in the Chinese Note. Therefore it is clear that the Government of China preferred these charges and assumed the right to protest about so called intrusions by Indian troops without any basis at all. Under these circumstances, the Government of India reject these protests which not only have no basis in fact but constitute unjustifiable interference in the internal affairs of India.

It has been noticed that the Government of China are increasingly taking recourse to such baseless allegations against the Government of India at a

4. Note, 6 June 1962. From *White Paper VI*, pp. 60-61.

time when Chinese forces are themselves making fresh encroachments into Indian territory

Such Chinese military activity has been noticed particularly in the vicinity of the Chinese Military Base illegally set up at 78° 12′ East 35° 10′ North, and at point 78° 13′ East 35° 15′ North.

Carefully verified reports from other sectors of Ladakh also show that Chinese troops are daily intruding into Indian territory, pushing forward on trucks and jeeps, blasting the mountainside with heavy explosives, constructing new military bases and extending military bases already set up.

It is on record that since 1960-61 Chinese intruders have set up no less than five new military bases on Indian territory at Nyagzu, Dambuguru at point 78° 12′ E, 35° 19 N on the Chip Chap river, at a point six miles west of Sumdo, and at 78° 52 30′ E, 33° 30′ N about 8/10 miles south-east of Spanggur.

Against the record of territorial aggression by Chinese forces, there is not even single case to show that Indian troops intruded into Chinese territory or set up a post there.

It seems clear that the Government of China are spreading rumours about the so-called "news reports disseminated from New Delhi" to prove that "Indian troops are preparing to make armed provocations against China when the thaw comes to the border areas" to cover up their aggressive activities. The Government of India have no wish to embroil themselves in hostilities with any country, far less to invade Chinese territory. They are, however, bound to do all they can to preserve the territorial integrity and sovereignty of the Republic of India.

The Government of India lodge an emphatic protest with the Government of China for the fresh encroachments into Indian territory by Chinese intruders and urge the Government of China to put an end to such dangerous and illegitimate activities.

The Ministry of External Affairs renew to the Embassy of the People's Republic of China the assurances of their highest consideration.

2. From MEA[5]

[Refer to item 399]

Note given by the Ministry of External Affairs, New Delhi, to the Embassy of China in India, 18 April 1962

The Ministry of External Affairs presents its compliments to the Embassy of the People Republic of China and has the honour to state that another instance of Chinese intrusion into Indian territory in the Eastern Sector of the border took place in the second week of January 1962. Two Chinese officials of Migyitun accompanied by an interpreter and two platoon commanders crossed the Sino-Indian border near Longju and visited the village of Roi, which is about half a mile South of Longju.

The Government of India have taken serious notice of this unlawful intrusion into Indian territory which is contrary to the repeated assertions of the Government of China that their personnel have never violated the Sino-Indian border in the Eastern Sector. The Government of India regret that despite these solemn assertions Chinese personnel have again intruded into Indian territory and caused fear and tension among the local inhabitants.

In lodging a firm protest with the Government of China in regard to this illegal activity on the part of Chinese personnel in the Tibet region, the Government of India hope that appropriate steps will be taken by the Government of China to ensure that similar intrusions into Indian territory do not occur in future.

The Ministry of External Affairs avails itself of this opportunity to renew to the Embassy of the People's Republic of China the assurance of its highest consideration.

5. Note, 18 April 1962. From *White Paper VI*, p. 27.

3. (a) From the Ministry of Foreign Affairs, China[6]

[See item 391]

Note given by the Ministry of Foreign Affairs, Peking, to the Embassy of India in China, 11 May 1962

Ministry of Foreign Affairs of the People's Republic of China presents its compliments to the Indian Embassy in China and with reference to another recent case of intrusion and provocation by Indian troops in the western sector of the Sino-Indian boundary, has the honour to state as follows:

Recently, Indian troops, about twenty in number, again intruded into Chinese territory in the area south of the Spanggur Lake in western Tibet, China. On May 2, 1962, they pressed forward to a place (approximately 33° 28′ 30" N, 78° 50′ 30" E) only about four kilometres from the Chinese outpost at Jechiung, and there they set up a military post and constructed fortifications in preparation for prolonged entrenchment. Moreover, on May 5, 1962, two of the above-mentioned Indian military men continued to sneak deeper into Chinese territory for about 600 metres and from there fired three shots at the Chinese outpost (two shots were fired at 12:11 hours and the third at 12: 23 hours). If the Chinese frontier guards had not put themselves on the alert in time and firmly would have led to very serious consequences.

The Chinese Government hereby lodges a serious protest with the Indian Government against the above-mentioned intrusion and provocative activities of the Indian troops and demands that India immediately withdraws its aggressive post and put an end to all its intrusions and provocations. As the Chinese Government pointed out in its note of April 30, 1962, India's encroachment on the border of Sinkiang and its provocations against a Chinese post there has already created a very grave situation on the border between the two countries. And now the Indian Government, in disregard of the warning of the Chinese Government, has furthermore stepped up its encroaching and provocative activities in western Tibet, threatening the security of another Chinese outpost. This shows that the Indian Government has set its mind on aggravating tension in the entire western sector of the Sino-Indian boundary and does not scruple to create incidents of bloodshed. The Chinese Government hereby reiterates, if India does not withdraw its aggressive posts and intruding troops from Chinese territory and continues to carry out provocative activities, the Chinese frontier

6. Note, 11 May 1962. From *White Paper VI*, p. 40.

guards will have to defend themselves, and the Indian side will be held wholly responsible for all the consequences arising therefrom.

The Ministry of Foreign Affairs of the People's Republic of China avails itself of this opportunity to renew to the Indian Embassy the assurances of its highest consideration.

3. (b) From the Ministry of Foreign Affairs, China[7]

[Refer to items 388, 390, 391 & 398]

Note given by the Ministry of Foreign Affairs, Peking, to the Embassy of India in China, 2 June 1962

1. The Ministry of Foreign Affairs of the People's Republic of China presents its compliments to the Indian Embassy in China and has the honour to acknowledge that the Chinese Government has received the Indian Government's note of May 14, 1962 in reply to the Chinese Government's note of April 30, 1962

2. The Indian Government in its note not only refuses to withdraw its military strong points and intruding troops, but fraudulently contends that it is responsible for the protection of the areas it has intruded. This further shows that India is determined to encroach on Chinese territory and, to this end, does not scruple to provoke bloody conflicts. The Chinese Government cannot but express its utmost regret at this.

3. The Indian note again repeats the fallacy that large tracts of territory in the western sector of the Sino-Indian boundary which always belong to China are part of Indian territory. The Chinese Government in its previous related notes has refuted in detail this completely groundless latitude. A lie is after all a lie and a truth a truth. A lie can never be turned into truth no matter how often the Indian Government repeats it. As a matter of fact, India admits in its reply note that it has set up strong points at approximately 35° 17′ N, 78° 06′ E and 35° 21′ N, 78° 02′ E and carried out activities around them, thus testifying to nothing but India's encroachment on Chinese territory. In order to cover up its own intrusions, the Indian Government slanderously counter-charges that the Chinese post at 35° 19′ N, 78° 12′ E, which was set up by China years ago, is a newly established one and describes the normal patrols by Chinese frontier guards as aggressive patrolling intended for encircling Indian soldiers. This is entirely a distortion of the fact and a reversal of right and wrong; it is like

7. Note, 2 June 1962. From *White Paper VI*, pp. 56-58.

the trick of a thief calling "stop thief" which serves all the more to reveal the offence he intends to cover up.

4. The Indian Government in its reply reiterates its proposal made in 1959 that in the western sector of the Sino-Indian boundary the Indian Government should withdraw its personnel to the west of the line shown in Chinese maps and the Chinese Government should withdraw its personnel to the east of the line claimed by India as shown by Indian official maps. The note further states that the Indian Government is prepared in the interest of a peaceful settlement, to permit, pending negotiations and settlement of the boundary question, the continued use of the Aksai Chin road for Chinese civilian traffic. Why should China need to ask India's permission for using its own road on its own territory? What an absurdity! As for the Indian Government's old proposal made in 1959, Premier Chou En-lai already pointed out in his letter to Prime Minister Nehru dated December 17, 1959 that it is unfair and that though "equitable" it may appear, it in fact would require China to make a one-sided withdrawal. The Indian Government knows this only too well. Prime Minister Nehru said in Parliament on May 14, 1962 that this proposal "applies entirely to the Ladakh area (it should be read as 'the western sector of the Sino-Indian boundary') and not the eastern area at all, because we are not going to withdraw in the east. In the Ladakh area, it meant a very small withdrawal for us—a few villages—and it meant a large withdrawal for them". That is to say, this "very fair" proposal bragged of by India means in essence that India wants to secure the Chinese side's withdrawal from large tracts of Chinese territory measuring more than 33,000 square kilometers which have always belonged to China in exchange for the Indian side's withdrawal from a few points, which always belong to China but have only recently been occupied by India, while the Indian side continues to occupy, exactly as before, Chinese territories in the eastern and middle sectors of the Sino-Indian boundary. This is of course unacceptable to the Chinese Government, unacceptable now as before.

5. There is reason to believe that the Indian Government is not serious in making the above-mentioned proposal. If it truly wishes the Chinese Government to give earnest consideration to its proposal, it should be prepared to apply the principle embodied in the proposal equally to the eastern section of the border, that is to say, to require both the Chinese and Indian sides to withdraw all their personnel from the area between the so-called McMahon Line and the section of the Sino-Indian boundary as shown on Chinese maps. However, judging from Prime Minister Nehru's May 14 speech in the Indian Parliament, the Indian Government has renewed this proposal on the pre-condition of not doing that. How can one assume that the Chinese Government would accept such unilaterally-imposed submissive terms? Is China a defeated

country? It is clear that the Indian Government in making the proposals did not expect earnest consideration from the Chinese Government. It is evident that, in doing so, it only attempted to divert people's attention.

6. But people's attention can in no way be diverted. The most urgent problem in the current Sino-Indian border situation is that the Indian side persists in changing by force the status quo of the Sino-Indian boundary and setting up military strong points on Chinese territory and is carrying on provocations, so that a border clash may touch off at any moment. As China pointed out in its note of May 28, since China lodged its protest on April 30, Indian troops have set up another new military strong point inside Sinkiang, China, and have continued their intrusions and provocations in Sinkiang and the Ari district. Facts speak louder than words. They show that what the Indian Government now seeks is to provoke bloody conflicts, occupy China's territory and change the status quo of the boundary regardless of consequences, and not at all to settle the Sino-Indian boundary question peacefully through negotiations.

7. The Chinese Government consistently stands for a peaceful settlement of the Sino-Indian boundary question through negotiations. Even now when the Sino-Indian border situation has become so tense owing to Indian aggression and provocation, the door for negotiations is still open so far as the Chinese side is concerned. However, China will never submit before any threat of force. What is imperative now is for the Indian Government to stop its military provocations and withdraw Indian military strong points and troops from Chinese territory. The Chinese Government renews its protest and demand made on April 30 and May 28. This is a serious test as to whether the Indian Government has the sincerity to settle peacefully the Sino-Indian boundary question and improve Sino-Indian relations.

The Ministry of Foreign Affairs of the People's Republic of China avails itself of this opportunity to renew to the Embassy of India in China the assurances of its highest consideration.

The Ministry of External Affairs renew to the Embassy of the People's Republic of China the assurances of its highest consideration.

4. From MEA[8]

[Refer to item 388 & 398]

Note given by the Ministry of External Affairs, New Delhi, to the Embassy of China in India, 14 May 1962

The Ministry of External Affairs presents its compliments to the Embassy of the People's Republic of China and has the honour to refer to the note handed over by the Chinese Ministry of Foreign Affairs to the Indian Embassy in Peking on 30th April 1962.

2. It is obvious that the allegations made in the Chinese note are misconceived and are based on an erroneous notion of the territorial boundary of the Sinkiang and Tibet regions of China. The Government of India have repeatedly tried to correct this erroneous notion but their patient and repeated efforts in this regard seem to have had no effect on the Chinese Government.

3. It is a [an] indisputable fact that, by stages, since 1957, the Government of China have occupied unlawfully a large area of Ladakh which has always been part of India. It is in this process of enlarging their occupation of Indian territory that the Chinese post on the Chip Chap river was established at 35° 19′ N, 78 ° 12′ E in 1961. The Government of India had, in their note dated 31st October 1961, drawn the attention of the Government of China to the fact of the establishment of this new post and had urged the Government of China to withdraw the post from Indian territory. This protest, like many others before and after it, has gone unheeded, and meantime, a further gradual change has been brought about in the territorial status quo in this region of the Sino-Indian border.

4. It is strange that in spite of this deep advance into Indian territory, the establishment of military strong points and the construction of roads through Indian territory linking these military strong points with rear bases, the Government of China continue to affirm "that they have stopped sending patrols within 20 kms on their side of the boundary". This claim as the Government of India's earlier notes have shown, is patently false and, in the context of further inroads into Indian territory pointed out in the various notes of the Government of India, absolutely meaningless.

5. The Chinese note alleges that the Government of India have set up two posts at 35° 16′ N, 78° 8′ E and 35° 22′ N, 78° 5′ E. No post at these points has been established by the Government of India although the Government of India have had posts at approximately 78° 06′ E, 35° 17′ N and at 78° 02′ E,

8. Note, 14 May 1962. From *White Paper VI.* pp. 41-43.

35° 21′ N. These latter posts which are well inside Indian territory have been in existence for some time.

6. The Chinese note cites 18 cases of alleged intrusion from April 11 to 27. This entire area into which Indian troops are alleged to have intruded is part of Indian territory and the Government of India are responsible for the protection of this territory. In compliance with this defence responsibility, the Government of India have certain posts in the area and men at these posts have been going out occasionally for essential purposes. These posts have been established there to defend Indian territory from further inroads. They are not there to attack anybody or for any aggressive activity as alleged in the Chinese note.

7. The Government of China are doubtless aware of the aggressive patrolling which Chinese troops in the Chip Chap river area have been carrying out. A few recent examples of such patrolling are cited below:--

(1) On 16th April 1962, 11 Chinese soldiers reached a point at approximately 78° 14′ E, 35° 16′ N and tried to encircle 4 Indian soldiers at 78° 13 E, 35° 15′ N.

(2) On 21st April 1962, 20 Chinese soldiers with 7 horses reached a point 2,000 yards to the north of the Indian post at 78° 11′ E, 35° 16′ N for reconnaissance.

(3) On 22nd April 1962, approximately 70 to 80 Chinese soldiers debussed from three 3-tons lorries immediately to the north of the Indian post at 78° 11′ E, 35° 16′ N. These men moved forward and occupied a hill feature at 78° 12′ E, 35° 15′ N, approximately 3,000 yards south-east of the Indian post.

(4) On 6th May 1962 at 0930 hours, approximately 20 Chinese soldiers came within 150 yards of the Indian post at 78° 07′ E, 35° 28′ N. They were supported by a party of another 100 Chinese soldiers, who were approximately 1,000 yards away. When the 20 Chinese soldiers moved to closer to the Indian post, the Indian post commander walked up to within 100 yards of the Chinese party and asked them to withdraw.

The examples cited above show which of the two sides is pursuing an aggressive course in the area. The fact is that not only have Chinese soldiers been carrying on aggressive patrolling deep inside Indian territory and systematically violating India's territorial integrity and security but the Government of China have themselves been constantly threatening to extend these activities along the entire Sino-Indian boundary. Such threats and aggressive activities are not indicative of peaceful intentions.

8. In the context of the position stated in paras 3, 4 and 7 above, the Government of India must point out that the order which has now been issued by the Chinese Government to their frontier guards to resume patrolling in the sector from Karakoram pass to Kongkala and the further threat that Chinese troops in certain contingencies will resume patrolling along the entire border can only mean that far from maintaining "tranquility on the border" the Chinese Government propose to adopt further aggressive measures and precipitate clashes. The Government of India hope that the Chinese authorities will consider the grave consequences of what they have threatened to do and act with circumspection.

9. The Prime Minister of India stated in Parliament on 2nd May 1962, "India does not want and dislikes very much a war with China. But that is not within India's control".[9] The Government of India hope that Government of China are earnest about maintaining peace. If so, the two Governments should take necessary steps to prevent armed clashes on the border, ease the tension now existing in the northern sector of Ladakh and lay a proper foundation for peaceful negotiations or the boundary question between the two Governments. In this connection the Government of India would urge the Chinese Government to give serious consideration to the offer made in the Indian Prime Minister's letter dated 16th November 1959 to Premier Chou En-lai,[10] which inter alia proposed as an interim measure that, in the Ladakh region, the Government of India should withdraw their personnel to the west of the line shown in the 1956 Chinese map and the Government of China should withdraw their personnel to the east of the international boundary shown in Indian official maps. This will apply not only to armed but also to unarmed and administrative personnel which should be withdrawn and the entire area between the boundaries claimed by the two sides left unoccupied. The adoption of this suggestion will lead to the relaxation of tension in this border region and create the necessary atmosphere for settlement of the Sino-Indian boundary problem by negotiations and discussions. The Government of India are prepared in the interest of a peaceful settlement to permit, pending negotiations and settlement of the boundary question the continued use of the Aksai Chin road for Chinese civilian traffic. In renewing the Prime Minister of India's offer of 16th November 1959 and also providing for the continued use of the Aksai Chin road, pending negotiations and settlement the Government of India are solely motivated by their earnest desire to settle the boundary question by peaceful methods. The Government of India hope that the Chinese Government will give serious consideration to

9. See SWJN/SS/76/item 8 p. 65.
10. See SWJN/SS/54/item 154.

this proposal and avoid threatening and aggressive postures, which solve no problem but only create a climate of conflict.

5. (a) From the Ministry of Foreign Affairs, China[11]

[Refer to item 386]

Note given by the Ministry of Foreign Affairs, Peking, to the Embassy of India in China, 19 May 1962

The Ministry of Foreign Affairs of the People's Republic of China presents its compliments to the Indian Embassy in China and has the honour to state as follows:

At noon-time on April 28, 1962, ten fully armed Indian military personnel intruded into Chinese territory at Longju and disseminated the information that they would come for a prolonged stay; and they did not leave till they had carried out military reconnaissance there. Having made repeated verifications, the Chinese Government hereby lodges a serious protest with the Indian Government against the above-mentioned act of provocation by the Indian troops which constitutes a grave violation of Chinese territory.

Just as predicted by the Chinese Government, the slanderous charge made by the Indian Government on April 18, 1962 to the effect that Chinese personnel had gone south of Longju was indeed a foretoken of India's further encroachment on Chinese territory in that area. The Chinese Government already pointed out in its note of May 15, 1962 that the Indian side had recently been intensifying its military activities directed against China in the area unlawfully occupied by India close to Longju. The aforesaid new action of Indian troops was obviously taken to pave the way for their renewed occupation of Longju and precipitation of new armed clashes; and at the same time it clearly indicates that India intends to disrupt the status quo of the boundary and create tension not only in the western sector but also in the eastern sector of the Sino-Indian boundary. The Chinese Government demands that the Indian Government desist immediately from its intrusion into Longju; otherwise the Chinese Government will not stand idly by seeing its territory once again unlawfully invaded and occupied and the Indian Government must bear the responsibility for all the grave consequences arising therefrom.

11. Note, 19 May 1962. From *White Paper VI*, p. 46.

The Ministry of Foreign Affairs of the People's Republic of China avails itself of this opportunity to renew to the Indian Embassy in China the assurances of its highest consideration.

5. (b) From MEA[12]

[Refer to item 386]

Note given by the Ministry of External Affairs, New Delhi, to the Embassy of China in India, 28 May 1962

The Ministry of External Affairs present their compliments to the Embassy of the People's Republic of China and have the honour to refer to Note dated 19th May, 1962, of the Ministry of Foreign Affairs of the People's Republic of China.

It is apparent from the note that the Government of China are again wanting to create disturbance in the Eastern Sector of the border which has been peaceful since 26th August 1959 when Chinese troops crossed the internationally border and dislodged the Indian post from Longju by force. Since then, except for occasional intrusions by Chinese personnel, the international border in the Eastern Sector has been quiet although the Government of China in their recent notes dated 30th November 1961 and 30th April 1962 have held out the threat of extensive military action in the Eastern Sector in the event of the Government of India adopting measures for the defence of their territories in the Western Sector of the border.

In their note dated 18th April 1962, the Government of India have drawn the attention of the Government of China to the intrusion by Chinese officials and army personnel into the village of Roy (Ruyu), half a mile south of Longju on the 2nd week of January 1962. In the face of threats held out by the Government of China and the aggressive activities pursued by their personnel on the border it is absurd for the Government of China to make false allegations of planning aggression in the Eastern Sector against the Government of India.

As to Longju, the past facts would bear reiteration. Longju which is south of the McMahon Line has always been a part of Indian territory. It is about two miles south of the international border and at about the same distance south of the Tibetan village of Migyitun.

Longju has always been under the administrative jurisdiction of india and the Government of India maintained a border check post there. As the Chinese Government are aware, in July 1959, the officer-in-charge of the Indian

12. Note, 28 May 1962. From *White Paper VI*, pp. 52-53.

Checkpost at Longju fell seriously ill. The Government of India informed the Government of China on 24th July 1959 in a note verbale that they proposed to paradrop a doctor at the post. While communicating this information to the Government of China, the Government of India gave the Grid Reference of the post. This was done as Longju was near the border, and lest the pilot of the aircraft by error of judgment intruded into Chinee airspace. There was no objection from the Chinese Government.

Yet, on the 25th August 1959, a strong Chinese detachment crossed into Indian territory south of Migyitun and fired without notice on an Indian picket. They arrested the entire picket. Thereafter on the 26th August 1959, Chinese forces encircled the post at Longju and opened heavy fire on it. The Indian personnel at Longju had in the circumstances, to abandon the post. The Government of India lodged a strong protest with the Chinese Ministry of Foreign Affairs on 28th August 1959. In their note dated 10th September 1959, the Government of India had offered to discuss with the Chinese Government the exact alignment of the McMahon Line at Khinzemane, Longju and Tamaden areas on condition that the status quo was maintained at all these places. As far as Longju was concerned, the Government of India had expressed their willingness not to send their personnel back to the area provided the Chinese also withdrew their forces from Longju. This meant that neither side would have their personnel at Longju pending discussions.

Thereafter, the Prime Minister of India had reiterated this proposal, and although there was news that the Chinese personnel at Longju had withdrawn sometime in 1961, the Government of India made no attempt to re-enter Longju.

The specific allegation made in the Chinese note that 10 armed Indian soldiers had intruded into Longju on 28th April 1962 is completely false. There are Indian checkposts in the area adjoining Longju but in accordance with the directive given by the Prime Minister, Indian forces have not re-entered Longju since 26th August 1959.

The Chinese note under reference suggests that Chinese troops have again trespassed into Longju and their forward patrols are engaged in reconnaissance around Longju. The Government of India register an emphatic protest against these aggressive activities on the part of Chinese troops in Indian territory. It should be clear to the Government of China that Longju is in Indian territory and that the Government of India will not allow any foreign aggression in Longju. If the Chinese Government have any doubt about the precise alignment of the border in this area, the Government of India would be glad to discuss the matter with them and clarify their doubt.

The Ministry of External Affairs renew to the Embassy of the People's Republic of China the assurance of their highest consideration.

6. From Humayun Kabir: An Academy of Sciences for India[13]

[Refer to item 348]

May 27, 1962

My dear Jawaharlalji,

Thanks to your vision and enlightened leadership, Indian science has in the last few years received a degree of encouragement and support which is perhaps without parallel so far as State action is concerned. This has led to remarkable achievements in many fields, but in spite of your unprecedented support, many, especially among the younger scientists, complain that they do not find a congenial atmosphere for work.

I have been thinking for some time why such complaints should at all be made. The reason seems to be the existence of a kind of hierarchy in the world of science. Seniority, rather than merit and present achievement often determines status, and those in higher positions do not always give the necessary encouragement to their younger colleagues. In fact, a certain absence of sympathy between older and younger scientists is one of the banes of Indian science. Another reason is the tendency to build up close preserves and keep scientific enquiry and research confined among one's own associates or protégés. Lack of adequate discussion and assessment by one’s compeers tends to flourish under such an arrangement.

One manifestation of these divisions is seen in our failure to develop a scientific society for India more or less on the lines of the Royal society in London or the Soviet Academy. There is of course the National Institute of Science which was intended to serve the purpose. It has not been able to do so fully, even though it is perhaps the most representative scientific organisation we have today. There is, in addition, the Indian Academy of Science at Allahabad, but neither of these can claim even the representative character which the Institute has. The Science Congress cannot perform these functions, as it must be, from the nature of the case, more a forum than a scientific society.

I have been thinking of the matter and have come to the conclusion that none of the existing institutions can be developed into the national organisation. We could however make a new beginning if we can get together a select body of representative scientists from the recognised All India Associations, Universities and the various Government sponsored organisations into a small conference where we may be able to evolve a scheme which will give us the desired body.

13. Letter from the Minister for Scienftic Research and Cultural Affairs. PMO, File No. 17(504) 62-66-PMS, Sr. No. 1-A.

I am therefore planning to call a small conference of scientists where I propose to invite ten distinguished scientists like Professor Raman, Dr Bhabha, Prof. Mahalanobis, Dr Kothari, Prof Satyen Bose and others in their personal capacity, three representatives each from the established All India Associations and two representatives each from Universities and Government organisations. I am enclosing a list which gives the scheme of invitation I have in view.

I feel that such a conference of about 40 outstanding scientists of India would enable us to frame proposals which would ensure the development of Indian science on the lines desired by you. Perhaps these forty could be the Foundation Members of the proposed body, and help to break the barriers which now exist between different organisations. My view, subject to what the conference may decide, is that the proposed body should have a limited membership, not exceeding a hundred, but there should be provision for Associate Members and Corresponding Members to bring in a larger number of promising scientists.

Obviously, such a body could not be set up without your blessing and we feel that the strongest guarantee of its success would be if you would kindly agree to inaugurate the proposed conference. Subject to your approval, I would like to call the conference towards the end of September, preferably in some place away from Delhi. If you are going on a holiday to Kashmir or Manali, I wonder if we could come and take one morning out of your vacation.

Yours sincerely,
Humayun Kabir

7. (a) From the Ministry of Foreign Affairs, China[14]

[Refer to item 393]

Note given by the Ministry of Foreign Affairs, Peking, to the Embassy of India in China, 28 May 1962

The Ministry of Foreign Affairs of the People's Republic of China presents its compliments to the Embassy of India in China and with reference to India's establishment of a new military strong point in Chinese territory in the western sector of the Sino-Indian boundary and further intrusions and provocations there, has the honour to state as follow:

14. Note, 28 May 1962. From *White Paper VI*, pp. 54-55.

1. India not only gave no heed to China's protests and refused to evacuate its new aggressive strong point in the Chip Chap River Valley area in Sinkiang, China, but has recently set up another military strong point at Hongshantou (approximately 35° 18′ N, 78°, 05′ 30′ E), which is barely some eight kilometers west by south of the Chinese post (approximately 35° 19′ N, 78° 12′ E) in that area, and built fortifications there. In addition, Indian troops have repeatedly intruded into the areas west, northwest and southwest of the Chinese post for harassment. It has been established through repeated check-ups that in the period from April 28 to May 17, 1962 alone, 18 such cases involving 131 person-times occurred. What is more, the intruding Indian troops and aircraft have kept on conducting reconnaissance and making provocations against the said Chinese post. For instance, at about 18:30 hours on May 1, 1962, 11 Indian military men intruded into the area around height 5,500 metres in proximity to the Chinese post and conducted reconnaissance for as long as over 40 minutes; at 9:15 hours on May 10 an Indian aircraft intruded into the air space over the Chinese post, flying audaciously at such a low altitude as no more than 400 metres from the ground, and circled there for reconnaissance for as long as 30 minutes or so.
2. In the Ari district in Tibet, China, Indian troops have continued to make intrusions and made another provocative firing. Here are the outstanding cases:
    (1) At about 14:00 hours on May 7, 1962, five Indian military men, three of whom were mounted, intruded into the area around 34° 16′ N, 79° 01′ E, that is, the place where Indian troops had provoked the Kongka Pass incident of bloodshed in October, 1959, and carried out armed reconnaissance there. On the same day, another group of Indian military men numbering about 20 intruded into the area at 34° 18′ N, 79° 01′ E for illegal activities there.
    (2) At about 17:30 hours on May 9, 1962, Indian troops again fired three shots at the Chinese post at Jechiung from the Indian military strong point only about 4 kilometres away, which was set up recently in Chinese territory at a place south of the Spanggur Lake. This is another serious armed provocation by Indian troops since their firing at the same Chinese post on May 5.
    (3) On May 3, 1962, four mounted Indian soldiers intruded deep into Chinese territory and even went beyond the boundary line claimed by the Indian side itself for about four kilometers and arrived at

Goro (approximately 32° 38′ N, 79° 34′ E) in Tibet and conducted reconnaissance for quite some time.

The Indian Government, having remained indifferent to the repeated protests of the Chinese Government, has not only refused to withdraw its aggressive strong point newly set up on Chinese territory and put an end to its intrusions and provocations, but even set up new aggressive strong points on Chinese territory, expanded the scope of its encroachments and continued its intrusions and provocations. The Chinese Government hereby lodges a strong protest with the Indian Government against these actions, and demands that the Indian Government, in the interest of peace, evacuate immediately its military strong points set up recently in Chinese territory and put an end to all its unlawful intrusions into China. Otherwise the Indian side must bear the responsibility for the consequences of such intrusions.

The Ministry of Foreign Affairs of the People's Republic of China avails itself of this opportunity to renew to the Indian Embassy the assurances of its highest consideration.

7. (b) From MEA[15]

[Refer to item 393]

Note given by the Ministry of External Affairs, New Delhi, to the Embassy of China in India 22 June 1962

The Ministry of External Affairs present their compliments to the Embassy of the People's Republic of China and have the honour to refer to the Chinese Government note dated the 28th May 1962.

The Government of India have not established any strong points in any part of Chinese territory. It is the Chinese who have unlawfully established various posts in Indian territory and violated India's territorial integrity. If the Government of India have, in the light of these Chinese intrusions, taken measures to prevent further intrusion by the Chinese, this is what any sovereign government would and must do in the exercise of its responsibility for maintaining the integrity of its territory. It is preposterous, therefore, for the Government of China to allege that not only Indian territories which have been illegally occupied by the Chinese forces in Ladakh are part of Chinese territory but some Indian areas beyond these are also Chinese territory. There seems to be no limit to Chinese expansionist aims.

15. Note, 22 June 1962. From *White Paper VI*, pp. 68-70.

The specific instances of alleged intrusions cited in the Chinese note are dealt with seriatim below:

Allegation (1):

India has recently set up another military strong point at approximately 35° 18′ N 78° 05′ 30" E, 8 Kms. west by south of the Chinese post at 35° 19′ N 78° 12′ E on the Chip Chap river.

Comments:

This is a repetition of an allegation made earlier in the Chinese note of 30th April 1962. It was then alleged that India had set up a new military post at 35° 16′ N 78° 08′ E. The Government of India in their note of 14th May 1962 had pointed out that there was no post as alleged at 35° 16' N 78′ 06 E. It was made clear then that this Indian post which was well inside Indian territory had been in existence for some time. Nevertheless the allegation, already refuted, has reappeared in the Chinese note under reference with a new Chinese name given to the location and with a small change in the map reference of the post.

This allegation of intrusion into Chinese territory is entirely baseless.

Allegation (2):

Between 28th April and 17th May Indian troops repeatedly intruded into this area. There were 18 cases of such intrusions.

Comments:

The Chinese note of 30th April 1962 carried more or less the same allegations, viz, that in 17 days Indian troops had intruded 18 times into the area. This time the number of intrusions remains the same although the period during which they took place has been extended by 3 days. In refuting the earlier allegation, Government of India had observed in their note of 14th May 1962 that "the entire area into which Indian troops are alleged to have intruded is part of Indian territory and the Government of India are responsible for the protection of this territory. In compliance with this defence responsibility, the Government of India have certain posts in the area and men at these posts go out occasionally for essential purposes. These posts have been established there to defend Indian territory from further inroads. They are not there to attack anybody or for any aggressive activity as alleged in the Chinese note".

This allegation of intrusion into Chinese territory is not only baseless but is merely a repetition of an earlier allegation which had been dealt with fully.

Introduction of phrases like "131 persons – times'[16] does not alter the fact that it is a baseless repetition.

The two specific instances of intrusion cited in the Chinese note to illustrate the general allegation, viz., (1) that on 1st May 1962 11 Indian soldiers had gone to the area near Height 5500 metres and (2) that on 10th May 1962 at 9:15 hours Indian aircraft flew over the Chinese post unlawfully set up in Indian territory at 35° 19′ N 78° 12′ E are both unfounded.

The truth behind these Chinese allegations is that

(1) Chinese troops are illegally posted in this area where they have no right to be;
(2) They have built a strong military base with fortifications in the area which is Indian territory;
(3) They are extending this fortified area and
(4) Strong patrols from this Chinese military base are threatening the adjoining areas and the Indian posts located there.

Allegation (3):

On 7th May 1962 at about 14:00 hours, five Indian soldiers intruded into the area at 34° 16′ N 79° 01′ E. On the same day another 20 men intruded into the area at 34° 18′ N 79° 01′ E.

Comments:

Although both the locations are inside Indian territory there is no truth in the Chinese allegation that Indian soldiers had been there on the 7th May 1962. On the contrary on the 7th May 1962, 20 Chinese soldiers had intruded into this very area at 15:20 hours. What is more, there is evidence to show that Chinese troops are daily intruding into this area and are carrying out various illegal activities.

Allegation (4):

On 9th May 1962 at 17:30 hours Indian soldiers again fired 3 shots at the Chinese post at Jechiung.

16. As in the original.

Comments:

A similar allegation was made in the Chinese note dated 11th May 1962 which said that on 5th May 1962 Indian soldiers had reached the same location and fired 3 shots at the Chinese outpost. That allegation as pointed out in the Government of India's note dated 21st May 1962 was untrue. An earlier allegation about firing by Indian troops made in the Chinese note of 12th August 1961 had also proved unfounded. The present allegation about firing at the Chinese post on 9th May 1962 has been checked, and it has been found to be untrue. The fact is that Chinese intruders have set up a new military base at 'Jechiung' in Indian territory and are covering this up by resorting to baseless allegations against Indian troops.

Allegation (5):

On 3rd May 1962, 4 mounted Indian soldiers intruded into Gore at 32° 38′ N 79° 34′ E for carrying out reconnaissance.

Comments:

The Government of India firmly repudiate this entirely baseless allegation. Indian soldiers did not visit Gore on 3rd May 1962 or on any other day. Unlike Chinese intruders, Indian soldiers are strictly forbidden to cross the international frontier. The Government of India are fully satisfied that there has been no case where Indian soldiers trespassed into Chinese territory across the international border.

The Government of India are constrained to observe that these and other baseless allegations are being repeated by the Chinese Government as part of their planned propaganda against India to further Chinese expansionist aims and to lay fresh claims to Indian territory and to divert attention from the unlawful activities which are being ceaselessly pursued by Chinese forces in Indian territory. The Government of India, therefore, cannot but reject the Government of China's protest note based on these false allegations.

The Ministry of External Affairs renew to the Embassy of the People's Republic of China the assurance of their highest consideration.

8. (a) From Ministry of Foreign Affairs, China[17]

[Refer to item 397]

Note given by the Ministry of Foreign Affairs, Peking,
to the Embassy of India in China, 31 May 1962

The Ministry of Foreign Affairs of the People's Republic of China presents its compliments to the Embassy of India in China and, with reference to the note of the Ministry of External Affairs of India dated May 10, 1962, has the honour to state the following:

1. The Indian Government in its note has gone to the length of lodging a protest with the Chinese Government against Sino-Pakistan negotiations for a provisional boundary agreement and want only slandering and intimidating China. The Chinese Government categorically rejects the unjustifiable protest of the Indian Government and, from the Indian Government's completely unreasonable attitude of imposing its will on others, cannot but draw with regret the conclusion that the Indian Government is bent on making use of the Sino-Pakistan negotiations to whip up anti-Chinese sentiments and aggravate the tension between China and India.
2. The Indian note alleges that the Chinese Government accepted without reservation the position that Kashmir is under Indian sovereignty, that there is no common boundary between China and Pakistan, and that therefore China has no right to conduct boundary negotiations with Pakistan. This allegation is totally untenable. When did the Chinese Government accept without any reservation the position that Kashmir is under Indian sovereignty? The Indian Government could not cite any official Chinese document to prove this arbitrary contention but, basing itself solely on the guesswork and impression of Indian diplomatic officials who have been to China, insisted that Chinese Government authorities had made statements to that effect. This is not only a unilateral misrepresentation of the fact but a conclusion imposed on others, to which the Chinese Government categorically objects. There is a boundary of several hundred kilometers between China's Sinkiang and the areas the defence of which is under the control of Pakistan, and it has never been formally delimited and demarcated. If one does not shut his eyes to the facts, how can he assert that there is no common boundary between China and Pakistan? Since both

17. Note, 31 May 1962. From *White Paper VI*, pp. 99-102.

China and Pakistan are sovereign states, why cannot China conduct negotiations with Pakistan to settle the question of the actually existing common boundary so as to maintain tranquillity on the border and amity between the two countries? Long before it agreed with the Government of Pakistan to negotiate the boundary question, the Chinese Government had repeatedly proposed, and now still proposes, to conduct negotiations with the Indian Government for the settlement of the Sino-Indian boundary question. But the Indian Government has again and again turned down China's proposal, consequently the Sino-Indian boundary question remains unsettled and the situation on the Sino-Indian border becomes increasingly tense. Now the Indian Government not only refuses itself to negotiate a settlement of the boundary question with China, but object to China's negotiating a boundary settlement with Pakistan. Does it mean that the Indian Government, after creating the Sino-Indian boundary-dispute, wishes to see a similar dispute arise between China and Pakistan?

3. The boundary negotiations between China and Pakistan do not at all involve the question of the ownership of Kashmir. The agreement between the Governments of China and Pakistan made it crystal clear that after the settlement of the dispute between Pakistan and India over Kashmir, the sovereign authorities concerned shall reopen negotiations with the Chinese Government on the question of the Kashmir boundary so as to conclude a formal boundary treaty to replace the provisional agreement to be signed after the Sino-Pakistan negotiations. The signing of such an agreement will only help maintain tranquillity on the existing boundary between China and Pakistan, and will in no way prejudice a peaceful settlement of the Kashmir dispute between India and Pakistan. The Indian Government is wholly unjustified in objecting to boundary negotiations between China and Pakistan on the pretext of the Kashmir dispute.

4. With regard to the Kashmir dispute, it has been the consistent position of the Chinese Government to be impartial and to wish that India and Pakistan will reach a peaceful settlement. This has been and still is the Chinese position. The Indian Government is clearly aware of this. Suffice it to point out the fact that Premier Chou En-lai declared at a press conference in Calcutta on December 9. 1956, that the Chinese Government considered the Kashmir question "an outstanding issue between India and Pakistan". Furthermore, Premier Chou En-lai, together with the late Prime Minister Bandaranaike of Ceylon, made an appeal in their joint statement issued on February 5, 1957, to India

and Pakistan to strive further for a peaceful settlement of the Kashmir question. This attitude of the Chinese Government of never getting involved in the dispute over Kashmir can in no way be distorted and is well-known throughout the world.

5. The Chinese Government has always refrained from making any remarks on the historical background of the Kashmir question. Nevertheless, the Kashmir question is after all a dispute between two legal governments, those of India and of Pakistan. China has diplomatic relations with India and also with Pakistan, and India, too, has diplomatic relations with Pakistan. The Chinese Government only hopes that this dispute between India and Pakistan will be settled by them peacefully, and has always been against anyone taking advantage of it to sow discord in the relations between the two countries. So far as China is concerned, nothing would be better than a peaceful settlement of this dispute by India and Pakistan through negotiation. However, more than ten years have passed and despite the best wishes and expectations all along cherished by China, this dispute between India and Pakistan remain unsettled. In these circumstances, anyone with common sense can understand that the Chinese Government cannot leave unsettled indefinitely its boundary of several hundred kilometres with the areas the defence of which is under the control of Pakistan merely because there is a dispute between India and Pakistan over Kashmir. It is entirely necessary, proper, legitimate and in accordance with international practice for the Chinese Government to agree with the Government of Pakistan to negotiate a provisional agreement concerning this boundary pending a final settlement of the Kashmir question. What fault can be found with this? Yet in the note the Indian Government rudely slanders the Chinese Government's agreeing to open negotiations with Pakistan as taking advantage of the difference between India and Pakistan and committing aggression against India. But unreasonable assertions can never hold water. The fact, on the contrary, is that the Indian Government itself is seeking to make use of the boundary question to sow discord in the relations between China and Pakistan. On May 7, 1962, Prime Minister Nehru openly admitted in the Indian Parliament that "we treated the Pakistan Government in a friendly way in these matters because we thought that any action which they might take should be in line with the action we were taking in regard to this border and should not conflict".[18]

18. See SWJN/SS/76/item 460 p. 501.

Small wonder that the Indian Government should get so excited about Sino-Pakistan negotiations. Its scheme to sow discord in the relations between China and Pakistan has failed.

6. The excitement of the Indian Government will only bring results contrary to its expectations. Anyone in the world with common sense will ask: Since the Burmese and Nepalese Governments can settle their boundary questions with China in a friendly way through negotiations and since the Government of Pakistan has also agreed with the Chinese Government to negotiate a boundary settlement, why is it that the Indian Government cannot negotiate and settle its boundary question with the Chinese Government? Such a commonsense query is indeed rather embarrassing. But it is useless to get furious with China. As in the past, the Chinese Government still stands for a friendly settlement of the Sino-Indian boundary question through peaceful negotiations. The Indian Government's unenviable situation on this matter is of its own making. For example, the Indian Government's note says: "It is the India-China boundary which starts from the tri-junction of the boundaries of India, China and Afghanistan.......... and runs eastward upto the tri-junction of the boundaries of India, Burma and China". Pray, what kind of an assertion is that? Not only are the areas the defence of which is under the control of Pakistan negated, but even Nepal no longer exists, Sikkim no longer exists, and Bhutan no longer exists. This is out-and-out great-power chauvinism. The Indian Government should realise that it is now in the sixties of the 20th century and that the cursed era in which great powers controlled everything has gone forever. Anyone who persists in an attitude of great-power chauvinism in international affairs will always knock his head against a stone wall.

7. The Chinese Government is deeply convinced that it is a good thing to hold boundary negotiations between China and Pakistan, which are in the interests of both friendship among Asian countries and peace in Asia. No slander of any kind can ever distort this fact the position of the Chinese Government is not difficult for any reasonable person to understand. One who tries to make use of Sino-Pakistan negotiations to whip up anti-Chinese sentiments will only be lifting a rock to crush his own toes in the end. The Chinese Government hopes that the Indian Government will coolly think it over: Would it not be better to make some earnest effort towards a peaceful settlement of the Sino-Indian boundary question, rather than wasting its strength in such fruitless quarrel?

The Ministry of Foreign Affairs of the People's Republic of China avails itself of this opportunity to renew to the Embassy of India in China the assurances of its highest consideration.

8. (b) From MEA[19]

[Refer to item 397]

Note given by the Ministry of External Affairs, New Delhi, to the Embassy of China in India, 10 May 1962

The Ministry of External Affairs present their compliments to the Embassy of the People's Republic of China and have the honour to state that according to a communiqué issued by the Governments of China and Pakistan have entered into an agreement "to locate and align their common border".

As the Government of China are aware there is no common border between Pakistan and the People's Republic of China. It is the India-China boundary which starts from the tri-junction of the boundaries of India, China and Afghanistan at approximately long 74° 34′ E and Lat. 37° 3′ N and runs eastward upto the tri-junction of the boundaries of India, Burma and China.

There has never been any doubt that the sovereignty over the entire State of Jammu and Kashmir including that part which is under Pakistan's unlawful occupation vests solely in the Indian Union. The Government of India had so far believed that the Government of the People's Republic of China had accepted this basic position without any reservation. This was confirmed by Premier Chou En-lai when he stated to the Indian Ambassador in Peking on March 16, 1956 "that the people of Kashmir had already expressed their will" on the issue of Kashmir's accession to India. The same impression was gained at the meeting between the Secretary General of the Indian Ministry of External Affairs and the Chinese Prime Minister in July 1961. At that time it seemed that the Government of China still acknowledged the final accession of the State of Jammu and Kashmir to the Indian Union. The Government of India are, in view of this background surprised that the Government of the People's Republic of China should have suddenly decided to enter into an international agreement to negotiate the boundary of that part of the State of Jammu and Kashmir which is under the unlawful occupation of Pakistan with the Government of Pakistan. This is a reversal of the attitude of the Government of the People's Republic of China in regard to India's sovereignty over the entire State of Jammu and

19. Note, 10 May 1962. From *White Paper VI*, pp. 96-97.

Kashmir and is obviously a step in furtherance of the aggressive aims that China has been pursuing towards India in recent years.

In lodging an emphatic protest with the Government of the People's Republic of China for this interference with the sovereignty of India over the State of Jammu and Kashmir, Government of India solemnly warns the Government of China that any change provisional or otherwise in the status of the State of Jammu and Kashmir brought about by third parties which seeks to submit certain parts of Indian territory to foreign jurisdiction will not be binding on the Government of India and that the Government of India firmly repudiate any agreements provisional or otherwise regarding her own territories arrived at between third parties who have no legal or constitutional locus standi of any kind.

It is clear that the Government of China are in this matter acting in furtherance of their aggressive designs and are seeking to exploit the troubled situation in Kashmir and India's differences with Pakistan for their advantage. The Government of India will hold the Government of China responsible for the consequences of their action.

The Ministry of External Affairs avail themselves of the opportunity to renew to the Embassy of the People's Republic of China the assurances of their highest consideration.

9. From J.D. Bernal: World Congress in Moscow[20]

[Refer to item 364]

World Congress for General Disarmament and Peace
Moscow, 9-14 July, 1962

Preparatory Committee
Chairman: J.D. Bernal

94 Charlotte Street,
London
25th May 1962

Dear Mr Prime Minister,
I have the honour to write to you on behalf of the International Preparatory Committee for the World Congress for General Disarmament and Peace, to be held in Moscow from 9 to 14 July.

20. Letter from the Chairman of the International Preparatory Committee for the World Congress for General Disarmament and Peace. MEA, File No. A(3)-DISARM/1962/, p. 12/corr.

The Congress will be attended by representatives of, and observers from, many different organisations working for disarmament and peace and by persons of all shades of opinion interested in peace, drawn from every part of the world.

It is clearly desirable that in its discussions the Congress should start from the fullest and most authoritative expression of the policies on disarmament held by the eighteen governments invited by the United Nations General Assembly to form the Disarmament Committee now meeting in Geneva.

At its meeting in Eskilstuna, Sweden, on 19-20 May, the Preparatory Committee accordingly asked me to request the heads of these Governments to convey to the World Congress, in writing or by sending a representative, their views on the problem of general and complete disarmament and on how the obstacles to it may best be overcome.

We are confident that the opportunity to learn directly your government's views on these problems will be deeply appreciated by all the participants at the Congress as a most important contribution to more widespread understanding, and the eventual solution, of the problem of disarmament.[21]

I have, Sir, the honour to be,

Yours faithfully,
J.D. Bernal
Chairman, Preparatory Committee

10. From M.C. Chagla: Indians in Trinidad[22]

[Refer to items 427 & 428]

London W.C. 2
May 29, 1962

My Dear Panditji,

Sir Leary Constantine, who is likely to become the High Commissioner for Trinidad when that country attains freedom, came to see me this afternoon. He apprised me of the progress that the Constitutional Conference is making in London and drew my attention to the unfortunate role that the representatives of the Indian community are playing at the Conference. The Indian community constitutes 36 per cent of the population of Trinidad and they are emphasising their separateness, insisting on separate representation in services, etc., and even going to the length of claiming a partition of the country so as to give

21. See also item 365.
22. Letter from the High Commissioner in London. MEA, File No. SII/104-5/62, p. 37/Corr.

a separate homeland to the Indians. This is a picture so reminiscent of what happened in our own country. The British played the same part in Trinidad as they did in India. The principle was the same—rally the minorities—and the minorities having been rallied and strengthened, they now feel that they have a stake in the country which is as important as that of the majority community and that their interests and rights should be permanently safeguarded. I told Sir Leary that the policy of our Government, not only in India itself but outside also, was to set its face against any partition of a newly emerging independent country. We, having experienced the horrors of partition, would not like any other country to suffer the same. My suggestion to him was that he should follow the principle we have accepted in our own Constitution—fundamental rights guarantee to all citizens; no distinction between one citizen and another; and an independent Judiciary to act as the custodians of these rights. He told me that they are thinking on the same lines but it was difficult to satisfy the so-called minority interests.

He expects that the date for independence of Trinidad will be fixed either in September or December this year and he is most keen that you should go to Trinidad for the Independence Day. Your presence may be of great help in persuading the Indian community to work shoulder to shoulder with the Negroes in working the constitution of a free country with the object of improving the lot of the people. I pointed out to him that you will be coming here in September for the Prime Ministers' Conference, and perhaps, it will be difficult for you to go to Trinidad. He suggested that failing you, perhaps, the President, Dr Radhakrishnan might be persuaded to go there. I think this will be an excellent idea if our President could undertake this journey. It will be a very fine gesture on the part of India to a small country which has become free, and it will emphasise the bonds that should exist between the Negroes and Indians in Trinidad.

With kind regards,

Yours sincerely,
M.C. Chagla

11. From Krishna Dev Tripathi: Farmers' Cooperatives[23]

[Refer to item 272]

30 May 1962

Respected Panditji,

Excuse me for taking some of your time. I have been feeling that much headway is not being made in cooperative farming even though it has become an accepted policy of the Government. Various schemes of land reforms executed by the Congress Governments must culminate in widespread cooperative farming which is the only way to provide better and modern means to farming and to bring a substantial increase in food production. During the last general elections, parties in opposition indulged in intensive false propaganda against Congress on the issue of cooperative farming. It is unfortunate that while much was said against us on this issue, we failed to put forward our point of view. I feel that the rightist opposition is making a lot of noise on this issue against us while we are not making effective attempts to demonstrate advantages of cooperative farming.

I therefore, suggest that steps should be taken in the immediate future to organise cooperative farming in one village per Community Development Block covering the entire area of cultivated land of the village. In order to ensure that people brought under cooperative farming do not oppose its introduction, the government should convince them that it is going to be on experimental basis, that the ownership of the land will continue to vest in them which is already our avowed policy, that they will get, irrespective of the yield, a minimum which will be equal to the average yield per plot and in case actual yield under cooperative farming goes down the government would make the deficit good in produce by paying an equal amount of subsidy on the basis of the average yield of the years preceding cooperative farming. Government should provide all possible facilities to villages brought under this scheme and, to start with, the scheme may be undertaken for a period of five years. I am sure, given a good organisation and government help, we should be able to demonstrate obvious superiority of cooperative farming over individual farming. Once the scheme becomes successful at the experimental stage, other villages of the Block will feel inspired follow suit.

This scheme should be taken up as a national drive and prominent Congressmen along with legislators may be asked to organise this drive. I remember the good old days of zamindari abolition Fund drive organised in UP

23. Letter from Lok Sabha MP, Congress. PMO, File No. 31(93)/59-70-PMS, Sr. No. 54-A.

of which my late father Shri V.D. Tripathi[24] happened to be the in charge. All Congressmen were mobilised and the scheme was a grand success. This scheme will give opportunity to Congressmen not engaged in legislative activities to render useful service to the country and they will have a feeling of usefulness. As an incentive to work with zeal for this drive it should be made clear that at the time of selection of Congress candidates for legislative and local bodies, contribution to the drive of cooperative farming would be the most important criterion.

If you think it proper I may raise this question in the Congress Parliamentary Party meeting and also in the Lok Sabha by a motion.

I hope you will consider my humble suggestion.

With respects, I am,

Yours obediently,
Krishna Dev Tripathi

12. From B.K. Sunthankar: Marathi Speakers in Mysore[25]

[Refer to item 157]

We beg to request that the following subject may kindly be taken up for consideration at the meeting of the National Integration Council to be held on 2nd and 3rd June, 1962, as it vitally concerns the question of national integration.

The Marathi-speaking people residing in the areas in dispute between the Maharashtra and Mysore States and numbering about seven lacs have been passionately pleading for their inclusion in Maharashtra ever since the idea of linguistic States was mooted. The States Reorganisation Commission no doubt took some other factors besides language into consideration while making their recommendations, but it cannot be denied that language was the principal factor in determining the boundaries of the States. That we form the majority of the population in the disputed areas and that we wish to join Maharashtra has been abundantly proved by our winning all the elections right from the Gram Panchayats to the Mysore Legislative Assembly solely on this issue. We know that you as a true democrat, attach considerable importance to the

24. Member, UP Assembly, 1937-40, and Lok Sabha, 1952-57.
25. Copy of letter of 31 May 1962 from MLA, 328 Tilakwadi, Belgaum. Salutation and signature not available.

popular wishes as expressed through elections and we fail to understand why this wholesome democratic principle has been ignored in our case.

We are being treated as inferior citizens in a pre-dominantly Kannad State and have been subjected to severe police repression in the hope of breaking down our resistance. In fact, when our President, Dr Radhakrishnan, was told of these atrocities when he visited Belgaum last year, he expressed surprise that such things should happen in India after independence.

Over five years were wasted in vainly seeking a settlement through negotiations between the two Governments concerned, though it was obvious that such a settlement was not possible due to the intransigence of the Mysore Government. As the boundary disputes are an offshoot of the reorganisation of the States, the Centre cannot evade its responsibility of settling them in a just and fair manner.

The apathy of the Union Government to settle this problem has encouraged the Mysore Government to ride roughshod over the feelings, culture and language of the Marathi people in the border areas. When the question of teaching Kannad in the Marathi schools in the border areas was raised in the Mysore Assembly some time back, the then Chief Minister Shri Jatti,[26] remarked that the Maharashtrians were free to get out of Mysore. He was further pleased to say that Mysore was a Kannad State and that all the people of the State were Kannad people. Similarly when a deputation of the Belgaum Municipality waited upon Shri Jatti, when he was the Chief Minister to plead for the withdrawal of the notice served on the Municipality to show cause against suspension, he told them that he would not suspend the Municipality and would also give them financial aid only if they passed a resolution favouring retention of Belgaum in Mysore State. It is for you to consider how far such utterances of a Chief Minister who was on the National Integration Council would help promote the cause of National Integration.

It is widely recognised that even after 14 years of independence, the country has not been emotionally integrated and has remained weak and disunited. We are all very grateful to you for taking the initiative in combating this danger by focusing attention on the need of national integration. The non-settlement of the boundary dispute is coming in the way of integration by poisoning the relations between the two neighbouring peoples.

We have patiently waited for over five years, and there is no point in asking us to have still more patience when the problem can easily be solved now.

We earnestly urge that the National Integration Council should take up this Maharashtra-Mysore border dispute and settle it satisfactorily.

26. B.D. Jatti.

13. From Sooryakant Parikh[27]

[Refer to item 441]

31st May 1962

With a desire to understand, may I ask you one thing about Shri Mahesh Kothari from Gujarat? He poses to be very very close to you, travels along with you and represents you at certain high level. He tells us that he had been twice to Mozambique and would go to see Salazar for certain problems about Indians in Portuguese territories. He also tells us that you desire that he should go round to Europe, as your personal representative and meet informally, top politicians to ascertain their views on economic and political policies of India.

In this context, we fail to understand how could he be your personal representative and on what qualities and ground? No doubt, he is a good worker of Bhoodan Movement, our colleague, but this type of activities, flying from one place to another, with lot of expenses, seem contrary to Bhoodan work and is beyond our understanding.

Without going into the details, I as an humble citizen, I would like to request you to educate me for my query.

I shall be highly grateful if my letter will be treated confidential.

With kindest regards,

Sooryakant Parikh

14. From Padmaja Naidu to S. Radhakrishnan: Malda Riots[28]

[Refer to item 50]

In my last letter I had referred to reports having reached me of stray incidents that had occurred recently in the district of Nadia and in the North Bengal Districts of West Dinajpur, Jalpaiguri and Cooch Behar. Before going into the details of these incidents I would like to give you the general background as reported to me by the Home (Police) Minister of the Government of West Bengal[29] who toured extensively in each of the districts where incidents had taken place and came to Darjeeling to discuss the situation with me.

27. Letter. NMML,Sooryakant Parikh Papers, Acc. No. 434. Salutation not available.
28. Extracts from letter from Governor of West Bengal to the President of India, 31 May 1962.
29. Kalipada Mukherjee.

The communal tension which resulted in these incidents was apparently the effect of the reports published in the Calcutta press describing in horrid details of murder, arson and looting in East Pakistan in which the Hindus had been the victims and partly the result of letters received recently from East Pakistan by refugees in the border areas of West Bengal, many of whom lost their relations and friends. The Home (Police) Minister showed me the copies of the reports, which the Home Secretary of West Bengal[30] is sending to the External Affairs Ministry based partly on statements of Hindus who have migrated from East Pakistan and partly on Pakistan Government's wireless messages intercepted by us. I gathered the impression that even making allowances for a certain percentage of exaggeration due to panic and sorrow, some terrible things have been happening in East Pakistani particularly Pabna, Rajshahi and Dacca.

One significant feature about the incidents in the three North Bengal districts is that they started on precisely the same date, namely, the night of 11 May. This leads one to conclude that the incidents were not just sporadic ones but were the result of a concerted move by a group of persons displaced from the Mymensingh district in East Pakistan. So far as Cooch Behar, where the largest number of these incidents took place, is concerned, a local incident appears to have aggravated the situation. On the 9th May, a young girl belonging to a family displaced from Mymensingh district which had settled in Kotwali PS was kidnapped by some local Muslims and appears to have been kept in hiding in different places and later taken away to Pakistan. Many of the incidents, which occurred, were connected with those places, households or persons apparently involved in the affair.

The Commissioner of the Presidency Division who visited the areas in Cooch Behar where the incidents took place in joint planning with the Deputy Inspector General of Police, Northern Range, has constituted 25 new Police Posts there, with 17 civil zones in charge of responsible civil officers who will be in active, constant and close touch with the Police Force not only to ensure, as far as possible, that no further untoward incidents occur but also to restore a feeling of security among the local people. Night patrols in jeeps have been organised and steps taken for the speedy rehabilitation of the people affected by the recent incidents. The Police had been active and mobile from the beginning, the number of arrests in Cooch Behar alone being 216. Vigorous Police patrolling is continuing and Police pickets have also been posted in places where incidents have occurred. Village resistance parties are being revived and peace squads are being organised in every Anchal and village.

30. M.M. Basu.

No further reports have been received of incidents having taken place in these districts and the situation is now absolutely normal and peaceful. There has been no exodus of minorities to Pakistan on account of the disturbances. My Government has asked the District officers to remain especially vigilant until the Muharrum, which ends on 13th June. I intend visiting the three North Bengal districts of West Dinajpur, Jalpaiguri and Cooch Behar immediately after the Muharrum to see things for myself, to instill confidence among the minorities and to impress upon the population that all acts of lawlessness will be firmly dealt with.

I give below a brief summary in chronological order of the incidents that have occurred between 3rd May and 17th May in Nadia, West Dinajpur, Jalpaiguri and Cooch Behar.

Nadia

On 3rd May following the publication of the news of communal incidents in the district of Pabna in East Pakistan, a few young Hindus assaulted four Muslim labourers at Saktinagar in Kotwali Police Station. On 13th May, some Hindus raided and set fire to 6 Muslim houses in the village of Betna-Dangapara in Hanskhali Police Station and also assaulted 6 Muslims. On May 14th at night, 5 Muslim houses at Bogoola and 12 Muslim huts at Pyradanga in Hanskhali P.S. were set on fire.

West Dinajpur

On 11th May at night, a Muslim was stabbed to death at Raiganj town. On 14th May, 4 Muslim houses in village Sahapur in Raiganj PS were raided and set on fire and 3 Muslims who were running away were attacked and injured. On 17th May, one Muslim was murdered, two of his sons injured in village Hasahar in Tapan PS and his house set on fire.

Jalpaiguri

On 11th May, an unknown person trespassed into the house of a Muslim at Adaagarpatty in Jalpaiguri town. He ran away after a scuffle between him and the house owner had taken place, and the mother-in-law of the house owner who came to his rescue had sustained knife injuries. On 12th May, 11 Muslim huts in Kotwali PS were set on fire and 3 Muslims seriously injured in Paharpur. On 13th May, a large number of young men attacked some Muslim houses at Fakirpara in Kotwali PS killed two children, injured 5 Muslims and set fire to two houses. These children, one aged 4 and one aged 8 were dragged away from their mother and killed before her eyes. On 14th May at night, an attempt was made to set fire to the house of a Muslim in Jalpaiguri town. On 15th May at night, two persons of Khoprabandi in Kotwali PS trespassed into the houses of Muslims and threw away the beef that was being cooked. On 16th May, three unknown persons entered the house of a Muslim at Sannyashipara in Raiganj PS at night and severely assaulted two inmates.

Cooch Behar

On 11th May, there was an altercation between some Hindus and Muslims and Muslims at Nazirhat in Dinhata PS, which subsequently took a communal turn. 5 Muslims and one Hindu shop were looted. Trouble spread to the adjoining villages and six Muslim houses were raided. In all, 19 Muslims received injuries. On 12th May, Hindus at Maruganjhat assaulted 6 Muslims in Toofanganj PS over a minor issue. The same night, two Muslim houses were set on fire at Sheoraguri in Toofanganj PS and a Police patrol party fired one round to disperse the mob. No casualties took place. The same night, six Muslim houses were burnt in village Nawabganj Balashi in Kotwali PS. On the morning of 13th May, the dead body of a Muslim was found on a public road at Chakchaka in Kotwali PS. On the morning of 14th May, also another dead body of a Muslim and an injured Muslim were found at Dodiarhat in Kotwali PS while one Muslim was stabbed at Khagrabari in the same PS that same evening and 3 Muslim huts were gutted at Kechuarkhuti in the same PS at night. 17 Muslim huts were also gutted at Soladanga in the Tufanganj PS the same night. On 15th May, 12 Muslim houses were raided by a mob at Panisila in Kotwali PS. The inmates of the houses ran away at the sight of the mob and the mob looted the household property. The same night, a Muslim woman of Dudkura was kidnapped from her house. She was recovered the next morning. On 15th May at night again, three Muslim huts at Chekarpara were set on fire and some Muslim houses at Krishna Panishala, both in Tufanganj PS were raided and looted. On 16th May, refugees raided a Muslim house at Jiranpur in Kotwali PS and were looting paddy when a mobile Police party arrested two of the miscreants on the spot. The same day a mob fatally assaulted a Muslim at Singra in Tufanganj PS. Some policemen, who came to his rescue, were injured. Another Muslim was also stabbed at Pundibarihat in Kotwali PS the same night. On 17th May, a Muslim house was looted at Soladanga in Tufanganj PS, another Muslim house was raided and looted at Satkura in Dinhata PS and a Muslim was fatally stabbed at Bamanpara in Kotwali PS.

Every form of relief was provided at once—shelter, food, clothing, etc—

and, as in the case of Malda where relief was given on a very generous scale, similar measures will be taken in these districts.

15. From Morarji Desai: Foreign Exchange Crisis[31]

[Refer to item 245]

2nd June 1962

My dear Jawaharlalji,

You will have noticed from Bijju's[32] cables that the World Bank Consortium, which met in Washington at the end of May, adjourned without making any definite commitments of additional assistance to us. When we made the foreign exchange allocations to different Ministries for the current half year, it was our expectation that substantial relief to our balance of payments position during the current year would be forthcoming at the Consortium meeting. The main object of the Consortium meeting was to get us 220 million dollars of additional assistance from non-American sources, mainly European countries. The USA had already promised an additional contribution of a like amount subject to matching assistance from Europe. When the USA had made this stipulation about an equal amount being available from Europe, it was really using it as a lever to exert pressure on Europe. However, as things are and in view of the tussle between the US Administration and Senate on the subject, the shortfall of 156 million dollars in the target of non-US assistance will mean a similar drop in US assistance. We are, therefore, as Bijju's telegram pointed out, likely to get 312 million dollars or about Rs 155 crores less of external assistance during this year than we were counting on.

2. While we may, and indeed must, take such steps as may be possible to ensure that this short fall is made good, it is clearly necessary that we should, for our part, adopt such measures as will enable us to safeguard our currency and reserve even if no further external assistance was forthcoming during the year. When proposing the allocations for the different Ministries, which the Cabinet approved a few weeks ago, we had indicated that they would result in our sterling balances going down from 126 crores at the beginning of the year to 91 crores at the end of the year. As explained above, we were hoping, with the new external assistance which we expected, to avert this fall. Now that there seems to be no certainty about the quantum of new assistance, there

31. Letter from the Finance Minister. PMO, File No. 37(35)/56-63-PMS, Volume III, Sr. No. 156-A.

32. B.K. Nehru, Ambassador to the USA.

is no alternative but to make sizable cuts in the allocations we approved in the Cabinet earlier. The Economic Secretaries are discussing the matter next Monday and we hope to submit a paper to the Cabinet next week on the subject. These cuts in imports will undoubtedly place a strain on the economy but we must face them. In addition, other measures would be necessary.

3. The Governor of the Reserve Bank has particularly urged that we must now put a stop to people travelling abroad without any foreign exchange being released to them by the Reserve Bank. Although they all pretend to be going as guests, in actual fact most of them obtain foreign exchange in the black market, which means that they find ways of diverting the foreign exchange which would have otherwise come to the country. It will, therefore, be necessary to be very strict about letting people go abroad even when they say that they are going as guests. I hope you will agree that such strictness would be fully justified in our present conditions. A number of other measures will also have to be taken but I do not propose to worry you with them.

4. One of the disturbing features of the present situation is that our sterling balances have already come down to about Rs 100 crores. The Reserve Bank of India Act prescribes that these balances should not fall below Rs 82 crores unless Government issues a Notification and gives a waiver. We are trying to see whether by accelerating the disbursement of aid, particularly from the UK and Germany, we can avert a decline in our sterling balances below the prescribed minimum. I am not sure how successful we shall be in our efforts. We could also have recourse to a temporary borrowing from the International Monetary Fund. There is, however, a danger in this. We have already borrowed from the IMF what we could borrow as of right and any further request for a loan might make the IMF seek to impose certain conditions in regard to our economic policies which we should avoid being subjected to. Anjaria[33] is making tentative enquiries on the subject. Meanwhile, it seems advisable that we should issue a Notification which will enable the Reserve Bank to allow the sterling balances to fall below the legal minimum.

5. As I have said above, we would bring a paper to the Cabinet on the subject next week. Thereafter, I think it will be desirable to make a statement in Parliament also on this subject. Meanwhile, I thought I would share my thoughts and anxieties with you and I would welcome any comments or suggestions that you might have in respect of the various measures referred to above.

Yours sincerely,
Morarji Desai

33. J.J. Anjaria, Executive Director for India at the IMF.

16. From B.V. Keskar[34]

[Refer to items 7 & 8]

4 June 1962

I understand that during discussion about Press Code in the National Integration Council, adverse remarks were made about the Ministry of I& B's inactivity in the formation of the Press Council. It is regrettable that the representatives of the I& B Ministry did not care to present correct facts and dispel a wrong impression.

The question of the Press Council had been discussed often in Parliament, more especially during budget discussions and I have had the opportunity of explaining the reasons for non-formation of the Council. I would here very briefly give the main reasons.

On the basis of the recommendations of the Press Commission, the Ministry of I & B had prepared and brought forward a Press Council Bill. It was taken up in the Rajya Sabha, I think, in 1957. During the discussion the Bill ran into active controversy amongst journalists.

The principle of the Press Council is resolutely opposed by the proprietors of newspapers who contend that there should be no statutory Press council. The working journalists wanted this council, but they opposed the composition and structure as proposed. Their main opposition was that the number of 13 representatives of journalists should not include editors, who ought not to be categorised with other working journalists. This was clearly a fundamental point and could not be accepted by Government. The working journalists carried on such a lobbying even in the Congress Party that the Bill had to be dropped for the time being.

Careful consideration was given to the situation. A Press council, as envisaged by the Press Commission, is a body with only moral authority and it was felt that its moral value will be nullified unless a large number in the journalistic profession were agreed and would support the measure. However, as a matter of fact both the wings of the Press were opposed to the Bill on account of different reasons. The proprietors because they were opposed to the principle of a statutory Council and working journalists because they were opposed to the composition of the Council. A Council formed under such auspices would not have delivered the goods.

I had discussions with the Working Journalists Federation regarding this question and once I invited them to revise their stand regarding the composition

34. Letter from the Minister of Information and Broadcasting. Salutation not available.

of the Council, which we broadly wanted to conform to the recommendations of the Press Commission. I had also informed Parliament a few times that a minimum measure of agreement in the Press circles is necessary for proceeding with the Bill. You might yourself have observed that the British Press Council, a voluntary body, has not given the results expected from it. In fact, decisions of the Council have been in recent years defied quite openly by the leading Papers and there have been comments in the British Papers about the usefulness of the Council.

While a council would be a useful moral authority, it would not be wise to create the body without a minimum understanding with the different wings of the Press. I hope that would be tried by the Ministry now. In any case, unnecessary blame should not be attached to the Ministry for non-compliance with this recommendation of the Press Commission. We tried our very best to carry out as many recommendations of the Press Commission as possible and in the course of that had even to earn a hostility of the big proprietorial Press.

17. From Sushila Nayar: Examinations of the Royal College of Surgeons[35]

[Refer to items 280 & 281]

June 5, 1962

My dear Panditji,

I have your letter dated June 1st along with the enclosures sent by Dr Roy. I am enclosing herewith a copy of my letter dated May 2nd, 1962, together with the draft reply from the office, that I sent to Dr Roy. I would have expected Dr Roy to mention it to you. A copy of Dr Roy's reply dated May 9th is also enclosed.

I find from the files that the Ministry of Health had decided to stop the Primary FRCS Examination from being held in India some years ago after very careful consideration. The idea was to build respect for the Indian Degrees and to discourage Indian students from going abroad for the purpose of obtaining degrees and diplomas. The Mudaliar Committee Report has also emphasised this point.

Dr Roy seems to be under the impression that a student can sit for the Primary FRCS Examination soon after his First Professional – Anatomy and Physiology Examination. That used to be the case when Dr Roy took this Examination. Nowadays student has to graduate and then take the Primary FRCS Examination. I think it is a good idea. The object of the Primary FRCS

35. Letter from the Health Minister. PMO, File No. 40(230)/ 61-70-PMS, Sr. No. 7-A.

Examination is to ensure that a student who is going to specialise in surgery has fully refreshed his knowledge of Anatomy and Physiology and this object can be served better by the present system. The President of the Indian Medical Council has assured me that England does not allow anyone to sit for the Primary FRCS now unless he has passed MBBS.

The President of the Indian Medical Council, Dr C.S. Patel in his talk with me a few days ago said he was in agreement that the restarting of the Primary FRCS Examination in India was undesirable. I would not mind Dr Roy and others to put their heads together to institute an Indian Examination of a similar kind as a pre-requisite to our students taking say for instance Master of Surgery Examination. But to restart Primary FRCS Examination in India would mean that our boys would rather sit for FRCS than for MS. Further those who take the Primary would want to go for Secondary FRCS and we will not be justified in refusing them the necessary permission and foreign exchange. We have been trying to persuade the UPSC and everyone else to give equal status to Indian Degrees, if not a better one, as compared with foreign degrees. By allowing Primary FRCS Examination to be held in India we would be tacitly admitting that foreign degrees are better than our own. The truth of the matter is that boys who take FRCS hardly ever touch the knife to do the operations in England. MS in India gives them better practical training. We have very competent experts in all the fields. We can improve it still further and make the post-graduate training and examination in India of as high a standard as may be considered necessary. But we should do nothing which will discourage our students from taking post-graduate degrees in India, though they may go abroad for gaining wider experience as is done by students from several other countries.

I hope you will agree with me that we should stick to the resolve that has already been taken by the Ministry of Health several years ago that we should do everything possible to foster respect for the Indian Degrees and discourage our students from running after foreign degrees. Restarting of the Primary FRCS Examination in India will go counter to this idea.

With kindest regards,

Yours affectionately,
Sushila Nayar

18. From Mehr Chand Khanna: The Khanna Nagar[36]

[Refer to item 80]

5th June 1962

My dear Panditji,

Please refer to your letter No. 775-PMH/62 dated the 4th June 1962 regarding Khanna Nagar. I had no idea that there was a Khanna Nagar in Delhi. Khanna, as you know, is a caste and there must be hundreds of Khanna in Delhi alone. I am writing to the Chief Commissioner to find out where this Khanna Nagar is and how it has come to be named as such, though even after getting the requisite information, I wonder whether we can do anything about it unless it be a Government colony.

With kind regards,

Yours sincerely,
Mehr Chand Khanna

19. From T.R. Deogirikar: G.K. Gokhale after Bankipore Congress[37]

[Refer to item 443]

June 7, 1962

My dear Panditji,

Kindly excuse me for the troubles. While writing Biography of Honorable G.K. Gokhale,[38] I came across the following incident described by you, in your *Autobiography*.

> "A characteristic incident occurred when Gokhale was leaving Bankipore. He was a member of the Public Service Commission at the time and, as such, was entitled to a first class Railway Compartment to himself.[39] He liked to be left alone by himself and after the strain of the Congress Session,

36. Letter from the Minister of Works, Housing and Supply. PMO, File No. 45(12)/59-69-PMS, Sr. No. 8-A.
37. Letter from the biographer of G.K. Gokhale. NMML, T.R. Deogirikar Papers, Acc No. 411 (a).
38. *Gopal Krishna Gokhale*, by T.R. Deogirikar was published by Government of India, Ministry of Information and Broadcasting, Publications Division, 1964.
39. The first edition (London: John Lane The Bodley Head, 1936) of *An Autobiography* has another sentence here : " He was not well and crowds and uncongenial company upset him." The Penguin edition (2004, page 30).

he was looking forward to a quiet journey by train. He got his compartment but the rest of the train was crowded with delegates returning to Calcutta". (Page 27, first edition).[40]

While I was going through Gokhale's correspondence in the Servants of India Society, I found a letter dated the 21st November 1914 written to Mrs Annie Besant, marked Private, by Honorable G.K. Gokhale. I reproduce the relevant portion.

"At Bankipore, I was unfortunately not present at the discussion which took place as I had to hurry to Madras after the first day of the Congress to join the Public Service Commission & I saw later on etc."

From this letter, it seems (1) that Mr Gokhale was not present for the whole of the Bankipore Session; (2) that though he was entitled to the first class compartment, it was kept at his disposal only while undertaking journeys in connection with the work for the Commission; (3) He was not going to Calcutta but via Calcutta to Madras.

From your writing it appears that Mr Bhupendranath Basu and the delegates were returning to Calcutta after ... finishing[41] the session and not on the first day of the session.

I have tried to find out whether Bankipore is a Railway Station, where this incident as described by you happened. I do not know whether the old name of the Station is charged or Bankipore is some suburb of Patna. But in the All-India Railway Time Table, I do not find "Bankipore".

40. The remaining part of the paragraph read: "After a little while, Bhupendra Nath Basu, who later became a member of the India Council, came up to Gokhale and casually asked him if he could travel in his compartment. Mr Gokhale was a little taken aback as Mr Basu was an aggressive talker, but naturally he agreed. A few minutes later Mr Basu again came up to Gokhale and asked him if he would mind if a friend of his also travelled in the same compartment. Mr Gokhale again mildly agreed. A little before the train left, Mr Basu mentioned casually that both he and his friend would find it very uncomfortable to sleep in the upper births, so would Gokhale mind occupying an upper berth so that the two lower berths might be taken by them? And that, I think, was the arrangement arrived at and poor Mr Gokhale had to climb up and spend a bad night."
41. Ellipsis in the original.

The main incident as narrated by you is very typical. But the details need minor corrections. If you think it worthwhile kindly do so in the next edition as nothing incorrect should go in the History.

With respects,

Yours sincerely,
T.R. Deogirikar

20. From Sushila Nayar: Army Medical College[42]

[Refer to item 283]

June 7th 1962

My dear Panditji,

I received a telephone call from the Defence Minister[43] this morning. He said that he was starting an undergraduate Medical College for (I think he said) 150 students at Poona and enquired whether I would make any money available from the funds for starting Medical Colleges. I was not sure that running Medical Colleges was the function of the Defence Ministry. Without saying anything about it, I very politely suggested to him that he might make use of the Health Ministry for starting the College for the training of necessary medical personnel. The Health Ministry would be glad to do the needful with his help and guidance. He turned down the suggestion in words that I would not like to repeat. He said there was a lot of money with the Health Ministry for the starting of medical college and there was shortage of doctors in the country. He would need Rs 40 lakhs against a crore required by the Health Ministry for a Medical College. I said I would like to meet him and discuss the whole matter with him. The money for medical colleges was earmarked for certain medical colleges in different States. I shall have to look into the whole thing before I could give him a definite reply. He did not like this and said, "This means a no". He did not require any money from me. He would do it out of his own funds. I again suggested to him that I would like to discuss the matter with him. He said, he was leaving India and did not know when he would return. I concluded the telephone conversation by saying that I would see him in the Lok Sabha today. He was, however, not there during the question hour.

I am reporting this to you because the matter will have to be considered carefully as a matter of policy. Should every department of the Government

42. Letter from the Health Minister. PMO, File No. 23(84)/62-71-PMS, Sr. No. 1-A.
43. V.K. Krishna Menon.

of India which requires doctors such as Railways, Labour (ESI Scheme) train them for themselves? Should every department of the Government of India be self-sufficient in every way? If that is the case, is there need for different Ministries?

I had hoped to work out some kind of a close collaboration with the Defence Minister and his department so that their hospital and some of their medical experts could be available for teaching purposes if a medical college was started at Poona or elsewhere. They could even be posted to some of the civil hospitals from time to time to gain a wider experience and, in the converse, some of the civil doctors could be sent to the military hospitals on a short-term or long-term basis to benefit from military discipline. As it is the doctors employed by the Military, generally speaking, do not get a wide variety of cases to practice on. The Army, by and large, keep fit. That is as it should be and that is why in the old days, the IMS Officers used to be posted to the civil hospitals for a certain number of years periodically. Their skills would be kept up to date by enabling them to practice in civil hospitals. This is in the interest of the Army. The benefit to the civil population would be an additional gain. But his telephone this morning has upset me.

I feel unhappy to have to trouble you with these matters, but I need your guidance and advice. I am going out of Delhi tomorrow and will be back on the 14th afternoon. I shall come and see you, if you like, at your convenience.

With kindest regards,

Yours affectionately,
Sushila Nayar

21. (a) From Bakhshi Ghulam Mohammed[44]

[Refer to item 136]

Kindly refer to your letter of 22nd May 1962 regarding the request of Chinese Turks to become Indian nationals.[45] I have had the position looked into. These persons are holding Chinese Republic passports issued by the Government in Taiwan (Formosa) and as such the Government of India, Ministry of Home Affairs, advised us that they should be treated as "stateless persons" of Chinese origin because the Government in Taiwan has not been recognised by the

44. Copy of letter, 7 June 1962, from the Prime Minister of Jammu and Kashmir. Salutation and signature not available. MEA, File No. P.V.1021 (F)/62, p. 4/corr. Also available in the JN Collection.

45. See SWJN/SS/76/item 223 also item 224.

Government of India and that the State Government should register them in accordance with the instructions conveyed by the said Ministry in their Circular letter No. 6/10/60-F.I. dated 23rd April 1960. The residential permits of these persons were accordingly renewed for a period of one year as advised by the Union Home Ministry. The State Government would very much like that these persons should be recognised as Indian nationals as they have been residing here for more than fifteen years and some of them for over two decades and have for all practical purposes adopted this country as their home. I would suggest in this connection that the Union Ministry of Home Affairs may consider the question and communicate to us the action that should be taken in this matter.

21. (b) From Turkistan Refugee Committee[46]

[Refer to item 136]

Copy of letter dated May 16th, 1962 to the Prime Minister from Shri Haji Mohd. Kasim, President, Turkistan Refugee Committee, Sarai Safa Kadal, Srinagar, Kashmir.

> Sub: Request to consider the Turkistan Refugees (males, females, and minors less than one hundred) as the Indian nationals who have been living here in Srinagar, Kashmir (India) for the last 30/35 years having matrimonial relations with the Indians.

We beg to bring to your worship's kind notice the following few lines for your honour's favourable consideration and orders.

1) That we are the genuine residents of the Eastern Turkistan (Sinkiang) and come from Kashgar, Khatan and Yarkand. Our mother tongue is Turki and we are Mohammadans.
2) That we are businessmen from the ancient times and our way to Haj Ziarat Baat and Sherfa was via Ladakh through India. And so we had come to India for trade and Ziart Baat Ahad Sherief. [Probably, Haj Ziyaarat Bait-Allah Sharif].
3) That we are residing in Srinagar (Kashmir) for the last 30/35 years. And we could live at any place in the undivided India without any legal binding on account of our simplicity and for the last some years

46. Copy of letter. MEA, File No. P.V.1021 (F)/62, pp. 2-3/corr. Also available in the JN Collection.

on account of the Democratic Government of the Republic of India we are passing our days quite happily.

4) That in 1960 a law was formulated for the aliens to obtain residential permits and under this law we also were forced to obtain such permits. And in order to obtain the said residential permits every alien was directed to obtain first a fresh passport of his own Government and since we have no Ambassador or Council of our own country in India (we have no Government of our own) since our country was taken over by force by the Chinese Communists and we have been living in India as refugees and so it is quite clear that we have no Government of our own from which to get new passport.

5) That on being forced we would obtain passports from the Government of Formosa with great difficulty and at present it is difficult and impossible.

6) That we may point out, Sir, that we are old and decrepit and our wives are mostly Indians and our number—males, females and minors is 100 (one hundred) or so, and as stated our business is trade and industry.

7) That for the last so many years we were desirous of becoming Indian nationals, but on account of our being ignorant, illiterate and without knowing any medium of the Indian origin to talk, we could not find out a way to become Indian nationals.

8) That we request your worship to issue an order for considering all of us as the Indian nationals and to free us from all the troubles we are encountering, which will, Sir, be the human sympathy with the poor refugees.

In view of the above, we hope our request in question will find a favourable consideration and thus administering justice in our case.

22. From G.M. Sadiq:Political Sufferers in Princely States[47]

[Refer to item 137]

We were invited by the Union Ministry of Education in 1959 to participate in the scheme for grant of scholarships and other educational facilities to the children of political sufferers. The scheme was examined by us and we found that its scope was extremely limited as such political sufferers as had participated in the

47. Copy of letter, 7 June 1962, from the Minister of Education, Jammu and Kashmir. Salutation and signature not available.

struggle for responsible government in the Princely States had been excluded from its purview. We accordingly proposed amendment of this definition so that the cases in our State could be included in the scheme. We have now been informed by the Union Ministry of Education that the matter was examined by them in consultation with the Union Ministry of Home Affairs and it was felt that as far as Central assistance was concerned, it would be advisable to adhere to the uniform definition of the term "Political Sufferer" as approved by the Government of India.

Apart from the fact that our State will not be able to participate in the scheme, this matter touches an important issue and I apprehend that the distinction sought to be made will certainly be construed as an unfair discrimination. As such the limitations imposed in the scheme has wider implications. For this reason I thought I should draw your attention to this matter. Of course, the State Government is willing to institute a scheme of its own for extending benefits contemplated in the All India Scheme to the political sufferers in our State. Even so, the reasons for our inability to take advantage of an All India scheme of this nature may give rise to unpleasant questions. I do not know what the reaction of the other erstwhile Princely States has been; but here we do feel that this distinction, even for the limited purpose for which the scheme is intended, would be unfortunate.

23. From Sooryakant Parikh: Why Mahesh Kothari[48]

[Refer to item 125]

Patdi Building, Ellisbridge
Ahmedabad – 6
June 8, 1962

[Dear Panditji,]
It is very kind of you to give me prompt reply for my query about Shri Mahesh Kothari. But, I regret to state, that it does not convince me on two points.

(1) Did you sanction that Shri Kothari should act as your personal representative at Peace Conference in Japan, and for investigation in Diu, Daman and Goa and then meeting with Dr Salazar at Lisbon?

(2) Have you thought any time, where from all these expenses comes from?

48. Letter. NMML, Sooryakant Parikh Papers, Acc No. 434. The letterhead carries the name of Geeta Parikh along with that of Sooryakant Parikh.

I may be wrong, but it seems that he uses your goodwill for him in creating an impression amongst all concerned, that you desire to convey certain things through him. Those who know him fail to understand that on what basis you desire that Shri Kothari is competent to represent you. As you know, your name is enough to create sacred sensational tie in the hearts of all people, which works in above question.

Please try to understand me. We earnestly desire that he should build up his substantial constructive ability rather than his influence.

May I say without any comparison, that the example of Shri Cherian Thomas is worth considering.[49]Though he commands your confidence and love, he prefers to work on his own ability. Incidentally, I had the honour to see you twice along with him after All Party Elwal [Yelwal] Conference in 1957.[50]

With kindest regards,

Respectfully yours,
Sooryakant Parikh

24. From R.K. Nehru: Speculation and Building Crisis in Delhi[51]

[Refer to items 343, 344 and 345]

I spoke to PM this morning about the land problem in Delhi. I would like to place my ideas before PM. Delhi has grown enormously and has a cosmopolitan population. There are hundreds of foreigners who can pay almost any rent that is demanded. There are also thousands of Indians who can only pay a reasonable rent. In addition, there are thousands more—workers, servants and others—who have crowded into the city, which lacks low-priced accommodation.

2. Vast areas of land were handed over in the past to some individuals for purposes of development. These individuals have become millionaires as the value of land has gone up. Part of the land has been built over, but a great many plots are being bought and sold by speculators in land. They are not merely speculators, but also evaders of income tax. I have some personal experience of this. Two years ago, I was anxious to buy a plot and build a house as the Government Servants' Cooperative of which I am a member was

49. A social worker, see SWJN/SS/76/ items 83-84, 95 and 97-98.

50. All Party Conference at Yelwal, 21-22 September 1957, on Gramdan movement. See SWJN/SS/39/pp. 12, 114-115, 347.

51. Note, 10 June 1962, from the SG, MEA.

making slow progress. I wished to withdraw from the Cooperative, but when I made enquiries about a plot belonging to a speculator though building agency, I was told that part of the price would have to be paid in cash. I was also told that this is a common practice and I suppose the reason is that the speculator wishes to evade income tax. Naturally, I refused to buy the plot.

3. The speculators will not build houses as they are waiting for land values to go up. Some also own houses and as there are not enough houses, rents are also going up. Thus, the speculators gain both ways and people like us have to suffer.

4. As for foreigners, I understand that fantastic rents are being charged, partly in cash, which is not shown in the agreement with the landlord. This too, I suppose, is for evading income tax. The foreigner has to agree as otherwise he cannot get a suitable house. It is not only rich speculators who are involved, but also Government officials. Some high officials have built private houses for which they charge fantastic rents. Some member of the family is shown as owner of the house. The official concerned gets Government accommodation as there is no house in his own name and he collects a high rent for his private house in the name of the member of his family.

5. I think the time has come to put an end to these scandals. I would like to make some suggestions for PM's consideration. The suggestions are somewhat tentative, as I have not yet examined all the facts. I shall do so if the broad approach is agreed to in principle:

i) Delhi should have a high-powered Development Authority. This should be separate from the local administration and the Chairman should be a senior official of high standing. The other members should be representatives of various Ministries and the local administration. The Chairman should have the widest possible executive authority and the power to give decisions. I would place the Authority directly under PM.

ii) No one should be included in the Authority—not even officials working under the Chairman—if he, or any dependant of his, owns a house, or land, in Delhi, except as a member of a cooperative society. There should be town planning experts under the Chairman and the Authority should be responsible for the further development and planning of Delhi.

iii) All vacant land whether freehold or leasehold not belonging to Cooperative Societies should be frozen immediately. Sale, or building, should be subject to the approval of the Authority. If the Authority is satisfied that the land was bought for purposes of speculation and there are no adequate grounds for delay in building a house the land should be re-acquired by Government, or allotted to some cooperative society. Naturally, reasonable compensation should be paid to the owner. The Authority should allot land to a society, or individual applicant, at a reasonable price. If land is sold by auction, the rich speculators will again come in. No one who has a house, or land, either in his own or a dependant's name, should ordinarily be allowed to buy any more land.

iv) We might also examine the possibility of introducing a rent control law. Some other cities in India have such a law and I do not know why Delhi has not, although the situation here is much more serious. A tenant whether a foreigner, or an Indian, should be entitled to apply to the Development Authority for re-fixation of his rent. The Authority should fix a fair rent for the house, irrespective of agreements entered into in the past. Some drastic legislation will be needed to prevent charging of surreptitious rent in addition to the fair rent.

v) The law might also make provision for renting of houses with the approval of the Development Authority. This would ensure that no owner could rent his house to another person on rent exceeding a fair rent. If he does not wish to accept a fair rent, he can live in the house himself, or keep it empty. In most cases, he will have to accept a fair rent. If he prefers to keep his house empty, the law might provide for some sort of compulsory renting of the house to a person in the Development Authority's waiting list of applicants for houses, or building plots.

6. In the past, we have requisitioned houses for which a fair rent was fixed. I suppose it is difficult now to revive requisitioning, but some drastic rent control law might serve the same purpose. In any case, we should take steps to re-acquire all vacant land held by Delhi's rich speculators.

7. An impossible situation has been created for honest people with moderate incomes. In Cairo, there was a similar shortage and Government put an end to all speculation. Land was allotted to a number of societies and hundreds of houses and workers' flats were built. Surely, we in Delhi could take some similar measures. Why should we remain at the mercy of these rich speculators who have dozens of plots in various names and are keeping them for purposes of speculation, while thousands of others—both foreigners and Indians—are experiencing the most acute difficulties?

8. As I have said, these are some tentative ideas, which need fuller examination. I suppose there will be a clamour that all this legislation is expropriatory. If these rich landlords and speculators are indulging in

malpractices and exploiting the situation, I think expropriation is justified. However, compensation, etc. will be paid and, in any case, the measures proposed will be in the interest of the people.

9. Steps should also be taken to ensure that Government official and others who have private houses in their own name, or in the name of a dependant, give up their Government accommodation, go, and live in their own houses. It is my belief that the highest officials are violating this rule.

25. From Rajendra Prasad: Pensions for Governors[52]

[Refer to items 88 and 89]

When I was in Delhi I learnt that the Government would be introducing legislation to make provision for a secretariat for me and medical attendance on my retirement. Since then I have read that a Bill has already been introduced. I thank the Government for their kindly thought. But at the same time I confess to a feeling of embarrassment also. You will recollect that on several occasions I have suggested to you that some provision for pension etc. might be made for Governors also, but you felt that Parliament would not take kindly to a proposal like that. I have always felt that there might be some provision for a man who has served the country and reached the distinction of Governorship of a State for the period after his retirement and I am still of the some opinion. But if it is felt that on account of the number of Governors the financial implications would be heavy, I would suggest a way out. There is a salary provided for Governors; if the Government is unable to make pensionary provision for them, it can very well set apart a portion of the salary, say, Rs 500/- per month in some sort of provident fund which they will be able to withdraw only after cessation of their services. If Rs 500 a month is deducted for five years, it will come to Rs 500 x 12 x 5=Rs 30,000 plus such interest as the deposit may earn. If the Government could make some contribution, the amount would be enhanced to that extent. But even if the Government is not prepared to make any contribution in the case of Governors, their own compulsory saving would give them a decent sum at the time of their retirement. I would ask you to consider this question, and, if required, the necessary amendment in the Constitution may be made and other steps taken to put this proposal on a sound legal basis.

Considering the provision that is being made so generously by the Government I feel, as I have said, a little embarrassed and I have therefore

52. Copy of etter from the former President, 10 June 1962. Salutation and signature not available.

taken the liberty of writing to you on this point. If you like to refer to their cases you will see that there are some Governors who are more or less utterly unprovided and in one case at least you were good enough to put him in the Rajya Sabha to enable him to assist the Government with his experience and, on the other hand, have a provision for him after his retirement.

26. From Chaman Lall: Delegation to Moscow Peace Congress[53]

[Refer to item 365]

30, Prithviraj Road,
New Delhi
June 11,1962

My dear Jawaharlalji,

Thank you very much for the note sent to me by M.J. Desai[54]regarding the delegation to Moscow.[55] I think about the involvement of foreign exchange. No foreign exchange is involved not even one penny. The Reserve Bank people have also told me that there is no difficulty where expenses of stay etc. are guaranteed by another country. Even fares come under the agreement between Aeroflot and Air India which stipulates rupee payment. Two hundred invitees are going from Japan and a similar number from Italy. A large number is going from the United States. If the Indian Delegation is to make a mark and support our own foreign policy, it must be a substantial Delegation consisting of substantial people.

In view of the fact that no foreign exchange is involved, I suggest that at least 125 people should be permitted to go as it will be cheaper to charter a plane than to buy individual tickets.

Please be kind enough to ask M.J. Desai to let me have your sanction.

I feel worried even to write to you as it involves an unnecessary strain but the matter is of some urgency.

Yours affectionately,
Diwan Chaman Lall

53. Letter from Congress Rajya Sabha MP. MEA, File No. A(3)-DISARM/1962, p. 26/Corr.
54. Foreign Secretary.
55. The Peace Congress was to be held 9-14 July 1962.

27. From Ajit Singh Bhatinda: Restoring Political Career[56]

[Refer to items 192 & 193]

June 11, 1962

May I take the liberty of inviting your attention to my letter of the 3rd March 1962, regarding my political rehabilitation. I had presented that letter along with:

1. a copy of my resignation from the Akali Party in 1954 against their hooliganism when you visited the Fatehgarh Sahib Gurdwara in Pepsu.
2. a copy of my speech in the Parliament on the 29th August 1961 on the demand of Punjabi Suba and,
3. a copy of the memorandum submitted to the Dass commission (I led the deputation).

While appreciating the spirit of accommodating our defeated colleagues, I very humbly wish to be enlisted in the same category.

You will very kindly remember when you last gave me an interview, you had promised to talk to the high ups in the Punjab Administration to get me fixed honourably.

These days I am doing nothing, I am simply wasting my time. I have already told you the reasons of my defeat. I am the follower of your great ideals and personality. I cannot knock any other door except yours.

I shall feel obliged if you could get me fixed honourably where ever you deem fit.

28. World Press Review No. 5896, Monday 11 June 1962[57]

[Refer to item 353]

UK Press, London, 8 June 1962

Daily Telegraph Report on Geneva Conference on Disarmament

The *Daily Telegraph*'s correspondent from Geneva reported on June 7, under caption "Zorin[58] Rejects Control Plan—Indian Backing At Geneva."

56. Copy of letter, salutation and signature not available; address: Civil Station, Bhatinda.
57. Copied by the MEA, External Publicity Division, Hyderabad House, New Delhi. MEA, File No. B(104)-DISARM/62 Vol-II, pp.1-2/ corr.
58. Valerian A. Zorin, Soviet Permanent Representative to the United Nations until 1962; Soviet Representative to the Eighteen-Nation Disarmament Committee, 1962.

"With the help of India, Russia rejected, at the 17-nation disarmament conference in Geneva, today a British proposal for technical studies on control problems. She accepted an Indian 'compromise' proposal which would bring the British idea to nothing.

Mr Zorin, Russia, said it might even be harmful to study the details of control at the present stage of political decisions. He was replying to a proposal made yesterday by Mr Godber, Britain, who had stressed the ease with which nuclear weapons could be hidden.

The Indian delegate, Mr Lall, proposed studies in the plenary conference, meeting formally or informally. Political aspects could not be divorced from technical ones, he said.

Mr Godber did not accept India's proposal, as Mr Zorin did with alacrity. He maintained that technical studies by experts should be made outside the plenary conference.

Western sources said there was a taut 'undertone' in the exchange between Mr Godber and Mr Lall. The Indian delegate repeatedly interrupted Mr Godber when he replied to what was patently a pro-Russian speech by Mr Lall.

The Indian kept claiming that he had been misunderstood, or that he had not said this or that which implied basic opposition to the American Disarmament Plan. Mr Godber kept his temper in spite of this most unusual behavior at an international conference.

In fact, Mr Godber was at last reacting forthrightly to Mr Lall's increasingly obvious espousal of the Russian cause. Protestations of Indian impartiality now ring very hollow indeed in the ears of Western delegates.

Replying to Mr Godber's speech of yesterday and to his proposal for technical studies, Mr Lall remarked tartly that disarmament inspectors would clearly have to have a good look at Britain. Mr Godber had thought up many ways of avoiding control, he said.

Tomorrow the conference will debate the issue of nuclear tests, the prospects for a test ban treaty are now dismal in the extreme."

29. (a) From Sudhir Ghosh: Admission to Congress[59]

[Refer to item 25]

12 June, 1962

My dear Panditji,

I venture to enclose a copy of the formal application for my admission to the Party which I submitted on the 20th March last. So far I have not received from the Party office an acknowledgment or a reply. The application has been pending for quite some time and I very much hope that it may be possible to consider it now.

As an Independent I am really wasting my time; if I am a member of the Party I may be able to do some useful work here and there. I shall be very grateful if you take a little interest in this matter.

With regards,

Yours sincerely,
Sudhir Ghosh

29. (b) From Sudhir Ghosh: Admission to Congress[60]

[Refer to item 25]

95, South Avenue,
New Delhi

14th June, 1962

My dear Panditji,

I am grateful to you for your letter of the 12th June.

I am very sorry to hear that I have created the impression on some people in the Party that I have on several occasions opposed Congress policies and programmes. No intelligent man can oppose your basic policies—domestic or foreign—but in the details of the execution of these policies there are things that are done or left undone by individual Ministers which can be legitimately criticised. And after all when a man sits in the opposition it is a part of his job to oppose some of these things, isn't it? When he becomes a member of the Party it is his duty to uphold what the Government does.

59. Letter from Rajya Sabha MP, Independent. NMML, Sudhir Ghosh Papers.
60. Letter from Independent Rajya Sabha MP. NMML, Sudhir Ghosh Papers.

The meaning of Congress policies and programme also varies from individual to individual—even among Ministers. For instance, a major matter like public enterprises and our concentrated investment on the big steel plants, which are obviously in trouble. I made a speech on this subject in Parliament and also said the same thing in an article which I wrote at the request of the Editor of the *Manchester Guardian*. I venture to enclose a clipping; I hope you will some time have a look at it. To the previous Steel Minister[61] this meant opposition to Government policy and programme; to the present Steel Minister[62] this means support of Government policy and programme. I had a long talk with the new Steel Minister and gave him a transcript of what I said in Parliament and he has recently said in the Lok Sabha almost everything I said.

However, I give you my assurances that even when I become a member of the Party I will faithfully support the policies of the Party.

With regards,

Yours sincerely,
Sudhir Ghosh

30. From S.D.D. Nichols-Roy: An Eastern Frontier State[63]

[Refer to item 180]

We thank you for your letter of May 3, 1962[64] in reply to our representation dated 4th April 1962. Your letter was placed before the Council of Action of the APHLC[65] which met at Jowai on the 9th and 10th May 1962, which, after considering all that you have said in your letter and also your statements in Parliament on the 4h May 1962, felt it necessary to reply as follows:

The two main objections to the creation of a separate State which you mentioned are economic difficulties and communications. We admit that the formation of the Eastern Frontier State would initially place some financial burden on the Government of India, but we are confident that when the hill areas, which have enormous natural resources, have been developed, this

61. Swaran Singh, Minister of Steel, Mines and Fuel till 10 April 1962.
62. C. Subramaniam, Minister of Steel and Heavy Industries from 10 April.
63. Copy of letter from S.D.D. Nichols Roy, the General Secretary of the Council of Action, APHLC, Shillong. Salutation and signature not available. MHA, File No. 4/1/62-SR(R)-A., pp. 50-51/c.
64. See SWJN/SS/76/item 259.
65. All Party Hill Leaders' Conference.

burden will not only be eliminated, but the hill areas will be able to contribute their share in the development of the country as a whole. This confidence is based on the fact that the people of these hills are industrious, hard working and progressive, but it is only in a separate state that their pent-up energies will be released and mobilised toward development. Moreover, the revenue resources from the hill districts as shown in the budget of the Government of Assam might have given you a wrong picture of the financial position of the hill areas. In fact, certain substantial sources of revenue which accrue from the hill districts have not been shown as such by the Government of Assam, thus resulting in an unreal and adverse picture of the financial position of the hill districts. In any case financial viability has not been the main criterion for the formation of any State. The happiness of a people does not depend only on economic factors but also to a greater extent on the measure of real freedom of the people providing them with opportunities of self expression, self rulé and self improvement.

As regards the difficulty of communications as referred to by you in your statements in Parliament, we would like to point out that the proposed eastern frontier State would be part and parcel of India and, as such, there should be no real difficulty of communications between the different parts of the State through other parts of India or of communications with the rest of India.

You have also mentioned in your letter that your proposals had met everyone of the points raised by us. Similarly you said in Parliament that your offer had met 99% of what we wanted. We assume that the "99% of what we wanted" had reference to the demands embodied in our draft plan and pattern of the Eastern Frontier State already submitted to you in November 1960. With all due respect, we are constrained to state that your proposals did not come anywhere near our demands. However, we are glad that you have reaffirmed your recognition of our grievances as legitimate and so, since you are prepared to meet 99% of our demand, we would request you to clarify what the remaining 1% is.

So far as the language question is concerned all you have stated in your letter may be true only upto the district level. At the State level, with the Assam Official Language Act as already passed, making "Assamese" as the official language of the State, all areas and people in the State cannot but be affected and the Assamese language will be imposed in one way or another.

In view of the above we reaffirm our conviction that the best and simplest solution of the problems of the hills people of Assam lies in the creation of the Separate Eastern Frontier State.

We note that you could not accept the verdict of the people as given in the general elections because you thought that your proposals had not been placed fully before the electorate. We would like to inform you that your proposals had been fully placed before the electorate as the main issue in the elections and they were thoroughly explained, for and against, by both the Congress and our Conference leaders during the election campaign. Pamphlets and newspaper articles were widely circulated on the merits and demerits of the Scottish Pattern proposals. We may also remind you that your public speech of January 1, 1962 at Shillong which was printed and widely circulated by the Publicity Department of the Government of Assam, had very clearly focused attention of the electorate on your proposals and had called upon the people to vote for the candidates supporting the Scottish Pattern proposals. The elections were thus clearly fought on the issue of the Separate State versus the Scottish Pattern proposals of administration. That was why we stated in our representation to you dated 4th April 1962 that the general elections in these hills may be considered as a referendum on this issue.

In conclusion we regret to note from your letter that you gained the impression from our talks that we had largely agreed with your proposals except, to some extent, on the language question. We do not really understand how you gained such an impression but can only state that this impression is incorrect. It is true that we listened and discussed your proposals in our talks but did not at any time ever say that we agreed to them or express our readiness to accept them. All we stated then was that we would place your proposals before our Conference. Our 4th Conference held in Shillong in April 1961 clearly expressed our inability to accept your proposals and our 2nd delegation to Delhi in May 1961 placed before you the Conference resolution to that effect in which it was stated that we wanted to meet you to explain why we could not accept the proposals. Then again, our 5th Conference held at Tura in the beginning of July 1961 had clearly rejected the proposals which were reexamined along with the policy statements made on June 6, 1961 by the Union Home Minister and the Chief Minister of Assam on the language question.

We request you, therefore, to reconsider the whole position in the light of the special circumstances prevailing in these frontier hill districts of Assam.[66]

66. See item 190.

31. From Mani Ram Bagri: Farmers' Misery[67]

[Refer to items 194 & 195]

श्री मनीराम बागड़ी,
मैम्बर लोकसभा,

हिसार, (पंजाब)
तारीख 12 जून, 62

आदरणीय प्रधान मंत्री जी,

जय हिन्द।

मौजा रावढ़ हैडा तहसील कैथल जिला करनाल (पंजाब) वाहिद मलगुजार सरदार गुरबख्शसिंह, जी आई० जी० पंजाब व मुख्यमंत्री पंजाब के रिश्तेदार हैं, का था और वहां के पुराने मुजारे जो सिर्फ हरिजन थे उनकी जबरदस्ती उजाड़ दिया गया था। उन्होंने डी०सी० करनाल से बसाने की मांग की लेकिन बेकार। आखिर उन दिनों जब दलाई लामा और पंचेन लामा भारत में आये थे वे सब गरीब उजड़े हुए बाल बच्चे समेत आपकी कोठी के आगे आकर पड़े थे। 12 दिन पड़े रहते के बाद आपने दया कर के डी०सी० करनाल को चिट्ठी लिखी थी कि इनको आबाद किया जाये। मैं भी उस वक्त उन किसानों के साथ आपकी कोठी के आगे पड़ा रहा करता था। उस वक्त 25 कुनबों को सिर्फ 25 किला जमीन मिली थी। इस उम्मीद पर हमने सब्र किया था कि कभी न कभी तो देश में मालगुजारी प्रथा खत्म होगी और यह जमीन किसानों को मिलेगी परन्तु यह देखकर बड़ा दुःख हुआ है कि इस वाहिद मालगुजार की जमीन वैलफैयर महकमे ने इसलिये खरीद ली कि मालिक जमीन को पूरा मुनाफा मिल जाये और इन किसानों ने जो जमीन लेने के लिये पं० नेहरु तक रुसवाई की थी उनको सख्त सजा मिले। मैं आगे उमीद करूगा कि आप पंजाब गवर्नमेंट से इस गांव के साथ संबंधित कागजात जांच कराने के लिये मंगवाकर करे और उन किसानों को जमीन सरप्लस से लेकर बंटवायें।

आपका
मनीराम बागड़ी

67. Letter from Socialist Lok Sabha MP; address: Hisar, Punjab. He had sent copies of this letter to the Chief Minister and Revenue Minister of Punjab, D.C., Karnal and Kundanlal of Rawal Heda, P.O. Faral, Distt Karnal.

[Translation begins:

Maniram Bagri
Member Lok Sabha

Hisar
(Punjab)
12 June 1962

Honourable Prime Minister,

Jai Hind!

Mauja Rawad Heda, Tehsil Kaithal, District Karnal (Punjab), belonged to Wahid Malguzaar Sardar Gurbaksh Singh who is a relative of IG Punjab and Chief Minister of Punjab; and the old settlement where only Harijans lived was forcibly laid bare. They requested the D.C., Karnal for a place to settle in but it was vain. Ultimately, when the Dalai Lama and Panchen Lama came to India, all these poor evicted men and women with their children sat in a dharna in front of your house. After eleven days, you took pity and wrote to D.C., Karnal to settle them. I was also sitting with those poor peasants in front of your house those days. At that time, 25 families were given only 25 kila of land. At that time we bore it patiently in the hope that at some time or the other land reforms will happen and the system of malguzari will be ended with the farmers getting their own land. But it is very painful to see that the land of Wahid Malguzaar was bought for welfare purposes so that the landlord may get full compensation and the farmers who had sat in front of Pandit Nehru's house to get their land back may be punished severely. I hope that you will ask the Punjab Government to send you all the papers related to this village and have them examined and distribute the land in surplus to these farmers.

Yours sincerely,
Maniram Bagri

Translation ends]

32. From Sudhavati Narayan: Help from Maharashtra[68]

[Refer to item 338]

Date 12-6-62

Respected Pandit Chacha,

It was indeed very gracious of you to have sent such an inspiring message which has greatly encouraged me and my colleagues in our efforts for collection of funds for the new building we are creating for the Kendra at Bhagalpur.

You will be glad to know that I met with a fair share of success in my efforts, thanks to the warm support and encouragement I received from Shri Y.B. Chavan, Chief Minister of Maharastra, and also because of the hard and efficient work put in by such friends as Shri Navin T. Khandwala and others. The variety entertainment show, which the Bombay Committee presented in aid of the fund, was a great success. I know that you have a soft corner for the Institution to which I am devoting my full time, and I have no doubt that on future occasions also I will be blessed with your gracious support and kind help.

I am to find from the newspapers that your health is better now, for which I thank God, because you are so absolutely necessary for years to come to our nation for her progress and prosperity. I hope you have already received the mango parcel.

With kind regards,

Yours affectionately,
Sudhavati

33. From Kashi Ram Gupta: Party Symbols[69]

[Refer to item 90]

137, Constitution House,
New Delhi
13th June 1962

Respected Shri Jawaharlalji Nehru,

On the 31st ultimo I had written you a letter in reply to your No. 257-PMO/62 dated the 30th ultimo. That letter of mine remains unreplied upto this day. Your

68. Letter from the daughter of Sri Prakasa. PMS, File No. 8/217/62-PMP. Nehru's letter item 338 refers to her letter of 13 June; but her letter, appendix 32 has the date 12 June.
69. Letter from Independent MP from Alwar. PMO, File No. 2(397)/61-70-PM, Vol. II, Sr. No. 104-A.

remaining over busy can be the main reason of not giving reply or also the letter may have been misplaced and thus lost catch of your eye.

However, I humbly request you to please see to it and let me have a reply, specially in regard to items No. 4, 6 and 7 of my letter. Regarding No. 4 and 6, I have sought your permission to send my own views on the subject raised. As for no. 7, I have again to request and lay stress on the point that the matter of Election Symbols is a very important one and hence the best remedy is Separate Elections for Vidhan Sabhas and Lok Sabha or in the alternative separate party symbols for Vidhan Sabha and Lok Sabha if elections take place simultaneously. I hope you will kindly give further consideration to this matter and express your views on the matter.

An early reply is solicited.

Yours sincerely,
Kashi Ram Gupta

34. From Gulzarilal Nanda: Backward East UP[70]

[Refer to item 203 & 204]

June 14, 1962

My dear Jawaharlalji,

Will you kindly refer to your letter No.842-PMH/62 dated June 12, 1962 regarding the speech delivered in the Lok Sabha by Viswanath Singh Gahmari in which he referred to economic conditions in Ghazipur, Ballia and Azamgarh?

2. In the Planning Commission we have been deeply concerned with the problem presented by areas in different States which are markedly less developed. In preparing the Third Plan, we requested State Governments to indicate such areas and to show their development programmes and the financial provisions for them separately. This has been done in several States, for instance, UP, Maharashtra, Punjab, Andhra Pradesh and Jammu & Kashmir.

3. With a view to working out programmes for more intensified development of the less developed areas in the country we have tried to collect information about these areas from all States. You will be interested to see the enclosed statement in which the available information has been summarised. The main responsibility for the more rapid development of these areas has to be undertaken by State Governments, but there are many ways in which the Central Government and, in particular, the Planning Commission, can and must

70. Letter from the Deputy Chairman of the Planning Commission. Planning Commission, File No. PC(P)17/4/61/I/A), Programme Administration Division.

assist. What we contemplate is a study by the State Government, supported by the Planning Commission, of the problems and programmes of development in each area both during the Third Plan period and to a meeting over a longer period. I think it would be useful if you could come to a meeting in the Planning Commission at which we could consider this subject more fully. I shall have a paper prepared for consideration.

4. The development of Eastern UP has been followed fairly closely in the Planning Commission over the past four or five years. You may recall that the Asoka Mehta Committee which studied the food problem was specially asked to examine the problem of scarcity areas in UP where, on account of floods and other factors, the food problem was one of recurring nature. During 1959-61 the Central Government allotted Rs 4 crores in addition to the provisions in UP's Plan for the backward areas of the State, which included the Eastern districts, Bundelkhand and the hill districts. In addition, during the Second Plan, the Central Government spent more than Rs 8 crores of flood control in UP, most of the amount being for the Eastern districts.

5. The UP Government has divided the State into six zones with a view to securing balanced regional development. These are as follows:

Zone	Districts
Eastern Zone	Deoria, Gorakhpur, Basti, Azamgarh, Gonda, Bahraich, Faizabad, Sultanpur, Pratapgarh, Ballia, Ghazipur, Varanasi, Jaunpur, Mirzapur and Allahabad.
Central Zone	Kheri, Sitapur, Lucknow, Rae Bareli, Unnao, Hardoi, Kanpur, Fatehpur and Bara Banki.
Western Zone	Saharanpur, Muzaffarnagar, Meerut, Bulandshahr, Aligarh, Agra, Etah, Mainpuri, Mathura, Bijnor, Moradabad, Budaun, Rampur, Bareilly, Pilibhit, Shahjahanpur, Etawah and Farrukhabad.
Hill Zone	Tehri-Garhwal, Garhwal, Almora, Naini Tal and Dehra Dun.
Uttarakhand	Uttar Kashi, Chamoli and Pithoragarh.
Bundelkhand	Jhansi, Jalaun, Hamirpur and Banda.

Out of a total outlay in the Third Plan of about Rs 500 crores, Rs 360 crores have been distributed in terms of regions, the rest being accounted for by power projects, major irrigation works, State highways and schemes which benefit more than one region. The development programmes specifically assigned for the Eastern districts entail an outlay of Rs 110 crores, of which Rs 47 crores are for agricultural development, Rs 24 crores for irrigation and power, Rs 28 crores for education and other social services and a little over Rs 10 crores for industry and transport. Perhaps the major weakness of the present plans lies in the lack of industrial and non-agricultural employment and in inadequate transport and communications. Power development also requires much more attention.

6. Under the Rural Works Programme, 21 projects have been taken up in the second series initiated three months ago. Of these Azamgarh has 4, Ballia 2, Ghazipur 1, Varanasi 4, Deoria, Faizabad and Bahraich 2 each, and Basti and Gonda 1 each. We should be quite prepared to increase the number of rural works projects in Eastern UP and I am asking C.B. Gupta to prepare an expanded programme for areas which require special and urgent attention.

7. In his speech Viswanath Singh Gahmari referred particularly to lack of industries and lack of irrigation and the impact of increasing population on the landless sections. There is no doubt that the pressure of population greatly accentuates the economic situation. Gahmari's statement that the ordinary agricultural labourer in Ballia gets two annas a day and a lot of sugarcane juice, while the labourer who ploughs the land receives 2½ seers of cereals may be true of certain pockets or of certain seasons, but should be verified. The information that we have from the UP Government for each of the districts in which the Rural Works Programme is being taken up is that during the slack agricultural season the wage rate is Rs 1.50 NP per day, and during the busy season about Rs 1.50 NP per day. We shall go further into this matter.

8. The National Council of Applied Economic Research is engaged in undertaking a survey of economic conditions in UP. The Planning Commission is in touch with the National Council. Three years ago the Council undertook a survey of Basti District in collaboration with the All India Cooperative Union. This was intended to be a case study in the economics of depressed areas. Surveys of other districts on these lines would be useful and we propose to go further into this matter.

9. When we have the meeting in the Planning Commission which I have suggested, we can go more fully into the questions of policy and the measures involved in securing accelerated development of the less developed areas in the country.[71]

Yours sincerely,
G. L. Nanda

71. For Nehru's response, see item 204.

35. From Amar Nath Sehgal: Select Art Works Properly[72]

[Refer to item 321]

June 16, 1962

Respected Sir,

Your will kindly forgive me for sending this note and encroaching upon your most valuable time. But I could not refrain myself since a press news containing extract of your letter to Shri Mani Ram Bagri, MP, regarding statues to be put up on the last Mughal King and Martyrs Raja Nahar Singh[73] and Nawab of Jhajjar, has somewhat disappointed me as a sculptor.

Sir, I agree that not too many good statues have been erected. For this I do blame the sculptors and also the sponsors and the judges. The sponsor must in the first instance select someone of experience and knowledge and after having awarded the particular commission they should appoint a committee of judges, the majority of whom may include art critics of standing. Once these judges feel that a particular work is not being made of a standard and does not bring out salient features of the personality whose memory is to be commemorated, they should outright reject the work.

However, I do feel that sculptors may be given a chance to show their talent and worth in executing the works for monuments and memorials. Unless this is done I do not see a hope for their survival or for the development of arts and aesthetics which is vital....

Love and respects.

Yours sincerely,
Amar Nath Sehgal

72. Extracts of letter from sculptor, only paragraphs 1-3 available here. PMO, File No. 2(433)/62-70-PMS, Sr. No. 16-A.
73. Of Ballabhgarh, as indicated in the subject of the file.

36. From Sampurnanand: K.M. Panikkar's Offensive Behaviour[74]

[Refer to item 9]

Raj Bhawan,
Mt. Abu
17th June, 1962

My dear Jawaharlalji,

A Sub-Committee of the Emotional Integration Committee[75] recently visited Srinagar. In fact their visit coincided with yours. The Committee has rather an unusual experience and I think you will find it interesting particularly as there is a reference to you personally.

As in other places, the Committee requested Sardar Panikkar, the Vice-Chancellor of the Local University, to let it have the benefit of his knowledge and experience. He refused to do so. A similar request was made to him for a second time and met the same fate. He was the only Vice-Chancellor in the country whose cooperation was not available to the Committee. The Members had the privilege of meeting him at a large At Home given by the Government and later at a dinner given by Bakhshi Ghulam Mohammad. On the former occasion he spoke very disparagingly of the Committee, its work and its purpose, bluntly asking why an effort should be made for integration in India when there were countries in Europe like France, Germany, Spain, etc. all independent living separate lives and making no effort to come together. The whole talk of integration in his opinion was silly and bound to fail. On the second occasion he was, if anything, more offensive. He said that he had met you and that you knew nothing about the Committee or its work. When it was pointed out to him that Indiraji is herself a member and that therefore you must be aware of the existence of the Committee and its work, he became, if anything, more violent. Apparently he made very offensive remarks about me which the Members have not repeated to me. They have only referred to them. He said clearly that he did not believe in integration. As he became more violent in his denunciation, Bakhshiji had to snub him publicly. He said since you do not believe in integration where is the use of your saying anything more. These are my honoured guests and I do not want you to insult them.

74. Letter from the Chairman of the Emotional Integration Committee. PMO, File No. 2(397)/61-70-PM, Vol. III, Sr. No. 108-A.

75. The Emotional Integration Committee was set up under the chairmanship of Sampurnanand on the recommendations of the Education Ministers' Conference, held in November 1960.

It is not a thing of pleasure to me to report this unpleasant incident to you but Sardar Panikkar occupies an important position in public life and has often been put by the Government of India in responsible positions. The way that his mind functions on the very important question of national integration cannot in my opinion be ignored. The approach of a person who can compare the various parts of India to the independent States of Europe will be radically different from most nationalist-minded Indians.

Yours sincerely,
Sampurnanand

37. From B.P. Chaliha: Assam Oil Revenues[76]

[Refer to item 181]

Shillong
18th June 1962

My dear Prime Minister,

I am constrained to trouble you once again regarding the oil royalty question which has continued to remain unresolved despite our repeated efforts to arrive at a mutually-acceptable solution. Shri Fakhruddin Ali Ahmed[77] briefly apprised you of the latest position in this regard last week. Shri Ahmed and Shri Tripathy[78] have met Shri Malaviya[79] more than once in this connection but to no avail as the Union Minister is not willing to consider any modification of the royalty calculation as provided for in the Supplemental Agreement between the Government of India and the BOC.[80] We had always been assured, over the last few months, that the royalty question would be satisfactorily settled, but no solution appears to be in sight. Shri Malaviya has himself described the situation by saying that there seems to be no meeting ground between his Ministry and Assam Government.

While I do not wish to trouble you with the details of the royalty dispute, I should like only to recapitulate that, prior to the Supplemental Agreement, the State Government were receiving royalty at the rate of Rs 10.8 per ton,

76. Letter from the Chief Minister of Assam. PMO, File No. 17(490)/62-70-PMS, Sr. No. 20-B.
77. Minister of Finance, Law, Panchayats and Community Projects in Assam.
78. K.P. Tripathy, Minister of Power (Electricity), Industries (including Cottage Industries), Planning and Development, Town and Country Planning, Labour and Statics.
79. K.D. Malaviya, Minister of Mines and Fuel.
80. Burmah Oil Company.

on the basis of 10% of wellhead value, the actual payments by the Assam Oil Company averaging at about Rs 7 per ton as the AOC had certain earlier leases which provided for royalty payment at 5% of wellhead value, together with others where the rate was 10%. Under the formula devised in the Supplemental Agreement, the reduced rate of royalty, on the basis of a greatly reduced wellhead value, would come to Rs 4.8 per ton only which would be further reduced with a reduction in price of crude and other variable factors. Given the cost of the pipeline (present or future) together with interest on loan and other charges have been set off against wellhead value instead of against the final price to be paid by the Indian Refineries Ltd., the loss to the State Government on the basis of the earlier royalty calculation of Rs 10.8 per ton, would come to Rs 1.65 crores annually when the two public sector refineries went on stream. The Assam Oil Company had never found the necessity of such revision in the royalty rate downwards all these years. Now, they are also demanding such revision in terms of the new formula suggested. Hence, while against the average rate paid by the Assam Oil Company till last year, the loss would come to Rs 60 lakhs annually. Both the Planning and Finance Commissions had included the royalty income to the extent of the latter figure, in assessing financial resources of the State for Plan and non-Plan purposes. The very heavy reduction in royalty revenue that would result to the State Government as a result of the Mines and Fuel Ministry's policy would undoubtedly affect the economy of this underdeveloped State very adversely. During the last meeting between the Union Minister and the State Minister, a general offer of 15% participation in the Gauhati Refinery was made by the Union Minister on the lines of the offer made to the Gujarat Government. In view of the very small returns likely from this arrangement, this would hardly be anywhere near adequate recompense for our losses on account of reduced royalty revenue and it would not be possible for the State Government to accept this offer. The position of Assam as an oil-producing State for many decades must be taken into account and any decision about royalty payable to this State Government should be made against the background of the royalty rate and payments that we have been receiving all through this period.

The stand taken by the Union Minister virtually amounts to this that the Central Government has the authority to dispose of the mineral and oil resources situated within a State in its absolute discretion and may also modify the terms of a subsisting lease or license granted by the State Government without any reference to the grantor and that the State Government comes nowhere in the picture except for the purpose of signing the lease or license as drawn up by the Central Government. As the owners of oil resources situated within the State in terms of the Constitution we are unable to accept the position; and our contention is that within the framework of the Constitution, it is the State Government that has the right and the power to dispose of its own minerals and oil resources. The issues involved in this dispute are, therefore, very fundamental and of vital importance to us. We recognise that the development of our oil resources is also of vital interest to the nation and it is far from our intention to be obstructive in this regard.

May we therefore look up to you to have the matter re-examined in the light of the contentions put forward by us? We assure you that once our legitimate rights are recognised, we shall be prepared, by and large, to be guided by the advice given to us by the Central Government in the broad context of our national policy. We cherish the hope that the difference of opinion that has so far emerged on the royalty question and in respect of wellhead value may yet be settled by mutual consultation under your kind auspices. If, however, no meeting ground can unfortunately be found between the two view points, we would be grateful for your advice regarding the forum through which these differences may be resolved, so that we are not obliged to move the Supreme Court.

I must mention, in this context, that we still have not received any reply to the official communication addressed to the Mines and Fuel Ministry more than six months ago on the question of the Supplemental Agreement entered into between the Government of India and the BOC and the lease to be issued to Oil India Ltd with regard to new areas in Assam.

I should like to take this opportunity to refer to another proposal of the Mines and Fuel Ministry which envisages bringing crude oil under the purview of Central Sales Tax. The State Government had imposed the tax on crude oil sold within the State since 1960, which the Assam Oil Company have been paying on their purchases of Naharkatiya crude since the last 1½ years. The revenue estimated from this tax when the Gauhati Refinery went on full stream was Rs 91 lakhs annually. This revenue was also fully taken into account by the Planning and Finance Commissions in assessing our resources. If, however, crude oil is brought within the ambit of Central Sales Tax, the State tax would no longer be leviable and we would get only Rs 10 lakhs as share of Central Sales Tax. The loss on this account would come to Rs 80 lakhs annually.

We are very concerned at these developments in the oil sector which seek to affect the State revenues so adversely. The interests of an oil-producing State such as Assam, which is contributing so much to national wealth, should not be sacrificed in this manner and I would earnestly request your intervention in the matter.

In respect of new areas to be leased to Oil India Ltd., we had sent a draft on 30th March, 1962 to be issued to Oil India Ltd., to the Mines and Fuel Ministry for approval, which authorised OIL to go ahead with the plans and programme of oil exploration in the new areas. The Central Ministry have, however, on 5th May, 1962 insisted that a formal license should be issued by the State Government. In our view this is neither necessary for the purposes of starting exploration by the Company nor would it be in the interest of State Government to issue such a license till the difference of opinion regarding the royalty is nearer solution.

In the above circumstances, we seek your guidance in this matter.

With regards,

Yours sincerely,
B.P. Chaliha

38. From V.K. Krishna Menon: UN Debate on Kashmir[81]

[Refer to items 409 and 432]

Kashmir debate is following an unusual course. Instead of Pakistan who wanted the meeting, either opening it or saying anything, this role was assumed by the US (Stevenson)[82] followed by UK. The US statement already enclaired will indicate that it is based on basic fallacies of this being a territorial dispute on which the two are misbehaving. The speech itself is very Pakistan oriented.

2. Talks about resolutions have continued. But nothing has emerged. We have made it clear that we do not see any room for any resolutions. One that refers to bilateral talks is (a) unnecessary as we have always been ready to talk, (b) unwarranted in equal appeal to both because we came here after Pakistan President refused to meet you, (c) that mention of bilateral talks at the UN is intended to lay the foundation for renewed meeting.

3. Ghana's position has been disappointing and unjustified. It was forceful against us in content and in the tone of delivery. It was quite contrary to what Nkrumah[83] had stated to Kakar[84] and also to impression given by Quaison-

81. Telegram No. 272, 20 June 1962, from the Defence Minister, then at the UN. NMML, V.K. Krishna Menon Papers (Official) File No. 4.
82. Adlai Stevenson, US delegate to the UNO.
83. Kwame Nkrumah, President of Ghana.
84. J.C. Kakar, Indian High Commissioner to Ghana.

Sackey[85] at interview he had with me when I explained our position. At that time he was most friendly and had stated that he would go very easy. The UAR delegate[86] told us afterwards that Quaison-Sackey was now sorry that he made the speech he did. It appears that either Nkrumah is speaking with two voices or Quaison-Sackey here has a view of his own.

4. Irish speech also while milder in tone was pushing us back to UNCIP resolutions[87] and equating the two parties.[88]

5. UAR has made no proposals beyond saying that this could only be settled by the two parties, but like all others except the Eastern bloc, they also equated the two of us. Impression left by the UAR speech was that Riad was under direction from Cairo to behave but within that direction he was willing to lean as much to the other side as he could.

6. Romanian made a very restrained and factual speech.

7. An attempt to drag out proceedings by not having a meeting today was stopped by the Russians with great courtesy which surprised the Council.

8. We are now really on the horns of a dilemma. If the President says after Venezuela and Chile have spoken this afternoon that there are no further speakers listed and therefore he adjourns the meeting or declares it to have ended we may regard the session as talked out. This may happen. In that event, the harmful statements made by US and to a lesser degree by UK, China and Ghana will remain uncontradicted and may be used against us on a future occasion. If we continue the debate by intervening, proceedings will be prolonged and give time to US to put further pressure to bring out resolutions against us. It is possible, however, that US or its friends may not permit the President to let the meeting fizzle out as he himself would perhaps like to do, in which case we have no alternative but deal with the matter fully. Pakistan is remaining silent but appears to have taken steps in Washington yesterday through US Ambassador to Pakistan[89] who met President Kennedy. (For your information,

85. Alex Quaison-Sackey, Ghana's permanent representative at the UN.
86. Mohamed Riad, UAR delegate to the UN.
87. Resolutions of 13 August 1948 and 5 January 1949 adopted by the United Nations Commission for India and Pakistan.
88. Frederick H. Boland, Ireland's Representative to the Council, had submitted a draft resolution that made reference to earlier resolutions adopted by the Council concerning Kashmir and urged India and Pakistan to enter into direct negotiations to seek a settlement to the dispute.
89. Walter Patrick McConaughty.

we gather that Kashmir policy is directed largely by Pentagon). This is openly mentioned here by all delegations and some of our friends have also told us that they are under great pressure, particularly Chile. In fact the original draft resolution prepared by "small five" was under US instigation and pressure. This having failed US is now using all efforts to pressurise Latins to table a pro-Pakistan resolution.

9. We are keeping prepared either to intervene or to keep quiet. If silence is more eloquent or serves our purpose better and even if it may be misunderstood in India, we may adopt it. The attempt on the part of the US is to force the position back to the pre-1957 period. If this is further continued then we shall, at least for the purpose of the record, have to establish by argument and precedent: (1) the doctrine of changed conditions, (2) the uncontroverted issue of Indian sovereignty over the whole of Jammu and Kashmir, (3) the tentative character of UNCIP resolutions, (4) that resolutions have on the one hand to be read as one piece and on the other cannot be considered except in the context of explicit assurances given to the Prime Minster of India in writing.

10. You may perhaps find it difficult to accept it from me, but the role of the US in this matter is vicious, partisan and calculated to injure us. While I would agree it is necessary and one should not be provoked into unrestrained language, it would be against our interests if occasion compelled it to let the position go unchallenged. Pakistan though more silent has a larger delegation and is insisting upon her position as an ally of the West. Furthermore, even some of the friends of the West are surprised that her negotiations with China and the whole of that context is not provoking even a mild observation from the West.

11. It is impossible to say now whether the debate will terminate this week, (I hope it will), or will go on. I do not rule out the possibility of the silent role for us. On yesterday's showing, however, and pressures that are being built up in Latin Capitals, Ghana's duplicity and Riad's "working to rule" anything can happen. Privately everyone except UK and US come to us and express sympathy and say "you know we have to say these things."

39. From Sophia Wadia: Grant for PEN Conference[90]

[Refer to item 318]

The PEN All-India Centre
Theosophy Hall
40 New Marine Lines
Bombay-1

Sixth All-India Writer's Conference, Mysore

20th June 1962

Dear and Esteemed Friend,

I am approaching you on behalf of the PEN All-India Centre for Financial assistance for our Sixth All-India Writers' Conference which is going to be held at Mysore in August, from the 3rd to the 6th, at the kind invitation of the Mysore University. This Conference, as the other five we have held in the past years, will be a meeting ground for writers from all over India and abroad. Four subjects of much importance in Indian literature, also culture, will be discussed at the Conference. The main theme will be "How Writers see Contemporary India." The other subjects chosen are "East-West Dialogue," "Ideas in Modern Poetry" and "Humour in Modern Indian Literature." We have asked distinguished writers to participate and there is every hope that many from abroad will also take active part. Dr Radhakrishnan has agreed to preside at the inaugural session and we are very much hoping that it will be possible for you to inaugurate it.

Though the Mysore University will offer the delegates accommodation at a nominal fee, there will be many other incidental expenses. We shall have to pay delegates' travelling expenses for those participating in the Conference and also token honorariums for each paper. I need not add how much we of the PEN will appreciate any financial help from the Sahitya Akademi to us on this occasion.

I shall await an early reply.

With kind regards,

Yours sincerely,
Sophia

90. Letter from Founder-Organiser of PEN All India Centre. Sahitya Akademi Records, File No. S.A.2, Part. V, Executive Board, 1962.

40. (a) From S.K. Dey: Publicity in USA[91]

[Refer to item 374]

June 21, 1962

My dear Panditji,

Although it was not an officially sponsored programme, I thought, you would be interested in some of the spontaneous reactions I felt on my recent visit to the USA and Japan. The attached notes are an effort to put these briefly for your ready use.

I would like very much to discuss the subject at a greater length with you. A new vista appears to have opened with far-reaching potentialities. Because the matter relates to External Affairs, I can express and act only through you.

Yours sincerely,
S.K. Dey

40. (b) From S.K. Dey: Publicity in USA[92]

[Refer to item 374]

A Note on My Recent Visit to America

With PM's approval, I visited the USA for a little less than three weeks in response to an invitation from the Michigan State University, East Lansing, for participation in their Land Grant centenary celebration (Hundredth anniversary of the Morrill Act signed by Abraham Lincoln in 1862 which provided through extension for the mass education of farmers and factory workers both in the wider humanities and the subject matter of their avocations).

This was my first visit to the USA since I came back from there after my engineering education, in 1932. It would be difficult to compress in the body of this brief note my reactions to what I saw after this interval of thirty years in the physical development of the African people and the distinct change in their attitude to life which I could perceive without effort. I would like to attempt this in the form of a book by way of wider understanding between our two

91. Letter from the Minister of Community Development and Cooperation. MEA, File No. XPP/302-(21)/7/62, pp. 2/ -25.
92. Note from Minister of Community Development and Cooperation, 21 June 1962. MEA, File No. XPP/302-(21)/7/62, pp. 21-25.

countries, before the end of the year. I would like to indicate here briefly the main features which I thought might be of immediate interest to PM.

(1) The country is unrecognisable compared to what I saw in 1932. Highways have changed beyond recognition. Almost every adult has an automobile. The telephone system is a superlative. Shops are bursting with merchandise.
(2) Farming has reached the height of mechanisation and threatens soon to grow into joint stock or cooperative enterprises as against individual operation.
(3) Affluence is there even for the average man. Strangely, pursuit of dollars has ceased to be the be-all and end-all which was the case in the thirties. America is in genuine quest of a soul behind this life of automation.
(4) America recognises, a leadership has been thrust on her which she cannot evade. There is a warm-hearted willingness in her to understand other people's point of view and to accept the validity of a different way of life.
(5) America is desperately earnest to come to the help of others but is eager to ensure that her support promotes the growth of the common people and that Kuomintang experience will not repeat.
(6) Universities in America have grown to be even more vital nerve centres for propagation of knowledge and ideological motivations.
(7) There is an increasing allergy to tendentious knowledge doled out through the newspapers. There is eagerness to hear people over the radio, television or directly in meetings, forums and seminars.
(8) The average American is opposed to concentration of power, whether communistic, capitalistic or feudalistic.
(9) The American is hungry to learn about himself and other people and to receive a pat on occasions for his allegiance to the cause of freedom and the sacrifices he makes and is asked to make.

I did all I could while in the University to project the image of India struggling for attainment of the objective of a political, economic and social democracy through the method of Community Development. I felt agreeably shocked to see the extent of the impact.

At the invitation of our Ambassador in Washington,[93] I visited New York and Washington and spent three packed days meeting individually and in groups some of the prominent people. The impression gathered at the University was

93. B.K. Nehru.

further confirmed by the experiences at New York and Washington. I had also an unmistakeable impression that President Kennedy had brought in a vitality in the new administration which was causing a churning in the whole system. A planning organisation is already in the process of growth in the State Department. The purpose obviously is to bring about coordination between the different agencies of Government and also to extend some control over things happening outside of Government. Even in matters of foreign aid, a realisation seems to have dawned on all that a new approach is called for as against the cold war one. Those who know, are clear that the American way of life can apply only to the affluent American soil; other people will have to be left free to forge their own way of life best suited to their geography. Aid programme in future has necessarily to be designed more to act as a catalyst such as will offer an organised voice to the dumb and mute in the population and work up a pressure on those who rule, to initiate programmes of development of the people. I had a clear impression that America expected India to give in this matter a lead to the underdeveloped sections of the world. She seems to admire India as much as she is jealous of her. She realises nevertheless she will have to seek increasing leadership from India in helping herself extending her resources for effective use in other areas of the underdeveloped world. Just as America has been thrust with a leadership not of her own choice, but which she cannot escape, so also is India thrust with a leadership in "Developmental Science" consistent with democracy, which she cannot escape. India has to be prepared for it. It is high time. From this point of view India and USA will have a common ground on which the two will be called upon to work increasingly together.

The world having grown to be an open forum where each nation's progress in the midst of others will depend more and more on the goodwill of all others, presentation of an image of a nation faithfully against the movement of time grows to be a new imperative in world diplomacy. The present context of the world calls for a "Developmental diplomacy" to supplement "Political diplomacy" which is already taking a second place. Our missions abroad will have a new growing role thrust on them. They should act as catalysts in the new dispensation. Our real Ambassadors should be the very large number of students - boys and girls - who are studying in foreign universities, the businessmen and the vast number of leaders of thought in the countries concerned who are supporters of what India stands for. We cannot get all these groups of people to do their assignment on our behalf unless we go out of our way to mobilise and equip them with uptodate interpretation of our programmes and our new philosophy. Statements of our industrial progress, the growth of our production in steel, water and electricity, etc. are important. But, these do not signify much to the developed countries; even to Japan, What matters almost fantastically "is what we are trying to do with the masses of our people, be it family planning, children's education, primary health services, midday meals for school children and last but not the least the slow but steady growth of Panchayati Raj and Sahakari Samaj from the roots.

I consider it of the utmost importance in this behalf that the following steps should be taken forthwith:

(1) Our missions abroad should be furnished with adequate quantities of literature on all programmes of development taking place in India, particularly the ones relating to the people with which they can inform themselves, which they can distribute in adequate quantities to others interested in India.

(2) Our missions should maintain close contact with our students and businessmen and Indians settled in the respective countries, furnish them with literature and provide for discussions on India periodically, with the collaboration of the Embassy staff specially earmarked for this educational campaign.

(3) Some members of the Embassy staff should, as a routine practice, be brought back to India periodically and carried through a systematic course of orientation in various aspects of development taking place in India. The Ministry of Community Development, Panchayati Raj and Cooperation should be happy to organise a programme like this for every officer if we can have him for a period of approximately two months.

(4) Our Ambassadors and others should be encouraged to go and organise study circles on India in different universities, these being the most potent centres from where progressive ideas flow in most western countries.

(5) Ministers in the Government of India should, as a matter of course, be encouraged to meet our Embassy staff whenever they go abroad, discuss in details about the development in their respective spheres and talk broadly about other development programmes in India. They should also be encouraged to talk before audiences like Institutes and forums of foreign relations at strategic centres in the countries they visit and also have engagements in universities.

(6) We should go out of our way to invite people who matter in foreign countries to come to India and go through organised programmes of visits covering both sightseeing and contacts with people at the roots. Carefully chosen delegations should also be sent out from India to visit foreign countries with the deliberate object of reflecting the image of

India at strategic points. There should also be other approaches all of which should be explored.

I recognise that what will ultimately matter is what we achieve here in India. I cannot help feeling, however, that we cannot do what we wish to do in India, unless the world is with us in what we do. We have therefore to sell the image of our effort. I am afraid, our modesty in this behalf is already proving a heavy disability. I believe, all Ministries can make a contribution in this behalf. Ours certainly can and will, if PM approves.

S.K. Dey
21.6.1962

41. (a) From C. Subramaniam: Orissa Police Inaction on Narayanaswami Murder[94]

[Refer to items 260 and 261]

June 23, 1962

My dear Jawaharlalji,

Your letter, dated 22nd June, 1962. I had not bothered you about the incident mentioned in your letter, as I did not wish to trouble you with what is essentially a detail of administration. Now that you are seized of the matter, I may be pardoned for acquainting you with my difficulties.

2. The unfortunate incident in which Narayanaswami was fatally injured has been exercising us for quite some time. I have discussed the details of further action on this with Shri Patnaik and his officers. When I went to Rourkela recently, I had discussions with the Chief Secretary, Orissa[95] and the General Manager, Rourkela.[96] I must confess that the Orissa Police have not been as cooperative in this matter as one would expect. They have been taking a very rigid and legalistic line, as, for instance, arguing that Shri Narayaswami had not himself made any complaint against the suspect when he was first hit on the head with a stone on the 6th May, as a result of which he eventually died on the 19th May.

3. I have myself gone into the details of the case at considerable length and I am convinced that there is strong reason to suspect that the death was caused through assault by a disgruntled employee who is related to a known

94. Letter from the Minister of Steel and Heavy Industries. PMO, File No. 17(12)/61-65-PMS, Sr.No.30-A.

95. B. Sivaraman.

96. S.T. Raja.

goonda of the place. The least that the Orissa police should have done was to have acted on the General Manager's complaint and taken the suspect into custody—a procedure with which the police is not unfamiliar.

4. It is nearly a month since the death of Shri Narayanswami and, in spite of repeated reminders, we have not heard of any action taken by the Orissa Government and the police against the suspect. Meanwhile, I have received a pathetic and moving letter from the parents of the deceased officer complaining that no action has been taken against the culprits who caused the death of their only son. This may be an individual case; but it has had wide repercussions and upset the morale of the managerial personnel, many of whom we have trained at considerable cost and who represent some of the best of our engineering executives.

5. On our part, we have been taking steps to improve the security inside the Steel Plant itself. One of the steps which has been suggested is to replace the present unsatisfactory organisation in the Rourkela Plant by men borrowed from the Orissa Police. Although I had been enthusiastic about this, I am afraid that, if the present inaction of the Orissa Police is any indication, I should hesitate to entrust this vital function of internal security to the men borrowed from the Orissa Police. I am, therefore, also considering whether we could borrow some men from the Armed Forces, who could be drafted into the security force of the plant.

6. Meanwhile, I am writing a letter (copy enclosed) to Shri Patnaik,[97] drawing his attention to the widespread feeling of insecurity in the plant and requesting him to take some action in the matter.

Yours sincerely,
C. Subramaniam

97. C. Subramaniam's letter of 23 June 1962 to B. Patnaik: "My dear Patnaik, You may remember my discussions with you in regard to the unfortunate case of Shri Narayaswami, Foreman of the Rourkela Plant. When I was at Rourkela recently, I had discussions on this with your Chief Secretary and the General Manager. I suggested to the Chief Secretary that action should be taken against the suspect even though Shri Narayanswami has not named anybody in his complaint as the assailant. There is already a complaint on file from the General Manager, Rourkela, which should be a good enough basis for taking the suspect into custody. I understand that the Chief Secretary and the Inspector-General of Police are taking the attitude that no further proceedings are possible against the suspect. This failure to take any action has completely upset the morale of the managerial personnel. If only the police could move in the matter and take the suspect into custody or take at least security proceedings against the suspect, it would improve the morale of the Plant considerably. Yours sincerely, C. Subramaniam." PMO, File No. 17(12)/61-65-PMS, Sr. No. 30-3.

41. (b) From B. Patnaik: Conflict in Rourkela[98]

[Refer to items 261 and 263]

Bhubaneshwar
26th June 1962

Respected Panditji,
Your letter No. 925-HMH/62 dated the 23rd June, 1962 enclosing a copy of Subramaniam's letter to you.[99] I shall certainly take effective steps to book the bad lot in Rourkela inspite of severe legal and constitutional restrictions.

In the meantime I would recommend that the morale question need not be too much emphasised by Subramaniam so that management at Rourkela may not tend to become more inefficient under this excuse. Such things happen in Calcutta industrial areas every day without any loss of morale.

The internal strife amongst the different sections of management at Rourkela has been the root cause of various group clashes which has substantially subscribed to the inefficiency of Rourkela management. Since Raja[100] has come as General Manager, he is trying his best to put the house in order and I am backing him fully. While I was discussing Rourkela matters with Subramaniam at Delhi recently, he suggested use of third degree methods to put the fear of God into the rowdy elements. Perhaps that may be the only answer.

In this connection I am thinking of bringing in the Goonda Act or Security Act as prevalent in Bengal and some other States during the next Assembly session. Without adequate powers it is very difficult for the Police to round up the anti-social elements and extern them, which has been already weakened by separation of Judiciary. The passage of such a Bill as proposed above is bound to arouse a great deal of indignant opposition from various quarters. Consequently, I seek your advice whether I should push through such a Bill in the Orissa Legislature, as political complexion is likely to be given to such powers being vested with Government.

In the meantime I am taking stern action in that area, as other incidents have also been brought to my notice which need certain amount of ruthlessness.

Personal regards,

Yours sincerely,
B. Patnaik

98. To the Chief Minister of Orissa. PMO, File No. 17(12)/61-65-PMS, Sr. No. 33-A.
99. Appendix 41 (a); See also item 260.
100. S.T. Raja.

42. From M.L. Bazaz: Bhakt Darshan on UP Mountain Development[101]

[Refer to item 209]

Shri Bhakt Darshan, MP, has sent a note containing his suggestions about the development of mountainous regions in Uttar Pradesh. He has sent copies of this note to Shri Lal Bahadur Shastri and Shri Chandrabhanu Gupta also.

2. His suggestions in regard to the intensive administration and accelerated development of the recently created three border districts of Uttar Kashi, Chamoli and Pithoragarh are summarised below:

i) Disbursement and utilisation of Rs 28 crores allotted for development of this region during the 3rd Plan, should be so managed that all the amount is utilised and that no part of it is allowed to lapse.

ii) As separate figures for the amount being spent for the developments in each of the three districts are not available there is a feeling that the amount is neither being spent equitably nor on the basis of intensity of backwardness of each district. (Evidently he means that separate figures for the amount being spent in each of the three districts should be made available to public to remove this feeling.)

iii) Number of Government officials should be reduced and only local people or persons experienced to work in mountainous regions, should be recruited to work in these districts.

iv) There is discontentment due to the powers of the District Boards being given to Collectors. To remove this Zila Parishads should be established with non-official Chairman to allow public men to take part in the Administration.

v) The Collectors should be instructed to act normally on the advice of the District Advisory Committees. A Committee consisting of MLAs and MPs representing the three border districts should be established under the Chairmanship of the Chief Minister of UP. Similarly an Advisory Committee with MPs from the border districts and the Chief Ministers concerned, as its members, should be constituted under the Chairmanship of the Home Minister.

3. Shri Bhakt Darshan suggests that besides these three districts special attention should be paid to the development of the rest of the mountainous regions of UP. He says that the Union Government should give special aid to

101. Note, 24 June 1962, from PS. PMO, File No. 2(242)/58-64-PMS, Vol. I, Minute No. 65.

the States for implementation of the recommendations made by the inaccessible Areas Committee.

4. Although Shri Bhakt Darshan has sent copies of his letter direct to the Chief Minister of UP and the Home Minister, PM may perhaps like to have the Chief Minister's comments on the various suggestions made. I shall merely acknowledge Shri Bhakt Darshan's letter telling him that the suggestions made by him are being considered.

M.L. Bazaz
24 June 1962

43. From K. D. Malaviya: Orissa Development Plans[102]

[Refer to item 191]

En Route: Dehra Dun,
June 24, 1962

My dear Jawaharlalji,

Manubhai[103] along with Patnaik[104] held a Conference with the Ambassador of Japan[105] on the 13th June and committed the Government to certain schemes which include many complicated schemes like the exploitation of mineral ore, the transport on the proposed Express Highway of Orissa and some others. His Department was asked to prepare a scheme in consultation with the Railways and my Ministry for being considered by the Cabinet. The Working Group under the Department of International Trade is already seized of the matter and have circulated to us a paper for our comments and they are at present considering working out the relative cost of road/rail link between Paradip and the mining areas before construction of the road is undertaken. Under these circumstances, I do not understand how Manubhai could convey such intentions of the Government to a foreign Government. I suggest for your consideration that this matter along with the question of the construction of the Highway may immediately be discussed in the Cabinet. The Department of International Trade have already obtained the comments on the draft paper for the Cabinet from us and so the question can immediately be considered by the Cabinet.

102. Letter from the Minister of Mines and Fuel. PMO, File No. 17(43)/56-64-PMS, Sr. No. 107-A.
103. Manubhai Shah, Minister of State for International Trade in the Ministry of Commerce and Industry.
104. Bijoyananda Patnaik, Chief Minister of Orissa.
105. Koto Matsudaira.

2. I have in this connection sent a letter to Morarjibhai[106] whose copy I am enclosing along with this. I have also sent a copy to Shri T.T. Krishnamachari.[107] But for the fact that a lot of confusion has been created on this account, I would have not bothered you and others with my views on the matter.

Yours affectionately,
Keshava Deva Malaviya

44. From V. K. Krishna Menon: Kashmir at the UN[108]

[Refer to items 431 & 432 pp. 703-708]

I have just seen press reports of extracts from your statement on Kashmir in foreign debate. The attitude of the United States is both obstinate and vicious. The resolution and the speeches go further and are much harder in implications than the ones hitherto attempted. I explained our position to Ambassador Plimpton[109] fully and objections to resolution para by para prior to its introduction, on the only occasion when it was shown to us by the US, not by Ireland, on plebiscite obligation undertaken, virtues and sanctity of resolutions, arbitration, international agreements and all kinds of things. They have campaigned as though their existence was threatened and spoken to us only on the eve of introduction of resolution, while they were masterminding the whole operation in every detail. Graham[110]functioned openly almost as Pakistan lobbyist with US support. Secretary-General[111] had no influence whatever. Neither US nor President[112] ever consulted Soviets as customary.

2. Even B.K. Nehru[113] who was here expressed himself privately about the attitude of the US being "foolish". It is clear that further economic and political pressures and threats and of military consequences etc. are on the way. They

106. Morarji Desai, Finance Minister.
107. Minister without Portfolio.
108. Telegram No. 277, 24 June 1962, from the Defence Minister then at the UN. NMML, V.K. Krishna Menon Papers (Official) File No. 4.
109. Francis T.P. Plimpton, Deputy United States Representative to the United Nations.
110. Frank P. Graham, UN mediator on Kashmir issue between India and Pakistan.
111. U. Thant.
112. Armand Berard, French representative, was the president of the Security Council for June 1962.
113. Ambassador to USA.

want to break non-alignment. Stevenson's[114]speech, entirely on the veto, was intended to frighten us about reference to the Assembly. Some background and foreground of this problem is best personally discussed and not by telegram. This long indictment of the veto is generally regarded not merely as anti-Russian tirade but as giving us notice about reference to General Assembly.[115] I prefer to suspend my judgment on this although we should keep our power dry.

3. Also seen some reference, as quoted, of your having stated in Parliament that we will not adopt the MIGs or other planes if Sabre Jets are withdrawn. Respectfully request that we make no further statements of this kind because we will walk into a trap. The other side has now been trained on these machines and even if withdrawn as a ruse they and even more numbers can be delivered any time. Furthermore, the making, not the buying, of the MIGs has considerable and crucial advantages and consequences to us in the basic production of aeroplanes, not only military craft, ally material, design, and technology of a character which would change fundamentals of production. Same applies to guided weapons, air, land and sea, of which till now we have only our unaided resources. I beg of you therefore to refrain from further general statements, i.e., if the report is true because you will begin to feel that you have made some commitment. Furthermore, I have also communicated to Benedictov[116]on the lines I spoke to you before I left. We do not want to fall between two stools. As requested the DCC[117] may kindly be called soon after my return and our team should go. Against our unpreparedness preparations are going on the other side and we should make no more unilateral commitments or walk into various traps. Hope you will forgive my saying this. For your information, both US and UK have been withholding equipment and know-how even on simpler matters and dragging things out.

4. Also during the last three or four days reports have been pouring in here that Duncan Sandys[118]has obtained some undertaking, all indicating postponement of a decision. I have not accepted this for myself as I know the ways of the press.

5. The British have played a sinister part here. For your information, Patrick Dean[119] has not had the courtesy even to come and say "how do you do"

114. Adlai Stevenson, US representative in the UN.
115. The Security Council voted in favour of the Irish resolution by a vote of 7-2, with 2 abstentions and the United States voting in favour of the resolution, which was vetoed by the USSR Representative.
116. I.A. Benediktov, USSR Ambassador to India.
117. Defence Committee of the Cabinet.
118. British Secretary of State for Commonwealth Relations.
119. UK Representative in the UN.

to a Minister of a State of the Commonwealth of which he speaks so much in public. I believe they are sore about Rhodesia more than anything else and are always with Pakistan. Africans and Arabs will require all our efforts to keep them at least neutral.

6. Am reaching Bombay on Wednesday 27th.

45. From Humayun Kabir: Delegation to the ECOSOC[120]

[Refer to item 433]

25th June 1962

I have just seen the proposed Delegation to the ECOSOC 1962. I had wanted to speak to you in this connection, but it appears I am too late.

You have for the last few years introduced an innovation of associating a Minister from a State Government with such delegations. Shri Venkataraman[121] from Madras and Shri Moinul Haque Chowdhury[122] from Assam have attended some of the meetings of the UN. Shrimati Sucheta Kripalani from UP has also gone to Labour Conference. If I may so, this is an excellent measure, for it gives Ministers in State Governments an opportunity to come into contact with world movements and thus broaden their outlook.

In this connection, I would like to suggest for your consideration the name of Shri Tarun Kanti Ghosh[123] from West Bengal for the UN Delegation this year or any other delegation which you may suitable. Shri Ghosh is about forty but has already been a Minister for about 10 years and a full member of the Cabinet for about 4 years. He was in charge of Food Production and is now in charge of Small Scale Industries and Cooperation.

Humayun Kabir

120. Letter from the Minister for Scientific Research and Cultural Affairs. NMML, Humayun Kabir papers, File No. 16/1962-64. Salutation not available.
121. R. Venkataraman, Minister of Industries in Madras Government.
122. Minister of Agriculture in Assam Government.
123. Minister of Commerce and Industry in West Bengal Government.

46. (a) From the Nawab of Malerkotla[124]

[Refer to item 65 & 66]

I have recently received a letter from the Ministry of Home Affairs No. 10/46/61-F.111 dated Nil on the above subject, which was a special request I made to you personally and through a letter dated 29th June 1961. The matter was evidently referred to the Punjab Government for opinion and comments. Permission seems to have been given to my step-mother Her Highness Ruqia Begum Sahiba and my uncle Sahibzada Raja Jafar Ali Khan Bahadur, to return to Malerkotla for which I am very grateful, but it has been withheld in the case of my younger brother Sahibzada Altaf Ali Khan and his two children Sahibzada Kazim Ali Khan and Sahibzadi Sarwar Jehan Begum. I think my mother and uncle would be reluctant to return to Malerkotla and leave Sahibzada Kazim Ali Khan who is their only grandson behind in Lahore.

I quite see the point of doing so in the case of my brother, probably because he took up military service in Pakistan. As I have said before, I do not wish to do anything that may be embarrassing to Government, although I shall always be anxious about my brother who will be in Pakistan, but I am still specially interested in my nephew Sahibzada Kazim Ali Khan returning to Malerkotla permanently. I did not give reasons for this earlier, as I thought it would be better to take up the matter with you when my nephew returned permanently to India. I am now giving you the reasons as to why I am keen to seek your help to permit him to return permanently. I am confident that you will realise the reasonableness of my request and accede to it, by again giving it sympathetic consideration.

I have no children of my own, and as long as my brother Sahibzada Mumtaz Ali Khan was alive he was a source of strength to me, not only as my brother but also as a successor. On his death, I have as I have said felt extremely lonely. Naturally an anxiety lingers when one has completely over 50 years, when there is no heir upon whom the responsibilities and interests of the family can devolve. As you know the Malerkotla State was founded by my ancestor well over five centuries ago, and the family has existed for those five centuries, and is probably one of the oldest in the Punjab. It would really be a tragedy if it became extinct, when it could be perpetuated through my nephew Sahibzada Kazim Ali Khan, who is only separated from me by an artificial barrier, created on the Partition of India which I have always considered as an unpardonable crime. Succession in my family is governed by primogeniture. Sahibzada

124. Copy of letter, 1 July 1962. Salutation not available. MHA, File No. 10/40/62-F.IIIpp.2-3/c.

Kazim Ali Khan is the only male issue amongst us three brothers, and he left Malerkotla with his parents when only a child.

I hope I have now been able to explain why I am so very keen to request you Sir, to very kindly give sympathetic consideration to my request of permitting my nephew to return to Malerkotla permanently as a special case, as in the instance of my late brother Sahibzada Mumtaz Ali Khan. His sister Sahibzadi Sarwar Jehan Begum is engaged to my nephew Sahibzada Zafar Ali Khan, eldest son of my cousin Nawab Sahib of Kurwai, and will be getting married in March 1963.

I am also attaching a copy of the letter received from the Ministry of Home Affairs on the subject for your perusal.

I am prepared to take full responsibility on behalf of my nephew when he returns to Malerkotla permanently that nothing should impair the traditional loyalty of my Home towards my country and its Government.

I would suggest that in the first instance Sahibzada Kazim Ali Khan may kindly be granted a temporary visa allowing him to visit Malerkotla. To enable him to continue his stay here he may then kindly be given permission to stay indefinitely as was done in the case of my late brother Sahibzada Mumtaz Ali Khan, until such time elapses that he can be given Indian citizenship. All other issues can be taken up after that for consideration of the Government of India. I do hope that this suggestion will also receive your approval.[125]

46. (b) From Ministry of Home Affairs to the Nawab of Malerkotla[126]

[Refer to item 65]

2/22/53/F. 111. Your letter December 12th and telegram February 16th to Dr Katju. Sahibzada Mumtaz Ali Khan. Orders allowing him stay in India for indefinite period issued to Chief Secretary Pepsu today – Home.

125. See summing up of problem by Home Ministry, appendix 46 (d).

126. Copy of telegram, 22 February 1952, and copy of letter, 9 March 1954, from K.N. Katju, Minister of Home Affairs, New Delhi, to Nawab Iftikhar Ali Khan, Nawab of Malerkotla, Malerkotla.

Copy of a letter No. 2/22/53-F-111 dated 9th March 1954 from Dr K.N. Katju, Minister of Home Affairs, New Delhi, to His Highness Nawab Iftikhar Ali Khan, Nawab of Malerkotla, Malerkotla.

Please refer to your letter dated the 2nd March 1954 regarding Sahibzada Mumtaz Ali Khan.

I am afraid that, under the existing provisions of Part 11 of the Constitution, which alone at present regulate the acquisition of Indian Citizenship, Sahibzada Mumtaz Ali Khan cannot be treated as an Indian citizen. He will, therefore, have to await the enactment of the new Citizenship Law before he can reacquire Indian Citizenship. Meanwhile, he will be allowed to stay on in India with an undefined status. This will not, however, stand in the way of his doing any work independently or to proceed out of India on short visits for which he will be granted a suitable travel document.

46. (c) V. Vishwanathan to the Nawab of Malerkotla[127]

[Refer to item 65]

I am writing this with reference to your letter No. HHS/MK786, dated the 29th June 1961, to the Prime Minister, regarding permanent resettlement in India of your uncle, step-mother and youngest brother and his two children.

2. The case has been carefully considered in consultation with the Government of Punjab and other Ministries of the Government of India. It is regretted that it has not been found possible to grant permanent resettlement facilities in India to Sahibzada Altaf Ali Khan and his two children. As regards, however, your uncle Sahibzada Raja Jafar Ali Khan and step-mother, Her Highness Ruqia Begum Sahiba, we have issued instructions to the Indian High Commission, Karachi, to grant them necessary visas. You may kindly advise them to contact the Indian High commission in the matter.

127. Copy of letter, 11 April 1962, from the Secretary, Ministry of Home Affairs, Government of India. Salutation not available.

46. (d) Nawab of Malerkotla's Demands[128]

[Refer to item 65]

The summary at flag "A" fully explains the history and the facts of this case.

2. It will be observed that a good number of close relatives of the Nawab of Malerkotla migrated to Pakistan after the partition of the country. The Nawab has been making efforts to bring back these relatives one by one. In 1953, he succeeded in getting back his younger brother Nawabzada Mumtaz Ali Khan on the ground that he was in great domestic trouble on account of his wife who had in fact dragged him to Pakistan. Since he had divorced his wife, he should be given facilities to resettle in India. This request of the Nawab was acceded to as a very special case.

3. In June, 1961,[129] the Nawab of Malerkotla again represented to the Prime Minister that his uncle Sahibzada Raja Jafar Ali Khan, step mother, Her Highness Ruqia Begum, his second brother Shri Altaf Ali Khan, and his two children Sahibzada Kazim Ali Khan and Sahibzadi Sarwar Jehan Begum should be granted facilities for permanent resettlement in India as was done earlier, in the case of his brother Nawabzada Mumtaz Ali Khan. After detailed examination of these cases in consultation with the Government of Punjab, the Directorate of Military Intelligence, Ministries of Defence and External Affairs, the conclusion arrived at was that while permanent resettlement facilities might be granted to the Nawab's uncle Sahibzada Jafar Ali Khan and step mother, Her Highness Ruqia Begum, there was no case for the grant of such facilities to his brother, Shri Altaf Ali Khan and his two children Sahibzada Kazim Ali Khan and Sahibzadi Sarwar Jehan Begum. This was approved by the PrimeMinister and the Nawab of Malterkota was informed of this decision in April, 1962.[130]

4. It appears from the present letter addressed by the Nawab of Malerkotla to the Prime Minister that his uncle and step mother are reluctant to return to Malerkotla as they do not like to leave behind Sahibzada Kazim Ali Khan, who is the son of the Nawab's younger brother, Shri Altaf Ali Khan. It also appears from the Nawab's letter that he is thinking of adopting Sahibzada Kazim Ali Khan as his successor. We do not seem to have anything specific in our papers against this boy. But his father who is a retired officer of the Pakistan army is still reported to have active association with the Pakistan army. It was also reported by the Punjab Government in December, 1961 that Shri Altaf Ali Khan was a

128. Note, 6 July 1962, by Fateh Singh, Joint Secretary, MHA, to the Secretary, MHA. MHA, File No. 19/40/62-F.III, pp. 2-5/Note.

129. See SWJN/SS/69/item 167 and appendix 67.

130. See appendix 46 (c).

thoroughly undesirable character. He was a staunch communalist who instigated the Muslims in the State Forces of the Malerkotla State to remain prepared for fighting against India in support of the cause of Pakistan. His activities were anti-national and prejudicial. They were, therefore, strongly opposed to his return to India. It was mostly because of these reasons and of the opposition of the Defence Ministry and the Directorate of Military Intelligence that it was decided as recently as in April, 1962 that he and his two children should not be allowed, to return to India for permanent settlement. The question now is whether we should grant such facilities to Sahibzada Kazim Ali Khan as requested by the Nawab of Malerkotla. Apart from anything else, it is almost certain that once one of the children of Shri Altaf Ali Khan is allowed to come to India along with the uncle and the step mother of the Nawab of Malerkotla, we would be approached on humanitarian and compassionate grounds to allow the father and the other child also to return to India. It may then be difficult to resist this request. But what is more importantis that Sahibzada Kazim Ali Khan, who is now stated to be about 22 years old, has spent the most impressionable part of his life in Pakistan. It is, therefore, almost certain that he must have imbibed the ideology of Pakistan and the communal outlook of his father. To allow such a person to return to India on a permanent basis against the wishes of the Punjab Government and also the considered views of the Defence Ministry and the Directorate of Military Intelligence will not be advisable. His return to India will also raise the delicate question of a Pakistani national being recognised as a successor to the present Nawab of Malerkotla. In these circumstances, it is for consideration whether we should agree to grant facilities to return to India to Sahibzada Kazim Ali Khan in addition to the uncle and the step mother of the Nawab. It will perhaps be desirable to consult the Government of Punjab and the Ministry of Defence before taking a final decision.

(Fateh Singh)
Joint Secretary
6.7.1962

Secretary

47. From C. Subramaniam: Reorganisation in Rourkela[131]

[Refer to item 266]

1st July, 1962

My dear Jawaharlalji,

I am herewith enclosing a note, which explains the scheme of decentralisation, which is being introduced in the Hindustan Steel Limited. As stated in the note, this reorganisation is being undertaken as an immediate short term measure. I had the advantage of discussing this matter with some of our Senior Secretaries (Ranganathan,[132] Jha,[133] Swaminathan,[134] Wanchoo[135] and Bhoothalingam[136]) before finalising these proposals. A good deal of study and thinking is necessary before it is possible to take decisions regarding the final shape and pattern of the Steel Organisation. But the present steps will, I hope, solve many of the immediate problems and perhaps also show the way for final decisions in the matter.

2. I would like, particularly, to draw your attention to the proposal at "A" on page 3 of the note, which refers to appointments to posts in the Hindustan Steel Limited carrying a salary of Rs 2,000 and above. A procedural change is indicated therein, which I hope, will be accepted.

With my respectful regards,

Yours sincerely,
C. Subramaniam

131. Letter from the Minister of Steel and Heavy Industries. PMO, File No. 17(12)/61-65-PMS, Sr. No. 35-A.
132. S. Ranganathan, Secretary, Department of International Trade and Industry, Ministry of Commerce and Industry.
133. L.K. Jha, Secretary, Department of Economic Affairs, Ministry of Finance.
134. T. Swaminathan, Additional Secretary, Department of Heavy Industries, Ministry of Steel and Heavy Industries.
135. N.N. Wanchoo, Secretary of Iron and Steel, Ministry of Steel and Heavy Industries.
136. S. Bhoothalingam, Department of Expenditure, Ministry of Finance.

48. From Arjun Arora: Arbitration on Assam Royalty[137]

[Refer to item 186]

15/79, Civil Lines
Kanpur
1st July, 1962

Revered Pandit Ji,

As a humble Congressman I have felt unhappy at the newspaper report that the Oil Royalty differences between the Union Government and the Assam Government will be referred to the Supreme Court. Both of them are governments manned and run by our glorious party. As is well known, Congress exercises some control over the various governments in the country through the Working Committee and other bodies. It is also well known that where formal bodies may not usefully do the task, what is known as the High Command guides Congressmen in office. I have wondered why these authorities of the organisation have not attempted to find a solution of the issue between the Union Ministry of Mines and Fuel and the Assam Government when both are Congress Governments. Our party should not be incapable of resolving such differences and taking steps to avoid the spectacle of our two governments fighting it out in a law court. In all humility I suggest that as the supreme leader of the Congress you may please give this matter a little more personal attention and arrange that the differences are not taken to a court of law.

Yours sincerely,
Arjun Arora

49. From E.M.S. Namboodiripad[138]

[Refer to item 151]

I am writing this in order to draw your attention to the case of Mr C.A. Balan, a prisoner serving his sentence in Kerala. He was a Trade Unionist in Coimbatore and was convicted and sentenced in Madras State. He would ordinarily have been released along with other long term prisoners whose case was considered by the Government of Madras in pursuance of a memorandum submitted to

137. Letter from Congress Rajya Sabha MP. PMO, File No. 17(490)/62-70-PMS, Sr. No. 29-A.

138. Copy of letter, 2 July 1962, from the Secretary of the CPI, New Delhi. Copy, salutation not available.

you by a delegation of our Party led by the late Ajoy Ghosh.[139] He was not included in it only because, being a Malayalee, he was transferred to the Kerala Government to be kept under their custody after the formation of the State of Kerala. There was some doubt regarding the legal position—whether it is for the Government of Madras or for the Government of Kerala to consider his case. It appears now that the doubt has been cleared by both the Governments—that it is for the Government of Kerala to do so. It is, at the same time, certain, that if he had been in Madras jail, he would have been released along with the rest.

I myself wrote to Mr Chacko[140] drawing his attention to this case and requesting him that he should be released. The reply I received from the Government of Kerala was that the Board considered the case and has decided not to recommend his name for release and that, therefore, the Government do not propose to do so. I would, therefore, request you to advise the Kerala Government to take all aspects of the case and do what the Government of Madras would have done if the prisoner had been kept in Madras.

50. From K.C. Reddy: Malerkotla's Plans for Industry[141]

[Refer to item 264 & 265]

This is with reference to your letter No. 1016-PMH/62, dated July 1, 1962, regarding the Nawab of Malerkotla's proposals to start some industry in Punjab. As you have yourself stated, we cannot consider any proposal which will involve foreign exchange expenditure. The only proposal of this kind in the various alternatives he has put forward is the setting up of 100 power looms for the manufacture of worsted fabrics. Unfortunately, however, we are not nowadays sanctioning the setting up of power looms for the manufacture of woollen fabrics. The reason for this decision is that even for the existing looms, supply of yarn from indigenous sources is exceedingly difficult. I might mention here that even this yarn has to be produced form imported wool. Most of even the existing looms are occupied only to 50% of their capacity. In the circumstances, if these power looms are sanctioned to the Nawab, it will add to the strain on the available supplies of yarn, and what the Nawab has asked for – "only the supply of worsted yarn from the Indian Mills should be ensured" – will not be possible. It would, therefore, result in wasteful expenditure of his capital. In

139. General Secretary of the CPI, until January 1962.

140. P.T. Chacko, Minister of Home, Police and Jails in Kerala.

141. Copy of letter from the Minister of Commerce & Industry, 3 July 1962, salutation and signature not available.

the circumstances, I am afraid even this request of the Nawab Saheb cannot be acceded to.

51. From K. L. Shrimali: B.F.H.B. Tyabji as Vice-Chancellor at Aligarh[142]

[Refer to items 306 & 307]

I have given careful consideration to the question of appointing a new Vice-Chancellor at the Aligarh Muslim University when the present Vice-Chancellor[143] retires within a couple of months. I have discussed the matter both with the President and the Vice-President and the only name that is generally acceptable is that of Shri B.F.H.B. Tyabji. I have talked to Tyabji also and he seems to be inclined to go over to the University if you agree. Aligarh University is one of our most important national institutions and we should try to select the best man available in the country to guide this University. Having considered all the aspects of the question I have come to the conclusion that Tyabji should be spared for a few years for this work.

It would take some time to finalise the arrangements with regard to his emoluments, pension contribution etc. I would, therefore, be grateful if you kindly give your, approval so that we can discuss the matter with the Finance Ministry.

According to the present Act of the University, Tyabji will have to be formally elected by the Executive Council of the University.

52. From Kaoru Yasui: Conference against Atomic and Hydrogen Bombs[144]

[Refer to item 356]

Tokyo
July 5, 1962

Your Excellency,

In recent years, the peoples of the world have become more and more aware of the terrible danger with which they are confronted. At the same time they

142. Letter from the Education Minister, 4 July 1962. Salutation and signature not available.

143. Syed Bashir Husain Zaidi.

144. Letter from the Chairman of the Japan Council against Atomic and Hydrogen Bombs. PMO, File No. 9/2/62-PMP, Vol. V, Sr. No. 12-A.PMO, File No. 9/2/62-PMP, Vol. V, Sr. No. 12-A.

have come to realise that in order to avert this danger the people themselves must act, both nationally and internationally.

For this reason, the Japan Council against Atomic and Hydrogen Bombs has convened the Eighth World Conference against A and H Bombs and for Prevention of Nuclear War, in Tokyo, August 1-6. This will be a Conference of persons from all over the world who will meet together, fully conscious of the responsibility they bear, to bring about a ban on nuclear weapons, to prevent nuclear war, and to ensure world peace.

In conjunction with the World Conference, the Fifth Nationwide Peace March, covering the whole of Japan, will converge on Tokyo while the Conference is in session, and on Hiroshima and Nagasaki on August 6 and 9, to coincide with the meetings commemorating the atomic bombing of these two cities.

The forces for peace are strong. They are becoming stronger and more united every day, and words and actions of solidarity and encouragement will make them more so.

We would greatly appreciate, if you will kindly send a message to both the Eighth World Conference and to the Fifth Nationwide Peace March.

Yours very truly,
Prof. Dr Kaoru Yasui

53. From B. Gopala Reddi: Press Consultative Committee[145]

[Refer to item 7 & 8, 239]

7th July '62

My dear Sri Panditji,

You will recall that at the last meeting of the National Integration Council, one of the points considered was the question of evolving codes of conduct for the Press.[146] The decision of the Council was to recommend to Government the setting up of a Committee to confer with the different sections of the Press and to examine and formulate a Press Code with due regard to the Press Commission's recommendations.

145. Letter from the Minister of Information and Broadcasting. PMO, File No. 43(186)/62-63-PMS, Sr. No. 1-A.

146. On 3 June 1962. See items 7 & 8.

2. I have given this matter my careful consideration. I am in the process of setting up a Press Consultative Committee as a prelude to the setting up of a Press Council in accordance with the recommendations in the report of the Press Commission (1954). The Consultative Committee would be an advisory body and its main purpose would be to create a liaison between the Press and the Government. Tentatively, I am proposing to put on it, apart from five eminent persons not directly concerned with the Press, representatives of the proprietors of newspapers, both in English and Indian languages, the editors and the working journalists. My suggestion in connection with the recommendation of the National Integration Council is that the responsibility for formulating a Press Code should be entrusted not to an ad hoc Committee but to a Sub-Committee of the proposed Consultative Committee of the Press. The advantage of this would be that the Code would be formulated by representatives of the persons whom it will seek to govern. If, on the other hand, an ad hoc Committee is set up, there it likely to be a feeling amongst members of the Press that Government are trying to impose a Code on them. I hope the procedure, which I have proposed above, has your approval.

3. I hope I would also be right in inferring that the Code which has to be evolved on the recommendations of the Integration Council has to relate only to the question of emotional integration with which this Council is concerned. The Press Commission's recommendations in this regard covered a wider area and these could in due course be considered by the Press Council which it proposed to be set up at an early date.

With kind regards,

Yours sincerely,
B. Gopala Reddi

54. From S. Radhakrishnan: Nehru's Hyderabad Visit[147]

[Refer to item 114]

July 8, 1962

My dear Prime Minister,

Thank you for your letter of the 5th of July.[148]

I left Delhi on the 7th and I am now here. I saw Dr Rajendra Prasad[149] yesterday evening. He looks better but his wife is in the same condition.

147. Letter from the President. PMS, File No. 8(226)62-PMP.

148. Item 100.

149. The previous President.

As for the small house, I have not made up my mind. While I feel it would be more convenient, I do not wish to do anything which may not be agreeable to my successors.

I am glad you are having some rest and that Indira and her sons are there with you.

I am expecting you here on the 18th. You may spend two or three days quietly. All that I propose to do when you are here is to have a lunch when I shall invite Rajenbabu,[150] the Governor,[151] the Chief Minister[152] and a few others. I won't make any other engagement for you. A day – 19th or 20th – may be fixed to suit your convenience.

Yours affectionately,
S. Radhakrishnan

55. From B.L. Jani: School for Adivasis[153]

[Refer to item 77]

Bombay,
9th July, 1962

Respected Panditji,

The above Society, viz. the Sabarkantha Education Society is registered with the Charity Commissioner of Bombay and is giving Scholarships to the deserving students of the Sabarkantha district in Gujarat State, without any restriction of cast or creed.

Since last year, the Society is conducting one Adivasi School, in an Adivasi Village "Dhichania", which is about 15 miles from Idar Station in Sabarkantha District (Gujarat State). This School is run in a broken *jupdha* (hut) by engaging two teachers. More than 80 Adivasi half-naked and half-starved children are taking advantage of this School, free of charge. This Society is also providing books to the students. The monthly expenses of the School comes to about Rs 200/-. The photos of the hut in which the School is run and the conditions of the students is enclosed herewith for your information. This School is registered with the Education Department of the Sabarkantha District and Government

150. Rajendra Prasad.
151. Bhimsen Sachar.
152. N. Sanjiva Reddy.
153. Letter from the President of the Sabarkantha Educational Society, 1st Floor, Bhanabhai Chawl, Bhuleshwar, near Kabutarkhana, Bombay-2. PMO, File No. 9/2/62-PMP, V, Sr. No. 27-A.

is giving grants. Now, Government has sanctioned 2 acres and 19 gunthas of land free of charge for the construction of the building, etc. After 14 years of independence, such is the case in rural India. Of course, the Government is trying its best to improve the conditions of these people in all respects.

Mr K.K. Shah, the General Secretary of the Congress, who hails from Sabarkantha District, is serving the nation for the last 23 years. We feel there is no better man in this District than Mr K.K. Shah who has served the nation, and so our Society has decided to give the name of the School as "Shri K.K. Shah Adivasis Sanskar Kendra" as a token of love and goodwill towards him.

Now, we are deciding to raise a fund for the School, say about Rs 50,000/- for the construction of the building.

We are also pleased to inform you that Mrs K.K. Shah has consented to become the Chairman of the Society.

Please give your blessings for our venture for the upliftment of these Adivasis in the cause of education.

Yours obediently
B.L. Jani

56. From V.K. Krishna Menon: Northeast Problems[154]

[Refer to item 189]

Reference your note of 26 June about the Mizo Hills District.

You may recall that I brought up this matter at the last meeting of the Border Roads Board. The Board took a decision to participate in, and if necessary to undertake, the construction of this road having regard to its importance both internally for the Mizo Hills District and inside Assam and externally in our relations with Pakistan.

The Director General of Border Roads assures me that the survey has begun and I have asked that the work should be proceeded without avoidable delay if the Assam Government gives its cooperation at all stages. The first stage of construction of the road or most of it should be completed in the course of the year or soon after. I do not think more can be done in regard to this.

With regard to the landing strips the only way of dealing with this matter is for the Border Roads itself to construct the landing strip for emergency purposes.

154. Letter from the President of the Sabarkantha Educational Society, 1st Floor, Bhanabhai Chawl, Bhuleshwar, near Kabutarkhana, Bombay-2. PMO, File No. 9/2/62-PMP, V, Sr. No. 27-A.

This may have to be after the monsoon. It is not possible to place this strip under Air Force works as Air Headquarters are unlikely to give priority to it.

The Governor has made some reference to ex-Servicemen. This is dealt with in the Directorate for ex-Servicemen which I am doing my best to get to the tempo and dimensions that it should have without much encouragement.

The Governor is quite competent to discuss the problem of ex-Servicemen through his local Sailors, Soldiers and Airmen Board within the terms of its function and I have no objection to the reference to the Adjutant General, and if anything can be done in that sphere I shall be glad. The general problem, however, is much larger and is sought to be tackled as best as possible and will come before you in due course.

The Governor has also referred to those dismissed from the Assam Regiment. I am afraid in regard to these men it would not be take any action which does not take into account the enormity of their offence. It would be a bad day for the Army when mutineers obtained protection. However, I will have talk with the COAS and CGS who are mainly concerned in this matter.

(V.K. Krishan Menon)
9.7.62

57. From N. Sanjiva Reddy: Reservations in Government Jobs[155]

[Refer to item 79]

Hyderabad
9th July 1962

My dear Panditji,

Subject: Reservation of Government posts on communal basis

I am writing to seek your advice on the subject of reservation of posts on the basis of community which has been a matter of controversy in this State for the last one year or more besides being a subject of considerable divergence of view in the then State Cabinet. In fact, I gather, almost all the then Ministers were opposed to an order of this Government, G.O. Ms. No.559, dated the 4th May 1961, of which I enclose a copy.

155. Letter from the Chief Minister of Andhra Pradesh. Only extract available in the NMML. PMO, File No. 33(76)/62-64-PMS, Sr. No. 11-A.

XXX XXX XXX

Immediately after orders were passed, some Ministers called for the file and asked that the matter be brought before the Cabinet but the Chief Minister thought it unnecessary to bring up the matter before the Cabinet.

I would invite your attention to the fact that –

1. the proposal based on caste and not on economic or social conditions is *prima facie* unsound and besides being unfair to the so-called forward communities is likely to affect the efficiency, incentive and morale of the services;
2. the manner of transfer of posts unfilled by Scheduled Caste and Scheduled Tribe candidates to the so-called Backward Classes gives the latter an extra undue advantage which amounts to discrimination and therefore offends the Constitution;
3. the Public Service Commission had advised against the proposal;
4. the matter though important was not brought before the Cabinet despite requests for such consideration by a number of Ministers, the majority of the Cabinet was opposed to the proposal and that the order would not have issued if, in fact, the matter had been considered by the Cabinet.

To my humble mind the sections of the Constitution quoted by my predecessor do not bear the interpretation given by him though some concessions to the Scheduled Castes sad Tribes is doubtless justified. It would also appear that one of the reasons for the view taken by him is the application of the communal rotation rule to promotions in the Railway Ministry of the Government of India.

I feel that G.O. Ms.No.559, dated the 4th May 1961, in this State is likely to seriously affect the efficiency and contentment of the Services.

With regards,

Yours sincerely,
N. Sanjiva Reddy

58. From Muni Lal: Be Constructive not Factionalist[156]

[Refer to item 40]

11-7-62

Respected Pandit Ji,

Last month at Ludhiana meet, the younger progressive element in Congress formed a "Congress Socialist Forum" with a view to fight out the reactionary forces and revitalise the Congress.

This unit, as others in the Country, requires your guidance and lead in accelerating the activities of this forum. We trust that you will shower upon us your affection and wisdom in the matter of carrying out the onerous job of coming up to the expectations of the masses and making the Congress strong in the province through the signal service of the forum.

We therefore, request you to kindly grant us an interview at Delhi, so that we may seek your guidance in this matter. The deputation would consist of seven persons.

With respects and kindest regards,

Yours affectionately,
Muni Lal
Convener,
Punjab Congress Socialist Forum
Camp Office, Saran Lodge
Solan (Simla Hills)

59. From V.K. Krishna Menon: Malerkotla's Nephew[157]

[Refer to items 66 & 73]

12 July 1962

My dear Prime Minister,

I am grateful to you for your letter of 1 July about the nephew of the Nawab of Malerkotla. His father's brother being a member of the Pakistan Army has created the difficulty. I do not, however, think that it would be insurmountable.

Without giving all the consideration that this requires I think the appropriate and prudent thing to do would be to let him return on a visa which could

156. Letter from the Convenor of Punjab Congress Socialist Forum, Ludhiana. PMO, File No. 17 (502)/62-66-PMS, Sr. No. 7-C.

157. Letter from the Defence Minister. MHA, File No. 10/40/62-F.III, p.9/c.

automatically be renewed and do the same as in the case of others. While he is here *de facto* as an Indian we would be able to assure ourselves and consider what step can be taken. Giving Indian nationality no doubt creates precedents but after all rules have to be construed in the light of circumstances. To enable us to do so if we took the first step as a temporary measure we could consider what we can do later.

I will ascertain Service and Ministry views on this matter discreetly and write to you further.

Affectionately,
V.K. Krishna Menon

60. From Humayun Kabir: Punitive Tax[158]

[Refer to item 75]

12th July 1962

My dear Panditji,

Thank you for your letter of July 10, 1962 which reached me last evening.[159]

I am very thankful that you found time to read this long note and I am happy to know that you agree broadly with the suggestions.

The use of punitive police and punitive tax would be an ultimate measure but if the other steps are enforced, I hope the occasion for punitive police and punitive tax may not arise at all. As I told you, I had discussed some of the points with Shastriji[160] and he was in general agreement. Since then I have heard from some of the Chief Ministers and several of them agree generally.

Since the prevention of group conflicts must be a preliminary step before we can think of emotional integration of committees, I wonder if you would one day have a meeting of the Cabinet devoted exclusively to the discussion of short and long term measure in this behalf.

Yours sincerely,
Humayun Kabir

158. Letter from the Minister of Scientific Research and Cultural Affairs. MHA, File No. 7/21/62-Poll. II., Sr. No. 2.
159. Item 72.
160. Lal Bahadur Shastri, the Home Minister.

61. From Lal Bahadur Shastri: All Party Hill Leaders' Conference[161]

[Refer to item 190]

13th July, 1962

My dear Panditji,

I have been thinking about the advisability of sending a reply to the letter of General Secretary of the Council of Action, All Party Hill Leaders' Conference,[162] a copy of which you had sent to me with your letter No. 908-PMH/62 of June 21, 1962.[163] Some of the hill tribe leaders are encouraging their people to resort to direct action and Nichols-Roy has spoken about setting up of a parallel Government etc. It seems to me that a reply might do some good and that, in any case, it would do no harm. The Scottish pattern of autonomy offered to them will give them all the opportunity to develop the Hill districts, and to administer them, which they desire. They will be free to develop their culture and to carry on the administration in their local languages and English until it is replaced by Hindi with which they themselves agree. While having all this opportunity and freedom they would, under the Scottish pattern, share the larger, political and economic life of Assam, and would be able to exercise influence on the policies and programmes of the Government of the whole State.

Particular mention has been made of the question in the Council of Action's letter. It has been said that Assamese having been made the official language of the State all areas and people in the State cannot but be affected, and that the Assamese language would be imposed in one way or another. If the Council of Action really entertains these fears, we ought to consider, in consultation with the Assam Government, how these fears can be removed. I do not myself think that this should be impossible, and if you think it proper you may perhaps specifically enquire in your reply what precisely their fears are.

Yours affectionately,
Lal Bahadur

161. Letter from the Home Minister. MHA, File No. 4/1/62-SR(R)-A., p.56/c.
162. S.D.D. Nichols-Roy.
163. Item 180.

62. From Mohan Singh: Succession to Nehru[164]

[Refer to item 4]

For the past so many years, the big question which most Indians visiting some of the countries in Europe and USA were usually asked was who will succeed your Prime Minister, if anything happened to him. Of late, however, this has become an important topic of discussion in India as well I was recently in Bombay and at almost every party I attended the conversation ultimately veered round to this question. A prominent industrialist asked me to tell him in confidence what was the latest thinking in Delhi about the successor of Mr Nehru. Although my answer to him was that life in the official capital was much too busy and people there had very little time to indulge in idle talk or wild conjectures and that gossip mongering was the privilege of big cities like Bombay where the appearance of a person like T.T.K.[165] upsets the stock exchange, yet I heard all sorts of wild rumours about your possible successor. I heard a person saying that if anything happened to Panditji, Indira will take over as Prime Minister and that she will lean heavily on Krishna Menon. Another remarked why not take T.T.K. out of the control room and seat Krishna Menon in a controlled room. We all wish, and pray that you may live long and guide the destinies of our dear country for many many years to come. However, it was time this sort of idle talk stopped. I have a humble suggestion to make in this regard by which you can be to the world tomorrow what you are to India today. No one man can shoulder and discharge efficiently even half the responsibilities that you have taken on yourself. So let these responsibilities be shouldered by a team consisting of Sarvshri Lal Bahadur Shastri, Morarji Desai, T.T. Krishnamachari and Mrs Indira Gandhi, under your guidance and supervision for say six months or so. Thereafter you should apply your mind to the world problems. The humanity today needs an intellectual giant of your calibre and stature to save it from total annihilation the way it is heading towards a sure catastrophe. You alone with the powerful impact of your great personality and the tremendous prestige you enjoy, can save the world.

People who have had occasion recently to come into close contact with T.T.K. of late say that he has now gone very much more sober, amiable and cooperative. If Morarji Bhai and T.T.K could work and pull together they would team up wonderfully with Lal Bahadurji and Indiraji. They would be the most appropriate answer to "After Nehru Who".

164. Letter from the General Manager, Punjab National Bank Ltd., New Delhi. NMML, T.T. Krishnamachari Papers, File 1962. Copy, salutation and signature not available.

165. T.T. Krishnamachari, the Minister without Portfolio and former Finance Minister.

Praying for your long life and still greater achievements in the international plane, 1 remain.

63. From Humayun Kabir: M.S. Thacker for Planning Commission[166]

[Refer to items 105 and 351]

14th July 1962

My dear Jawaharlal ji,

Thank you very much for your secret letter No. 1051-PMH/62 of July 13, 1962.

While I am sorry to lose Professor M.S. Thacker, I agree with you that he would make a very good Member of the Planning Commission. He has imagination and vision and also a quick grasp of things. In addition, he is very well balanced and I think his inclusion will strengthen the Commission.

I understand from Dr Khosla that he is planning to make over charge about the 10th or 11th of September. I do not know if Thacker would like to have a few weeks before he joins, but there should be no difficulty in letting him join the Commission from the beginning of September.

It will now be necessary to look for a new Director-General. Ever since I spoke to you I have been thinking over the matter. It seems to me that it would be a good thing to introduce the principle of tenure for the post of Director-General. If one of the outstanding Directors from the National Laboratories came as Director-General for a period of three years or so, this would establish closer contact between the Laboratories and the Central Office. He would come with the knowledge of the difficulties which the Laboratories face and when he went back to his own laboratory, he would also know the all-India implications of what the Laboratories do. We need not of course confine ourselves to the Directors and if a very eminent man is available from outside, he should certainly be selected.

If you agree, I would like to appoint a small Informal Committee consisting of:

(1) Professor P.C. Mahalanobis;
(2) Professor H.J. Bhabha;
(3) Dr A.N. Khosla;
(4) Professor M.S. Thacker; and
(5) Dr D.S. Kothari

166. Letter from the Minister for Scientific Research and Cultural Affairs. NMML, Humayun Kabir Papers, F. No. 5/1958-62.

to suggest two or three names from among the Directors of National Laboratories or from outside for appointment as Director-General. I will then discuss these names with you and make our choice.

Yours sincerely,
Humayun Kabir

64. From Jayaprakash Narayan: Miscellaneous[167]

[Refer to item 418]

July 15, 1962

Dear Bhai,
It is good that you have had that holiday in Kashmir. A picture of you that I saw in the papers showed a very refreshed and rested face. I hope you will pay some heed to Bidhan Babu's last advice. You have such a resilient constitution that if you give it half a chance it is sure to carry you across the century boundary.

I am enclosing a few documents you may glance through if you get the time. About one of them, I would like to have your advice. Do you think it would help if the Sarva Seva Sangh published Badshah Khan's wonderful statement before the High Court.

I had thought of preparing a short note on my East African visit, but, unfortunately, I have not had the time. But there is one thing, however, which I should bring to your notice. Young African leaders almost everywhere that I met wanted India to provide more scholarships for African students. This ought to be considered.

Yours affectionately,

65. From Moolchand Deshlahra: Intrigues in Madhya Pradesh Congress[168]

[Refer to item 155]

17th July 1962

Respected Panditji,
I request you to kindly excuse me for this lengthy note. When I met you some time back, I explained to you in brief the circumstances that led to the unhappy

167. Copy of letter from Sarvodaya leader. Signature not available. Sent from Simultala, Monghyr, Bihar. MEA, File No. A-IV/102/13/62, pp.48-63/Corr.
168. Letter from the President of the Madhya Pradesh PCC. Sent from Bhopal.

results of the Third General Elections in MP and the situation that developed as an outcome thereof. Dr Ramkrishna Rao has sent his report. I regret, I have not been furnished with a copy of the report.

Shri K.K. Shah, General Secretary AICC, has sent me some abstracts from Dr Rao's report. From the extracts supplied to me, I understand that even a Prima Facie Case has not been made out against me. In spite of this finding Dr Rao has suggested that I should step down for the only reason that I have become unpopular with an important section of the Congress. I have been denied a simple right to know the extent and nature of the alleged unpopularity and the persons constituting the said important section. I presume that it is the same section which is known to you as well for its false and malicious propaganda against me in Press and public. It is the same section some leading members of which have been found guilty of sabotage and indiscipline by Dr Rao according to his report, but it is surprising that no action has been suggested against any of them and I alone have been singled out for punishment and that too for the only reason that these gentlemen are not pleased with me. In a democratic set up nobody can become unpopular with a certain section but I still claim the confidence of a major and substantial section of the PCC, and Congressmen.

I am at a loss to understand as to why Dr Rao suggested that I should resign, after having found nothing against me in his inquiry. This does not appear to be judicious, from the abstracts that have been supplied to me. It is just possible that the decision taken by the Seven-men Committee that I should resign, even before the enquiry was entrusted to Dr Rao, influenced the mind of Dr Rao and he gave the suggestion which is not sustained by his own findings.

For various reasons, unhappy selection of candidates, apprehension of non co-operation from Ministers, paucity of funds, existence of public discontent and grievances and all that, I did not expect good results and I offered to resign on the eve of elections, but I was not allowed to do so. I did my best in a trying situation. I toured and collected funds as much as I could. Funds and materials were given without discrimination. Cash aid was given to 168 candidates out of whom 90 belonged to the other group. Not a single complaint was made about any negligence, partiality or sabotage on my part during the course of Elections while against the other group serious complaints were received even during Elections, especially from Rajgarh and Morena districts. The reverses generally in reserved seats and especially in the Indore Parliamentary and Budni Assembly seats cannot be excused. All the five rebels of the PCC group were expelled and defeated. There were about forty rebels in the other group. The other group had a decent election fund which was collected individually by some Ministers and spent for themselves and their groupmen. Many Ministers did not stir out of their constituencies during elections.

The circumstances and causes of reverses that obtained in Madhya Pradesh before and during the General Elections of 1962 never existed in the General Elections of 1946 of the then Madras State. Therefore the Madras analogy does not apply in my case. Moreover there is no precedent where an elected office bearer was punished after an inquiry was held and he was exonerated of the charge.

Under the present set up of our organisation the PCC only reaps to a great extent the crop that is sown by the administrative wing. Dr Rao has admitted, though in a different context, that the PCC is well organised. I do not know what Dr Rao has said about the administration during the last term. I think, his observation in this connection may not be happy. It was very unfortunate that the reactionary element could utilise the good name of Dr Katju[169] for ventilating their own grievances against me. I always valued the age and experience of Dr Katju, but he allowed himself to be misled by my opponents. If I can be said to be guilty of intolerance, Dr Katju had his own share of the same.

I may be pardoned for a line about myself. I decided to take to active and serious politics just on the day when Shri D.P. Mishra, Ex-Home Minister, read his post-resignation address in the Legislative Assembly of Ex-Madhya Pradesh [Madhya Bharat] about twelve years back. At the cost of my personal career, I came to the PCC with a purpose and that purpose was to keep away Shri D.P.Mishra and his supporters, casteists, princes and bidi magnates, from gaining supreme leadership in the State of Madhya Pradesh.

Whatever be the mind and whatever be the decision of the High Command but on my part I may submit that my conscience is clear. I have not yet been able to convince myself that I should leave my post, especially at the present juncture and in the present political situation. I have been facing trials and tribulations all these years because of your goodwill and I hope that I have not lost it.

Awaiting a word from you and with best respects,

Yours sincerely,
Moolchand Deshlahra

169. Kailas Nath Katju, former Chief Minister of Madhya Pradesh.

66. The Indian President[170]

[Refer to item 23]

A year ago, Dr Rajendra Prasad, the President of India, delivered a speech to the Indian Law Institute,which caused a good deal of controversy. In that speech,[a] he called upon the Institute to examine, "purely as a subject of study and investigation in a scientific manner," how far the powers and functions of the President under the Indian Constitution were identical with those of the British monarch, whether it would be right to incorporate into our written Constitution the conventions of the unwritten British Constitution or to invoke them in interpreting our Constitution. It has been so widely assumed that the Indian Constitution provides for a parliamentary system on the model of the United Kingdom that the President's suggestion came as something of a shock. As a matter of fact, however, the debate over the position of the President, which was first touched off on the promulgation of the Constitution in 1950, has never been satisfactorily settled. But the political experience of the country led to a general belief that the functions and powers of the President were quite clear and further, that these were in extent almost non-existent.

What the President's speech did was to revive an interest that had lain dormant. Several people, following his suggestion, called upon the Government to examine the exact position of the President in the governance of the country. Others suggested that the Supreme Court be called upon to advise in the matter. In Parliament itself, attempts were made at a definitive amendment to the Constitution which would clarify the issue. The Government, however, maintained that the position of the President was akin to that of the British Crown and there was therefore no need for an inquiry or constitutional amendment of any kind. For the time being, it would seem that the issue has been settled, but the doubt persists—what is the precise position of the President? The necessity for a clear statement on the controversy will become apparent when we examine the two views that are held regarding the position of the President.

The Analogy of the British Monarchy

One view which is widely propounded has been voiced by Mr M.C. Setalvad, the present Attorney-General of India, and the late Mr B.N. Rau,

170. Article by B.A.V. Sharma, a lecturer in Bombay University, and N.M. Valecha, a political commentator in *The Political Quarterly*, Vol. 33, 1962, pp. 59-73.
Footnotes of the original appear as letter numbering as a, b, c and so on.

a. See *The Hindu*, November 29, 1961. [Rajendra Prasad spoke on 28 November 1960].

Constitutional Adviser to the Constituent Assembly, which was responsible for the framing of the Indian Constitution. According to these authoritative sources, the position of the Indian President is analogous to that of the British monarch. The President is a titular executive; his functions and powers are purely ornamental and nominal. The office carries prestige but no power. Real power is exercised by the Council of Ministers responsible to a Parliament elected by the nation. The President is merely a "working hypothesis" a "magnificent cypher" without the right to exercise his independent judgment.

Equally impressive is the opposite view held by Mr Patanjali Sastri, former Chief Justice of the Supreme Court of India, and Mr N.C. Chatterjee, a well-known constitutional lawyer, who maintain that the President is endowed with enormous powers and that the only limitation on this power is the Constitution itself. Conventions are foreign to a written constitution; they cannot fetter the exercise of powers granted under the Constitution. These constitutional powers accord to him a prominent place in the governance of the country. The Indian President cannot be equated with the British monarch. The two are dissimilar and hence non-comparable.

The Implications of Cabinet Government

What are the distinguishing features of a Cabinet form of government? Sir Ivor Jennings, in his book on *Cabinet Government*, observed that if the British Constitution were to be set out in a written document, the Cabinet would be accorded a central place and the Prime Minister would emerge as the most important person.[b] It is submitted that the type of executive provided for or envisaged by the Indian Constitution is totally unlike that described by Sir Ivor as typical of Cabinet government. Neither the Cabinet nor the Prime Minister occupies a position of prominence in it; rather, the central place is accorded to the President.

The chapter on the Executive bears eloquent testimony to the importance attached to the President vis-a-vis the Cabinet and the Prime Minister. Except for two articles wherein a reference is made to the Council of Ministers, the entire chapter deals with the President. It is curious that those who claim that the Indian Constitution provides for a Cabinet type of government should find support only in a couple of articles—which are themselves by no means definitive. The Ministers are, in fact, described as officers "subordinate" to the President[c] in the exercise of executive power.

b. W.I. Jennings, *Cabinet Government*, 3rd ed., p.1.

c. Art. 53 (1), Constitution of India.

The most important factor determining the nature of the Executive is the powers and functions of the President and the Council of Ministers under the Constitution. In a Cabinet system of government, the Cabinet should possess supreme policy-making and executive powers. The Indian Constitution, on the other hand, not only denies to the Council of Ministers supreme control over the government of the country but gives to the President the right to interfere in the policy-determining functions of the Cabinet.

Article 53 (1) of the Indian Constitution declares that the executive power of the Union shall be vested in the President. The only limitation on the President's constitutional powers is the Constitution itself. Parliament has no right to regulate or restrict the exercise of these powers. In this respect, the Indian President bears comparison with his American counterpart. The executive power, however, may be exercised by the President of India either directly by himself or through officers subordinate to him.

The Indian Constitution

The Constitution confers on the President the power to interfere in the working, of the Cabinet. Article 77 (3) enables the President to encroach on the right of the Council of Ministers to frame its own rules of business as also on the Prime Minister's right to allocate portfolios among his colleagues. In the United Kingdom, on the other hand, the selection of the Cabinet and the distribution of portfolios are left entirely to the Prime Minister; the Crown has no voice in these matters.

Where a decision has been taken by a Minister on a matter not considered by the Cabinet as a whole, the President has the right to demand that the matter be placed for consideration before the Council of Ministers for a collective decision.[d] In the United Kingdom, it is left to the Ministers to decide whether or not a matter should be referred to the Cabinet according as it involves a question of policy or is a departmental act.

The Indian President can influence the judgment of Parliament—and hinder the law-promoting functions of the Cabinet—by the constitutional power to send messages to both the Houses of Parliament even with regard to Bills pending before Parliament.[e] It is incumbent on Parliament to consider his message with all dispatch. The power to send messages to Parliament which has fallen into disuse in the United Kingdom has been expressly provided for in the Indian Constitution.

d. Art. 78 (c).
e. Art. 86 (2).

The President possesses certain other important powers.[f] He has the power to dissolve the Lower House of Parliament. He can summon either of the Houses or a joint meeting of both Houses at any time and require the attendance of the members of Parliament for this purpose. Certain legislative measures require his sanction or recommendation prior to their introduction in Parliament. His assent is essential for a Bill to become law. If he so chooses, he may return a non-Money Bill duly passed by Parliament to either of the Houses for reconsideration with or without proposals for amendment. Of all legislative powers, his ordinance-making power is the most important. Its ambit is co-extensive with the legislative powers of Parliament and an ordinance has the same force and effect as an Act of Parliament.

In the financial sphere, it is the President who causes the annual financial statement (and the statement of supplementary, additional, or excess grants) to be laid before Parliament. The demand for grants and the introduction of Money Bills in Parliament can be made only on his recommendation.

The President is the Supreme Commander of the Defence Forces. He has important powers of appointment. For instance, he appoints ambassadors and diplomatic representatives to foreign countries. At home, he is responsible for the appointment of the Governors of States, the Attorney-General, the Comptroller and Auditor-General, the judges of the Supreme Court and High Courts, the members of the Union Public Service Commission, the Commissioner for Linguistic Minorities, etc.

He has besides, certain extraordinary powers to deal with emergencies. He can proclaim a state of emergency if (i) the security of India or any part thereof is threatened by war, external aggression, or internal disturbances, (ii) the constitutional machinery breaks down in any state, (iii) the financial stability or credit of India is threatened. When a proclamation of emergency—made on the initiative of the President[g]—is in operation, the President can suspend the Fundamental Rights guaranteed to the citizens by Article 19 of the Constitution and declare them unenforceable by the courts.

The Constitution thus confers enormous and extraordinary powers on the President. But in spite of its formidable length the Constitution nowhere expressly lays down that the President, in the exercise of his powers, shall act on the advice of the Council of Ministers. Whereas certain other conventions of the British Constitution—like the collective responsibility of the Cabinet and the appointment of Ministers by the Head of the State on the advice of

f. For a detailed account of the powers and functions of the Indian President refer to D.D. Basu, *Introduction to the Constitution of India*, Chap. X.

g. Art. 352.

the Prime Minister—have been incorporated into the Indian Constitution, the convention that the Head of the State shall always act on the advice of the Council of Ministers has been left out.

The Irish and Burmese Constitutions, framed consciously on the model of the British Constitution, have a special provision that makes it obligatory for the President to exercise his powers on the advice of the Cabinet.[h] The Indian Constitution, on the other hand, while it provides for a Council of Ministers with the Prime Minister as its head to aid and advise the President in the exercise of his functions, does not compel the Indian President either to seek the advice of the Council of Ministers or to follow it where it has been sought.

Further, the Constitution does not declare that the President shall be competent to act only when a decree, regulation, or other document issued by him bears the counter-signature of a Minister. Rather, it is the President who makes rules as to the manner in which his orders and instruments shall be authenticated. In practice, Presidential orders are authenticated by the Secretary of the Department and not by a Minister.[i]

Article 74 (2) of the Indian Constitution expressly states that the President is under no legal obligation to act on the advice of his Ministers. As Mr B.N. Rau pointed out: "... the Indian Constitution leaves no doubt . . . that the question whether any, and if so what, advice was tendered by Ministers to the President shall not be inquired into in any court. It follows that even if in any particular instance the President acts otherwise than on ministerial advice, the validity of the act cannot be challenged in a court of law on that ground."[j]

Discussions in the Constituent Assembly

Those who subscribe to the view that the Indian Constitution provides for a Cabinet system of government based on the model of the United Kingdom maintain that the President is merely a titular executive. They seek the support of the Constituent Assembly debates which leave no room for doubt that the position of the President was visualised as a purely ornamental one carrying few powers.

In the course of the debates, the President of India, who was then President of the Constituent Assembly, expressed the hope that the convention which in England compelled the sovereign to act always on the advice of the Cabinet would be established in this country so that the President in India would become

h. D.D. Basu, *Commentary on the Constitution of India*, 2nd ed., p. 289.
i. *Ibid*, p. 306.
j. B.N. Rau, *India's Constitution in the Making*, p. 375.

a constitutional President in all matters.[k] In the recent debate in the Lok Sabha (Lower House of the Indian Parliament) the Union Law Minister maintained that the President's words were not only to be considered as conclusive but as an authoritative interpretation of the President's functions under the Constitution.

Sentiments similar to those expressed by the President in the Constituent Assembly were supported by the arguments of other participants in the debates. The Draft Constitution of India had provided for a Schedule of Instructions which said: "In all matters within the scope of the executive power of the Union, the President shall in the exercise of the powers conferred upon him be guided by the advice of his Ministers."[l] The proposal, to include this Schedule of Instructions was dropped. The apprehensions created in the minds of the members of the Constituent Assembly by its exclusion were sought to be laid at rest by the argument that as the Constitution stood, there was no cause for any doubts on the issue and the Schedule was therefore superfluous. To a specific question, "if in any particular case the President does not act upon the advice of the Council of Ministers, will that be tantamount to a violation of the Constitution and will he be liable to impeachment?" Dr Ambedkar, the then Law Minister, categorically replied: "There is not the slightest doubt about it."[m]

The provision for the indirect election of the President is also cited to prove that the Constitution visualises the Head of the State as a mere figurehead. Justifying the provision, Mr Nehru had observed: "If we had the President elected on adult franchise and did not give him real powers, it might become a little anomalous."[n] The implication of this statement is clear: that since the President was not to be endowed with real powers, the Cabinet would be the effective executive.

It is submitted, however, that though the intentions of the framers of the Constitution as seen in the Constituent Assembly debates have immense value,[o] it would be foolish to use the arguments put forward therein when the express letter of the Constitution militates against their conclusions. As for Dr Ambedkar's statement that the President's disregard of ministerial advice would be tantamount to a violation of the Constitution, it is clearly not tenable in the light of what the Constitution itself has to say. Mr B.N. Rau, cited earlier, is firm on this point.

k. M.V. Pylee, *Constitutional Government in India*, p. 336.
l. B.N. Rau, *op. cit.*, p. 378.
m. *Ibid*, p. 378.
n. *Ibid*, p. 378.
o. C.H. Alexandrowicz, *Constitutional Developments in India*, Chap. 1.

Certain provisions in the Constitution itself are cited to support the claim that the President must act on the advice of the Council of Ministers. Article 74 (1) provides for a Council of Ministers to aid and advise the President in the exercise of his powers. Since no reservations or provisions to the contrary have been made, it is clear that on all matters within the sphere of the Union Government, the President must seek the advice of the Council of Ministers. Article 163 (1) relating to the States of the Union provides that "There shall be a Council of Ministers with the Chief Minister at the head to aid and advise the Governor in the exercise of his functions, *except in so far as he is by or under this Constitution required to exercise his functions or any of them in his discretion*."[p] It is evident, then, that whereas the Governor has been allotted an area of discretion where he is specifically permitted to disregard ministerial advice, no such exception has been made in the case of the President. It follows that the President has no discretionary powers vested in him under the Constitution.

Where Does "Responsibility"Lie ?

Further, the phrase "aid and advise" is taken to be the expression in a statutory form of the British convention that the monarch should act in conformity with the advice of the Cabinet. In Canada, the British North America Act has a similar provision which also omits any express obligation on the part of the Governor-General to follow ministerial advice. Yet Canada has developed a "responsible government"and the Governor-General has been transformed into a ceremonial head.[q] However, it should be noted that the Preamble in the Canadian Constitution clearly implies that its government is to be modelled on that of the United Kingdom. There is no such provision in the Indian Constitution.

Article 75 (3), which states that the Council of Ministers shall be collectively responsible to the Lower House of Parliament, is held to indirectly bind the President. For, if the President were to disregard the advice of the Cabinet, the Cabinet would resign. If an alternative government enjoying the confidence of the Lower House could not be formed, the President would have to dissolve Parliament. The ensuing elections might result in a return of the previous government to power and this would certainly put the President into an acutely embarrassing position and drag him into unpleasant political controversy. Since the consequences of disregarding ministerial advice is fraught

p. Our italics.

q. D.D. Basu, *Commentary on the Constitution of India*, p. 290.

with dangerous possibilities, a politically wise President would necessarily act on the advice of the Cabinet.

Further, the constitutional responsibility of the Council of Ministers to the Lower House elected by the people on the basis of universal adult franchise implies the acceptance of the concept of "responsible government." The Council of Ministers is responsible immediately to Parliament and ultimately to the nation; the President is responsible to none. He holds his office for a fixed term of five years and can be removed from office only by impeachment for violation of the Constitution. If the power to ignore ministerial advice were to be given to the President, Parliament, it is argued, would have no control over the executive. Mr B.N. Rau points out that this would "result in the reduction of the sphere of responsible government" and that such a diminution of the sovereignty of the people could not be justified in the absence of any express provision in the Constitution.[r] The Preamble to the Indian Constitution, it may be added, proclaims India a "Sovereign, Democratic Republic." In a republic, the real powers ought to vest in a Cabinet representative of, and responsible to the people and not in a President installed in office by indirect election and responsible to none.

Article 78, which requires the Prime Minister to communicate to the President all "decisions" of the Council of Ministers relating to the proposed legislation and administration of the affairs of the Union, implies that the President is merely to be "informed" of such decisions. These are, then, the decisions of the Cabinet, not of the President. Like his British counterpart, he is to be informed of decisions made but does not participate in their making.

Articles 74 and 75, taken together, are said to provide for a parliamentary form of government. It is implicit in such a scheme that real power vests in a Cabinet responsible to Parliament. The exercise of effective power by the Head of the State would be contrary to the spirit of such a scheme.

Arguments of this sort based on inferences can never be a substitute for the clear expression in the Constitution of the relations that ought to obtain between the Cabinet and the President. A matter of such fundamental importance in the governance of the country should have been expressed in unambiguous terms as in the case of the Irish and Burmese Constitutions. For the interpretation of a constitution flows from its clearly expressed provisions and to draw from it implications which contradict the letter of the constitution would be incapable of justification.

r. B.N. Rau, *op. cit.*, p.380.

The Place of Conventions

The most important argument put forward by those who claim that the Indian Constitution provides for a Cabinet system is that a written constitution does not—and, indeed, should not—embody all matters relating to the governance of the country. Something should be left to conventions and the growth of constitutional practice. The Indian Constitution contains no express provision to the effect that the President shall appoint as Prime Minister the leader of the majority party in the House of the People; or that the Cabinet shall resign when it ceases to enjoy the confidence of the Lower House. And yet these propositions are unanimously accepted. There is, therefore, no reason to insist that in the case of the relations that should exist between the President and his Cabinet, a constitutional provision is absolutely necessary. The development of these relations, too, could be left to conventions. Moreover, a provision that specifically bound the President to follow ministerial advice would introduce an element of rigidity into the Constitution besides detracting from the dignity and prestige attached to the office of the President.

The Attorney-General's Advice

In the course of the last ten years, the President has on several occasions raised the question of his powers and functions. On all such occasions, the Government sought the views of the Attorney-General, who has consistently maintained that the President has no independent powers to exercise or functions to perform and that he was to be guided by the Council of Ministers in whichever capacity he functioned.[s] The President's plea to be allowed direct communication with the Secretaries of the Departments was turned down as unconstitutional. His powers in respect of the appointment of judges, the Attorney-General, the Election Commissioner, and members of the Union Public Service Commission—independent authorities outside the control of the Executive—were held by the Attorney-General to be subject to ministerial advice and the independent exercise of these powers was held to be untenable. The accrediting of diplomatic representatives did not confer any power of appointment. Similarly, the President's status as Supreme Commander-in-Chief did not give him the right to interfere in the affairs of the Defence Ministry. He seems to have acquiesced in, if not endorsed, the stand taken by the Attorney-General that he is a titular head with no powers or functions. Not least is the fact that the Indian President has hitherto so functioned as to leave little doubt that he regards his position as one of only ceremonial importance.

s. *The Hindu*, December 5, 1960.

Those who claim that the Constitution envisaged a Cabinet type of Executive look for support to opinions similar to those expressed here and to conventions which they claim have been established that the President should abide by the advice of his Cabinet. However the Indian political experience is too short to have conclusively established any convention The fairly even tenor of government so far has meant that this "convention" has yet to be tested in the crucible of a political crisis. And if such a convention were to be questioned, it is difficult to see how it could stand against a clear provision to the contrary in the Constitution itself.

An examination of the two views on the nature of the Indian Executive reveals that those who look upon the President as the seat of power base their arguments on clear and explicit provisions in the Constitution. On the other hand, their opponents rely on the intentions of the framers of the Constitution and a few provisions in the Constitution with their indirect implications. But by and large they must look for the vindication of their position to the political experience of the country. For, on strictly legal and constitutional grounds, it must be admitted that their position is untenable.

The President as a Political Power

The "constitutionalists"—as we may call those who regard the President as the real executive—can point to a few cases in which the President did function effectively, to strengthen their case. On one occasion, the President used the power to express his opinion when he differed from ministerial policy. This was in connection with the Hindu Code Bill when the President threatened to appeal to Parliament by sending a message recommending the postponement of the Bill till after the completion of the General Elections.[t] The Government was forced to give way and postpone consideration of the Bill. In yet another instance, the President sought to influence Cabinet policy. On at least two occasions, the President wrote to the Prime Minister to express his disagreement with Government policies in the matter of state trading in food grains and the ceiling on landholdings. This action became known to the Press, and the knowledge of Presidential opposition to Government policy "strengthened the hands of the State governments which were reluctant to undertake trading," and slowed down the allegedly hasty legislation on land

t. Since the Bill contemplated far-reaching changes in certain Hindu laws dealing with inheritance of property and marriage the President felt that the verdict of the electorate ought to be sought. See K.L. Panjabi, *Rajendra Prasad*, p. 163.

ceilings.[u] On an earlier occasion, the President exercised his power of veto in respect of the PEPSU Appropriation Bill, passed by Parliament in 1954. He held that the Bill was beyond the competence of Parliament and contrary to the provisions of the Constitution. Hence, to act on the advice of the Council of Ministers would result, in this case, in the violation of the Constitution and make him liable to impeachment, under Article 61.[v] Here the President used his discretion, and it might be added that the President has certain specific powers which are exercised independently of ministerial advice. Article 111 empowers the President to return to Parliament a Bill for reconsideration and adoption of such amendments as he suggests. It must be conceded, however, that if Parliament should again pass the Bill with or without the suggested amendments, he cannot withhold assent. Where a dispute arises as to the qualification for membership of Parliament under Article 102, the question is referred to the President who decides it on the basis of the advice of the Election Commissioner. His decision in the matter is final. Recently—after the formation of Maharashtra and Gujerat—the President has been given the right to provide by order for special responsibilities of the Governors of these States in respect of certain matters. These powers clearly show that his position is unlike that of the British monarch who has no special or discretionary powers.

But in a period of ten years, the few examples cited above have been the only known instances when the President has sought to exercise his powers. For the rest, he has conducted himself in a manner befitting one in his high position. He has scrupulously eschewed party politics. He has succeeded in laying down precedents of "constitutional" behaviour which his successors will find difficult to ignore. In other words, the President has so functioned as to give credence to the belief that he is just a titular head.

The Influence of Mr Nehru

A point of considerable significance is that, during the last decade, the Prime Minister has emerged as the most powerful figure on the Indian political scene. How much of this can be attributed to the charisma of Mr Nehru and to the personal loyalty that he is able to command among all sections of the Indian people, it is difficult to say. Due to a variety of factors, not least of which are the charm and accessibility of the Prime Minister, he has come to be identified, in the eyes of the people, with the Government of the country. At home he is the spokesman of Government policy—and abroad he represents the Indian nation.

u. Ibid, pp. 189-190.
v. Ibid, p. 164.

The political history of the country's struggle for freedom and its aspirations for the future are uniquely centred in a single personality who has dominated and continues to dominate the political arena. The leadership which he has been able to offer has made at least one thing certain: that in India today it is the Prime Minister and not the President who wields power. Will this endure? It is difficult to give a categorical answer to such a question. Much depends on the changes that are likely to take place in the not too distant future. Let us assume that Mr Nehru—for whatever reason—ceases to be the Prime Minister but that the Congress continues to be the majority party. The most likely choice for the leadership of the Congress Party, and therefore for the Prime Ministership, seems according to present indications to be Mr Morarji Desai. With the retirement of Dr Rajendra Prasad as President of India, the almost certain choice in his place is the present Vice-President, Dr S. Radhakrishnan. What we know of these two men would seem to indicate that there will be no appreciable change in the President-Prime Minister relationship. Mr Desai, it is true, does not evoke the same personal devotion as Mr Nehru. Nevertheless, he is known to be a first-rate administrator and it is extremely unlikely that while the administration rests in his hands, there will be any reversal of the present trends. It can be equally confidently claimed that, both by inclination and by virtue of the position he holds, Dr Radhakrishnan will not act in a manner likely to give rise to conflict. If anything, the tradition laid down by Dr Rajendra Prasad will be strengthened by the predictable political behaviour of Mr Desai and the present Vice-President.

Future Possibilities

But there are other possibilities to be considered. The first is the possibility of a change in the political complexion of the country. To date, the Congress has been able to secure a majority at the centre and in the states.[w] This position of strength is not likely to continue. If the opposition parties were to secure power in one state or some of the states, there is every reason to believe that a conflict will arise between the state(s) and the centre. If, for instance, a state were to introduce changes in its educational system, changes not in conformity with the national policy, there is bound to be a clash. The state's Bill which embodied the contemplated changes in the educational structure might have to

w. The two exceptions are Kerala and Orissa. In Kerala, the Communist government was ousted by popular agitation, to be followed by a coalition government. In Orissa, till recently, the state was ruled by a coalition of the Congress and the Ganatantra Parishad. The coalition broke down a few months ago and Congress was returned to power in the ensuing election.

receive Presidential assent. The Cabinet might advise the President to refuse assent to the Bill, and his veto is final. Mr Asok Chanda maintains that if in such a case the President on ministerial advice did refuse assent, he would be abdicating his responsibility. To quote: "If such a legislature were to pass a Bill, within its legislative competence, which was not in harmony with the ideologies of the majority party in Parliament, and the Governor exercised his option of reserving the Bill for consideration of the President, should the President, acting on the advice of the Council of Ministers, refuse to give his assent to the Bill ? If he were to do so, he would be surrendering the position of being above party politics."[x] On the other hand, it is scarcely conceivable that the Union Government should contemplate with equanimity a radical departure from its policies. In case of a conflict, the ambiguity of the President's position will become embarrassingly apparent. If he accepts the Cabinet's advice, he will lay himself open to the charge of being partisan. If he supports the state(s) he will be accused of disregarding the advice of the Cabinet and thus acting in contravention of Government policy. In either case, he will be dragged into undesirable political controversy.

Another possibility which cannot be entirely ruled out is that at the centre no single party in the future will have a majority that will enable it to form a government without the support of some other party. If a coalition government were to come into being at the centre, it might become difficult for the President to keep aloof from politics. If the experiments in coalition government in the states are any indication, a like government at the centre will not be a very happy state of affairs. The chances are then equal that in such a situation, the President will act either as a stabilising influence which will ensure continuity of government, or alternatively, that he will exploit the situation to take power into his own hands. Here again, his right to engage in politics may at any time be called into question.

The Need for Clarification

If there is a possibility—however remote it may seem at present of a political crisis in which the position of the President becomes a matter of considerable significance, it can be argued that a clarification of his status is necessary to avoid any difficulties in the future. Attempts have, in fact, been made to exploit the ambiguous position of the President. Mr C. Rajagopalachari recently suggested to the President that the question of land ceilings be referred to the Supreme Court for opinion on its constitutional validity. This suggestion

x. A. Chandra, *Indian Administration*, p. 76.

was rejected by the Home Ministry. Mr Rajagopalachari saw in this a usurpation of the President's right to exercise his independent judgment. Again, during the linguistic agitation in Assam, opposition parties called upon the President to dismiss the ruling Congress Party and impose the President's rule. The feeling was that no Congress Cabinet at the centre would advise the President to depose a Congress Ministry in a state. There is thus a clear tendency on the part of the opposition parties to go over the head of the Government and appeal directly to the President, to exercise what they believe to be his constitutional powers. Whether such a belief arises from a feeling of political futility or is the result of a consciously held conviction on the nature of the Executive it is not easy to determine. But it is at least an indication that even in Parliament there is no unanimity regarding the true function of the President. From this point of view, those who clamour for an amendment to the Constitution are on firm ground.

An amendment could be made to the effect that the President shall be bound by the advice of the Cabinet. Or, it could be framed so as to leave certain areas of discretion to the President wherein he can exercise his independent judgment. An amendment of the first sort would imply that the President's authority is purely nominal,[y] and would solve, once and for all, the riddle of the nature of the Indian Executive. But with an amendment that reserved to the President certain special powers to be exercised at his discretion, the unique position of the President could impart a significant stabilising and restraining influence in politics. There is, however, one difficulty. The definition of the area of discretion is no easy task. A general description would be of little use, for, while it would silence those who see in him a figurehead, its very generality would be dangerous. A specific list of discretionary powers would be almost impossible to draw up since it could hardly foresee the matters in which the use of the President's discretion would be advisable. We are forced to conclude that if an amendment is to be definitive it can be so only if it decides to embody in the Constitution a Cabinet system of government—i.e., if it reduces the President to a nonentity.

Can an amendment be avoided? Perhaps. If no political crisis intervenes and the country continues to be governed by a party determined to uphold responsible Cabinet government—and a President who is inclined to co-operate—we feel that an amendment might not become necessary. Besides, it is necessary to remember that the man who will normally be chosen President will

y. The British monarch's position is slightly different. For though in theory the Queen possesses no power, the influence of the Crown cannot be ignored. In India, however, there is no "aura" comparable to that surrounding the Queen. To deprive the President of all powers is to reduce him effectively to a nonentity.

have to be one who has had experience in public life, who commands respect from more than one party, who is believed to be capable of rising above politics. There is no absolute guarantee that such a man will not be also power-hungry. The risk involved is the price we have to pay for having a President who will be more than a "cypher."

We would conclude by saying that the decision whether to amend the Constitution or not will depend upon one's conception of the role of the President under the Constitution. Whether, in other words, one should bind the President forever and remove any doubts as to his constitutional position but lose whatever advantages there are in his present position. Or, whether the ambiguity should be retained for its possible benefits despite the political risks involved in such a situation.

67. T.N. Kaul's Article on Non-Alignment[171]

[Refer to item 437]

THE "PHILOSOPHY" OF NON-ALIGNMENT[a]

It is not easy, at the best of times, to write about philosophy. It is even harder to write about the philosophy of "non-alignment". And when the writer himself is anything but a philosopher, the task is made doubly difficult.

I shall, therefore, at the very outset, disclaim the high sounding title of a philosophy for non-alignment. A philosophy is perhaps associated in our minds with a system of thought that holds good for all times and in all circumstances. I do not wish to press that claim for non-alignment – not yet at any rate – when it has not stood the test of time or survived the stresses and strains of war. And yet it would, perhaps, not be presumptuous to claim for it the merit of a policy that has shown some strength to sustain itself in the midst of a period of acute international tension that has become known as "cold war". Also, perhaps, it holds some attraction for an increasing number of countries that are backward economically and socially and are peacefully but rapidly emerging into political freedom. It is possible that this policy has something more in it than meets the eye and the ear, that it has developed some quality which makes it look now less disreputable and immoral in the eyes of the power blocs that seem to hold the destinies of mankind in their shaky hands than it did ten years ago.

Non-alignment may not, after all, be a purely negative concept but may also contain some seeds of positive growth and dynamic development. It may hold some fascination for countries and peoples who are not yet overgrown with political power and economic prosperity and are trying desperately to keep their heads above water. These newly independent countries need most urgently to give social and economic content to their political independence. While in the West economic development preceded the transfer of political power to the people through universal suffrage, the reverse process has taken place in these new countries. They have to telescope centuries into decades and

171. Reproduced from T.N. Kaul, *Ambassadors Need Not Lie*, Volume 2, Non-Alignment (New Delhi: Lancer International, 1989), pp.7-20. This article seems to have been republished as follows: T.N. Kaul, "The Philosophy of Non-alignment" *India 1962* (New Delhi, 1963).

Footnotes of the original appear as letter numbering as a, b, c and so on.

a. Based on a speech and article by the author in *India Annual*, London, 1962, which was approved by Jawaharlal Nehru.

fulfil the hopes and aspirations, the urgent needs and demands for a reasonable standard of living of their people.

The danger of war breaking out in any corner of the globe and spreading to the whole world is compelling the great powers and their allies to recognise non-alignment as a better way, a more practical way, of preventing local conflicts from engulfing the whole world. A convincing example is the 14-Power agreement about Laos which has shown the relative futility of military alliances like SEATO and the comparative merit of a policy of non-alignment.

Each country has its own history, geography and national interests which determine its outlook and policy and which are, therefore, bound to vary in some important aspects from the outlook and policy of its neighbours. Just as there are differing emphases and nuances in the policy of alignment between various members of a group of aligned countries, so are there differences in emphasis and orientation in the policy of non-alignment among the non-aligned countries; in fact, more so, because the very concept of non-alignment precludes any idea of alignment even between the non-aligned countries inter se. The essence of non-alignment consists in the freedom and independence of a country to judge each question as it arises not on the basis of a pre-determined attitude because of alignment with other countries, but on its own merits as it affects the interests of the country concerned and the world at large.

Non-alignment is not neutrality, though it is often confused with it. Neutrality is perhaps a more preconceived attitude than alignment, because it is an attitude of non-participation or not taking sides on an issue, irrespective of its merits. Alignment, on the other hand, is an attitude of openly declaring in advance that the country concerned will take the side of other countries aligned with it. Non-alignment differs from both these attitudes in that it does not declare in advance that it will or will not take one side or the other – but that it will judge each issue as it arises on its merits, according to its own perspective and not necessarily as others see it. Non-alignment at the state level may be compared with the concept of liberty and freedom at the individual level. Just as an individual should have the right of freedom of thought and expression and action as long as he does not violate any law, similarly, sovereign and independent countries and nations should have the right to decide for themselves their conduct in any particular situation as long as they do not violate the laws of peace or the laws of war.

Neutrality is a concept essentially applied to a state of war while non-alignment is a concept that has significance and relevance in times of peace as well as war. A neutral country declares in advance that it will not be an ally of either belligerent in case of war. A non-aligned country, on the contrary, retains the freedom to participate on either side or neither as it deems proper when the choice has to be made. Non-alignment, therefore, does not preclude belligerency or neutrality – but differs from both inasmuch as one cannot take a non-aligned country for granted in advance as either neutral or belligerent.

Why should a country adopt a policy of non-alignment? Often it is smeared as a policy of opportunism or expediency trying to take advantage of both sides and have the best of both worlds. It is sometimes dubbed as a policy of least resistance and the easiest way out of a dilemma. Members of the two main power blocs in the world have in the past often criticised it as leaning more to one side or the other. Some people have even called it "immoral", on the self-righteous assumption that "those who are not with us are against us". Non-alignment is anything but the easiest way out of a dilemma. It often brings the wrath of both power blocs on the non-aligned government. It needs courage and conviction to resist the pressure of bigger and greater powers and follow an independent policy.

Such criticism is understandable though not justifiable when one considers the fact that most of the countries that have adopted a policy of non-alignment are economically and militarily weak and have yet had the courage to disagree with and even criticise in national and international forums much more powerful and prosperous countries and blocs. Although the UN proclaims the equality of membership of all sovereign countries, big or small, even the UN Charter gives the right of veto and permanent membership in the Security Council to only the so-called "Big Five". No wonder then that the Big Five and those aligned with them did not, at first, like the independence and open defiance of these "upstart" nations who till yesterday were mere colonies.

This resentment is even greater among some of the smaller countries who are aligned with the big powers when they find that the non-aligned countries are being wooed and respected by their own "big brothers" and given economic aid and loans. They naturally begin to wonder whether, in the circumstances, it would have been wiser for them to have remained non-aligned too to get a bigger share of military and economic aid from their allies, or at least so they say. They conveniently forget that, apart from military aid, the per capita economic aid received by any country aligned with the East or the West is more than twice the aid received by any non-aligned country from both. Those who had prophesised that non-alignment was a short-sighted policy, doomed to failure, are, however, more than a little surprised when they find more and more countries in Asia, Africa and Latin America adhering to that policy – especially among those countries which have gained independence after World War II.

What are the essential qualities of non-alignment that have gained for it more and more adherents in recent years? What are its advantages and disadvantages, from the national and international points of view? Is it a philosophy that has some permanent value and has come to stay, or will it meet the same fate as other political policies propounded from time to time, such as "splendid isolation", "enlightened self-interest", "balance of power", "spheres of influence", etc.?

I shall confine myself to merely answering the first question, namely, what the main characteristics of non-alignment are. I shall not be so bold or rash as to predict its future in a world that is rapidly changing because of tremendous scientific and technological advances, where horizons are widening ever more into outer space and where the relative importance of national interests may soon be overshadowed by global interests and developments. Another important factor that inhibits looking far into the future is the fact that non-alignment tends, in the popular mind, to be associated with a policy confined mainly to the military field and arising of necessity because of the division of most of the world powers into two main militarily aligned blocs. Should the present alignment of military powers be replaced by a World Authority on the completion of a total disarmament agreement, the need for military non-alignment may not exist anymore. Non-alignment has relevance in a situation where alignment exists. When there is no need for alignment and military alignments disappear, non-alignment, in a military sense, would disappear too. This is an important aspect of non-alignment which limits its scope and future development or, in a manner of speaking, presents a possibility of its total fulfilment. When or whether such a time will come to pass, must be left to the judgement of prophets, poets and philosophers – and future diplomatists.

Let us confine our attention then, for the present, to the main ingredients of non-alignment, as seen during recent yeas Non-alignment, in general, means keeping aloof from and remaining outside military affiliations and alliances with great powers. Hence its frequent confusion with neutrality. Non-alignment does not preclude cultural or economic alignment, or rule but even the possibility of military alignment with others, not permanently or in advance, but when a particular situation arises and is considered on its merits. All it precludes is the assumption, in advance, that a non-aligned country will necessarily align itself with one side or the other in any dispute that may arise in the future. Precluding this assumption makes it necessary to convince a non-aligned country as to the merits of your case in order to gain its support. This in one sense leads to uncertainty, as the attitude a non-aligned country will adopt cannot be taken for granted in advance. And yet, in another sense, it creates a confidence that issues will be considered on their merits, as they affect the world at large and not only a particular group of powers. It raises the discussion and settlement of international questions from a partisan basis to one of fundamental principles. This naturally increases the faith of peoples and powers that the larger interests of humanity will not be sacrificed in international forums where non-aligned countries have a voice. To this extent, therefore, non-alignment has introduced a healthy tendency in international affairs.

The capacity of non-aligned countries to play an effective or influential role, however, depends not entirely on themselves but mainly on the willingness of the great powers and their allies to be influenced by them. This willingness, in turn, depends on the impartiality and powers of persuasion, of the non-aligned countries, on the extent to which their attitude represents world public opinion, and the relative unanimity and agreement with which this attitude is adopted by the bulk of the non-aligned powers.

A democratic country, even if it belongs to an alliance, is likely to be more sensitive to the opinion of non-aligned countries than a totalitarian regime, which is not always responsive even to the opinions of its own people. This sometimes leads to the erroneous impression among the former that they are at a disadvantage and that non-alignment operates only against them. This, however, is not true. If a totalitarian regime defies non-aligned opinion in one case, it prejudices non-aligned countries against itself. What is more, it creates a stiffening of attitude in the opposite camp which becomes less prone to non-aligned opinion in other cases.

There is, however, universal recognition of the fact that the presence of non-aligned powers in the UN Disarmament Committee at Geneva has produced a sobering effect on both sides and made their discussions less vituperative than in the past. That may not be a great achievement in itself but it is an improvement that is likely to lead to other improvements in the future.

The motivating force of non-alignment thus seems to be a positive influence in favour of world peace and lessening of world tension. Its strength springs from this and from the fact that it represents the feelings of humanity at large. If it did not do so, or where it does not do so, its influence is practically non-existent.

Non-alignment, therefore, implies an attitude of impartiality, based on larger world interests rather than on the narrow and limited interests of one power or group of powers. Where the two conflict, the former must take precedence – that in brief is the *raison d'être* of non-alignment. Where these interests do not conflict so obviously, or where each side has a point to make, where the issue is not pure white or pure black, but contains many shades of grey – as in most international disputes – non-alignment takes on the role of the "honest broker" and is useful as a sort of bridge between two contending sides. But its effectiveness or usefulness depends on the willingness of contending parties to compromise, their faith in the motives and honesty of the non-aligned powers, on the impartiality of the non-aligned powers and last but not the least, on the strength of world opinion on a particular issue.

This explains why non-alignment has come to the fore in international affairs only recently — mainly after World War II. Before World War II, international bodies and even the League of Nations were dominated by powers or groups of powers who had imperial or colonial interests and were governed by the doctrines of Spheres of Influence and the Balance of Power. Their interests were often at variance with each other and their usual method of compromise was at the expense of the weaker and smaller powers or by a re-distribution of spheres of influence and the sharing of spoils. The Open Door policy in China and the carving out of colonies on the continent of Africa are two glaring examples, apart from others in Asia, Latin America and Central and Eastern Europe.

After World War II, the pattern of international discussion underwent a radical change. This period saw the beginning of the process of dissolving empires and the freeing of colonies, a process in which Great Britain gave a lead, and America and the Soviet Union played the role of catalytic agents. The emergence into freedom of countries like India, Burma, Indonesia and Ceylon, who refused to be browbeaten into military alliances, the democratization of regimes in countries like Egypt, the emergence of Yugoslavia as a Communist country non-aligned to the East or West, after 1948, created the possibility, for the first time in history, of putting across an independent and, as it were, disinterested point of view in international forums.

This tendency was naturally looked upon with suspicion by both the power blocs at first — because it presented a challenge to their erstwhile domination in their respective spheres of influence. But, this trend had come to stay and was further strengthened by the emergence into freedom of other Asian and African countries which felt more and more inclined to follow a policy of non-alignment. This development was helped also by the existence of two powerful blocs or groups of powers whose policies and ideologies clashed on almost every international issue and made it necessary and desirable for each to win and woo this new group of countries. And all this was helped by the fact that there was an international forum like the UN where each new country, big or small, that became free and independent, was admitted as a member with a right of vote equal to that of older and bigger powers. The latter still retained effective control in the Security Council by virtue of their permanent membership and right of veto. But even in the Security Council the presence of six elected non-permanent members whose votes could not always be counted upon by one or the other bloc created a new situation. In the General Assembly and its various Committees the voice of this new group of non-aligned powers was more effective and they seemed to hold the balance between the two sides. They compelled attention on such issues as colonialism, non-self-governing territories, disarmament, banning of nuclear tests, etc. which were sometimes to the liking of one bloc or the other and sometimes of neither. Here was non-alignment playing a positive role in hastening the process of liberation of colonies and non-self-governing territories, condemning aggression and interference in the internal affairs of small countries by bigger ones or their allies.

And yet, in spite of this positive role, the non-aligned countries did not and could not become a Third Force. Why? First and foremost, such a development would go against the very fundamental basis of non-alignment. Non-alignment is not confined only to the two power blocs but is, by its very definition, against alignment even between non-aligned countries inter se. This tendency may be seen to have asserted itself between the Bandung and Belgrade Conferences. At Bandung an attempt was made by certain powers to exploit the non-aligned countries to favour one bloc's point of view against the other. The non-aligned countries realized, however, that their force and influence depended on their ability to keep themselves aloof from both blocs and not allow themselves to be exploited by either. They were not afraid of coming down on the side of a particular point of view, whether it favoured one bloc or the other, but in doing so they used the language of conciliation rather than of condemnation, they talked in terms of peace rather than war, of discussion and negotiation rather than threats and coercion. Each bloc made, between Bandung and Belgrade, various attempts to woo this new ideological influence, but both realized that non-alignment was not a tool they could mould through fear or favour. Thus, non-alignment came to be accepted as a policy and an attitude, a philosophy and an outlook that could be adopted by various countries of the world that did not wish to get involved in the cold war and wanted desperately to prevent a shooting war.

Military alliances are necessarily against some actual or potential enemy. To join them means practically naming the enemy and thus, in a sense, weakening ourselves. Even from the strictly narrow point of view of defence, it does not add to our strength but rather weakens it and makes little difference to the "balance of terror" prevailing between the two mighty blocs. Perhaps this may not apply in the case of all countries but it certainly applies to India. Military alliances mean thinking and planning for war. They are opposed fundamentally to the search for peace. They add to the dangers of war and create an atmosphere opposed to peace. In fact, anything but non-alignment would be basically opposed to the policy we have followed and to all our thinking on this subject. It would create bitter conflicts in India.[b]

b. This paragraph was inserted on the advice of Jawaharlal Nehru.

If Bandung was the beginning of this trend, albeit with certain doubts and reservations, Belgrade was its vindication. While Bandung proved that non-alignment as a policy had a basis and was necessary, Belgrade showed that it was a dynamic concept that was not divorced from the realities of the world situation but deeply affected by and concerned with them. It also proved the maturity of this concept. While it was essential to abolish colonialism, it was equally important to preserve the peace of the world and save humanity from self-destruction by nuclear weapons and tests.

One may, perhaps, hope that non-alignment will one day shed its passive role and be able to concentrate entirely on its active aspect of keeping the peace, increasing cooperation for productive purposes and bringing the various countries of this globe closer to the concept of One World, That would be the fulfilment of the philosophy of non-alignment, its withering away in its own Nirvana.

This may sound like a distant dream but it is the only hope for the future survival of humanity. Even when this goal of One World is achieved, we cannot expect all countries to be alike in their social, political or economic systems. I hope each country and its people will have the freedom and opportunity to develop according to its own genius and its peculiar needs. There will, of course, have to be greater cooperation and less friction on inter-state and world problems. It is in this field that the positive aspects of non-alignment will then come into greater play.

As non-alignment in a military sense disappears with the achievement of total and complete disarmament and the creation of a World Authority, non-alignment as a philosophy of live and let live will, it is hoped, not only survive but get stronger and more universal.

POSTSCRIPT
(written soon after the Sino-Indian conflict of 1962)

Until the invasion of India by China in September-October 1962, the policy of non-alignment had not been tested by the stresses and strains of war. It is, therefore, pertinent to consider what effect the Chinese invasion has already had on a non-aligned peaceful democratic country like India and is likely to have on non-alignment in the future. The following tentative conclusions may be worth considering:

(a) Non-alignment will be successful and useful to the extent that it is observed by non-aligned powers themselves and respected by other powers, particularly by the aligned power blocs.

(b) In order to gain such respect and acceptance, non-alignment must be based on strength and not weakness. Obviously, this strength cannot be mainly of a military character because the very basis of non-alignment is military non-alignment. At the same time, however, those non-aligned countries like India who have been invaded, or are open to such threats and invasions from another country, must make necessary and adequate military preparations to defend their territorial integrity and security. India must, therefore, seek military equipment and assistance from such countries as are willing to give it without any strings, political or military, and without giving up her policy of non-alignment. For this purpose it is necessary that leading countries of both power blocs give, without any political or military strings, necessary military equipment to a non-aligned country that is threatened, as India is.

(c) If, however, such assistance is not forthcoming and a non-aligned country has to choose between survival and non-alignment, naturally survival will take precedence. Non-alignment is a means to an end and not an end in itself. It is a means to the lessening of tensions in the world and the preservation of world peace, so that underdeveloped countries that have recently emerged into freedom may be able to devote all their energies and resources towards economic and social development. If, however, the very existence of a country is threatened and non-alignment is not respected by a powerful neighbour and other powerful countries merely look on, then non-alignment will have to undergo a radical change.

(d) If this should happen – and it will be very unfortunate – then a conflict in any part of the world may lead to a world conflagration which may mean a thermonuclear war and thus destroy the bulk of humanity and human civilization. It is from this point of view that non-alignment in a military sense has its importance and must be accepted and respected by both the power blocs and maintained and supported effectively by the non-aligned countries themselves.

(e) Although the non-aligned countries are not militarily strong, they exercise a moral influence in the world, through such international organs as the United Nations and the Belgrade-type conferences. While non-aligned countries may be non-aligned inter se, in a military sense, they should not remain neutral, when the very concept and existence of non-alignment is threatened as happened in the Suez in 1956 and as in the case of India's invasion by China in 1962.

(f) All non-aligned countries should frequently consult and cooperate with each other, try to take a united stand on the major problems facing the world today and thus mould public opinion and world opinion in favour of peace and peaceful coexistence. This coming together should no longer be based on geographical considerations alone – like the Asian countries, the African countries, the Latin American countries, grouping separately and together but should rather be based on common ideas, interests and attitudes which cut across geographical, racial and regional divisions. The non-aligned countries of Asia, Africa, Europe, Latin America and other areas should group together, in and outside the United Nations, to put moral pressure on any country that does not respect non-alignment and peaceful coexistence. They must come closer to each other politically, economically, culturally and socially in so far as their ideologies and attitudes are common.

(g) This does not mean that they will gang up and form a "third force" in the world but it does mean that, within the United Nations and outside – they will, in their efforts to preserve peace and peaceful coexistence, represent the sentiments, hopes and aspirations of large sections of the world, and of the majority of the world population. This does not mean that they need come in physical conflict with the aligned countries, but it does mean that they represent a third trend of political thought in the world which must be taken notice of.

(h) It is significant that the countries that have given military assistance to India to meet the Chinese threat have not laid down any conditions compelling India to give up her policy of non-alignment. It is also significant that even the countries of the socialist camp have remained neutral, perhaps for the first time in their history, in a dispute between a member of their camp and a non-aligned country like India. What is even more significant is that they disapproved of China's use of force against a peaceful, non-aligned country like India, as a violation of the 1957 Declaration and the 1960 Statement which supported the doctrine of peaceful co-existence.

(i) Whatever the ultimate aims and objects of one bloc or the other may be, it must be recognize that countries differing from them in social, political and economic ideologies must not be forced, through military pressure or otherwise, to join one camp or the other. It is for each country to evolve its own salvation through methods suited to its needs, the genius of its people, its culture, its social system and its history. As long as there is s single powerful country in the world that does not accept the right of other countries to live their own way of life, there will be a threat to peace. As long as there is a single country in either bloc which threatens to solve disputes with her neighbours through force and aggression, there will be a serious threat to peace.

(j) It is, therefore, necessary that non-aligned countries solidly and unitedly come out with one voice against such threats of aggression and invasion. The existence of non-alignment and peaceful co-existence is in danger. A heavy responsibility, therefore, lies on the shoulders of the non-aligned countries themselves, as well as on the aligned countries and, in particular, on the Big Powers, to see that the methods adopted by China in 1962 in dealing with India are not allowed to be used again by any power in the world. The initiative taken by the Colombo Powers is, therefore, commendable. But the Big Powers must also support the Colombo proposals and compel China to accept them in toto, as India has done, or to settle this border question by a reference to international arbitration as India has offered.

If the above conditions are made possible, then non-alignment will not only survive but develop into a positive philosophy of closer cooperation between the non-aligned countries inter se and between them and others in the more fruitful fields of economic development, cultural enrichment, social progress and political understanding in an atmosphere of peace, of goodwill and respect for each other's ways of life. If, however, the non-aligned countries do not take a firm and united stand among themselves towards the threat to non-alignment, or the Big Powers exploit it for purposes of the cold war, then the future of non-alignment will be threatened and its ability to preserve peace and thus enabling underdeveloped countries to devote their resources and energy for peaceful development, will be diminished. It is, therefore, in the interests of the non-aligned countries themselves and of the world at large, to see that non-alignment is respected by all countries of the world, big and small, and that through it peaceful coexistence and the peace of the world are safeguarded.

P.P.S. (September 1988)

In the post-Nehru period Indira Gandhi tried to have a dialogue with China and restored ambassadorial relations with Peking in 1976. The Janata Foreign Minister, Atal Behari [Bihari] Vajpayee, paid a visit to China in early 1979 but had to cut it short when China invaded Vietnam in February of that year. Now Rajiv Gandhi is trying to restart a dialogue with China and eight rounds of talks have been held at the official level. If they create a basis for raising the dialogue to a higher political level, Rajiv Gandhi may well send one of his senior Ministers to Peking or even consider a visit by himself. It is good to have a dialogue but summit talks are not usually held unless there is some basis for their positive outcome. It seems unlikely that the border problem will be resolved at this stage, but tension along the border could be defused and relations in the commercial and cultural fields improved, as the USSR is trying to do.

If China and the Soviet Union succeed in normalizing their relations, it might help rather than hinder the normalization of Sino-Indian relations and vice versa. However, one should be realistic and not euphoric or unduly pessimistic about such possibilities. The time has come, perhaps, for both China and India to realize that they will have to settle the border question peacefully and by mutual accommodation and not by an eyeball-to-eyeball confrontation on the border which may lead to incidents.

In dealing with the Chinese one has to be patient and persevering, realistic and pragmatic. At the same time, China must also realize that in dealing with India she has to respect the Indian sensibilities and historical, traditional, cultural factors which had made the Sino-Indian border one of peace and good neighbourliness for centuries. It is possible to revive that provided there is mutual trust and political will to have a fair and equitable settlement on both sides.

GLOSSARY

(Including abbreviations and names of places)

Allahabad	Prayagraj
AICC	All India Congress Committee
AIIMS	All India Institute of Medical Sciences
AIR	All India Radio
AMU	Aligarh Muslim University
AOC	Assam Oil Company
AOC	Assam Oil Company
APHLC	All Party Hill Leaders' Conference
Bangalore	Bengaluru
BOC	Burmah Oil Company
Bombay	Mumbai
Burma	Myanmar
Calcutta	Kolkata
Ceylon	Sri Lanka
CGS	Chief of General Staff
COAS	Chief of Army Staff
CPI	Communist Party of India
CPP	Congress Party in Parliament/Congress Parliamentary Party
CPWD	Central Public Works Department
CS	Commonwealth Secretary
CSIR	Council of Scientific and Industrial Research
CW & PC	Central Water and Power and Commission

CWC	Congress Working Committee
Dacca	Dhaka
DCC	District Congress Committee
DMK	Dravida Munnetra Kazhagam
DPCC	Delhi Pradesh Congress Committee
DVC	Damodar Valley Corporation
ECM	European Common Market
ECOSOC	Economic and Social Council
ESI Scheme	Employees' State Insurance Scheme
FICCI	Federation of Indian Chambers of Commerce and Industry
FRCS	Fellow of the Royal College of Surgeons
FS	Foreign Secretary
GOI	Government of India
IAF	Indian Air Force
ICSC	International Commission of Supervision and Control
IFAS	Indian Frontier Administration Service
IMF	International Monetary Fund
IMS	Indian Medical Service
INTUC	Indian National Trade Union Conference
Jubbulpore	Jabalpur
J & K	Jammu and Kashmir
Madras City	Chennai
Madras State	Tamil Nadu
MBBS	Bachelor of Medicine and Bachelor of Surgery
MCC	Mandal Congress Committee
MEA	Ministry of External Affairs
MHA	Ministry of Home Affairs
MLA	Member of Legislative Assembly
MLC	Member of Legislative Council
MP	Member of Parliament

MS	Master of Surgery
Mukhia	Village Head
MPCC	Madhya Pradesh Congress Committee
Mysore State	Karnataka
NDA	National Defence Academy
NEFA	North East Frontier Agency
NMML	Nehru Memorial Museum and Library
OAS	Organisation de l'Armée Secrète/ Secret Army Organization
OIL	Oil India Limited
Orissa	Odisha
PCC	Pradesh Congress Committee
PEN	Poets, Essayists and Novelists
PEPSU	Patiala and East Punjab States Union
PIB	Press Information Bureau
PIDE	Policia Internationale por Defesa do Estado (International Police for Defence of the State)
PMO	Prime Minister's Office
PMS	Prime Minister's Secretariat
Pondicherry	Puducherry
Poona	Pune
PPS	Principal Private Secretary/Post Post Script
PS	Police Station/Private Secretary
PSP	Praja Socialist Party
Rajya Sabha Debates	*Parliamentary Debates. Rajya Sabha. Official Report*, various volumes and years (New Delhi: Rajya Sabha Secretariat)
RECI	*Report on the Third General Elections in India 1962, Volume II (Statistical) (Election Commission India, n.d.)*
RSS	Rashtriya Swayamsevak Sangh
Rumania	Romania
SDO	Sub Divisional Officer

SEATO	South East Asian Treaty Organisation
SG	Secretary General
SS	Special Secretary
SWJN/FS	*Selected Works of Jawaharlal Nehru/First Series*
SWJN/SS	*Selected Works of Jawaharlal Nehru/Second Series*
UAR	United Arab Republic
UGC	University Grants Commission
UK	United Kingdom
UNCIP	United Nations Commision for India and Pakistan
UN/UNO	United Nations Organisation
UP	Uttar Pradesh
UPCC	Uttar Pradesh Congress Committee
UPSC	Union Public Service Commission
US/USA	United States of America
USSR	Union of Soviet Socialists Republics
Ministry of WH & S	Ministry of Works, Housing & Supply
White Paper No. VI	Notes, Memoranda and Letters and China, November 1961-July 1962 Exchanged Between the Governments of India

INDEX

I

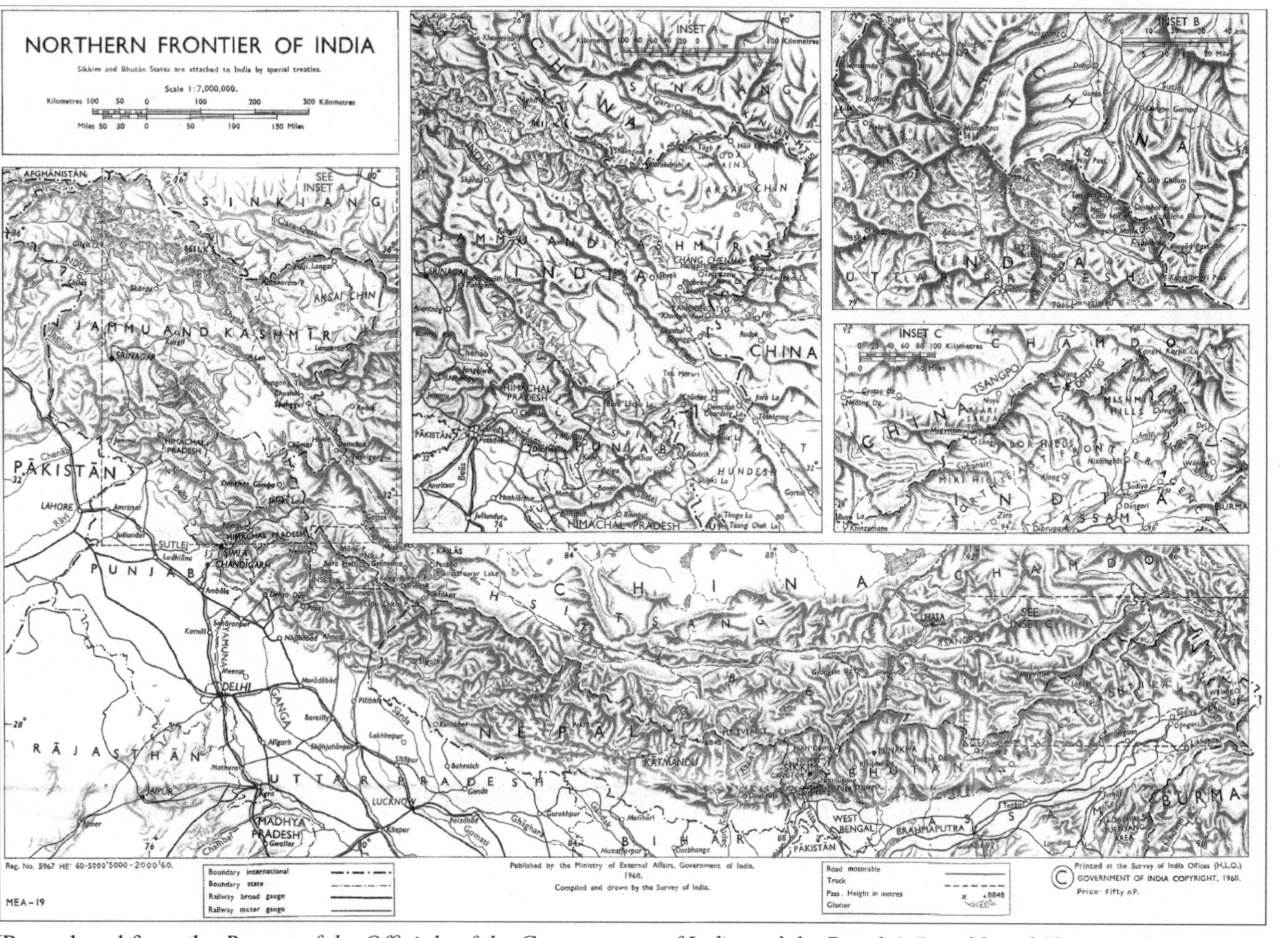

[Reproduced from the *Report of the Officials of the Governments of India and the People's Republic of China on the Boundary Question*, prepared by the Ministry of External Affairs and tabled in Parliament on 14 February 1961. Insets follow]

II

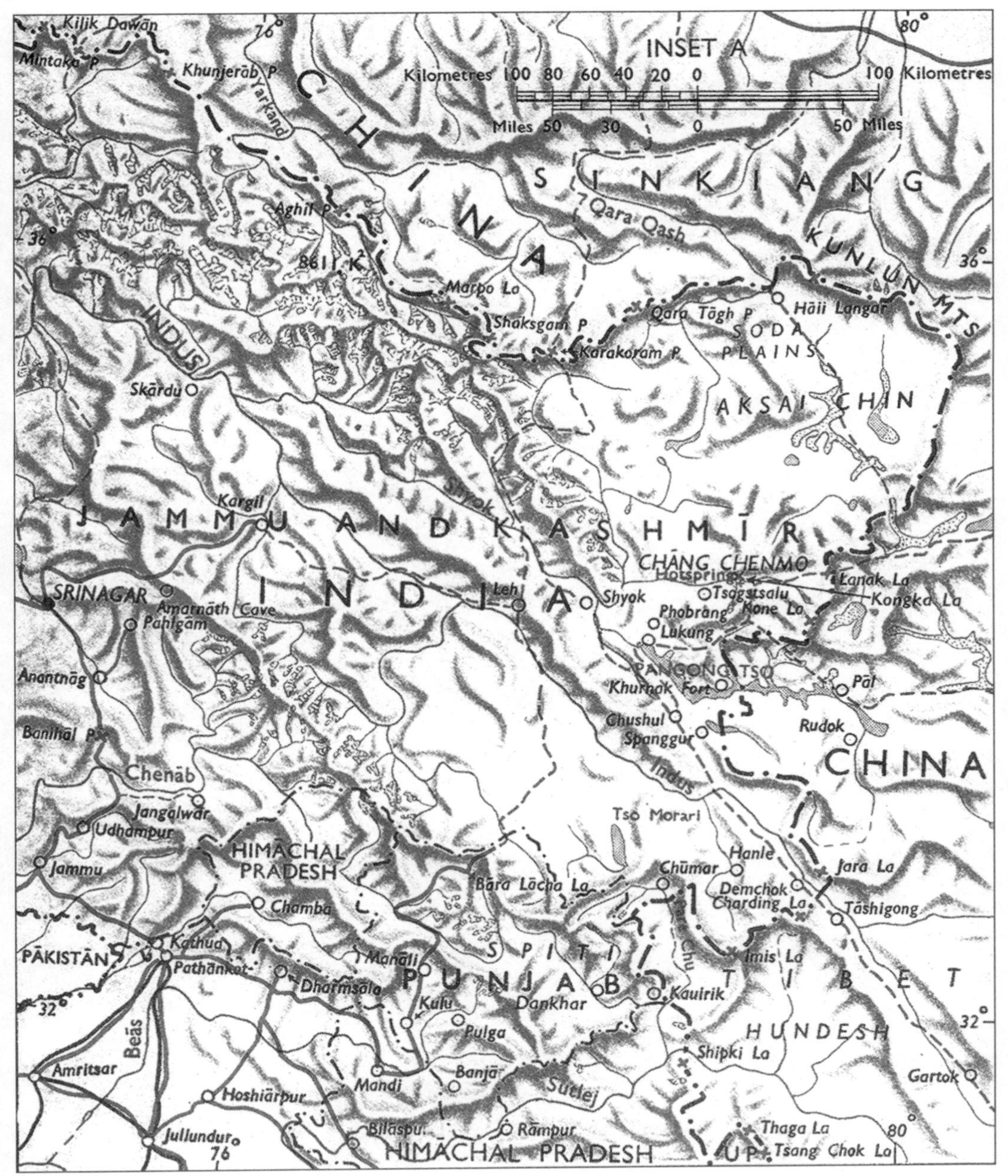

[Inset A, from map in *Report of the Officials of the Governments of India and the People's Republic of China on the Boundary Question*, prepared by the Ministry of External Affairs and tabled in Parliament on 14 February 1961]

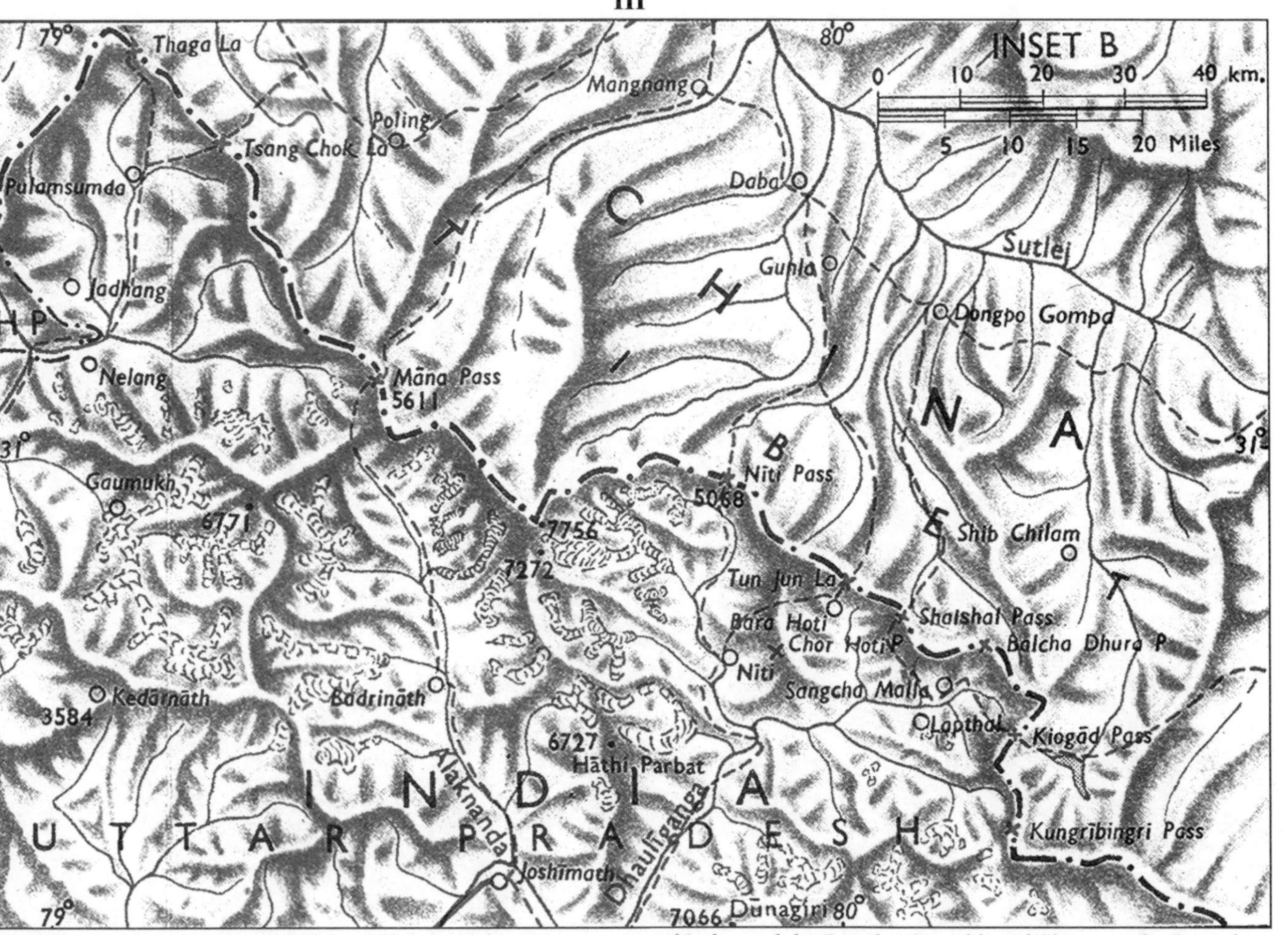

[Inset B, from map in *Report of the Officials of the Governments of India and the People's Republic of China on the Boundary Question*, prepared by the Ministry of External Affairs and tabled in Parliament on 14 February 1961]

IV

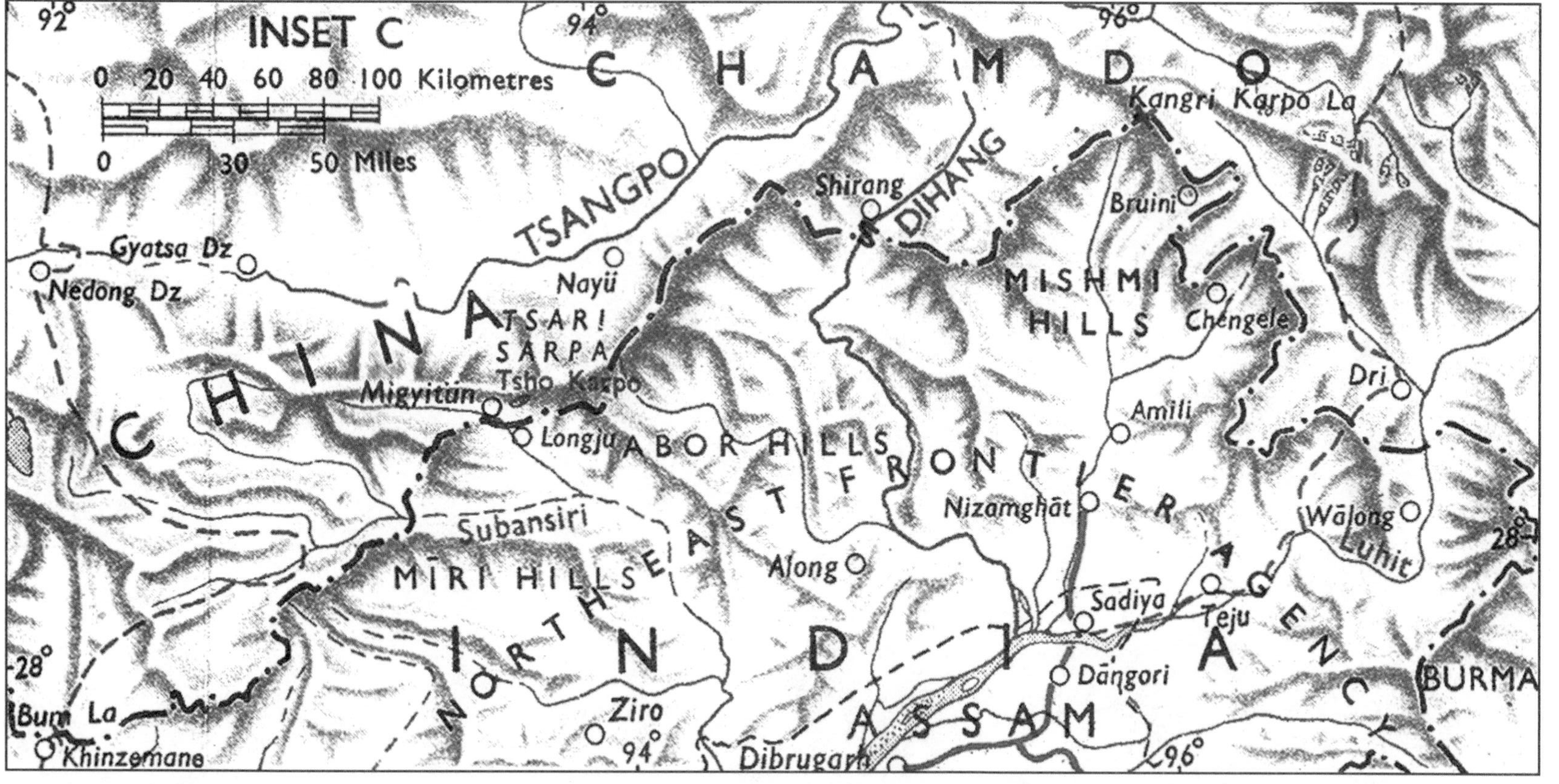

[Inset C, from map in *Report of the Officials of the Governments of India and the People's Republic of China on the Boundary Question*, prepared by the Ministry of External Affairs and tabled in Parliament on 14 February 1961]